International Aircraft Directory

The World's Most Popular Aircraft

International Aircraft Directory

The World's Most Popular Aircraft

Third Edition

By the Editors of **PLANE&PILOT** Magazine

Aviation Supplies & Academics, Inc.
Newcastle, Washington

International Aircraft Directory
Third Edition
By the Editors of Plane & Pilot Magazine

Aviation Supplies & Academics, Inc.
7005 132nd Place SE
Newcastle, Washington 98059-3153
Email: asa@asa2fly.com
Web: www.asa2fly.com

Published 2005 by Aviation Supplies & Academics, Inc.

Printed in the United States of America

09   08   07   06   05   9   8   7   6   5   4   3   2   1

Library of Congress Number 95-8613

ASA-ACD
ISBN 1-56027-590-1
        978-1-56027-590-9

Contents

Preface

No one at our company really imagined the stir that the first edition of the *Plane & Pilot International Aircraft Directory* would create. We knew that in our business, a simple-to-use, yet complete listing of the world's most popular aircraft would be a valuable asset, but we were surprised to find so many other people in the world liked the idea as well. So here we are, more than two decades later, offering a new Third Edition.

This latest edition of the Aircraft Directory is revised to include the up-to-date specification figures, performance data, design changes, and new models of current production aircraft. Also of special note are the greatly expanded homebuilt/kitbuilt, and sailplane/motorglider sections that provide specifications and performance data. As with each edition, more significantly interesting airplanes from the years past, as well as current aircraft developments, are added to this collection. New information on the aircraft included in this and past editions is added to when it becomes available.

This Third Edition of the *International Aircraft Directory* contains many of the private and commercial airplanes, whether of domestic or foreign manufacture, that are in active service or currently found on the United States FAA registry. This broad category includes new and late production models, current and discontinued homebuilts, military surplus, antiques, and some foreign makes. There are also a select number of classics, warbirds, and prototypes no longer in active service, in an effort to better acquaint pilots with the past so that they can better appreciate the present — and to pay tribute to those airplanes that have played such an important role in our aviation heritage.

Aviation enthusiasts will find the *International Aircraft Directory* to be a handy portable reference tool for spot-checking facts about a particular model, identifying unusual aircraft, and recognizing the trends in airplane design. The directory is a thorough collection of performance data, airframe and powerplant information and historical facts to help answer the questions most commonly asked by pilots.

While the aircraft found on the following pages are mostly produced or designed in the United States, they nevertheless represent the majority of civilian aircraft in service throughout the world. This is not to say that foreign aircraft abroad do not abound, but rather that the aircraft wholly designed and produced by them amount to a relatively small number.

How to use the Directory

The standard data and performance figures given for each airplane are in the following terms:

All weights are given in pounds with the gross weight representing the maximum takeoff weight and the empty weight representing the standard equipped weight. Fuel capacity is in total, not usable, U.S. gallons, and where two figures are given, they represent the standard and the standard plus optional capacities. Engines are rated in horsepower or maximum continuous horsepower (hp) for normally aspirated piston and turbocharged piston models, or shaft horsepower (shp) for turboprops and pounds of thrust (lbs s.t.) in the case of jets and fanjets. Speeds are in miles per hour (mph) with cruise speeds generally computed at 75 percent power of the particular aircraft's optimum operational altitude.

The initial climb rate is in feet per minute (fpm), usually computed at sea level. The range is given in statute miles (sm), and where two figures are given, they apply to the standard and optional fuel loads. Wherever possible, range is quoted for 65- or 75-percent power at optimum altitude allowing for reserves. Ceiling loosely refers to maximum service ceiling (all engines operating for multi-engine airplanes). Takeoff and landing distance refer to the total distance in feet needed to clear a 50-foot obstacle, unless otherwise specified as takeoff run or landing roll when only the runway length is measured (older airplanes were often rated this way).

Introduction

ON DECEMBER 17, 1903, THE WORLD WAS CHANGED FOREVER. The events of that day on a sandy beach in Kitty Hawk, North Carolina, brought forth by two brothers from Dayton, Ohio, ushered in a new era in technology, one that would change the course of history, the technology of the flying machine. In 1903, the idea and experimentation of man flying was nothing new. In fact, man had been enamored with flight ever since he first saw a bird take to the skies. The trick, of course, was to devise how man could emulate the bird and take leave of the earth's surface and soar on the winds and currents of air.

In the fifteenth century, Leonardo DaVinci built models and drew working drawings for manned flying machines and helicopters. The models proved that a heavier-than-air craft could indeed ride on currents of air. In 1783, the first successfully manned hot-air balloons were brought into vogue by Jacques and Joseph Montgolfier. These two French aeronaut brothers showed the world that man could indeed rise above the Earth and travel great distances in a relatively short time. The only drawback with balloon flight soon proved to be the lack of directional controllability. Nonetheless, man could fly.

Otto Lilienthal, in nineteenth-century Germany, constructed man-controlled gliders that greatly resembled our modern hang-gliders. Through his experimentation, Lilienthal proved that aircraft direction could be altered by the shifting of weight—in this case, the weight of the pilot. Gliders proved that man could indeed fly, but the real puzzle was how to get man to fly under his own controlled power. Also, to make manned flight really practical, he would have to be able to get airborne from level ground, fly to a destination, and land safely again on level ground.

Many different power supplies were tried, and many failed for one reason or another. At this point in the late nineteenth century, technological advancement in aviation began to take off, so to speak. Through their extensive experimentation, Orville and Wilbur Wright—the two brothers from Dayton who were proprietors of a bicycle shop—invented the first practical engine to power the first aeroplane. Centuries of the combined efforts of hundreds of inventors, scientists, mechanics, and dreamers finally became a reality on that windy and chilly day in December 1903.

Never in the history of man has a technology and its related sciences evolved so rapidly and in so many directions. In a hundred years, man has pushed the aviation envelope from a scant 100-yard straight-line flight to putting man and machinery into space, on the Moon, and beyond. We have seen aviation and the airplane shrink our planet by closing travel time from place to far-off place. We have seen the airplane become an instrument of leisurely joy, of hard-fought competition, and of terrifying war and destruction. Through every one of these avenues, the airplane and its form has progressed and in some cases regressed, but it has always evolved.

Advancements have made their way through by way of necessity and by way of luck through mistake. In peacetime, aircraft design and evolution progressed as a result of competitions and sport. The will of man to go farther and faster lead aircraft development through racing and record-setting. In the early years of aviation, there was a record to be set at every turn and a world of never-ending turns. When peacetime turned to wartime, worldwide government intervention accelerated aviation technology to a head-spinning pace as the need to gain the technological upper hand was always the difference between winning and losing in a given conflict. In times of postwar peacetime, technology took the form of creative checks and balances between nations and superpowers with surveillance and intelligence becoming the thrust of direction for aviation to take. Peeking into our neighbor's backyard became a dangerous game of cat and mouse.

Throughout the good times and the bad times, every aspect of the airplane has advanced in leaps and bounds. Engines and power systems have evolved.

Redundant systems have improved; building a better, stronger, lighter, more efficient, and safer system has become the norm. Navigational systems and avionics have become so advanced as to actually fly the aircraft themselves in order to reduce the in-cockpit workload for the pilot, so that his or her attentions can be more efficiently utilized.

With the skies becoming steadily crowded, the military technology of global positioning system (GPS) was made available to all general aviators to make navigating the skies more precise, less arduous, and safer in congested airspace. Now full glass-panel cockpits are showing up in even the most simple piston aircraft. Over the coming years, technologies in the cockpit and ahead of the firewall will surely continue to transform all levels of aviation.

We at Plane & Pilot Magazine have compiled the *International Aircraft Directory* to celebrate the technology of the airplane and aviation and to provide for readers an overview of aircraft history and its evolution. We say "overview" because it is not meant to be a comprehensive work. Of the tens of thousands of flying machines throughout history, here we only scratch the surface. We have indeed compiled the most popular and recognizable, as well as the most influential designs of the twentieth century from around the world to provide a reference tool for the aviation enthusiast.

We hope that this *International Aircraft Directory* will become a well-read, useful, and enjoyable addition to your aviation library.

The Editors of Plane & Pilot Magazine

Single-Engine Aircraft

The single-engine aircraft has remained throughout the history of aviation as the preeminent platform for airframe design. In the beginning, one engine was the logical choice for weight considerations. Also, engine technology was not advanced to the point of providing decent power-to-weight ratios that were attractive for the flying machines of that time. As engine power technology continued to develop, manned, powered flight and the single-engine aircraft were a natural combination as an economical and practical mode of personal transportation. For the sportsman aviator in today's world, it has remained the logical choice.

Today, the single engine airplane has become a showpiece for the modern technology boom. New designs have begun to flow again, many made of light-weight carbon fiber composite materials. Singles now come with a flurry of innovation, including airframe parachutes and all-glass flight decks. One-engine aircraft have also made substantial inroads into the business aircraft market, a domain previously occupied almost exclusively by multi-engine airplanes. Turboprop engines have proven themselves a reliable and significantly less costly way to get from point A to point B, guaranteeing single engine airplanes an important part of the future. Other jet-fuel operated singles, now with diesel engines, are growing in popularity around the world as the availability of aviation 100LL avgas becomes less certain. And the most prolific aircraft designer of all time, Burt Rutan, is building rocket-powered single-engine aircraft that fly to sub-orbital space. The following section is a testimonial to those aircraft which make up the past and the future of single-engine aircraft.

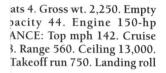

ats 4. Gross wt. 2,250. Empty
pacity 44. Engine 150-hp
ANCE: Top mph 142. Cruise
3. Range 560. Ceiling 13,000.
Takeoff run 750. Landing roll

a division of North American
he Lark in April 1968. It was
eeds of both the business and
asonable price. Equipped with
ne and a fixed-pitch prop, this
r unspectacular cruise perfor-
apability for its class. The his-
began in 1961 when Volaircraft
type approval for the Volaire
type version. The production
), received type certification in
d 150-hp. This design was ac-
nder 100. With the merger of
North American Rockwell the
is time to "Darter." The Lark
lution of the line featuring a
:, a more powerful engine, de-
e drag, and deluxe furnishing
troduction of the Aero Com-
ly Rockwell Commander 112),
went out of production in the

the automobile and powers the pusher propeller aft of the tail unit. When the flight section is detached, it can be towed by means of wheels inset in the wings. The Model I was replaced by a Model III that incorporated an improved fiberglass body and retractable wheels. The Model II was a non-roadable version that made use of the same wing and tail assembly as the Model I.

AERO COMMANDER "LARK"
1968–71

STANDARD DATA: Seats 4. Gross wt. 2,475. Empty wt. 1,532. Fuel capacity 44. Engine 180-hp Lycoming. PERFORMANCE: Top mph 138. Cruise mph 132. Stall mph 59. Initial climb rate 718. Range 525. Ceiling 11,000. Takeoff distance (50') 1,250. Landing distance (50') 1,280.

AERO COMMANDER 200
1958–67

STANDARD DATA: Seats 4. Gross wt. 3,000. Empty wt. 1,940. Fuel capacity 80. Engine 285-hp Lycoming. PERFORMANCE: Top mph 235. Cruise mph 215. Stall mph 54. Range 1,060. Ceiling 18,500. Initial climb rate 1,450. Takeoff run (50') 1,200. Landing distance (50') 1,150.

STANDARD DATA: Seats 4. Gross wt. 3,000. Empty wt. 1,870. Fuel capacity 80. Engine 260-hp Continental. PERFORMANCE: Top mph 208. Cruise mph 204. Stall mph 55. Range 1,300. Initial climb rate 1,350. Ceiling 21,000.

The Aero Commander 200 began as a product of the Meyers Aircraft Co. In its hands, the airplane evolved from the two-place Meyers 145 to the Meyers 200 that was initially produced with a 240-hp engine. Small numbers of this model were produced until the design was acquired by Aero Commander in 1965. On the part of Aero Commander, it was an apparent move to acquire a foothold in the single-engine retractable field with a design that had already established a reputation for high performance for its size and power. During its nine years of production, the Aero Commander 200 was upgraded in horsepower from 260 hp to 285 hp. With the larger engine, the airplane had a top speed of 235 mph and a cruise speed of 215 mph. Fuel consumption was only 12 gph. Takeoff and landing distances were also minimal, and the gear was sturdy enough to extend up to speeds of 210 mph. Though the airplane was high-spirited and somewhat temperamental, it achieved a strong following for its speed and outstanding flight characteristics. An interesting modification of this design, called the Interceptor 400, was tested by the Interceptor Corp. Equipped with an AiResearch turboprop powerplant flat-rated at 400 shp, cruising speeds in excess of 280 mph were reported.

AERONCA C-2
1929

STANDARD DATA: Seats 1. Gross wt. 700. Empty wt. 426. Engine 26-hp Aeronca two-cylinder. PERFORMANCE: Top mph 75. Cruise mph 60. Range 200. Initial climb rate 450.

Cincinnati's Aeronautical Corp. of America debuted the Aeronca C-2 at the Los Angeles Air Races of 1929. It was the first truly light plane to be manufactured in quantity. Despite the obvious limitations of its 26-hp engine, specifically designed for use in the company's light aircraft, performance was said to be good. Construction of the C-2 was conventional, utilizing a high-braced wing with two spruce spars and a welded steel-tube fuselage covered with fabric. Production totaled 112, including the C-2 Deluxe version, which featured a 36-hp Aeronca powerplant. The increased horsepower added about 20 mph to the C-2's top speed and cruise speed but limited its range to 175 miles.

AERONCA C-3
1934

STANDARD DATA: Seats 2. Gross wt. 1,005. Empty wt. 569. Engine 40-hp Aeronca two-cylinder. PERFORMANCE: Top mph 95. Cruise mph 87. Range 200. Ceiling 12,000. Initial climb rate 450.

The Aeronca C-3 was an offshoot of the C-2 Deluxe. Introduced in 1934, it was similar to the C-2 in structure but was expanded to accommodate side-by-side seating for two. The C-3 was produced in two versions. The Master was changed to an enclosed cabin design. The Collegian retained the open cockpit styling and is easily confused with its C-2 predecessor. By this time, the production of both the engine and airframe of the Aeronca took place in Britain where several are still active. In this country, roughly 17 are still flying with the original Aeronca engine. Others in use have Lycomings and Continentals installed.

AERONCA L
1935

STANDARD DATA: Seats 2. Gross wt. 1,680. Empty wt. 1,036. Engine 70-hp Le Blond radial. PERFORMANCE: Top mph 115. Cruise mph 100. Initial climb rate 500.

The Aeronca L cabin monoplane was the Aeronautical Corporation of America's first attempt at constructing a low-wing side-by-side cabin airplane. It was produced in four versions: the LA with a 70-hp Le Blond, the LB using an 85-hp LeBlond, the LC using a 90-hp Warner Scarab Junior, and the LD powered by a 90-hp Lambert. The airframe of the Model I is of conventional mixed construction. The wings were built around a structure of spruce spars and ribs. The fuselage was a framework of welded steel tubing. Both the fuselage and the wings were covered with fabric.

AERONCA 65TC & L-3
1939

STANDARD DATA: Seats 2. Gross wt. 1,260. Empty wt. 793. Fuel capacity 12. Engine 65-hp Continental. PERFORMANCE: Top mph 95. Cruise mph 87. Landing mph 42. Range 225. Initial climb rate 450. Ceiling 10,000.

STANDARD DATA: (Model K) Seats 2. Gross wt. 1,040. Empty wt. 590. Fuel capacity 10. Engine 36-hp Aeronca E-113C. PERFORMANCE: Top mph 80. Cruise mph 70. Stall mph 35. Initial climb rate 400. Ceiling 12,500. Range 175.

The Aeronca C-3 evolved into the Aeronca K Scout in 1937. In turn, the K evolved into the SOC Chief in 1938. The latter was propelled by 50-hp Franklin or Lycoming engine options. In 1939, the 65-series appeared and featured the 65hp Continental option. The 65-series is currently the most abundant version. The 65TC Defender, a tandem two-seat trainer, was widely used throughout the war, particularly in the Civilian Pilot Training Program. The Model L-3, the military version of the same airplane, featured a wider fuselage and larger window area to facilitate its role as an observation plane. Although provided with dual controls, the L-3 was designed to be flown from the front seat. The observer's seat might face forward or aft. Many of the planes reached civilian hands after World War II.

AERONCA 7AC CHAMPION
1945–48

STANDARD DATA: (7AC) Seats 2. Gross wt. 1,220. Empty wt. 740. Fuel capacity 13. Engine 65-hp Continental. PERFORMANCE: Top mph 95. Cruise mph 85. Stall mph 38. Initial climb rate 370. Range 270. Ceiling 12,500. Takeoff distance (50) 632. Landing distance (50') 885.

STANDARD DATA: (7AC) Seats 2. Gross wt. 1,300. Empty wt. 810. Fuel capacity 18.5. Engine 85-hp

Continental. PERFORMANCE: Top mph 102. Cruise mph 92. Stall mph 44. Initial climb rate 750. Range 315.

STANDARD DATA: (7EC) Seats 2. Gross wt. 1,450. Empty wt. 820. Fuel capacity 18.5-24. Engine 90-hp Continental. PERFORMANCE: Top mph 135. Cruise mph 100. Stall mph 40. Initial climb rate 315.

Though similar to the prewar L-3, the Champion is in reality a tandem version of the Chief series. The original Champ, which first flew in 1944, was powered by a 65-hp Continental engine and was designated the 7AC. The design proved to be popular, and Aeronca increased the plane's power rating to 85 hp before the Champion Aircraft Corp. acquired the tooling and rights to the design in 1951. Over 10,000 Model 7s were turned out by Aeronca between 1946 and 1951. In 1955, the Champion firm reinstituted production of the 90-hp version, the Model 7EC Traveller. Production continued with minor refinements until 1964 when production tapered off in favor of the 7ECA, a further improved version of the original airframe.

AERONCA 11AC/11CC
1938–46

STANDARD DATA: (Chief) Seats 2. Gross wt. 1,155. Empty wt. 675. Fuel capacity 12. Engine 65-hp Lycoming. PERFORMANCE: Top mph 105. Cruise

mph 95. Stall mph 37. Initial climb rate 600. Ceiling 14,000. Range 240.

STANDARD DATA: (Super Chief) Seats 2. Gross wt. 1,350. Empty wt. 820. Fuel capacity 23. Engine 85-hp Continental. PERFORMANCE: Top mph 110. Cruise mph 97. Stall mph 43. Initial climb rate 650. Ceiling 14,500. Range 370. Takeoff (50') 620. Landing (50') 860.

After World War II, the Chief was introduced as the Model II AC. It was a variation of the Model 7 Champion and differed primarily by having increased fuselage width to permit side-by-side seating and a lowered cowling line to permit better visibility. The wings and engine are identical to and interchangeable with those of the Champion. The IIAC was powered by a 65-hp Continental. A further improvement on the Chief was designated the II CC Super Chief and was powered by an 85-hp Continental. It featured new balanced elevator surfaces to meet new trim requirements called for in the Civil Air Regulations. Its cruise speed was 95 mph, and its climb rate was 600 fpm. The Chief is the version that is still present in the greatest numbers.

AERONCA 15AC "SEDAN"
1948–50

STANDARD DATA: Seats 4. Gross wt. 2,050. Empty wt. 1,150. Fuel capacity 40. Engine 145-hp Continental. PERFORMANCE: Top mph 120. Cruise mph 105. Stall mph 53. Initial climb rate 650. Range 430. Ceiling 12,400.

The last civilian airplane to be produced by the Aeronca Manufacturing Corp., the 15AC Sedan, was also Aeronca's first four-seater airplane. A prototype appeared in 1947, and production began in 1948. The Sedan soon became a familiar sight at civilian fields. A large number of Sedans were built, and over 200 of them are still active today. It featured an all-metal construction with a metal-skinned single-spar wing and fabric-covered, welded, steel-tube fuselage. Optional Franklin 165-hp engines were fitted into a few 15AC Sedans. Another option put the Aeronca on floats, and that version was called the S15AC.

ALL AMERICAN "ENSIGN"
1945

STANDARD DATA: Seats 2. Gross wt. 1,150. Empty wt. 900. Engine 85-hp Continental. PERFORMANCE: Top mph 125. Cruise mph 112. Initial climb rate 700. Ceiling 14,000. Range 400.

All American Aircraft, Inc., originally specialized in subcontract work but eventually designed and built the two-place Ensign. The plane subsequently took to the air for the first time in 1945. The original plans called for engines ranging from 85 to 125 hp. Seating was side-by-side fashion under an unusually large, blown plexiglass canopy on the prototype. Full dual controls were optional. The Ensign was of all-metal construction with a semi-monocoque fuselage with low wings and fixed landing gear.

AMERICAN CHAMPION "CITABRIA"/ "SUPER DECATHALON"/"SCOUT"
1988–Present

Citabria

Citabria Explorer

Super Decathlon

Scout

STANDARD DATA: Citabria Aurora Seats 2. Gross wt. 1,750. Empty wt. 1,120. Fuel capacity 36. Engine 118-hp Lycoming 0-235-K2C. PERFORMANCE: Top Cruise 109 KTAS. Initial climb rate 740 fpm. Ceiling 11,500. Stall 47 kts. Takeoff distance ground roll 650'. Landing distance roll 520'.

STANDARD DATA: Citabria Adventure/Explorer Seats 2. Gross wt. 1,750/1,800. Empty wt. 1,200/1,250. Fuel capacity 36. Engine 160-hp Lycoming 0-320-B2B. PERFORMANCE: Top Cruise 127 KTAS. Initial climb rate 1,167/1,130 fpm. Ceiling 15,000/15,500. Stall 47/42 kts. Takeoff distance ground roll 430/412'. Landing distance roll 480/360'.

STANDARD DATA: Super Decathlon Seats 2. Gross wt. 1,950. Empty wt. 1,340. Fuel capacity 40. Engine 180-hp Lycoming AEI0-360-H1B. PERFORMANCE: Top Cruise 142 KTAS. Initial climb rate 1,280 fpm. Ceiling 15,800. Stall 48 kts. Takeoff distance ground roll 495. Landing distance roll 425'.

STANDARD DATA: Scout Seats 2. Gross wt. 2,150. Empty wt. 1,400. Fuel capacity 36-72. Engine 180-hp Lycoming 0-360-C1G. PERFORMANCE: Top Cruise 109 KTAS. Initial climb rate 1,075 fpm. Ceiling 17,000. Stall 45 kts. Takeoff distance ground roll 490'. Landing distance roll 420'.

American Champion became somewhat of a legend when it rescued the Bellanca Super Decathlon from extinction. The company now owns the type certificate to the Model 7 and Model 8 Champion Line (Champs, Challengers, Citabrias, Decathlons, Scouts). American Champion switched to metal wing spars, replacing the wooden ones championed by Giuseppe Bellanca, and now manufactures five models of the distinctive high wing aircraft—three Citabrias, the Aurora, Adventure and Explorer, as well as the Super Decathlon and Scout. American Champion aircraft are popular as tailwheel trainers, aerobatic trainers as well as backcountry bush aircraft.

AIRCRAFT MANUFACTURING & DEVELOPMENT "ALARUS"
1995–Present

STANDARD DATA: Seats 2. Gross wt. 1,692. Empty wt. 1,085. Engine 116-hp Lycoming 0-235-N2C. Fuel 28. PERFORMANCE: Cruise 99 kts. Stall 48 kts. Initial Climb Rate 750 fpm. Takeoff (50') 1,640'. Landing (50') 1,820'.

With its legacy in the kit plane industry, the Zenith CH2000 received FAA certification to become the Alarus. The all-metal airframe and carbine fiber cockpit is aimed at the flight training market, though the two-seater is approved for Day/Night VFR/IFR to satisfy personal transportation needs. In 2005, Alarus was redesigned to include a larger cabin, tougher landing gear and airbags for each seat.

AMERICAN EAGLE
1925

STANDARD DATA: Seats 3. Gross wt. 2,057. Empty wt. 1,227. Engine 90-hp Curtiss eight-cylinder, water-cooled. PERFORMANCE: Top mph 101. Cruise mph 85. Landing mph 30. Initial Climb Rate 575. Range 425. Ceiling 12,000.

The American Eagle Aircraft Corporation was established in 1925. Its president was E.E. Porterfield, who later founded the Porterfield Aircraft Corp. The American Eagle open-cockpit, three-seat biplane was powered by a 90-hp, water-cooled Curtiss engine; its radiator was fitted under the fuselage and featured adjustable shutters. A later model of the biplane was powered by a 100-hp Kinner five-cylinder aircooled radial engine. The three occupants are seated with one in the rear seat and two side-by-side in the front seat. Its construction made use of wooden wings and a steel-tube fuselage. It originally sold for $2,995.

AMERICAN EAGLECRAFT "EAGLET"
1929–66

STANDARD DATA: (1930) Seats 2. Gross wt. 922. Empty wt. 509. Engine 45-hp Szekely, three-cylinder radial. PERFORMANCE: Top mph 90. Cruise mph 75. Landing mph 25. Initial climb rate 700. Ceiling 14,500.

STANDARD DATA: (1965) Seats 2. Gross wt. 1,050. Empty wt. 638. Engine 50-hp Continental. PERFORMANCE: Top mph 92. Cruise mph 75. Landing mph 28. Initial climb rate 700. Range 225. Ceiling 14,500.

The Eaglet, a light two-seat monoplane, endured several changes in ownership during its lifetime. It was originally built by the American Eagle Aircraft Corp. In 1931, its production was taken over by the American Eagle-Lincoln Aircraft Company when its parent company merged with the Lincoln Aircraft Company. In the same year, the company changed its name to the Victor H. Roose Aircraft Co. The Roose company continued the production of the Eaglet powered by a Szekely radial engine. Its braced high-wing structure was of the conventional wooden two-spar type with fabric covering. The fuselage utilized a rectangular structure of welded steel tubes and was also covered with fabric. Its single large cockpit had room for two to sit in tandem fashion with dual controls. The Eaglet's production was taken over by the American Eaglecraft Co. in the 1960s. The company built an aircraft that was basically a modernized version of the famous Eaglet of the 1930s.

ANDERSON GREENWOOD
1950

STANDARD DATA: Seats 2. Gross wt. 1,400. Empty wt. 850. Fuel capacity 23. Engine 90-hp Continental. PERFORMANCE: Top mph 120. Cruise mph 110. Ceiling 19,000. Initial climb rate 750. Landing speed 49.

The Anderson Greenwood enjoyed an extremely short production life. First produced in 1950, only four aircraft were completed before production was terminated. Today, only two are active. The twin-boom tail assembly and pusher design of the Anderson Greenwood made for easy cabin entry (like that of an automobile), propeller safety, and excellent visibility. The aircraft was designed in the late 1940s by three engineers, Anderson, Greenwood, and Slaughter, the latter being left out of the plane's name for obvious reasons. Cessna later imitated the Anderson Greenwood's design with the one-time experimental XMC. Occupants are seated in side-by-side fashion, and the cockpit has dual controls. There is a door on each side of the cabin.

APEX AIRCRAFT "ROBIN"/"CAP 10"
1957–Present

Robin

Cap 10

STANDARD DATA: Robin 140 Seats 4. Gross wt. 2,204. Useful Load 926. Fuel capacity 29. Engine 160-hp Lycoming 0-320. PERFORMANCE: Top Cruise 128 kts. Initial climb rate 870 fpm. Range 500 nm. Take off (50') 1,591'. Landing (50') 1,541'.

STANDARD DATA: CAP10C Seats 2. Gross wt. 1,830. Empty wt. 1,190. Fuel capacity 32. Engine 180-hp Lycoming AEIO-360 B2F. PERFORMANCE: Top Cruise 153 kts. Stall mph 53 kts. Initial climb rate 1,600 fpm. Ceiling 16,400'. Range 600 nm. Load limit +6g/-4g.

Apex International is a French-owned holding company, manufacturing the Robin and the CAP series of aircraft. Due to the legacy of both designs, more than 4,000 of those airframes are already on the market. The CAP10 is a two-place side-by-side low wing that has been a mainstay aerobatic aircraft for more than three decades, and variants of the original design, most notably the CAP232, have logged a number of world championships. In 2004, the CAP10C received FAA certification in the United States. Earlier that year, Apex modified the wing to improve the roll rate and overall strength. The original Robin got its name from Pierre Robin, who initiated development in 1957. Because he was not only a pilot but also a cabinetmaker, Robins are part wood, part composite. Construction of the Robin moved from Europe to New Zealand, with the first aircraft rolling off the production line in mid-2005. Three models, the 120, 135CDI and Robin 140 vary primarily in horsepower, accompanied by the expected performance changes.

AQUILA AERO "A210"

STANDARD DATA: Seats 2. Gross wt. 1,654. Empty wt. 1,080. Fuel capacity 32. Engine 100-hp Rotax 912S. PERFORMANCE: Top Cruise 130 kts. Stall mph 43 kts. Initial climb rate 750 fpm. Ceiling 14,500. Range 535 nm. Takeoff roll 820'. Landing Roll 650'.

The Aquila A210 is a German-made fiber composite construction. The two-seater is designed for cruising, training and aero-tow applications. Electric Fowler flaps and a constant speed prop give it excellent low-speed control, and short landing capabilities. The canopy configuration offers exceptional visibility. The aircraft is FAA-certified for DAY/VFR.

ARROW SPORT F
1936

STANDARD DATA: Seats 2. Gross wt. 1,675. Empty wt. 1,172. Fuel capacity 20. Engine 82-hp Ford V-8. PERFORMANCE: Top mph 100. Cruise mph 95. Stall mph 38. Initial climb rate 700. Ceiling 12,000. Range 300.

The Arrow Sport F came about when the Bureau of Air Commerce awarded the Arrow Aircraft and Motor Corp. a contract to design and build a lightplane that could be powered by a modified eight-cylinder automobile engine. It was the fourth such airplane to be ordered by the Development Section to investigate the possibilities of using cheap, mass-produced automobile engines. The resulting Arrow Sport F (or V-8) was a side-by-side monoplane of mixed construction with a two-spar fabric-covered wing and a fabric-covered steel-tube fuselage. It was available in three models: "The Master," which was a standard open-cockpit type; "The Master Coupe," which was fitted with a coupe top; and the "De Luxe Coupe," which had a deluxe finish and was fitted with blind-flying instruments, wheel pants, and other accessories. The engine chosen was a converted Ford V-8 air-cooled powerplant. Several Arrow Sport Fs are still registered.

ARCTIC "TERN"

STANDARD DATA: Seats 2. Gross wt. 1,900. Empty wt. 1,073. Fuel capacity 40. Engine 160-hp Lycoming. PERFORMANCE: Top mph 117. Cruise mph 112. Stall mph 34. Initial climb rate 1,275. Ceiling 21,000. Range 650. Takeoff (50') 500. Landing (50') 350.

The old tandem Interstate trainer was reborn when the Arctic Aircraft Co. decided to develop the Tern bush plane. The Interstate's rugged design and construction make it ideal for operating in remote areas on unimproved fields, sandbars, and beaches. Manufactured in Alaska, there are several features that bring the old trainer up to date. The Tern features a high gross weight (1,900 pounds under State of Alaska commercial requirements) and large balanced control surfaces. Its NACA 23012 airfoil design affords a wide center of gravity range with the famous floating characteristic of the Taylorcraft. A semi-Fowler slotted flap gives the pilot complete control and allows the slowest flight and slowest stall speed available in the lightplane field. The Tern is also designed for the mechanic because all components are readily accessible for inspection and maintenance. It can be easily fitted with floats, skis, or high-flotation tires to meet the bush pilot's choice of terrain.

AUSTER
1942–68

STANDARD DATA: Seats 2. Gross wt. 2,200. Empty wt. 1,480. Fuel capacity 19. Engine 145-hp de Havilland Gipsy Major. PERFORMANCE: Top mph 122. Cruise mph 107. Stall mph 34. Initial climb rate 660. Range 315. Ceiling 12,000. Takeoff run 375. Landing roll 270.

The Auster was a continuation of the British Taylorcraft Model D, which was in turn produced under license from Taylorcraft in the United States. The first Austers were produced in 1942 as air observation-post monoplanes powered by 130-hp Gipsy Major engines. Later versions were fined with various powerplants including: 130, 160, and 180-hp Lycomings; 75hp Continental; 145-hp Gipsy Major; and 100-hp Blackburn Cirrus Minor. Most had accommodations for two seated in tandem fashion, but some were converted to three- and fourseaters. In 1962, Auster Aircraft, Ltd. was absorbed into Beagle Aircraft, Ltd. and became Beagle Auster. The Husky was introduced in 1960 with a 160-hp Lycoming and then in 1962 with a 180-hp Lycoming. The Terrior, a redesigned version of the early MK 6, was produced in 1961 with the same 145-hp de Havilland powerplant.

AVIAT AIRCRAFT "HUSKY"/"PITTS"
1987–Present

Husky

Pitts S-2C

STANDARD DATA: Husky A-1B Seats 2. Gross wt. 2,000. Empty wt. 1,155. Fuel capacity 29. Engine 180-hp Lycoming 0-360-A1P . PERFORMANCE: Top speed 126 kts. Cruise 121 kts. Stall 37 kts. Initial climb rate 1,500 fpm. Range 686 nm. Ceiling 20,000. Takeoff distance 200'. Landing distance 350'.

STANDARD DATA: Pitts S-2C 2. Gross wt. 1,700. Empty wt. 1,090. Fuel capacity 29. Engine 260-hp Lycoming AEIO-540. PERFORMANCE: Max Cruise 169 kts. Stall 56 kts. Initial climb rate 2,900 fpm. Range 284 sm. Takeoff distance 554'. Landing distance (50') 1,430.

Located in Afton, Wyoming, Aviat specializes in sport and utility aircraft. The company manufactures two certified aircraft, the Husky and the Pitts, as well as the kit-built Eagle II. The Husky A1-A was certified in 1987 and based loosely on Piper's talented Super

Cub. The tandem two-seater quickly became one of the world's most popular bush planes. The latest generation, the Husky A-1B continues the tradition. The sturdy taildragger has tremendous short and soft field abilities even with a healthy load and functions on wheels, floats or skis. Aviat refined the design in 2005, improving the ailerons and flaps, as well as offering the Husky with an optional 200-hp powerplant and composite 82" propeller.

The Pitts is one of the world's great aerobatic aircraft and in fact the only FAA certified competition airplane made in the U.S. Designed by the legendary Curtis Pitts in the mid-1940s, an early version of the unlimited category biplane now hangs in the Smithsonian Air and Space Museum in Washington, DC, as well as other museums around the world. The most current model of the +6G/-5G Pitts is the S-2C.

BEAGLE "PUP"
1968–71

STANDARD DATA: Seats 2-4. Gross wt. 1,900. Empty wt. 1,090. Fuel capacity 29-41. Engine 150-hp Lycoming. PERFORMANCE: Top mph 139. Cruise mph 129. Stall mph 56. Initial climb rate 840. Range 417-605. Ceiling 14,000. Takeoff distance (50') 1,350. Landing distance (50') 1,430.

An aerobatic lightplane, the Pup was built by Beagle Aircraft in England. The Pup was sold in three models: the Pup-100, -150, and -180. The Pup-100 model carries two seats and two optional children's seats. It is powered by a 100-hp Rolls-Royce/Continental four-cylinder engine. Production of the Pup-100 began in February 1968. The Pup-150 is quite similar to the Pup-100. The fuselage is only three inches longer while wingspan dimensions of the low-wing tricycle gear airplane remain the same. A 150-hp Lycoming engine allows optional seating for four. The Pup-150 also offered a larger 34-Imperial-gallon fuel tank as opposed to the standard 24 Imperial-gallon tank installed as standard equipment in the -100 and -150 models. A large rudder on the -150 allows full aerobatics including unlimited spinning. The Pup-180 is also very similar to the Pup-100 but has a full four seats and is fitted with a 180-hp four-cylinder Lycoming engine. Many of the Pup-180s produced were exported.

BEECHCRAFT "STAGGERWING"
1932–48

STANDARD DATA: (G-17S) Seats 4-5. Gross wt. 4,250. Empty wt. 2,800. Fuel capacity 170. Engine 450-hp Pratt & Whitney Wasp Junior. PERFORMANCE: Top mph 212. Cruise mph 201. Stall mph 60. Initial climb rate 1,500. Ceiling 20,000. Range 1,300. Takeoff distance (50) 1,130. Landing distance (50) 980.

One of the all-time classic airplanes produced in the United States is the Beech Staggerwing. The original version of the Model 17 was first flown in 1932 and was powered by a 420-hp Wright Whirlwind. The next preproduction model was fitted with a 690-hp Wright Cyclone, but although the basic design would appear to give stable flight characteristics, the horsepower was excessive, resulting in "porpoising" due to the short fuselage. The first production model, built from 1934 to 1936, was the B17 powered by a 285-hp Jacobs (B17B), a 285-hp Wright (B17E), a 225-hp Jacobs (B17L), or a 420-hp Wright (B17R). In fact, throughout the Staggerwing's production, no less than eight different engines ranging from 225 hp to 690 hp were used. The most popular model was the D17S with a 420-hp Pratt & Whitney R-985 Wasp Junior nine-cylinder air-cooled radial engine built from 1937 to 1945. The C17 was produced from 1936 to 1937; the E17 was built from 1937 to 1944; the F17 was built for the military from 1938 to 1944; and the last in the series was the G17 built from 1946 to 1948.

An early refinement of this classic five-seater was the installation of the retractable landing gear system, but the most significant feature was the negative stagger of the wings. There are many reasons for this design, beginning with the fact that automatic stability in a stall is achieved because the lower wing stalls first and, since it's in a forward position, lowers the nose of the airplane before the upper wing has a chance to stall. The upper wing retains its lift, and that wing's position above the center of gravity provides pendulous stability at stall speeds. Additionally, the negative stagger permits good pilot visibility to the side and back and allows for a flat bottom on the fuselage, which enables belly landings to be made without any possibility of nosing over. Cabin doors can be entered without interference from the lower wing, and servicemen can stand on the lower leading wing to reach the fuel ports in the upper wing.

After World War II, approximately 20 G17 models were built and sold new for $29,000. They were fitted with enclosed gear fairings, cowl flaps, a longer windshield, larger vertical fin, and the engine was moved forward 12 inches. At 9,700 feet, pulling 65% power, the G17 exceeds 200 mph. Most of the time it cruises at 53% power at 185 mph, burning around 22 gph with its 450-hp radial. Six fuel tanks (two in the upper wing, two in the lower wing, one forward fuselage tank, and one rear fuselage tank) carry 179 gallons to yield a 7-hour endurance or 1,300-mile range. A total of 781 Staggerwings were built, of which 353 were commercial and 428 were for the military.

BEECHCRAFT "SKIPPER"
1979–81

STANDARD DATA: Seats 2. Gross wt. 1,675. Empty wt. 1,100. Fuel capacity 30. Engine 115-hp Lycoming. PERFORMANCE: Top mph 122. Cruise mph 121. Stall mph 54. Initial climb rate 720. Ceiling 12,900. Takeoff distance (50') 1,280. Landing distance (50') 1,313. Range 447.

Originally designated the PD 28'S, this single-engine trainer was first delivered in early 1979. A low-wing T-tail model, it was powered by a four-cylinder Lycoming engine rated at 115 hp at 2,700 RPM. The Skipper's canopy-type cabin gives the instructor and student pilot optimum, all-around visibility, while both left and right doors provide for convenient entry. An external tunnel on the bottom of the fuselage houses primary controls and makes for additional cabin room, as well as allowing for easy maintenance.

A new concept in airfoil design was utilized by the Skipper. Its airfoil section is an outgrowth of NASA's high-speed, super-critical airfoil technology and provides a lower drag, higher lift capability. The T-tail configuration places the horizontal stabilizer above the slipstream in undisturbed air to give smoother flight and more positive control during landing maneuvers.

The Skipper is the third Beechcraft T-tail model, following the Super King Air and Duchess. A substantial portion of its construction is bonded metal, including the lower cabin section of the fuselage, the entire wing, the leading edge of the vertical stabilizer, the trim tabs, and the rudder.

The landing gear is a low-maintenance, spring system designed for sturdiness and utility. Control response is superbly balanced, and the ailerons are quite frisky in all speed ranges right down to the stall. Stalling the Skipper is almost fun. The wings give lots of prestall buffetto let you know that it is about to quit flying. For cross-country flights, the 29 gallons of usable fuel combine with a 65% power setting to yield a 4.6-hour endurance. Only 312 of these two-place trainers were built before production was halted abruptly in 1981.

BEECHCRAFT SPORT 150
1966–78

STANDARD DATA: (Sport) Seats 2-4. Gross wt. 2,150. Empty wt. 1,423. Fuel capacity 57. Engine 150-hp Lycoming. PERFORMANCE: Top mph 127. Cruise mph 123. Stall mph 57. Initial climb rate 680. Ceiling 11,650. Range 622. Takeoff distance (50') 1,635. Landing distance (50') 1,693.

STANDARD DATA: (Sport III) Seats 2-4. Gross wt. 2,350. Empty wt. 1,365. Fuel capacity 60. Engine 150-hp Lycoming. PERFORMANCE: Top mph 140. Cruise mph 13 1. Stall mph 55. Initial climb rate 740. Ceiling 11,900. Range 883. Takeoff distance (50') 1,255. Landing distance (50') 1,220.

Primarily designed as a two-place trainer, the Sport III was introduced in 1965 along with the Super III as a complement to the existing Musketeer A23/Custom III. It was powered by a 150-hp Lycoming engine turning a fixed-pitch prop and could be outfitted with an optional rear seat for two additional passengers but not without a loss in maximum range. With four adults (and no baggage aboard) the range was reduced by more than half due to fuel weight limitations. The Sport III was also available in an aerobatic version.

Like all Musketeers, the Sport made use of a honeycomb wing structure and bonded skins that reduce rivet-head drag and add to the plane's sleek appearance. In 1972, Beech changed the names of its other Musketeers but retained the Sport. The term Musketeer was dropped and the line of light Beechcrafts was known as the Aero Center line. Later, fuel capacity in all models was increased by five gallons and for the first time all three Aero Center models could be equipped with EdoAire Mitchell Century III autopilots. In 1979, this 150-hp version of the original Musketeer design was replaced by the Skipper 77 as Beechcraft's trainer model in its Aero Center line.

BEECHCRAFT CUSTOM 180 "SUNDOWNER"
1962–83

STANDARD DATA: (Sundowner) Seats 4. Gross wt. 2,450. Empty wt. 1,505. Fuel capacity 57. Engine 180-hp Lycoming. PERFORMANCE: Top mph 141. Cruise mph 127. Stall mph 59. Initial climb rate 792. Ceiling 12,600. Range 670. Takeoff distance (50') 1,955. Landing distance (50') 1,484.

STANDARD DATA: (Musketeer Custom III) Seats 4. Gross wt. 2,450. Empty wt. 1,365. Fuel capacity 60. Engine 165-hp Lycoming. PERFORMANCE: Top mph 146. Cruise mph 138. Stall mph 58. Initial climb rate 728. Ceiling 11,870. Range 906. Takeoff distance (50') 1,460. Landing distance (50') 1,260.

The first of Beech's "Three Musketeers" was introduced to the flying public in 1962 as a four-place, 160-hp Model 23. More than 500 of these 23s had been sold when a redesigned model, the A-23, went into production in 1964. The A-23, powered by a 165-hp fuel-injected Continental engine, had an increased landing flap angle and a restyled interior. This Musketeer became the Custom III in 1966 when it was joined by the Super III and the Sport III. An acrobatic version of the Musketeer Sport III joined the fleet in 1968, and an acrobatic version of the Custom made its debut in 1969. Beech redesigned the Musketeer fuselage in 1970, giving it rounded sides and more cabin room. The panel was improved extensively and a third side window was added. When names were changed in 1972, the Cus-

tom became the Sundowner. Like other models, the Sundowner is also available with an autopilot, and its useful fuel has been boosted to 57 gallons. This extra gasoline translates into greater range and 30 pounds of additional useful load. The Sundowner is equipped with a fixed-pitch propeller and non-retractable landing gear. An Aerobatic version was available and approved for rolls, Immelmann turns, loops, spins, chandelles, and the like.

BEECHCRAFT "SIERRA"/"SUPER"/ "SUPER 200"
1966–83

STANDARD DATA: (Sierra) Seats 6. Gross wt. 2,750. Empty wt. 1,701. Fuel capacity 57. Engine 200-hp fuel-injected Lycoming. PERFORMANCE: Top mph 163. Cruise mph 158. Stall mph 69. Initial climb rate 927. Ceiling 15,385. Range 744. Takeoff distance (50') 1,561. Landing distance (50') 1,462.

STANDARD DATA: (Super III) Seats 4. Gross wt. 2,450. Empty wt. 1,365. Fuel capacity 60. Engine 200-hp Lycoming. PERFORMANCE: Top mph 158. Cruise mph 150. Stall mph 61. Initial climb rate 880. Ceiling 14,850. Range 823. Takeoff distance (50') 1,380. Landing distance (50') 1,300.

The classiest of the Musketeers in 1966 was the Super III with 200 hp, six seats optional, a constant-speed prop, and non-retractable landing gear. In 1970, a retractable version was added to the Musketeer line, the Super R. Both models were continued through the next year, when the fixed-gear model was dropped. As part of the Aero Center line, the 200-hp retractable version became known as the Sundowner. The name changes and the "cleaning up" of the Musketeer line was all part of a major corporate redirection by Beech management to devote more attention to the small airplanes. Beech Aero Centers were set up around the country, franchised just to sell the Sport, Sundowner and Sierra. More recent Sierras benefit from increased useful fuel, an optional autopilot, a larger diameter propeller, and wheel well fairings. The result is increased range, a greater rate of climb, and a higher cruise speed and service ceiling.

BEECHCRAFT T-34 MENTOR
1953–58

STANDARD DATA: Seats 2. Gross wt. 2,950. Empty wt. 2,156. Fuel capacity 50. Engine 225-hp Continental. PERFORMANCE: Top mph 189. Cruise mph 173. Stall mph 53. Initial climb rate 1,120. Range 975. Ceiling 20,000. Takeoff distance (50') 1,200. Landing distance (50') 960.

An outstanding buy in a military surplus aircraft, when you can find one, is the Beech T-34 Mentor. Built originally for the U.S. Air Force and Navy pilot training programs, a few are found now in civilian life. In Japan, the Fuji Company built 176 T-34s for Japanese and Philippine military forces. The Canadian Car and Foundry produced 125 Mentors, and an additional 75 were assembled in Argentina. The tandem two-seaters are today highly prized for civilian use since they are fully aerobatic if all FAA maintenance advisory bulletins have been followed. A series of in-flight wing failures has led to a number of airworthiness directives as well.

The Mentor makes wide use of standard parts from the Beech Bonanza. The landing gear was designed to survive the hard simulated carrier landings practiced by student pilots. Mentors are often found in military flying clubs and, due to top military maintenance, are usually in top condition. If you can find a T-34 with all airplane logs complete, you're no doubt getting an excellent plane for your money. Under a U.S. Navy development program, Beech has upgraded T-34 Mentors to turbine-powered YT-34s. Using only 400-hp from the 715-hp turbine engine, the modified aircraft have exceeded 275 mph. The ultimate objective was to provide all-new turbine-powered aircraft in the Navy pilot training program.

BEECHCRAFT MODEL 33 "BONANZA"/ "DEBONAIR"
1960–94

STANDARD DATA: (F-33A) Seats 6. Gross wt. 3,400. Empty wt. 2,125. Fuel capacity 74. Engine 285-hp fuel-injected Continental. PERFORMANCE: Top mph 209. Cruise mph 198. Stall mph 59. Initial climb rate 1,167. Ceiling 17,858. Range 824. Takeoff distance (50) 1,769. Landing distance (50') 1,324.

STANDARD DATA: (Debonair) Seats 4-5. Gross wt. 2,900. Empty wt. 1,730. Fuel capacity 64. Engine 225-hp Continental. PERFORMANCE: Top mph 195. Cruise mph 185. Stall mph 60. Initial climb rate 930. Range 650. Ceiling 17,800. Takeoff distance (50') 1,288. Landing distance (50') 1,298.

The Model 33 Debonair flew for the first time in September 1959. It was basically similar to the Model 35 Bonanza, but had a conventional tail assembly in place of the "V"-type tail. The Debonair was produced in four-seat versions with a 225-hp Continental, six-cylinder engine. It had a simplified interior and less elaborate equipment than the Model 35. In 1961, the aileron and elevator trim tabs were improved, and larger rear windows and a restyled cabin interior with bucket-seats were featured. In 1966, the option of a 285hp powerplant was added.

The Debonair name was dropped in 1967 and the subsequent aircraft, now a part of the Bonanza family, were simply designated E33, F33 and G33. During these years all model numbers ending in "A" featured the 285-hp Continental. All others retained the 225-hp engine. In 1972, the G33 was introduced with a 260-hp Continental. Currently, only the F-33A remains in production. Since its introduction as the Beechcraft Debonair, approximately 3,100 Model 33s have been produced.

Recent standard features for all Bonanza models are a 15-degree approach flap setting and a 28-volt electrical system. The approach flaps are identical to the Baron models and will allow for a maximum extension speed of 175 mph. An improved electrical system speeds up the landing gear cycle and allows Bonanzas to be equipped with propeller deicing. Also, all late model Bonanzas offer increased oxygen capacity. Single-piece headliners and redesigned cabin sidewalls make for a clean appearance and reduced cabin sound levels. As of 1981 airspeed indicators read in knots only, and an electronic fuel-flow sensor has replaced the mechanical sensor to ensure greater gauge accuracy.

BEECHCRAFT MODEL 35 "BONANZA"
1947–81

STANDARD DATA: (V-35B) Seats 4. Gross wt. 3,400. Empty wt. 2,106. Fuel capacity 74. Engine 285-hp Continental. PERFORMANCE: Top mph 209. Cruise mph 198. Stall mph 59. Initial climb rate 1,167. Ceiling 17,858. Range 824. Takeoff distance (50) 1,769. Landing distance (50') 1,324.

STANDARD DATA: (C-D35) Seats 4. Gross wt. 2,725. Empty wt. 1,675. Fuel capacity 359. Engine 205-hp Continental. PERFORMANCE: Top mph 190. Cruise mph 180. Stall mph 55. Initial climb rate 1,100. Ceiling 18,000. Range 775. Takeoff distance (50') 1,375. Landing distance (50') 970.

STANDARD DATA: (E-35) Seats 4. Gross wt. 2,775. Empty wt. 1,722. Fuel capacity 39. Engine 225-hp Continental. PERFORMANCE: Top mph 194. Cruise mph 184. Stall mph 55. Initial climb rate 1,300. Range 775. Ceiling 19,000. Takeoff distance (50') 1,300. Landing distance (50') 970.

STANDARD DATA: (N-P35) Seats 4-5. Gross wt. 3,125. Empty wt. 1,855. Fuel capacity 49-78. Engine 260-hp Continental. PERFORMANCE: Top mph 205. Cruise mph 195. Stall mph 60. Initial climb rate 1,150. Ceiling 19,200. Range 690-1,215. Takeoff distance (50) 1,050. Landing distance (50) 840.

The Beechcraft Bonanza remains one of the most outstanding aircraft in its class. It has been described as the best aerodynamically designed airplane ever offered to general aviation. The Bonanza was introduced as a production model in 1947 and was labeled the Model 35. Subsequent aircraft were designated A35, B35, C35, and the like until the S35, after which the letter V was placed in front of the model number and

the lettering process began all over again. Early models were fitted with 185-hp powerplants and seated four persons. In 1952, the C-model appeared with enlarged tail surfaces and a 205-hp engine. The 225-hp Continental was first used in 1954 with the E35. The H35 utilized a 240-hp engine and the J through M models were fitted with 250-hp Continentals. The 260-hp engine was introduced in the N35, and the 285-hp engine first appeared in 1964 in the S35.

Early model Bonanzas are still highly competitive on the used-plane market and are highly prized as personal transportation aircraft. All were four-seaters until the S35, after which all have accommodations for up to six. Like other Bonanzas, the V35B model benefits from the new 15-degree flap setting and the 28-volt electrical system to support optional propeller deicing equipment. For improved soundproofing and a neat appearance, the interior sidewalls and the one-piece headliner are constructed of sound-absorbing foam.

BEECHCRAFT A36/A36TC/B36TC "BONANZA"
1968–Present

STANDARD DATA: (A36) Seats 6. Gross wt. 3,600. Empty wt. 2,195. Fuel capacity 74. Engine 285-hp Continental. PERFORMANCE: Top mph 206. Cruise mph 193. Stall mph 60. Initial climb rate 1,030. Ceiling 16,600. Range 802. Takeoff distance (50') 2,040. Landing distance (50) 1,450.

STANDARD DATA: (A36TC) Seats 6. Gross wt. 3,650. Empty wt. 2,278. Fuel capacity 74. Engine 300-hp Turbocharged Continental. PERFORMANCE: Top mph 246. Cruise mph 223. Stall mph 66. Initial climb rate 1,165. Ceiling 25,000. Range 774. Takeoff distance (50) 2,012. Landing distance (50') 1,449.

The biggest single-engine Bonanza, the model 36, was introduced in 1968 to compete with Piper's Cherokee Six and the 200-series haulers from Cessna. It remains the only retractable in the single-engine, six-seater utility class. The A36 was developed by lengthening the fuselage of the Model 33 and using the same durable wing, landing gear and Continental engine of the Bonanza family. Six seats were available, and with club seating arrangements and a foldout table, it became a flying office. In 1975, the A36 outsold all other Bonanza models for the first time.

With a longer cabin and wide double doors, the Bonanza A36 offers greater utility and convenience without sacrificing performance and economy. In 1977, for the first time, the A36 was offered with factory-installed electric trim, formerly available only on aircraft equipped with an autopilot. The A36 accounted for 50% of the total Bonanza production in 1977, and that percentage increased in 1978. Beech added a turbocharged version of its Bonanza A36 in mid-1979. The aircraft is certified to a maximum operational altitude of 25,000 feet and has approximately the same takeoff distance as the A36. Power is supplied by a 300-hp Continental engine, which conforms to the minimum horsepower concept introduced on the Baron 58P and 58TC in 1977. The A36TC has a gross weight of 3,650 pounds, which is 50 pounds more than the standard A36. A shortened three-blade propeller reduces tip speed, increases ground clearance, and reduces noise.

In 1982, Beechcraft replaced the A36TC with the B36TC. The new design mated the longer Baron wing to the model 36 fuselage, and fuel capacity was increased from 74 gallons to 102 gallons. Service ceiling for the A36TC and B36TC remained at 25,000'. The final year of production for turbocharged Bonanzas was 2001. The B36TC's production run ended in 2001.

Of all the Bonanza models, only the normally aspirated A36 remains. Beginning in 2005, the six-seat Beech came to market with an all glass panel.

BELL P-63 "KING COBRA"
1942–45

STANDARD DATA: Seats 1. Gross wt. 8,800. Empty wt. 6,375. Fuel capacity 136. Engine 1,325-hp Allison. PERFORMANCE: Top mph 410. Cruise mph 378. Initial climb rate 3,500. Ceiling 43,000.

Bell began development of the P-39 Aircobra in 1937 to meet the need for a fighter with great firepower. The design was quite radical for its time, featuring tri-

cycle gear and an engine that was mounted behind the pilot. The propeller was driven by a drive shaft that ran between the pilot's legs. Mounted in the nose was a 37mm cannon. Though nearly 10,000 of this type were built, it was unspectacular as a fighter and eventually found a role as a tank-buster on the Russian front. A greatly modified development of the P-39, the P-63 King Cobra, was designed in 1942. Easily recognized by its larger tail surface and more prominent airscoop, the King Cobra also met with an unenthusiastic reception. Of those that weren't lend-leased to Russia, many were converted into target planes for use with dummy bullets. A few King Cobras have been altered for racing. Several exist in flying condition.

BELLANCA "AIRCRUISER"
1932–38

STANDARD DATA: Seats 11-17. Gross wt. 11,400. Empty wt. 6,300. Fuel capacity 300. Engine 875-hp Wright Cyclone. PERFORMANCE: Top mph 165. Cruise mph 137. Initial climb rate 620. Range 610-1,100. Ceiling 17,500.

The Aircruiser single-engine commercial sesquiplane entered production in 1932 as a refinement of the Airbus and was designed to carry 11 to 17 passengers. It could be fitted with either wheel or float undercarriage and was powered by either a Wright Cyclone or Pratt & Whitney Hornet engine. The Cyclone produced 760 hp with 875 hp available for takeoff. The Hornet was rated at 750 hp. The Aircruiser made use of an unusual wing configuration. The top plane was of conventional design; however, the lower airfoils consisted of inner sections with a coarse anhedral and outer sections that sloped up from the extremities of the inner sections to the top wing to form airfoil-sectioned bracing struts. While the top wings had solid spruce spars, the lower wings were built from welded steel-tube spars and ribs. The Aircruiser also featured electrical wing flaps. In 1935, an Aircruiser was purchased by the Mackenzie Air Service of Edmonton, Alberta. In three weeks the plane carried 30,537 pounds of radium and silver ore over the 900-mile route from the Eldorado Mining Co. to the railhead at Fort McMurray.

BELLANCA "PACEMAKER"/ "SKYROCKET"
1928-47

STANDARD DATA: (Senior Pacemaker) Seats 6-8. Gross wt. 5,600. Empty wt. 2,900. Fuel capacity 100. Engine 420-hp Wright Whirlwind radial. PERFORMANCE: Top mph 170. Cruise mph 145. Initial climb rate 900. Ceiling 18,000. Range 1,180.

STANDARD DATA: (Senior Skyrocket) Seats 6-8. Gross wt. 5,600. Empty wt. 3,520. Engine 550-hp Pratt & Whitney Wasp. PERFORMANCE: Top mph 190. Cruise mph 175. Initial climb rate 1,240. Ceiling 25,000. Range 1,280.

The Model 300 Pacemaker was first produced in 1928 and versions of this basic design were built until 1936. The first derivative was the Model 400 whose major difference was the swapping of a 420-hp Wright Whirlwind for the original 300-hp Wright Whirlwind nine-cylinder radial engine. Production of the Pacemaker continued throughout the 1930s. The Skyrocket was evolved from the Pacemaker and first flew in 1930. Aside from minor changes, the Skyrocket differed by its 550-hp Pratt and Whitney Wasp nine-cylinder radial engine and an increased seating capacity from the Pacemaker's six to eight persons. Production of the Skyrocket continued until 1936. In 1946, license for production of the airplane was taken over by a Canadian firm, Northwest Industries, and the aircraft's designation was changed from the Bellanca 31-42 to the Bellanca 31-55A. Under the new license, the Skyrocket remained substantially the same as the prewar model.

BELLANCA 7AC "CHAMP"
1970-72

STANDARD DATA: Seats 2. Gross wt. 1,220. Empty wt. 750. Engine 60-hp Franklin. PERFORMANCE: Top mph 91. Cruise mph 86. Stall mph 28. Range 310. Initial climb rate 460. Takeoff run 450. Landing roll 300.

During the period between 1946 and 1948, Aeronca built some 7,200 Model 7AC Champs, but the 7AC was dropped from the line when Champion Aircraft Corp. acquired manufacturing rights to the airframe in 1951; however, when Champion merged with Bellanca in 1970, it was decided to reinstate the design in an improved version. Production began sporadically due to the loss of the main production facility in a fire, but soon the Champ was coming off the assembly in increasing numbers. The primary difference in the new 7AC was the use of a 65-hp Continental four-cylinder engine as a replacement for the original 60-hp Franklin two-cylinder, which was no longer in production. Use of the new engine allowed for a redesigned cowling and air scoop that substantially improved forward visibility. Other new features included a lightweight cantilever spring-steel main landing gear and modern materials in interior design.

BELLANCA 8GCBC "SCOUT"
1970-80

STANDARD DATA: (8GCBC) Seats 2. Gross wt. 2,150. Empty wt. 1,315. Fuel capacity 35. Engine 180-hp Lycoming. PERFORMANCE: Top mph 128. Cruise mph 123. Stall mph 52. Initial climb rate 1,080. Takeoff distance (50') 525. Landing distance (50') 690.

STANDARD DATA: (7GC8C) Seats 2. Gross wt. 1,650. Empty wt. 1,037. Fuel capacity 35. Engine 150-hp Lycoming. PERFORMANCE: Top mph 128. Cruise mph 125. Stall mph 45. Initial climb rate 1,145. Ceiling 17,000. Range 537. Takeoff distance (50') 525. Landing distance (50') 690.

The basic utility version of the Citabria is known as the 8GCBC Scout. Its predecessor was the 7GCBC Scout that was powered by the smaller 150-hp Lycoming. The new multipurpose 180-hp Scout was introduced early in 1974 and enjoyed a high demand for the first production models. The Scout can be used for power line patrol, forestry work, cargo hauling, and training. When fitted with Sorensen spray equipment, it becomes a highly efficient and economical agricultural plane. The Scout can also be equipped with EDO 2000 floats and with skis for north-country flying. Its 180-hp engine provides good short-field performance.

BELLANCA "CITABRIA"
1964–80

STANDARD DATA: (Bellanca) Seats 2. Gross wt. 1,650 Empty wt. 1,110. Fuel capacity 35. Engine 150-hp Lycoming. PERFORMANCE: Top mph 130. Cruise mph 129. Stall mph 51. Initial climb rate 1,120. Range 560. Ceiling 17,000. Takeoff distance (50') 630. Landing distance (50') 755.

STANDARD DATA: (Champion) Seats 2. Gross wt. 1,650. Empty wt. 980. Fuel capacity 26. Engine 100-hp Lycoming. PERFORMANCE: Top mph 117. Cruise mph 112. Stall mph 50. Initial climb rate 725. Ceiling 12,000. Range 728. Takeoff distance (50') 890. Landing distance (50') 755.

The name "Citabria" is actually "airbatic" spelled backward. The Champion 7ECA Citabria was a modernized version of the Champion Model 7EC Traveler. Champion's first Citabria flew as a prototype in May 1964. Its production as a replacement for the Traveler began in August of the same year. The Champion two-seat aircraft was powered by a 108hp Continental four-cylinder engine. When Bellanca introduced its version

of the 7ECA, the airplane was fitted with a 1... Lycoming. The Citabria's basic wing, fuselage, and u... dercarriage are similar to previous tandem two-seaters. Major changes to the aerobatic, high-winger include the enlarged rear cabin windows, the square-cut vertical tail surfaces, and low-drag wheel spats similar to those on the Champion 7KC Olympia. Models 7GCAA, 7KCAB, and 7GCBA are generally similar to the Citabria 7ECA, with the exception that they are all powered by a 150-hp Lycoming engine. In addition, the 7KCAB has special fuel and oil systems for inverted flying, and the 7GCBC is fitted with flaps. The Citabria was the country's first aircraft certified for aerobatic flight by the FAA and is still the lowest priced production aircraft with these capabilities. Production of the Citabria was discontinued in 1980 when Bellanca Aircraft Corp. declared bankruptcy.

BELLANCA 8KCAB "DECATHLON"
1964–80

STANDARD DATA: Seats 2. Gross wt. 1,800. Empty wt. 1,275. Fuel capacity 40. Engine 150-hp Lycoming. PERFORMANCE: Top mph 145. Cruise mph 135. Stall mph 53. Initial climb rate 1,025. Range 550. Ceiling 16,000. Takeoff distance (50') 650. Landing distance (50') 755.

Following the acquisition of the Champion Aircraft Corp. in September 1970, Bellanca Aircraft continued the production of the Citabria. The fully aerobatic Citabria, model 8KCAB, is now named the Decathlon. Designed for loads of +6G and -5G, it can be flown in inverted flight for periods up to four minutes without loss of oil or oil pressure. Generally similar in all respects to the 150-hp Model 7 Citabria, the high-wing aerobat was, for a time, the only unlimited acrobatic competition aircraft produced in the United States. Although maximum speed is limited to 138 mph, a retrofit of the windshield will increase top speed. Some claim that with the Decathlon's standard top speed, it

necessary vertical speed to com-
:ompulsory unlimited sequence,
off the top of the vertical snaps
n Bellanca Aircraft Corp. declared
, production of the Decathlon

BELLANCA "JUNIOR"/"CRUISAIR"/ "CRUISEMASTER"
1937–59

Bellanca 14-23 Cruisair

Junior Cruisair

Bellanca 14-19 Cruisemaster

STANDARD DATA: (1413) Seats 4. Gross wt. 3,000. Empty wt. 1,850. Fuel capacity 60. Engine 260-hp Continental. PERFORMANCE: Top mph 208. Cruise mph 203. Stall mph 62. Initial climb rate 1,500. Ceiling 22,500. Range 1,000. Takeoff distance (50') 1,000. Landing distance (50) 800.

STANDARD DATA: (1419-2) Seats 4. Gross wt. 2,700. Empty wt. 1,640. Fuel capacity 40. Engine 230-hp Continental. PERFORMANCE: Top mph 206. Cruise mph 196. Stall mph 48. Initial climb rate 1,500. Range 624. Ceiling 20,000. Takeoff distance (50) 1,060. Landing distance (50) 935.

STANDARD DATA: (Cruisemaster 1419) Seats 4. Gross wt. 2,600. Empty wt. 1,525. Fuel capacity 20. Engine 190-hp Lycoming. PERFORMANCE: Cruise mph 180. Stall mph 43. Initial climb rate 1,400. Ceiling 22,500. Range 680.

STANDARD DATA: (Cruisair 149) Seats 3. Gross wt. 1,750. Empty wt. 1,050. Fuel capacity 20. Engine 90-hp Ken Royce radial. PERFORMANCE: Top mph 133. Cruise mph 120. Stall mph 43. Initial climb rate 750. Ceiling 12,500. Range 410.

STANDARD DATA: (Junior 149) Seats 3. Gross wt. 1,650. Empty wt. 943. Fuel capacity 22. Engine 90-hp LeBlond radial. PERFORMANCE: Top mph 137. Cruise mph 120. Stall mph 45. Initial climb rate 800. Ceiling 14,760. Range 500.

STANDARD DATA: (Junior 147) Seats 3. Gross wt. 1,650. Empty wt. 912. Fuel capacity 22. Engine 75-hp LeBlond radial. PERFORMANCE: Top mph 115. Cruise mph 105. Stall mph 45. Initial climb rate 600. Ceiling 12,000. Range 500.

The earlier versions of the Bellanca, produced from shortly after the end of World War II until 1962, are sometimes humorously referred to as the "Cardboard Constellations." This friendly remark refers to the tail surfaces that in earlier versions featured twin vertical fins outboard from the central vertical stabilizer and rudder. The first Bellancas of this series were produced between 1937 and 1940 and were known as the Junior. The 147 had a 75-hp LeBlond engine and fixed landing gear; the 149 was fitted with a 90-hp of the same make and retractable gear. Cruisair became the name applied to the 147 and 149 when they received 75-hp and 90-hp Ken Royce engines, respectively.

In 1946, the first 1413 Cruisairs were introduced with 150-hp Franklin engines, and in the following years updated versions, the 1413-2 and 1413-3, were built. This latter plane stayed in production, along with the first 190-hp Cruisemaster 1419 introduced in 1948 until 1956. In 1958, Northern Aircraft Inc. took over production and built the Cruisemaster 1419-2 with its 230-hp Continental engine. Northern Aircraft became the Downer Aircraft Company in 1959, and introduced the 1419-3 "260," a considerably more powerful Cruisemaster with a 260-hp Continental, tricycle landing gear, and other refinements. Inter-Air acquired production rights in 1962, and the 260A received its first conventional tail section. Shortly afterwards, Inter-Air became known as the Bellanca Sales Company, a subsidiary of Miller Flying Service.

BELLANCA 300 "VIKING"
1971–80

STANDARD DATA: Seats 4. Gross wt. 3,325. Empty wt. 2,217. Fuel capacity 60-75. Engine 300-hp Continental. PERFORMANCE: Top mph 226. Cruise mph 188. Stall mph 70. Initial climb rate 1,170. Range 734. Ceiling 17,000. Takeoff distance (50') 850. Landing distance (50') 1,100.

The modern Bellanca first flew in 1962. At that time, under the name of Inter-Air, the design was revised to eliminate the triple tail and replace it with a large, single, vertical fin. There were several other new design features, but many of the earlier features of the Cruisemaster were retained, including the laminated wood wing of spruce and mahogany, which is pressure sealed in plastic. The fuselage and tail surfaces, however, are constructed of metal tubing covered with Dacron. In addition to changing the tail surfaces, the cabin was extensively redesigned and enlarged, along with the cowling and landing gear. This radically revised Bellanca entered quantity production in 1964 and was produced in increasing numbers until 1980. A 260-hp engine powered the Bellanca 260C Viking; however, the standard engine in the 300 series was rated at 300-hp. The buyer can choose between a Continental IO-520D six-cylinder engine or the Lycoming IO-540.

The standard fuel tanks hold 58 gallons or 72 gallons in the Super 300 Viking, although optional long-range tanks provide a total fuel capacity of 92 gallons. The Super 300 Viking is the same airplane, only equipped with a more luxurious cabin and the larger fuel tanks. Bellanca also produced the Turbo Viking 300, similar to the Standard Viking 300, but fitted with a 310-hp Lycoming turbocharged engine. All Vikings have retractable tricycle gear. The main gear retracts forward into the wing, and the nosewheel retracts rearward. When retracted, the wheels protrude slightly to reduce danger in a gear-up landing. Bellanca made it a practice to offer many extra features normally considered as standard equipment. A good example is the standard installation of an autopilot. After about 43 years of production, it looked as if Bellanca's family of single-engine wooden-winged retractables would be laid to rest when the company declared bankruptcy in 1980. The type certificate and tooling have traded hands several times and the aircraft remains in irregular and limited production.

BELLANCA T-250 "ARIES"
1978–80

STANDARD DATA: Seats 4. Gross wt. 3,150. Empty wt. 1,888. Fuel capacity 76. Engine 250-hp Lycoming. PERFORMANCE: Cruise mph 208. Stall mph 64. Initial climb rate 1,240. Ceiling 18,100. Range 1,170.

The title of fastest normally-aspirated single has been bandied back and forth for years. Throughout the late 1950s and early 1960s, the V-tail Bonanza was the often challenged but undefeated champ. Then there was the exercise in horsepower overkill known as the Comanche 400, followed by the Aero Commander 200 and the Waco Meteor. The trouble was that all except the Bonanza were economic failures. The Bellanca Axies T-250 was initiated by Anderson, Greenwood and Company when it assumed financial control of Bellanca. Unfortunately, the Aries did not get into production before Bellanca declared bankruptcy in 1980.

For lower-cost production, the Aries utilized flat skins wherever possible and simple rather than compound curves. The wings and T-tail are laminar-flow constant-chord airfoils. Power is supplied by a carbureted six-cylinder Lycoming that is roughly the same engine that powered the old 250 Comanche, delivering 250 hp at 2,575 RPM. Other hints that the T-250 is fast are the use of flush riveting, sealed nosegear doors, butt skin joints and flush vents, drains, and engine breather. The cabin accommodates four, but there is enough room so the Aries could be configured to handle one more.

BOEING/STEARMAN "KAYDET" SERIES (PT-13,17-1827 AND N2S)
1934–45

STANDARD DATA: Seats 2. Gross wt. 2,717. Empty wt. 1,936. Fuel capacity 43. Engine 220-hp Lycoming

R-680 or 220-hp Continental R-670. PERFOR-
MANCE: Top mph 124. Cruise mph 106. Landing
mph 52. Initial climb rate 840. Range 505. Ceiling
11,200.

In 1934, the Stearman Aircraft Co. became a Boeing
subsidiary and placed in production its Model 73. It
was a variation of both the Stearman Model C series
that was produced between 1926 and 1930 and the
Model 70 prototype that was completed in 1933. Out
of this biplane grew a family of primary trainers, of
which over 2,000 were produced by 1945. The Model
76 was simply a larger version of the Model 75, which
was the most prominent member of the family.

The Model 75 was powered by a 215-hp Lycoming
and was designated by the military as the PT-13. The
series that was produced in the largest numbers was
the Model A75NI. It was similar to the PT-13 but was
powered by a 220-hp Continental radial engine; its
military designation was PT-17. The Royal Canadian
Air Force ordered 300 winterized versions of the PT-17
and unofficially changed the name to Kaydet, a name
that has come to apply to the entire family of Stearmans.

The last of the 75 series to be produced was the
Model E-75 powered by a 220-hp Lycoming engine.
When production was terminated on VJ-Day, its production totaled over 1,700 as both the PT-13D and the
N2S-5. Thousands of Model 75s have become available for civilian use and are extremely popular, both as
a warbird and classic open cockpit biplanes. In some
cases, their original engines have been replaced by the
Pratt & Whitney Wasp juniors providing twice the
power.

BUCKER BU131 "JUNGMANN"
1939–56

STANDARD DATA: Seats 2. Gross wt. 1,474. Empty
wt. 836. Engine 105-hp Hirth. PERFORMANCE: Top
mph 115. Cruise mph 106. Stall mph 51. Initial
climb rate 650. Range 400. Ceiling 14,000.

The Bucker Jungmann, which first appeared in
Germany in 1934, has proved to be one of the most
popular two-seat, tandem aerobatic biplanes in the
world. Several thousand were produced at the Bucker
factory near Berlin during the 1930s and 1940s and
many others were constructed under license in Spain,
Switzerland, and Czechoslovakia. Originally, the
Jungmann was powered by an 80-hp Hirth engine.
Later in 1936, the 105-hp Hirth became the standard
engine. Several Jungmanns have found their way into
the United States, and some have been adapted to larger
American engines. The biplane is capable of performing remarkably graceful and precise aerobatics and is
in great demand.

BUCKER "JUNGMEISTER"
1935, 1967–75

STANDARD DATA: Seats 1. Gross wt. 1,290. Empty
wt. 925. Engine 160-hp Siemens. PERFORMANCE:
Top mph 137. Cruise mph 125. Initial climb rate
1,150. Stall mph 54. Range 310. Ceiling 19,500.

The Jungmeister, first introduced in 1935, quickly
developed an international reputation for its outstanding aerobatic capabilities. Until recently, Jungmeisters
were heavily involved in world acrobatic competition
and were widely used by exhibition pilots. Most of the
700 or so Jungmeisters built were constructed in Germany, but others of the type were built in Spain and
Switzerland. Several examples are currently registered
in the United States, at least three of which have been
reengined with Warner radials. In 1968, the Aero
Technik Canary in Munich, Germany, began production of the BU-133 D-1, also called the Jungmeister. Its

engine is a remanufactured Siemens-Halske Sh-14A4; however, due to this engine's limited availability and demand for more power, a new version, the BU-133F, was built by WolfHirth-GmbH with a 220-hp Franklin engine.

BUHL LA.1 "BULL-PUP"
1930

STANDARD DATA: Seats 1. Gross wt. 850. Empty wt. 550. Engine 40-hp Szekely. PERFORMANCE: Top mph 95. Cruise mph 76. Initial climb rate 800. Ceiling 14,000.

The LA Bull-Pup, produced by the Buhl Aircraft Company in 1930, was powered by a 45-hp A.H.C. (Szekely) SR-3 three-cylinder radial engine. The wire-braced wooden wing is fabric covered and has two spars. The fuselage is an oval metal monocoque. The wing is supported by a turnover pylon mounted in front of the single-seat cockpit. Some Bull-Pup owners have modified their planes with 65-hp Continental engines that help performance considerably.

CALLAIR
1941–57

STANDARD DATA: (A-1) Seats 2-3. Gross wt. 1,550. Empty wt. 1,000. Fuel capacity 25. Engine 100-hp Lycoming. PERFORMANCE: Top mph 115. Cruise mph 105. Stall mph 40. Initial climb rate 500. Ceiling 13,000. Range 260.

STANDARD DATA: (A-2, A-3). Seats 2. Gross wt. 1,550. Empty wt. 975. Fuel capacity 30. Engine 125-hp Lycoming. PERFORMANCE: Top mph 120.

Cruise mph 109. Stall mph 45. Initial climb rate 1,000. Ceiling 17,500. Range 456. Takeoff run 426. Landing roll 300.

The first CallAir flew in 1941 and was designated the Model A. The last version was introduced in 1957 and was named the A-6. Throughout the years of its existence, the basic difference between any of the models was the powerplant; otherwise, the Model A-4 differed little externally from the original Model A. The CallAir was built with mixed construction: fabric-covered wooden wings and a fabric-covered steeltube fuselage. The Model A-2, with a 125-hp Lycoming, and the Model A-3, with a 125-hp Continental, were produced during the years between 1946 and 1948. The first production models of the A-4 appeared in 1955, and the major refinement was the addition of 25 more horsepower with the installation of a 150-hp Lycoming. All models shared the same two-to three-seat cabin and low wing with exposed struts.

Another version of the CallAir was introduced in 1956 and was basically an agricultural development of the Model A-4. Designated the A-S, it was normally flown as a singleseater with the cockpit offset to the starboard side due to the inclusion of the dust hopper. The Model A-6 flown in 1957 was identical, apart from another jump in horsepower to a 180-hp Lycoming. The Intermountain Manufacturing Co. developed a series of low-priced agricultural aircraft from the CallAir, and the first airplane rolled off the production line in 1963. The A-9 featured a 235-hp Lycoming; its top speed was now 130 mph, and its climb rate was now 650 fpm. The dust hopper was moved to a position in front of the cockpit.

CESSNA "AIRMASTER"
1933–42

STANDARD DATA: Seats 4. Gross wt. 2,450. Empty wt. 1,380. Engine 145-hp Warner Scarab radial. PERFORMANCE: Top mph 162. Cruise mph 150. Stall mph 50. Initial climb rate 1,000. Range 472. Ceiling 18,000.

Clyde Cessna first entered the light plane market on his own in 1927. Between the years of 1928 and

1930 he produced a series of airplanes that were remarkably clean and efficient. The final manifestation of this series was the Cessna AW, a four-seat cabin monoplane utilizing the 125-hp Warner Scarab engine followed by the BW. The Depression caught up with Cessna in 1930, forcing the factory to suspend production; however, in 1933, Cessna was back in business again, this time with a much improved version of the AW, featuring an improved landing gear and a 145-hp engine. This first model, designated the C-34, was possibly the most efficient airplane in its class, and nearly 100 were built. The C-145 Airmaster is basically a modified C-34 featuring revised flaps and a wider gear. In 1932, the Airmaster was made available with the 165-hp Super Scarab, and the line continued in production until 1942.

CESSNA 120/140
1946–50

STANDARD DATA: Seats 2. Gross wt. 1,450. Empty wt. 770. Fuel capacity 21. Engine 80- to 90-hp Continental. PERFORMANCE: Top mph 119. Cruise mph 103. Stall mph 53. Initial climb rate 680. Range 439. Ceiling 15,600. Takeoff run 650. Landing roll 460.

Cessna's 140 was a somewhat more deluxe version of the 120 model when both debuted in 1946. Along with a few cabin refinements, the 140 had a starter, generator, battery, and manually operated plain-hinge flaps. Both were powered by the Continental C85-12, which developed a lusty 85-hp at full RPM, but the 140 could accept the additional surge of a 90-hp Continental up front. A grand total of 2,164 120s were produced by Cessna before this model was phased out in 1948. The side-by-side two-seat 140 continued in production with a choice of the 85-hp or 90-hp engine.

Introduced in 1949 as the 140A, the 90-hp version had a metal skin in place of fabric covering on the wings. It featured single wing struts in place of the earlier "Y" struts. More than 5,500 140s and 140As were built before the series was permanently discontinued in 1950. Although the 150 with its tricycle gear was later designed as a replacement for the 120/140 series, there are many pilots who continue to favor the lovable old

tail-draggers. A Cessna 140 owned by a flying school in Canada logged more than 17,500 hours of flight time before being respectfully retired. Along with the Aeroncas, Cubs, and Luscombes, the Cessna 140 did its share in making general aviation what it is today.

CESSNA 150 "COMMUTER"/ "AEROBAT"
1959–77

STANDARD DATA: (150) Seats 2. Gross wt. 1,600. Empty wt. 1,111. Fuel capacity 26-38. Engine 100-hp Teledyne Continental. PERFORMANCE: Top mph 125. Cruise mph 123. Stall mph 48. Initial climb rate 670. Ceiling 14,000. Range 591-667. Takeoff distance (50') 1,385. Landing distance (50') 1,075.

STANDARD DATA: (Aerobat) Seats 2. Gross wt. 1,600. Empty wt. 1,093. Fuel capacity 26-38. Engine 100-hp Teledyne Continental. PERFORMANCE: Top mph 124. Cruise mph 121. Stall mph 48. Initial climb rate 670. Ceiling 14,000. Range 385-656. Takeoff distance (50') 1,385. Landing distance (50) 1,075.

The Cessna 150 is one of the leading examples of the light civilian pilot trainer and personal aircraft. It is basically unchanged since it was introduced in 1959, and the only differences in model years are in minor styling, equipment, and accessories. As a trainer, it is very easy to learn to fly in and can be used in all stages of instruction from solo through instrument and commercial ratings. As a personal plane, it is limited by two seats in the normal arrangement, although there is quite ample baggage space. The three versions (standard, trainer, and commuter) vary only in deluxe extras.

A pilot new to the Cessna 150 will find it as easy to handle as anything with wings. Its light weight makes it somewhat bouncy in rough air. There are no tricky characteristics, and recoveries from any attitude are gentle and steady. Operational costs are about the rock bottom of the price lists. As a new or used airplane, the Cessna is not topped in its class by another make or design as a good, general all-purpose light two-seater.

In 1970, Cessna introduced the Model A150K Acrobat, a 150 with structural changes to allow aerobatics. It is rated at +6G to -3G, which permits most standard acrobatic maneuvers such as snap rolls, barrel and aileron rolls, Cuban eights, loops, etc. Empty weight of the Aerobat is slightly higher than the standard 150, and speed is reduced by two mph.

CESSNA 152/152 "AEROBAT"
1978–81

STANDARD DATA: (152) Seats 2. Gross wt. 1,670. Empty wt. 1,107. Fuel capacity 26-39. Engine 110-hp Lycoming. PERFORMANCE: Top mph 126. Cruise mph 123. Stall mph 49. Initial climb rate 715. Ceiling 14,700. Range 368-794. Takeoff distance (50') 1,340. Landing distance (50') 1,200.

STANDARD DATA: (Aerobat) Seats 2. Gross wt. 1,670 Empty wt. 1,135. Fuel capacity 26-39. Engine 110-hp Lycoming PERFORMANCE: Top mph 125. Cruise mph 122. Stall mph 49. Initial climb rate 715. Ceiling 14,700. Range 362-788. Takeoff distance (50') 1,340. Landing distance (50) 1,200.

In 1978, Cessna Aircraft introduced a new training airplane to "replace" the Model 150 after a 19-year production run that amounted to almost 24,000 airplanes. Though to most eyes the new Model 152 still looked like the original 150, it was introduced with the intention of providing an airplane that burns 100-octane fuel with lower sound levels, better fuel consumption, and an increased payload. The Lycoming "Blue Streak" engine produces 110-hp at a low 2,500 rpm. Possibly the most remarkable improvement is the increase of the trainer's maximum useful load by over 100 pounds to 589. With full fuel, the 152 has 433 pounds of payload for people, baggage, and/or accessories. Contributing to the impressive useful load is an unusable fuel quantity of only 1-1/2 gallons. Cessna's 69-inch prop teams with the derated engine to produce more efficient climb and cruise performance at a reduced RPM.

The 152 Aerobat is also available. It meets requirements for aerobatic maneuvers of 6Gs positive and 3Gs negative load. The most recent improvements include a system that injects fuel evenly into all four cylinders for prompt ignition and even combustion. With the 152's optional fuel tanks, it can cover 794 miles while traveling at 122 mph at 7,000 feet and carrying a useful load of 1,101 pounds.

Cessna offered a training version for the first time in 1981; the Trainer included a package price for the most frequently ordered avionics and accessories for training purposes. Main gear tires are 15-6.00 x 6 to reduce frontal area and save weight.

CESSNA 170
1948–56

STANDARD DATA: Seats 4. Gross wt. 2,200. Empty wt. 1,205. Fuel capacity 42. Engine 145-hp Continental. PERFORMANCE: Top mph 140. Cruise mph 120. Stall mph 52. Initial climb rate 690. Range 540. Ceiling 15,500. Takeoff distance (50) 1,820. Landing distance (50) 1,145.

The conventional-gear Cessna 170 was the forerunner of the 172/Skyhawk series in production until 1986. Basically, the 170 was a four-place, 145-hp version of the 140 series. It remained unchanged until 1953 when the engine cowling was redesigned and lengthened. Final alterations, made in 1955, increased the size of the rear windows, revised the tailwheel, and added an additional flap position. Of the 5,171 Cessna 170s that were built, more than 3,000 are found on the active list in the United States today while many others are still flying in Canada, Europe, and Latin America. Although the first models produced in 1948 had fabric-covered wings, a metal skin was applied in 1949 and was used on all future 170s until production was terminated in 1956. Although not speedy, it is still a good buy on the used aircraft market. It represents one of the lowest-priced four-seaters available.

CESSNA 172 SKYHAWK
1956–86

STANDARD DATA: (1986) Seats 4. Gross wt. 2,400. Empty wt. 1,414. Fuel capacity 43-68. Engine 160-hp Lycoming. PERFORMANCE: Top mph 142. Cruise mph 138. Stall mph 53. Initial climb rate

700. Ceiling 13,000. Range 506-869. Takeoff distance (50) 1,825. Landing distance (50') 1,280.

STANDARD DATA: (1976) Seats 4. Gross wt. 2,300. Empty wt. 1,387. Fuel capacity 42-52. Engine 150-hp Lycoming. PERFORMANCE: Top mph 144. Cruise mph 138. Stall mph 41. Initial climb rate 645. Range 657. Ceiling 13,100. Takeoff distance (50') 1,525. Landing distance (50') 1,250.

STANDARD DATA: (1963) Seats 4. Gross wt. 2,300. Empty wt. 1,260. Fuel capacity 42. Engine 140-hp Continental. PERFORMANCE: Top mph 138. Cruise mph 130. Stall mph 49. Initial climb rate 645. Range 595. Ceiling 13,100. Takeoff distance (50') 1,525. Landing distance (50') 1,250.

The Cessna 172/Skyhawk has undoubtedly been the most popular four-place aircraft among general aviation pilots for close to three decades. First produced in 1956, the 172 was initially a revision of the model 170 with a tricycle landing gear and redesigned tail surfaces. It didn't take long for the 172 to "catch on," and in 1960 a more deluxe version, the Skyhawk, was introduced. The 1960 models incorporated the swept vertical fin, an external baggage door, and a shorter undercarriage for easier cabin entry. The large wraparound rear window was installed in 1963, providing a full 360-degree field of vision.

Other than a few wingtip and cabin refinements, the 172/Skyhawk series remained unchanged until 1968 when a 150-hp four-cylinder Lycoming replaced the 145-hp Continental 0-300-C engine. The 1970 models offered conical-camber wingtips, a light gray instrument panel, and other small refinements. A wider, softer spring-steel gear called Land-O-Matic was fitted onto the 172 in 1971, similar to the main legs on the 150 and Cardinal. The 172/Skyhawk featured an increased vertical fin, which was now a standard item on all new Cessnas. More recent versions sport the redesigned camber-lift wing introduced on the 1972/182 model, as well as improved soundproofing and a new instrument panel arrangement.

The Skyhawk/100, introduced in 1977, had more horsepower and speed, greater climb performance, and a higher service ceiling—all this with less fuel con-

sumption than previous models. Using a 160-hp Lycoming, the Skyhawk has at its disposal 10 additional horsepower to yield a 1-1/2 mph increase in cruise speed and a 5% improvement in fuel consumption. It will clear a 50-foot obstacle in 1,440 feet, 85 feet less than earlier model Skyhawks. In addition, the modern engine is designed to use the readily available 100-octane fuel. Other refinements include improved instrument visibility, a flap control with infinite settings, a vernier mixture control and optional rudder trim.

Air conditioning was added as an option in 1978, and in 1979 the Skyhawk's flap extension speed was increased from 98 mph to 127 mph, permitting earlier use of the flaps. For 1981, the Skyhawk offered increased useful load, a new engine, improved handling, and a new avionics cooling system. The ramp weight was increased 100 pounds, allowing for 89 pounds of extra useful load after 11 pounds are subtracted as a result of a heavier engine. The new engine was a 160-hp Lycoming 0-320-D2J with an oil cooler and full-flow oil filter as standard accessories. Also, a rounded leading edge on the elevator reduced elevator forces required during landing flare.

CESSNA SKYHAWK
1997–present

STANDARD DATA: (Model 172R) Seats 4. Gross wt. 2,450. Empty wt. 1,620. Fuel capacity 56 gallons. Engine 160-hp Textron Lycoming IO-360-L2A. PERFORMANCE: Max Cruise 123 kts. Cruise 122 kts. Stall 47-51 kts. Rate of climb, sea level 720 fpm. Service ceiling 13,500'. Takeoff distance (50') 1,685. Landing distance (50') 1,295.

As the general aviation market regained momentum in the 1990s, Cessna re-entered the single engine piston aircraft with the Skyhawk 172. Changes to the new aircraft were modest as the manufacturer sought to improve upon a winning design. Leather seats, a quiet cockpit, and modern avionics led the Skyhawk into the 21st Century. In 2004, Cessna introduced the "most popular airplane in the world" with an all glass panel. Optional equipment for 2005 included pilot and copilot airbags.

CESSNA SKYHAWK SP
1998 – Present

STANDARD DATA: (Model 172S) Seats 4. Gross wt. 2,550. Empty wt. 1,626. Fuel capacity 56 gallons. Engine 180-hp Textron Lycoming IO-360-L2A. PERFORMANCE: Max Cruise 126 kts. Cruise 124 kts. Stall 48-53 kts. Rate of climb, sea level 730 fpm. Service ceiling 14,000. Takeoff distance (50') 1,630. Landing distance (50') 1,335.

This popular version of Skyhawk comes with same engine as the classic 172, but is rated for an additional 300 rpm and develops a corresponding 20 more hp. Consequently the SP produces a touch better rate-of-climb, a shade higher cruise speed, and 500' more service ceiling. That edge in performance has made the Skyhawk SP a big seller over its more conventional Skyhawk.

CESSNA CUTLASS RG
1979 – 86

STANDARD DATA: Seats 4. Gross wt. 2,650. Empty wt. 1,555. Fuel capacity 66. Engine 180-hp Lycoming. PERFORMANCE: Top mph 167. Cruise mph 161. Stall mph 58. Initial climb rate 800. Ceiling 16,800. Range 828. Takeoff distance (50') 1,775. Landing distance (50') 1,340.

A retractable version of Cessna's ever-popular Skyhawk was introduced in late 1979. Designated the Cutlass RG, it carries 180-hp in the nose, 20-hp more than its sister ship. Even with the addition of retractable gear mechanisms, the Cutlass achieves an impressive 14.7 pounds/hp power loading ratio, compared to

14.4 for the Skyhawk or the Piper Arrow IV and Beech Sierra at 13.75 pounds/hp. Everything from the firewall back and the belly upward is 172. The gear is the same used in the Skylane RG and can be operated at anytime under 161 mph, taking about five seconds to cycle.

The Cutlass fit into the airplane market as the lowest-priced four-place retractable and was economical to operate with a fuel consumption rate of 10 gph at 75% power. Cruise at 9,000 feet and 75% power is 161 mph. With a maximum usable fuel capacity of 62 gallons, range at that power setting is 829 miles. The useful load of 1,092 pounds and four seats allows the Cutlass to achieve 64 seat-miles per gallon. Because it was built from the time-tested Skyhawk airframe, proven Skylane RG landing gear, and the reliable Lycoming 0-360 engine, people at Cessna liked to joke that it was "a new Cessna that already withstood the test of time."

CESSNA HAWK XP
1970 – 81

STANDARD DATA: Seats 4. Gross wt. 2,550. Empty wt. 1,538. Fuel capacity 52-68. Engine 195-hp Teledyne Continental. PERFORMANCE: Top mph 153. Cruise mph 149. Stall mph 54. Initial climb rate 870. Ceiling 17,000. Range 506-73 1. Takeoff distance (50') 1,360. Landing distance (50') 1,345.

The Hawk XP is a single-engine airplane introduced by Cessna in 1977. Utilizing a 195-hp fuel-injected powerplant turning a constant-speed propeller, it offers the pilot 1,000 pounds of useful load and a 150-mph cruising speed for cross-country transportation. It was Cessna's attempt to add another option to the four-place airplane market. The Hawk combines optimum payload, speed, and climb performance for the moderate price bracket. Its 76-inch propeller delivers takeoff thrust at a low 2,600 RPM, thus reducing internal and external noise levels. Even with full fuel (49 useful gallons), the plane has 707 pounds of useful load remaining. At gross weight it can clear a 50-foot obstacle in 80 feet less than the Skyhawk/100 and 40 feet less than the Cardinal.

Like most other single-engine Cessnas, the Hawk incorporates flap control with multiple settings, a vernier fuel mixture control and a reengineered instrument panel. Rudder trim was included as standard equipment. In 1979, optional integral fuel cells increased usable fuel to 66 gallons for a range of 938 miles with a 45-minute reserve. Flap extension is permitted at 127 mph (110 knots) compared to 98 mph (85 knots) on pre-1979 models. In addition to the standard four seats, an optional child's seat could be added for extra seating capacity. With the 1981 model year, handling characteristics of the XP were significantly improved by the addition of rounded leading edges on the elevators. The forces required during landing flare were reduced, balked-landing climb capability was enhanced, and trim requirements during flap-setting changes were reduced.

CESSNA 175 "SKYLARK"
1958–62

STANDARD DATA: Seats 4. Gross wt. 2,350. Empty wt. 1,312. Fuel capacity 52. Engine 170-hp Continental. PERFORMANCE: Top mph 147. Cruise mph 139. Stall mph 62. Initial climb rate 850. Ceiling 15,900. Range 595. Takeoff distance (50') 1,340. Landing distance (50') 1,155.

Originally introduced in 1958, the Skylark was intended to fill the gap between the 145-hp Skyhawk and the 230-hp Skylane. It featured numerous refinements on the basic 172 configuration. A 175-hp geared Continental boosted the maximum cruise speed from 124 mph for the Skyhawk to 139. The Skylark boasted a 210-fpm increase in initial climb rate over its sister ship. Other improvements included a free-blown windshield, electric fuel gauges, fiberglass speed-fairings, a new panel design, and a redesigned interior decor; otherwise, the Skylark handled and flew much like the Skyhawk. In fact, the only way to tell them apart was that the Skylark had a bump in the cowl to allow for the engine gearing mechanism. Cessna discontinued the 175 after about five years because it earned a reputation for engine problems. This was possibly due to the fact that near 3,000 RPMs for cruise and takeoff were required, but pilots were hesitant to follow the manual; they cut back and caused the engine to overheat. Even

during runup, the tach needle slid easily down to 2,600 RPM, redline for most planes. Because pilots often failed to fly up to the Skylark's potential, they tended to be skeptical about its performance claims over the Skyhawk.

CESSNA 177 "CARDINAL CLASSIC"
1968–78

STANDARD DATA: Seats 4. Gross wt. 2,500. Empty wt. 1,533. Fuel capacity 50-61. Engine 180-hp Lycoming. PERFORMANCE: Top mph 160. Cruise mph 150. Stall mph 53. Initial climb rate 840. Ceiling 14,600. Range 636-776. Takeoff distance (50') 1,400. Landing distance (50') 1,220.

Don't confuse the 1968 and 1969 Cardinal with the 1970 through 1973 models. The original 1968 Cardinal was powered by a 150-hp Lycoming engine. It soon became obvious that the 150 hp just couldn't do the job, so a replacement 180-hp Lycoming was installed in 1969. Cessna made a major change on the Cardinal for 1970 with a revised airfoil that much improves low-speed handling. The airplane also has a constant-speed propeller and cowl flaps, moving it out of the Skyhawk class and into the realm of the Skylane. It could be fitted with optional children's jump seats and offered a range of more than 800 miles. The new wing allowed safe low-speed approaches, and the engine/prop combination yielded fine takeoff, climb, and go-around performance. The 1970 models replaced the earlier straight wingtips with drooping conical camber tips.

CESSNA "CARDINAL RG"
1970–78

STANDARD DATA: Seats 4. Gross wt. 2,800. Empty wt. 1,707. Fuel capacity 61. Engine 200-hp Lycoming. PERFORMANCE: Top mph 180. Cruise mph 170. Stall mph 57.5. Initial climb rate 925. Range 823-1,030. Ceiling 17,100. Takeoff distance (50') 1,585. Landing distance (50') 1,350.

First announced by Cessna on Dec. 3, 1970, the Cardinal RG (retractable gear) has become the choice for many who look for a single-engine plane with good cruising speed yet with a reasonable price tag. With no wing struts to create drag and a hydraulically retractable tricycle landing gear, the RG can reach a cruise speed of 171 mph while burning only eight gph at 9,500 feet. Since its introduction, the RG has been handed some important changes, such as an improved propeller that has increased the airspeed about six mph and the removal of the foot step under the cabin door. The sleek-looking high-winger is powered by a 200-hp four-cylinder fuel-injected Lycoming engine.

The landing gear is retracted by an electrically powered hydraulic pump in a self-contained hydraulic system. When the gear is retracted, the main gear is flush with the fuselage using no wheel doors; the nose gear is faired by wheel doors. On late models, the landing gear has improved hydraulics, wheel doors, wheels, brakes, and nose gear trunion. The instrument panel was completely redesigned to provide more space and better locations for key instruments and avionics.

CESSNA L-19 "BIRD DOG"
1950–63

STANDARD DATA: Seats 2. Gross wt. 2,400. Empty wt. 1,614. Fuel capacity 41. Engine 210-hp Continental. PERFORMANCE: Top mph 115. Cruise mph 104. Stall mph 54. Initial climb rate 1,150. Range 530. Ceiling 18,500. Takeoff distance (50') 560. Landing distance (50') 600.

The Cessna L-19 "Bird Dog" was adopted by the U.S. Army for liaison and observation work in 1950. The airplane was used extensively in Korea and later in Vietnam in these and other capacities. A total of 3,381 L-19 series aircraft were built by Cessna, the last in 1963. Some have reached civilian hands and are prized

as short-field utility aircraft. Ector Odessa, Texas, marketed an extensivel version of the Bird Dog under the nam eer." It is powered by a 213-hp engine stant-speed prop. A "Super" version is also produced with a 240-hp Lycoming.

CESSNA 180 "SKYWAGON"
1953–81

STANDARD DATA: Seats 4-6. Gross wt. 2,800. Empty wt. 1,643. Fuel capacity 88. Engine 230-hp Teledyne Continental. PERFORMANCE: Top mph 170. Cruise mph 163. Stall mph 55. Initial climb rate 1,100. Range 903. Ceiling 17,700. Takeoff distance (50') 1,205. Landing distance (50') 1,365.

Cessna's 180 represents another well-designed airframe that has withstood the test of time. Production deliveries of the 180 started in 1953, and it was produced through 1981 with several minor changes in design and increased engine power. Early models of this conventional-gear high-wing aircraft were powered by a 225-hp Continental engine but were otherwise similar to a Cessna 170. Although the dimensions of the 180 have been altered only a scant three inches, models since 1966 seat six persons. In 1956, a 230-hp powerplant was swapped for the original engine. The last 180s retain this engine as well as conventional gear for operation from short or rough landing strips. Also, the original vertical fin is still used in place of the swept-fin introduced on all other Cessnas (except the 185) in 1960.

The same high-compression powerplant used for the Skylane was also used for the Skywagon 180 in 1977. It achieves 230 hp at 200 RPMs less than before and adds over 50 miles to the airplane's range. In addition, takeoff performance is improved along with reduced sound levels. In 1979, wheel fairings were added as an option and were claimed to raise both maximum and cruise speeds by one knot. Both Skywagons can be converted quickly from six-place seating to provide more than 721 cu. ft. of cargo area. For agricultural uses, 1980 improvements included the option of a 151-gallon, fan-driven Sorenson spray system, deflector cable plus windshield, and landing-gear wire cutters. Also, the 20-degree flap speed was increased from 90 mph to 110 mph.

CESSNA 182 "SKYLANE"
1956–86

STANDARD DATA: Seats 4. Gross wt. 3,100. Empty wt. 1,720. Fuel capacity 92. Engine 230-hp Continental. PERFORMANCE: Top mph 168. Cruise mph 163. Stall mph 56. Initial climb rate 865. Ceiling 14,900. Range 945. Takeoff distance (50') 1,515. Landing distance (50') 1,350.

STANDARD DATA: (Turbo 182) Seats 4. Gross wt. 3,100. Empty wt. 1,725. Fuel capacity 92. Engine 235-hp turbocharged Lycoming. PERFORMANCE: Top mph 193. Cruise mph 181. Stall mph 56. Initial climb rate 965. Ceiling 20,000. Range 857. Takeoff (50') 1,475. Landing (50') 1,350.

Because of its extra size and power, many consider the 182 Skylane as the best all-round Cessna ever built. The only other fixed-gear four-place airplane that has chalked up more sales is its little brother, the 172 Skyhawk. Using the 180 series airframe, Cessna installed a tricycle landing gear, and the 182 came into being. The deluxe Skylane model appeared in 1958 and, along with most of the Cessna line, the swept vertical fin was added in 1960. The wrap-around rear window and electric flaps were new features in 1962.

With a constant-speed prop in front of a 230-hp Continental engine, the 182 Skylane carries four adults, their luggage, and a full load of fuel at 160 mph for more than 600 miles. A spacious panel provides ample room for installation of full IFR equipment for the instrument-rated owner. The 1969 features included a restyled panel with electro-lummescent lighting and a revised flap control indicator that retained the preselect feature. In 1972, a tubular spring-steel gear was installed on the 182 Skylane, bringing what was formerly a maximum landing weight of 2,800 pounds up to the gross weight of 2,950. Other changes included the addition of cuffed leading edges similar to the Robertson wing; restyled gear fairings, wing root fairings, fuel tank covers, fin tip, and rudder fairings to improve airflow and reduce drag; new stronger wheels and brakes; and optional electric elevator trim.

For 1977, the Skylane made use of a new powerplant that is capable of providing 230 hp at 200 RPMs less than the previous engine. Also, its higher compression ratio makes more efficient use of readily available 100-octane fuel. The Skylane will fly about 52 miles farther than its predecessors. A bonded wing added in 1979 provides an added standard fuel capacity of 12 gallons more than the previous year's optional long-range tanks, or 1,013 miles at 166 mph compared to 599 miles with the earlier standard tanks. There is also the added benefit of a decrease in unusable fuel.

For 1981, the Skylane was joined by a turbocharged stablemate powered by the same turbocharged 235-hp Lycoming engine found in the Turbo Skylane RG. Both the Skylane and Turbo Skylane now have a 3,100-pound maximum takeoff weight. That gives the normally aspirated Skylane 150 pounds of extra takeoff weight. The Turbo 182 has a top speed of 168 knots and cruises at 158 knots at 75% power and 20,000 feet and 145 knots (167 mph) at 75% power and 10,000 feet. When production of Piper's Turbo Dakota discontinued, the Turbo Skylane was the only player in its class.

CESSNA 182 "SKYLANE"
1997–Present

STANDARD DATA: (182T) Seats 4. Gross wt. 3,100. Empty wt. 1,897. Fuel capacity 92. Engine 230-hp Textron Lycoming IO-540-AB1A5. PERFORMANCE: Top 149 kts. Cruise 145 kts. Stall 4-54 kts. Initial climb rate 924 fpm. Service Ceiling 18,100'. Takeoff distance (50') 1,514. Landing distance (50') 1,350.

STANDARD DATA: (T182T) Seats 4. Gross wt. 3,100. Empty wt. 2,017 lbs. Fuel capacity 92. Engine 235-hp turbocharged Textron Lycoming IO-540-AB1A5. PERFORMANCE: Cruise Max 175 kts. Cruise 158 kts. Stall 49-54 kts. Initial climb rate 1,040'. Service Ceiling 20,000. Takeoff (50') 1,475. Landing (50') 1,350.

The reintroduction of both the normally aspirated (182T) and in 2001 the turbocharged (T182T) Skylane was eagerly awaited. Despite putting on a little weight with age, the new Skylanes equaled or surpassed their predecessors in every category except useful load. As with all the newest Cessna models, the emphasis was on refinement. The new batch of Skylanes came with a noticeable increase in creature comfort and weather capable instruments and avionics. In 2004, Cessna introduced Skylanes with all glass panels, and in 2005, airbags became standard equipment on all four of the C-182's seats.

CESSNA "SKYLANE RG"
1978–86

STANDARD DATA: (RG) Seats 4. Gross wt. 3,100. Empty wt. 1,750. Fuel capacity 92. Engine 235-hp Continental. PERFORMANCE: Top mph 184. Cruise mph 180. Stall mph 58. Initial climb rate 1,140. Ceiling 14,300. Range 972. Takeoff distance (50') 1,570. Landing distance (50') 1,320.

STANDARD DATA: (Turbo RG) Seats 4. Gross wt. 3,100. Empty wt. 1,797. Fuel capacity 92. Engine 235-hp turbocharged Lycoming. PERFORMANCE: Top mph 215. Cruise mph 199. Stall mph 58. Initial climb rate 1,040. Ceiling 20,000. Range 949. Takeoff distance (50') 1,570. Landing distance (50') 1,320.

The Skylane RG is the most recent addition to Cessna's high-performance retractable single-engine lineup. It retains all the features that have made the Skylane the most popular 200-hp plus single-engine airplane ever built. Without the drag of nonretractable gear, speed and climb performance have been greatly improved. The Skylane RG has a maximum speed of 184 mph and a climb speed of 1,140 fpm that puts the airplane at 7,500 feet in less than 10 minutes. Despite the addition of retractable gear, the useful load has actually been increased by 145 pounds. The retractable gear has been designed with simplicity in mind. Retraction time is seven seconds, with the main gear retracting

into the wheel wells in the fuselage and the nose gear rotating forward.

In 1979, Cessna added a turbocharged version of the Skylane RG to its line. The turbocharged model provides sea-level performance at altitude. Its rate of climb at 10,000 feet is 890 fpm, while at 20,000 feet it's 660 fpm. Above 10,000 feet, the Turbo RG will climb twice as fast as the normally aspirated model. The only noticeable external difference between the two is the one exhaust pipe instead of the two pipes on the non-turbocharged version. In 1980, both Skylane RG models added air conditioning as an option. Although not certified for flight into known icing, an optional anti-ice system includes propeller anti-ice, windshield anti-ice, heated pitot and stall warning, plus an ice detection light. Also, 1981 and later models can be fitted with three-blade propellers and an autopilot as options.

CESSNA 185 "SKYWAGON"
1961–81

STANDARD DATA: (1961-65) Seats 5-6. Gross wt. 3,200. Empty wt. 1,520. Fuel capacity 84. Engine 260-hp Continental. PERFORMANCE: Top mph 176. Cruise mph 165. Stall mph 62. Initial climb rate 1,000. Ceiling 17,300. Range 885-1,005. Takeoff distance (50') 1,510. Landing distance (50') 1,267.

STANDARD DATA: (1966-80) Seats 6. Gross wt. 3,350. Empty wt. 1,688. Fuel capacity 88. Engine 280-hp Teledyne Continental (300-hp at takeoff). PERFORMANCE: Top mph 178. Cruise mph 169. Stall mph 56. Initial climb rate 1,075. Ceiling 17,900. Range 742. Takeoff distance (50') 1,430. Landing distance (50') 1,400.

Based upon the 180 airframe, the Skywagon 185 is famous for its size, speed, and ease of flying. For the first five years, it was powered by the 260-hp Continental. That engine was replaced the following year by the 520-cu. in., six-cylinder powerplant rated at 300 hp for takeoff at 2,850 RPM. The 185 will take off in 1,025 feet, climb out at better than 1,000 fpm, and cruise at 167 mph while carrying a 1,663-pound useful load. Fuel injection enhances its all-weather reliability and economical operation. Its high-lift wing with modified Frise all-metal ailerons and 28.8 sq. ft. of Para-Lift flaps afford easy handling over obstacles. A full six-place aircraft, its seats are easily removable to provide fast change to all-cargo configuration. Its rugged interior and reinforced floor allow it to handle heavy loads, and its double cargo doors facilitate loading. Like the 180, the 185 is easily transformed into a skiplane, float-plane, or amphibian. In 1979, optional wheel fairings were offered to increase speeds by one knot, and a McCauley three-blade propeller could be ordered for smoother, quieter flight and more ground clearance. In addition to the same spray system option offered for the 180, the 185 received a three-blade propeller for lower vibration and a quieter cabin in 1980. Also, the 20-degree flap speed was increased from 90 mph to 110 mph.

CESSNA AG "CARRYALL"
1972–79

STANDARD DATA: Seats 2. Gross wt. 3,350. Empty wt. 1,895. Fuel capacity 88. Engine 300-hp Teledyne Continental fuel injected. PERFORMANCE: Top mph 148. Cruise mph 140. Stall mph 56. Initial climb rate 845. Range 650. Ceiling 13,400. Takeoff distance (50') 1,450. Landing distance (50') 1,400.

Based on the Model 185, the AG Carryall was introduced in 1971 as a multipurpose aircraft capable of performing both agricultural and general purpose duties. It is perfect for farmers who require both spraying capabilities and transportation. The AG Carryall is fitted with dual seating but has optional arrangements for four to six. It also features spray booms and a 151-gallon chemical tank. The most recent models have been equipped with an improved electrical system and an increased flap-extension speed. In 1979, the fuel tanks were enlarged to carry up to 88 gallons for extended range. Removable spray booms allow conversion from sprayplane to transportation airplane. Its Camber-Lift wing Land-O-Matic gear and Para-Lift flap give the AG Carryall the stability, maneuverability, and performance required for agricultural flying.

CESSNA 190/195
1947–54

STANDARD DATA: (190) Seats 5. Gross wt. 3,350. Empty wt. 2,015. Fuel capacity 80. Engine 240-hp Continental. PERFORMANCE: Top mph 170. Cruise mph 160. Stall mph 63. Initial climb rate 1,050. Ceiling 16,000. Range 750. Takeoff distance (50') 1,670. Landing distance (50') 1,495.

STANDARD DATA: (195) Seats 5. Gross wt. 3,350. Empty wt. 2,030. Fuel capacity 80. Engine 300-hp Jacobs Radial. PERFORMANCE: Top mph 180. Cruise mph 165. Stall mph 63. Initial climb rate 1,210. Range 750. Ceiling 18,300. Takeoff distance (50') 1,670. Landing distance (50') 1,495.

The model 190 and 195 have become Cessna classics. Some 995 of the 195s were produced between 1947 and 1954, and more than half of this number are still rated airworthy. Easily identified by their gleaming spinners and large cowlings encasing the nine-cylinder radial engines, these high-wing five-place airplanes have seen many years of service since production was discontinued. Both the 190 and 195 entered production in 1947. The 190 was powered by a 240-hp Continental radial driving a Hamilton Standard constant-speed airscrew. The 195 was virtually the same, with the exception of a more powerful 300-hp Jacobs. Engine variations resulted in two other versions, the 195B and the 195A. The 195B was fitted with the 275-hp Jacobs; the 195A, the last to be built, was powered by a Jacobs 245-hp radial and had a 50% increase in flap area on the huge, strutless wings. With an oil capacity of five gallons (minimum recommended is three gallons) the stock 195s with steel-cylinder engines will gulp about two quarts per hour, but chrome barrels will decrease the radial's consumption.

CESSNA 205/206/"STATIONAIR"
1963–86

STANDARD DATA: (Stationair 6) Seats 6. Gross wt. 3,600. Empty wt. 1,927. Fuel capacity 92. Engine 285-hp Continental (300 hp at takeoff). PERFOR-

MANCE: Top mph 179. Cruise mph 169. Stall mph 62. Initial climb rate 920. Ceiling 14,800. Range 783. Takeoff distance (50') 1,780. Landing distance (50') 1,395.

STANDARD DATA: (Turbo Stationair) Seats 6. Gross wt. 3,600. Empty wt. 2,003. Fuel capacity 92. Engine 285-hp turbocharged Continental (310 hp, at takeoff). PERFORMANCE: Top mph 200. Cruise mph 192. Stall mph 62. Initial climb rate 1,010. Ceiling 27,000. Range 737. Takeoff distance (50') 1,640. Landing distance (50') 1,395.

STANDARD DATA: (205) Seats 6. Gross wt. 3,300. Empty wt. 1,750. Fuel capacity 84. Engine 260-hp Continental. PERFORMANCE: Top mph 165. Cruise mph 158. Stall mph 57. Initial climb rate 965. Ceiling 16,100. Range 915. Takeoff distance (50') 1,465. Landing distance (50') 1,510.

STANDARD DATA: (U206) Seats 4-6. Gross wt. 3,600. Empty wt. 1,710. Fuel capacity 65-84. Engine 300-hp Continental, PERFORMANCE: Top mph 174. Cruise mph 164. Stall mph 61. Initial climb rate 920. Ceiling 14,800. Range 650-830. Takeoff distance (50') 1,780. Landing distance (50') 1,395.

STANDARD DATA: (P-206) Seats 6. Gross wt. 3,600. Empty wt. 1,820. Fuel capacity 65. Engine 285-hp Continental. PERFORMANCE: Top mph 174. Cruise mph 164. Stall mph 61. Initial climb rate 920. Ceiling 14,800. Range 650-830. Takeoff distance (50') 1,780. Landing distance (50') 1,395.

STANDARD DATA: (TU206) Seats 4-6. Gross wt. 3,600. Empty wt. 1,795. Fuel capacity 65-84. Engine 285-hp turbocharged Continental. PERFORMANCE: Top mph 200. Cruise mph 182. Stall mph 61. Initial climb rate 1,030. Ceiling 26,300. Range 700-890. Takeoff distance (50') 1,810. Landing distance (50') 1,395.

STANDARD DATA: (TP206) Seats 6. Gross wt. 3,600. Empty wt. 1,915. Fuel capacity 65. Engine 285-hp turbocharged Continental. PERFORMANCE: Top mph 200. Cruise mph 182. Stall mph 61. Initial climb rate 1,030. Ceiling 26,300. Range 700-

890. Takeoff distance (50') 1,810. Landing distance (50') 1,395.

The Cessna 205 was introduced in 1962 as an advanced version of the Skylane. It had an enlarged cabin to house six passengers and a 260-hp Continental engine. In 1964, this aircraft evolved into the Model 206, which was in turn available in three versions: U206 Super Skywagon, P206 Utility, and P206 Super Skylane. All three were powered by the 285-hp Continental engine. The Super Skywagon featured conical-camber wingtips, a tailplane of greater span, larger flaps, and double cargo doors for easy loading. The Utility version had only the usual passenger door, while the Super Skylane was the deluxe six-seat version with passenger doors on both sides in the front and a third on the rear portside. Starting in 1966, these versions also became available with turbocharging, and in 1968 the Super Skywagon's horsepower was boosted to 300. The 300-hp turbosystem Super Skywagon provided excellent over-the-weather capability with its 26,300-foot service ceiling. To permit full use of its high-altitude performance, a 76 cu. ft. oxygen system (three to four hours) included a pilot's mask with built-in microphone, five passenger oxygen masks, and other essentials.

By 1971, Cessna replaced the 206 series with the Stationair and Turbo Stationair in order to emphasize the difference between these streamlined cargo/utility aircraft and the conventional-geared 180/185 models. The Stationair and the Turbo Stationair retained the 285-hp Continental used in all previous models. All Stationairs were fitted with double cargo doors on the starboard side and could be converted easily from cargo to passenger configuration. The doors can accommodate a 4 x 3 x 3-foot crate and can also be removed for photography missions or air drops. Though the basic Stationair engine is rated at 285 hp for maximum continuous operation, it delivers up to 300 hp for takeoff.

For 1977, the turbocharged Continental powerplant was refined to deliver the same continuous power at 100 RPMs less, while its available takeoff horsepower was increased from 300 to 310. Just as before, the normally aspirated engine in the Stationair provides 300 hp for takeoff. In 1978, the Stationair 6 and Turbo Stationair 6 introduced club seating in the Cessna single engine line, replacing the 206 and Turbo Stationair. In 1979, the major change was the addition of 16 gallons of fuel, with the change to 92-gallon fuel tanks as standard equipment.

In 1980, anti-icing was added as an option. The same as used on the Skylane RG, it included propeller anti-ice, windshield anti-ice, heated pitot tube and stall warning, plus an ice detector light. Standard features for 1981 models included improved avionics cooling, a new muffler for the normally aspirated model, and an anti-precipitation static antenna when factory installed radios were ordered.

CESSNA 206 "STATIONAIR"
1998–Present

STANDARD DATA: (206H) Seats 6. Gross wt. 3,600. Empty wt. 2,179. Fuel capacity 92. Engine 300-hp Textron Lycoming IO-540-AC1A5. PERFORMANCE: Max Cruise 151 kts. Cruise 142 kts. Stall 54-62 kts. Initial climb rate 988 fpm. Service Ceiling 15,700. Takeoff distance (50') 1,860. Landing distance (50') 1,395.

STANDARD DATA: (T206H Turbo) Seats 6. Gross wt. 3,600. Empty wt. 2,279. Fuel capacity 92. Engine 300-hp turbocharged Textron Lycoming IO-540-AC1A5. PERFORMANCE: Max Cruise 178 kts. Cruise 150 kts. Stall 54-62 kts. Initial climb rate 1,050 fpm. Service Ceiling 27,000. Takeoff distance (50') 1,740. Landing distance (50') 1,395.

The 206 Stationair had been such a Cessna success story that many thought it was only a matter of time before it came back into production. The aging fleet of big piston singles was still coming and going from virtually every type of runway in the world, polishing its reputation as the world's best heavy hauler. Though the pressurized versions of the Stationair did not make the cut for the new production schedule, an audience built over more than forty years of service quickly applauded the return of both the normally aspirated and turbocharged C-206.

Though the new Stationairs did suffer a loss in useful load, they could still best the overall performance figures turned in by the older legacy fleet. The modern turbocharged 206 could now climb all the way to 27,000' and turn in an honest 170+ knots. No piston single in product can match the Stationair's combination of speed, altitude and load lifting talent.

Cessna also markets a luxury version of the big single, emphasizing its capabilities of carrying executives or families for short to medium trips. Adjustable leather seats, state-of-the-art avionics, pilot and passenger air bags, reading lights, individual climate control vents and passenger-friendly double doors can deliver surprising creature comfort to an airplane revered for its bare-knuckled utility.

CESSNA "STATIONAIR 8"/7/ "SKYWAGON" 207
1969–86

STANDARD DATA: (Stationair 8) Seats 8. Gross wt. 3,800. Empty wt. 2,110. Fuel capacity 61-80. Engine 285-hp fuel-injected Continental (300 hp at take-off). PERFORMANCE: Top mph 173. Cruise mph 165. Stall mph 67. Initial climb rate 810. Ceiling 13,300. Range 403-604. Takeoff distance (50') 1,970. Landing distance (50') 1,500.

STANDARD DATA: (Turbo Stationair 8) Seats 8. Gross wt. 3,800. Empty wt. 2,183. Fuel capacity 61-80. Engine 285-hp turbocharged Continental (310 hp at takeoff). PERFORMANCE: Top mph 196. Cruise mph 185. Stall mph 67. Initial climb rate 885. Ceiling 26,000. Range 345-547. Takeoff distance (50') 1,860. Landing distance (50') 1,500.

STANDARD DATA: (Stationair 7) Seats 7. Gross wt. 3,800. Empty wt. 2,076. Fuel capacity 61-80. Engine 285-hp Continental (300 hp at takeoff). PERFORMANCE: Top mph 173. Cruise mph 165. Stall mph 67. Initial climb rate 810. Ceiling 13,300. Range 449-650. Takeoff distance (50') 1,970. Landing distance (50') 1,500.

STANDARD DATA: (Turbo Stationair 7) Seats 7. Gross wt. 3,800. Empty wt. 2,157. Fuel capacity 61-80. Engine 285-hp turbocharged Continental (310 hp at takeoff). PERFORMANCE: Top mph 196. Cruise mph 185. Stall mph 67. Initial climb rate 885. Ceiling 26,000. Range 403-604. Takeoff distance (50') 1,860. Landing distance (50') 1,500.

Cessna seemed willing to go to any length to sell airplanes. The company went to a length of 31 feet, 9 inches on the Model 207. The 165 cubic feet of fuselage can accommodate almost a ton of cargo or a starting basketball team and two substitutes. Power is the Continental IO-520F equipped with fuel injection to deliver 300 hp for takeoff and 285 hp max continuous. The Turbo model is outfitted with the TSIO-520G and delivers the same power for takeoff and continuous flight.

CESSNA 208 "CARAVAN"
1985–Present

Caravan

Super Caravan

Caravan on floats

STANDARD DATA: (Model 675) Seats 2-14. Empty wt. 3,973 lbs. Maximum Useful Load 4,062 lbs. Fuel capacity 335 gallons. Engine Pratt & Whitney PT6A-114A, 675 shp. PERFORMANCE: Cruise 186 kts. Stall 61 kts. Initial climb rate 1,234 fpm. Service Ceiling 25,000. Takeoff distance (50') 2,053. Landing distance (50') 1,655 ft.

STANDARD DATA: (Grand Caravan) Seats 2-14. Empty wt. 4,285 lbs. Maximum Useful Load 4,500 lbs. Fuel capacity 335 gallons. Engine Pratt & Whitney PT6A-114A, 675 shp. PERFORMANCE: Cruise 184 kts. Stall 61 kts. Initial climb rate 975 fpm. Service Ceiling 25,000. Takeoff distance (50') 1,365. Landing distance (50') 1,795 ft.

Cessna's biggest single was in a class all by itself from the very beginning. The square-cabin design was roomier than many twins, and the bulletproof Pratt & Whitney turboprop up front made the Caravan 675 reliable and comparatively inexpensive to operate. It could haul a staggering amount of people or cargo, land on virtually any runway surface and gleefully take to the water on floats (the Caravan Amphibian).

In 1987, Cessna introduced the Super Cargomaster, with an additional 340 cubic feet of space, and 720 more pounds of load carrying capacity. The same fuselage would eventually appear as the more refined Grand Caravan in 1990. At 15 feet tall, 41.6 feet long with a 52.1-foot wingspan, it remains the largest Cessna single ever. In 2004, the Caravan was optionally available with an Oasis interior, which allowed the single engine turboprop to compete with the luxuries of any pure jet on the market.

CESSNA "AG WAGON"/"AG TRUCK"/ "AG HUSKY"
1965–83

STANDARD DATA: (AG Husky) Seats 1. Gross wt. 4,400. Empty wt. 2,293. Fuel capacity 54. Engine 310-hp, turbocharged Continental. PERFORMANCE: Top mph 126. Cruise mph 118. Stall mph 67. Initial climb rate 510. Ceiling 14,000. Range 245. Takeoff distance (50') 1,975. Landing distance (50') 1,265.

STANDARD DATA: (AG Wagon) Seats 1. Gross wt. 4,000. Empty wt. 2,164. Fuel capacity 54. Engine 285-hp fuel-injected Continental (300 hp at takeoff). PERFORMANCE: Top mph 151. Cruise mph 112. Stall mph 63. Initial climb rate 550. Ceiling 9,100. Range 260. Takeoff distance (50') 1,885. Landing distance (50') 1,265.

STANDARD DATA: (AG Truck) Seats 1. Gross wt. 4,200. Empty wt. 2,222. Fuel capacity 54. Engine 285-hp fuel-injected Continental (300 hp at takeoff). PERFORMANCE: Top mph 120. Cruise mph 111. Stall mph 65. Initial climb rate 490. Ceiling 8,100. Range 250. Takeoff distance (50') 2,140. Landing distance (50') 1,265.

Especially designed for agricultural use, the AG Wagon incorporates a variety of features to improve both the effectiveness and safety of spraying and dusting operations. The AG Truck is basically similar to the AG Wagon except that it carries a 280-gallon hopper rather than the former's 200-gallon hopper. Both airplanes are equipped with extra-heavy springsteel landing gear with oversized tires; camber-lift wings and wing fences for

33

Cessna AG Wagon

Cessna AG Truck

Cessna AG Husky

better slow-speed control and smooth airflow; ample cockpit safety padding, wire cutters, and cable deflector; and various chemical dispersal systems. The cockpit features 360-degree vision and an airscoop that develops slight pressurization to keep out dust and chemicals.

Both the AG Wagon and AG Truck are powered by a 300-hp Teledyne Continental turning a constant-speed propeller. The AG Pickup, which was discontinued in 1972, and previous AG models housed smaller 230-hp Continentals. Cessna introduced the turbocharged AG Husky to its agricultural line in 1979. The highly efficient turbocharged Husky has a 310-hp engine to provide extra performance at varying operating altitudes. Standard equipment on the AG Husky is a 280-gallon hopper, an exclusive dispersal system, special lighting package, and a three-blade wide-chord prop. A new high-volume dispersal system that was standard on 1981-83 models allowed capability for up to 25% more chemical flow. Also, a redesigned emergency dump control gives fast, more convenient operation. Standard equipment on the AG Truck was an 86-inch two-blade threadless retention propeller. An 80-inch three-blade prop was an option.

CESSNA 210 "CENTURION"
1960–86

Cessna Turbo Centurion II

Cessna Pressurized Centurion

STANDARD DATA: (Centurion) Seats 4-6. Gross wt. 3,800. Empty wt. 2,133. Fuel capacity 90. Engine 300-hp Teledyne Continental (at takeoff). PERFORMANCE: Top mph 201. Cruise mph 198. Stall mph 64. Initial climb rate 950. Ceiling 17,300. Range 926. Takeoff distance (50') 2,030. Landing distance (50') 1,500.

STANDARD DATA: (Turbo) Seats 4-6. Gross wt. 4,000. Empty wt. 2,221. Fuel capacity 90. Engine 310-hp turbocharged Teledyne Continental (at takeoff). PERFORMANCE: Top mph 235. Cruise mph 226. Stall mph 67. Initial climb rate 930. Ceiling 27,000. Range 869 (80%). Takeoff distance (50') 2,160. Landing distance (50') 1,500.

STANDARD DATA: (Pressurized) Seats 4-6. Gross wt. 4,000. Empty wt. 2,340. Fuel capacity 90. Engine 310-hp turbocharged Continental (at takeoff). PERFORMANCE: Top mph 237. Cruise mph 230. Stall mph 67. Initial climb rate 930. Ceiling 23,000. Range 926 (70%). Takeoff distance (50') 2,160. Landing distance (50') 1,500.

STANDARD DATA: (Early 210) Seats 4. Gross wt. 2,900. Empty wt. 1,735. Fuel capacity 84. Engine 260-hp Continental. PERFORMANCE: Top mph 199. Cruise mph 190. Stall mph 59. Initial climb rate 1,300. Ceiling 20,700. Range 985. Takeoff distance (50') 1,135. Landing distance (50') 1,190.

Until the introduction of the Cardinal RG in 1971, the Cessna 210 Centurion was the only single-engine, high-wing, retractable gear airplane manufactured by the largest maker of light aircraft. The Centurion was introduced in 1960, and the early versions had a top speed of about 195 mph. A gain in horsepower to 185 increased the top speed by five mph, but it was not until 1966, when a turbocharged engine was made available, and 1967, when the strutless wing was installed, that the Centurion became a truly high-speed aircraft. Service ceiling with the turbocharged engine is high enough to get over most weather problems. The maximum takeoff and landing weight had been increased to 3,800 pounds, with almost half of that in useful load. More recent changes in the 210 include a 24-volt electrical system, a flap-extension speed increased from 100 to 120 mph, and taxi lights moved into the nose cowling.

Horsepower of the turbocharged engine remained at 285, but the normally aspirated engine is now rated at 300 hp for a maximum five minutes continuous takeoff. Like other Cessna models employing the turbocharged version of the basic 285-hp Continental, the Turbo Centurion makes use of 310 hp on takeoff. Overall, the 1977 T210 climbs and cruises faster and more efficiently than its 1976 counterpart. Maximum cruise speed is up by approximately six mph at altitudes between 10,000 and 20,000 feet. Also, the reduction in takeoff distance is a significant 130 feet less than before. Other refinements included power switch/circuit breakers, simplified wiring, improved ventilation, and a redesigned vernier mixture control. In 1978, Cessna introduced the world's first pressurized single-engine aircraft, the Pressurized Centurion with standard seating for six, the economy of up to 77 seat-miles per gallon, and a payload of more than 1,100 pounds with full fuel. The pressurized differential provides a 12,000-foot cabin at 23,000 feet. A special high-capacity turbocharger on the Continental powerplant supports the pressurization system.

Improvements for 1979 included elimination of the main landing gear doors to decrease the empty weight of the aircraft by 25 pounds, dropping gear-retraction time to less than eight seconds, and simplifying maintenance. For the Turbo Centurion, takeoff weight was increased by 200 pounds to 4,000 pounds so that it now equaled the figures for the pressurized model. In 1980, air conditioning and deice became an option for all Centurion models. Newer standard features were an improved avionics cooling system and an anti-precipitation antenna.

Though many believed that the pressurized Centurion had evolved into a nearly perfect high altitude single, the model was shelved when Cessna ceased all single engine production after the 1986 model year and has never reappeared.

CHAMPION "TRAVELLER"/ "CHALLENGER"
1955–65

STANDARD DATA: (Traveller) Seats 2. Gross wt. 1,450. Empty wt. 820. Fuel capacity 24. Engine 90-hp Continental. PERFORMANCE: Top mph 135. Cruise mph 112. Stall mph 40. Initial climb rate 700. Range 500. Ceiling 15,500. Takeoff run 890. Landing roll 755.

STANDARD DATA: (Challenger) Seats 2. Gross wt. 1,650. Empty wt. 1,050. Fuel capacity 39. Engine 150-hp Lycoming. PERFORMANCE: Top mph 162. Cruise mph 125. Stall mph 36. Initial climb rate 1,145. Range 510. Ceiling 17,500. Takeoff distance (50') 493. Landing distance (50') 580.

Champion Aircraft, formed in June 1954, acquired the manufacturing rights to Aeronca's Model 7 Champ and put the monoplane back into production as the 7EC Traveller. The Traveller was powered by a 90-hp Continental four-cylinder engine. The first Champion-built models were marketed in 1955, and several revised versions soon followed. The Tri-Traveller was introduced in 1957 with tricycle landing gear added to the Traveller airframe. In 1958, the 7GC entered production as the Sky-Trac with a 140-hp Lycoming. From this evolved the 7GCB Challenger powered by a 150-hp Lycoming. The 7ECA Citabria was a refinement of the Traveller Deluxe, which was in turn a further development of the 7EC Traveller. The Challenger was out of production by 1965, but the Citabria was continued until 1970, when it was bought by Bellanca.

CHAMPION 7FC "TRI-TRAVELLER"
1956–64

STANDARD DATA: Seats 2. Gross wt. 1,500. Empty wt. 910. Fuel capacity 26. Engine 90-hp Continental. PERFORMANCE: Top mph 135. Cruise mph 105. Stall mph 40. Initial climb rate 800. Range 500. Ceiling 12,000. Takeoff run 250.

The Champion 7FC Tri-Traveller is derived from the Model 7EC Traveller, and production began in 1956. The Tri-Traveller differed from its predecessors by em-

ploying a tricycle fixed undercarriage. This tandem two-seater is powered by a single 90-hp Continental C912F four-cylinder engine. It is of mixed construction with a fabric-covered welded steel-tube fuselage. The wings are built with two wooden spars, aluminum ribs, and fabric covering. The Tri-Traveller was widely used by flying schools as a trainer.

CHANCE-VOUGHT F4U "CORSAIR"
1941–57

STANDARD DATA: Seats 1. Gross wt. 12,309. Empty wt. 8,694. Engine 2,250-hp Pratt & Whitney. PERFORMANCE: Top mph 425. Cruise mph 350. Stall mph 80. Initial climb rate 3,120. Range 1,560. Ceiling 44,100.

The prototype XF4U4 was delivered to the Navy in 1940, and after extensive testing the Corsair entered quantity production in the fall of 1941. The Corsair was the first United States fighter to exceed 400 mph, and the airplane achieved an outstanding record as a carrier fighter during World War II and as a ground attack weapon in Korea. During the record period of production that extended from 1941 to 1957, over 12,000 of the type were built, several of which are currently active in civilian hands.

CIRRUS SR20/SR22/SRV
1999–Present

STANDARD DATA: (SR20/SRV) Seats 4. Gross wt. 3,000 lbs. Empty wt. 2,070/2,050 lbs. Usable fuel capacity 56 gallons. Engine 200-hp Continental IO-

Cirrus SR20

Cirrus 2R22

Cirrus SRV

360-ES. PERFORMANCE: Cruise 150 kts. Stall 54 kts. Initial climb rate 900 fpm. Takeoff distance (50') 1,958'. Landing distance (50') 2,040'.

STANDARD DATA: (SR22) Seats 4. Gross wt. 3,400 lbs. Empty wt. 2,250 lbs. Usable fuel capacity 81 gallons. Engine 310-hp Continental IO-550-N. PERFORMANCE: Cruise 185 kts. Stall 54 kts. Initial climb rate 1,400. Takeoff distance (50') 1,575'. Landing distance (50') 2,325'.

When aviation suffered serious economic setbacks in the first half of the 1980s, Cessna, the world's largest general aviation manufacturer simply stopped producing single-engine aircraft. Other manufacturers, such as Piper and Mooney and Beechcraft, saw their production runs dwindle to a mere fraction of what it once was. Needless to say, very little innovation came from the traditional airplane manufacturers.

Instead the innovations began to come from homebuilders. Free from the financial burdens of certifying their airplanes, experimental/home built/kit plane builders were free to explore new methods of construction and aerodynamic design.

Two of the new players were brothers, Dale and Alan Klapmeier, who established Cirrus Design Corporation in 1984. Three years later they debuted their first airplane, the VK-30, interesting in that it was made of carbon composite fiber, instead of aluminum. By 1994, the Klapmeiers were showing off a new composite airplane, the Cirrus SR20, which boasted two new important firsts in general aviation: an airframe parachute, and large multi-function display screen on the instrument panel.

By 1998, Cirrus had been awarded a FAA type certificate for the SR20, and in 1999 delivered their first aircraft. By 2001 they introduced a new version of their composite, the SR22, this time with more power and a slightly longer wing. In less than a decade, Cirrus Design developed into one of the world's major aircraft manufacturers.

In 2002 the company began production of the SRV, the "V" signifying VFR only. The aircraft was a simplified version of the SR20 and took its place as the Cirrus entry-level aircraft.

LANCAIR COLUMBIA 300/350/400

STANDARD DATA: (Columbia 300/350) Seats 4. Gross wt. 3,400. Empty wt. 2,300. Fuel capacity 98. Engine 310-hp TCM IO-550-N. PERFORMANCE: Top Speed, 190 KTAS. Cruise 165 KTAS. Stall mph 50. Ceiling 18,000'. Rate of Climb 1,225 fpm. Takeoff roll/50 ft, 1250'. Landing roll/50 ft, 2,350'. Range 1,320 nm.

STANDARD DATA: (Columbia 400) Seats 4. Gross wt. 3,600. Empty wt. 2,350. Fuel capacity 98. Engine 310-hp TCM TSIO-550. PERFORMANCE: Cruise 223 kts. Stall mph 59. Initial climb rate 1,635. Ceiling 25,000'. Takeoff/50 ft, 1,800'. Landing/50 ft, 2,350'.

Company founder Lance Neibauer began designing aircraft more like a sculptor than an engineer, carving his signature flowing fuselage designs out of stacks of foam. His resulting kit models quickly garnered a reputation for unmatchable speed and performance. In 1994, Neibauer announced his entry into the certified light aircraft category, the Columbia, which was made entirely of composite fiber materials. Four years later, the FAA awarded type certification to the Columbia 300, now the basis for the Lancair family of four-seat singles.

The Columbia 300 was one of the first aircraft to employ large LCD multi-function display screens, and the yoke was replaced by a side-stick control. Perhaps the most remarkable feature was its speed — 220 mph despite fixed gear.

The Columbia 350 transformed its predecessor into an all-electric airplane, replacing gyro-driven systems with dual redundant electrical systems to power an all-glass cockpit. Dual turbocharging was added in 2004, creating the Columbia 400. That raised the Columbia's operating envelope up to 25,000' and delivered 288 mph at FL240, again with the gear down and welded.

COMMANDER AIRCRAFT 114/115

STANDARD DATA: (114) Seats 4. Gross wt. 3,260. Empty wt. 2,102. Fuel capacity 68. Engine 260-hp Lycoming IO-540-T4B5. PERFORMANCE: Cruise

160 kts. Stall mph 54 kts. Initial climb rate 1,160. Range 705. Ceiling 16,800'. Takeoff distance 1,145'. Landing distance 720'.

The first examples of this airframe came from aerospace giant Rockwell Aircraft. Their model 112 first flew in late 1970 and continued to evolve through a number of engine changes. In 1976, a six-cylinder 260-hp powerplant was installed and the model became the Rockwell Commander 114. When Gulfstream purchased the rights to Rockwell designs in 1979, the 112 and 114 models were taken out of production. The Commander Aircraft Company acquired the manufacturing rights in 1991, and by the next year, the first Commander 114 rolled off the line, now designated the 114B. The new Commander had a few enhancements, primarily in the way of modernized avionics. The Bethany, Oklahoma manufacturer also produced a turbocharged version, the 270-hp 114TC. In 2000, Commander replaced the 114 models with the 115 and 115TC. Changes included extended fuel capability, upgraded standard avionics, and a series of system refinements.

CONSOLIDATED VULTEE (CONVAIR) L-13
1945

STANDARD DATA: (L-13) Seats 3. Gross wt. 2,900. Empty wt. 2,070. Fuel capacity 60-112. Engine 245-hp Franklin. PERFORMANCE: Top mph 115. Cruise mph 92. Stall mph 43. Initial climb rate 1,050. Ceiling 15,000. Range 368-750. Takeoff distance (50') 561. Landing distance (50') 483.

STANDARD DATA: (Centaur) Seats 6. Gross wt. 3,550. Empty wt. 2,300. Engine 300-hp Lycoming. PERFORMANCE: Top mph 121. Cruise mph 100. Stall mph 46. Initial climb rate 750. Ceiling 13,100. Range 850. Takeoff distance (50') 725. Landing distance (50') 700.

First built in 1945, the L-13 was intended to meet military requirements for a general-purpose liaison, observation, photographic, and ambulance aircraft. By 1947, 300 aircraft were delivered; twenty-eight were adapted for Arctic use on wheels, skis, or floats. Standard seating was for one pilot, an observer, and a third member aft. As an ambulance airplane, the L-13 carried a pilot, medical attendant, and two casualty stretchers. Power was supplied by a 245-hp Franklin flat six-cylinder engine. The aircraft payload was 833 pounds. As is often the case with military observation/liaison aircraft, several companies have produced civilian versions. Most conversions are fitted with 300-hp Lycoming radial engines, such as the Centaur 101 (originally the Longren Centaur). This model can seat up to six persons and has double loading doors in the starboard side. The Caribbean Traders Husky Mk 11 is similarly powered but makes use of an extended vertical stabilizer and can accommodate up to eight persons. Another firm, L-13 Inc., built a 300-hp version that could carry up to one ton of cargo in addition to the pilot. Its structure is reinforced, but otherwise it is similar to the Centaur 101 and the Husky.

CONSOLIDATED VULTEE BT-13 "VALIANT"
1941–45

STANDARD DATA: Seats 2. Gross wt. 4,360. Empty wt. 3,345. Fuel capacity 120. Engine 450-hp Pratt & Whitney. PERFORMANCE: Top mph 166. Cruise mph 140. Stall mph 75. Initial climb rate 1,562. Range 516. Ceiling 16,500.

Almost 10,000 BT-13 basic trainers were manufactured for the Army Air Corps before and during World War II, but relatively few remain active. Designed by the Vultee Aircraft Division of the Aviation Manufacturing Corp., the airplane soon took the parent name of Convair as the former company merged with the Consolidated Aircraft Corp. to become Consolidated Vultee Aircraft Corp. (Convair). The airplane was officially named the Valiant, universally dubbed the "Vibrator," but fly it did, behind a 450-hp Pratt & Whitney Wasp Junior nine-cylinder engine or a Wright Whirlwind of the same power. Similar in many respects to the much more prevalent T-6, except for fixed landing gear and generally lower performance, the BT-13 was used by the Air Corps as a "halfway house" on the training road between biplane and civilian lightplane training and the advanced instruction given in the AT-6. Those who enjoy restoring older aircraft can have a field day with the Valiant, several hundred of which exist in out-of-license condition and needing major repair. Plenty of airframes exist for parts sources, and the Wasp that powered most Valiants is one of the best engines ever built; parts and service are available almost anywhere in the free world. The Valiant is relatively easy to fly but weighs almost as much as the Cessna 310 or Beech Baron when everything is full, so it can't be treated like an Aircoupe.

CULVER DART MODEL G
1938–41, 1946

STANDARD DATA: Seats 2. Gross wt. 1,550. Empty wt. 910. Engine 90-hp Lambert. PERFORMANCE: Top mph 132. Cruise mph 112. Initial climb rate 850. Range 580. Ceiling 14,800.

The Dart Model G two-seat light cabin monoplane, designed by Al Mooney, was originally produced as the Lambert Monosport by Lambert Aircraft Corp., which later became the Monocoupe Corp. Designs and rights were later acquired by the Dart Manufacturing Corp. and then ultimately held by Culver Aircraft. Production of the Model G began in 1938. A 90-hp Lambert five-cylinder radial air-cooled engine provided the power. Variations of the Dart were designated by engine type and an alpha code after the G prefix. For example, the Dart GK was powered by a 90-hp Ken Royce five-cylinder radial, and the Dart GW was equipped with a 90-hp Warner Scarab Junior radial swinging a Hamilton Standard aluminum prop. The Model GC was subsequently produced with a 100-hp Continental. All Dart Model Gs were of mixed construction with welded steel-tube fuselages and wooden wings. Seating was for two in side-by-side fashion with dual controls. In all, 51 Darts were manufactured.

CULVER CADET
1939–41

STANDARD DATA: Seats 2. Gross wt. 1,305. Empty wt. 730. Fuel capacity 20. Engine 80-hp Franklin or 75-hp Continental. PERFORMANCE: (LFA) Top mph 140. Cruise mph 120. Stall mph 45. Initial climb rate 800. Range 600. Ceiling 17,500.

The Culver Aircraft Co. was formed to take over Dart Manufacturing Corporation's production of the Dart Model G in 1939. A new aircraft, similar to the Dart in appearance, but smaller, was designed and soon became known as the Cadet. The aircraft was modified and in 1940 became the Model LCA. Production of the wooden aircraft lasted until the next year when the Culver company closed its civilian works to concentrate on military contracts. The LCA was powered by a 75-hp Continental engine, while a similar version, the LFA, was powered by an 80-hp Franklin four-cylinder engine.

CULVER NR-D

STANDARD DATA: Seats 1. Gross wt. 1,830. Engine 150-hp Franklin. PERFORMANCE: Top mph 175. Cruise mph 160. Initial climb rate 800. Range 512.

The Culver NR-D was initially a radio-controlled target airplane intended to simulate enemy attacks. Its design was derived from that of the Culver Cadet. A unique feature in comparison to other target planes was that it was built with a single-seat cockpit and could be flown manually. When the surplus planes became available to private owners, the cockpit made the conversion to conventional private use very easy. The radio-controlled equipment was removed, and the interiors were refinished.

CULVER MODEL V
1946–62

STANDARD DATA: Seats 2. Gross wt. 1,600. Empty wt. 1,030. Fuel capacity 32. Engine 90-hp Continental. PERFORMANCE: Top mph 135. Cruise mph 130. Stall mph 55. Initial climb rate 750. Range 700. Ceiling 13,100. Takeoff run 800. Takeoff distance (50') 1,600.

The Model V was introduced in 1946 by the Culver Aircraft Corp., but few were produced before the company went bankrupt in the same year. In those years, power was supplied by an 85-hp Continental engine. In 1956, Superior Aircraft Co. was founded to acquire Culver Aircraft and reinstate production of the Model V under the name Superior Satellite. The Satellite used a 90-hp Continental engine, but otherwise retained the same basic structure as the Model V. The fuselage and wings were constructed from resin-bonded spruce and plywood.

CURTISS JN-4D "JENNY"
1914

STANDARD DATA: Seats 2. Gross wt. 2,130. Empty wt. 1,580. Engine 90-hp Curtiss OX-5. PERFORMANCE: Top mph 75. Cruise mph 65. Stall mph 35. Initial climb rate 250.

The Curtiss Jenny was America's first mass-produced commercially viable airplane. Designed in 1914 to lower the accident record for pusher airplanes, the Jenny went on to become the standard U.S. military trainer throughout World War I and for five years thereafter. Nearly 7,000 were built, and surplus Jennies began showing up in civilian hands by 1919. For around $6,000 you could buy a crated Jenny, put it together, and start your own barnstorming business. Many took up the challenge with varying degrees of success. The fatal flaw of the Jenny (aside from a vicious stall-spin characteristic) was the powerplant. Literally dozens of things could (and did) go wrong with the OX-5, and an engine failure every 10 hours was not uncommon. By the close of the 1920s, wrecks, and rot had begun to take a toll on the original 7,000.

CURTISS-WRIGHT C1 "ROBIN"
1928–30

STANDARD DATA: Seats 3. Gross wt. 2,620. Empty wt. 1,710. Fuel capacity 35. Engine 90-hp Curtiss OX-5 or 225-hp Continental W-670K. PERFORMANCE: (90 hp). Top mph 100. Cruise mph 84. Initial climb rate 400. Range 800. Ceiling 10,200. PERFORMANCE (225 hp): Top mph 126. Cruise mph 104. Initial climb rate 800. Range 410. Ceiling 14,250.

The design and production of the first Curtiss Robin three-seat monoplanes was begun by the Curtiss Aeroplane and Motor Co. in Garden City, New York. It was soon decided that producing a commercial machine in a factory primarily equipped for military aircraft was impractical; thus, the Curtiss-Robertson Airplane Manufacturing Corp. was formed in 1928 to take over production of the Curtiss Robin C-1. The first Robin's modest price was primarily due to its use of cheap, surplus 90-hp OX-5 engines. Sales were excellent, and the type became the first cabin three-seater to be mass-produced. During the plane's production life, several variations were produced with different engines, but today about half of the Robins still in service are powered by 225-hp Continentals. As the supply of the OX-5 engines diminished, the Robin was introduced with the new Curtiss Challenger 165-hp engine. This combination proved to be the most popular of the last several Robin models, and over 750 were sold. In the last year of production, a four-place variant of the type was introduced as the Robin 4C-1A but failed to achieve much of a following; only 25 of this type were produced.

CURTISS-WRIGHT P-40 "HAWK"
1938–44

STANDARD DATA: Seats 1. Gross wt. 6,789. Empty wt. 5,381. Engine 1,200-hp Allison liquid-cooled V-12. PERFORMANCE: Top mph 365. Cruise mph 315. Landing mph 72.5. Range 945. Ceiling 35,000.

The P-40 Warhawk saw wider service than any other fighter during World War II. It was present on every front throughout the world from 1939 to 1945, and it flew under the colors of 28 allied nations. The Warhawk was the only Army Air Corps fighter in service during the first month of the war, and it (along with the British Spitfire and the Grumman Wildcat) bore the bulk of the responsibility for meeting the enemy's attack until late in 1942. The Warhawk fought in Africa, England, Australia, China, and Russia. A total of 13,783 P-40s were produced during the war. Power was supplied by a single 1,200-hp Allison 12-cylinder liquid-cooled engine.

DAVIS D1-W
1930

STANDARD DATA: Seats 2. Gross wt. 1,460. Empty wt. 925. Engine 125-hp Warner Scarab. PERFORMANCE: Top mph 142. Cruise mph 122. Initial climb rate 1,360. Ceiling 14,800.

Davis Aircraft Corp. produced three models of the D4 series two-seat light monoplanes in the early 1930s. Neither of the first two models, the D-1-85 with an 85-hp Le Blond engine or the D-1-K with a 100-hp Kinner engine, can be found active today. The third model, the D1-W was equipped with a 125-hp Warner Scarab seven-cylinder radial air-cooled engine. Very few D1-

W models can be found still active. Easily identified by the large "Parasol" type wing and what looks like an over-sized engine for its small, open-cockpit fuselage, the Dl-W features complete dual controls for its tandem seats. The aircraft has a steel-tube fuselage covered with fabric and a two-spar wing.

DE HAVILLAND DH-4
1917–24

STANDARD DATA: Seats 2. Gross wt. 3,740. Empty wt. 2,440. Engine 420-hp Liberty. PERFORMANCE: Top mph 124. Cruise mph 115. Stall mph 55. Initial climb rate 1,000. Range 350.

The DH-4 was the first combat plane to go into production in the United States. Over 3,400 of the type were built before production ceased at the war's end in 1918. Armed with two Vickers guns on the cowl, two Lewis guns at the rear cockpit and 220 pounds of bombs in the wing racks, it became the first and only American-built plane to fly over enemy territory in World War I. After the Armistice, variations of the DH-4 remained with the military services as observation or transport planes until 1932. During the 1920s, DH-4s also achieved prominence as airmail carriers piloted by such luminaries as Charles Lindbergh. Generally, the type was very serviceable with tremendous load-carrying capability and good reliability; however, its early versions quickly achieved the inglorious title of "Flaming Coffins" because the fuel tanks had a habit of exploding. Though the problem was satisfactorily resolved after the first year of production, the title stuck. Scant few exist today.

DE HAVILLAND DH-60 "GIPSYMOTH"
1925–32

STANDARD DATA: Seats 2. Gross wt. 1,750. Empty wt. 920. Engine 120-hp de Havilland Gipsy II. PERFORMANCE: Top mph 107. Cruise mph 85. Initial climb rate 720. Range 320. Ceiling 18,000.

The de Havilland Moth series of two-seat light biplanes began with the flight of the DH-60 in 1925. The original Moths had a wooden fuselage structure and

were powered by engines ranging from the 60-hp A.D.C. Cirrus I to the 105-hp Cirrus Hermes. As production of the early models tapered off, the improved DH-60 GM Gipsy Moth was introduced in 1928. The Gipsy featured a welded steel-tube fuselage, folding wings, and engine options up to 120-hp. About 1,700 DH-60s were built in England during the seven years of production, with an additional 150 built by Moth Aircraft Co. of Lowell, Massachusetts.

DE HAVILLAND DH-82
"TIGER MOTH"
1931–45

STANDARD DATA: Seats 2. Gross wt. 1,825. Empty wt. 1,115. Engine 130-hp Gipsy Major 1. PERFORMANCE: Top mph 109. Cruise mph 90. Stall mph 43. Initial climb rate 673. Range 300. Ceiling 13,600.

The Tiger Moth was the final refinement of the two-place Moth series. Distinguished in part from its predecessors by its swept-back folding wings and more powerful Gipsy Major engine, the Tiger Moth first flew in October 1931, and more than 1,000 had been delivered by the outbreak of World War II. During the war, the British government adopted the biplane as a primary trainer for military flying schools throughout the Commonwealth. Between 1939 and 1945, de Havilland built 4,005 Tiger Moths in the United Kingdom and 1,747 in Canada. After the plane was declared surplus in 1947, it became perhaps the most widely operated biplane in Canada and Europe. Several examples have recently been imported into the United States and are finding great favor for their acrobatic capability and antiquated appearance.

DE HAVILLAND CANADA
DHC-1 "CHIPMUNK"
1946–53

STANDARD DATA: Seats 2. Gross wt. 1,930. Empty wt. 1,158. Fuel capacity 30. Engine 145-hp D.H. Gipsy Major. PERFORMANCE: Top mph 139. Cruise mph 124. Stall mph 50. Initial climb rate 900. Range 485. Ceiling 17,200. Takeoff distance (50') 870. Landing distance (50') 930.

The Chipmunk was designed by the Canadian de Havilland company for use as a primary trainer in both Canada and the United Kingdom. Slightly over 200 machines were produced in Canada, but over 1,000 were manufactured in Britain. A further 60 Chipmunks were produced in the late 1950s under license in Portugal. Few of these airplanes have made their way into the United States, but of those that have, most have been extensively modified for acrobatic and airshow work. Seating is tandem fashion under a sliding bubble canopy. A 145-hp Gipsy Major four-cylinder engine turns either a fixed-pitch wood propeller or a metal Fairey-Reed airscrew. The fuselage and wings are of all-metal construction, but the ailerons, elevators, and rudder are fabric covered.

DE HAVILLAND CANADA
DHC-2 "BEAVER"
1948–69

STANDARD DATA: (Mk I) Seats 7. Gross wt. 5,100. Empty wt. 3,000. Fuel capacity 95-138. Engine 450-hp Pratt & Whitney. PERFORMANCE: Top mph 140. Cruise mph 135. Stall mph 60. Initial climb rate 1,020. Range 778. Ceiling 18,000. Takeoff distance (50') 1,015. Landing distance (50') 1,000.

STANDARD DATA: (Mk III) Seats 7-9. Gross wt. 5,370. Empty wt. 2,760. Fuel capacity 191. Engine

578-eshp Pratt & Whitney turboprop. PERFOR-MANCE: Top mph 170. Cruise mph 157. Stall mph 60. Initial climb rate 1,185. Range 677. Ceiling 20,500. Takeoff distance (50') 920. Landing distance (50') 870.

The Beaver first entered production in March 1948 and was the first in a family of STOL utility aircraft designed primarily for use in the Canadian bush. Since that time it has found great favor in a variety of civilian and military roles throughout the world. Beavers have had an excellent reputation of performing under the most difficult conditions, especially in Northern Canada, Alaska, Korea, and Vietnam and are noted for their ruggedness and short-field capability. The Mark I Beaver was the first in the series and was powered by a 450-hp nine-cylinder radial. The Mark III, which first became available in 1964, was designated the TurboBeaver. Accommodations were altered to seat up to nine passengers, and a 578-eshp (estimated shaft horsepower) turboprop with increased fuel capacity was installed. The starboard seat in the pilot's compartment is removable, and the cabin floor is stressed to handle freight. The Beaver's controls feature dual rudder pedals and a Y-type control column with a throw-over wheel.

DE HAVILLAND CANADA DHC-3 "OTTER"
1952–67

STANDARD DATA: Seats 9-10. Gross wt. 8,000. Empty wt. 4,431. Fuel capacity 214. Engine 600-hp Pratt & Whitney. PERFORMANCE: Top mph 160. Cruise mph 132. Stall mph 58. Initial climb rate 850. Range 875. Ceiling 18,800. Takeoff distance (50') 1,155. Landing distance (50') 880.

The Otter began production in 1951 as a larger complement to the Beaver. Like the Beaver, it has found favor with military as well as civilian operators who demand a great deal from their airplanes. By early 1966, a total of 460 Otters had been produced, many of which went to the U.S. Army under the U-IB designation. The R.C.A.F. uses Otters in Arctic search and rescue missions, paratroop drops, and aerial photographic duties. The United States has employed them in a wide range of areas from the Antarctic to Vietnam.

DIAMOND AIRCRAFT DA-20 C1 "KATANA"
1995–present

STANDARD DATA: (DA-20) Seats 2. Gross wt. 1,764 lbs. Empty wt. 1,166 lbs. Usable fuel 24 gallons. Engine 125-hp Continental IO240B3B. PERFOR-MANCE: Top mph 199. Cruise 135 kts. Stall mph 53. Initial climb rate 1,000 fpm. Takeoff distance (50') 1,106'. Landing distance (50') 1,280'.

Originally introduced to the United States as the Diamond DV-20, the Katana is an all-composite, two-place, side-by-side training aircraft that was designed and produced in Europe by the Hoffman Öesterreische Aircraft Company (HOAC), later to be renamed Diamond Aircraft. The company's original entry into aircraft production was with the HK-36R motorglider, so it's no accident the Katana came out of the same factory with a 36' wingspan. The Austrian-based company opened engineering and production facilities in London, Ontario, and is now the third largest general aviation manufacturer of single engine aircraft in Canada.

The Katana and its several iterations (including the Katana 100, which utilizes a Bombardier Rotax engine) remain focused on the training market. The exception is the C1 Eclipse (beginning in 1999), which features extra creature comforts and advanced avionics to reach beyond the student pilot category.

DIAMOND AIRCRAFT DA-40 DIAMOND STAR

STANDARD DATA: (DA-40) Seats 4. Gross wt. 2,535 lbs. Empty wt. 1,641 lbs. Fuel capacity 41 gallons. Engine 180-hp Lycoming IO-360-M1A. PERFOR-MANCE: Cruise 145 kts. Stall 49 kts. Initial climb rate 1,070 fpm. Takeoff distance (50') 1,150'. Landing distance (50') 1,190'.

Building on the success of the Katana C1, Diamond began development of the four place DA-40 Diamond Star in 1997. The all-composite airplane would not only get a spacious fuselage, but a whole new wing (39.4'). The Diamond Star not only offered a customer upgrade to the Katana, it also sent the Austrian/Canadian company deep into new territory as a single engine, four seat, general aviation competitor. By 2000, the first DA-40s were rolling off the line. The company later intro-

duced a variant, the DA-40FP (fixed pitch propeller), and by 2004, Diamond continued its full court press by equipping the Diamond Star with all glass instrument panels.

DOUGLAS "DAUNTLESS"
1941–44

STANDARD DATA: Seats 2. Gross wt. 10,500. Empty wt. 6,450. Engine 1,200-hp Wright Cyclone. PERFORMANCE: Top mph 255. Cruise mph 185. Stall mph 78. Initial climb rate 1,428. Ceiling 25,200. Range 773.

The Dauntless was produced in land-based and shipboard attack bomber variations. The two scout and dive bomber aircraft differed from each other only in minor items of equipment and in the elimination of carrier arrester gear on the land-based versions. The A-24 was built for the U.S. Army Air Force from 1941-43, and 863 were delivered for service. The Dauntless was powered by a 1,200-hp Wright Cyclone nine-cylinder radial engine and could achieve a top speed of 255 mph at 14,000 feet. Seating was in tandem fashion, and the rear cockpit was fitted with two machine guns on flexible mounts. Other armament included two fixed .50-caliber guns mounted in the fuselage, which were synchronized to fire through the propeller. A swinging bomb cradle for one bomb in the 500-1,000-pound class was carried underneath the fuselage, while other bomb racks were attached under the wing roots. Hydraulically operated dive brakes above and below the trailing edges of the outer wings and the center section of the fuselage set it apart as a dive bomber. By

1944, 5,936 Dauntlesses had been built and put into service. It was replaced by other advanced aircraft in the middle 1940s, but many stayed active.

DRIGGS DART I, II
1928

STANDARD DATA: Seats 2. Gross wt. 820. Empty wt. 450. Engine 35-hp Anzani. PERFORMANCE: Top mph 85. Cruise mph 80. Landing mph 30. Initial climb rate 550. Range 250. Ceiling (absolute) 18,000.

The Driggs Dart was a light two-seat biplane first built in 1928. Original power was supplied by a French-built Anzani three-cylinder radial engine fed by a main fuel tank in the fuselage just behind the engine. Its tandem cockpits were fitted with dual controls, and its airfoils were of unequal span. The Driggs Aircraft Corp. was founded in Lansing, Michigan, by Ivan Driggs who had been previously associated with the Dayton-Wright Co. and the Johnson Airplane and AA Supply Co. In addition to the Dart, Driggs also built a lightplane designated the Skylark, which was fitted with a 60-hp Rover four cylinder in-line inverted powerplant and could achieve a top speed of 110 mph.

EAGLE 150
2001–Present

STANDARD DATA: Seats 2. Gross wt. 1439 lbs. Empty wt. 953 lbs. Fuel capacity 26 gallons. Engine TCM IO 240, 125 hp. Performance: Max Cruise 130 kts, cruise 120 kts at 2000'. Range 500 nm.

The Eagle 150 originated in Perth, Australia. The two-seat forward canard all composite design was ideal for flight training. Later models, including the 150B, came optionally equipped with leather seats and color moving maps to attract broader recreational and light business applications. Manufacturing of the Eagle 150 has now moved to Malaysia.

EMIGH "TROJAN"
1948–51

STANDARD DATA: Seats 2. Gross wt. 1,450. Engine 90-hp Continental. PERFORMANCE: Top mph 130. Cruise mph 115. Landing mph 48. Range 550. Ceiling 13,000.

The Emigh Trojan was built in small numbers between 1948 and 1950 by the Emigh Aircraft Corp. and later the Emigh Trojan Aircraft Co. Its unique feature is the simplified construction methods used in its assembly. The metal fuselage of the Trojan is made up of two identical halves that are joined along their horizontal centerline. Its wingtips, tail surfaces, and ailerons are all interchangeable. This side-by-side two-seat cabin airplane can still be seen at airports around the country.

ERCOUPE, AIRCOUPE
1937–67

STANDARD DATA: (Aircoupe) Seats 2. Gross wt. 1,450. Empty wt. 930. Fuel capacity 25. Engine 90-hp Continental. PERFORMANCE: Top mph 129. Cruise mph 114. Stall mph 48. Initial climb rate 640. Range 615. Ceiling 17,300. Takeoff run 540. Landing roll 350.

STANDARD DATA: (Ercoupe) Seats 2. Gross wt. 1,400. Empty wt. 838. Fuel capacity 25. Engine 85-hp, Continental. PERFORMANCE: Top mph 12. Cruise mph 110. Stall mph 47. Initial climb rate 560. Ceiling 11,000. Range 430.

STANDARD DATA: (Mooney Cadet) Seats 2. Gross wt. 1,450. Empty wt. 950. Fuel capacity 24. Engine 90-hp Continental. PERFORMANCE: Top mph 118. Cruise mph 110. Stall mph 46. Initial climb rate 835. Ceiling 12,500. Range 480. Takeoff distance (50') 953. Landing distance (50') 1,016.

In the late 1930s, the Ercoupe was designed as a stallproof, spinproof airplane that had no rudder pedals. An interconnection between the ailerons and limited-travel rudders made flying the Ercoupe as easy as steering a car. Prevention of stalls was accomplished by blocking elevator travel before stall angle was achieved. Dubbed the Model 415, the low-wing two-seater was produced from 1937 until World War II. None of the twin-tailed models were built during the war, but production resumed in 1945 with models 41 SE, F, and G appearing between 1947 and 1949. Finally, in 1951, production ceased, but in 1955, Fornaire Aircraft resurrected the Ercoupe calling it the F-I Aircoupe. Air Products took over production between 1960 and 1962, and then it passed to Alon Aircraft in 1964.

Alon called its airplane — still virtually unchanged from the original Ercoupe — the Aircoupe A-2. The Alon version did, however, have rudder pedals and a modified landing gear, which on some models is a backward-bending spring-steel gear leg rather than an oleo strut. The Alon A-2 also featured a blown sliding-bubble canopy instead of the lift-up type fitted on earlier models. Alon Aircoupes had extremely attractive upholstery, and all flight gauges were shock-mounted on a floating subpanel in front of the pilot. Dual toe brakes were standard, operated by a bar running across and above the rudder pedals. Alon was not the end of the Ercoupe history, Mooney Aircraft purchased the Aircoupe rights in 1968, changed the double tail to a single tail and sold the airplane with the name of Mooney Cadet. The A-2 Cadet and MIO Cadet were produced until 1970 when Mooney sold out to Aerostar.

EXTRA AIRCRAFT "400/500"

STANDARD DATA: Extra 400 Seats 6. Gross wt. 4,409. Empty wt. 2,974. Fuel capacity 124. Engine 475-shp Continental TSIOL-550-C. PERFORMANCE: Max Cruise 235 kts. Initial climb rate 1,400 fpm. Ceiling 25,000. Range 2,100 nm. Takeoff distance 1,475'. Landing distance 1,000'.

German designer Walter Extra ruled the aerobatic aircraft world with his Extra 200 and 300 series low wing singles, but in late 1990s he began work on a larger idea — the Extra 400. The mostly composite six-seater was imagined to be direct competition to the Piper

Extra 400

Extra 500

Malibu and other cabin class singles. Pressurization differential was 5.5 psi, providing an 8,000' cabin at 25,000', and max gross was set at just over 4,400 lbs (or 1,999 kilograms because users of the European airway system pay progressively higher charges to operate aircraft weighing 2,000 kilograms or more). Power was supplied by the Continental Voyager TSIOL-550-C water-cooled engine. Despite the rugged, high-tech German engineering, only a handful of Extra 400s have made their way across the Atlantic to the American market. In parallel to the piston model, the company also developed a turbine version of the super-single, with a compact 450-shp Rolls Royce/Allison engine.

FAIRCHILD 71 MONOPLANE

1928

STANDARD DATA: Seats 6. Gross wt. 5,500. Empty wt. 3,135. Fuel capacity 160. Engine 410-hp Pratt & Whitney Wasp radial. PERFORMANCE: Top mph

138. Cruise mph 102. Landing mph 55. Initial climb rate 900. Range 850. Ceiling 17,000.

The Fairchild 71 was designed as an improved version of the popular FC-2W2 and was first introduced in 1928. In the following year, Fairchild Aviation Limited began building this six-passenger lightweight commercial airplane in Canada and designated it the Model 71C and 71CM. The Model 71CM differed from the 71C by its metal fuselage skin rather than the standard fabric covering. All Fairchild 71s are of mixed construction with wooden wings and steel-tube fuselage structures. The enclosed cabin houses six passengers and a pilot. The pilot is in a single seat at the front of a cabin that narrows considerably at the nose.

FAIRCHILD F-45

1936

STANDARD DATA: Seats 5. Gross wt. 4,000. Empty wt. 2,474. Fuel capacity 90. Engine 370-hp Wright Whirlwind. PERFORMANCE: Top mph 170. Cruise mph 164. Stall mph 49. Initial climb rate 1,140. Range 840. Ceiling 19,000.

First introduced in 1936, the F-45 was a five-seat cabin monoplane intended as a high-performance personal transport aircraft. Primarily used as an executive aircraft, it was built with a mixed construction that made use of a fabric-covered steel-tube fuselage and a wooden outer wing section. While the prototype was powered by a 220-hp Jacobs radial engine, subsequent production models received the 370-hp Wright Whirlwind seven-cylinder radial engine. Many reengined versions are still in active service powered by 450-hp Pratt & Whitney Wasp Juniors and 475-hp Wright Whirlwinds.

Original Model 45s were capable of cruising at 164 mph at 75% power and 8,000 feet. Accommodations provided for two at the controls and three on a cross-seat in the back of the cab. A door on each side of the cabin made for easy entry.

FAIRCHILD PT-19/-23/-26
1939–45

STANDARD DATA: (PT-26) Seats 2. Gross wt. 2,741. Empty wt. 2,022. Fuel capacity 45. Engine 200-hp Ranger. PERFORMANCE: Top mph 126. Cruise mph 114. Stall mph 53. Initial climb rate 675. Range 450. Ceiling 17,300.

The Fairchild PT-19 was designed as a tandem two-seat primary trainer for use in the United States and Canada. Full scale production began early in 1940, and by the end of the war 5,401 PT-19s had been built in Canada, the United States, and Brazil. PT-19s were operated by Civilian Pilot Training schools throughout the war in conjunction with the Army Air Force, the principal user. In Canada, the aircraft was known as the Cornell. The PT-19 was powered by a 175-hp six-cylinder in-line inverted Ranger engine and could cruise at 113 mph for about 430 miles. Two other versions of the basic airframe also were produced. These were the PT-26, which featured an enclosed cockpit and a 200-hp Ranger engine, and the PT-23, which resembled the original PT-19 but utilized a 220-hp Continental radial engine. A few civilian models of the Cornell were also produced and were known as M-62s.

FAIRCHILD F-22
1931–36

STANDARD DATA: Seats 2. Gross wt. 1,750. Empty wt. 1,102. Engine 145-hp Warner Scarab. PERFORMANCE: Top mph 133. Cruise mph 115. Initial climb rate 900. Ceiling 20,000. Range 350 mph.

The Kreider-Reisner Division of Fairchild produced this tandem two-seat parasol monoplane in 1931. It has the distinction of being one of the first successful light monoplanes that was built in quantity. During the five years that it was produced, a variety of engines were used. One of the most common powerplants was the 145-hp Warner Scarab seven-cylinder radial air-cooled engine; other engines included the 125-hp Warner Scarab, the 95-hp A.C.E. Cirrus, and the 90-hp Wright Gipsy.

FAIRCHILD F-24
1939–46

STANDARD DATA: Seats 4. Gross wt. 2,882. Empty wt. 1,813. Fuel capacity 60. Engine 200-hp Ranger. PERFORMANCE: Top mph 124. Cruise mph 112. Landing mph 57. Range 465. Ceiling 12,700.

Fairchild's 24R four-seat cabin monoplane first appeared in 1939 and was produced for the civilian aircraft market until the United States entered World War II. In 1942, production of the F-24R was shifted to a military version, which was designated UC-61K. The F-24R is equipped with a 175-hp Ranger six-cylinder, air-cooled engine that delivers a near 120-mph cruise speed for more than 600 miles. Other versions of the F-24 were powered by 145- or 165-hp Warner Super Scarab radials, 200-hp inline Ranger, and 450-hp Pratt & Whitney Wasp Junior.

A close look at the landing gear assembly reveals Fairchild's wide stance. Turns while taxiing are accomplished through the use of a steerable tailwheel, a point which challenges some of the F-24's pilots because of the rearward location of the center of gravity. Construction of the F-24 is a steel-tube fuselage, heavily faired to shape with formers and spruce longerons. Wings are wooden with fabric covering.

HILLER TURBO-PORTER 'ORTER)

STANDARD DATA: (PC-6/132) Seats 10. Gross wt. 4,850. Empty wt. 2,601. Fuel capacity 170. Engine 550-shp Pratt & Whitney turboprop. PERFOR-MANCE: Top mph 174. Cruise mph 161. Stall mph 52. Initial climb rate 1,580. Range 634. Ceiling 30,025. Takeoff distance (50') 620. Landing distance (50') 560.

STANDARD DATA: (PC-6/C) Seats 10. Gross wt. 4,850. Empty wt. 2,612. Fuel capacity 170-270. Engine 575-shp AiResearch turboprop. PERFOR-MANCE: Top mph 174. Cruise mph 164. Stall mph 52. Initial climb rate 1,607. Ceiling 27,875. Range 683-1,044. Takeoff distance (50') 600. Landing distance (50').

Fairchild Hiller produced the first series of Pilatus Turbo-Porters under license from the Pilatus Flugzeugwerke AG of Switzerland. This single-engine utility STOL aircraft was originally called the Heli-Porter and was powered by a 575-shp Pratt & Whitney. Other models produced by both the Fairchild Hiller and Pilatus companies include the PC-6/131 Turbo-Porter and the PC-6/C Turbo-Porter. The PC-6/B I utilizes a 550-shp Pratt & Whitney. The PC-6/IC is the later version of the first Heli-Porters and is now powered by a 575-shp AiResearch turboprop engine. The Turbo-Porter's STOL characteristics enable it to operate from small airfields.

Its easily removable seats allow it to be rapidly changed from a passenger carrier to a cargo carrier. Other jobs performed by the Pilatus are ambulance duties, aerial photography, supply dropping, parachute training, and agricultural dusting. Current models of the Turbo-Porter have forward-opening doors on both sides of the cockpit, a large sliding door on the starboard side of the fuselage, and a double door on the portside. Currently, Fairchild continues to produce the Porter utility aircraft for agencies of the United States government. This version is powered by a Pratt & Whitney turboprop flat rated at 550-shp with 680-shp available for takeoff. Also under production is the Peacemaker, housing a 650-shp Garrett turboprop and used primarily for counter-insurgency operations. Fairchild Hiller discontinued building and marketing the Turbo-Porter in the United States; however, the airplane continues to be produced by its parent company in Switzerland.

FLEET MODEL 1 AND 2
1929-41

STANDARD DATA: Seats 2. Gross wt. 1,530. Empty wt. 976. Fuel capacity 24. Engine 110-hp Warner Scarab seven-cylinder radial. PERFORMANCE: Top mph 111. Cruise mph 90. Stall mph 46. Initial climb rate 930. Range 350. Ceiling 16,000.

The Fleet Aircraft Division of the Consolidated Aircraft Corp. was formed in Buffalo, New York, in 1929 specifically to undertake production of the Fleet Trainer. Prior to 1932, the Fleet I (110-hp Warner), the Fleet 2 (100-hp Kinner), and the Fleet 7 (125-hp Kinner) outsold any other make in their class and also proved to be popular overseas, particularly in China and Latin America. In all, about 600 Fleets were produced in the United States before production was terminated in 1935.

In the late 1930s, Fleet Aircraft of Canada acquired the manufacturing rights to the design and began producing an improved version of the Fleet I under the designation Fleet 16B Finch 11. These models were equipped with 125-hp Kinners, and over 600 were delivered to the R.C.A.F. as basic trainers during the early part of the war. Most of these Canadian models are equipped with a sliding canopy to replace the open cockpit of the earlier models. Perhaps 30 Fleets exist today in the United States, with a few more active in Canada and other countries.

FLEET 80 "CANUCK"
1945-47

STANDARD DATA: Seats 2. Gross wt. 1,480. Empty wt. 858. Engine 85-hp Continental. PERFORMANCE: Top mph 111. Cruise mph 100. Range 400. Ceiling 12,000.

A favorite with Canadian pilots, this lightweight side-by-side two-seater can be fitted with wheels, floats, or skis. The sturdy all-metal fabric-covered frame is powered by a Continental four-cylinder 85- or 90-hp engine. A total of 210 Canucks were built in two years by Fleet Manufacturing, Ltd. in Fort Erie, Ontario, and of those a healthy percentage are still in flying condition. Most of the Fleet 80s flying today have been modified with improved heaters and cowling systems, updated Ceconite covering, and additional gyros and radios. Designed especially for Canadian flying conditions, the Canuck is still traded fairly regularly in Canada, and many a Canadian pilot has received primary pilot training in this Fleet airplane.

FLEETWINGS "SEABIRD"

STANDARD DATA: Seats 4. Gross wt. 3,750. Empty wt. 2,450. Fuel capacity 70. Engine 285-hp Jacobs. PERFORMANCE: Top mph 150. Cruise mph 135. Initial climb rate 900. Range 540. Ceiling 14,500. Takeoff run 29 seconds.

The "Sea Bird" amphibian was the first stainless-steel airplane to receive approved certification in the United States. In 1929, Fleetwings, Inc. began design and research work in stainless-steel construction. In 1934, the firm acquired Keystone Aircraft Corp. and built all-stainless-steel wings for the U.S. Army's Douglas "Dolphin." The "Sea Bird" is powered by a single

285-hp 7-cylinder radial engine in a nacelle mounted above the fuselage on steel-tube struts. A hatch on the port side provides entrance to both the forward stowage area and the cabin, where seating is for four in two pairs. The landing lights, water rudder, tail wheel, and main gear are all retractable.

FOKKER D VII
1917–29

STANDARD DATA: Seats 1. Gross wt. 1,984. Engine 185hp BMW or 160-hp Mercedes. PERFORMANCE: Top mph 117. Cruise mph 100. Stall mph 45. Range 150. Ceiling 19,680.

Only a few of the original single-seat German World War I fighters exist today. The Fokker D VII was chosen by the chief of the German air service, General Von Hoeppel, as the plane that could outmaneuver the Spad and the Sopwith in aerial combat. Fokker delivered the first D VII to the Von Richthofen unit within two months after the original order of 400 had been placed. Although the famous Von Richthofen chose to stick with the Fokker Triplane, eventually he was shot down while flying a D VII. The D VII ultimately became the favorite of many a German pilot.

Fitted with twin Spandau guns, the thick-winged fighter could almost hang by its prop at 45 degrees yet maintain excellent controllability. Its fuselage was made of welded and braced steel tube in box girder structure and covered with metal panels forward and a fabric-ply combination in the rear. The wooden cantilevered wings required no external wire bracing, and struts really weren't needed but were added to give the pilots some moral support. Both the 160-hp Mercedes D III and the BMW III 185-hp engines were six-cylinder in-line water cooled.

Perhaps the easiest to fly of all the World War I fighters, the Fokker D VII could execute rapid, smooth turns and was quite sensitive on the elevators. After the war, Fokker continued to build the D VII selling the coveted plane to Holland, Belgium, Poland, Sweden, Italy, and Spain. The United States received 142 D VIIs that served with the military until the mid-1920s when a lack of spare parts forced their grounding.

FOUND "BUSH HAWK XP"
1996–Present

STANDARD DATA: Seats 5. Gross wt. 3,500. Empty wt. 1975. Engine 300-hp IO-540-L1C5. PERFORMANCE: Cruise 145 kts. Stall 52 KCAS. Initial climb rate 1,120 fpm. Range 880 nm. Ceiling 18,000. Takeoff roll 750'.

The Bush Hawk-XP, designed and manufactured by Found Aircraft, is perhaps the ultimate bush plane. Variants are equally at home on floats or skis as on wheel. It is certified to Canadian Regulation AWM 523 and U.S. 14 CFR Part 23 regulations to carry passengers and freight in day and night VFR and IFR conditions. The Bush Hawk-XP is a rugged, all-metal, high cantilever wing, single-engine airplane equipped with a tail wheel landing gear and designed for general utility purposes.

FUNK MODEL B
1939

STANDARD DATA: Seats 2. Gross wt. 1,350. Empty wt. 890. Fuel capacity 20. Engine 75-hp, Lycoming or 85-hp, Continental. PERFORMANCE: (85-hp). Top mph 115. Cruise mph 100. Stall mph 37. Initial climb rate 800. Range 350. Ceiling 15,000. Takeoff run 348.

Originally produced by Akron Aircraft Co., the Model B was kept in production by the Funk Aircraft Co. after the latter company replaced Akron in 1941. The two-seat cabin monoplane, first made in 1939, had been equipped with a 65-hp Funk four-cylinder engine but in 1941 featured a 75-hp Lycoming engine and the designation 75L. After World War II, production continued on the Model B, this time with a Continental 85-hp engine and called the B-85C. The Model B has fabric-covered wooden wings and a steel-tube fuselage, also covered with fabric. Many present-day Funk owners have replaced the original fabric with strong Ceconite fabric and added other features such as hydraulic brakes and wheel pants.

GRANDVILLE BROTHERS "GEE BEE"
1931

STANDARD DATA: Seats 1. Gross wt. 2,280. Empty wt. 1,400. Fuel capacity 103. Engine 535-hp, supercharged Pratt & Whitney Wasp Jr. PERFORMANCE: Top mph 270. Cruise mph 230.

During the Great Depression of the early 1930s, almost all American businesses felt the strain, including aviation. The Grandville Brothers decided to take a shot at substantial prize money offered at air racing events. With an engine borrowed from Pratt & Whitney and propeller borrowed from Curtiss, the Gee Bee Model Z Sportser entered the competition. In one race, the Gee Bee averaged 267.342 miles per hour, the fastest speed ever recorded for a land plane. Later in the year with a upgraded 800-hp Pratt & Whitney R-1340, the model Z was clock in at 281.75 mph. None of the original Gee Bees survive, but replicas still fly at a variety of air shows.

GREAT LAKES SPORT TRAINER
1929–32/1974–78/1980–94

STANDARD DATA: (1932) Seats 2. Gross wt. 1,580. Empty wt. 910. Engine 90-hp Cirrus. PERFORMANCE: Top mph 116. Cruise mph 100. Stall mph 40. Initial climb rate 1,035. Range 400. Ceiling 21,000.

STANDARD DATA: Seats 2. Gross wt. 1,800. Empty wt. 1,230. Fuel capacity 26. Engine 180-hp Lycoming. PERFORMANCE: Top mph 132. Cruise mph 118. Stall mph 54. Initial climb rate 1,150. Ceiling 17,000. Range 300. Takeoff distance (50') 825. Landing distance (50') 825.

The original Great Lakes Model 2T-I Sport Trainer was built by the Great Lakes Aircraft Corp. in Cleveland, Ohio, in 1929. Between 1929 and 1932, the company built more than 200 of them, and they quickly became a great favorite of aerobatic pilots. The designer, Charles W. Meyers, raced a customized Great Lakes with considerable success during the early 1930s, and the legendary Tex Rankin flew one in airshows throughout the country before World War II setting records for both inside and outside loops. After the war, enthusiasm for the airplane continued and many airframes were converted to accept larger engines, particularly Warner radials. During the past several years, factory blueprints of the design have been available to homebuilders from the resurrected Great Lakes Aircraft Co., also of Cleveland, and several are under construction utilizing various modern engines.

In 1972, the design rights were sold to the Great Lakes Aircraft Co. of Wichita, Kansas, and Enid, Oklahoma. In 1973, the Model 2T-IA-1 was certified with a 140-hp Lycoming, and the Model 2T-IA-2 (with a 180-hp Lycoming) was produced for the first time in 1974. In 1980, after more than 50 years, the legendary Great Lakes biplane found a new home in Eastman, Georgia. R. Dean Franklin, a Great Lakes pilot, set up a modern production facility after acquiring production rights, type certificates, and other assets of the Great Lakes Aircraft Co. The Great Lakes is the oldest certificated airplane still in production, and its manufacture closely follows the basic specifications of the original design.

GRUMMAN J2F "DUCK"
1933–45

STANDARD DATA: Seats 2. Gross wt. 7,290. Empty wt. 5,445. Fuel capacity 150. Engine 1,050-hp Wright Cyclone nine-cylinder radial. PERFOR-

MANCE: Top mph 190. Cruise mph 106. Initial climb 1,330. Range 850. Ceiling 21,000.

Production of this general utility amphibian began in 1933 when the first prototype flew, and production continued until 1945. In all, nine series of the Duck were built. The J2F6 was by far the most common. It featured aerodynamic improvements over the previous models, including a long-cord engine cowling. Only two Ducks are known to be active, though several more are registered. The amphibian was originally used for photography, target-towing, scouting, and rescue work. Although the Duck is normally flown as a two-seater in tandem fashion, a folding floor in the rear cockpit gives access to a lower compartment for use in rescue work and the like; the lower compartment could house either two extra crew members or a stretcher. Some models of the Duck were powered by the 725-hp Wright Cyclone engine.

GRUMMAN F4F "WILDCAT"
1941–45

STANDARD DATA: Seats 1. Gross wt. 5,876. Empty wt. 4,425. Fuel capacity 160. Engine 1,000-hp Wright Cyclone or 1,050-hp Pratt & Whitney Twin Wasp. PERFORMANCE: (Wright Cyclone) Top mph 325. Cruise mph 285. Landing mph 66. Initial climb rate 3,300. Range 1,150. Ceiling 28,000.

Designed in 1937 by Robert L. Hall, designer of the famous Gee Bee racers of the early 1930s, the Wildcat first entered production in 1941. By 1942, Wildcats equipped all carrier fighter squadrons and remained our sole carrier fighter in action until mid-1943. Of all the U.S. wartime fighters, Wildcats were the slowest, even among the carrier-based varieties, yet they compensated for this defect in part by their good rate of climb and maneuverability. Though inferior to the Mitsubishi Zero in performance, Wildcats managed to score many crucial victories over the Japanese in the Pacific. This was due to good armament, firepower, and outstanding piloting techniques. At first, Wildcats were powered by 1,000-hp Wright Cyclones and 900-hp Twin Wasps. Those craft were designated F4F-4 and F4F-3 respectively. Later, the FM-2 Wildcat standardized the use of the 1,350-hp Cyclone engine. It was the last version to be built.

GRUMMAN F6F "HELLCAT"
1942–45

STANDARD DATA: Seats 1. Gross wt. 12,500. Empty wt. 9,153. Engine 2,000-hp Pratt & Whitney. PERFORMANCE: Top mph 400. Initial climb rate 3,000. Range 1,800. Ceiling 37,800.

The Hellcat single-seat shipboard fighter is easily recognizable by its landing gear that retracts into the center section as opposed to the Wildcat with gear that retracts into the fuselage just forward of the wings. It also differs from the later Bearcats in that it lacks the Bearcat's 360-degree vision canopy. The prototype of the Hellcat first flew in 1942. The shipboard fighter saw its first action in an attack on Marcus Island in 1943. Later Hellcats differ from their predecessors by having a redesigned engine cowling, improved windshield and tail surfaces, additional armor, and a waxed glossy skin. Bulletproof fuel tanks were housed in the wings, and an auxiliary drop tank could be added. Armament included six .50-caliber machine guns in the wings.

GRUMMAN F8F "BEARCAT"
1944–49

STANDARD DATA: Seats 1. Gross wt. 9,300. Empty wt. 7,070. Fuel capacity 185, two drop tanks 150 gals. each. Engine 2,100-hp Pratt & Whitney 18-cylinder radial. PERFORMANCE: Top mph 425.

Cruise mph (economy) 163. Initial climb rate 5,700. Range 1,105. Ceiling 42,300.

The Grumman F8F Bearcat was originally designed as a replacement for the Hellcat, and it was hoped that the Bearcat would have better maneuverability and be able to operate from the smallest Navy carriers. The Bearcat was small, limited in weight and armed with four .50-caliber guns and external fittings for two 1,000-pound bombs, drop tanks, or four rockets. It was powered by a 2,100-hp Pratt & Whitney 18-cylinder radial engine, which accounts for an exceptional climb rate. Contracts for 2,023 Bearcats were approved in October 1944, and deliveries started in February 1945. The end of the war reduced the contract for the F8F-1D, and a total of 1,263 were produced. Surplus Bearcats designated F8F-ID and fitted with a modified fuel system were used in the Indochina war by the French Armee de l'Air. A number of Bearcats were later transferred to the Vietnam Air Force. The Bearcat was the last of Grumman's piston-engine carrier fighters.

GRUMMAN AMERICAN TRAINER
1967–79

STANDARD DATA: (Trainer) Seats 2. Gross wt. 1,560. Empty wt. 975. Fuel capacity 24. Engine 108-hp Lycoming. PERFORMANCE: Top mph 138. Cruise mph 124. Stall mph 60. Initial climb rate 705. Range 435. Ceiling 12,750. Takeoff distance (50') 1,590. Landing distance (50') 1,100.

STANDARD DATA: (Yankee) Seats 2. Gross wt. 1,500. Empty wt. 963. Fuel capacity 24. Engine 108-

hp Lycoming. PERFORMANCE: Top mph 144. Cruise mph 134. Stall mph 66. Initial climb rate 710. Ceiling 11,000. Range 515. Takeoff distance (50') 1,615. Landing distance (50') 1,245.

The American AA-I Yankee and its improved version, the AA-IA Trainer, started out as the James Bede-designed BD-I. After acquiring the design from Bede in 1964, American Aviation did some extensive redesign work and put the two-place Yankee into production in 1967. Conceived as a low-cost sport or utility aircraft, the Yankee incorporated several new construction techniques, including the use of aluminum honeycomb panels as the primary structural members and metal-to-metal bonding instead of rivets or bolts. The wing spar is a heavy aluminum tube that also houses the fuel supply. The wing ribs are bonded to the spar. Large bonded-on skin panels virtually eliminate all seams, and there are no protruding rivet heads to create drag.

The AA-IA Trainer was introduced in 1971 and soon replaced the Yankee. It incorporated a modified wing with improved low-speed characteristics, some changes in optional equipment, and a propeller with improved cruising performance. Grumman American Aircraft Corp. ultimately took over the production of the Trainer and added more versions based on the basic airframe design.

GRUMMAN AMERICAN TR-2
1971–79

STANDARD DATA: Seats 2. Gross wt. 1,560. Empty wt. 1,039. Fuel capacity 24. Engine 108-hp Lycoming. PERFORMANCE: Top mph 144. Cruise mph 133. Stall mph 60. Initial climb rate 660. Range 463. Ceiling 11,550. Takeoff distance (50') 1,590. Landing distance (50') 1,100.

Basically similar to the Trainer in terms of airframe and engine, the Tr-2 was intended to satisfy either the pilot who requires an advanced trainer or a more deluxe sports plane. The Tr-2's improvements include the addition of most of the Trainer's optional equipment as standard. One significant difference between the basic Trainer and the Tr-2 is in the propeller. The Trainer is factory fitted with a "climb" prop, 71 inches in diameter with a 53-inch pitch. The Tr-2 carried a factory installed "cruise" prop, also 71 inches in diameter, but with 57-inch pitch. This cruise propeller accounts for

the increase in top and cruise speed plus about 30 additional miles in total range; however, the Tr-2 suffers in the climb department with a 660-fpm capability compared to the Trainer's 705-fpm climb speed. Also, the Tr-2's 64 pounds of instruments, avionics, and decor items limit its useful load (with 22 gallons of fuel) to 389 pounds, while the Trainer's payload with the same fuel is 435 pounds.

GULFSTREAM AMERICAN "CHEETAH"
1972–79

STANDARD DATA: (Cheetah) Seats 4. Gross wt. 2,200. Empty wt. 1,362. Fuel capacity 38-52. Engine 150-hp Lycoming. PERFORMANCE: Top mph 157. Cruise mph 147. Stall mph 60. Initial climb rate 660. Range 589-830. Ceiling 12,650. Takeoff distance (50') 1,600. Landing distance (50') 1,100.

STANDARD DATA: (Traveler) Seats 4. Gross wt. 2,200. Empty wt. 1,180. Fuel capacity 37. Engine 150-hp Lycoming. PERFORMANCE: Top mph 150. Cruise mph 140. Stall mph 61. Initial climb rate 660. Ceiling 12,650. Range 627. Takeoff distance (50') 1,420. Landing distance (50') 1,052.

The AA-5 Traveler is essentially an enlarged version of the AA-IA Trainer. Given an increased wingspan and 32 more horsepower on an extended fuselage, the Traveler is a full four-place airplane. Production first began in late 1971 and was facilitated by the fact that the Trainer and the Traveler share nearly two thirds of their parts in common. Introduced by Grumman American, the Cheetah includes as standard equipment that which is usually optional on the Trainer. Also added were: electric flaps, increased tailplane dimensions, a baggage allowance of 120 pounds, and optional fuel capacity of 52 gallons (as opposed to the standard 38-gallon tanks).

At 75% power at 8,500 feet, the Cheetah will true 147 mph. Drop down to a more normal 6,500 feet and a more economical 65% power setting, and it will pull a true of 133 mph. Clean surfaces and clean design are behind the Cheetah's super speed figures. A rugged, chemical, metal-to-metal bonding process is used in place of rivets. It was a fairly new manufacturing process that other manufacturers were beginning to use on their expensive twins. Grumman American redesigned the old AA-5 Traveler's engine cowling for reduced drag, streamlined the main gear fairings and eliminated the ventral fin, all of which were speed-helping changes. Other improvements over the old AA-5 were engine cooling baffles, a long-range fuel tank option, a better exhaust system, a redesigned nose strut, and a 30% larger tail surface. The larger tail surface allowed the aft center-of-gravity loading to be extended and markedly improved control response. The Cheetah was finally manufactured by Gulfstream American Corp.

GULFSTREAM AMERICAN "TIGER"
1975–79 (AA-5B)
1990–1993 (AG-5B)
2001 to present (AG-5B)

Grumman Tiger

Tiger Aircraft

STANDARD DATA: Seats 4. Gross wt. 2,400. Empty wt. 1,400. Fuel capacity 52. Engine 180-hp Lycoming. PERFORMANCE: Top mph 170. Cruise mph 160. Stall mph 61. Initial climb rate 850. Range 752. Ceiling 13,800. Takeoff distance (50') 1,550. Landing distance (50') 1,120.

If cats have nine lives, Tigers have at least three. For the most part, the first Tiger was a new-engine version of the four-seat Traveler. Its cruise speed, rate of climb, and 110-pound useful load put it in the class of many higher priced aircraft, including some light retractables. The Tiger features fold-down rear seats for increased baggage space and a redesigned engine cowl for easier removal. Still in use are the honeycomb box section and the extruded tubular alloy spar in the wing, the virtually rivetless resin-bonded skin, and free-

castering nose wheel to facilitate steering in tight places. Airflow has been smoothed by adding new wheel fairings and a recontoured spinner cowl area. Though the year 1979 saw the company name change from Grumman American to Gulfstream American, there were no significant changes in the Tiger itself. Production was halted during 1980.

In 1990 the Tiger came to market again as the American General Tiger, designated as the AG-5B. The newest Tiger had remarkably few changes, except the price tag. Because of the rough economic conditions of the early 1990s, American General ceased production in 1993.

In late 2001 the Tiger made a third entrance into the market, this time from facilities in Martinsburg, West Virginia and backed by foreign investors. While most of the airplane remains unchanged, the newest Tigers have an advantage over legacy AA-5B and AG-5Bs simply because of avionics upgrades. New Tigers are available with an all-glass flight deck.

GULFSTREAM AMERICAN "SUPER AG-CAT"
1957–81

STANDARD DATA: Seats 1. Gross wt. 4,500. Empty wt. 2,690. Fuel capacity 80. Engine 450-hp Pratt & Whitney radial. PERFORMANCE: Top mph 147. Cruise mph 90. Stall mph 67. Initial climb rate 1,800. Range 400. Ceiling 14,000. Takeoff distance (50') 1,360. Landing distance (50') 750.

After Gulfstream acquired the Grumman designs, they started producing the Grumman Super AG-Cat, a beefed-up version of the regular G-164 AG-Cat built under contract by Schweizer Aircraft in Elmira, New York. The specialized agricultural sprayer flew for the first time in 1957, with first deliveries in 1959. Designed with a maximum-lift wing using minimum wingspan, the powerful biplane can make a continuous 1.5G turn at dusting speed even at gross weight. The wings are constructed of Duralumin with fabric covering, and the fuselage is made with steel tube covered with Duralumin sheet metal. The upper and lower wings of the biplane are interchangeable. An enclosed cockpit canopy is optional; otherwise, the single-seat cockpit is open and a reinforced fairing aft of the cockpit provides "turnover" protection. The Super AG-Cat will carry up to 2,000 pounds or 247 gallons of agricultural chemicals in a fiberglass hopper. Power was originally supplied by a 220-hp Continental. Until 1969 the 220-hp Continental, 300- or 275-hp Jacobs, or 450-hp Pratt & Whitney were used. Since 1969, engine options have been limited to the 600 or 450-hp Pratt & Whitneys.

HARLOW PJC-2
1938–41

STANDARD DATA: Seats 4. Gross wt. 2,600. Empty wt. 1,700. Engine 145-hp Warner Super-Scarab seven-cylinder radial. PERFORMANCE: Top mph 150. Cruise mph 135. Landing mph 53. Initial climb rate 660. Range 500. Ceiling 15,500.

The Harlow Engineering Corp. of Alhambra, California, began production of the Harlow PJC-2 in 1938. In the following year, the company changed its name to the Harlow Aircraft Co. The Model PJC-2 was a four-seat cabin-monoplane of all metal construction and was fitted with retractable landing gear. The Harlow was under development for three years and submitted to over a year of flight testing before it was placed on the market. Production was continued in small numbers until 1941. In that same year, a two-seat training version was produced under the designation of PC-5A. It differed mainly by having a narrower fuselage and a 165-hp Warner SuperScarab engine. PC-5A production lasted until 1942.

HAWKER "HURRICANE"
1937–44

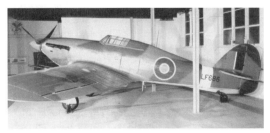

STANDARD DATA: (Hurricane II) Seats 1. Gross wt. 7,014. Empty wt. 5,454. Engine 1,195-bhp, Rolls-Royce Merlin II. PERFORMANCE: Top mph 320. Initial climb rate 2,950. Ceiling 33,000.

During the Battle of Britain, Hurricanes accounted for more victories over Luftwaffe aircraft than any other fighter 1,500 in all. The first Hurricane flew in October 1937. Designated the Hurricane I, it was outfitted with a Rolls-Royce Merlin II or III engine, fabric-covered wings, and a wooden prop. It lacked armor and self-sealing fuel tanks. Hurricanes saw action throughout the war from the skies over Great Britain to Norway, Italy, North Africa, and Burma. They carried out missions as fighters, fighter-bombers, tank-busters, catapult fighters, and carrier fighters. The first Hurricane II went into production in 1940 and was powered by a Merlin XX V-12-cylinder liquid-cooled engine. Improvements included wing alterations for increased armament, redesigned engine mount, strengthened fuselage, and tanks protected with self-sealing rubber. In all, over 15,000 Hurricanes were built by the time production ceased in 1944.

HAWKER "SEA FURY"
1944–53

STANDARD DATA: Seats 1. Gross wt. 12,350. Empty wt. 9,240. Fuel capacity 240. Engine 2,560-hp Bristol Centaurus 18-cylinder radial. PERFORMANCE: Top mph 450. Cruise mph (30,000 ft.) 415. Initial climb rate 4,320. Range 1,630. Takeoff run 960.

The Hawker Sea Fury was the last piston-engine fighter to serve the Royal Navy. It was designed in 1942, primarily as a lighter version of the Tempest although it didn't enter production in time to see action in World War II. Sea Fury airplanes were used in Korea where they often had to engage Soviet-built MiG 15 jet fighters and succeeded in scoring a few victories against their faster opponents. A total of 860 Sea Fury airplanes were built, including a number of tandem two seat trainers. This type exists in very small numbers in the United States where modified versions have scored notable wins on the air-racing circuit.

URIER H-295/395/391

STANDARD DATA: (H-295) Seats 4-6. Gross wt. 3,400. Empty wt. 2,080. Fuel capacity 120. Engine 295-hp Lycoming. PERFORMANCE: Top mph 167. Cruise mph 165. Stall mph 30. Initial climb rate 1,150. Range 660. Ceiling 20,500. Takeoff distance (50') 6 10. Landing distance (50') 520.

STANDARD DATA: (H-250) Seats 6. Gross wt. 3,400. Empty wt. 1,890. Fuel capacity 120-270. Engine 250-hp Lycoming. PERFORMANCE: Top mph 160. Cruise mph 152. Stall mph 31. Initial climb rate 830, Ceiling 15,200. Range 644-1,288. Takeoff distance (50') 750. Landing distance (50') 520.

The Helio Courier, which has the ability to take off and land at 30 mph on unimproved landing strips less than 500 feet long, has established itself firmly in the general aviation market. A certificated STOL (Short Take Off and Land) aircraft, the Courier series displays an aptitude for safe, almost stall-proof, slow-speed flight, as well as the range and cruising speed of comparable conventional aircraft. Leading-edge wing slats automatically extend or retract in response to changes in air pressure to prevent stalls or spins. Aileron-linked airflow interceptors provide excellent lateral control while large slotted flaps on the trailing edge, working in conjunction with the slats on the leading edge, double the lift of the wing.

Also, its full cantilever construction eliminates the wasteful drag created by strut braces. With an all-moving stabilator for pitch control and a tall, swept fin, and rudder for its direction control, the two Courier models possess maximum stability during slow flight. The original Courier prototype was a converted Piper Vagabond, from this was created the H-391, which was powered by a 260-hp Lycoming and offered seating for four to five. The H-395 followed in 1959 with its 295-hp engine and five seats. The H-295 first appeared in 1965 and featured increased seating and the same 295-hp engine. Its counterpart was the H-250 powered by the 250-hp Lycoming.

The two current commercial versions of the Helio are the Super Courier H-295 with nonretractable con-

ventional landing gear and the Tri-gear 54-Courier HT-295 with nonretractable tricycle gear. Three models are flown, by the U.S. Air Force: the U-10A with a fuel capacity of 60 gallons; the U-1013, a long-range version with tankage for 120 gallons; and the U-10D, an improved long-range version with a fuel capacity of 120 gallons and a gross weight boosted to 3,600 pounds.

HELIO H-550A "STALLION"
1966–76

STANDARD DATA: Seats 8-10. Gross wt. 5,100. Empty wt. 2,860. Fuel capacity 120. Engine 680-hp United Aircraft of Canada turboprop. PERFORMANCE: Top mph 216. Cruise mph 206. Minimum mph 42. Initial climb rate 2,200. Range 445. Ceiling 25,000. Takeoff distance (50') 660. Landing distance (50') 750.

The Stallion is specifically designed for operation from unprepared fields and is equipped with a full complement of STOL devices. Design of the Stallion began in 1963, and the first models were produced in 1966. The Helio Aircraft Corp. was founded in 1948, and its first prototype was a converted Piper Vagabond. Then Helio became a part of the General Aircraft Corp. and produced the Super Courier and the Stallion. Both aircraft are similar in construction. The Stallion is powered by a single 680-ehp turboprop engine driving a three blade reversible-pitch prop and fed by wing tanks with a capacity of 120 gallons.

Its all-metal cantilevered wings are equipped with high lift slotted all-metal flaps, fabric-covered balanced ailerons, and full-span automatic leading-edge slats. The tail unit features a one-piece horizontal surface with combined trim and antibalance tab. The cabin is protected by a crash-resistant tubular frame. The Stallion's accommodations provide for a pilot and copilot up front with either eight passengers on bench seats or six passengers seated individually. Access is made through a door on the port side near the pilot, an optional starboard door, and a double cargo door on the port side. The double door is in two sections—the forward half hinges and the rear half slides. The rear half can be opened during flight for cargo drops or parachutists.

HOWARD DGA-15P
1939–42

STANDARD DATA: Seats 5. Gross wt. 4,350. Empty wt. 2,700. Fuel capacity 150. Engine 450-hp Pratt & Whitney Wasp Junior 9-cylinder radial. PERFORMANCE: Top mph 201. Cruise mph 191. Landing mph 61. Range 1,263. Ceiling 21,500.

First produced by the Howard Aircraft Corp. in 1939, the DGA-15 was modeled after the Bendix Trophy winner DGA-6 "Mr. Mulligan" of 1934-35. It was a progressive development of the DGA-8 and the DGA-9. Four variations of the DGA-15 were the DGA-15P with a 450-hp Wasp Junior, the DGA-15W with a 350-hp Wright engine, the DGA-15J with a 350-hp Jacobs engine, and finally the GH-1 produced for the U.S. Navy as a four seat personnel transport.

INTERSTATE S1B "CADET"
1940/1969–80

STANDARD DATA: (102 hp) Seats 2. Gross wt. 1,650. Empty wt. 1,103. Fuel capacity 15. Engine 102-hp Franklin. PERFORMANCE: Top mph 114. Cruise mph 105. Stall mph 38. Initial climb rate 900. Range 540. Ceiling 16,500.

STANDARD DATA: (150 hp) Gross wt. 1,900. Empty wt. 1,100. Fuel capacity 40. Engine 150-hp Lycoming. PERFORMANCE: Top mph 115. Cruise mph 110. Stall mph 39. Range 650. Initial climb rate 1,000. Takeoff run 350.

In 1940, the Interstate Aircraft & Engineering Corp. began production of the Interstate Cadet. The S1B was a member of a family of taildraggers, such as the Piper Cub, Taylorcraft, Luscombe, and Aeronca Champ that served many a weekend pilot with fun-filled hours during the late 1930s and early 1940s. The original Cadet was produced in a number of versions using engines from 65 hp to 102 hp. Most popular was the S513 using a 102-hp four-cylinder Franklin. The tandem two-seater was modified for the military at the beginning of the war and called the L-6 liaison plane. This version was equipped with a glazed canopy that extended well aft toward the tail.

In 1969, production of the Interstate Cadet was resurrected by Bill and Jan Diehl, owners of Arctic Aircraft Co. in Anchorage, Alaska. The one family operation has modified the Cadet to become a lightweight bush plane. Installation of a 150-hp Lycoming engine has markedly increased performance and useful load. Large, high flotation tires permit safe landings on beaches or riverbeds. Construction is of chromoly tubing covered with Dacron. All control cables, brake cables, fuel lines, and the like are completely exposed. The revived Cadet, now dubbed the S2132, has been certificated for aerobatics, and even snap maneuvers are approved.

JOHNSON "ROCKET 185"/ "TEXAS BULLET"
1946–51

Johnson "Rocket"

Johnson "Texas Bullet"

STANDARD DATA: Seats 4. Gross wt. 2,250. Empty wt. 1,550. Fuel capacity 55. Engine 185-hp Lycoming/185-hp Continental. PERFORMANCE: Top, mph 207. Cruise mph 185. Stall mph 50. Initial climb rate 900. Ceiling 24,500. Takeoff run 600. Landing roll 400.

1-performance, three-seat, cabin mono-
:st built in 1946 by Johnson Aircraft, Inc.
.nately manufactured in small numbers. The
.ght aircraft was built of all-metal construction w.... i fabric-covered fuselage. Two persons are
seated side-by-side with full dual controls while the
third is seated centrally just behind the front seats. In
1950, Aircraft Manufacturing Co. acquired the rights
to produce a refined four-seat version of the Rocket,
which it called the Texas Bullet.

The original Rocket was powered by a 185-hp four-
cylinder Lycoming engine; the Texas Bullet changed over
to a Continental of the same rating. Also, the fabric
covering of the Rocket was traded for an all-metal, flush-
riveted skin, and a redesigned tail was added. The Bullet sported a top speed of 210 mph, a cruise speed of
183 mph, and a climb rate of 900 fpm. Overall, the
new refinements added only 100 pounds to the empty
weight, and 50 pounds were added to the fully loaded
weight. Exhaust gasses from the engine of the Rocket
and Bullet were led into a unique "jet assist" cylinder
below the fuselage. It was claimed that the device converted engine exhaust into useful thrust at speeds faster
than 40 mph. Also, both aircraft made use of a Hartzell
hydro-selective two-blade variable-pitch propeller.

KINNER "SPORTSTER"
1932

STANDARD DATA: Seats 2. Gross wt. 1,875. Empty
wt. 1,218. Engine 100-hp Kinner. PERFORMANCE:
Top mph 104. Cruise mph 90. Initial climb rate 800.
Ceiling 14,000. Range 340.

Kinner Airplane and Motor Corp. is better-known
for radial engines used in many World War II primary
trainers, including the Meyers OTW and the Ryan PT-
22, but Kinner also introduced an airplane of its own
design in 1932. As might be expected, the side-by-side
two-seat Sportster series of low wing taildraggers was
powered by 100-hp Kinner five-cylinder radial engines.
Some of the Sportsters that are still active have opted
for the 125-hp Kinner. The aircraft employed a mixed
construction with the conventional fabric-covered
wooden wings and fabric-covered steel-tube fuselage
combination. Another version, named the Playboy, was
a cabin model powered by a 160-hp Kinner. It featured

wire-braced rather than strut-braced wings; otherwise,
construction was essentially the same.

LAKE "AMPHIBIAN / BUCCANEER /
RENEGADE / SEAFURY"
1957–2004

Lake Buccaneer

Lake Renegade

STANDARD DATA: (LA-4) Seats 4. Gross wt. 2,400.
Empty wt. 1,600. Fuel capacity 40. Engine 180-hp
Lycoming. PERFORMANCE: Top mph 135. Cruise
mph 131. Stall mph 51. Initial climb rate 800. Ceiling 14,000. Range 627. Takeoff run (land) 650. Takeoff run (water) 1,125. Landing roll (land) 475.
Landing run (water) 600.

STANDARD DATA: (Buccaneer) Seats 3-4. Gross wt.
2,690. Empty wt. 1,555. Fuel capacity 54. Engine
200-hp Lycoming. PERFORMANCE: Top mph 154.
Cruise 150. Stall mph 45. Initial climb rate 1,200.
Range 825. Ceiling 14,700. Takeoff run (water)
1,100. Takeoff run (land) 600. Landing run (water)
600. Landing roll (land) 475.

STANDARD DATA: (LA-250-270) Seats 4-6. Gross
wt. 3,140. Empty wt. 1,850. Fuel capacity 90. Engine
250-hp Lycoming IO-540-C4B5/ 270-hp TIO-540-
AA1AB. PERFORMANCE: Cruise 122 kts./128 kts.
Stall mph 53. Initial climb rate 900. Ceiling 14,000/
23,800'. Takeoff run (land) 650. Takeoff run (water)
1,125. Landing roll (land) 475. Landing run (water)
600.

The Lake Amphibian takes it heritage from the development of a plane formerly known as the Skimmer,
which was built by Colonial Aircraft Corp., founded in

1946 by David B. Thurston and Herbert P. Lindbad. Both had worked for the Grumman Company on the Goose and the Widgeon. Their entry into general aviation was a design called the Skimmer. Various versions of the Skimmer were produced in the 1950s in limited quantities. In 1959, the name of the plane was changed to the Lake, and improvements were introduced. From 1958 to 1970, the standard engine was a 180-hp Lycoming, and the airplane was designated the LA-4 Amphibian. In 1970, Lake removed the retractable gear from some LA-4s and offered them as seaplanes with detachable beaching gear.

Also in 1970, Lake fitted a 200-hp fuel-injected Lycoming engine to the LA-4 and renamed it the Buccaneer. Performance increased substantially, as did the price tag. Lake has since discontinued the LA-4 and the Seaplane and is concentrating on production of the Buccaneer and the Renegade. Standard fuel tanks in the Lake were 40 gallons until someone decided that the pontoons could also be used as fuel links. The new auxiliary tanks took 7-1/2 gallons on each side, and the total capacity increased to 55 gallons. The extra 20 hp in the 200-hp Buccaneer has increased cruising speed by 12 mph and top speed by 14 mph. Allowable gross weight also increased an additional 200 pounds.

During the sagging economic times for general aviation during the 1980s, Lake aircraft played musical chairs with powerplants. In 1984 the Buccaneer's engine was upgraded to a 250 hp Lycoming IO-540-C4B5, creating the LA-250 Renegade in a modestly enlarged airframe. The model offered four to six passenger seating, improved useful load and 90 gallons of fuel on board. In 1987 turbo charging was added via the Lycoming TIO-540-AA1AB, resulting in 20 more horses to the Renegade and a ceiling of up to 23,800'. That same year the Buccaneer model was put into retirement.

Latest models of the 250 and 270 hp Lakes are all marketed under the name Seafury, and incorporate improvements in corrosion protection for operation in salt water. There are also two military variants, the SeaWolfe and Ranger, which use 290 hp engines and feature hardpoints for mounting ordnance.

LIBERTY AEROSPACE "XL2"

2002–Present

STANDARD DATA: Seats 2. Gross wt. 1,653. Empty wt. 1,065. Fuel capacity 29.5. Engine 125-hp Continental IOF 240-B (FADEC). PERFORMANCE: Top Cruise 132 kts. Stall 43 kts. Initial climb rate 682 fpm. Range 500 nm. Takeoff roll 822'. Landing roll 841'.

This two-seater was the first aircraft to be certified with FADEC, or Full Authority Digital Engine Control. A single lever combines throttle and mixture allowing a computer to control ignition and fuel injection, as

well as other vital engine parameters. The aircraft owes much of its design history to the Europa kit plane, though the metal winged, all-composite fuselage XL2 has evolved considerably, and is now one of the most advanced light general aviation aircraft on the market.

LINCOLN-PAGE

1928

STANDARD DATA: Seats 3. Gross wt. 2,500. Empty wt. 1,380. Fuel capacity 67. Engine 150-hp water-cooled Hispano Suiza 8-cylinder. PERFORMANCE: Top mph 127. Cruise mph 111. Landing mph 38. Initial climb rate 1,000. Ceiling 18,400.

The Lincoln-Page LP-3 was the principal product of the Lincoln Aircraft Co. located in Lincoln, Nebraska. Its president, Victor H. Roos, later named the company when Lincoln and American Eagle merged. The LP-3 was a three-seat open-cockpit biplane in the same class as the Lairds, Swallows, and Eaglerocks. It was powered by any of three different engines: the 150-hp Hispano Suiza eight-cylinder water-cooled engine, the 150-hp Axelson seven-cylinder radial air-cooled engine, or the 90-hp Curtiss OX-5 engine. Its tandem cockpits sat two occupants in the front and one in the rear. The Lincoln-Page featured mixed construction with wooden wings and a steel-tube fuselage. Kin to the LP-3 was the Trainer, a two-seat training biplane. It housed the OX-5 powerplant and could attain a top speed of 105 mph.

LOCKHEED "VEGA"
1927–33

STANDARD DATA: Seats 5-7. Gross wt. 4,750. Empty wt. 2,725. Engine 450-hp Pratt & Whitney Wasp SC-1. PERFORMANCE: Top mph 195. Cruise mph 170. Stall mph 59. Initial climb rate 1,250. Range 550. Ceiling 55,000.

During the late 1920s and early 1930s, the Vega was the favorite of many of the world's most renowned aviators. Such greats as Roscoe Turner, Wiley Post, and Charles Lindbergh used the Vega and its variations to break all existing records for speed, altitude, distance, and endurance. Post, flying his beloved "Winnie Mae," climbed to the astonishing altitude of 55,000 feet in 1935. He pioneered the pressure suit to make the record-setting flight. Meanwhile, Lindbergh and his wife Anne were busy flying a Sirus, which is a sistership to the Vega, setting distance records that would stand for 30 years. Turner and his faithful lion cub flew a Vega to new transcontinental victories in the United States. Several offshoot versions of the Vega were also named for stars such as Orion and Sirus. The Vega was the first airplane to be produced by the Lockheed Aircraft Co. and stands in front of a long line of great Lockheed airplanes to follow. Lockheed first produced the high-wing cabin monoplane in 1927 and by the time production ceased in 1933 a total of 131 had been made. Only a few of the great record-makers are still active today.

LUSCOMBE "PHANTOM"
1934–37

STANDARD DATA: Seats 2. Gross wt. 1,725. Empty wt. 960. Fuel capacity 30. Engine 145-hp Warner "Super-Scarab" seven-cylinder radial engine. PERFORMANCE: Top mph 132. Cruise mph 120. Stall mph 40. Initial climb rate 850. Ceiling 15,000. Range 600.

The Phantom was a side-by-side, two-seat cabin monoplane that first appeared as a product of the newly formed Luscombe Airplane Corp. Its president was Donald A. Luscombe, formerly president and chief engineer of the Monocoupe Corp., which pioneered the development of die-cut metal construction. This method helped to make production with interchangeable parts possible. The Phantom is of all-metal construction and was an advanced airplane for its time, making use of a stressed-skin Duralumin fuselage. Its production was also unusual in that Luscombe subcontracted all components from specialist manufacturers; only assembly and finish work were performed by the parent company. Power was supplied by a single 145-hp Warner "Super-Scarab" seven-cylinder radial engine, and dual controls were standard.

LUSCOMBE 8A–8F "SILVAIRE"
1937–60

STANDARD DATA: (817) Seats 2. Gross wt. 1,400. Empty wt. 870. Fuel capacity 25. Engine 90-hp Continental. PERFORMANCE: Top mph 128. Cruise mph 120. Stall mph 40. Initial climb rate 900. Range 500. Ceiling 17,000. Takeoff run 550. Landing roll 450.

STANDARD DATA: (8-A) Seats 2. Gross wt. 1,200. Empty wt. 650. Fuel capacity 14. Engine 65-hp Lycoming. PERFORMANCE: Top mph 110. Cruise mph 104. Stall mph 37. Initial climb rate 900. Ceiling 15,000. Range 350. Takeoff distance (50') 1,950. Landing distance (50') 1,540.

Luscombe's Model 8 Silvaire first appeared in 1937, and the first 50-hp production models were on the market in 1938. In March 1939, the 8A, with a 65-hp Lycoming, and the 813, with a 65-hp Continental engine, were introduced. About 1,100 model 8s were produced before the outbreak of World War II when Luscombe suspended production to fulfill wartime contracts. Production was resumed after the war with all-metal versions of the Silvaire, the 8E and 8F. Side-by-side two-seaters, the postwar models used a Continental 90-hp engine and were claimed to be acrobatic. Over 6,000 postwar Silvaires were built, and more than 2,000 are currently rated airworthy. Luscombe was acquired by Temco Aircraft Corp. in 1948, but only some 50 Silvaires were manufactured before the line was suspended for a second time due to military commitments. The final models of the 8F were produced by Silvaire Aircraft Co. between 1946 and 1960 when their production was discontinued permanently.

LUSCOMBE 11-A "SEDAN"
1948–50

STANDARD DATA: Seats 4. Gross wt. 2,280. Empty wt. 1,280. Fuel capacity 42. Engine 165-hp Continental. PERFORMANCE: Top mph 145. Cruise mph 130. Landing mph 58. Initial climb rate 900. Range 500. Ceiling 17,000. Takeoff run 800. Landing roll 500.

In 1948, the four-place, 165-hp Luscombe Silvaire ll-A Sedan was introduced and then discontinued the following year. The ll-A was essentially a four-seat re-development of Luscombe's Model 8 with a deeper fuselage. Constructed of all-metal, the Sedan can be used to carry cargo. The rear seats are removable, and tie down straps are provided to hold a maximum 600 pounds of cargo in place. The Sedan was manufactured in only limited numbers both under Luscombe and Temco Aircraft Corp., the company that purchased Luscombe in 1948.

LUSCOMBE 11E
2002–Present

STANDARD DATA: Seats 4. Gross wt. 2,280. Empty wt. 1,350. Fuel capacity 40. Engine 185-hp TCM IO-360-ES. PERFORMANCE: Cruise 126 kts. Stall mph 43. Initial climb rate 1,050 fpm. Ceiling 13,000. Takeoff run 900'. Landing roll 866'.

Luscombe Aircraft Corporation in Altus, Oklahoma was awarded an amended type certificate to reintroduce the classic Luscombe 11A "Sedan." The new aircraft, now the Luscombe 11E, is a 4-place, single engine, high wing, aircraft with new tricycle landing gear, a more powerful fuel injected engine, and modern avionics. A memo issued by the FAA after testing the 11E stated, "In spite of exhaustive attempts, it has not been possible to cause the airplane to enter a spin condition."

MAULE M-4 THROUGH M8
1962–Present

STANDARD DATA: (M-4 Jetasen) Seats 4. Gross wt. 2,100. Empty wt. 1,100. Fuel capacity 42. Engine 145-hp Continental. PERFORMANCE: Top mph 157. Cruise mph Stall mph 40. Initial climb rate 700. Ceiling 12,000. Range 750. Takeoff distance 585. Landing distance (50') 600.

STANDARD DATA: (M-4 Rocket) Seats 4. Gross wt. 2,100. Empty wt. 1,190. Fuel capacity 42. Engine 210-hp Continental. PERFORMANCE: Top mph 170. Cruise mph 165. Stall mph 40. Initial climb rate 1,250. Range 680. Ceiling 18,000. Takeoff distance (50') 585. Landing distance (50') 600.

STANDARD DATA: (M-5-210C) Seats 4. Gross wt. 2,300. Empty wt. 1,350. Fuel capacity 42. Engine 210-hp Continental. PERFORMANCE: Top mph 158. Cruise mph 150. Stall mph 56. Initial climb rate 1,250. Ceiling 18,000. Range 600. Takeoff distance (50') 600. Landing distance (50') 600.

STANDARD DATA: (M-5-235C) Seat 4. Gross wt. 2,300. Empty wt. 1,400. Fuel capacity 40-63. Engine 235-hp Lycoming. PERFORMANCE: Cruise 150 kts. Stall mph 33 kts. Initial climb rate 1,350. Range 360 nm. Ceiling 20,000. Takeoff distance (50') 600. Landing distance (50') 600.

Maule M-5

Maule M-7

STANDARD DATA: (M-7-235) Seat 4-5. Gross wt. 2,500. Empty wt. 1,500. Fuel capacity 40-70. Engine 235-hp Lycoming O-540-J3A5. **PERFORMANCE:** Cruise 148 kts. Stall 40 kts. Initial climb rate 1,350. Range 478. Ceiling 20,000. Takeoff distance (50') 600. Landing distance (50') 600.

STANDARD DATA: (M-7-420AC) Seat 5. Gross wt. 2,500. Empty wt. 1,570. Fuel capacity 85. Engine 420-shp Allison 250-B17-C turbine. **PERFORMANCE:** Cruise 168 kts. Stall 50 kts. Initial climb rate 2,800 fpm. Ceiling 20,000. Takeoff distance (50') 600. Landing distance (50') 500.

Belford D. (B.D.) Maule began a family airplane manufacturing business that received its first FAA type certificate in 1961. The first production model, known as the Jetasen M-4 was delivered in April 1962. Then, as now, all Maules are constructed in Moutrie, Georgia. The welded steel-tube fuselage is covered with fiberglass, and the shortspan wing is all-metal with a thick, high-lift airfoil. The airplane accomplishes its short-field performance with two-position flaps of an unusually high-lift capability and without the elaborate spoilers, slots, and other items normally associated with STOL design.

The original M-4 was powered by a 145-hp Continental engine, and in 1965, the Rocket entered pro-

duction with a 210-hp Continental powerplant and a constant-speed propeller. The Astro-Rocket was a deluxe version of the Jetasen, housing a 180-hp Franklin. In 1967, the Strata-Rocket was introduced into the line. Basically similar to the Rocket, it was powered by a 220-hp Franklin. All aircraft mentioned thus far shared the same M-4 designation.

The first M-5 Lunar-Rockets were delivered in 1974 as M-5-210Cs with 210-hp Continental engines. As expected, the M-5-220C houses a 220-hp Franklin. These models differ from the earlier M-4s by having four cabin doors for hauling cargo as the "C" in the model number implies; otherwise, the M-5 has a 30% increase in flap area and enlarged tail surfaces to enhance its short-field performance. The 220-hp version was discontinued when the Franklin engine was no longer available, and the M-5-235C was added to the line in 1976 employing a 235-hp Lycoming.

In 1981, Maule installed an IO-540-W1A5D out front and began delivering the M-6, also available with EDO floats. Two years later the model would morph into the M-7 and in 1989, the M-8. In 1991, the company experimented with a turbine Maule, installing an Allison 420 shp 250-B17-C and eventually offered the design in both taildragger and tricycle gear configurations. The family continues to create endless variations and improvements on the original airframe, with the original fuselage jig designed by founder B.D. Maule still in use.

MESSERSCHMITT BF-108 "TAIFUN"
1934–44

STANDARD DATA: Seats 3. Gross wt. 3,087. Empty wt. 1,887. Engine 240-hp Argus. **PERFORMANCE:** (240 hp) Top mph 189. Cruise mph 161. Initial climb rate 1,030. Range 620. Ceiling 20,340.

The BF-108 Taifun (Typhoon) is a three-seat cabin monoplane built by the Bayerische Flugzeugwerke. The design by Prof. Willy Messerschmitt in 1933 was the forerunner of the famous BF-109 Messerschmitt fighter that ruled Axis skies during World War II. A few of the all-metal Taifuns were owned by wealthy Europeans before the war, but most of the 885 airplanes built entered service in Luftwaffe training schools. They were also extensively used for liaison and communication missions. After the war, France continued production of the BF-108 (by then Me 108 and Me 208), using the designation of Nord 1000 for the Me 108 and Nord 1100 for the Me 208. Both were fitted with 220-hp Renault engines, and the Me 208 featured a tricycle landing gear.

MESSERSCHMITT BF-109
1935–44

STANDARD DATA: Seats 1. Gross wt. 6,090. Empty wt. 4,180. Fuel capacity 106. Engine 1,200-hp Mercedes-Benz inverted 12-cylinder. PERFORMANCE: Top mph 390. Cruise mph 310. Initial climb rate 3,320. Range 440. Ceiling 37,000.

The Messerschmitt 109 was Germany's primary frontline fighter throughout World War II. Designed between 1933 and 1935, the first production models began reaching Luftwaffe units in mid-1937. By the outbreak of the war, there were only 235 in service, but within a short time production was drastically accelerated. By the war's end, around 35,000 of the type had been manufactured, making it the most numerous fighter of the conflict.

Performance and maneuverability were outstanding and proved generally superior against all types of opposing fighters in the European Theater, with the probable exception of the Spitfire. Some later models, particularly the 109G, suffered performance problems due to design changes, and in the later stages of the war, Allied fighters succeeded in effectively dealing with the type. After the war, Czechs undertook production of the design, and 109s served in the Czechoslovakian Air Force until 1952. The Israel Defense Force also made good use of the Czech-made 109s during the late 1940s. Few of the original 35,000 survive today, and anyone showing up at a fly-in these days in a Messerschmitt can count on gathering a crowd.

MESSERSCHMITT 209 "MONSUN"
1970–80

STANDARD DATA: Seats 2. Gross wt. 1,807. Empty wt. 1,067. Fuel capacity 37. Engine 150-hp to 160-hp Lycoming. PERFORMANCE: (160 hp). Top mph 170. Cruise mph 158. Stall mph 62. Initial climb

rate 1,180. Range 745. Ceiling 18,100. Takeoff run 590. Landing roll 655.

The 209 Monsun is built by the largest aerospace company in Germany, the Messerschmitt Bolkow-Blohm Gmbh. The Messerschmitt part of the name comes from the company that produced the famous ME-109 during World War II. MBB's light two-seater called the Monsun (Monsoon) is produced in three versions: the B0209-150 with a 150-hp Lycoming engine, the B0209-160 with a 160-hp fuel-injected Lycoming, and the B0209S, which is the trainer model with a non-retractable nose wheel and the choice of a 125-hp Lycoming or a 130-hp Rolls-Royce/Continental engine.

Flown for the first time in 1969 and produced in 1970, the low-wing Monsun features tricycle gear with retractable nose gear as an option. The main gear is non-retractable. Wings on the 150 and 160 models can be unbolted and folded back along the fuselage for ease in storage or for towing the airplane behind a car. The control lines to the ailerons and flaps automatically dismount and reconnect when the wings are folded and unfolded. With a large clear bubble canopy, the visibility in the 209 is excellent. Construction is all metal except for a fiberglass cowling.

MEYERS OTW
1939–44

STANDARD DATA: Seats 2. Gross wt. 1,910. Empty wt. 1,340. Fuel capacity 26. Engine 160-hp Kinner five-cylinder radial. PERFORMANCE: Top mph 120. Cruise mph 105. Landing mph 40. Initial climb rate 1,200. Range 400. Ceiling 17,500.

This popular two-seat biplane was introduced in 1939 as a primary trainer. The first model was the OTW-125, powered by a 125-hp Warner Scarab engine and constructed with a metal fuselage and wooden wings. A year later, Meyers installed a 145-hp Scarab and gave the tandem-seat airplane the OTW-145 designation. The OTW-160 soon followed and featured a 160-hp Kinner. In 1943, the entire production of the Meyers plant in Tecumseh, Michigan, was concentrated on the Model OTW160, and the total output was delivered to schools operating under C.A.A. War Training Service. All three models of the OTW can still be found flying in the United States and Canada.

MICCO AIRCRAFT "SP20"/"SP26"

Micco SP20

Micco SP26

STANDARD DATA: (SP20) Seats 2. Gross wt. 2,600. Empty wt. 1,800. Fuel capacity 73. Engine 200-hp Lycoming IO-360-C1E6. PERFORMANCE: Cruise 140 kts. Stall 43 kts. Initial climb rate 950 fpm. Ceiling 12,000. Takeoff roll 600'. Landing roll 700'.

STANDARD DATA: (SP26) Seats 2. Gross wt. 2.850. Empty wt. 2,040. Fuel capacity 68. Engine 260-hp Lycoming IO-540-T4B5. PERFORMANCE: Cruise 155 kts. Stall 49 kts. Initial climb rate 1,500 fpm. Range 800 nm. Ceiling 18,000'. Takeoff roll 800'. Landing roll 700'.

The Micco Aircraft Company acquired the type certificate for the original two-place Meyers 145 in 1994. The company invested in a substantial effort to redesign and improve the aircraft, and eventually won an amended type certificate for the SP20 in early 2000. The 200-hp, all-metal low wing sports plane had retractable gear and was fully aerobatic. Looking to push the envelope even further, Micco put a 260-hp SP26 into production in 2002. The more advanced designed allowed for +6 Gs and –3 Gs at its maximum gross weight.

MITSUBISHI NAVY "ZERO"
1942

STANDARD DATA: Seats 1. Gross wt. 5,140. Engine 1,100 hp Nakajima. Sakae 21 14-cylinder radial. PERFORMANCE: (Zeke) Top mph 325. Cruise mph 265. Range 590. Ceiling 36,000.

The Mitsubishi Navy ZERO was a single-seat fighter powered by a 1,100-hp Nakajima powerplant of 14-cylinders in two rows. It had three unprotected fuel tanks, one in the fuselage and one in each wing. The pilot's cockpit was located over the center section of the wing and was under a raised transparent canopy with no armor protection. The ZERO fighter was produced in two versions, the Mk. I, code-named "Zeke," and the Mk. II, code-named "Hamp." The only difference was that the Mk. II had a redesigned wing with smaller span and blunt wingtips. Both fighters' armament consisted of two 20mm cannon in the leading edge of the wings, outboard of the prop disc, and two 7.7mm machine guns mounted in the top cowling, firing through the airscrew. One 500-pound bomb could be carried in place of a drop fuel tank.

MONOCOUPE 90A
1930–42/1947–50

STANDARD DATA: Seats 2. Gross wt. 1,610. Empty wt. 1,000. Fuel capacity 14. Engine 115-hp Lycoming. PERFORMANCE: Top mph 156. Cruise mph 135. Stall mph 40. Initial climb rate 1,100. Range 600.

Introduced by the Monocoupe Corporation in 1930, the Model 90A two-seat cabin monoplane was progressively improved until production was suspended in 1942. These early Monocoupes were powered by various engines, including the 90-hp Lambert, the 90-hp Franklin, and the Warner 125-hp Scarab or 145-hp Super Scarab. The main tanks were mounted in the wing roots, providing gravity feed to the engine. Seating was for two in side-by-side fashion with access by means of doors on either side. The fuselage was of welded steel-tube construction, while the wings were of wood. All surfaces, save the aluminum leading wing edges, were fabric covered. After a five year lapse in production, the Monocoupe was again built utilizing the same basic airframe but changing to either the 125- or 115-hp, Lycoming horizontally opposed air-cooled engine.

MOONEY M-18 "MITE"
1947

STANDARD DATA: Seats 1. Gross wt. 780. Empty wt. 520. Fuel capacity 14. Engine 65-hp Continental. PERFORMANCE: Top mph 138. Cruise mph 125. Stall mph 43. Initial climb rate 1,090. Range 440. Ceiling 19,400. Takeoff distance (50') 525. Landing distance (50') 860.

The Mooney Mite, first flown in 1947, was constructed by Mooney Aircraft, a company formed by two former executives of the defunct Culver Aircraft Corp. This single-seat monoplane was originally powered by a converted 25-hp Crosley automobile engine. With this engine, the Mite had a top speed of over 100 mph, a cruising speed of 85 mph, and a climb rate of 400 fpm. To improve the aircraft's takeoff and initial rate of climb performance, the company installed 55 and 65-hp Lycoming engines and designated it the M-18L. The final engine was the 65-hp Continental in the M-18C.

The Mite included "safe-trim," a trim-control system that consisted of a gear linking the tail trim with the wingflaps. It automatically established proper settings for takeoff climb, approach, and landing. The little personal plane was constructed with a single spruce-and-plywood D-spar wing structure with fabric covering aft of the spar. It had a metal-covered steel-tube fuselage forward and a wooden structure aft.

MOONEY MARK 20/21 SERIES
1955–Present

Mooney Ranger

Mooney Chaparral

Mooney 201

Mooney 231

STANDARD DATA: (Ranger) Seats 4. Gross wt. 2,575. Empty wt. 1,525. Fuel capacity 52. Engine 180-hp Lycoming. PERFORMANCE: Top mph 169. Cruise mph 165. Stall mph 57. Initial climb rate 800. Ceiling 16,500. Range 1,047. Takeoff distance (50') 1,395. Landing distance (50') 1,550.

STANDARD DATA: (Chaparral) Seats 4. Gross wt. 2,575. Empty wt. 1,600. Fuel capacity 52. Engine 200-hp Lycoming. PERFORMANCE: Top mph 195. Cruise mph 182. Stall mph 57. Initial climb rate 1,400. Ceiling 18,800. Range 1,015. Takeoff distance (50') 1,010. Landing distance (50') 1,360.

STANDARD DATA: (201) Seats 4. Gross wt. 2,740. Empty wt. 1,640. Fuel capacity 64. Engine 200-hp Lycoming. PERFORMANCE: Top mph 201. Cruise mph 195. Stall mph 61. Initial climb rate 1,030. Ceiling 18,800. Range 1,295. Takeoff distance 870. Landing roll 770.

STANDARD DATA: (231) Seats 4. Gross wt. 2,900. Empty wt. 1,800. Fuel capacity 75.6. Engine 210-hp turbocharged Continental. PERFORMANCE: Top mph 231. Cruise mph 210. Stall mph 66. Initial climb rate 1,080. Ceiling 24,000. Range 1,258. Takeoff distance (50') 2,060. Landing distance (50') 2,280.

Like the B.D. Maule's M-4 design, Al Mooney's M20 airframe has evolved as the basis for virtually the entire line. In 1955, Mooney introduced the Mark 20 as a low-wing aircraft with retractable landing gear. This early version was powered by a 150-hp Lycoming. Its wings were constructed of wood and fabric, while its tail unit was a plywood structure with steel-tube framed control surfaces. The Mark 20A entered production in 1958 offering a 180-hp Lycoming engine as an option. These two aircraft continued in production until 1960, when the Mark 20 was discontinued, and 1961, when the Mark 20A was replaced by the Mark 21.

The Mark 21 was the first Mooney to feature all-metal construction but was otherwise the same airplane. In 1963, the Master was offered as a non-retractable version of the Mark 21, and in 1964, the Super 21 entered production with its fuel-injected 200-hp Lycoming. The Ranger replaced the Mark 21 and Master in 1967. It differed from earlier models by the addition of a one-piece windshield and the elimination of the dorsal fin. That same year the Statesman was added to the line with its longer fuselage and extra passenger windows; the Executive 21 was also introduced, utilizing the Statesman's fuselage with a 200-hp fuel-injected engine.

Production of all aircraft ceased for a while in 1972, but resumed in 1974. The airframe was put through an extensive aerodynamic clean-up program by aerodynamicist Roy Lopresti. The previously uncovered gear wells were fitted with complete doors. A McCauley paddle-blade prop yielded increased efficiency at the blade extremities. A super-slick engine cowling shape provided minimum drag at cruise, while new cowl flaps were reworked to open wide during climb to keep down engine temperatures. The windshield was streamlined. The use of flush riveting was expanded to the leading 60% of the wing chord, and fiberglass fairings were used on all hinges. The result was the Mooney 201, the first aircraft in history to fly 200mph with 200hp.

The addition of turbocharging might seem a rather meager justification for calling an airplane "new," but in the case of the Mooney 231, turbocharging was a big deal. When the 201 was first introduced in 1976, there was little question that a turbo version would follow. Like Rajay's Piper Lance system, the Mooney installation is a sea-level unit designed to deliver 30 inches of manifold pressure right up to the critical altitude. Maximum operation altitude for the 231 was established at 23,000 feet. It flies at approximately 207 mph at 75% power. Of special note is the fact that 1980 was the first year Mooney surpassed Piper Arrow in sales since the single-engine retractable-gear Piper took the number one sales position away from Mooney.

For 1981, the Model 201 featured sculptured wingtips with integral navigation and strobe lights. First introduced on the 231, the new tips reduce parasite drag and help provide better roll response. They're made of tough and resilient fiberglass. Improvement to range and payload for the Turbo 231 results from redesign of the fuel tanks. Eight gallons of unusable fuel have been reduced to three gallons; this and other changes result in a 35-pound increase in payload. Total usable fuel is up from 72 to 75.6 gallons.

In 1986, the 231 morphed into the Mooney 252TSE. The model added such exotics as speed brakes and an intercooler, but couldn't survive the sour economy of the early 1990s, nor Mooney's off again/on again financial woes. Production on the 252 ended in 1990.

MOONEY M20 "PFM, MSE, TLS, EAGLE, ENCORE, OVATION, BRAVO"

STANDARD DATA: (Ovation) Seats 4. Gross wt. 3,368. Empty wt. 2,205. Fuel capacity 89. Engine 280-hp Continental IO-550-G. PERFORMANCE: Cruise Speed 190 KTAS. Stall 59 kts. Initial climb rate 1,250. Ceiling 20,000. Range 1,240. Takeoff distance (50') 2,060. Landing distance (50') 2,280.

STANDARD DATA: (Bravo) Seats 4. Gross wt. 3,368. Empty wt. 2,268. Fuel capacity 75.6. Engine 270-bhp Continental TIO-540-AF1B. PERFORMANCE: Cruise Speed 220 KTAS. Stall mph 59. Initial climb rate 1,130. Ceiling 25,000. Range 1,050. Takeoff distance 2,050'. Landing distance 2,600'.

Mooney PFM

Mooney Ovation

Mooney Bravo

In 1988-89 Mooney offered the PFM (M20L), a regular M20 airframe with a Porsche engine up front. It was a first in many ways, primarily because it offered a high performance automobile manufacturer's variant for an aircraft, and second, the PFM was the first airplane to have a single-engine power control, the precursor to what is now called FADEC (Fully Automated Digital Electronic Control). Porsche placed limits on their liability exposure by setting a finite availability for the PFM Mooney engine, all of which were eventually removed from their M20 airframes and returned to Porsche.

Also in 1989, Mooney addressed a common complaint about comfort in the M20 airframe, and extended the fuselage by 18 inches. The first mode vantage of the new dimensions was the With a 350-hp Lycoming, derated 270 turned in an effortless 223-knot high-speed high-altitude cruise speed. The aircraft would ultimately be renamed the Mooney Bravo.

After testing a model-name change to Mooney 205, the venerable Mooney 201 was christened the MSE (Mooney Special Edition M20J) in 1990. That name would continue until 1998 when the 200-hp M20 was laid to rest in favor of more powerful newcomers.

Beginning in the mid-1990s Mooney began to search for a replacement for the 201, arriving first at the Ovation (M20R), with a 280-hp Continental. In 1997, Mooney searched for a lower-costing, entry level design, offering the 220-hp Encore (M20K). In 1999 they tried again with the 244-hp Eagle (M20S). Neither the Encore nor the Eagle remain in production, however the M20 airframe will doubtlessly continue to evolve for years to come.

MOONEY MARK 22 "MUSTANG"
1967–69

STANDARD DATA: Seats 5. Gross wt. 3,680. Empty wt. 2,440. Fuel capacity 52. Engine 310-hp fuel-injected Lycoming. PERFORMANCE: Top mph 256. Cruise mph 230. Stall mph 67. Initial climb rate 1,125. Range 1,493. Ceiling 24,000. Takeoff distance (50') 1,870. Landing distance (50') 1,520.

The Mooney Mark 22 was the most radical in its class in that it offered the only pressurized cabin in a commercial single-engine plane. The Mustang was first introduced in 1967 and was dropped when Butler Aviation took over the Mooney line. The engine is a 310-hp Lycoming that is turbocharged for high-altitude operation and adequate power. The Mustang has flight characteristics similar to other Mooneys; however, special pilot training is required to assure proper management of the cabin pressurization system. Mooney had engineered all the necessary safety features into the cabin and door, which had to provide a good seal against the loss of air. Because the Mark 22 can be operated so easily and so high, it offers very fast airspeeds at very reduced fuel consumption. Though an important first, the Mooney Mustang Mark 22 enjoyed only meager success. Only 30 aircraft were sold before the model was withdrawn from production.

MOONEY M30 "301"
1983

STANDARD DATA: M30 Seats 6. Gross wt. 4,000. Useful Load. 1,600. Fuel capacity 100 gallons. Engine 360-hp Lycoming TSIO-540. PERFORMANCE: Top Cruise 262 kts. Initial climb rate 1,400 fpm. Range 986 nm. Ceiling 25,000'.

In response to Cessna's success with the pressurized 210 Centurion, and with similar pressurized products on the drawing boards at Piper and Beech, Mooney began work on a pressurized single called the Mooney 301. The design was to have a 360-hp Lycoming TSIO-540 for a speed of 262 knots, or 301 mph, and was the responsibility of the renowned Roy LoPresti. The first prototype flew on April 7, 1983, overweight and slower than expected. Mooney's financial troubles hobbled the continuing research and development. The company entered a joint venture with the Socata division of French Aerospatiale, and in 1987 the Mooney 301 was shipped to the factory at Tarbes, France. Ultimately much of the aircraft's design was incorporated into Socata's TBM 700, the 'TB' standing for Tarbes, France, and the 'M' for Mooney.

NAKAJIMA NAVY 97 "KATE"
1942

STANDARD DATA: Seats 2-3. Engine 700-hp Nakajima Hikari nine-cylinder radial. PERFORMANCE: Top mph 225. Cruise mph 205. Range 600.

The Nakajima Navy 97 was a single-engine torpedo bomber and was code-named "Kate." Housing a 700-hp nine-cylinder air-cooled radial engine, the Model 97 is easily identified by its continuous canopy under which two to three crewmen were seated. This torpedo plane also featured cantilevered wings with taper on both the leading and trailing edges and dihedral on the outer sections only. Its flaps were exceptionally short. The main landing gear were inward-retractable, and the tail wheel was nonretractable. Armament consisted of two 7.7mm machine guns mounted in the cowling and one or two movable machine guns of the same caliber in the rear cockpit. An 18-inch torpedo or bombs up to 1,100 lbs. could be carried under the fuselage.

NAKAJIMA "OSCAR"
1937–43

STANDARD DATA: Seats 1. Gross wt. 5,500. Empty wt. 1,150-hp Nakajima Type 2. PERFORMANCE: Top mph 333. Cruise mph 265. Range 1,000.

The Japanese Army designation for this single-seat fighter was Type I fighter, Model 2; the popular name was "Haya-busa" meaning peregrine falcon, and the Americans call it "Oscar." Its wings taper in chord and thickness, and the landing gear retracted inward into recesses in the underside of the wings. The powerplant was one 1,150-hp Nakajima Type 214-cylinder twin-row radial engine. It was fitted with a two-speed supercharger and turned a three-blade constant-speed propeller. The fuel tanks were in the wings, protected by self-sealing rubber. Standard armament was two 12.7mm machine guns in the fuselage that were synchronized to fire through the prop. The pilot sat under a sliding "bubble" canopy and was protected by armor to the rear.

NAVAL AIRCRAFT FACTORY N3N-3
1940–52

STANDARD DATA: Seats 2. Gross wt. 2,780. Empty wt. 2,050. Engine 235-hp Wright Whirlwind. PERFORMANCE: Top mph 118. Cruise mph 98. Initial climb rate 800. Range 470. Ceiling 13,700.

In 1935, the Naval Aircraft Factory in Philadelphia began design of the N3N primary trainer. The govern-

ment-owned company finally began production in April 1940 and produced a total of 816 two-seaters before production ceased in 1942. The tandem biplane, nicknamed the "Yellow Peril," was built both as a landplane and floatplane; many of the latter were used at Annapolis until retired in 1959. The original Yellow Peril was powered by a 235-hp seven-cylinder Wright Whirlwind radial engine although many of the trainers that found themselves in civilian hands were fitted with other engines such as the 459-hp Pratt & Whitney Wasp Junior, the 600-hp Wasp, or smaller Continental engines of 220 to 250 hp. Almost 150 N3N biplanes are active today, many of them serving faithfully as agricultural aircraft.

NAVION "RANGEMASTER"
1961–78

STANDARD DATA: (285 hp) Seats 5. Gross wt. 3,315. Empty wt. 1,950. Fuel capacity 108. Engine 285-hp Continental. PERFORMANCE: Top mph 197. Cruise mph 191. Stall mph 59. Initial climb rate 1,375. Range 1,800. Ceiling 21,500. Takeoff distance (50') 920. Landing distance (50') 980.

The Rangemaster is a refinement of the earlier North American/Ryan Navion design. It is quite a different airplane despite the fact that it retains the original Navion wing, undercarriage, and fuselage. In the early 1960s, the production of Navions was taken over by the Navion Aircraft Corp., which was made up of mem-

bers of the American Navion Society. The first Rangemaster took to the air in 1960, and production began in 1961. The first model was designated the Rangemaster G and retained the 260-hp Continental. The Rangemaster G-1 followed in 1962 with redesigned smaller tail surfaces. Rangemasters get their name from the excellent range provided by the extra fuel that can be carried in the two centerline fuel tanks mounted on the tip of each wing. These 34-gallon tip tanks are in addition to the main 40-gallon tank. In 1966, the Rangemaster II was unveiled with its 285-hp powerplant. It quickly became known for its speed, short-field performance, and of course its exceptional range.

NEW STANDARD D-25
1929

STANDARD DATA: Seats 5. Gross wt. 3,400. Empty wt. 2,010. Fuel capacity 62. Engine 200-hp Wright Whirlwind. PERFORMANCE: Top mph 105. Cruise mph 85. Stall mph 40. Initial climb rate 800. Ceiling 17,800.

The D-25 was a further development of the Gates-Day GD-24. This five-seat general-purpose commercial biplane accommodated four persons in side-by-side pairs in the forward of two tandem cockpits; the pilot sat in the aft cockpit. Power was supplied by a 200-hp Wright Whirlwind J-5 radial fed by a 62-gallon fuel tank. In 1929, a fleet of D-27 Mail Planes was delivered to Clifford Ball who operated the Cleveland-Pittsburgh-Washington mail route. Another version was the D-26, in which two of the front four seats were removed.

The D-27 Mail Plane differed by having all four seats removed and the forward cockpit covered ᵒᵛᵉ⁻ ⁻ 28 was a twin-float seaplane. M have survived have been put in tural aircraft with the dust hopp placing the forward cockpit. The fu Duralumin angles and channels gether. The wings were made from wood and covered with fabric.

NOORDUYN "NORSEMAN" (C.C.F.)
1935–59

STANDARD DATA: Seats 6-8. Gross wt. 7,540. Empty wt. 4,700. Fuel capacity 120. Engines 550-hp Pratt & Whitney Wasp. PERFORMANCE: Top mph 155. Cruise mph 141. Stall mph 68. Initial climb rate 714. Range 464. Ceiling 17,000.

The Norseman was designed by Robert B.C. Noorduyn in 1934 and entered production in Montreal, Canada, in 1935. Designed primarily for use in the Canadian bush as a lightweight freighter and transport, the Norseman IV with the Pratt & Whitney Wasp engine was used during World War II by both the R.C.A.F. and the U.S. Air Corps as a utility transport and navigational trainer. Altogether 759 aircraft were supplied to the Air Corps under the UC-64 designation. After the war, the Canadian Car and Foundry Co. acquired the assets of the Noorduyn Co. and continued production of an improved Norseman until 1959.

NORTH AMERICAN AT-6 "TEXAN"
1941–54

STANDARD DATA: Seats 2. Gross wt. 5,300. Empty wt. 4,158. Fuel capacity 111. Engine 550-hp Pratt & Whitney Wasp. PERFORMANCE: Top mph 205. Cruise mph 170. Landing mph 67. Initial climb rate 1,600. Range 750. Ceiling 21,500.

This is one of the most popular and widely used of military surplus aircraft in general aviation. It was manufactured in greater quantities than any other basic trainer plane. One of the great virtues of the AT-6 is the that it is an all-metal plane, which eliminates any over deterioration. The AT-6 is not difficult to fly and generally is the first step in ratings for any pilot who wishes to move up to faster surplus military aircraft. It is known under a variety of names and designations, including Texan, Harvard, AT-6, and SNJ-4. More than 10,000 were built by the United States and allied countries during the span of its lifetime. AT-6 was the army designation, and SNJ-4 was the navy designation. The name Harvard applied to those built by the Noorduyn factory in Canada; the Harvard differed only in its lack of armament equipment. The AT-6 was later modernized and used in Korea as a spotter plane. It had slightly more power and better visibility from both seats.

NORTH AMERICAN T-28 "TROJAN"
1950–58

STANDARD DATA: Seats 2. Gross wt. 6,759. Empty wt. 5,111. Fuel capacity 125. Engine 800-hp Wright radial. PERFORMANCE: Top mph 288. Cruise mph 190. Stall mph 72. Initial climb rate 2,570. Range 1,008. Ceiling 29,800. Takeoff distance (50') 1,308.

The North American T-28 was the first U.S. military trainer to be outfitted with tricycle landing gear. It was designed for the U.S. Air Force as a replacement for the AT-6 as an advanced trainer. Production began in 1950 and was discontinued eight years later. Several different versions of the T-28 exist. Some of the original T-28s were built for the air force, while others were constructed for the navy. A number of them were subsequently supplied to foreign countries. Finally, the latest version with a 1,425-hp engine was constructed for counterinsurgency warfare in the early 1960s. Another version produced during the same period was powered by a 2,450-shp Lycoming turboprop engine to increase the aircraft's maximum speed to 360 mph and gross weight to 15,530. The T-28 is considered to be easy to fly so long as the engine is operating at full power. When power is reduced, the rate of descent is spectacular.

NORTH AMERICAN P-51 "MUSTANG"
1943–46

STANDARD DATA: (P-51D) Seats 1-2. Gross wt. 11,600. Empty wt. 7,125. Fuel capacity 269-489. Engine 1,720-hp Rolls-Royce/Packard Merlin. PER-

FORMANCE: Top mph 437. Cruise mph 362. Initial climb rate 3,475. Range 2,300. Ceiling 41,900.

Many experts agree that the North American P-51 Mustang is the world's finest fighter plane in its class. Most air races around closed circuits include a large percentage of Mustangs. Quite a few P-51s have been converted to seat two persons. Although the Mustang went out of production in 1946, it is still in service in some places in the world. By civilian aircraft standards, the Mustang is a difficult plane to fly; it is considered especially tricky on takeoffs when the engine torque requires expert pilot handling. Designed originally for the V-12 Allison engine, the P-51's high-altitude and power performance did not live up to expectations. So, the 1,450-hp Packard Merlin became the standard powerplant.

There are several models of the Mustang, but the F-51 D was the first version to feature the trimmed-down rear fuselage and bubble canopy. Earlier Mustangs looked similar to the Spitfire. Today many Mustangs have been modified to handle engines with an output of over 2,000 hp. An interesting mutation of the P-51 was the F-82 "Twin Mustang." Essentially, it was two Mustang fuselages joined by a constant-chord center section and a rectangular tailplane. It was used as a two-seat long-range escort fighter and had a maximum speed of over 475 mph.

NORTHWEST "RANGER"
1961–72

STANDARD DATA: Seats 6-8. Gross wt. 4,700. Empty wt. 2,848. Fuel capacity 91. Engine 520-hp Lycoming. PERFORMANCE: Top mph 170. Cruise mph 166. Stall mph 62. Initial climb rate 1,475. Range 530. Ceiling 20,000. Takeoff distance (50') 915. Landing distance (50') 920.

Originally designed by Lockheed Aircraft as the Model 60 light utility transport, the eight-seat Ranger was also manufactured under license by Aeronautica Macchi of Italy with the name "Conestoga." In 1968, marketing and production rights were acquired by Northwest Industries, Ltd. of Edmonton, Alberta. The versatile high-wing airplane was certified as either a land plane with tricycle or conventional gear, or a floatplane on EDO floats, or a ski plane on Fluidyne wheel skis. The original model was powered by a large 400-hp eight-cylinder fuel-injected Lycoming and had a maximum speed of 156 mph. Without the drag brought about by floats, the Ranger can climb at 1,080 fpm at sea level. Entrance to the large cabin is through a giant passenger/cargo door or through the pilot's door beside the left front seat. In 1970, the Ranger received a 520-hp Lycoming engine to increase its climb rate and cruise speed when used with floats.

PACIFIC AEROSPACE CORPORATION "PAC 750XL"
2004–Present

STANDARD DATA: Seats 2-8. Gross wt. 7,500. Empty wt. 3220. Engine 750-hp Pratt & Whitney PT6-34. Fuel 221 gallons. PERFORMANCE: Cruise 169 kts. Stall 58 kts. Initial climb rate 1,600 fpm. Ceiling 20,000'. Takeoff roll 880'. Landing roll 866'.

PAC manufactures aircraft parts for Boeing, Airbus and others. Their success with the CT/4 civilian and military trainer and the Cresco agricultural plane led to testing the growing market for turbine utility singles. The New Zealand company ultimately built the 750XL, an extremely versatile, fixed-gear Pratt & Whitney-powered aircraft, and quickly found a niche in personal, passenger and freight hauling applications. FAA certification now welcomes the PAC 750XL into the U.S. market.

PASPED "SKYLARK"
1936

STANDARD DATA: Seats 2. Gross wt. 1,885. Empty wt. 1,288. Engine 125-hp Warner Scarab. PERFORMANCE: Top mph 139. Cruise mph 125. Stall mph 35. Initial climb rate 850. Ceiling 16,000. Range 650.

In 1936, the Pasped Aircraft Co. of Glendale, California, introduced a two-seat side-by-side cabin monoplane called the Skylark. Its engine was a 125-hp Warner Scarab radial engine housed in a low-drag cowling. The fuselage was a rectangular steel-tube welded structure covered with Duralumin metal panels forward and fabric aft. The wings were wire-braced from above, had plywood leading edges, and were covered with both fabric and Duralumin (the latter only at the center section). The single surviving example still flying is fitted with a 175-hp Warner Super Scarab.

PILATUS "PC-12"
1994–Present

STANDARD DATA: Pilatus PC-6 Seats 6-8. Gross wt. 9,920. Standard Empty Weight 5,867 lbs. Usable Fuel 402. Engine 1,200 shp Pratt & Whitney PT6A-67B. PERFORMANCE: Cruise 300 KTAS. Initial climb rate 1,587 fpm. Stall 72 kts. Range 2,489 nm. Ceiling 30,000'. Takeoff run 1395'. Landing roll 900'.

The biggest of the single-engine turbines, the PC-12 has a 53' wing and stands 14 feet tall. Despite its size, the PC-12 can come and go from the shortest of runways. The popularity of the Pilatus comes not only from its mission versatility, but the variety of configurations. PC-12 huge cabin door allows the aircraft to serve as luxury personal transportation as easily as cargo or air ambulance application.

PIPER J-3 "CUB"
1938–47

STANDARD DATA: Seats 2. Gross wt. 1,200. Empty wt. 680. Fuel capacity 9. Engine 40-hp to 65-hp Continental. PERFORMANCE: (65 hp). Top mph 87. Cruise mph 75. Stall mph 38. Initial climb rate 450. Range 206. Ceiling 11,500. Takeoff run 700. Landing roll 800.

The Piper J-3, developed in 1937, made the name "Cub" a household word. It became one of the most popular of the inexpensive "flivver" aircraft that were intended to bring amateur flying within the reach of the average man. The J-3 was a classic learn-to-fly plane that was originally derived from the similar J-2 Cub of 1936 vintage. The 40-hp J-3 first appeared in 1938, and more than 5,500 of these tandem two-seat fabric-covered flying machines were built before production was temporarily suspended in 1942. The J-3s were back in production again in 1945 powered by a 65-hp Continental. In 1947, several revisions changed the nomenclature to PA-11 Cub Special. Although parts for the old J-3s are becoming harder to obtain, many of these aircraft are changing hands every year. It is one of the lowest priced used airplanes on the market, but is rapidly gaining appeal as a near-classic.

PIPER J-4 "CUB COUPE"
1939–42

STANDARD DATA: Seats 2. Gross wt. 1,400. Empty wt. 865. Fuel capacity 16. Engine 75-hp Continental. PERFORMANCE: Top mph 100. Cruise mph 96.

Landing mph 40. Initial climb rate 450. Range 455. Ceiling 12,000.

The J-4 Coupe was the first Piper monoplane to have side-by-side seating. First flown in 1938 and produced from 1939 to 1942, the light high-wing monoplane with enclosed cabin was often used in flight training schools and in the Civilian War Training Program. Very similar in structure to the J-3 Cub, the J-4 was powered by a 75-hp four-cylinder Continental engine. Cub Coupe features included hydraulic brakes, a more complete instrument panel, and navigation lights. Fuel capacity and overall size of the J-4 was also increased over its predecessor, the J-3. Construction is a welded steel-tube fuselage, and wings are made from spruce spars and aluminum alloy. Almost 200 Coupes are still active.

PIPER PA-15 "VAGABOND"/ PA-16 "CLIPPER"/PA-17 "PACER"
1948–49

STANDARD DATA: (PA-15) Seats 2. Gross wt. 1,100. Empty wt. 620. Fuel capacity 36. Engine 65-hp, Continental. PERFORMANCE: Top mph 100. Cruise mph 90. Stall mph 45. Initial climb rate 510. Range 250. Ceiling 10,000. Takeoff run 900. Landing roll 300.

STANDARD DATA: (PA-16) Seats 4. Gross wt. 1,500. Empty wt. 800. Fuel capacity 36. Engine 115-hp Lycoming. PERFORMANCE: Top mph 125. Cruise mph 112. Stall mph 50. Initial climb rate 600. Range 480. Ceiling 11,000. Takeoff run 720. Landing roll 600.

STANDARD DATA: (PA-17) Top mph 100. Cruise mph 90. Stall mph 45. Initial climb rate 530. Ceiling 10,500. Range 250. Takeoff run 800. Landing roll 300.

The PA-15 entered production in 1948 and was one of the first to appear after Piper had temporarily suspended its activities. Originally powered by a 65-hp Lycoming engine, the PA-15 Vagabond was a side-by-side two-seater and a forerunner of a new series that would come to include the Clipper, Pacer, and ultimately the Tri-Pacer. The PA-17, introduced in 1949,

was primarily intended to serve as a trainer and with a 65-hp, Continental installed. The PA-15 and PA-17 were not built in large quantities, perhaps due to the four-seat PA-16 Clipper, which was also produced in 1949. The PA-16 housed a 115-hp Lycoming engine and subsequently evolved into the PA-20 Pacer.

PIPER J-5 "CUB CRUISER"/ PA-12 "SUPER CRUISER"
1946–48

STANDARD DATA: (Super Cruiser) Seats 3. Gross wt. 1,390. Empty wt. 490. Fuel capacity 30. Engine 108-hp Lycoming. PERFORMANCE: Top mph 115. Cruise mph 105. Stall mph 49. Initial climb rate 600. Range 600. Ceiling 12,600. Takeoff distance (50') 720. Landing distance (50') 470.

STANDARD DATA: (J-5) Seats 3. Gross wt. 1,450. Empty wt. 830. Fuel capacity 25. Engine 75-hp Continental. PERFORMANCE: Top mph 100. Cruise mph 85. Landing mph 39. Initial climb rate 450. Range 450. Ceiling 10,000.

The Piper J-5 Cruiser, one of the many J-3 derivatives, entered production in 1946. It differed from the earlier Cub by having increased seating with a single forward seat and a side-by-side seat aft. Also featured was increased engine size from the J-3's 65-hp engine to either a 75-hp or 100-hp Lycoming engine. The PA-11 was similar to the J-5 but was powered by a 90-hp engine. The PA-12 Super Cruiser was powered by a 108-hp Lycoming four-cylinder engine and was also designed to carry three persons. A later version of the Cruiser line was the PA-14 Family Cruiser, which was designed to carry four persons and sported flaps on its wings. The PA-12 Super Cruiser, typical of the J-3 Cub derivatives, is still extremely common throughout the United States.

PIPER PA-18 "SUPER CUB"
1949–94

STANDARD DATA: Seats 3. Gross wt. 1,750. Empty wt. 930. Fuel capacity 36. Engine 150-hp Lycoming. PERFORMANCE: Top mph 130. Cruise mph 115.

Stall mph 43. Initial climb rate 960. Range 460. Ceiling 19,000. Takeoff distance (50') 500. Landing distance (50') 725.

STANDARD DATA: Seats 2. Gross wt. 1,500. Empty wt. 800. Fuel capacity 18. Engine 90-hp Continental. PERFORMANCE: Top mph 112. Cruise mph 100. Stall mph 42. Initial climb rate 710. Ceiling 15,750. Range 360. Takeoff distance (50') 750. Landing distance (50') 800.

Piper's PA-18 Super Cub first appeared in 1949 as a replacement for the J-3 and PA-11 series. It follows the same basic design as the older Cubs while offering a more powerful engine. Between 1949 and 1955, the power was gradually increased through several different engines from 90 hp to 150 hp. Some of the earlier models of the Super Cub (PA-18A) had dusting and spraying equipment installed and were used as agricultural aircraft. Other versions, designated L-18 and L-21, were designed for the military as liaison aircraft and have been used as observation planes in Southeast Asia. Along with the increase in engine power, the fuel capacity was quadrupled over that of its predecessor, extending the maximum range to more than 400 miles.

Although its top speed leaves something to be desired, the design of this airplane meets the purpose for which it was intended. After 45 years of production, Piper decided to leave the Super Cub well enough alone. Piper sells every one that it makes, particularly in South America, Asia, and Africa-anywhere a pilot needs to lift off from an unimproved airstrip in 500 feet carrying 820 pounds of people, fuel, and baggage. The PA-18 has earned the distinction of being the longest production run of any single model airplane in the history of aviation. As of 1980, over 30,000 had been built.

PIPER PA-20 "PACER"
1950–54

STANDARD DATA: Seats 4. Gross wt. 1,950. Empty wt. 1,010. Fuel capacity 36. Engine 135-hp Lycoming. PERFORMANCE: Top mph 139. Cruise mph 125. Stall mph 48. Initial climb rate 620. Range 580. Ceiling 15,000. Takeoff distance (50') 1,600. Landing distance (50') 1,280.

The PA-20 Pacer was first introduced in 1949 as the PA-16 Clipper, a development of the PA-15 Vagabond. The "Clipper" name lasted only a year because Pan Am owned rights to that trademark. As the first four-seater to be built on the "short" Piper wing, the PA-16 featured a 115-hp Lycoming engine. In 1950, the PA-20 Pacer appeared with a larger tail, larger fuel tanks, wheel controls (versus a stick), and balanced elevators. The PA-20 was then produced in several versions, each featuring slight differences in engine size. Between 1950 and 1951, it was built with either the 115-hp or 125-hp Lycoming engine. From 1952 until production ceased in 1954, the 125-hp and 135-hp Lycoming powerplants were used.

PIPER PA-22 "TRI-PACER"
1951–60

STANDARD DATA: Seats 4. Gross wt. 2,000. Empty wt. 1,104. Fuel capacity 36. Engine 150-hp Lycoming. PERFORMANCE: Top mph 140. Cruise mph 130. Stall mph 49. Initial climb rate 536. Ceiling 16,000. Takeoff distance (50') 600. Landing distance (50') 1,280.

STANDARD DATA: Seats 4. Gross wt. 1,950. Empty wt. 1,040. Fuel capacity 36. Engine 135-hp Lycoming. PERFORMANCE: Top mph 137. Cruise mph 132. Stall mph 48. Initial climb rate 620. Ceiling 15,000. Range 580. Takeoff distance (50') 1,600. Landing distance (50') 1,280.

STANDARD DATA: Seats 4. Gross wt. 2,000. Empty wt. 1,110. Fuel capacity 36. Engine 160-hp Lycoming. PERFORMANCE: Top mph 141. Cruise mph 134. Stall mph 48. Initial climb rate 800. Ceiling 16,500. Range 536. Takeoff distance (50') 1,480. Landing distance (50') 1,280.

Piper's Tri-Pacer came to life in 1951 as a redesigned PA-20 Pacer. The conventional-gear Pacer had a tendency to swerve when landing in a crosswind, so Piper Aircraft went to the drawing boards and came up with a tricycle landing gear version. Originally equipped with a 125-hp engine, the power was increased on subsequent models approximately every two years: 135 hp, 150 hp, and 160 hp. When the 160-hp version was introduced in 1958, the 150-hp model also remained in production. To distinguish the two models, the 150-hp version was called the "Caribbean" during 1959 and 1960. The four-seater (really a three-placer) proved very popular with pilots during the 1950s and is continuing to serve faithfully today.

Of fabric-covered tubular construction, the Tri-Pacer was never known for outstanding speed, but it does perform surprisingly well against newer aircraft in its class. In comparison with Piper's 180 and Cessna's 172, the Tri-Pacer takes off in less distance, climbs faster, carries almost as much weight, and cruises a little faster than the 172. In spite of its stubby appearance, there are many pilots/owners who speak fondly of these sturdy little birds. Besides, they weren't designed to win any beauty contests; they were designed to carry four people through the sky from point A to point B, and they do just that very well.

PIPER PA-22-108 "COLT"
1961–63

STANDARD DATA: Seats 2. Gross wt. 1,650. Empty wt. 940. Fuel capacity 36. Engine 108-hp Lycoming. PERFORMANCE: Top mph 120. Cruise mph 108. Stall mph 54. Initial climb rate 610. Range 648. Ceiling 12,000. Takeoff distance (50') 1,570. Landing distance (50') 1,250.

The Piper Colt, introduced in 1961, is primarily intended for use by clubs and flying schools. It is identical in many ways to the Tri-Pacer and employs the same undercarriage, engine mounts, seats, windshield, door, tail surfaces, struts, and instrument panel. This two-seater aircraft is powered by a 108-hp Lycoming four-cylinder engine. The Colt features an all-metal airframe with fabric covering and was available in many Custom and Super Custom versions. Over 2,000 Piper Colts were built during the two years of production, and many of those are still very active.

PIPER "TOMAHAWK"
1978–82

STANDARD DATA: Seats 2. Gross wt. 1,670. Empty wt. 1,064. Fuel capacity 32. Engine 112-hp Lycoming. PERFORMANCE: Top mph 130. Cruise mph 125. Stall mph 53. Initial climb rate 718. Ceiling 12,000. Range 502. Takeoff distance (50') 1,460. Landing distance (50') 1,374.

The sleek all-metal Tomahawk was the first trainer to meet all FAA requirements of 14 CFR Part 23, Amendment 16. It combines a number of innovative design elements, including a jet-age T-tail that positions the fixed horizontal stabilizer and interchangeable elevators in air undisturbed by propeller slipstream. The T-tail facilitates quieter, smoother, and more stable flight with minimal pitch change at any speed. As an end plate for the vertical fin, the "T" also provides more positive rudder control. The "T" permits precise spin training, and the positive response gives the student excellent conditions for practicing stalls.

The Tomahawk's modern low-wing design is an adaptation of NASA's Whitcomb airfoil and provides optimum inflight visibility, ground handling, safety, and landing ease. The design consists of a constant thickness and a rectangular platform with a high aspect ratio chosen for its low drag that permits excellent speed and high lift. The Tomahawk also features a bubble canopy and a door both sides of the cabin. For cost- and time-efficient maintenance, the Tomahawk's engine is accessible through a wide double opening cowling, and if necessary, the engine can be removed without detaching the propeller. The most significant refinement for the Tomahawk in 1980 was the reduction in the forces necessary to extend the flaps, carried out with the intention of reducing the student pilot's workload. In keeping with the T-tail design, there is no pitch-up tendency with flap extension.

PIPER "CHEROKEE"/"CRUISER"/ "CADET"/"WARRIOR"
1964–Present

Piper Cherokee Cruiser

Piper Warrior II

STANDARD DATA: (Warrior) Seats 2. Gross wt. 2,325. Empty wt. 1,342. Fuel capacity 50. Engine 160-hp Lycoming. PERFORMANCE: Top mph 146. Cruise mph 141. Stall mph 58. Initial climb rate 710. Ceiling 13,000. Range 730. Takeoff distance (50') 1,490. Landing distance (50') 1,115.

STANDARD DATA: (140) Seats 2. Gross wt. 1,950. Empty wt. 1,180. Fuel capacity 36-50. Engine 140-hp Lycoming. PERFORMANCE: Top mph 144. Cruise mph 134. Stall mph 52. Initial climb rate 820. Ceiling 15,000. Range 560-780. Takeoff distance (50') 1,700. Landing distance (50') 1,080.

STANDARD DATA: Warrior (PA-160) Seats 4. Gross wt. 2,200. Empty wt. 1,215. Fuel capacity 36-50. Engine 160-hp Lycoming. PERFORMANCE: Top mph 146. Cruise mph 137. Stall mph 55. Initial climb rate 730. Ceiling 15,800. Range 545-735. Takeoff distance (50') 1,660. Landing distance (50') 1,090.

STANDARD DATA: Warrior (PA-28-161) Seats 4. Gross wt. 2,440. Empty wt. 1,348. Fuel capacity 50. Engine 160-hp Lycoming 0-320D3G. PERFORMANCE: Top mph 146. Cruise mph 140. Initial climb rate 644. Ceiling 11,000. Range 640. Takeoff distance (50') 1,650. Landing distance (50') 1,160.

The Cherokee 140 was introduced in 1964 to meet the demand for an efficient low-wing trainer. Initially powered by a 140-hp Lycoming engine, the smallest Cherokee graduated to 150 hp in 1966, and an optional two-passenger rear seat was also made available. Licensed in the utility category, Piper's learn-to-fly airplane is also approved for aerobatic maneuvers such as lazy eights, chandelles, steep turns, and spins when operating below 1,950 pounds gross weight. When trimmed properly, the Cherokee is a very stable airplane and can be flown with aileron control alone.

The plane was sold in three versions: the Cherokee 140D, the Custom Cherokee 140D, and the Executive Cherokee 140D. The versions differed in the amount of optional equipment added. The 1973 models of the 140 were called the Cruiser and the Flite Liner, the latter being the trainer version. In 1975, the names were again changed. The Cruiser became the trainer version and the Warrior is the spacious sportster. The Warrior differs from the trainer by having a longer range, higher gross weight, longer wingspan, and more room. Because the same engine is used, the Warrior's performance suffers a little by comparison.

Mechanically, the Cruiser has changed little from 1976; however, 1977 refinements include new easy-to-close doors, a one-piece stabilator, and a sophisticated power console with a T-shaped throttle. In 1978, the Warrior flew almost seven mph faster as a result of overall drag reductions, a refined powerplant, and new high-performance speed fairings for the gear. An additional benefit is an increase in range by five percent.

By 1979, the Cruiser was discontinued as Piper's trainer airplane, replaced by the T-tail Tomahawk. Virtually unchanged, the Warrior continued as the airplane with the greatest useful load and lowest base price in its class. The Warrior boasts 983 pounds of useful load. As for fuel economy, the Warrior's 160-hp Lycoming sips only 6.6 gph at 55% power. When set up for best economy at 75% power, the four-seater can cover 679 miles with a 45-minute reserve.

In 1977, Piper replaced its 'Hershey Bar Wing' with a new semi-tapered design that added speed and performance to the Warrior II. The new airplane was the PA-28-161. With an almost simultaneous introduction of the two-seat Tomahawk trainer, the Warrior became Piper's entry level four-seater. But when Piper ran into hard times in the early 1990s, the PA-38 was discontinued, and the Warrior II and a stripped-down trainer version, the Cadet, were being sold. The Cadet is essentially the same aircraft minus the creature comforts and two seats. With a standard useful load of 1,099 pounds, the Warrior II continues to be a rugged sportplane capable of carrying four 180-pound adults and 80 pounds of baggage. As a trainer, the Cadet sold for around $100,000 in early 1995, and well-appointed versions of the Warrior II started at around $130,000.

Today New Piper Aircraft offers the Warrior III, still with its PA-28-161 heritage, enhanced interiors and state-of-the-art avionics.

PIPER CHEROKEE "180"/"ARCHER"
1963–Present

Piper Cherokee 180

New Piper Archer III

pounds of people, luggage, and fue
Archer got an upgraded designat
because of a new semi-tapered wing
much of the credit for the 181's
increases. The modernized Arche
still sporting the original 180 hp.

PIPER CHEROKEE "ARROW"
1967–Present

Piper Arrow IV

New Piper Arrow

STANDARD DATA: Archer (PA-28-180) Seats 4. Gross wt. 2,450. Empty wt. 1,395. Fuel capacity 50. Engine 180-hp Lycoming. PERFORMANCE: Cruise 129 kts. Stall 53 kts. Initial climb rate 725 fpm. Range 507 nm. Ceiling 14,150. Takeoff distance (50') 1,625. Landing distance (50') 1,185.

STANDARD DATA: Archer (PA-28-181) Seats 4. Gross wt. 2,550. Empty wt. 1,414. Fuel capacity 50. Engine 180-hp Lycoming. PERFORMANCE: Cruise 129 kts. Stall 49 kts. Initial climb rate 667 fpm. Range 565 nm. Ceiling 13,236. Takeoff distance (50') 1,210. Landing distance (50') 1,390.

The 180-hp Cherokee 180 was unveiled in 1963, one year before the Cherokee 140 made its debut. It uses the same basic Cherokee airframe and wing that serves the entire series from the 140-hp two-seat trainer to the 300-hp fuel-injected Cherokee Six. The Model 180 utilizes a slightly longer wing, a wider horizontal stabilator, and a more spacious cabin. In recent models, handling and stability improved, while the heavy airliner feel changed to a light control response. The first year in which the Cherokee 180 received a name was 1973, it was dubbed the Challenger. The following year it was renamed Archer, and in 1976 it became Archer II. The 1976 Archer can carry up to 1,160

STANDARD DATA: (Arrow) Seats 4. Gross wt. 2,750. Empty wt. 1,593. Fuel capacity 77. Engine 200-hp Lycoming. PERFORMANCE: Top mph 175. Cruise mph 165. Stall mph 63. Initial climb rate 831. Ceiling 17,000. Range 932. Takeoff distance (50') 1,600. Landing distance (50') 1,525.

STANDARD DATA: (Turbo Arrow) Seats 4. Gross wt. 2,900. Empty wt. 1,638. Fuel capacity 77. Engine 200-hp turbocharged Continental. PERFORMANCE: Top mph 205. Cruise mph 198. Stall mph 66. Initial climb rate 940. Ceiling 20,000. Range 897. Takeoff distance (50') 1,620. Landing distance (50') 1,555.

First introduced in 1967 with a 180-hp Lycoming, Piper offered a 200-hp Arrow in the latter half of 1969. Both the 180-hp and 200-hp Arrows were sold through 1971, but in 1972 an all-new Arrow II was announced in Lock Haven. The Arrow II had a number of refinements over the former Arrows. The fuselage was stretched for more passenger leg room, a bigger stabilator was added for stability and better control, a modified upswept rudder was added, and the wing span was increased by two feet to increase gross weight, takeoff run, and rate of climb. Wider cabin windows, a wider n door, and a new paint job improved the exterior osmetics of the Arrow II.

In 1977, the Arrow got the newest Piper wing, making it the Arrow III. In 1979, Piper introduced the Arrow with a T-tail. Models were given the Arrow IV and Turbo Arrow IV designators. Piper claimed, the long popular, high-performance Arrow benefited from the new tail with advanced handling characteristics and reduced cabin noise. But moving the stabilator out of the prop wash also created a decrease in pitch control at slower landing approach speeds. Piper abandoned the Arrow's T-tail by the end of the 1980s, and from then on relied on a more conventional empennage.

PIPER CHEROKEE 235 "PATHFINDER/DAKOTA"
1964–94

STANDARD DATA: (Dakota) Seats 4. Gross wt. 3,000. Empty wt. 1,633. Fuel capacity 77. Engine 235-hp Lycoming. PERFORMANCE: Top mph 170. Cruise mph 166. Stall mph 64. Initial climb rate 965. Ceiling 17,900. Range 800. Takeoff distance (50') 1,300. Landing distance (50') 1,740.

STANDARD DATA: (Pathfinder) Seats 4. Gross wt. 3,000. Empty wt. 1,565. Fuel capacity 84. Engine 235-hp Lycoming. PERFORMANCE: Top mph 161. Cruise mph 153. Stall mph 65. Initial climb rate 800. Range 915. Ceiling 13,550. Takeoff distance (50') 1,410. Landing distance (50') 1,740.

This middle-of-the-line Cherokee (formerly the Charger) is powered by a 235-hp engine and ranks between the Archer and the bigger Cherokee Six. Piper apparently planned the entire Cherokee series so that even a student could work his or her way up the line progressively to constant-speed-prop retractables with a minimum of transitioning difficulty. The 235 is of fixed-gear variety, but a constant-speed prop is offered as one of the many factory options.

The main difference between the Pathfinder and the other Cherokees is its powerful 540 cu. in. Lycoming beneath the fiberglass cowl. It is a true four-place airplane in every sense of the word and excels in the fixed-gear category with a capability of carrying a useful load that is greater than its empty weight. The 235 Path-

finder can take off with four adults, 200 pounds of baggage, 84 gallons of fuel, and still be under the approved gross weight limitations. Couple this with its range of just under 1,110 miles at 55% power, and it can readily be seen why the 235 Pathfinder outranks many other aircraft in the same class.

In 1979, Dakota became the name of Piper's 235-hp four-seater. Along with its new name, the Dakota came outfitted with the same semi-tapered wings that had graced earlier model Arrow IIIs, Warrior Is, and Archer IIs. The Dakota boasts more useful load and range plus a shorter takeoff distance and faster cruise than any plane in its class. Further aerodynamic streamlining is also accomplished with the introduction of the same speed fairings used on several other single-engine models. The Dakota's cowl design includes a streamlined close-fitting cowl and oversized spinner to better cut through the air.

PIPER CHEROKEE SIX "260/300"
1965–79

STANDARD DATA: (260) Seats 6-7. Gross wt. 3,400. Empty wt. 1,779. Fuel capacity 84. Engine 260-hp Lycoming. PERFORMANCE: Top mph 170. Cruise mph 158. Stall mph 63. Initial climb rate 775. Ceiling 12,800. Range 828. Takeoff distance (50') 1,800. Landing distance (50') 1,000.

STANDARD DATA: (300) Seats 6-7. Gross wt. 3,400. Empty wt. 1,846. Fuel capacity 84. Engine 300-hp Lycoming. PERFORMANCE: Top mph 180. Cruise mph 170. Stall mph 63. Initial climb rate 1,050. Ceiling 16,250. Range 840. Takeoff distance (50') 1,350. Landing distance (50') 1,000.

The big Six is a prodigious people packer. Resembling a stretched version of the basic Cherokee airframe, it provides slight twin performance with single-engine economy. The Six was introduced in 1965 with a 260-hp engine, which some pilots seem to feel was not quite enough power. So the people at Piper decided to offer the option of the 300-hp powerplant up front in 1970. Basically a six-seater, the largest of the Cherokees is easily converted to handle a large amount of cargo loaded through its spacious rear double doors; thus it performs as a double-duty passenger utility airplane. Besides the standard six-seat arrangement with center aisle, there is a seventh-seat option.

In 1978, increased speeds of 7 mph made the Cherokee Sixes the fastest planes in their class. A 5% increase in range is also a product of overall drag reductions, a refined powerplant, and new Piper-engineered speed fairings. In 1979, the single-engine workhorse was fitted with a 98-gallon capacity fuel tank and structurally integrated fuel system popularized by the Lance. The new fuel system increased the Six's range by over 100 miles at many power settings. At 65% best power, the Six's range is 923 miles.

PIPER "LANCE"/"TURBO LANCE"
1977–84

STANDARD DATA: (Lance) Seats 6-7. Gross wt. 3,600. Empty wt. 2,011. Fuel capacity 98. Engine 300-hp Lycoming. PERFORMANCE: Top mph 190. Cruise mph 181. Stall mph 80. Initial climb rate 1,000. Ceiling 14,600. Range 994. Takeoff distance (50') 1,690. Landing distance (50') 1,710.

STANDARD DATA: (Turbo Lance) Seats 6-7. Gross wt. 3,600. Empty wt. 2,071. Fuel capacity 98. Engine 300-hp turbocharged Lycoming. PERFORMANCE: Top mph 222. Cruise mph 201. Stall mph 80. Initial climb rate 1,000. Ceiling 20,000. Range 937. Takeoff distance (50') 1,660. Landing distance (50')1,710.

Piper's Lance is essentially a Cherokee Six with retractable landing gear. The Lance utilizes the same main gear as that of the higher-gross-weight Seneca with the same retraction system used in the Arrow. The Lance's 1,690-pound useful load is a healthy allowance for passengers, fuel, and luggage. As with the Cherokee Six 300, the dependable 300-hp engine is fuel injected. Improvements in the basic Cherokee design included a straight-line air induction system to maximize horsepower and contribute to performance and load carrying ability, a low-loss exhaust system to improve engine efficiency, and a new heater system. The Lance's distinction is that it is the first airplane to make

the step from fixed-gear super-hauler mance retractable.

Because the Six's strongest selling po load, Piper had to look for ways to impro carrying ability in order to make room f weight of the new gear without sacrificing pa did this by refining the intake and exhaust systems to achieve more horsepower from the venerable Lycoming engine. With added effective power and the increased aerodynamic efficiency of retractable gear, it was possible to up the gross from 3,400 to 3,600; thus, the Lance still retains a 114-pound useful-load advantage over the Six, even with its retractable gear.

Lance changes in 1978 included the addition of a turbocharged version as well as the use of a T-tail on both models. The Turbo Lance, with its turbocharged 300-hp Lycoming cruises at 201 mph at 16,000 feet. Maximum continuous power is provided to 15,000 feet. The T-tail design reduces noise and vibration levels, increases stability by diminishing longitudinal trim changes as power and flap settings are changed, and increases the center-of-gravity envelope.

PIPER "COMANCHE"
1958–72

Comanche 260

Comanche 400

STANDARD DATA: (260) Seats 4-6. Gross wt. 3,100. Empty wt. 1,728. Fuel capacity 90. Engine 260-hp Lycoming. PERFORMANCE: Top mph 195. Cruise

_.nph 185. Stall mph 61. Initial climb rate 1,370. Range 1,190. Ceiling 20,000. Takeoff distance (50') 1,040. Landing distance (50') 1,015.

STANDARD DATA: (250) Seats 4. Gross wt. 2,900. Empty wt. 1,690. Fuel capacity 60. Engine 250-hp Lycoming. PERFORMANCE: Top mph 190. Cruise mph 180. Stall mph 61. Initial climb rate 1,350. Ceiling 19,800. Range 748. Takeoff distance (50') 1,650. Landing distance (50') 1,015.

STANDARD DATA: (400) Seats 4. Gross wt. 3,600. Empty wt. 2,110. Fuel capacity 130. Engine 400-hp Lycoming. PERFORMANCE: Top mph 233. Cruise mph 202. Stall mph 68. Initial climb rate 1,600. Range 1,540. Ceiling 19,500. Takeoff distance (50') 1,500. Landing distance (50') 1,820.

STANDARD DATA: (180) Seats 4. Gross wt. 2,550. Empty wt. 1,475. Fuel capacity 60. Engine 180-hp Lycoming. PERFORMANCE: Top mph 167. Cruise mph 150. Stall mph 61. Initial climb rate 910. Ceiling 18,500. Range 705. Takeoff distance (50') 2,240. Landing distance (50') 1,015.

The Comanche was once the top of Piper's single-engine lineup. It was introduced in 1958 as the PA-24 with a 250-hp Lycoming powerplant. A 180-hp version was also offered as an option. The Comanche continued to be produced in these two models until 1964 when a third Comanche option was introduced as the Comanche 400 powered by a 400-hp eight cylinder engine, it was claimed to be the world's fastest single, piston-engine airplane of the day. The airframe was basically the same except for structural allowances for catering to its higher gross weight and increased airspeed. Its larger tail unit had horizontal surfaces similar to those used on the Aztec. By 1966, the single-engine Comanche line was limited to the Model 260 version only; the 180 was discontinued in 1964, the 250 was replaced by the 260 in 1965, and the 400 was discontinued in 1966. Also in 1966, the seating was increased by adding an optional third row of seats, and the gross takeoff weight was boosted from 2,900 pounds to 3,100 pounds.

PIPER "PAWNEE"/"BRAVE"
1959–81

Piper Pawnee II

Piper Brave 300

STANDARD DATA: (Brave restricted category) Seats 1. Gross wt. 4,400. Empty wt. 2,225. Fuel capacity 89. Engine 300-hp Continental. PERFORMANCE: Top mph 125. Cruise mph 106. Stall mph 67. Initial climb rate 355. Range 515. Takeoff distance (50') 2,600. Landing distance (50') 1,470.

STANDARD DATA: (Pawnee D with duster) Seats 1. Gross wt. 2,900. Empty wt. 1,479. Fuel capacity 38. Engine 235-hp Lycoming. PERFORMANCE: Top mph 110. Cruise mph 100. Stall mph 46. Initial climb rate 500. Range 255. Takeoff distance (50') 1,470. Landing roll 850.

Piper's version of an agricultural duster-sprayer is the PA-25 Pawnee. First produced in August 1959, the single-seat chemical applicator was designed especially to give maximum pilot safety. The pilot sits high, gaining good visibility both forward and rearward. Safety exits are installed on both sides of the specially strengthened enclosed cockpit, and a steel tube "turnover" structure is built in. A wire cutter is mounted on the center of the windshield, and there is a cable from the top of the cockpit to the top of the rudder to deflect wires or cables. Inside the cockpit, a rounded sheet-metal cushion above the instrument panel protects the pilot's head in case of a crash. The Pawnee is built with rectangular-section welded steel tube with fabric covering and Duraclad plastic finish. The chemical hopper in the Pawnee D carries 150 gallons or 1,200 pounds of chemicals, and the power to deliver it comes from either a 235- or 260-hp Lycoming. In 1975, the Pawnee Brave entered the lineup with its 285-hp Continental, a hopper with a capacity of 1,900 pounds or 225 gallons, and a larger sprayer.

PIPER "SARATOGA"
1980–Present

Piper Saratoga

Piper Turbo Saratoga

Piper Saratoga SP

Piper Saratoga II HP

STANDARD DATA: (SP) Seats 6. Gr[...] Empty wt. 1,986. Fuel capacity 107. [...] Lycoming. PERFORMANCE: Top m[...] mph 183. Stall mph 66. Initial clin[...] Ceiling 16,700. Range 995. Takeoff[...] 1,759 (two-blade), 1,573 (three-blade). Landing distance (50') 1,612.

STANDARD DATA: (Turbo SP) Seats 6. Gross wt. 3,600. Empty wt. 2,073. Fuel capacity 107. Engine 300-hp turbocharged Lycoming. PERFORMANCE: Top mph 224 (three-blade), 220 (two-blade). Cruise mph 204. Stall mph 64. Initial climb rate 1,120. Ceiling 20,000. Range 971. Takeoff distance (50') 1,590 (two-blade), 1,420 (three-blade). Landing distance (50') 1,640.

STANDARD DATA: (Saratoga) Seats 6. Gross wt. 3,600. Empty wt. 1,920. Fuel capacity 107. Engine 300-hp Lycoming. PERFORMANCE: Top mph 176. Cruise mph 173. Stall mph 66. Initial climb rate 990. Ceiling 15,900. Range 972. Takeoff distance (50') 1,740. Landing distance (50') 1,700.

STANDARD DATA: (Turbo) Seats 6. Gross wt. 3,600. Empty wt. 2,000. Fuel capacity 107. Engine 300-hp turbocharged Lycoming. PERFORMANCE: Top mph 209 (threeblade), 205 (two-blade). Cruise mph 190. Stall mph 66. Initial climb rate 1,075. Ceiling 20,000. Range 1,001. Takeoff distance (50') 1,590 (two-blade), 1,420 (three-blade). Landing distance (50') 1,700.

In order to organize and improve its "workhorse" lineup, Piper introduced the Saratoga models in 1980 to replace the Cherokee Six and Lance models. The Saratoga brand actually applies to four separate airplanes. Beginning with the junior model in the brood, we have the basic Saratoga, a six-place fixed-gear 300-hp version. Next is the Saratoga SP, which is everything the basic Saratoga is except that the feet tuck away in flight. For the rare-air set, there is the turbocharged version of the stiff-legged model, designated the Turbo Saratoga. With retractable gear, the high-sky version becomes the Saratoga SP. Possibly the most significant aerodynamic change is the move from the stubby airfoil of the Cherokee line to a state-of-the-art semi-tapered wing that is gracefully slender and powerfully long.

After all the hoopla that surrounded the introduction of the T-tail on the Lance, returning to the full-span stabilator was a move for which a variety of reasons were offered. According to Piper, the new wing is so aerodynamically efficient and docile that it simply doesn't need the T-tail to help, and since the T-tail is inherently more expensive to produce, there was no need to keep it. An optional three-blade propeller for all models reduces cabin noise, delivers peak performance on takeoff and climb out, and offers better cle[...]

ance when taxiing. Double rear doors make loading easy and helps owners take advantage of the Saratoga's substantial cargo capacity.

While the designation SP basically means retractable gear, it literally translates to "Special Performance." The aerodynamic profile is exceptionally clean by combining tuck-away gear with semi-tapered wings, which cut parasite drag to a minimum, and flush riveting on the leading edge. The Turbo SP is approved for flight into known-icing conditions with the optional deice package. The Saratoga provides a remarkably quiet and comfortable environment, closer to that usually associated with large multi-engine aircraft.

In 1994, the 'SP' changed to 'HP' when New Piper introduced the Saratoga II HP (high performance), in both normally aspirated and turbocharged models. The basic airframe remains unchanged, however interiors and avionics have remained continuously upgraded.

PIPER 6X/6XT
2004–Present

STANDARD DATA: (6XT) Seats 6. Gross wt. 3,600. Empty wt. 2,160. Fuel capacity 102. Engine 300-hp Lycoming TIO-540-K1G5. PERFORMANCE: Top speed 155 KTAS. Cruise mph 150. Stall mph 61. Initial climb rate 910. Ceiling 17,200. Takeoff distance (50') 2,028. Landing distance (50') 1,822.

Reborn in the body of the straight-legged Saratoga, the normally aspirated 6X and turbocharged 6XT, entered New Piper's production schedule in 2003. The fixed-gear, six-seater has impressive load capabilities reasonable speed given its size. It's typically cheaper to insure due to the absence of retractable gear. Newest models feature an all-glass cockpit.

PIPER MALIBU/MIRAGE
1984–Present

STANDARD DATA: Malibu/Mirage Seats 6. Gross
‍ ,300. Empty wt. 2,460/2,790 lbs. Fuel
0. Engine 310-hp Continental/350-hp
'ERFORMANCE: Cruise 203/232 KTAS.
kts. Initial climb rate 1,143/1,218 fpm.
)00. Range 1,261. Takeoff distance (50')
). Landing distance (50') 1,800/1,964'.

New Piper Malibu

New Piper Mirage

The cabin class Malibu set the single-engine piston market on its ear when it first came to market in 1984. The big pressurized Piper was the first aircraft to demonstrate that comfort in the flight levels did not require a second engine. After moving away from early troubles with its 310-hp Continental to a 350-hp Lycoming, the PA-46 Malibu transformed itself into the even better performing PA-46 Mirage. The original gamble Piper took with the Malibu would ultimately spawn a number of successful big cabin singles, albeit with turbine engines, including Piper's own Meridian. In 2005, the Mirage became available with an all-glass flight deck.

PIPER MERIDIAN
2001–Present

STANDARD DATA: (180) Seats 4. Gross wt. 2,550. Empty wt. 1,475. Fuel capacity 60. Engine 500-shp Pratt & Whitney PT6A-42A. PERFORMANCE: Top mph 167. Cruise mph 150. Stall mph 61. Initial climb rate 910. Ceiling 18,500. Range 705. Takeoff distance (50') 2,240. Landing distance (50') 1,015.

The New Piper Meridian is for all intents and purposes a Malibu with a Pratt & Whitney 500-shp PT6A-42A up front. Though smaller that some of its competition, the Meridian compares favorably with the TMB 700 and PC 12. Within its niche, single engine turbines compare favorably with many smaller pure jets, and consequently new entries in the category are always being discussed. The Meridian suffered poor payload numbers in the beginning, but a string of improvements and modifications have allowed New Piper's biggest single to remain strong in the market.

PORTERFIELD 65 "COLLEGIATE"/ 90 "FLYABOUT"
1935–39

Porterfield 65 Collegiate

Porterfield 90 Flyabout

STANDARD DATA: (65) Seats 2. Gross wt. 1,200. Empty wt. 700. Fuel capacity 13. Engine 65-hp Continental. PERFORMANCE: Top mph 108. Cruise mph 103. Landing mph 40. Initial climb rate 900. Range 325. Ceiling 16,000.

STANDARD DATA: (90) Seats 2. Gross wt. 1,326. Empty wt. 823. Fuel capacity 18. Engine 90-hp Warner Scarab Junior. PERFORMANCE: Top mph 135. Cruise mph 120. Stall mph 40. Initial climb rate 1,050. Ceiling 20,000. Range 336.

The Porterfield Aircraft Corp. was founded in 1934 by E.E. Porterfield, once president of the American Eagle Aircraft Corp. In the following year, it began producing the Porterfield two-seat monoplane. Designations included the 35-70 (70-hp Le Blond), 35-90 (90-hp Warner Scarab Junior), 35-65 (65-hp engine), and 35-75 (75-hp engine). The company introduced the CP-

series in 1939, which included the CP-50, CP-55, CP-65, FP-65, and LP-65. The initials refer to the type of engine—Continental, Franklin or Lycoming—and the numbers refer to the horsepower. The Collegiate CP-65 was the most popular of the series. A substantial number of these two-seat training planes are still in flyable condition.

PORTERFIELD MODEL 35-70/35-90
1935

STANDARD DATA: Seats 2. Gross wt. 1,326. Empty wt. 823. Fuel capacity 18. Engine 90-hp Warner Scarab Junior. PERFORMANCE: Top mph 135. Cruise mph 120. Stall mph 40. Initial climb rate 1,050. Ceiling 20,000. Range 336.

Both Porterfield models entered production in 1935 and were powered by either the 70-hp LeBlond five-cylinder or the 90-hp Warner Scarab Junior five-cylinder radial engines; thus, the numerical designations 35-70 and 35-90 apply. The Porterfield Aircraft Corp. of Kansas City, Missouri, had been founded one year, and the development work was done by E.E. Porterfield, who was formerly president of the American Eagle Aircraft Corp. Other versions of the first Porterfields were built with 50, 65, and 75-hp Continental or Lycoming engines. The enclosed cabin for two persons had dual controls, but they were quickly removable from either seat. Wing construction was two spruce spars, spruce and plywood ribs, and fabric covering. The fuselage was a fabric-covered steel-tube structure.

PZL-104 WILGA "THRUSH"
1964–80

STANDARD DATA: Seats 4. Gross wt. 2,755. Empty wt. 1,624. Fuel capacity 51. Engine 230-hp Continental. PERFORMANCE: Top mph 127. Cruise mph 93. Stall mph 40. Initial climb rate 865. Range 390. Ceiling 12,075. Takeoff distance (50') 625. Landing distance (50') 780.

The PZL-104 Wilga (Wilga translates to Thrush) is built in Warsaw, Poland, by WSK-Okecie. (The WSK stands for a company name that no Westerner would even attempt to pronounce.) The first PZL-104 Wilga-I flew in 1962 and was immediately followed by the

Wilga-2 and Wilga-3 as design modifications were made. The Wilga-32 and 35 were further improvements to incorporate a redesigned landing gear, a more comfortable cabin, and a fiberglass-laminated tailwheel leg. The Wilga 32 is fitted with a six-cylinder 230-hp Continental engine, and the Wilga 35 has a 260-hp Ivchenko nine-cylinder radial engine. Various models were sold for various purposes, such as glider towing (32A), passengers (32P), or ambulance use (32S). The Polish tail-dragger features a cantilevered high wing without the need for wing struts. Construction is all metal with a beaded metal skin.

REARWIN 8135 "CLOUDSTER"
1940

STANDARD DATA: Seats 2 or 3. Gross wt. 1,800. Empty wt. 1,100. Fuel capacity 34. Engine 120-hp Ken Royce seven-cylinder radial. PERFORMANCE: Top mph 135. Cruise mph 120. Landing mph 48. Initial climb rate 910. Range 609. Ceiling 16,300.

The Cloudster was preceded by the 8090 and 8125 versions with two seats each. The 8090 and 8125 were powered by 90-hp and 120-hp Ken Royce engines respectively. The three-seat Cloudster 8135 was introduced in 1940 and was powered by the same 120-hp engine as the 8125. The two planes were produced side-by-side to provide buyers with a two or three-seat option. Another model of the Cloudster was the 8135T. This two-seat tandem trainer was specially designed for instrument training in cooperation with Pan American Airways. It had two separate compartments, one behind the other, each with its own door, flying controls, and instruments. Included was a set of blind-flying instruments such as the Sperry directional gyro, artificial horizon, and a Lear radio transmitter and receiver.

REARWIN 7000 "SPORTSTER"
1935–42

STANDARD DATA- Seats 2. Gross wt. 1,460. Empty wt. 861. Fuel capacity 24. Engine 70-hp Ken Royce five-cylinder radial. PERFORMANCE: Top mph 115.

Cruise mph 103. Landing mph 38. Initial climb rate 670. Range 500. Ceiling 15,000.

The first Rearwin 7000 Sportsters appeared in 1935 and were powered by 70-hp LeBlond radials. The Model 8500 Sportster with an 85-hp LeBlond was also introduced in 1935. The Model 9000 version of the Sportster was powered by either a 90-hp Warner, Ken Royce, or LeBlond, which increased the top speed of the aircraft to 123 mph. The tandem two-seat cabin monoplane was produced for five years. During this time, Rearwin Airplanes, Inc. was taken over by the Rearwin Airplanes partnership of R.A. Rearwin, Royce S. Rearwin, and Kenneth R. Rearwin. They bought all the assets of the LeBlond Aircraft Corp. in 1937 and began producing their own engines that carried their name, Ken Royce. From then on all Rearwin Sportsters were provided with Ken Royce engines. The Rearwin company was bought in 1942 and the name changed to the Commonwealth Aircraft Inc.

REARWIN 185 "SKYRANGER"
1940–47

STANDARD DATA: Seats 2. Gross wt. 1,450. Empty wt. 910. Fuel capacity 48. Engine 80-hp Continental. PERFORMANCE: Top mph 114. Cruise mph 103. Stall mph 40. Initial climb rate 650. Range 500. Ceiling 14,000.

Rearwin Aircraft and Engines introduced the Skyranger in 1940 as a side-by-side two-seat cabin monoplane. This aircraft was first produced in four versions: the 175 with a 75-hp Continental, the 180 with an 80-hp Continental, the 180F with a 80-hp

Franklin, and the 190F powered by a 90-hp Franklin engine. After World War II, the aircraft was reintroduced as the Skyranger 185 by Commonwealth Aircraft, a company created from Rearwin in 1941. Its production was terminated in 1947. The Skyranger 185 differs from its predecessors in only one respect, an 85-hp Continental engine.

REPUBLIC "SEABEE"
1944–47

STANDARD DATA: Seats 4. Gross wt. 2,600. Empty wt. 1,775. Engine 215-hp Franklin. PERFORMANCE: Top mph 120. Cruise mph 103. Landing mph 53. Initial climb rate 700. Range 560. Ceiling 12,000.

About 200 Seabees are currently flying in the United States, with approximately 130 others active in other countries. First made in 1944 and placed into full-scale quantity production in 1946, a total of 1,060 aircraft were produced before Republic Aviation abandoned civilian aircraft production in 1947. The relatively low-cost amphibian is still a favorite among sea-rated pilots, and current used prices reflect its popularity. Design of the four-seat flying boat is unique. The RC-3 Seabee's single six-cylinder engine is mounted behind and on top of the cabin so that the pusher propeller spins about halfway back the length of the fuselage. The original Seabee prototype used a 175-hp Franklin engine and first flew in 1944. Numerous changes in design and components reduced empty weight and production costs before the final RC-3 model was approved.

REPUBLIC P-47 "THUNDERBOLT"
1942–45

STANDARD DATA: Seats 1. Gross wt. 12,500. Empty wt. 9,900. Fuel capacity 270-370. Engine 2,300-hp Pratt & Whitney Double Wasp. PERFORMANCE: Top mph 440. Cruise mph 350. Landing mph 100. Initial climb rate 2,500. Range 650. Ceiling 40,000.

The Thunderbolt had a reputation as the toughest, heaviest single-engine fighter used in World War II. It could take punishment like no other and packed a battery of eight .50-caliber machine guns along with a greater load of armament than any other fighter in its day. In the air, the P-47 had an outstanding record. For every one shot down, it destroyed five enemy aircraft. Because its size and rugged construction allowed it to survive heavy battle damage, all leading Thunderbolt aces survived the war. The product of several years of development, the P-47 first flew in May 1941 and entered production the following year. It was initially employed chiefly for long-range fighter sweeps and escort duty, but later models also saw action as fighter-bombers. More P-47s were produced than any other Army Air Force fighter, with the final total numbering 15,600.

ROCKWELL COMMANDER 112/112TC
1973–94

Rockwell Commander 112

STANDARD DATA: (112) Seats 4. Gross wt. 2,800. Empty wt. 1,173. Fuel capacity 48-68. Engine 200-hp Lycoming. PERFORMANCE: Top mph 173. Cruise mph 163. Stall mph 62. Initial climb rate 1,020. Range 592-880. Ceiling 13,900. Takeoff distance (50') 1,585. Landing distance (50') 1,310.

STANDARD DATA: (112TC) Seats 4. Gross wt. 2,950. Empty wt. 1,834. Fuel capacity 48-68. Engine

Rockwell Alpine Commander

Rockwell Gran Turismo Commander

210-hp turbocharged Lycoming. PERFORMANCE: Top mph 195. Cruise mph 181. Stall mph 58. Initial climb rate 1,023. Range 510-823. Ceiling 20,000. Takeoff distance (50') 1,780. Landing distance (50') 1,221.

STANDARD DATA: (Alpine) Seats 4. Gross wt. 2,950. Empty wt. 2,035. Fuel capacity 48-68. Engine 210-hp turbocharged Lycoming. PERFORMANCE: Top mph 197. Cruise mph 188. Stall mph 62. Initial climb rate 914. Ceiling 20,000. Range 529-764. Takeoff distance (50') 1,750. Landing distance (50') 1,275.

STANDARD DATA: (Gran Turismo) Seats 4. Gross wt. 3,272. Empty wt. 2,070. Fuel capacity 68. Engine 260-hp Lycoming. PERFORMANCE: Top mph 191. Cruise mph 181. Stall mph 62. Initial climb rate 1,030. Ceiling 16,500. Range 722. Takeoff distance (50') 2,150. Landing distance (50') 1,200.

The first deliveries of the Model 112 began in the summer of 1972 under the name of Aero Commander. A product of extensive consumer research, it was a four-seat, retractable gear aircraft, originally powered by a 180-hp Lycoming engine. A fixed-gear version of this low-priced Aero Commander was called the Model 111, but its production life span was short. The Model 112 features the most spacious cabin of any four-seat, single-engine production aircraft, and for convenience it has a passenger access door on each side. Many new construction procedures were developed to facilitate assembly and reduce drag while retaining the plane's structural integrity.

The new manufacturing process included the use of large single assemblies rather than small pieces riveted together. The reduced number of rivets together with beaded skins improved airflow over the 112's surfaces. Subsequent additions to the line include the 112TC and the 114. The TC designation of the former means turbocharged, and the added boost helps the 112TC climb to 10,000 feet in 10 minutes. Even at 14,000 feet, the airplane can continue to climb at a rate of 900 fpm. The Model 114 utilizes a 260-hp normally-aspirated engine to provide a useful load with enough allowance for four persons, full fuel, a full radio package, and 100 pounds of baggage.

One change in the single-engine lineup was an emphasis on reduced drag by the elimination of certain scoops and the addition of several fairings. The result is a slight increase in speed for the 114, 112TC, and the 112B. The 112B also received new disc brakes and larger wheels. Both the 112 models were increased by over 100 pounds.

The 200-hp Rockwell 112 was dropped from the lineup of single-engine aircraft in 1979, and the names of the 112TC and the 114 were changed to the Alpine Commander and Gran Turismo Commander, respectively. These aircraft display slightly differing specification and performance figures, as reflected in the introductory summaries. The Gran Turismo is a three-blade 260-hp model, and the Alpine is a 210-hp turbocharged wide-body Commander. They were offered fully IFR-equipped by Rockwell with King avionics and a Century III autopilot. The McCauley three-blade prop improves sound and vibration levels.

Rockwell discontinued production of the single-engine line by 1980. In 1988, the fights for the Commander 112/114 were bought by a new company called Commander Aircraft, which allowed that company to maintain the existing fleet. Certification for a newly redesigned 114B was granted in 1991 and full production began once more with the 1992 model year.

ROCKWELL COMMANDER "THRUSH"
1965–80

STANDARD DATA: (600) Seats 1. Gross wt. 6,000. Empty wt. 3,700. Fuel capacity 100. Engine 600-hp Pratt & Whitney. PERFORMANCE: Top mph 140. Cruise mph 124. Stall mph 55. Initial climb rate 900. Range 402. Ceiling 15,000. Takeoff run 775. Landing roll 500.

STANDARD DATA: (800) Seats 1. Gross wt. 6,000. Empty wt. 4,100. Fuel capacity 100. Engine 800-hp Pratt & Whitney. PERFORMANCE: Top mph 155. Cruise mph 137. Stall mph 57. Initial climb rate 1,600. Range 330. Ceiling 25,000. Takeoff run 600. Landing roll 500.

Aero Commander's entries into the agricultural aircraft market were in three basic sizes. The Sparrow was the smallest of the lot with a payload of 1,400 pounds and utilizing a 235-hp engine. The Quail was an intermediate model using the same airframe as the Sparrow but with engine power increased to 290 hp. The Thrush Commander was not only the largest of the Aero Commander line but also was the largest specialty designed agricultural craft in production in the United States. With 600 hp, this impressive aircraft can carry a payload up to 3,280 pounds and fuel capacity double that of any other ag plane. With that big Pratt & Whitney pulling it along through the air, it can probably use all the fuel it can get.

The Thrush 800 utilizes an impressive 800-hp Pratt & Whitney radial engine. It has a useful load of 1,900 pounds and a hopper capacity of 400 gallons. Marsh Aviation Co. builds a modification of the Thrush, called the S2R-T Turbo Thrush, in which turbine power replaces piston power. For standard use, the AiResearch turboprop is derated to 600-shp; however, maximum 778-shp output is available for emergencies. One advantage other than additional power is that normal automotive diesel fuel can be used if jet fuel is not at hand. Top speed is increased to 205 mph, and climb rate is boosted to 3,000 fpm.

RYAN SC/SCW
1937–41

STANDARD DATA: Seats 3. Gross wt. 2,150. Empty wt. 1,350. Engine 145-hp Warner Super Scarab radial or 150-hp Supercharged Menasco. PERFORMANCE: Top mph 152. Cruise mph 140. Stall mph 45. Initial climb rate 900. Ceiling 19,400. Range 520.

The Ryan Aeronautical Co. was the successor to the old Ryan Company that produced Charles Lindbergh's Spirit of St. Louis. The original company, known as Ryan Airlines, began operations in 1922, and rapid expansion took place after their transatlantic success; however, the Depression took its toll, and in 1931 T. Claude

Ryan reentered the industry by forming the Ryan Aeronautical Co. Production of the SC all-metal three-seat cabin monoplane began in 1938. The aircraft was either fitted with the 145-hp Warner Super Scarab seven-cylinder radial or the 150-hp Menasco supercharged in-line engine. The wings were detachable, supported by an all-metal structure and covered by stressed Alclad metal. Accommodations were for three under a sliding canopy: two up front and one in the rear.

RYAN STM-2
1934–42

STANDARD DATA: Seats 2. Gross wt. 1,600. Empty wt. 1,027. Fuel capacity 24. Engine 125-hp Menasco C-4. PERFORMANCE: Top mph 150. Cruise mph 127. Stall mph 42. Initial climb rate 1,200. Range 350. Ceiling 17,500.

The Ryan Aeronautical Co. was a successor to the Ryan Co. that produced the airplane Charles Lindbergh used to cross the Atlantic. The company benefited from the airplane boom that followed but succumbed to the Depression in 1931. In 1934, the company was revived and began building the ST two-seat monoplane series. There were three models: the ST with a 95-hp Menasco, the STA with a 125-hp Menasco, and the STA Special with a 150-hp Menasco. For military purposes, the STM1 was built with the 150-hp engine and sold to many Latin American countries. It was followed by the STM2, which embodied several modifications specified by the U.S. Army Air Corps and was designated the PT-20. Numerous aircraft of this type are still active.

RYAN PT-22
1939–42

STANDARD DATA: Seats 2. Gross wt. 1,860. Empty wt. 1,313. Fuel capacity 24. Engine 160-hp Kinner. PERFORMANCE: Top mph 131. Cruise mph 123. Landing mph 54. Initial climb rate 1,000. Range 352. Ceiling 15,500.

The Ryan PT-22 is another surplus military trainer of the World War II era that is still reasonably available on the used market. It is quite easy to operate and maintain. The fuselage is metal, but the wings are covered with fabric. The earliest versions had a Menasco engine, but the PT-22 trainers available in the largest numbers are powered by a Mimer radial engine. Beginning in 1941, the first model was the PT-21 powered by a 132-hp Kinner five-cylinder radial. The later version with a 160-hp engine was designated as the PT-22. Although the performance and range characteristics of these planes are too limited to make them practical, they are still popular with weekend pilots. The 160-hp Kinner engine is also a five-cylinder type, and the supply of surplus parts for it are still ample.

RYAN "NAVION"
1946–51

STANDARD DATA: (205 hp) Seats 4. Gross wt. 2,750. Empty wt. 1,782. Fuel capacity 40. Engine 205-hp Continental. PERFORMANCE: Top mph 163. Cruise mph 155. Stall mph 75. Initial climb rate 1,110. Range 500. Ceiling 15,600. Takeoff distance (50') 1,100. Landing distance (50') 1,110.

STANDARD DATA: (Super Navion) Seats 4. Gross wt. 2,850. Empty wt. 1,930. Fuel capacity 40-60. Engine 260-hp Lycoming. PERFORMANCE: Top mph 174. Cruise mph 170. Stall mph 55. Initial climb rate 1,250. Ceiling 18,000. Range 415-640. Takeoff run 399. Landing run 468.

The Navion has been built at intervals by several companies. It began in 1946 as an original design by the North American Aviation Co. It is believed that many of the features were borrowed from North American's highly successful fighter plane, the P-51 Mustang. North American was involved in the production for a relatively short time, and manufacture was transferred to the Ryan Co. The Navion of this era was powered by a 185-hp Continental. The engine was later boosted to 205 hp in the Navion A and 260 hp in the Navion B. North American and Ryan turned out over 1,000 Navions each from 1946 to 1951. Further development of the Navion design was carried out by the Navion Aircraft Co. established in 1961.

SHINN 2150-A
1959–62

STANDARD DATA: Seats 2. Gross wt. 1,817. Empty wt. 1,125. Fuel capacity 35. Engine 150-hp Lycoming. PERFORMANCE: Top mph 148. Cruise mph 135. Stall mph 52. Initial climb rate 1,450. Range 525. Ceiling 22,000. Takeoff distance (50') 440. Landing distance (50') 450.

Originally designed and built by W.J. Morrisey of Morrisey Aviation, Inc. the Model 2150 was built and sold by Shinn Engineering in Santa Ana, California, after the latter company purchased manufacturing and sales rights from Morrisey in 1960. Morrisey's original prototypes were known as the Model 2000, using a 95-hp Continental engine or a 108-hp Lycoming engine. When Shinn began production of the tandem two-seater in May 1961, the airplane became known as the Shinn 2150-A. Shinn included a number of refinements over the Morrisey, yet production of the tricycle-gear airplane stopped in 1962.

SIAI-MARCHETTI PN 333 "RIVIERA"
1962–66

STANDARD DATA: Seats 4. Gross wt. 3,270. Empty wt. 2,300. Fuel capacity 37-64. Engine 250-hp Continental. PERFORMANCE: Top mph 177. Cruise mph 164. Stall mph 68. Initial climb rate 1,220. Range 560. Ceiling 18,500. Ground takeoff run (50') 1,400. Water takeoff run 1,565. Ground landing distance (50') 1,100. Water landing distance 625.

Originally developed by the Nardi Company, the Riviera amphibian first flew in December 1952. Siai-Marchetti purchased manufacturing rights from Nardi and placed the four-seater into production in 1960. A New Jersey firm handled all United States sales, and the Rivieras were assembled by Southwest Airmotive. The four-seater is powered by a 250-hp six-cylinder Continental engine mounted on top of the fuselage behind the cabin in a pusher-prop arrangement. For water use, the landing gear folds up into the fuselage behind the cabin, and the small nose gear is hidden behind nose gear doors. Forward visibility through a large bubblenose windshield is excellent. Production of the Riviera ended in early 1966 after 30 airplanes had been built.

SIAI-MARCHETTI S.205 (WACO S.220)/S.2018
1966–81

STANDARD DATA: (S.205-20/R) Seats 4. Gross wt. 2,755. Empty wt. 1,630. Fuel capacity 56. Engine 200-hp Lycoming. PERFORMANCE: Top mph 174. Cruise mph 159. Stall mph 52. Initial climb rate 865. Range 940. Ceiling 17,650. Takeoff distance (50') 1,340. Landing distance (50') 1,540.

STANDARD DATA: (S.202-22/R) Seats 4. Gross wt. 2,755. Empty wt. 1,653. Fuel capacity 56. Engine 220-hp Franklin. PERFORMANCE: Top mph 183. Cruise mph 175. Stall mph 52. Initial climb rate 1,160. Range 823. Ceiling 20,330. Takeoff distance (50') 1,240. Landing distance (50') 1,540.

STANDARD DATA: (S.208) Seats 4. Gross wt. 3,306. Empty wt. 1,785. Fuel capacity 117. Engine 260-hp Lycoming. PERFORMANCE: Top mph 199. Cruise

mph 187. Stall mph 58. Range 1,250. Ceiling 17,725. Takeoff distance (50') 1,640. Landing distance (50') 1,310.

The Siai-Marchetti S.205 was built in several versions, all differing in engine size and gear type. For this reason, the airplane's uses can range from the most economical touring craft to a high-performance executive craft. It is designed to house engines varying in size from 180 to 300 hp. All Siai-Marchetti aircraft make use of honeycomb panels to give the airframe an exceptionally rigid structure. The first examples were completed in 1965, and were all powered by 180-hp Lycoming engines.

Later models included the S.205-10/17, S.205-18/R, S.205-20/17, S.205-20/R, S.205-22/R, and S.202-221M. The numbers following the dash refer to the engine size (10 = 100 hp, 18 = 180 hp, etc.) and the letter refers to retractable, fixed, or military. The Model S.202-22/R was powered by a Franklin engine and utilized retractable gear; it was also assembled in the United States by Allied Aero Industries as the Waco Vela S.220. All the variations went out of production in 1972 except the 20/17 and 20/R. The S.208 entered production in 1968 and shared nearly 60% of the S.206's structural components. It is powered by a 260-hp Lycoming and features retractable landing gear.

SIAI-MARCHETTI SF.260
1967–81

STANDARD DATA: Seats 3. Gross wt. 2,430. Empty wt. 1,543. Fuel capacity 63. Engine 260-hp Lycoming. PERFORMANCE: Top mph 235. Cruise mph 214. Stall mph 65. Initial climb rate 1,770. Range 1,275. Ceiling 21,370. Takeoff distance (50') 1,390. Landing distance (50') 1,610.

The Siai-Marchetti SF.260 looks very much like the Procaer Picchio except for its wingtip fuel tanks and rearward one-piece sliding canopy. The prototype of the aircraft was built by Aviamilano and flew for the first time in 1964. It was powered by a 250 engine. Production of the airplane was taken over by the Siai-Marchetti Co. an was upgraded to a 260-hp Lycoming, thu tion SF.260. The cabin has accommodati occupants, one in the rear seat and two seats. Two small children can be carried in the back seat as long as their combined weight does not exceed 250 pounds. Construction of the Siai-Marchetti is all metal with four fuel tanks (two in the wings and two tip tanks). Its landing gear is a retractable tricycle type. The SF.260 holds two FAI speed records in the C-I-b class and are listed under the aircraft's United States designation: Waco Meteor.

SOCATA "RALLYE"/WACO "MINERVA"
1966–81

STANDARD DATA: (150) Seats 4. Gross wt. 1,920. Empty wt. 1,170. Fuel capacity 47. Engine 150-hp Lycoming. PERFORMANCE: Top mph 134. Cruise mph 124. Stall mph 52. Initial climb rate 870. Ceiling 13,000. Range 622. Takeoff run 420. Landing roll 390.

STANDARD DATA: (180) Seats 4. Gross wt. 2,315. Empty wt. 1,260. Fuel capacity 60. Engine 180-hp Lycoming. PERFORMANCE: Top mph 150. Cruise mph 140. Stall mph 57. Initial climb rate 760. Ceiling 11,800. Range 805. Takeoff run 445. Landing roll 425.

STANDARD DATA: (235) Seats 4. Gross wt. 2,640. Empty wt. 1,525. Fuel capacity 71. Engine 230-hp Lycoming. PERFORMANCE: Top mph 171. Cruise mph 152. Stall mph 58. Initial climb rate 980. Ceiling 14,800. Range 810. Takeoff run 490. Landing roll 425.

SOCATA (Societe de Construction d'Avions de Tourisme et d'Affaires), a subsidiary of Aerospatiale, had reintroduced its Rallye line of airplanes to the American market. In 1963, development of the Rallye series was taken over by S.E.E.M.S. (Societe d'Exploitation des Establissements Morane-Saulnier). This company was soon taken over by G.E.M.S. (Gerance des Establissements Morane-Saulnier), which was controlled by Sud-Aviation, and Sud-Aviation ultimately became Aerospatiale and formed the SOCATA subsidiary to produce the Rallye. Then in the late 1960s and early 1970s, the Waco Aircraft Co., a subsidiary of Al-'ied Aero Industries, produced and marketed the Rallye ¬mmodore (220hp Franklin) in the United States as the Waco Minerva. After 1971, Waco discontinued its involvement.

The entire Rallye line consists of 12 models:

- 100S (Sport) has a 100-hp Rolls-Royce Continental, two seats, and is cleared for spins.
- 100T (Tourisme) has the same Rolls-Royce engine and three to four seats.
- 100ST can be operated as a two-seater cleared for spins or a four-seater not cleared for spins.
- 150CT has a 150-hp Lycoming and improved design.
- 150T is similar to the 100T except for its 150-hp Lycoming.
- 150ST is a high-performance version for flying clubs.
- 180CT has a 180-hp Lycoming and constant-speed prop.
- 180T is specialized for towing.
- 235CT has seating for four and a 235-hp Lycoming. 235CA is an agricultural version.
- 235C is a taildragger.
- 235G is a military variant.

Only the 150ST, 18OCT, and 235CT were marketed in the United States.

All Rallyes have full STOL capabilities as a result of full-span automatic anti-stall leading-edge slats plus slotted Fowler flaps and generously sized control surfaces. The 150 is one of the few trainers with seats for four, and all Rallyes feature sliding canopies for easy entrance. Both the 180 and 235 have larger airframes, a strengthened structure, wheel fairings, more prop clearance, larger rudder and ailerons, modified cockpit canopy, and larger baggage compartment.

SOCATA "TAMPICO" TB9 GT
1990–Present

STANDARD DATA: Seats 4. Gross wt. 2,332. Empty wt. 1,428. Fuel capacity 40. Engine 160-hp Lycoming 0-320-D2A. PERFORMANCE: Top mph 127. Cruise mph 122. Initial climb rate 738. Ceiling 11,000. Range 505. Takeoff distance (50) 1,706. Landing distance (50') 1,378.

EADS, an acronym for European Aeronautic Defense and Space Company, is Europe's largest aerospace manufacturer, and the second largest aerospace and defense company in the world. Products range from Airbus airliners to Eurocopters to Ariane rockets. EADS Socata, a wholly owned subsidiary of EADS, specializes in general aviation aircraft, with models including the Tampico, Tobago, Trinidad and TBM700. The headquarters and production are located in the Toulouse region of Southwest France.

The Tampico is the Socata entry-level airplane and has been widely accepted as a viable training platform here in the United States. With 160 hp, the Tampico doesn't exactly burn up the skies, but it does supply plenty of power to haul around two average couples and 70 pounds of baggage on full fuel. Visibility in the Tampico is virtually unsurpassed by anything else in the training category, and because of the Socata's exclusive forward positioning of the vertical stabilizer and the rear-mount horizontal stabilizer, the aircraft can handle up to 25-mph crosswinds.

SOCATA "TOBAGO" TB10 GT/ "TOBAGO XL" TB200 GT
1986–Present

STANDARD DATA: Seats 4. Gross wt. 2,535. Empty wt. 1,532; (XL) 1,576. Fuel capacity 55.5. Engine (std.) 180-hp Lycoming 0-360-AIAD; (XL) 200-hp Lycoming 10-360AIB6. PERFORMANCE: Top mph 147; (XL) 161. Cruise mph 143; (XL) 150. Initial climb rate 787; (XL) 940. Ceiling 13,000. Range 580; (XL) 648. Takeoff distance (50) 1,657; (XL) 1,558. Landing distance (50') 1,509; (XL) 1,475.

The fixed-gear 180-hp Tobago and 200-hp Tobago XL are in the middle of the line. Designed as medium-performance cross-country cruisers, both Tobagos possess a good combination of speed, simplicity, luxury, and efficiency. All Socata aircraft are noted for having extremely spacious and comfortable cabins, and the attention to ergonomic design is well thought out. Access to the cockpit is gained through two gull-wing doors on either side of the fuselage. Both aircraft perform reasonably well in and out of short-field situations.

SOCATA TRINIDAD TB20 GT/ TRINIDAD TC TB21 GT
1984–Present

STANDARD DATA: Seats 4. Gross wt. 3,086. Empty wt. 1,763; (TC) 1,850. Fuel capacity 86. Engine 250-hp Lycoming 10-540 (TC) 250-hp Lycoming TIO-540. PERFORMANCE: Top mph 192; (TC) 230. Cruise mph 189; (TC) 215. Initial climb rate 1,200; (TC) 1,126. Ceiling 20,000; (TC) 25,000. Range 966; (TC) 962. Takeoff distance (50') 2,099; (TC) 1,953. Landing distance (50') 1,772; (TC) 1,750.

At the top of the Socata piston line is the Trinidad (TB20 GT) and turbocharged Trinidad TC (TB 21 GT). Improvements over the Tampico and Tobago are numerous, including retractable landing gear and horsepower, plus creature comforts such as leather seating, soundproofing, and trim packages. Of course, with the higher horsepower and the addition of retracts comes an increase in gross weight, useful load, and climb rate. Comfort and luxury levels are elevated, and cruise and max speed are substantially increased. The Trinidad can handle four full-sized adults and carry 143 pounds of luggage to boot. The combination of speed, comfort, roominess, great visibility, and sleek design make the Trinidad an exceptional cross-country machine. The turbocharged Trinidad, the TB21 GT, turns in about 190 kts at 25,000 feet.

SOCATA "TBM 700"
1991–Present

STANDARD DATA: Seats 6-7. Gross wt., depending on model, 5,911-7,430 lbs. Empty wt. 3,282-4,685. Fuel capacity 290 gallons Jet Al-JP4-JP5. Engine Pratt & Whitney PT6A 40-64 turboprop, 700 shp. PERFORMANCE: Top mph 345. Cruise mph 288. Initial climb rate 2,300. Ceiling 31,000. Range 1,565 miles at economy cruise.

The TBM 700 began as an international joint venture between Mooney Aircraft Corporation and EADS Socata, then operating as Aerospatiale General Aviation.

Now the aircraft is property of EADS and manufactured in France. The TBM 700 is a pressurized cabin-class turboprop that is capable of a 300-knot cruise at 26,000 ft. With a cabin pressure differential of 6.2 psi, which translates to a cabin altitude of only 6,400 ft., the TBM 700 has one of the most efficient pressurization systems available in general aviation. The big turbine single has enjoyed tremendous success as a private and corporate aircraft, as well as a key player in military and commercial applications.

SOLARIS AVIATION SIGMA "230, 250 AND 310"

2001–Present

STANDARD DATA: (230) Seats 4. Gross wt. 2,980. Empty wt. 1,876. Fuel capacity 66. Engine 230-hp Lycoming IO-540-C4D5. PERFORMANCE: Cruise 175 kts. Stall 57 kts. Initial climb rate 1,140 fpm. Ceiling 20,000. Range 870 nm. Takeoff roll 853'. Landing roll 1,329'.

STANDARD DATA: (310) Seats 4. Gross wt. 3,500. Empty wt. 2,317. Fuel capacity 88. Engine 310-hp Continental IO-550N. PERFORMANCE: Cruise 215 kts. Stall 60 kts. Initial climb rate 1,330 fpm. Ceil-)0. Range 1,488 nm. Takeoff run 817'. Land- 390.

composite design came from German engineer schmeyer. Solaris Aviation, Inc., a U.S.-based

company, purchased the assets of Ruschmeyer Aircraft, GmbH in 1999. Each model of the Sigma differs purely by horsepower. The tapering wings have a 6.97 aspect ratio, a laminar-flow airfoil, leading-edge stall strips and tilted wing tips. The small ailerons have slight differential action, with deflection limited by concealed mass-balances. Inboard are large, three-position, electric Fowler flaps with similarly shrouded hinges and mechanisms. All models feature retractable trailing link landing gear and gull wing doors. The airframe is designed to 9 Gs.

SOPWITH "CAMEL"

1917–19

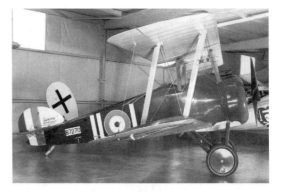

STANDARD DATA: Seats 1. Gross wt. 1,453. Empty wt. 929. Fuel capacity 31.5. Engine 130-hp Clerget, 110-hp Le Rhone Rotary, 150-hp Dentley, 100-hp Monosoupape. PERFORMANCE: (130 hp). Top mph 1,113. Initial climb rate 1,080. Range 300. Ceiling 19,000.

The Sopwith Camel holds the unique distinction of having achieved the highest number of aerial victories in World War I. This is especially amazing because the Camel entered combat during the latter part of 1917 when the war was just about over. During those final months, the Sopwith shot down 1,294 enemy fighters, bombers, and Zeppelins. The Camel received its nickname because the receivers of the two Vickers machine guns were covered by two humplike projections. It was the most highly maneuverable fighter of the war but quite tricky to master. The short and compact airframe coupled to the large torque-producing rotary engine made right-hand turns occur incredibly fast.

SPAD 5 XIII

1917

STANDARD DATA: Seats 1. Gross wt. 1,862. Engine 220-hp Hispano 8B. PERFORMANCE: Top mph 139. Initial climb rate 1,500. Range 185. Ceiling 21,800.

This famous World War I French fighter was designed and built by the Societes des Productions Armand Deperdussin and thus received the abbreviated nickname SPAD. The model S13 became available to French, British, American, and Italian squadrons in May 1917. It had considerable power and range for its time and carried two 7.65mm Vickers machine guns. The SPAD achieved numerous victories in the competent hands of such Allied aces as Eddie Rickenbacker, Guynemer, Rene Fonck, and Frank Luke. The total production of the SPAD XIII reached 8,440 before armistice.

SPARTAN C.3
1928

STANDARD DATA: Seats 3. Gross wt. 2,150. Empty wt. 1,310. Engine 120-hp Walter. PERFORMANCE: Top mph 105. Cruise mph 92. Landing mph 45. Initial climb rate 500.

The Spartan C-3 was one of the three-seat open-cockpit biplanes that were highly popular in the Midwest during the late 1920s. The tandem cockpits had accommodations for one pilot in the rear and two side-by-side passengers sitting in the front. The powerplant was a Walter nine-cylinder radial. The Spartan's wings were of equal-span design and utilized hollow box spars with spruce flanges and two-ply diagonal mahogany-planked sides. The main fuel tanks were housed in the top wings. The suspension was cushioned by a rubber shock-absorber cord. A later refinement of the C-3 called for either the 150-hp Wright Whirlwind J-6 or the 170-hp Curtiss Challenger. Improvements included increased cockpit protection, zippered inspection openings in the tail, the lower wings faired into the fuselage, a booster magneto, and a Hamilton Standard metal airscrew. The Challenger engine boosted the Spartan's maximum speed to 115 mph and climb rate to 900 fpm.

SPARTAN 7-W "EXECUTIVE"
1936–40

STANDARD DATA: Seats 5. Gross wt. 4,400. Empty wt. 2,987. Engine 450-hp Pratt & Whitney Wasp Junior. PERFORMANCE: Top mph 212. Cruise mph 200. Landing mph 65. Initial climb rate 1,430. Range 900. Ceiling 24,000.

This speedy low-wing cabin airplane received its performance from 450 hp supplied by a Pratt & Whitney nine-cylinder Wasp Junior radial engine. The Spartan 7-W Executive was produced during 1937 to 1940, and an attempted revival, called the Model 13 Executive, appeared in 1946. Only the prototype of the fixed-gear Model 12 flew; no production was ever undertaken. The Executive had a retractable conventional gear, a thick wing, and a relatively small tail for the amount of power it carried up front. Several Executives served during World War II using the "UC-7 1" designation.

SPORTAVIA AVION-PLANEUR RF4D
1966–80

STANDARD DATA: Seats 1. Gross wt. 804. Empty wt. 584. Fuel capacity 10. Engine 40-hp Volkswagen. PERFORMANCE: Top mph 122. Cruise mph 112. Stall mph 46. Initial climb rate 690. Range 422. Ceiling 19,700. Takeoff run 427. Landing roll 328.

Although the Sportavia RF4D had been around since 1966, it wasn't too widely known until May 1969 when

Mira Slovak flew one across the Atlantic to win the 1,000£ prize offered by the London Evening News for the best performance by a light aircraft under 5,000 pounds in the Daily Mail Air Race. Using a converted engine, the RF4D was preceded by models RF-01, RF-2, and RF-3 during the years 1960 through 1966. The all-wood single-seater is rated fully aerobatically and combines the characteristics of a sailplane and a small powered sportplane. A single main landing wheel retracts forward manually into a fiberglass cowling. The small tailwheel is steerable, and there is a manually operated brake on the main wheel.

STINSON (VULTEE) V-74/L-1 "VIGILANT"
1940

STANDARD DATA: (L-1) Seats 2. Gross wt. 3,332. Empty wt. 2,593. Fuel capacity 48. Engine 285-hp Lycoming radial. PERFORMANCE: Top mph 122. Cruise mph 110. Initial climb rate 1,160. Range 280. Ceiling 12,800.

The Stinson Vigilant is a two-seat liaison/observation plane powered by a Lycoming nine-cylinder radial engine rated at 285 hp. Its two occupants sit in tandem fashion surrounded by window side panels that slope outward to facilitate downward vision. The domed roof is made from transparent plastic material. In 1940, the Army Air Corps ordered better than 140 V-74s and gave them the designation of L-1. These were followed by a larger order of L-1As with their longer fuselage and increased gross weight. Other versions of the Vigilant were used as ambulances, glider pickup trainers, and floatplanes.

STINSON 76/L-5 "SENTINEL"
1941–44

STANDARD DATA: Seats 2. Gross wt. 2,158. Empty wt. 1,472. Fuel capacity 36. Engine 190-hp Lycoming. PERFORMANCE: Top mph 130. Cruise mph 112. Initial climb rate 975. Ceiling 15,800. Range 275. Maximum range 420.

The V-76 Sentinel two-seat liaison and observation airplane was developed from the Model 105 Voyager in 1941 by the Stinson Division of Consolidated Vultee. The first deliveries to the U.S. Army were made in 1942. Deliveries of the initial version, the L-5, totaled 1,731, and subsequent orders brought the total production to 3,283. In 1943, changes in the electrical system resulted in the designation L-5A. The L-5B version was an ambulance modification with the addition of a special downfolding door aft of and adjoining the standard backseat door. When both rear doors were opened, a single stretcher could be loaded. Other versions included the L-5C with a reconnaissance camera, the L-5F with drooping ailerons, and the L-5G with a 190-hp Lycoming. Fuel was carried in two tanks, one in each wing. The spruce wing spars and ribs were fabric covered. The same materials were used for the tail. The fuselage was fabric-covered steel tube.

STINSON "RELIANT"
1934–42

STANDARD DATA: (SR.10) Seats 5. Gross wt. 4,000. Empty wt. 2,810. Engine 290-hp Lycoming. PERFORMANCE: Top mph 141. Cruise mph 130. Initial climb rate 850. Ceiling 14,000.

The first model of the Reliant was the SR with a wingspan of 36 feet 3 inches; 88 were built. The Reliant underwent various minor changes that resulted in the SR-1 through SRA. The SR-S, still a four-seater, was introduced in 1934 with a 41-foot wingspan, and 145 subsequently were built. The SR-6 was next, and 50 ships were built. All these early Reliants had evolved from the Stinson S.M. series and had straight wings.

The first taper-wing (gull-wing) Reliant was the SR-7, which had a span of 41 feet. This characteristic wing also gave the Reliant the nickname of Stinson "Gullwing." The SR-8 was the first to feature five seats. The SR-9 was produced in 1937 making use of the same 285-hp Lycoming nine-cylinder radial engine as the SR-8, as well as a 450-hp Pratt & Whitney or a 350-hp Wright Whirlwind. The SR-10, introduced in 1938, was fitted with the same three engines. Vultee Aircraft bought the Stinson Aircraft Co. in 1940, and the Reliant became the V-77, and about 500 were completed.

STINSON 10A "VOYAGER"
1940–41

STANDARD DATA: Seats 3. Gross wt. 1,625. Empty wt. 948. Fuel capacity 20. Engine 90-hp Franklin. PERFORMANCE: Top mph 115. Cruise mph 109. Initial climb rate 600. Range 380. Ceiling 13,000.

The 10 Voyager was the improved successor to the 105 Voyager. Introduced in 1940, the new airplane differed only by its increased cabin width and other minor structural changes. Several versions of the Model 10 were built during its short life span. The 10 housed an 80-hp Continental, the 10A used the 90-hp Franklin, and the 1013 was powered by the 75-hp Lycoming. Wing construction consisted of spruce spars and aluminum ribs covered with fabric. The fuselage was built from a welded steel-tube frame covered with fabric. The enclosed cabin had seating for three, two side-by-side and one behind on the port side. Two doors provided access on either side of the plane. Though production of this light private plane ceased in 1941, it remained in wide use in the Civilian Pilot Training Program. The Voyager also formed the basis for the L-Sentinel liaison/observation plane.

STINSON 108 "VOYAGER"
1946–50

STANDARD DATA: Seats 4. Gross wt. 2,400. Empty wt. 1,300. Fuel capacity 50. Engine 150-hp to 165-hp Franklin. PERFORMANCE: Top mph 143. Cruise mph 121. Stall mph 65. Range 510. Initial climb rate 850. Takeoff run 1,400. Landing roll 1,500. Ceiling 16,500.

After the war, production of civil aircraft resumed, and the 108 Voyager appeared in 1946. It was an improved four seat version of the prewar Model 10 and was powered by a 150-hp Franklin engine. Subsequently, a 165-hp powerplant was used. The final version of the Voyager was produced in late 1948; the Model 108-3 with the larger fuel tank and increased vertical tail are symbolic of the Stinson line. Piper Aircraft acquired the tooling and manufacturing rights in December 1948, and a few additional Voyagers were built before production was discontinued in 1950. Piper also produced the Stinson Station Wagon that was a light freighter version of the Voyager. By removing the two rear seats, space was made available for up to 640 pounds of cargo. The Station Wagon had a slightly lighter empty weight.

SUPERMARINE "SPITFIRE"
1945

STANDARD DATA: (Spitfire 1) Seats 1. Gross wt. 5,332. Fuel capacity 102. Engine Rolls-Royce Merlin III. PERFORMANCE: Top mph 367. Initial climb rate 3,000. Range 500. Ceiling 40,000.

Six years of war proved the basic Spitfire design to be highly successful. In actuality, the first Spitfire was outfitted with a 600-hp Goshawk engine and fixed landing gear. The name was later transferred to the more familiar aircraft that was the product of high-speed design features borrowed from three successive Schneider Cup Trophy Contest winners that set three world speed records. Powered by one of the earliest Merlin engines turning a fixed-pitch prop, the prototype classed itself as the fastest military plane of its day.

The Spitfire I saw the early Merlin replaced by a Merlin III and the two-blade wooden prop exchanged for a three blade controllable-pitch metal prop. Subsequent Spitfires housed Merlin XII, 32, 45, 46, 47, 61-66, 70, 71, 77, Griffon III, IV, and 65 engines. Standard wings were elliptical in design; however, some were fitted with shorter square-tipped or pointed wings. Some later versions were equipped with a bubble-type rearview canopy.

SYPHONY AIRCRAFT INDUSTRIES "SYMPHONY 160"

2002–Present

STANDARD DATA: SYMPHONY 160 Seats 2. Gross wt. 2,150. Empty wt. 1,450. Fuel 30. Engine 160-hp Lycoming 0-320-D2A. PERFORMANCE: Top cruise 128 KTS. Initial climb rate 880 FPM. Range 430. Ceiling 16,500'. Stall 48 kts. Takeoff roll 919'. Landing roll 755'.

After a rocky start when European parent OMF GmbH declared bankruptcy, Symphony Aircraft Industries emerged from the fire as a standalone company with the 14 CFR Part 23 type certificate to resume production of the high-tech two-seater. The flying surfaces are of standard aircraft aluminum construction. The fuselage structure is steel tubing with a non-structural fiberglass shell. Variants of the Lycoming-powered aircraft are in testing.

TAYLORCRAFT

1939–58

STANDARD DATA: (Model 19) Seats 2. Gross wt. 1,500. Empty wt. 860. Fuel capacity 18. Engine

85-hp Continental. PERFORMANCE: Top mph 120. Cruise mph 110. Stall mph 38. Initial climb rate 700. Range 300. Ceiling 17,000.

STANDARD DATA: (Ranch Wagon) Seats 2. Gross wt. 1,150. Empty wt. 670. Fuel capacity 12. Engine 65-hp Lycoming. PERFORMANCE: Top mph 105. Cruise mph 95. Stall mph 35. Initial climb rate 450. Ceiling 17,000. Range 250.

STANDARD DATA: (Model 15) Seats 4. Gross wt. 21,200. Empty wt. 1,275. Fuel capacity 42. Engine 145-hp Continental. PERFORMANCE: Top mph 132. Cruise mph 120. Stall mph 136. Initial climb rate 700. Ceiling 16,000. Range 500. Takeoff run 500.

C.G. Taylor, who designed and developed what is now known as the Piper Cub, later formed another company and produced a second outstanding aircraft in the Taylorcraft series. All "T-Crafts" had welded steel-tube fuselages and wooden-spar wings. Most had fabric covering, but a few four-place Ranch Wagons (Model 20) were built with molded fiberglass wings and fuselage coverings. Power started with a Continental engine of 40-hp and in ensuing years Lycoming, Franklin, and Continental engines of 50, 65, and 85 hp were used in the two-seater models (Models A, B, and D).

The four-seat Tourist Model 15 (1950) had a 145-hp Continental, and the Ranch Wagon (1955) had a 225-hp Continental. Taylorcrafts were built in considerable numbers during World War II as military spotter aircraft, and most of T-Crafts seen flying today are ex-GI planes. These featured 65 hp, cruised at just over 90 mph, and were labeled 0-57. After the war, Taylorcraft slicked up the design, added an 85-hp Continental, and produced the Model 19 Sportsman version, which was good for a 110-mph cruise. A development of this model has been put back into production by Taylorcraft Aviation Corp. of Alliance, Ohio.

TEMCO/GLOBE "SWIFT"

1945–51

STANDARD DATA: Seats 2. Gross wt. 1,710. Empty wt. 1,139. Fuel capacity 26. Engine 125-hp Continental. PERFORMANCE: Top mph 150. Cruise mph 140. Stall mph 50. Initial climb rate 1,000. Range

420. Ceiling 16,000. Takeoff run 684. Landing roll 381.

In 1947, the Texas Engineering and Manufacturing Co. bought all tooling, patents, and manufacturing rights for the two-seat all-metal Globe Swift from the Globe Aircraft Corp. Before Globe had gone bankrupt, Temco had been building Swifts under a subcontract. After Globe collapsed, Temco continued to produce the Swift under its own name. Taking to the air for the first time in 1945, the Swift was originally powered by an 85-hp Continental. The later model Swift produced by Temco utilized a 125-hp Continental engine and was built from 1947 to 1951, when production ceased.

TEMCO "BUCKEROO"
1949

STANDARD DATA: (TE-18) Seats 2. Gross wt. 1,975. Empty wt. 1,350. Fuel capacity 32. Engine 165-hp Franklin. PERFORMANCE: Top mph 156. Cruise mph 145. Initial climb rate 1,000. Ceiling 17,000. Takeoff distance (50') 875. Landing distance (50') 740.

The Temco Buckeroo was built in two versions, the Model TE-1A using a 145-hp Continental and the TE-1B with a 165-hp Franklin. The Model TE-lA Buckeroo tandem two-seat basic trainer was introduced in 1949. It was a tandem-seat version of the Swift and made use of about 80% of the Swift's tooling. The Buckeroo was developed to meet the need for an airplane with a low initial cost and economical operation while maintaining the high-performance characteristics required of a military trainer. In 1951, after the Swift was discontinued to concentrate on emergency defense orders, Buckeroo production continued as the Model TE-113. Under the Air Force designation YT-35, this primary trainer also proved itself to be an adequate ground-support aircraft. Few Buckeroos remain active today.

THORP T211 "SKY SKOOTER"
1946–Present

STANDARD DATA: Seats 2. Gross wt. 1,270. Empty wt. 775. Engine 100-hp Continental 0-200. PERFORMANCE: Fuel Capacity 21. Cruise speed 107 kts. Initial Rate of Climb 750 fpm. Ceiling 12,500'. Takeoff Roll 450'. Landing Roll 495. Range 317 nm.

The two-seat low wing Thorp resembles Piper's Cherokee line for a reason: Both were designed by the same man, former Lockheed engineer John Thorp. The Sky Skooter featured external ribbing on the wing surfaces, which reduced the required number of internal ribs, saving weight and improving performance. The Thorp 211 earned FAA type certification in 1963. A Kentucky company, Thorp Aero, reengineered and recertified the airplane in 1990. T211s were manufactured under their production certificate for two years. The Thorp is now manufactured by InDUS Aviation, headquartered in Dallas, Texas. Examples of Sky Skooters are flying in both the certified and experimental categories.

TRAVEL AIR 6000
1928

STANDARD DATA: Seats 6. Gross wt. 3,725. Empty wt. 2,350. Engine 220-hp Wright Whirlwind. PERFORMANCE: Top mph 126. Cruise mph 108. Landing mph 53. Initial climb rate 750. Range 678. Ceiling 15,000.

Travel Air Manufacturing Co., of which Walter H. Beech was an officer, introduced the Travel Air 6000 in 1928. It was a six-seat commercial-cabin monoplane and a more recent development of the Travel Air 5000. The airplane housed either a 220-hp Wright Whirlwind, a 300-hp Whirlwind, or a 410-hp Pratt & Whitney. The 220-hp Whirlwind was the original powerplant. When Travel Air merged with the Curtiss-Robertson Division of Curtiss-Wright, the aircraft's designation was changed to Travel Air Model 6. Construction was mixed: fabric-covered wooden wings and a welded steel-tube fuselage covered by fabric. The wings utilized box spars with spruce flanges, plywood sides, and built-up Warren-truss-type ribs.

TRIDENT 320 "TRIGULL"
1977–79

STANDARD DATA: Seats 4. Gross wt. 3,800. Empty wt. 2,500. Fuel capacity 100. Engine 285-hp Continental Tiara. PERFORMANCE: Top mph 165. Cruise mph 154. Stall mph 56. Initial climb rate 1,030. Ceiling 16,000+. Range 795. Takeoff run (land) 520. Takeoff run (water) 790. Landing roll (land) 570. Landing (water) 490.

A product of Trident Aircraft Ltd., Vancouver, British Columbia, the Trigull 320 has been in the research, testing, and construction stage since 1971. The Trigull has been considered Canada's answer to the old Republic RC-3 SeaBee, the Lake Buccaneer, the Italian Riviera, and other amphibians that have been developed over the years. It is a pusher, which has many advantages over a tractor. The rearward location of the propeller and engine offers a more practical location of the center of gravity. Unique features include retractable wing floats that serve double duty as wing-lifting areas, a nose wheel that can act as a bumper, drooping ailerons with flap extension, Continental's tried and proven Tiara engine, retracting water rudder, and ample cabin and baggage space. The Trident's 285-hp powerplant turns a constant-speed reversible-pitch propeller and can produce up to 320 hp for five minutes. Seating is for a pilot and up to five passengers. Entrance is through three doors: one on each side of the cabin and one bow door.

VARGA 2150/2180 "KACHINA"
1977–1982

STANDARD DATA: Gross wt. 1,817. Empty wt. 1,125. Fuel capacity 35. Wingspan 30'. Length 21'2". Engine 150-hp Lycoming. PERFORMANCE: Top mph 148. Cruise mph 130. Stall mph 52. Climb rate 1,450. Ceiling 22,000. Takeoff distance (50') 440. Landing distance (50') 450. Range 525.

Veteran Douglas test pilot William Morrisey guessed that the thousands of returning World War II pilots would be eager to climb into a tandem sport plane that had all the charisma of a military trainer. After battling the FAA's red tape for some years, Morrisey sold out to Clifford Shinn, who built some 35 planes before quitting. The tandem two-seater was renamed Kachina and marketed by George Varga. The fuselage is built of chrome moly tubing with removable metal side and bottom panels for quick inspection. The left side of the greenhouse canopy swings open for entrance to the cockpit. The Kachina's big appeal is not only reasonable cost but sheer fun of flying.

In its last three years of production, Varga offered the more powerful 180-hp variant.

WACO OPEN COCKPIT BIPLANES
1931–42

Waco 1BA

STANDARD DATA: (UPF) Seats 2. Gross wt. 2,650. Empty wt. 1,870. Fuel capacity 50. Engine 220-hp Continental. PERFORMANCE: Top mph 138. Cruise mph 123. Climb to 9,000 in 15 minutes. Ceiling 15,800.

Waco UPF-7

Waco open-cockpit biplanes were first produced in 1923. The most popular and common survivor is the UPF-7 (PT-14) because it was produced in the largest numbers as a primary trainer from 1937 to 1942. The Waco F series was the replacement for the older 1928 0 series and was put into production in 1930. The F series airplanes represent the majority of Wacos still seen flying. The first to be assembled were the INF and the KNF, which housed 125-hp and 100-hp Kinners respectively. In subsequent years, numerous models were added, each differing for the most part by the powerplant: in 1931, the PCF (170-hp Jacobs) and QCF (165-hp Continental); in 1932, the PBF (170-hp Jacobs) and UBF (210-hp Jacobs); in 1934, the UMF (210-hp Continental) and YMF (225-hp Jacobs); and in 1935, the CPF (250-hp Wright) and YPF (225-hp Jacobs).

An explanation is necessary for an understanding of the Waco designation pattern. In the case of the UPF-7, the U stands for the 220-hp Continental engine, the P stands for the Waco wing that was used, the F indicates the model with twin open cockpits and seating for three, and the 7 means it is the seventh in the series of this basic type. After 1930, the third letter designations indicating year of introduction and style were as follows: F, 1930 with seating for three in two open cockpits; G, 1930 single-seat; C, 1931 standard cabin model until 1935 when it became the custom model (20 mph faster); M, 1931 mail plane version; A, 1932 single open cockpit with side-by-side seats; D, 1934 military export open or closed tandem cockpits; C-2, 1935 Standard model; S, 1935 Standard cabin model with four seats; F, 1939 cabin model with five seats; and N, 1939 tricycle version of the C.

The first letter engine designations are as follows: A, 330-hp Jacobs; 13, 165-hp Wright; C, 250-hp Wright; D, 285-hp Wright; F, 350-hp Wright; H, 300-hp Lycoming; 1,125-hp Kinner; J, 365-hp Wright; K, 100-hp Kinner; M, 125-hp Menasco; O, 210-hp Kinner; P, 170-hp Jacobs; Q, 165-hp Continental; R, 110-125-hp Warner Scarab; S, 420-450-hp Pratt & Whitney Wasp Junior; U, 220-hp Continental; V, 240-hp Continental; W, 450-hp Wright; Y, 225-hp Jacobs; and Z, 285-hp Jacobs.

Waco construction generally consisted of a wooden wing structure with metal leading edge covered in fabric and a steel-tube fuselage also covered with fabric.

WACO CABIN BIPLANES
1935–45

STANDARD DATA: (E) Seats 4. Gross wt. 4,200. Empty wt. 2,563. Fuel capacity 125. Engine 300-hp Jacobs radial. PERFORMANCE: Top mph 185. Cruise mph 177. Initial climb rate 1,170. Range 600. Ceiling 18,000.

STANDARD DATA: (S series) Seats 5. Gross wt. 3,250. Empty wt. 1,945. Fuel capacity 70. Engine 225-hp Jacobs. PERFORMANCE: Top mph 144. Cruise mph 135. Initial climb rate 750. Ceiling 12,500.

The heart of the Waco cabin biplane family is the C series. It was first introduced in 1935 and remained in production until 1939. The first models received the designation of PDC and employed a Jacobs radial rated at 170 hp. The subsequent model that was produced in the greatest numbers during 1931 was the QDC, which was powered by a 165-hp Continental. Other engines used were the 165-hp Wright, 210-hp Kinner, and 210-hp Continental. The design of the C series continued unchanged until 1935 when its constant-cord wing design was swapped for an elliptical design. After that, the various models were powered by the 320-hp Wright Whirlwind and the 330-hp and 285-hp Jacobs.

The N series appeared in 1937 and was essentially the same as the C series with the exception of tricycle landing gear. The F series was intended to replace the C series by virtue of its design refinements. The most noticeable of these changes was the elimination of the slanting wing struts and the use of wires instead. The S series was put into production in 1935 when the C series changed to the elliptical wing design. The S series was initiated to take the place of the old C series and retained the use of a constant-chord wing structure.

STANDARD DATA: Seats 4. Gross wt. 2,800. Empty wt. 1,690. Fuel capacity 65. Engine 230-hp Continental. PERFORMANCE: Top mph 160. Cruise mph 151. Stall mph 31. Initial climb rate 1,080. Range 1,150. Ceiling 19,200. Takeoff run 270. Landing roll 250.

Until the first part of 1972, the Wren Aircraft Corp. in Fort Worth, Texas, manufactured a STOL light aircraft using a new Cessna 182 airframe. With a design developed by James Robertson, the Wren 460 uses four Wren devices to provide the 182 with slow-flight and STOL capability. The four devices are (1) full-span double-slotted flaps to increase lift coefficient, (2) an increased wing section nose radius to postpone wing stall to 20 degrees angle of attack, (3) two small horizontal control surfaces-known as the Robertson ultralow-speed nose control system-mounted on both sides of the cowling immediately behind the propeller to use the propeller slipstream in slow flight pitch control, and (4) five feathering drag plates—known as "Wren's teeth"—added to each upper wing surface to overcome adverse aileron yaw and decrease lift and increase drag on the low wing during a turn.

An optional Hartzell/Wren Beta reversible-pitch propeller gives the 460 the ability to clear a 500-foot obstacle yet still come to a full stop in 1,000 feet. The added lift devices permit amazing slow-flight capability. In fact, the Wren is more maneuverable at slow speeds than at faster cruising speeds. With 20 degrees of flaps and an airspeed of 70 mph, the engine is at 21% power, thus allowing an endurance of over 15 hours.

WRIGHT FLYER
1903

STANDARD DATA: Wright Flyer Seats 1. Gross wt. 750. Empty wt. 605. Fuel capacity 24. Engine wt. 180 lbs & 12-hp. PERFORMANCE: Top mph 26. Range 120'. Ceiling 10'. Takeoff distance 60'.

December, 1903, Kitty Hawk, North Carolina. Orville and Wilbur Wright successfully flew the first powered aircraft.

Courtesy NASA

ZLIN Z 526 L & Z-242L
1966–77/1993–Present

STANDARD DATA: (526 L) Seats 2. Gross wt. 2,150. Empty wt. 1,521. Fuel capacity 24. Engine 200-hp Lycoming. PERFORMANCE: Top mph 158. Cruise mph 140. Stall mph 56. Initial climb rate 1,378. Range 310. Ceiling 22,300. Takeoff distance (50') 1,050. Landing distance (50') 1,345.

The Zlin's impressive record in aerobatic competition includes awards for first place in the World Acrobatic Championships of 1960, '62, '64, and '68, plus the Lockheed Trophy in Britain in 1957, '58, '61, '63, '64, and '65. Production of the Czechoslovakian training and aerobatic planes started in 1947 and includes the 726, 126, 226, 326 and 526. The Z 526 L is for all practical purposes a development of the Zlin Z 526 F Trener, the major difference between them being the 526 L's use of a 200-hp Lycoming in place of the usual 180-hp Avia M 137 engine. Both aircraft were designed to perform duties as ab initio or advanced trainers, acrobatic trainers, competition planes, and glider towplanes. The pilot and passenger are seated in tandem fashion under a continuous sliding canopy. The main landing gear retract backward into the wings, and the tires protrude slightly to reduce damage in the event of a wheels-up landing.

Zlin produces the 242 model primarily as a VFR/IFR trainer, operating in both normal and aerobatic categories with a +6/-3.5 G factor. It is powered by a Lycoming AEIO-360-A 1B6 with a three-blade propeller.

Multi-Engine Aircraft

As aircraft design evolved, the search for more power and greater performance led to multi-engine airframe formats. If one engine was good, two or more must be better. It was that enthusiasm for performance and power that ultimately allowed simple machines such as the Wright Flier to evolve into the airliners that begin stitching the world together. Rapidly progressing aircraft technology walked hand-in-hand with lightweight engine technology making possible aircraft that were increasingly fast and more powerful. The technological frontier was to find new ways to utilize the airplane. Then the goal became more people, more cargo, and greater distances.

In many designer's minds, multiple engines were the answer to safety concerns, their reasoning being that if one engine quit there would be another or more to keep the aircraft airborne. It didn't always work out that way, but multi-engine aircraft still became the natural progression from the limited performance available from a single engine. Though jet engines are becoming more efficient and more economical to operate, nothing yet has been able to replace the propeller driven multi-engine aircraft for short to medium range operations.

While commercial carriers continue with a heavy reliance on multi-engine aircraft, the private sectors of aviation are witness to a trend back toward single engines. Having only one engine to feed and care for produces significant reductions in fuel and maintenance expenses. And with the drastically improved reliability and performance of aircraft engines, new airframes built around a single powerplant have made a number of aircraft owners rethink multi-engine flying. Regardless of where you sit on the power curve, there will always be a huge number of historically significant multi-engine aircraft, and doubtlessly a good number yet to come.

ADAM AIRCRAFT "A500"
2005–Present

STANDARD DATA: A500 Seats 6. Gross wt. 6,300. Empty wt. 5,160. Fuel capacity 230. Engines two 350-hp Continental TSIO-550 E. PERFORMANCE: Top Speed 250 kts. Max Cruise 230 kts. Stall 70 kts. Initial climb rate 1,800 fpm. Ceiling 25,000'. Range 1,470 nm.

The basic design of this unique-looking pusher/puller came from Burt Rutan and Scaled Composites in Mojave, California. The A500 is a pressurized, twin-engine aircraft with centerline thrust and carbon composite construction. Control surfaces are aluminum and lead to a side-stick yoke for both the front-seaters. Each engine is intercooled and turbocharged, and has a 100-amp alternator to run the avionics. The A500 also has an emergency load-shedding feature that automatically shuts down non-essential electronics. Landing gear are electro-hydraulic actuated.

AERO COMMANDER L 3805
1948

STANDARD DATA: Seats 6-7. Gross wt. 4,600. Empty wt. 2,800. Fuel capacity 100. Engines two 190-hp Lycomings. PERFORMANCE: Top mph 181. Cruise mph 165. Stall mph 57. Initial climb rate 1,450. Ceiling 24,400. Range 850. Takeoff run 780. Landing roll 849.

The Aero Design and Engineering Corp., the predecessor of the Aero Commander Company, was formed in 1944, and its president was Theodore (Ted) R. Smith, more recently of Aerostar fame. The company's first production model was the Aero Commander 3805,

which first flew on April 23, 1948. In all, three prototypes of the six-seat light transport were built. The cabin accommodated six persons seated in side-by-side pairs with the full-width rear seat possibly being used for a seventh person. The wings were of all-metal construction with built-up spars and hydraulic flaps. The fuselage was also of all-metal construction. This first of a highly successful family of high-wing twins could cruise at 165 mph at 75% power at sea level. Its service ceiling was 24,400 feet, and its single-engine ceiling was 8,700 feet. Subsequently, the L 3805 underwent considerable design changes before going into production as the Aero Commander 520.

AERO COMMANDER 520
1951–54

STANDARD DATA: Seats 6-7. Gross wt. 5,400. Empty wt. 3,800. Fuel capacity 150. Engines two 260-hp Lycomings. PERFORMANCE: Top mph 211. Cruise mph 196. Stall mph 57. Initial climb rate 1,800. Ceiling 24,400. Range 850. Takeoff distance (50') 950.

By 1951, Ted Smith was general manager of the Aero Commander company and the Model 520 had entered into production. Its twin 260-hp Lycomings turning Hartzell two-blade props enabled the Commander to cruise at 196 mph at 10,000 feet and 60% power. Like its predecessor, it seated six to seven people, but the rear seat was optional. The landing gear was a retractable tricycle type, and fuel was carried in baglike wing cells. The company adopted a policy of assigning numbers to their aircraft that corresponded to the total horsepower of the model, and in 1952, the first Model 520 was delivered. By the time production subsided in 1954 and the Model 560 came into being, approximately 150 examples of the 520 were built.

AERO COMMANDER 560
1954–65

STANDARD DATA: Seats 5-7. Gross wt. 7,000. Empty wt. 4,690. Fuel capacity 223. Engines two 350-hp Lycomings. PERFORMANCE: Top mph 288. Cruise mph 230. Stall mph 73. Initial climb rate

1,587. Range 1,705. Ceiling 21,900. Takeoff distance (50') 1,350. Landing distance (50') 1,375.

STANDARD DATA: Seats 5-7. Gross wt. 6,500. Empty wt. 4,300. Fuel capacity 223. Engines two 295-hp Lycomings. PERFORMANCE: Top mph 222. Cruise mph 210. Initial climb rate 1,450. Stall mph 66. Ceiling 22,500. Range 1,625. Takeoff distance (50') 1,452. Landing distance (50') 1,625.

The Aero Commander 560 had a production run of 11 years, starting in 1954. It replaced the Model 520 in the Aero Commander line. For the first three years, it used the 44-1/2-foot wing, but in 1957 acquired the 49-1/2-foot wing now common to all the light Commander twins. The 560 featured a new tail unit with swept surfaces, more power, a greater all-up weight, and higher performance. Engine power was rated at 270 hp in 1954, increased to 295 hp in 1956, and boosted again in 1961 to 350 hp. It was the highest performance twin ever made in this Commander class. Top speed reached 248 mph, which is over 30 mph more than the Shrike Commander. Standard seating provided for five persons with optional seating for seven. Later, the 560F was available in an eight-seat high-density arrangement. The standard fuel tanks had a capacity of 223 gallons, but optional long range tanks with a capacity of 285 gallons could be installed.

In 1967 North American Rockwell purchased Aero Commander. The company changed the name of the Commander 500 to the Shrike Commander, which remained in production until 1980.

STANDARD DATA: Seats 5-11. Gross wt. Empty wt. 5,600. Fuel capacity 223. 380-hp Lycomings. PERFORMANCE: T Cruise mph 240. Stall mph 82. Initial climb ra. 1,285. Range 1,495. Ceiling 28,500. Takeoff distance (50') 1,560. Landing distance (50') 1,450.

STANDARD DATA: Seats 5-11. Gross wt. 7,000. Empty wt. 4,330. Fuel capacity 233. Engines two 340-hp Lycomings. PERFORMANCE: Top mph 260. Cruise mph 230. Stall mph 71. Initial climb rate 1,600. Ceiling 24,200. Range 1,480. Takeoff distance (50') 1,575. Landing distance (50') 1,630.

The Aero Commander 680 and Grand Commander are two of the larger versions of the basic Aero Commander design that appeared in profusion during the nearly two decades of type production. These particular models are king-sized with greater gross weight and more seating capacity. There is also a pressurized version. The basic characteristics, allowing for differences due to larger dimensions, are essentially similar to the more familiar, but smaller, Commander twins. Ease of handling in the air, exceptional short-field ability for the bulk and performance, and good economy at fast cruising speeds are notable, plus even greater pilot and passenger comfort. All Commander twins came off the same production line in Oklahoma.

The engines on the Commander 680 have always been supercharged, and the very earliest versions have some reputation for engine malfunctions if not operated with care. From 1955 to 1960, the Super and 680E were powered by 340-hp Lycomings. The 380-hp engines were first used in 1960, and the designation was changed to 680F or 680FL Grand Commander. In 1962, pressurization became available as an option. Another major option became available in 1967, a choice of turboprop power in place of the conventional reciprocating engines. Finally, in 1968, the 680 designation was dropped and the name changed to Courser for the last two years of production, 1968-69. The Rockwell 685 Commander was the final piston-powered model.

AERO COMMANDER 680/ "COURSER"
1955–69

AMERICAN JET INDUSTRIES "HUSTLER" 400/500
1978–81

STANDARD DATA: (500) Seats 7-9. Gross wt. 9,500. Empty wt. 4,681. Fuel capacity 500. Engines one 850-shp Pratt & Whitney Aircraft of Canada turboprop and one 2,200-lb s.t. Pratt & Whitney Aircraft of Canada turbofan. PERFORMANCE: Maximum cruise mph 460. Economy cruise mph 403. Stall mph 88. Initial climb rate 4,950. Ceiling (forward engine only) 25,000. Ceiling (both engines) 40,000. Range (both engines) 1,290. Range (forward engine only after reaching cruising altitude) 2,875. Takeoff distance (50') 1,500. Landing distance (50') 1,500.

STANDARD DATA: (400) Seats 7. Gross wt. 6,000. Empty wt. 3,500. Fuel capacity 290. Engines one 850-shp Pratt & Whitney Aircraft of Canada turboprop and one 640-lb s.t. Teledyne turbojet. PERFORMANCE: Maximum cruise mph 400. Economy cruise mph 292. Stall mph 68. Initial climb rate 3,500. Ceiling (forward engine only) 35,000. Range 2,400. Takeoff distance (50') 900. Landing distance (50') 1,000.

The prototype of the Hustler 400 first flew in 1978. Its unique powerplant setup allows the cruising economy of a single-engine turboprop with the safety of a twin and the landing/takeoff performance of a STOL airplane. Up front is a turboprop rated at 850-shp turning a four-blade constant-speed reversible prop. Aft is a standby power source in the form of a 640-pound s.t. turbojet intended to enhance safety by enabling the Hustler to maintain 170 mph at an altitude of 15,000 feet with the nose propeller feathered. Also, on takeoff, the aft jet is activated automatically by a torque-sensing device on the turboprop. In situations where a short-field forewarns of the need for extra boost, the aft jet can be left at idle.

The cabin is pressurized to permit operation at altitudes up to 35,000 feet. STOL operation is made possible by a supercritical wing with full-span Fowler trailing edge flaps and spoilers in place of ailerons for lateral control. For the Model 500, the fuselage was extended to make room for a larger, 2,200-pound s.t. turbofan engine, and wingtip tanks were added to augment the standard fuel supply. Also, ailerons were added, thereby requiring that the full-span flaps be trimmed. The larger aft turbofan makes it possible for the Model 500 to be certified as a twin-engine airplane.

ANGEL AIRCRAFT "ANGEL"
1992–Present

STANDARD DATA: Seats 2-8. Gross wt. 5,800. Empty wt. 3,880. Fuel capacity 222. Engines two 300-hp Lycoming IO-540 300. PERFORMANCE: Max Speed 180 kts. Max Cruise 175 kts. Range 1,139-1,720 nm. Initial rate of climb 1,345 fpm. Stall

57 kts. Ceiling 20,556'. Takeoff run 658'. Landing roll 585'.

The Angel was born to be a STOL bush plane, comfortable coming and going from rough, unimproved runways. The pusher twin received FAA certification in 1992 and has undergone continual refinement. The fuselage features two large cabin doors for easy cargo of passenger loading, and can carry enough fuel for a 13.5 hour endurance.

BAUMANN "BRIGADIER"
1947

STANDARD DATA: Seats 5. Gross wt. 3,500. Empty wt. 2,200. Fuel capacity 76. Engines two 145-hp Continentals. PERFORMANCE: Top mph 175. Cruise mph 155. Stall mph 55. Initial climb rate 1,250. Ceiling 18,000. Range 750.

From outside appearances, the Brigadier looks like an early Aero Commander with pusher engines. Baumann Aircraft Company was formed by J.B. Baumann in 1945, and its first product was the 250. This soon evolved into the B-290. Like the Aero Commander Company, the Baumann Company derived its numerical designations from the total horsepower of the aircraft; thus, the B-250 was powered by twin 125-hp Continentals and the B-290 was propelled by twin 145-hp Continentals. In both cases, the engines were installed in a pusher configuration. Construction was all-metal, and the landing gear were retractable tricycle type. The prototype of the five-seat B-250 was ultimately sold to Piper Aircraft for use as a test vehicle.

BEAGLE B.206 "BASSET"
1964–70

STANDARD DATA: Seats 5-8. Gross wt. 7,125. Empty wt. 4,380. Fuel capacity 234. Engines two 340-hp Rolls-Royce/Continentals. PERFORMANCE: Top mph 258. Cruise mph 220. Stall mph 80. Initial climb rate 1,590. Range 1,600. Ceiling 27,100. Takeoff distance (50') 2,390. Landing distance (50')

The Beagle B.206 was built in several versions, of which the most prominent are the Series I, Series II, and Basset C.C.I, the latter being the military version. The Series II differs from the Series I in that it is powered by twin 340-hp engines instead of the smaller 310-hp, engines used in Series I. This Beagle is basically a light twin-engine transport with accommodations for five to eight persons. The first prototype flew in 1961. The first flight of the Series II was in June 1965. The most current version of the Series II has an extended cabin with an additional rear window and a large passenger or cargo door on the port side. The Beagle B.218 closely resembles the B.206 but is considerably smaller in overall size. Accommodations provide for four (seated in pairs), and power is supplied by two 145-hp Rolls Royce/Continentals. Plastics are used extensively in the airframe where stress is not a problem.

BEECH "BARON"
1961–Present

Beech Baron B55

Beech Baron 58

Beech Jaguar Baron

STANDARD DATA: (B55) Seats 6. Gross wt. 5,100. Empty wt. 3,256. Fuel capacity 100-136. Engines two 260-hp Continentals. PERFORMANCE: Top mph 231. Cruise mph 216. Stall mph 84. Initial climb rate 1,693. Ceiling 19,300. Range 918. Takeoff distance (50') 2,154. Landing distance (50') 2,148.

STANDARD DATA: (E55) Seats 4-6. Gross wt. 5,300. Empty wt. 3,236. Fuel capacity 100-136. Engines two 260-hp Continentals. PERFORMANCE: Top mph 239. Cruise mph 230. Stall mph 84. Initial climb rate 1,682. Ceiling 19,100. Range 1,074. Takeoff distance (50') 2,050. Landing distance (50') 2,202.

STANDARD DATA: (56TC) Seats 4-6. Gross wt. 5,990. Empty wt. 3,700. Fuel capacity 142-204. Engines two 380-hp turbocharged Lycomings. PERFORMANCE: Top mph 290. Cruise mph 284. Stall mph 84. Initial climb rate 2,020. Ceiling 32,200. Range 1,070. Takeoff distance (50') 1,420. Landing distance (50') 2,080.

STANDARD DATA: (58P) Seats 4-6. Gross wt. 6,100. Empty wt. 4,018. Fuel capacity 160-190. Engines two 325-hp turbocharged Continentals. PERFORMANCE: Top mph 300. Cruise mph 290. Initial climb rate 1,475. Ceiling 25 1,160. Takeoff distance (50) 2,643. Landing (50) 2,427.

STANDARD DATA: (58TC) Seats 4-6. Gross wt. 6,200. Empty wt. 3,793. Fuel capacity 160-190. Engines two 325-hp turbocharged Continentals. PERFORMANCE: Top mph 300. Cruise mph 277. Stall mph 90. Initial climb rate 1,475. Ceiling 25,000+. Range 1,160. Takeoff distance (50') 2,643. Landing distance (50') 2,427.

STANDARD DATA: (58–1996 to present) Seats 4-6. Gross wt. 5,500. Empty wt. 3,890. Fuel capacity 194. Engines two 300-hp Continental IO-550-C. PERFORMANCE: Top Cruise 202 kts. Initial climb rate 1,700 fpm. Ceiling 20,688'. Range 1,287 nm. Takeoff distance 2,300'. Landing distance 1,300'.

The Beech Baron is a beautiful-to-fly airplane, outstanding even among other "royalty" in the Beechcraft line. The first Barons appeared in 1961 with 260-hp Continentals and a list price of only $58,000. The original 55 Baron became the A55 model and is still in production with the same engines as the B55. In 1966, the C55 was introduced with the 285-hp power-plants, and in the following year, the turbocharged 56TC entered production with its formidable 380-hp Lycomings. The C55 became the D55 and finally the E55, Beechcraft's high-performance, high-payload Baron. The Baron 58 became a part of the lineup in 1970, replacing the 56TC, and used the 285-hp Continental engine. In addition to these popular twins, Beechcraft has added two new versions, the 58P for over-the-weather pressurized comfort and the Baron 58TC for high-altitude performance. Both these additions use the same 310-hp turbocharged Continental engines, enabling them to have a service ceiling of 25,000 feet and above. All Baron 58s have accommodations for four to six passengers with optional club seating where the rear two pairs face each other. An increase in structural capacity allows the 58TC to carry 350 pounds more than the Baron 58.

In 1977, a new three-blade propeller was standard on the 58P. Two inches shorter, it improved maximum speed and increased the climb rate by more than 100 fpm. That year, club seating in all models, simplified fuel management, and increased optional fuel capacities were added. More than 4,700 Barons have been delivered. Optional equipment on the 58E55 and B55 are heavy-duty brakes that offer up to 50% greater stopping power.

In 1979, the pressurized Baron's performance was enhanced by an increase in horsepower from 310 to 325 with the Continental TSIO-52OWB six-cylinder engines. Providing a higher degree of performance, the turbocharged, fuel-injected engine is exclusively a Beech powerplant shared only by the 58TC. With the additional horsepower, the Baron 58P has a top speed approaching 300 mph. Maximum cruise speed for the 58TC was increased to 277 mph. Pressurization differential in the 58P was increased from 3.7 psi to 3.9 psi,

providing a sea-level cabin up to 8,350 feet. At 25,000 feet, the Baron's service ceiling, the cabin is a comfortable 11,900 feet. The latest improvements to the Baron line include 50-amp alternators as standard equipment, with 60-amp and 100-amp alternators for those aircraft fitted with abundant options. Redesigned sidewall panels and a one-piece headliner provide more headroom and elbowroom while reducing cabin noise levels.

The following year, 1980, Beech Aircraft Corporation is sold to the Raytheon Company, which continues making the Bonanza and Baron piston models. Raytheon ended production of the Model 55 Baron in 1982, and in 1984 the Model 58 Baron received a power upgrade to its current 300-hp configuration. In 2000, Raytheon joined with the Ford-owned Jaguar automobile company to offer the Jaguar Special Edition model of the Baron. A limited number of the six-seat twin sported British racing green paint scheme and a luxury interior.

BEECH 76 "DUCHESS"
1978–82

STANDARD DATA: Seats 4. Gross wt. 3,900. Empty wt. 2,460. Fuel capacity 100. Engine two 180-hp Lycomings. PERFORMANCE: Top mph 197. Cruise mph 191. Stall mph 69. Initial climb rate 1,248. Ceiling 19,650. Range 717. Takeoff distance (50) 2,119. Landing distance (50') 1,881.

This low-priced twin is fitted with two 180-hp Lycoming engines and is designed to carry four people with 180 pounds of luggage and optional equipment at 185 mph for more than 800 miles. The twin includes doors on both sides of the cabin. Optional avionics are similar to those on the Beechcraft Sierra. The Model 76 makes use of honeycomb-bonded wings for a smoother airfoil design with less drag and a lower manufacturing cost. Unlike other Beech twins, it was marketed through the Aero Centers because its economical and easy-to fly operation made it ideal for multi-engine training, charter, and personal transportation.

Outstanding design characteristics of the Duchess

include an aerodynamically advantageous T-tail, which places the horizontal surfaces above the propeller slipstream for better stability and handling, and opposite-rotating propellers to eliminate the "critical engine" aspect of multi-engine flying. In 1980, a 28-volt electrical system was added to provide increased cranking power in cold weather, more power for avionics, and improved parts commonality with other Beech products. The most recent improvements to the Duchess included a "Throttle Q Switch" that prevents the landing-gear warning horn from sounding when the throttle is retarded if the airspeed is kept above 99 knots; this allowed the pilot to reduce power during descent without having to listen to the gear horn. Also, RCA Weather Scout II radar was available as an option.

BEECH "TRAVEL AIR"
1958–68

STANDARD DATA: (E95) Seats 4-5. Gross wt. 4,200. Empty wt. 2,650. Fuel capacity 112. Engines two 160-hp Lycomings. PERFORMANCE: Top mph 240. Cruise mph 200. Stall mph 75. Initial climb rate 1,250. Range 1,035. Ceiling 18,100. Takeoff distance (50') 1,280. Landing distance (50') 1,590.

The Beechcraft Travel Air was the lowest priced light twin in the post-World War II lineup from the Wichita airframe maker. When the Model 95 Travel Air was in its prototype stage in 1956, it was known as the Badger. It entered production in 1958 with a factory list price of $49,500. In the 10 following years, the Travel Air was subject to a few major changes. Engine power output remained at 180 hp on all models, with carburetors being replaced by fuel injectors in 1964. In that same year, the cabin was stretched an additional 28 inches. The factory list price rose in 1968 to $153,500 including avionics. For this kind of money, the Travel Air, on a competitive basis, was an excellent value. In all these years and changes, the basic performance figures of the Travel Air differed only slightly. Top speed varied only by a mile per hour or so, cruise rose from 195 to 200, and range and altitude held constant. A limitation of the Travel Air to some pilots was the low single-engine ceiling of 4,400 feet. Obviously in some sections of the United States, mostly in the West, this would be inadequate for terrain clearance.

BEECH "TWIN BONANZA"
1950–63

STANDARD DATA: (150) Seats 6-7. Gross wt. 7,300. Empty wt. 4,460. Fuel capacity 230. Engines two 340-hp Lycomings. PERFORMANCE: Top mph 235. Cruise mph 223. Stall mph 82. Initial climb rate 1,270. Range 1,650. Ceiling 29,150. Takeoff distance (50') 1,450. Landing distance (50') 1,840.

STANDARD DATA: (D50A-E) Seats 6. Gross wt. 6,300. Empty wt. 3,981. Fuel capacity 180. Engines two 295-hp Lycomings. PERFORMANCE: Top mph 214. Cruise mph 203. Stall mph 71. Initial climb rate 1,450. Ceiling 20,000. Range 1,650. Takeoff distance (50') 1,260. Landing distance (50') 1,452.

STANDARD DATA: (C50) Seats 4-6. Gross wt. 5,500. Empty wt. 3,800. Fuel capacity 33. Engines two 275-hp Lycomings. PERFORMANCE: Top mph 205. Cruise mph 182. Stall mph 64. Initial climb rate 1,450. Ceiling 20,000. Range 920. Takeoff distance (50') 1,350. Landing distance (50') 1,210.

Not until late 1958 when the Queen Air flew did Beech introduce an airplane heavier than the Twin Bonanza, which began its life in 1949. It was the first postwar light twin to reach quantity production in the United States, and late models grossed 7,300 pounds. Built with 260, 275, 295, and 340-hp Lycoming engines, the Twin Bonanza design has proved highly versatile. Beech produced the military U8 Seminole, the civil Queen Air and early King Airs from the Twin Bonanza wing. Swearingen marketed a conversion of the basic Twin Bonanza as the Caliber. The design started life as a six-seater, and a seventh seat was added on the model in 1960. There is so much room inside that numerous luxury executive interiors have been custom-installed. The aircraft has also been successful as an ambulance plane with room for a stretcher and medical attendants, in addition to the crew.

The weight it can haul seems limited only by power and federal regulation; the 65-90 King Air, with the same basic wings, grosses more than a ton heavier than the Twin Bonanza. The airplane did not have particularly sparkling climb performance on the smaller engines, and single-engine ceiling also was poor, but more power cures these faults and makes a used Twin Bonanza highly competitive in performance against later, smaller, and more expensive twins. With a useful load of up to 1,840 pounds and two separate baggage compartments, there's plenty of room for your personal gear.

BEECH "DUKE"
1968–82

STANDARD DATA: (1360) Seats 4-6. Gross wt. 6,775. Empty wt. 4,423. Fuel capacity 142-232. Engines two 300-hp turbocharged Lycomings. PERFORMANCE: Top mph 283. Cruise mph 275. Stall mph 84. Initial climb rate 1,601. Ceiling 30,000. Range 1,203. Takeoff distance (50') 2,626. Landing distance (50') 3,065.

If you need to operate at altitudes above 31,000 feet or travel 286 mph at 23,000 feet, the fully pressurized Beech Duke will meet your needs. You can have seating for four to six, and on some versions the center row of seats faces aft. Custom interiors might include a toilet, refreshment bar, and writing desk. Powered by turbocharged 300-hp Lycomings, the Duke uses turbo bleed air to obtain 4.6 psi cabin pressure, which will maintain a 10,000-foot cabin altitude all the way to 24,800 feet. Either engine can do the job alone if needed. Two separate baggage compartments in the nose and aft fuselage handle 500 and 315 pounds of luggage, respectively. The spacious Duke cabin provides a center aisle separating the seats, and dividers are between the flight deck and passenger cabin.

Pilots will like the Duke's single-engine ceiling of 15,700 feet at gross. This airplane has so much power (the loading is only 8.5 pounds/hp) that it can cruise for 1,021 miles at 210 mph on a mere 45% of its rated output. Improvements in 1976 were a 20-percent increase in range and new landing lights on the retractable gear. As an option, the pressurized twin can hold up to 232 gallons of usable fuel by adding wet wingtips; this boosts the fuel load by 90 gallons over the 142-gallon standard fuel load. The previous option allowed a maximum of 202. In 1977, the Duke adver-

tised a higher cruise speed, improved exterior lighting, and a standard Collins avionics package. In 1980, a Hoskins fuel-flow system indicated flow in gallons and pounds per hour, plus fuel remaining. Timing modes calculated flying time remaining and elapsed time since engine start. In 1981, the air-conditioning system was refined to provide for greater cooling capacity.

BEECH "QUEEN AIR"
1960–81

STANDARD DATA: (1380) Seats 6-11. Gross wt. 8,800. Empty wt. 5,312. Fuel capacity 214-264. Engines two 380-hp supercharged Lycomings. PERFORMANCE: Top mph 247. Cruise mph 225. Stall mph 81. Initial climb rate 1,275. Ceiling 26,800. Range 1,102. Takeoff distance (50') 2,556. Landing distance (50) 2,572.

STANDARD DATA: (70) Seats 7-11. Gross wt. 8,200. Empty wt. 4,995. Fuel capacity 214. Engines two 340-hp Lycomings. PERFORMANCE: Top mph 240. Cruise mph 209. Stall mph 79. Initial climb rate 1,375. Ceiling 26,800. Range 1,295. Takeoff distance (50) 1,675. Landing distance (50') 2,017.

STANDARD DATA: (65) Seats 6-7. Gross wt. 7,700. Empty wt. 4,640. Fuel capacity 230. Engines two 340-hp Lycomings. PERFORMANCE: Top mph 240. Cruise mph 209. Stall mph 80. Initial climb rate 1,300. Ceiling 27,000. Range 1,205. Takeoff distance (50') 1,700. Landing distance (50') 1,980.

The Beech Queen Airs come in a dizzying variety of models: 65, 80, and 88. The Model 65 is the original and least expensive version. It dates from 1960 when it emerged as a six- to nine-place light twin powered by 340 hp and offering good comfort and performance. Two years later, a 380-hp option was available and designated as the Model 80. The Model 88 is a pressurized version of the Model 80. The single-engine service ceiling of the Queen Air 65 is a truly remarkable 15,500 feet. Also notable are the relatively short takeoff and landing distances over 50-foot obstacles. Air-conditioning is optional equipment.

At only 45% power, a Model 65 will cruise at 171 for 1,660 miles at 10,000 feet using only 23 gph of fuel. This includes warmup, taxi, takeoff and climb, plus a reserve of 45 minutes. In 1971, the Excalibur Aviation Company and Swearingen Aircraft acquired the rights to build and market a modified version of the Queen Air. Called the Queenair 800, it employs two 400-hp Lycoming eight-cylinder engines with modified lowdrag engine nacelles and three-blade Hartzell propellers. Deliveries of Queen Airs became limited to overseas markets, and sales in the United States were essentially discontinued. But the Queen Air was be born again with turboprop engine as the Beechcraft King Air.

BEECH MODEL 18
1937–69

STANDARD DATA: (D18S) Seats 5-7. Gross wt. 8,750. Empty wt. 5,770. Fuel capacity 206-286. Engines two 450-hp Pratt & Whitney Wasp Juniors. PERFORMANCE: Top mph 230. Cruise mph 211. Stall mph 77. Initial climb rate 1,190. Range 985. Ceiling 20,500. Takeoff distance (50) 1,760. Landing distance (50') 1,460.

The Model 18 was introduced before World War II and was subject to so many modifications, both civilian and military, that its variety is almost infinite. Some later Model 18s were optionally equipped with tricycle gear, turbines, new nose sections, and the like to such a degree that they are identified under other names. Few aircraft, however, can boast of such dependability and comfort. Some pilots find the tailwheel version tricky, but there are still executives of major companies who have a choice of more modern aircraft and still prefer the Model 18. Beech thought several times it could quietly discontinue the Model 18, but demand warranted keeping it available. Finally, in 1969, the last 10 planes were sold to the Japanese, ending a 32-year production cycle. Military versions of the Model 18 were designated C-45 and were primarily used as utility transports.

BEECH H18 "SUPER-LINER"
1964–69

STANDARD DATA: Seats 9-10. Gross wt. 9,900. Empty wt. 5,845. Fuel capacity 198-318. Engines two 450-hp Pratt & Whitneys. PERFORMANCE:

Stall mph 87. Initial climb rate 2,09[...] 26,313. Range 1,035. Takeoff distance [...] Landing distance (50) 1,810.

STANDARD DATA: (99) Sea[...] 10,400. Empty wt 5,675. Fue[...] two 550-shp Pratt & Whit[...] MANCE: Cruise mph 25[...] rate 1,910. Ceiling 2[...] tance (50) 3,200 [...]

The Beech[...] powered retr[...] approval f[...] ered in 1[...] shp P[...] pr[...]

are borrowed from the Volpar-modified version of the Beech 18. Other options included fuel injection, air-conditioning, an autopilot, and weather radar. Several companies produced variations of the Model 18. Pacific Airmotive Corp. built the Tradewind, a remanufactured D-18 offering tricycle gear, new windscreen, increased fuel capacity, and other updated equipment. Volpar Inc. originally marketed tricycle landing gear kits and later introduced kits for installing 705-shp AiResearch turbine engines. Volpar also produced a stretched version called the Turboliner with accommodations for 15 passengers. The Dumod Corp. also built a 15-seat version with larger windows and glass-fiber control surfaces. Another reengined Model 18 is the Hamilton Westwind III powered by 579-shp United Aircraft of Canada turboprops.

BEECH 99 "AIRLINER"
1968–95

STANDARD DATA: (B99) Seats 15-17. Gross wt. 10,955. Empty wt. 5,777. Fuel capacity 368. Engines two 688-shp Pratt & Whitney reverse-flow freespool turbines. PERFORMANCE: Cruise mph 285.

. **Ceiling** (50') 2,480.

15-17. **Gross wt.** capacity 374. **Engines** ...ey turboprops. **PERFOR-** ... **Stall mph 75. Initial climb** ...5,000. **Range 960. Takeoff dis-** ...Landing distance (50') 2,470.

...aft 99 Airliner was the first turbine-...ctable-landing-gear aircraft to meet FAA ...r commuter air carrier service. First deliv-...1968, the Model 99 was powered by twin 550-...ratt & Whitney turboprops driving reversible ...opellers. The Beechcraft 99 cruises at more than 250 mph and pulls a gross load of 10,200 pounds or more. Introduced in 1969, the 99A Airliner housed 680-shp Pratt & Whitney free-shaft turbines flat rated at 550-shp. Except for the engines, the 99A is identical to the original 99. The 99B, announced in 1972, featured engineering improvements for increased reliability, maintainability, and passenger comfort. The ship has an air-conditioning unit as an option with its high-pressure continuous-flow oxygen system. Also, an optional cargo door and a cargo pod—the pod is installed beneath the fuselage—increase its cargo capability. Seating can be varied to suit specific needs. Production ceased in 1978, but renewed interest in turboprop aircraft and the subsequent rapid growth in the commuter airline field caused Beech to reinstate production of the 99 Airliner. Total production of the Beech 99 fell just shy of 700 aircraft, many of which are still operating throughout the world. The heritage of the 99 ultimately became the Beech 1900.

BEECHCRAFT 1900
1983–Present

STANDARD DATA: 1900D Seats 19+2. Gross wt. 17,120. Empty wt 10,650. Engines two 1,280-shp Pratt & Whitney PT6A-67D turboprops. Fuel 665. PERFORMANCE: Max Cruise 288 kts. Initial climb rate 1,910. Ceiling 25,000. Range 1,498 nm. Takeoff 3,813'. Landing 2,790'.

After Raytheon acquired Beechcraft, the company looked for a re-entry into the regional aircraft market. The Beech 1900 derived from the King Air 200 with nearly 18 more feet of fuselage to accommodate the 19 passengers. The first Beech 1900 flew in 1982 with FAA certification coming the next year.

The 1900C model was the first significant improvement, upping the fuel capacity another 245 gallons. In 1991, the 1900D began service with a taller fuselage to allow standup headroom and larger passenger doors. Winglets improved and bigger engines improved performance, and the aircraft was also offered in a 10+ seat ExecLiner business configuration. In 1997, Raytheon delivered their 500th Beech 1900.

BEECHCRAFT KING AIR 90 SERIES
1965–Present

Beechcraft King Air E90

Beechcraft King Air 100

Beechcraft King Air C90B

STANDARD DATA: (B90) Seats 0-40. Gross wt. 9,650. Empty wt. 5,685. Fuel capacity 384. Engines two 500-shp Pratt & Whitney turboprops. PERFORMANCE: Cruise mph 260. Stall mph 87. Initial climb rate 1,900. Ceiling 27,000. Range 1,480. Takeoff distance (50') 1,420. Landing distance (50') 2,300.

STANDARD DATA: (C90) Seats 6-10. Gross wt. 9,650. Empty wt. 5,765. Fuel capacity 384. Engines two 550-shp Pratt & Whitney reverse-flow, free turbines. PERFORMANCE: Cruise mph 256. Stall mph 87. Initial climb rate 1,955. Ceiling 28,100. Range 1,384. Takeoff distance (50') 2,261. Landing distance (50') 1,672.

STANDARD DATA: (E90) Seats 6-10. Gross wt. 10,100. Empty wt. 6,052. Fuel capacity 474. Engines two 550-shp Pratt & Whitney reverse-flow free turbines. PERFORMANCE: Cruise mph 287. Stall mph 89. Initial climb rate 1,870. Ceiling 27,620. Range 1,507. Takeoff distance (50') 2,024. Landing distance (50') 2,110.

STANDARD DATA: (F90) Seats 7-10. Gross wt. 10,950. Empty wt. 6,549. Fuel capacity 470. Engines two 750-shp Pratt & Whitney PT6A-135. PERFORMANCE: Cruise mph 307. Stall mph 89. Initial climb rate 2,380. Ceiling 29,802. Range 1,657. Takeoff distance (50') 2,856. Landing distance (50') 2,275.

STANDARD DATA: (A100) Seats 8-15. Gross wt. 11,500. Empty wt. 6,797. Fuel capacity 470. Engines two 680-shp Pratt & Whitney reverse-flow free turbines. PERFORMANCE: Cruise mph 285. Stall mph 86. Initial climb rate 1,963. Ceiling 24,850. Range 1,481. Takeoff distance (50') 2,681. Landing distance (50') 2,109.

STANDARD DATA: (B100) Seats 8-15. Gross wt. 11,800. Empty wt. 7,088. Fuel capacity 470. Engines two 715-shp AiResearch fixed-shaft turbines. PERFORMANCE: Cruise mph 305. Stall mph 96. Initial climb rate 2,139. Ceiling 28,138. Range 1,455. Takeoff distance (50') 2,694. Landing distance (50') 2,679.

STANDARD DATA: (C90B) Seats 6. Gross wt. 10,160. Empty wt. 6,803. Fuel capacity 384. Engines two 550-shp Pratt & Whitney PT6A-21. PERFORMANCE: Cruise 246 kts. Initial climb rate 1,073 fpm. Ceiling 30,000. Range 1,264 nm. Takeoff distance 2,710'. Landing distance 2,290'.

One out of every four turbine-powered aircraft—turboprop and pure jet—in business and executive use in the United States is a King Air. Many are in commercial airline, government, or military use in the United States and internationally. This impressive record is a tribute to the outstanding qualities of the King Air. A full range of optional avionics includes autopilot and complete Category II landing system capability. The 90, A90, and B90 are all powered by 500 shp. In 1970, the B90 was fitted with a 550-shp Pratt & Whitney, which

was subsequently used on the C90. The 100 series was introduced in 1969, and the E90 became part of the lineup in 1972. Both employed the same 680-shp Pratt & Whitney turboprops. All have full-feathering reversible propellers. The pressurized three-compartment interior can be maintained at sea-level atmosphere pressure to flight levels as high as 10,500 feet.

The C90 is one of the industry's lowest priced turboprops, and the E90 is virtually a more powerful version of the C90. The King Air F90 is a fuel-efficient version, thanks in part to the Pratt & Whitney engines with improved turbine blades that extract more power from the engine. At 300 mph true air speed, it burns less than 70 gallons per hour. Slower turning props also reduce interior noise levels. The F90 was the first King Air in the 90 series to make use of the T-tail. The dual-wheel gear are fitted with brake deice systems. The pressurization differential of 5.0 psi provides a sea-level cabin at 11,000 feet.

The King Air 100, technically a variant of the King Air 90, was announced in May 1969. It featured a stretched fuselage (slightly more than 4'). The model A was built for military use, and the B was for civilian aircraft. Only about 350 of the longer models were built before production ended.

Of all the iterations of the 90 series King Air, the latest model, C90B has stood the test of time. Though it is dimensionally unchanged since its birth in 1964, dramatic improvements have derived from all the previous models. The biggest change came in 1991 when Raytheon changed over to the four-blade McCauley propellers, which significantly reduced the level of cabin noise.

BEECHCRAFT KING AIR 200/300/350
1973–Present

Beech Super King Air

STANDARD DATA: (A200) Seats 6-13. Gross wt. 12,500. Empty wt. 7,437. Fuel capacity 544. Engines two 850-shp Pratt & Whitney reverse-flow free turbines. PERFORMANCE: Top mph 333. Cruise mph 328. Stall mph 86. Initial climb rate 2,450. Ceiling

Beech Super King Air 350

33,880+. Range 2,185. Takeoff distance (50') 2,579. Landing distance (50') 2,074.

STANDARD DATA: King Air B200 Seats 8. Gross wt. 12,500. Empty wt. 8,283. Fuel 544. Engines two 850-shp Pratt & Whitney PT6A-42. PERFORMANCE: Top Cruise 292 kts. Initial climb rate 2,460 fpm. Ceiling 35,000'. Range 1,818 nm. Takeoff distance 2,579'. Landing distance 2,845'.

STANDARD DATA: King Air 350 Seats 8-12. Gross wt. 15,100. Empty wt. 9,326. Fuel 539. Engines two 1,050-shp Pratt & Whitney PT6A-60A. PERFORMANCE: Top Cruise 359 kts. Initial climb rate 2,731 fpm. Ceiling 35,000'. Range 1,725 nm. Takeoff distance 3,300'. Landing distance 2,692'.

The King Air 200 was a big step up from the 100 series, with bigger engines, a bigger wing, more fuel capacity and more useful load. The B200 came along in 1980 with even more efficient Pratt & Whitney PT6A42 engines and another increase in load. In 1995, Raytheon rolled out its 1,500th King Air 200, complete with an EFIS avionics panel.

Beechcraft's top-of-the-line answer to the business propjet market is the King Air 350, an evolution from the Super King Air 300 and the Super King Air 350. With executive seating for 8-12 in many specified and custom arrangements, the King Air 350 can accommodate most business travel applications. The biggest of the King Airs continues to evolve with modern avionics, and in 2004—the King Air's 40th anniversary—Raytheon added two 16-cubic foot wing lockers in the aft portion of the engine nacelles to increase loading flexibilities. Since 1964, King Airs have flown more than 10 billion miles, the equivalent of 143 round trips to Mars.

BEECHCRAFT "STARSHIP"
1989–94

STANDARD DATA: Seats 8-10. Gross wt. 14,610. Empty wt. 10,085. Fuel capacity 534. Engine two 1,200-shp Pratt & Whitney PT6A-67A free turbines.

PERFORMANCE: Top mph 385. Cruise mph 377. Initial climb rate 2,969. Ceiling 34,800. Range 1,633. Takeoff distance (50) 4,093. Landing distance (50') 2,630.

The Beech Starship is perhaps the most technologically advanced aircraft to ever hit the business aviation scene. Its twin-turbine pusher and canard-wing configuration is a direct development from the innovative efforts of design pioneer Burt Rutan. Rutan is famous for his unconventional proof-of-concept aircraft that have become some of the most popular kit-built and plans-built airplanes to grace homebuilt aviation. Starship is built entirely of composites such as carbon-graphite, Kevlar, and E-glass, which make for an exceptionally strong and light aircraft that is not subject to the same inherent long-term weaknesses found in aluminum airframes. The structure will not fatigue, crack, rot, and is impervious to attack by most chemical substances. The composite makeup of the airframe does not transmit noise or vibration from its twin 1,200-shp Pratt & Whitney engines, thus keeping interior cabin sound levels extremely low. Because of its canard configuration, the design is virtually impossible to stall, and the stock aircraft was equipped with an impressive avionics suite. Starship was definitely a ground-breaking step into the future of business-aviation transportation; unfortunately production ceased approximately 10 years after its introduction.

BOEING B-17 "FLYING FORTRESS"
1935–45

STANDARD DATA: Seats 5. Gross wt. 49,650. Empty wt. 30,620. Fuel capacity 1,700. Engines four 1,200-hp Wright Cyclone radials. PERFORMANCE: Top mph 323. Cruise mph 250. Climb to 25,000 ft. in 41 min. Range 3,400. Ceiling 37,000.

The tremendously tough B-17 flew the 8th Air Force's first combat mission out of England in August, 1942. The British were skeptical about daylight bombing, but the American strategy was made possible by the ruggedness built into high-flying bombers like the B-17 and by the deadly accuracy of the Norden bombsight. Used as the spearhead of the U.S. Army Air Force's attacks in Europe, the aircraft also saw combat duty in all theaters of war. Three days after Pearl Harbor, the Japanese convoys en route to Luzon in the Philippines were met by Flying Fortresses. Designed by Boeing in 1934, the four-engine bomber made its first flight in July 1935. The first model to see action was the B-17C, powered by Wright Cyclone nine-cylinder radial engines. Several versions of the basic B-17 were produced throughout the war, differing in armament, performance, and gross weight. A total of 12,731 Flying Fortresses were built between 1935 and 1945.

BOEING A-314 "CLIPPER"
1938

STANDARD DATA: Seats 74. Gross wt. 84,000. Empty wt. 48,400. Fuel capacity 5,408. Engines four 1,600-hp Wright Cyclone radials. PERFORMANCE: Top mph 210. Cruise mph 188. Range 4,900.

Boeing flying boats, known as "California Clippers," operated over the South Pacific Ocean routes for Pan American Airlines. One such "California Clipper" flew from Los Angeles Harbor to Auckland, New Zealand, an 8,000-mile, 50-hour route with night layovers at Honolulu, Canton Island, and Noumea, New Caledonia. On two decks, an upper or control deck and a passenger deck, there were accommodations for a crew of 11 and 68 passengers or 36 sleeping passengers. The passenger deck was divided into nine sections, including a lounge, six separate passenger compartments, a specially furnished deluxe compartment, a galley, and restrooms. The flying boat was propelled by four 1,600-hp Wright Cyclone twin-row 14-cylinder radial engines turning full-feathering constant-speed airscrews. The fuel tanks were housed in the wings and hydrostabilizers. In 1938, they were the largest airplanes built in the United States. They were tested to a maximum loaded weight of 82,500 pounds, the greatest weight ever carried aloft by any of the world's heavier-than-air craft to that date, with the exception of the German Dormer DO-X and the Russian Maxim-Gorky.

BOMBARDIER 415 "SCOOPER" AMPHIBIAN
1994–Present

STANDARD DATA: Seats 2-8. Gross wt. 43,850. Empty wt. 28,840. Fuel consumption 185-222/gal/hr. Engines two 2,380-shp Pratt & Whitney PW123AF turboprops. PERFORMANCE: Max Speed 203 kts. Firefighting Circuit Speed 150 kts. Rate of Climb 1,300 fpm. Range 1,310 nm. Takeoff (water) 2,770'. Landing (water) 2,210'.

Bombardier's unique firefighter can touch down in water as shallow as 6 feet, and in less than 12 seconds "scoop up" 1,621 gallons of water. The big amphib can even land on curved rivers or lakes to refill and quickly return for another water drop. The descendent of the firefighting CL-215 from the 1960s, the new B-415 is an all new airplane, with an air conditioned glass cockpit.

CAMAIR TWIN NAVION
1953–61

STANDARD DATA: Seats 4. Gross wt. 4,500. Empty wt. 3,000. Fuel capacity 188-200. Engines two 300-hp fuel-injected Continentals. PERFORMANCE: Top mph 215. Cruise mph 200. Stall mph 60. Initial climb rate 2,000. Ceiling 22,000. Range 900. Takeoff run 400. Landing roll 600.

The Camair flew for the first time in 1953 and was designed to meet the requirements of the Cameron Iron Works. The company was so pleased with the results of the prototype (powered by two 225-hp Continentals) that it decided to produce similar conversions of the Navion single-engine airplane on a commercial basis. The designation Camair 480 indicates the combined power of the twin 240-hp Continental powerplants used in the production model. Starting with a North American/Ryan Navion, structural modifications were carried out to allow for the increased horsepower and weight of the two engines, while aerodynamic, comfort, and styling refinements were added. Building of new aircraft has been suspended; however, the Camair Aircraft Corp. continues to supply spare parts to Twin Navion owners. In all, four models were built: the Model A prototype with two 225-hp Continentals, the Model B with twin 240-hp Continentals, the Model C with twin 260-hp Continentals, and the Model D with two 300-hp Continentals.

CASA "COMMUTER"
1975–Present

STANDARD DATA: Seats 26. Gross wt. 16,091. Empty wt. 9,072. Fuel capacity 555. Engines two 908-shp Garrett-AiResearch turboprops. PERFORMANCE: Top mph 242. Initial climb rate 1,730. Ceiling 28,000. Range 1,070. Takeoff distance (50') 1,588. Landing distance (50') 1,700.

The CASA Commuter is a product of Construcciones Aeronauticas, S.A. of Spain. It has been in service with several European and African airlines as well as the Spanish Air Force and is used by certain commuter airlines in the United States. The airplane's high-lift wing and 908-shp Garrett-AiResearch TPE331 turboprop engines allowed it to operate from unimproved 2,000-foot strips, yet the airplane can carry up to 28 passengers and a crew of two on stage lengths of 320 nm and cruise at 210 knots. Alternatively, the utilitarian CASA 200 may be converted to an all-cargo configuration that provides room for a small car plus other freight. The generous cabin dimensions allow a comfortable seating arrangement for passengers, and its height permits full stand-up headroom. The high wing design provides ample viewing for all 28 passengers.

The first civilian version of the aircraft was delivered in 1975. In 1978 CASA switched to more powerful engines and higher operating weights, and in 1984 produced the Series 300 Aviocar. The latest development is the C212-400, which was launched at the 1997 Paris Airshow. The cargo/passenger hauler uses TPE331-12JR engines and offers an EFIS flightdeck.

CENTURY "JETSTREAM III"
1966–81

STANDARD DATA: (Jetstream) Seats 4-18. Gross wt. 12,500. Empty wt. 8,450. Fuel capacity 456. Engines two 850-shp Turbomeca Astazou turboprops. PERFORMANCE: Top mph 345. Cruise mph 306. Stall mph 84. Initial climb rate 2,100. Ceiling 30,000. Range 1,900. Takeoff distance (50') 2,490. Landing distance (50) 2,300.

STANDARD DATA: (Jetstream III) Seats 4-18. Gross wt. 12,500. Empty wt. 8,200. Fuel capacity 426. Engines two 902-shp Garrett AiResearch turboprops. PERFORMANCE: Cruise mph 300+. Range 1,920. Takeoff distance (50') 2,500. Landing distance (50') 1,000.

The Jetstream was originally built by Handley Page in Great Britain. Work began in 1966 and 165 aircraft had been built by 1967. Powered by twin 850-shp Turbomeca Astazou turboprops in Europe or 895-shp Garrett AiResearch turboprops in the United States, the Jetstream had accommodations for a crew of two plus flight attendant and 4-18 passengers. With a diameter of 6 feet, a length of 24 feet, and 613 cu. ft. of usable cabin space, the Jetstream has the largest interior in its class. There is stand-up headroom, ample walk-around space, and 14 windows. The most recent version of the Jetstream was marketed by Century Aircraft Corp. of Amarillo, Texas, and was designated the Jetstream III. Powered by Garrett AiResearch turboprop engines delivering 904-eshp each, the Jetstream III is air-conditioned and pressurized at 6.5 psi. The conversion to Garrett engines allows the jet to squeeze 1,920 miles out of a 426-gallon fuel capacity. The engine conversions were performed by Volpar, Inc. in Van Nuys, California.

CESSNA T-50 "BOBCAT"
1939–44

STANDARD DATA: Seats 4-6. Gross wt. 5,700. Empty wt. 4,050. Fuel capacity 120-160. Engines two 245-hp Jacobs radials. PERFORMANCE: Top mph 179. Cruise mph 165. Landing mph 65. Initial climb rate 1,525. Range 750. Ceiling 15,000.

World War II is responsible for most of the Bobcats still flying. It is unlikely that the more than 5,000 of these five-passenger twins would have been built without a military requirement for twin-engine trainers. Several hundred remain on the United States civil register. Originally built with 245-hp Jacobs radial engines, some Bobcats later got 295-hp Lycomings, and others have since been re-engined with 300-hp Jacobs powerplants. With the addition of an exit-hatch window to meet safety requirements, some also have been converted to six-seaters, though normal seating is two pilots and three passengers on a single bench-type rear seat. The Bobcat is of fabric-covered steel-tube construction, the fuselage being faired with spruce stringers that gave way to the ship's nickname, "the Bamboo Bomber." The wing also is fabric-covered over heavy wooden spars. The landing gear retracts upward into the nacelles and remains partly exposed so that belly landings can be made with little or no damage if the flaps are up. An unusual feature of the Jacobs engine is that it operates on only one magneto, plus battery ignition. It is started on the battery, then switched to the mag. Both engines turn generators, and they run smoothly on ignition if a mag fails. Bobcats have a large rudder, but the vertical stabilizer is small and minimum single-engine control speed is 90 mph. At 10,000 feet, full throttle gives 20" of manifold pressure, and 1,900 RPM on the Hamilton Standard constant-speed props will yield 143 mph indicated.

CESSNA T303 "CRUSADER"
1981–84

STANDARD DATA: Seats 6. Gross wt. n/a. Empty wt. n/a. Fuel Capacity n/a. Engines two 250-hp turbocharged Continental TSIO520AE. PERFORMANCE: Top mph 247. Cruise mph 207. Stall mph n/a. Initial climb rate 1,400. Ceiling 25,000. Range n/a. Takeoff distance (50') 1,993. Landing distance (50') n/a.

When the Cessna 310 was nearing the end of its production years, Cessna began work on a brand new design, the model 303 light twin. It flew first in 1978, as a four-seater, but was ultimately released in late 1981 with two fuel-injected, turbocharged 250-hp and six seats. For a moment, Cessna called the new design the "Clipper," but ran into trouble with Pan Am who owned the name, and thus settled with "Crusader." In 1982 Cessna added anti-ice and the next year moved the rear cabin bulkhead to provide more baggage space and room for an access door. Crusader production ended when Cessna left the general aviation manufacturing business in the 1980s.

CESSNA 310
1954–81

STANDARD DATA: (310R) Seats 4-6. Gross wt. 5,500. Empty wt. 3,358. Fuel capacity 102-207. Engines two 285-hp fuel-injected Continentals. PERFORMANCE: Top mph 238. Cruise mph 224. Stall mph 81. Initial climb rate 1,662. Ceiling 19,750. Range 568-1,303. Takeoff distance (50) 1,700. Landing distance (50) 1,790.

STANDARD DATA: (T310R) Seats 4-6. Gross wt. 5,500. Empty wt. 3,467. Fuel capacity 102-207. Engines two 285-hp turbocharged Continentals. PERFORMANCE: Top mph 273. Cruise mph 231. Stall mph 81. Initial climb rate 1,700. Ceiling

27,400. Range 568-1,322. Takeoff distance (50') 1,662. Landing distance (50') 1,790.

STANDARD DATA: (310) Seats 5. Gross wt. 4,700. Empty wt. 2,695. Fuel capacity 102. Engines two 240-hp Continentals. PERFORMANCE: Top mph 232. Cruise mph 213. Stall mph 102. Initial climb rate 1,660. Ceiling 20,500. Range 800. Takeoff distance (50') 1,405. Landing distance (50') 1,720.

STANDARD DATA: (310/260-hp) Seats 4-6. Gross wt. 5,200. Empty wt. 3,110. Fuel capacity 184. Engines two 260-hp fuel-injected Continentals. PERFORMANCE: Top mph 237. Cruise mph 222. Stall mph 72. Initial climb rate 1,495. Range 1,082. Ceiling 19,500. Takeoff distance (50') 1,795. Landing distance (50) 1,697.

The 310 was the first twin engine model aircraft developed by Cessna after World War II. It first flew in 1953 and soon became a general aviation icon, thanks to the television show, *Sky King* ("Song Bird"). Models prior to 1960 have the square dorsal fin, the swept style having been introduced in 1960. Horsepower rating is 240 for each engine through 1958. In 1959, fuel-injected Continental engines rated at 260 hp were installed. From 1954 through 1957, the 310 had no alphabet designation. Starting in 1958 and continuing through 1971, each annual model was identified, beginning with the 310-B; however, there is no 310-E or 310-M in volume production due to engineering changes. The alphabet designation was dropped in 1972.

Two major changes in the 1956 model year were an increase in the number of windows and an improved Continental engine that was available. Earlier versions of the 310 are a little more difficult to pilot due to imbalance caused by fuel distribution. Since this has been revised, its maneuvering characteristics have improved. The 310 also yields more hard landings per pilot than other twins because flying speed is lost more quickly on the flare. The latest versions were available with turbocharged engines of the exhaust-driven type. The newer models featured a larger windshield and a new back window giving more cabin light and better passenger/pilot visibility. The nose of the most recent 310s has been extended 32 inches to add room for up to 350 pounds of avionics and/or cargo. Optionally available fuel tank capacity is up to 207 gallons and 285-hp injected powerplants provide a total of 50 horses more than before.

For 1977, the 310 was equipped with several new refinements, including improved cabin ventilation, a redesigned escape hatch, increased capacity of the circuit breaker panel by 30%, and simplified maintenance with a one-piece autopilot assembly. The wing locker fuel tanks now have tear-resistant bladders and a new metal containment canister. Newer model 310s benefited from a one-year warranty on the airframe, the avionics, and the engine. Also, new threadless blade propellers were standard; each is six pounds lighter than the previous prop, for a total of 12 pounds per aircraft. Cessna ended production of the 310 in 1980.

CESSNA 320 "SKYKNIGHT"
1962–68

STANDARD DATA: (320F) Seats 4-6. Gross wt. 5,300. Empty wt. 3,273. Fuel capacity 102-184. Engines two 285-hp turbo-supercharged Continentals. PERFORMANCE: Top mph 275. Cruise mph 256. Stall mph 78. Initial climb rate 1,924. Range 845. Ceiling 29,000. Takeoff distance (50') 1,190. Landing distance (50') 1,513.

STANDARD DATA: (320A-C) Seats 5. Gross wt. 4,990. Empty wt. 3,190. Fuel capacity 102-133. Engines two 260-hp Continentals. PERFORMANCE: Top mph 265. Cruise mph 245. Stall mph 77. Initial climb rate 1,850. Ceiling 27,200. Range 855-1,430. Takeoff distance (50') 1,470. Landing distance (50') 1,770.

The Cessna Skyknight, which has the numerical designation of 320, was an attempt by Cessna to establish a heavier version of the 310 design. The original Skyknight was developed from the 310 with supercharged engines giving increased performance. In 1963, the canted wingtip tanks were added. Horsepower was boosted in 1966 from 260 to 285. The more recent models also had extended engine nacelles to increase baggage capacity, a stretched cabin with greater glass area, and other refinements. Despite all these extras, the Skyknight actually has a gross weight of only 100 pounds greater than that of the comparable Cessna 310 and an empty weight differential of only 100 pounds more. Further, the fuel consumption at economical throttle settings was not substantially different. Yet the Skyknight offered a cruise speed almost 17% greater due to its ability to operate efficiently at higher altitudes. Starting in 1963, its second model year, the Skyknight also carried alphabetic designations, beginning as the 320-A and continuing without interruption through the 320-F in 1968.

CESSNA 335
1980

STANDARD DATA: Seats 6. Gross wt. 5,990. Empty wt, 3,749. Fuel capacity 102-207. Engines two 330-hp fuel-injected Continentals. PERFORMANCE: Top mph 265. Cruise mph 247. Stall mph 82. Initial climb rate 1,400. Ceiling 26,800. Range 429-1,168. Takeoff distance (50) 2,365. Landing distance (50) 1,950.

While the Cessna 310 celebrated its Silver Anniversary and the 1,000th Model 340 rolled off the assembly line, the Model 335 was introduced to challenge its two stalwart brothers on home turf. Billed as the lowest-priced cabin-class business twin, it offered six-place seating and a service ceiling of 26,800 feet to put it above weather situations. The Model 335 was powered by two 300-hp Teledyne Continental fuel-injected TSIO-520EB engines. Its cruise speed is judged to be 224 mph at 74% power and 10,000 feet. Maximum fuel range proves to be 1,372 miles at 194 mph and 20,000 feet. The 335 over powers the 310 by 30-hp and tags behind the 340 by 20-hp total. The 335 was expected to replace the 310s, Barons and Aztecs in the field, and possibly do the same for the 340 in years to come. Unexpectedly, its production was short-lived when it evidently didn't offer the flying/buying public what it wanted.

CESSNA 336/337 "SKYMASTER"/ "PRESSURIZED SKYMASTER"
1964–80

Cessna Skymaster

STANDARD DATA: (337) Seats 4-6. Gross wt. 4,630. Empty wt. 2,790. Fuel capacity 90-150. Engines two 210-hp fuel-injected Continentals. PERFORMANCE:

Cessna Pressurized Skymaster

Top mph 206. Cruise mph 194. Stall mph 70. Initial climb rate 1,100. Range 1,139. Takeoff distance (50') 1,675. Landing distance (50') 1,650.

STANDARD DATA: (Pressurized) Seats 5. Gross wt. 4,700. Empty wt. 3,061. Fuel capacity 150. Engines two 225-hp turbocharged Continentals. PERFORMANCE: Top mph 250. Cruise mph 236. Stall mph 71. Initial climb rate 1,250. Range 1,133. Ceiling 30,300. Takeoff distance (50') 1,500. Landing distance (50') 1,675.

STANDARD DATA: (T337) Seats 4-6. Gross wt. 4,500. Empty wt. 2,795. Fuel capacity 131. Engines two 210-hp turbocharged Continentals. PERFORMANCE: Top mph 231. Cruise mph 224. Stall mph 68. Initial climb rate 1,155. Ceiling 30,100. Range 1,200. Takeoff distance, (50) 1,595. Landing distance (50') 1,520.

The first Skymasters, the model designation 336, were a novel concept in that one engine was in front and other in the rear. This was an effort by Cessna to eliminate the asymmetric thrust problems that more conventional twins suffered in the event of an engine loss. These new airplanes were so unique that the FAA eventually created a new multi-engine rating for "centerline" thrust aircraft, a concept that the Cessna Skymaster originated.

A year into production, Cessna re-released the Skymaster 337 with more powerful engines and retractable gear. The following year turbocharging was added as an option, and pressurization became available in 1973. Both the standard and turbocharged Skymaster utilize the 210-hp engine; only the Pressurized Skymaster makes use of the 225-hp turbocharged Continental.

For both 1975 and 1976, Skymasters offered improved range plus the addition of two new specially-equipped IFR models, the Skymaster II and Pressurized Skymaster II. The "II" versions incorporated as standard equipment an extensive package of avionics and accessories usually ordered by owners. In 1976, flap extension speeds were reduced, and aerodynamics and soundproofing improved.

The 1977 Skymaster was the first general aviation aircraft with a nose-mounted engine to be radar-equipped. The Skymasters were fitted with a Bendix weather radar mounted in a fiberglass pod that is attached to the front and rear spars below the right wing. The pod is located just outboard of the wing strut and in no way alters flight characteristics.

Cessna also built more than 500 O-2s, a military version of the 337 used by the USAF as a Forward Air Control to search and mark targets for other aircraft to attack. Another military version of the 337, the FTB337 Milirole, was built in France.

CESSNA 340
1972–84

STANDARD DATA: Seats 6. Gross wt. 5,990. Empty wt. 3,921. Fuel capacity 102-207. Engines two 310-hp turbocharged Continentals. PERFORMANCE: Top mph 281. Cruise mph 231. Stall mph 82. Initial climb rate 1,650. Ceiling 29,800. Range 506-1,325. Takeoff distance (50) 2,175. Landing distance (50) 1,850.

The Cessna 340 is a pressurized six-place twin featuring center-aisle seating, an air-stair door, and top cruise performance. Developed from the 310, it utilizes a similar landing gear and tail unit. Its wings are borrowed from the Model 414. Until 1976, power for the 340 was generally quoted as 285 hp. It used the same turbocharged engines as the T310. But power in subsequent models is rated at 310 hp during takeoff for the 285-hp engine. Propellers with a shorter diameter were added in 1976 to reduce tip speeds, thereby lowering sound levels. In addition, a propeller synchrophaser maintains phase of the blades engine-to-engine by controlling prop RPM.

With a fuselage five feet longer than the 310, the 340's big selling point is a spacious interior with pressurization. It was the first light twin to offer pressurization, and it was Cessna's hope that the 340 would make this option accessible to light-twin owners. Allowable baggage in the airplane is 930 pounds with storage bins located in the nose, behind the seats, and in nacelle lockers. Since 1975, the Model 340 II and 340 III were added to the line with their packages of special avionics and instruments. For 1981, a McCauley threadless-blade propeller had become standard, resulting in a 12-pound weight saving per airplane.

In 1979, Cessna offered a less expensive version of the 340, the unpressurized 335. The model also featured a slight decrease in power with the 300hp TSIO-520-EB engines. The airplane enjoyed only modest success on the market, and it was taken out of production in 1980. The Cessna 340 would continue until 1984.

CESSNA 401/402
1966–85

STANDARD DATA: (402 C Businessliner) Seats 6-10. Gross wt. 6,885. Empty wt. 4,069. Fuel capacity 213. Engines two 325-hp turbocharged Continentals. PERFORMANCE: Top mph 266. Cruise mph 224. Stall mph 78. Initial climb rate 1,450. Ceiling 26,900. Range 461-1,101. Takeoff distance (50') 2,195. Landing distance (50') 2,485.

STANDARD DATA: (401) Seats 6-8. Gross wt. 6,300. Empty wt. 3,904. Fuel capacity 102-207. Engines two 300-hp turbocharged Continentals. PERFORMANCE: Top mph 263. Cruise mph 221. Stall mph 79. Initial climb rate 1,610. Ceiling 26,180. Range 489-1,242. Takeoff distance (50') 2,220. Landing distance (50') 1,765.

Derived from the Model 411, the Cessna 401 and 402 are essentially the same aircraft put to two different uses. The 401, introduced in 1966 and discontinued in 1972, was basically designed as a medium to light executive transport. The 402, introduced in conjunction with the 401 and in production until 1985, was intended for the third-level airline market and featured a cabin that was easily converted from cargo/utility to passenger seating. Both aircraft were aimed at owners/pilots who want to move up from the light twins to a somewhat heavier model. The 401/402 has excellent single-engine performance, yet can operate as a marginal small commercial feeder-type airliner. All versions are powered by twin 300-hp turbo-supercharged Continental engines, the smallest of all the 411 derivatives, turning three-blade constant-speed full-feathering propellers.

The 402 was available in two versions: the Utililiner and the Businessliner. The former features a 10-place high-density seating arrangement for commuter operations. These seats can be easily removed for conversion to an all-cargo configuration. The Businessliner has six- to eight-place executive seating in a variety of ar-

rangements. On lat
system powerplan
results in quieter o
maintains propelle
phase angles engi
level and vibratior

The 402C, int
useful load of 349
with added perfor
325-hp turbocharg
plishes its increa
bonded wet wing,
increased aspect r
wing also enables
gallons. The mc
increases single-er
fpm. Maximum cr
feet. Also, the eng
five inches for gre
resulting in a quie
landing gear from
traction time and s
hauls is extende
threadless-blade p
savings and requi

Ceiling 30,200. Takeoff distance (50') 2,323. Landing distance (50') 2,293.

The Cessna 421 evolved from the Cessna 411 design and represents the firm's effort to produce a pressurized light twin at a reasonable price. The pressurization system employed on the Cessna 421 is a standard type that operates off the engine turbochargers; it is not otherwise linked, either mechanically or hydraulically, to the Continental 375-hp powerplants. This system maintains sea-level pressure inside the cabin up to 9,000 feet. The 421B Golden Eagle, first produced in 1970, featured an increase in overall len principally due to an enlarged nose section to room for more baggage and avionics. The wing increased to maintain takeoff and cruise p

The 421B Executive Commuter mad to-remove seats to provide alternative capability; however, maximum fu creased standard fuel capacic duced to 225 gallons. For 1976 some 30 pounds to be ad turbocharger increased Wide-blade propelle tended vertical fir control. The Go cessfully com perior spe

Its
titud
27

CESSNA 411
1965–85

STANDARD DATA: (Chancellor) Seats 8. Gross wt. 6,750. Empty wt. 4,357. Fuel capacity 213. Engines two 310-hp turbocharged Continentals. PERFORMANCE: Top mph 275. Cruise mph 258. Stall mph 83. Initial climb rate 1,580. Ceiling 31,350. Range 600-1,507. Takeoff distance (50') 2,595. Landing distance (50') 2,393.

STANDARD DATA: (411) Seats 6-8. Gross wt. 6,500. Empty wt. 3,865. Fuel capacity 202. Engines two 340-hp turbocharged Continentals. PERFORMANCE: Top mph 268. Cruise mph 223. Stall mph 82. Initial climb rate 1,900. Ceiling 26,000. Range 1,284. Takeoff distance (50') 2,010. Landing distance (50') 1,815.

The Cessna 411, first delivered in 1965, was one of Wichita's first ventures into the "airliner" market. The

of the Golden Eagle gear and features a five-second retraction time. For 1981, Chancellor refinements included a heated fuel manifold, frost panes for cockpit side windows, and threadless-blade propellers.

CESSNA 421 "GOLDEN EAGLE" ⌃ 546P4
1967–85

STANDARD DATA: Seats 6-8. Gross wt. 7,450. Empty wt. 4,640. Fuel capacity 213-270. Engines two 375-hp turbocharged Continentals. PERFORMANCE: Top mph 297. Cruise mph 277. Stall mph 85. Initial climb rate 1,940. Range 1,099-1,377.

with exceptional fuel efficiency. Courier versions provide high-density seating that can be removed to allow room for cargo. Operators can choose the combination of seats and cargo space that suits their missions. The Ambassador executive versions of the Titan have luxurious interiors with room to work en route. The cabin volume of the Titan is 316 cu. ft., and its length is nearly 19 feet with 14 feet behind the crew.

Optional double doors allow for the loading of "D" size shipping containers and other oversized bundles. With a useful load of more than 3,500 pounds, the Ambassador can carry combinations of people (10 maximum), cargo, and fuel up to 2,040 pounds. A bonded wet wing holds 340 gallons of usable fuel. At 10,000 feet, 65% power, and peak exhaust gas temperature, the Titan Courier can carry up to 2,500 pounds of cargo 802 miles at 207 mph. With 2,000 pounds of passengers and baggage it will travel 1,308 miles at 208 mph. An optional propeller synchrophaser in recent models incorporates identical governors to eliminate the slaved combination used on previous systems. One significant change for 1981 was an extension of TBO time to 1,600 hours. The extension applied to engines on newer Titans and also to those previously manufactured.

CESSNA 441 "CONQUEST"
1978–86

Cessna Conquest

STANDARD DATA: Seats 11. Gross wt. 9,850. Empty wt. 5,687. Fuel capacity 481. Engines two flat-rated 635-shp Garrett AiResearch turboprops. PERFORMANCE: Top mph 339. Cruise mph 337. Stall mph 86. Initial climb rate 2,435. Ceiling 35,000+. Range 1,380-2,524. Takeoff distance (50') 2,465. Landing distance (50') 1,875.

Cessna entered the propjet market in 1977 with

---

gth, make span was rformance. e use of easy-cargo/passenger l capacity was re-, a wet-wing design in-y on the 421C and saved ded to useful load. A new critical altitude by 2,000 feet. rs reduced noise levels. An ex-and rudder improved directional lden Eagle distinguished itself by suc-peting with turboprops by providing su-d, useful load, and cabin size. uel efficiency is unmatched at low and high al-es. With six people on board, it typically cruises at mph over a distance of 1,118 miles at 25,000 feet. A new landing gear in 1980 gave the Golden Eagle a higher stance, a more level ground attitude, and softer touchdowns. An optional direct-current electric windshield was certified for service throughout the entire deice envelope. Improvements for 1981 were a refined fuel injection system, a heated fuel manifold, and frost panes for crew windows. The new injection system makes use of an engine-driven fuel pump that maintains pressure with a regulator referenced to the engine turbocharging system. A priming system independent of the fuel injection system enhances engine starting during temperature extremes.

CESSNA 425 "TITAN"
1977–81

STANDARD DATA: Seats 6-10. Gross wt. 8,400. Empty wt. 4,861. Fuel capacity 348. Engines two 375-hp turbocharged Continentals. PERFORMANCE: Top mph 267. Cruise mph 251. Stall mph 81. Initial climb rate 1,575. Ceiling 26,000. Range 739-1,755. Takeoff distance (50') 2,367. Landing distance (50') 2,130.

All-new planes added to the Cessna twin-engine lineup for 1977 were the Titan Ambassador, Titan Courier, and Freighter. All were designed to carry big loads

Cessna Caravan II

deliveries of the Conquest. Since the first flight of the Conquest in August 1975, it underwent a series of design improvements, including an increase in wing aspect ratio and improved engine performance. The Conquest is positioned at the top end of the turboprop market in performance; however, its modest price, low fuel consumption, and low operating costs make it competitive across the entire market of full-sized executive aircraft. The higher aspect-ratio wing also boosted fuel capacity to 475 usable gallons.

Its Garrett AiResearch powerplants are each flat-rated at 625-shp and yield a single-engine service ceiling of 21,380 feet and a single-engine climb rate of 715 fpm. Cruising at 33,000 feet with six people and baggage on board, the Conquest has a range of 2,237 miles plus reserves at an average speed of 312 mph.

Modification of the Conquest tail assemblies was necessary to comply with an airworthiness directive issued by the FAA in 1979. The company decided to provide all Conquest owners with a redesigned horizontal tail assembly and update all Conquests in the field to 1980 configuration. Ceiling also increased to 35,000 feet. When Cessna ended production in 1986, the French began building the Cessna F406 Caravan II, using the Conquest's wings mated to the unpressurized fuselage of the Cessna 425 Titan. The Caravan II remains in production today.

CESSNA CORSAIR
1980–86

STANDARD DATA: Seats 6-8. Gross wt. 8,200. Empty wt. 4,846. Fuel capacity 367. Engines two 450-shp Pratt & Whitney turbines. PERFORMANCE: Top mph 304. Initial climb rate 1,888. Ceiling 34,000. Range 1,621.

Cessna's second entry into the propjet market came in 1980 with the introduction of the Corsair. Its seating for up to eight and 8,200-pound maximum takeoff weight made it the lightest propjet on the market. Powered by two Pratt & Whitney PT6A-112 turbine engines flat-rated at 450 shp, the Corsair has a maximum cruise speed of 304 mph at 18,700 feet and can climb directly from sea level to 26,000 feet in less than 20 minutes. Service ceiling is rated at 34,000 feet. Its usable fuel supply of 367 gallons and useful load of 3,429 pounds allows the Corsair to carry eight adults plus baggage for 898 miles. With passengers and crew trimmed to four, the range is extended to 1,622 miles.

The Corsair's pressurized cabin makes high altitude travel quiet and comfortable. Cabin pressure differential is 5.0 psi, providing a 10,000-foot cabin at 26,500 feet or an 11,900-foot cabin at 30,000 feet. Slow-turning propellers along with propeller tip placement two feet from the fuselage combine to reduce cabin noise. The Corsair's trailing-link main landing gear allows wheels to pivot vertically and longitudinally for soft landings. Wide-chord three-blade propellers are reversible to aid shortfield landings and extend brake life. The props are equipped with deice protection, a synchronizer to minimize noise, and automatic feather to match blade angle to engine power.

CHAMPION LANCER
1963–65

STANDARD DATA: Seats 2. Gross wt. 2,450. Empty wt. 1,790. Fuel capacity 60. Engines two 100-hp Continentals. PERFORMANCE: Top mph 130. Cruise mph 120. Stall mph 62. Initial climb rate 642. Range 510. Ceiling 12,900. Takeoff run 500.

The Champion Lancer was (during its production run) the least expensive twin produced in this country. Champion's aim was to offer a twin with design simplicity, easy maintenance, and low operational costs.

The Lancer was also designed to handle unimproved landing strips. It flew for the first time in 1961, but production didn't start until 1963. Several revisions were made in the interim including the relocation of the engine nacelles to a position above the wing. Construction of the Lancer was all-metal with a fiberglass covering. Thirty-six Lancers rolled off the production line in the first year.

CONSOLIDATED VULTEE "PBY CATALINA"
1943–45

STANDARD DATA: Gross wt. 34,000. Empty wt. 17,564. Fuel capacity 1,750. Engines two 1,200-hp Pratt & Whitneys. PERFORMANCE: Top mph 196. Cruise mph 125. Stall mph 76. Initial climb rate 1,111. Range 2,520. Ceiling 15,800.

The PBY-5 flying boat went into service in the U.S. Navy in 1939 and was soon adopted by the RAF, which in turn dubbed it the "Catalina." This name was later recognized by the U.S. Navy in 1941. Over the years, numerous improvements were made to the design. An amphibious version, the PBY-5A, was developed in 1939, through the addition of a retractable tricycle undercarriage. The PBY-6A featured hydrodynamic improvements designed by the Naval Aircraft Factory. The Soviet Union produced a license-built version for their Navy called the GST and powered by Mikulin M-62 radial engines. Boeing Aircraft of Canada built the PB2B-1 and PB2B-2 ("Canso"), and a derivative of the PBY-5A was built by Canadian Vickers. In U.S. Army

Air Force service, the aircraft was known as the OA-10A (PBY-5A) and OA-10B (PBY-6A). The Royal Air Force's Coastal Command flew Catalinas under the designations Catalina Mk I/II/III/IV.

In addition to the aircraft's primary role as a patrol bomber, the Catalina has been used as a torpedo carrier, night bomber, antisubmarine weapon, long-range reconnaissance plane, and air/sea rescue plane. Catalinas also have exceptional load carrying ability with a cargo capacity of 15,000 pounds. Due to their versatility, PBYs have been widely used commercially and militarily throughout the world.

CONVAIR 240/340/440
1947–58

Convair CV-240

Convair 540

Convair 580

STANDARD DATA: (240) Seats 44. Gross wt. 41,790. Empty wt. 27,682. Fuel capacity 1,550. Engines two 2,100-hp Pratt & Whitney Twin-row Wasps. PERFORMANCE: Top mph 347. Cruise mph 291. Landing mph 88. Initial climb rate 1,520. Ceiling 30,000. Range 1,800. Takeoff distance (50') 2,760. Landing distance (50') 3,970.

STANDARD DATA: (340) Seats 44. Gross wt. 47,000. Empty wt. 29,486. Fuel capacity 1,750.

Engines two 2,400 Pratt & Whitneys. PERFOR-MANCE: Cruise mph 284. Range 2,015. Takeoff run 4,675. Landing roll 4,500.

STANDARD DATA: (440) Seats 44-52. Gross wt. 49,100. Empty wt. 31,305. Fuel capacity 1,730. Engines two 2,400 Pratt & Whitneys. PERFOR-MANCE: Top mph 309. Cruise mph 289. Stall mph 85. Initial climb rate 1,192. Range 1,040. Ceiling 25,500. Takeoff run 4,930. Landing roll 3,980.

Flown for the first time on March 16, 1947, the CV-240 was Convair's first postwar commercial transport. Three basic versions were produced in subsequent years, each differing in the location and type of passenger and loading facilities with the addition of minor refinements. The aircraft was originally designed to carry 44 passengers plus crew. It employed two Pratt & Whitney 18-cylinder radial engines rated at 1,900 hp in low blower, 1,700 hp in high blower, and 2,100 hp available at takeoff with water injection. The CV-240 with an increased wingspan and longer fuselage for a larger payload became the Convair-Liner 340, flown for the first time in 1951.

The CV-440 Metropolitan was merely a refinement of the CV-340 featuring modifications to increase speed, reduce the noise level in the cabin, and provide for up to 52 passengers. It was also available with twin Pratt & Whitneys that produced 2,500 hp at takeoff. The CV-580 was a conversion of the piston-engine CV-340 or CV-440 powered by Allison 501-D13 turboprops rated at 3,750 shp each. The conversion was developed by the Pacific Airmotive Corp. and received certification in 1960. Normal cruising speed was 348 mph, maximum range was 1,620 miles, and gross weight was increased to 53,200 pounds.

CURTISS-WRIGHT C46 "COMMANDO"
1940

STANDARD DATA: Seats 40. Gross wt. 45,000. Empty wt. 29,483. Fuel capacity 1,400-2,200. Engines two 2,000-hp Pratt & Whitney Twin Wasps. PERFORMANCE: Top mph 265. Cruise mph 227. Landing mph 71. Climb to 10,000 13.5 minutes. Range 2,994. Ceiling 24,500.

The first Curtiss-Wright C-46 production models

were delivered in 1941 to help fulfill the needs of the Air Transport Commands during World War II. In its military transport configuration, it can carry 16,000 pounds of cargo or 50 fully equipped troops. The civilian version contains 36 passenger seats. Nearly 400 commercial models remain in service in North and South America. A total of 3,180 "Commandos" were produced during World War II, and a large number of these serve in Chinese, Japanese, Korean, and South American Air Forces. In appearance, the C-46 is very similar to the Douglas DC-3, but the Curtiss's greater wing area, larger fuselage, and 1,600 extra horsepower made the C-46 a much more versatile workhorse.

DE HAVILLAND CANADA DASH 7-8

Dash 8 Q200

Dash 8 Q400

STANDARD DATA: Dash 7 Seats 52. Gross wt. 43,500. Empty wt. 25,800. Fuel capacity 1,480. Engines four 1,120-shp Pratt & Whitney Aircraft of Canada turboprops. PERFORMANCE: Top mph 271. Cruise mph 265. Initial climb rate 1,270 fpm. Ceiling 23,600. Takeoff run 5,700. Landing roll 3,040. Range 810-1,300.

STANDARD DATA: Dash 8 Seats 37-40. Gross wt. 36,300. Empty wt. 23,004. Engines four 1,120-shp Pratt & Whitney Aircraft of Canada turboprops. PERFORMANCE: Top Cruise 295 kts. Cruise mph 265. Initial climb rate 1,475 fpm. Ceiling 23,600.

Takeoff run 5,700. Landing roll 3,040. Range 970-1,100 nm.

Design of the Dash 7 STOL airliner began in 1972 in response to a market survey of short-haul transport requirements. The first production example took to the air in 1977, and certification followed within that same year. Each of the four turboprop engines (two on each wing) drives a Hamilton constant-speed full-feathering reversible-pitch four-blade propeller made from fiberglass. The props are slow-turning to reduce noise levels, so that the landing approach noise level on a three-degree glideslope is 92.4 EPNdB. Maximum seating is for 50 passengers divided on either side of a center aisle, a flightcrew of two, and two cabin attendants. Up to five standard pallets can be carried by the Dash 7 in an all-cargo configuration.

Development of the Dash 8 followed in the late 70s as De Havilland perceived a market for 30-40 seat airliners. Like the Dash 7, the aircraft features a high wing and T tail. The Dash 8 has been continually upgraded and comes in sizes to fit the mission. The Dash 8-Q200 holds 37 passengers, the -Q300 accommodates 50 passengers; the largest, the -Q400, can hold 70. The newest Dash-8s come equipped with a computer-controlled noise and vibration suppression system, indicated by the "Q" (standing for quiet) before the model/number designator.

DE HAVILLAND "DRAGON"/"RAPIDE"
1934–45

STANDARD DATA: Gross wt. 5,550. Empty wt. 3,230. Fuel capacity 76. Engines two 200-hp D.H. Gipsy-Sixes. PERFORMANCE: Top mph 157. Cruise mph 132. Initial climb rate 867. Range 556. Ceiling 16,700. Takeoff run 870. Landing roll 510.

The Dragon/Rapide was a twin-engine passenger or freight carrier designed by de Havilland Aircraft Company and flown for the first time in 1934. Production continued until 1945, and 737 of the airplanes were built including the D.H. 89A that was adopted by the R.A.F. and named the "Dominie." It was the radio training and communications version; 475 of these were built. It accommodated a pilot, who sat far up in the nose of the plane, and seats and freight space as de-

sired. You enter the main cabin by a large door on the port side. Construction consisted of a boxlike structured fuselage with plywood paneling on the inside and fabric covering on the outside. Wings had wooden spars and fabric covering. Dragons and Rapides still in service have usually changed to the Gipsy Queen 2 engines.

DE HAVILLAND DHC-6 "TWIN OTTER"
1965–94

STANDARD DATA: Seats 11-22. Gross wt. 12,500. Empty wt. 7,320. Fuel capacity 382. Engines two 652-shp Pratt & Whitney Aircraft of Canada turboprops. PERFORMANCE: Top mph 210. Stall mph 67. Initial climb rate 1,600. Range 794. Ceiling 26,700. Takeoff distance (50') 1,200. Landing distance (50') 1,050.

This popular STOL transport is used by a number of feeder airlines around the world. Its short- and soft-field capability gives the versatile Twin Otter room to spare on even the shortest of underdeveloped strips. Produced in Canada, the DHC6 300 series is powered by two Pratt & Whitney/United Aircraft of Canada turboprops, each capable of 652 shp. The 300S model features several improvements: high-capacity brakes, an antiskid system, wing spoilers, refined electrical and hydraulic systems, propeller automatic feather, and improved fire protection. In addition, six 300S enhanced STOL performance DHC-6-300s were built in the mid 1970s. Earlier models, the series 100 and 200, were fitted with 570-shp engines. Access to the two-man cockpit is through a car-like door on each side or through the cabin. The standard "Commuter" version will accommodate 20 passengers, but optional arrangements are available. During its run, more than 800 Twin Otters were built before production ended in 1988.

DIAMOND AIRCRAFT "TWIN STAR"
2005–Present

STANDARD DATA: DA-42 Seats 4. Gross wt. 3.637. Empty wt. 2,400. Fuel capacity 95. Engines two 136-bhp Thielert Centurion 1.7. PERFORMANCE: Max Cruise 181 kts. Stall 56 kts. Initial climb rate 1,730

fpm. Range 1,003-1,442 nm. Takeoff run 951'. Landing roll 950'.

Diamond's DA-42 Twin Star is an all-composite four-seater with twin turbocharged diesel engines that can operate on automotive diesel or Jet A1 fuel. At take-off the engines develop full power at a quiet 2,300 rpm, and feature automatic prop (FADEC) control and auto-feather. The Twin Star was designed to incorporate the Garmin G1000 all class cockpit from the beginning, and trailing landing gear give the twin a smooth transition to landing and taxi. Optional equipment available for the DA-42 include oxygen, anti/de-ice and air conditioning.

DORNIER DO 28 D-1 "SKYSERVANT"
1967–81

STANDARD DATA: Seats 12-13. Gross wt. 8,470. Empty wt. 5,066. Fuel capacity 236. Engines two 380-hp Lycomings. PERFORMANCE: Top mph 202. Cruise mph 170. Stall mph 65. Initial climb rate 1,180. Range 1,255. Ceiling 25,200. Takeoff distance (50') 1,020. Landing distance (50') 1,000.

Professor Claude Dornier started his first aircraft company in 1922 as the successor to the "Do" division of the Zeppelin Werke, GmbH. When aircraft manufacturing became forbidden in Germany after World War II, Dornier continued his design work in Spain. There he developed the Do 25, a general-purpose airplane that later evolved into the Do 27. The Do 28, a twin-engine version of the Do 27, was produced until 1971. The light utility transport Do 28 Skyservant was

required by the original specifications
military. In addition, it exceeded
guarantee and was 700 pound
empty weight. The Invader w
Ninth Air Force in the Eur
armament included six f
in the nose, eight pa
wings, and two tw
One turret was
fuselage; both
gun-sightin
turret co
by the
ex

STANDARD DATA: A-26-15-DL Seats 3. Gross wt. 37,000. Empty wt. 22,370. Engines two 2,000-hp Pratt & Whitney R-2800-2718-cylinder radials. PERFORMANCE: Top mph 355. Cruise mph 284. Initial climb rate 1,250. Range 1,400. Ceiling 22,100.

STANDARD DATA: A-26B-60-DL Seats 3. Gross wt. 41,800. Empty wt. 22,362. Engines two 2,350-hp Pratt & Whitney R-2800-79 air-cooled water injected radial engines. PERFORMANCE: Top mph 355. Cruise mph 284. Initial climb rate 1,250. Range 1,400-3,200 nm. Ceiling 22,100.

The A-26 Invader was originally built in three different prototypes, one as a light bombardment and attack airplane, one as a modification for use as a night fighter, and one as an attack bomber with a large-caliber mounted cannon. The prototype of the basic bomber and attack plane was flown for the first time in 1942. In testing, it actually carried nearly twice the bomb load submitted by the ... every performance ... under its designed ... ent into action with the ... opean Theater in 1944. Its ... xed .50-caliber machine guns ... red .50-caliber guns under the ... -gun electrically-operated turrets. ... above and one turret was below the ... turrets were remotely controlled from a ... g position behind the wings. The upper gun ... ld be locked in the forward position and fired ... pilot. The Invader also had internal bomb bays, ... rnal bomb racks, and self-sealing fuel tanks.

The A-26 featured a variety of configurations throughout the war, including a transparent nose. The A-26B-DL model was configured with eight machine guns in the nose, and six .50 inch guns were mounted in the wings. Bombs and rockets could also be attached to hard points. In 1948, the A-26B was redesignated the B-26B so as not to be confused with the Martin B-26 Marauder.

DOUGLAS DC-3

1936–46

STANDARD DATA: Seats 28-30. Gross wt. 25,200. Empty wt. 16,865. Fuel capacity 411. Engines two 1,200-hp Pratt & Whitney Twin-Wasps. PERFORMANCE: Top mph 230. Cruise mph 207. Stall mph 67. Initial climb rate 1,130. Range 2,125. Ceiling 23,200.

The DC-2 was developed from the DC-1. The DC-2 first flew in 1934, and production continued until 1936 when it was replaced by the DC-3. The DC-2 was powered by two Wright engines rated at 710 hp each. It was later modified by the U.S. Air Force under the designation C-39. The C-39 was essentially the DC-2 with DC-3 wing and tail assemblies and two 975-hp Wright engines. Construction was all-metal with a semimonocoque fuselage. In 1936, the first DC-3s rolled off the line and were an instant success. By 1941, more than 400 DC-3s had been sold to the airlines.

When the war broke out, the military designed the big airliner the C-47 Skytrain. More than 10,000 were built to transport troops back and forth across the oceans. And after the war ended, the demilitarized C47s

returned to the civilian designations, and created a bargain-priced backbone for the growing airline industry.

In 1949, Douglas created the Super DC-3 with a longer fuselage and more powerful engines. The updated, upgraded model was commercially unsuccessful. The original DC-3 remained the world's choice. Ultimately the greatest tribute to the DC-3 lies in the fact that after more than six decades, there are still hundreds of the big taildraggers still in operation around the globe.

DOUGLAS DC-4/C-54

1939

STANDARD DATA: Seats 42. Gross wt. 65,000. Empty wt. 35,000. Fuel capacity 2,100. Engines four 1,000-hp Pratt & Whitney Twin-Wasps. PERFORMANCE: Top mph 285. Cruise mph 222. Stall mph 80. Initial climb rate 1,200. Range 3,500. Ceiling 25,000.

The DC-4 design was the product of a group effort involving the technical departments of five of the largest airline companies in the United States in 1939. Its service tests were carried out under the supervision of United Airlines. The first model had seating for more than 50 passengers and was powered by Pratt & Whitney Twin-Wasp engines. Unfortunately, it was sold to Japan where it was involved in a crash. Its extensive service testing resulted in a somewhat smaller design with seating for approximately 40 passengers. This version was placed in production in 1940. At the outbreak of World War II, the military ordered large-scale production of the DC-4 and gave it the designation of C-54. The military version was powered by 1,350-hp Twin-Wasps and was outfitted to carry troops, trucks, and other heavy equipment. The C-54 was also provided with its own facilities for field loading.

DOUGLAS DC-6/DC-7

1947–58

STANDARD DATA: (DC-6) Seats 64-92. Gross wt. 106,000. Empty wt. 49,767. Fuel capacity 3,992-5,512. Engines four 2,500-hp Pratt & Whitney

Double Wasps. PERFORMANCE: Top mph 360.
Cruise mph 307. Landing mph 93. Initial climb rate
1,120. Range 3,860. Takeoff distance (50') 4,500.
Landing distance (50') 3,010.

STANDARD DATA: (DC-7) Seats 62-99. Gross wt.
143,000. Empty wt. 72,763. Fuel capacity 7,824.
Engines four 3,400-hp Wright Turbo Compound radials. PERFORMANCE: Top mph 406. Cruise mph
346. Stall mph 97. Climb rate (20,000 ft.) 240. Range
4,635. Ceiling 21,700. Takeoff distance (50') 6,360.
Landing distance (50') 5,100.

The Douglas DC-6 is essentially a stretched, more
powerful, and pressurized version of the DC-4 with
three-blade props. The DC-7 is merely a stretched DC-
6 with four-blade props and retaining all aerodynamic
and structural features. The only difference between the
DC-6 and the DC-4 in exterior appearance is that the
DC-6 is extended an additional seven feet and the windows are square instead of the earlier porthole style.
This new version also provides for up to 62 passengers, 20 more than the DC-4. The DC-7 was increased
3 feet 4 inches longer than the DC-6. It provided for
the accommodation of 69 first-class passengers or 95
coach passengers. The DC-7's engines further increased
its gross weight. The DC-7B, a later version, was basically an intercontinental aircraft.

EMBRAER "BANDEIRANTE"
1972–86

STANDARD DATA: Seats 21. Gross wt. 12,500.
Empty wt. 7,857. Fuel capacity 440. Engines two
750-shp Pratt & Whitney turboprops. PERFOR-
MANCE: Top mph 286. Cruise mph 259. Stall mph
82. Initial climb rate 1,788. Ceiling 24,100. Range
1,180. Takeoff distance (50') 2,215. Landing distance (50') 2,790.

The Bandeirante from Brazil is a commuter airliner
powered by two Pratt & Whitney PT6A-34 free-tur-
bine turboprop engines flat-rated at 750 shp maximum
continuous power at 2,200 propeller RPM. The propellers are three-blade Hartzells with automatic synchronization and full beta-control reversing. Standard
seating is for 18 passengers with maximum provisions
for 21. There is a crew/passenger door at the front and
passenger/baggage door at the rear, both on the port
side. The first prototype flew in 1968, with the first
production model flying in 1972. By the beginning of
1979, 219 Bandeirantes of various models had been
sold to some 40 operators around the world. The
Bandeirante is available in more than 14 versions, differing in their equipment for specialized missions.

EMBRAER "BRASILIA"
1985–Present

STANDARD DATA: Seats 24-32. Gross wt. 25,353.
Empty wt. 16,655. Engines two 750-shp Pratt &
Whitney turboprops. PERFORMANCE: Top Cruise
300 kts. Initial climb rate 2,500 fpm. Ceiling 29,000-
32,000'. Range 550-840 nm.

The Brasilia is an extremely successful regional turboprop that has continued to evolve. The first version
of the EMB 120 flew with Pratt & Whitney 118A
engines. The latest model, the EMB 120ER, is the basis
for Embraer's regional jets.

EVANGEL 4500 STOL
1969–76

STANDARD DATA: Seats 9. Gross wt. 5,500. Empty
wt. 3,530. Fuel capacity 111. Engines two 300-hp
Lycomings. PERFORMANCE: Top mph 230. Cruise

182. Stall mph 67. Initial climb rate 1,500. Range 637. Ceiling 21,030. Takeoff distance (50') 1,125. Landing distance (50') 1,140.

Few light twins can carry a full-sized refrigerator, two full 55-gallon drums, five adults, and a goat, and still fly in and out of 1,000-foot jungle strips. The Evangel 4500 STOL does it with ease. It derives its power from two direct-drive fuel-injected Lycoming engines rated at 300 hp each. Only rectangular sections are used for construction of the main fuselage; therefore, optimum utilization of space can be made. The Evangel's cargo doors, one on each side, are the full height of the fuselage side and twice as wide (compared to height). The main landing gear retracts rearward into the wings just below the engine nacelles, but the tires are allowed to protrude in order to provide some protection for wheels-up landings. A turbocharged version, the 4500-300-11, entered production in 1974 to increase the maximum takeoff weight to 5,700 pounds.

FAIRCHILD HILLER FH-227 (FOKKER)
1958–94

STANDARD DATA: (FH-227) Seats 44-52. Gross wt. 43,500. Empty wt. 22,923. Fuel capacity 1,364. Engines two 2,300-shp Rolls-Royce Dart turboprops. PERFORMANCE: Top 294. Cruise 270. Stall mph 87. Initial climb rate 1,560. Range 1,655. Ceiling 28,000. Takeoff run 3,950. Landing roll 4,100.

STANDARD DATA: (F27 Mk 600) Seats 44 plus crew. Gross wt. 45,000. Empty wt. 22,786. Fuel capacity 1,357-2,463. Engines two 2,140-shp Rolls-Royce Dart turboprops. PERFORMANCE: Cruise mph 298. Initial climb rate 1,480. Ceiling 29,500. Takeoff distance 2,310. Landing distance 3,290.

The original Fokker F-27 Friendship was built in Holland. Fairchild has built the F-27 under license from Fokker since 1958. The first F-27 models had a maximum gross weight of 40,500 pounds and seated 44 passengers. Power was supplied by twin 1,720-shp Dart turboprops. When Fairchild merged with Hiller Aircraft, the designation of the airplane was changed to FH-227 and the fuselage was stretched by six feet, giving increased cabin space for passengers and freight.

The stretched airliner will accommodate up to 52 passengers. In 1960, power was increased to 2,105-shp. The stretched version was fitted with 2,250-shp engines, and ultimately the FH-227 received a redesigned windshield, stronger landing gear, strengthened rear fuselage, heavier wing skin, propellers of increased diameter, and a more powerful 2,300-shp Dart turboprop. Fairchild discontinued building the FH-227 under license from Fokker in 1975.

FORD TRI-MOTOR
1926

STANDARD DATA: Seats 15. Gross wt. 13,250. Empty wt. 7,800. Engines three 425-hp Pratt & Whitneys. PERFORMANCE: Top mph 140. Cruise mph 115. Landing mph 60. Range 500. Ceiling 20,000.

The "Tin Goose" is perhaps the most important aircraft in United States airline history. The original Stout Metal Airplane Company was purchased in 1925 by Henry Ford. The new division of the Ford Motor Company produced three versions of the Tri-Motor monoplane. The 4-AT-E was fitted with three 300-hp Whirlwinds. The 6-AT utilized the same engine but had a larger wing area and accommodations for 13 instead of 11 passengers. The 5-AT-B was outfitted with the same wings and number of seats but differed by having the more powerful 425-hp Pratt & Whitney "Wasp" engines. The TriMotor's fuselage was constructed from a series of transverse duralumin bulkheads covered with corrugated metal skin. One engine was mounted in the nose, while the other two were suspended underneath the wings.

GAF NOMAD
1974–1984

STANDARD DATA: (N22B) Seats 13. Gross wt. 8,500. Empty wt. 4,613. Fuel capacity 269-363.

Engines two 420-shp Allison turboprops. PERFOR-MANCE: Cruise mph 193. Stall mph 75. Initial climb rate 1,460. Ceiling 21,000. Range 840. Takeoff (50') 1,180. Landing (50') 1,110. Takeoff run (STOL) 600. Landing run (STOL) 250.

STANDARD DATA: (N24A) Seats 17. Gross wt. 9,400. Empty wt. 5,241. Fuel capacity 269-363. Engines two 420-shp Allison turboprops. PERFOR-MANCE: Cruise mph 193. Stall mph 75. Initial climb rate 1,280. Ceiling 20,000. Range 840. Takeoff (50') 1,710. Landing (50') 1,380.

The Nomad is designed and built by the Government Aircraft Factories in Australia in two models. These are the short-takeoff-and-landing (STOL) Nomad N22B and the Nomad N24A commuter aircraft. Variations on the basic aircraft include the Mission Master, the Search Master for maritime surveillance work, and a photographic and mapping model. The aircraft have proven successful in many countries, often flying over rugged terrain in climates ranging from tropical to subarctic. Its STOL capability, originally developed for Australian military use, has made it ideal for operations in rugged areas such as the highlands of Papua, New Guinea.

The N22B, capable of carrying up to 12 passengers, can take off in only 800 feet. The larger N24A is a later development of the basic aircraft capable of carrying more passengers and cargo.

The Nomad is characterized by simplicity of construction and systems, which contribute to its economy of operation. Its two Allison 250-B17C turboprops are rated at 420 shp, producing more than two horsepower per pound of engine weight. The B17C offers an improved single-engine high-altitude performance capability and a more rugged gearbox. The GAF was renamed the ASTA (Aerospace Technologies of Australia) and later acquired by Rockwell in 1996.

GRUMMAN GOOSE/WIDGEON
1937–46

STANDARD DATA: (Goose) Seats 4-6. Gross wt. 8,000. Empty wt. 5,425. Fuel capacity 220. Engines two 400-hp Pratt & Whitney Wasp Juniors. PER-FORMANCE: Top mph 201. Cruise mph 191. Initial climb rate 1,100. Range 640. Ceiling 21,000.

Grumman Widgeon

Grumman Goose

STANDARD DATA: (Widgeon) Seats 4-5. Gross wt. 4,525. Empty wt. 3,240. Fuel capacity 108. Engines two 200-hp Rangers. PERFORMANCE: Top mph 153. Cruise mph 138. Initial climb rate 700. Range 920. Ceiling 14,600.

Seaplanes take a ferocious pounding, and it is a tribute to the way Grumman builds airplanes that these two continue to serve so well. More than 300 of the G-21A Goose series with 450-hp Pratt & Whitney engines were built just before and during World War II, of which about 80 remain active in the United States and Canada. Production of the smaller Widgeon, with 200-hp Ranger in-line engines, totaled more than 200, with a further 40 license-built in France and later resold to the United States.

The Goose has proved a popular "back country" airplane in Canada, where remote lakes and waterways serve as landing sites. A number had executive interiors installed by United States corporations whose vice presidents liked to fish in the northern woods. The Widgeon originally seated four, but the G-44A was built with five seats, and some have been converted to seat six with the middle row of seats facing aft and their backs against the wheel wells. The McKinnon Turbo Goose is a modified version of the Goose featuring twin 680-shp Pratt & Whitney powerplants, increased fuel capacity, retractable wing floats, plus other improvements. McKinnon also produces a "Super Widgeon" powered by 270-hp Lycomings.

GRUMMAN "GULFSTREAM I"
1959–68

STANDARD DATA: Seats 10-24. Gross wt. 35,100. Empty wt. 21,900. Fuel capacity 1,550. Engines two

2,210-shp Rolls-Royce Darts. PERFORMANCE: Top mph 348. Cruise mph 288. Initial climb rate 1,900. Approach speed 128. Range 2,540. Ceiling 33,600. Takeoff run 2,550. Landing roll 1,525.

The Gulfstream I is a business transport designed to carry a crew of two with 10 to 14 passengers. Power is provided by twin Rolls-Royce Dart turboprop engines turning four-blade Rotol constant-speed propellers. The Gulfstream I first flew in 1958 and was the first United States twin-engine business aircraft to be certificated to cruise at 30,000 feet. A later version received certification as a 24-passenger variation for feeder-line use. Two Gulfstream offspring were enlisted for military use: the VC-4A was a U.S. Coast Guard transport and the TC-4C was an "avionics classroom" for the U.S. Navy.

GRUMMAN ALBATROSS "HU-16"
1947–1961

STANDARD DATA: Seats 5-22. Gross wt. 37,500. Empty wt. 22,883. Engines two 1,425-hp Wright R-1820-76A radials. PERFORMANCE: Max Speed 236 mph. Cruise mph 191. Initial climb rate 1,100. Range 640. Ceiling 21,000.

The Albatross is the biggest of the Grumman flying boats and was designed for military service. Used originally by the U.S. Navy, the HUs flew a variety of missions, from reconnaissance to anti-submarine warfare and of course, search and rescue.

The unique capabilities of the big amphib have caused numerous attempts to modernize the basic hull. In the 1970s, Grumman reconfigured the military design to make room for 28 passengers, and added a galley for food and room for a fight attendant. The new airplane was designated the G111 and awarded FAA certification in 1980. Other Albatrosses have been converted to turbine power.

GRUMMAN MALLARD "G73"
1946–1951

STANDARD DATA: Seats 12. Gross wt. 12,750. Empty wt. 8,750. Engines two 600-715-hp Pratt & Whitney Wasp Juniors. PERFORMANCE: Max Speed 187-191 kts. Cruise 157-187 kts. Initial climb rate 1,290-1,350 fpm. Range 1,655 nm. Ceiling 23,000-24,500'.

The Mallard was Grumman's entry into the civilian/commercial use amphibian category. Based on the smaller Goose and Widgeon designs, the larger G73 featured tricycle landing gear. Only 59 Mallards were ever built, but some saw a new life as a turboprop with Pratt & Whitney PT6A out front. A supplemental type certificate was issued for the kerosene burning versions in 1960, but even the performance boost delivered by the more powerful engines was not enough to keep the Mallards in service.

GULFSTREAM "COUGAR"
1978–79

STANDARD DATA: Seats 4. Gross wt. 3,800. Empty wt. 2,588. Fuel capacity 80-118. Engines two 160-hp Lycomings. PERFORMANCE: Top mph 193. Cruise

mph 184. Stall mph 72. Initial climb rate 1,160. Ceiling 17,400. Range 609-966. Takeoff distance (50') 1,850. Landing distance (50') 1,330.

Several twins were called "light" in 1977, but only two were genuinely entitled to the term: the center-line-thrust Cessna Skymaster and the Piper Seneca. Grumman American (now Gulfstream American) entered this uncrowded field late in January 1977 with its Cougar. Competition had grown considerably by 1979. Gulfstream's fuel-stingy four-place retractable is powered by a pair of 160-hp Lycoming engines, long favored by pilots for their 2,000-hour recommended overhaul period. A single-engine minimum control speed that is slower than its stall speed at maximum gross weight with flaps extended puts the Cougar amongst the safest multi-engine airplanes.

Fully fueled and cruising at optimum altitude (8,500 feet) on 75% power, the Cougar can cover 970 miles while retaining a 45-minute reserve. The maximum-range power setting (45% power) yields 1,350 miles. Seating is for four, but the Cougar's cabin is easily large enough to accommodate six. Like single-engine models in the Gulfstream line, the light twin makes use of the same space-age metal-to-metal bonding construction techniques throughout. It also incorporates such sophisticated materials as a high-strength honeycomb "aluminum sandwich" slab that is extensively used in many high-performance military jets.

HAWKER SIDDELEY "DOVE"
1945

STANDARD DATA: Seats 117. Gross wt. 13,500. Empty wt. 6,325. Engines two 400-hp Bristol Siddeley Gipsy Queens. PERFORMANCE: Top mph 230. Cruise mph 187. Stall mph 74. Initial climb rate 1,135. Range 880. Ceiling 21,700.

Originally manufactured by the de Havilland Aircraft Company, the Dove took to the air for the first time in 1945. Since that time it has been made available in numerous variations, and its production was ultimately taken over by Hawker Siddeley. The light transport is powered by two six-cylinder air-cooled Gipsy Queen engines, each putting out 400 hp. The first Doves housed 340-hp Gipsy Queens that were later replaced by 380-hp models. Doves in the United States were marketed as the Custom 800 executive carriers and were equipped with all the usual appointments.

The R.A.F. and Royal Navy versions were called the "Devon" and "Sea Devon," respectively. The Dove utilizes a unique cockpit/canopy design in order to provide extra headroom and increase visibility for the pilots. For a time, Riley Turbostream Corp. of Waco, Texas, built a remanufactured Dove called the Turbo Exec 400 powered by twin turbocharged fuel-injected engines. Another version of the Dove was produced by Texas Airplane Manufacturing Co. that employed 705-eshp turboprops and a stretched fuselage.

HAWKER SIDDELEY "HERON"

STANDARD DATA: Seats 14-17. Gross wt. 13,500. Empty wt. 8,484. Fuel capacity 494. Engines four 250-hp Bristol Siddeley Gipsy Queens. PERFORMANCE: Top mph 190. Cruise mph 183. Stall mph 75. Initial climb rate 1,075. Range 1,550. Takeoff distance (50') 2,424. Landing distance (50') 2,065.

The Heron is basically an enlarged version of the Dove. The original Heron Series I had fixed tricycle landing gear, but that plane was soon replaced by the Series II, which was equipped with retractable gear. The Heron is equipped to seat 14 passengers in single seats on each side of the central aisle. Two alternative arrangements allow for either 17 passengers with no toilet facilities or luxurious executive appointments for six to eight. Four 250-hp Gipsy Queen six-cylinder inline direct-drive normally aspirated engines are fitted with bracket-type constant-speed two-blade airscrews. The Riley TurboSkyliner was one modification of the Heron; four 290-hp Lycoming engines with turbochargers were used in place of the originals.

LOCKHEED P-38 "LIGHTNING"
1939–45

STANDARD DATA: Seat 1. Gross wt. 21,600. Empty wt. 12,780. Engines two 1,425-hp Allisons. PERFOR-

MANCE: Top mph 414. Cruise mph 285. Range 460. Ceiling 35,000.

The P-38 Lightning was the first completely military air craft built by the Lockheed Aircraft Corp. It was produced in no less than 12 versions differing from each other by engine size, use, and armament. The most numerous model was the P-38L powered by the same 1,425-hp engine as the P-38H, but with improved performance ratings. When needed, the engine could produce a "war emergency" 1,600 hp. A bulletproof window was installed, the radiators in the twin tailbooms were increased in capacity, and fuel tanks were placed in the leading-wing edges. The Lightning's armament included one 20mm cannon and four .50-caliber machine guns in the nose along with racks to carry up to 1,600 pounds of bombs.

The P-38 was used as a single-seat fighter, a light bomber, a rocket carrier, and a photographic/reconnaissance plane. It utilized a unique fuel system with separate fuel tanks for each engine. Each tank was divided into three cells, all self-sealing. Two main tanks were in the center fuselage and one tank was in each leading wing edge. The entire system was interconnected so that fuel from any tank, except the outer wing tanks, could be routed to either engine.

LOCKHEED MODEL 10 "ELECTRA"/ MODEL 18 "LODESTAR"

STANDARD DATA: Seats 8-14. Gross wt. 24,000. Empty wt. (avg.) 15,000. Power two 1,200-hp Wright Whirlwind or 2,000-hp Pratt & Whitney Wasp engines. PERFORMANCE: Top mph 321. Cruise mph 280. Initial climb rate 1,494, Range 2,800. Ceiling 22,950.

In the 1930s and 1940s, Lockheed built a series of twins that still remain active in the general aviation fleet. Approximately 20 Model 10 Electras and 30 small

Model 12s remain registered in the United States, but several hundred of the big Model 18 Lodestars remain, many of which have been extensively modernized. Both of the smaller ships used Wasp Juniors; late models standardizing on the 450-hp version. The Electra carried 10 passengers, and the Model 12 carried six passengers, the latter being considerably faster with a 225-mph top speed and 202-mph cruise. The Lodestar and its derivatives were highly successful commercial carriers and served as the basis of the Hudson series of World War II lightweight bombers and the Model 37 Ventura patrol bombers. More than 100 converted Venturas also appear on the U.S. civil register. The Lodestar used 1,200-hp Pratt & Whitney Double Wasps.

A model 10E Lockheed Electra vanished along with Amelia Earhart and Fred Noonan in 1937.

LOCKHEED MODEL 12 "ELECTRA JR."
1936

STANDARD DATA: Seats 8. Gross wt. 8,650. Empty wt. 6,090. Fuel capacity 200. Engines two 420-hp Wright Whirlwinds. PERFORMANCE: Top mph 217. Cruise mph 220. Stall mph 65. Initial climb rate 1,460. Ceiling 21,300. Range 784.

Housing a crew of two and six passengers, the Model 12 was designed as a lighter, smaller version of the Model 10 Electra. It was first introduced in 1936 with a choice of two powerplants: twin 400-hp Wasp Juniors or twin 420-hp Wright Whirlwinds. The largest engine installed in later years was the 450-hp Pratt & Whitney Wasp Junior; this version of the lightweight Lockheed survives in the greatest numbers. In 1936, the Model 12 had the distinction of being the fastest airplane in its class (commercial twin) produced in the United States. The Model 212-A was a military version fitted with a dorsal gun turret and supplied to several foreign countries, including the Netherlands East Indies.

LOCKHEED "CONSTELLATION"
1943–58

STANDARD DATA: Seats 94. Gross wt. 133,000. Empty wt. 73,016. Fuel capacity 6,550. Engines four 3,250-hp Wright Turbo Compound radials. PERFORMANCE: Top mph 352. Cruise mph 331. Stall

mph 99. Initial climb rate 1,140. Range 4,820. Ceiling 23,000. Takeoff distance (50') 4,600. Landing distance (50') 3,550.

The Lockheed Constellation L.749 variation was a long-range version of the earlier L.049. The earliest Constellation was initially flown in January 1943. Designed for commercial transport, the first Constellations were produced for the U.S. Air Force as C-29s. The first Constellation placed in airline service was the L.749 series. This aircraft differed from earlier versions in its increased fuel capacity and takeoff weight. The L.749 provided for 44 to 64 passengers and was powered by four 2,500-hp Wright Cyclone 18-cylinder air-cooled engines.

A stretched version of the L.749, the L.1049 Super Constellation, was introduced in 1950. Gross weight was increased substantially when the fuselage was expanded by 18.4 feet and 3,250-hp Wright engines were fitted. The stretched "Connie" held up to 91 passengers; with tip tanks, range was increased to 5,840 miles. The L.1049C model had structural modifications to allow a gross weight of 150,000 pounds, provided that more powerful engines were available. Lockheed built 286 Super "Connies," then followed with production of the L.1619 Starliner, the ultimate in Constellation design. With a range of 7,200 miles, the Starliner became popular on long international routes for TWA and Air France. Only 43 Starliner Constellations were built, and most of those were short lived, bowing out gracefully for the introduction of the jet age. A historical note about the Connie's heritage: the tri-tailed airliner was the first Air Force One.

LOCKHEED L.188 "ELECTRA"
1958–63

STANDARD DATA: Seats 74-98. Gross wt. 116,000. Empty wt. 57,300. Fuel capacity 5,520. Engines four 3,750-shp Allison turboprops. PERFORMANCE: Top mph 448. Cruise mph 405. Stall mph 107. Initial climb rate 1,970. Range 2,770. Ceiling 28,400. Takeoff run 4,720. Landing roll 4,300.

Electras were produced in two versions, the L.188 and the L.188C. The L.188C was fitted with new tanks for increased fuel capacity and longer range. Initially developed according to specifications ordered by American Airlines to meet its need for a medium-range airliner, the Electra first took to the air in 1957. Most were equipped to carry about 74 passengers, but 98 could be packed in if necessary. Several crashes occurred in 1959 that caused Lockheed Corp. to make a few improvements including a stronger wing structure and engine nacelles plus thicker wing skins. The Electra is still used by many airlines around the world on their shorter routes.

MARTIN M-130, 156
1936

STANDARD DATA: (M-156) Seats 46. Gross wt. 63,000. Empty wt. 30,414. Engines four 1,000-hp Wright Cyclones. PERFORMANCE: Top mph 190. Cruise mph 156. Takeoff mph 70. Range 2,410. Ceiling 15,500.

The first aircraft to span the Pacific Ocean in scheduled commercial operations was the Martin 130 flying boat. It became famous in 1936 as the "China Clipper" when it was used to open Trans-Pacific service by Pan American World Airways. The giant Martin Clipper carried 10 passengers on overseas flights with a range of 3,200 miles. On shorter routes, its capacity was 48 passengers. The M-130 had a cruising speed of 163 mph, weighed 53,000 pounds when fully loaded, and a wingspan of 130 feet. The Model 156, a later development, was built for Pan American Airways. Lateral buoyancy was provided by seawings rather than conventional sponsons or outboard floats. Interior furnishings provided for either a maximum of 46 passengers or a more luxurious arrangement allowing for night sleeping for a reduced number of passengers. Four 1,000-hp nine-cylinder radial engines were mounted in nacelles on the leading edge of the center section.

MARTIN 202
1946–50

STANDARD DATA: Martin 202 Seats 40. Gross wt. 39,900. Empty wt. 26,930. Engines two 2,100-hp Pratt & Whitney. PERFORMANCE: Top mph 311. Cruise mph 286. Stall mph 76. Initial climb rate 2,200. Range 635. Ceiling 33,000. Takeoff distance (50') 1,565. Landing distance (50') 1,720.

STANDARD DATA: Martin 404 Seats 52. Gross wt. 44,900. Engines four 2,400-hp Pratt & Whitney R-2800. PERFORMANCE: Top Cruise 312 mph.

The prototype of the Martin 22 flew in 1946. Power was provided by twin Pratt & Whitney 18-cylinder air-cooled radial engines capable of developing a normal output of 1,800 hp, 2,100 hp for takeoff or 2,400 hp with water injection. The engines turned Hamilton Standard three-blade reversible-pitch airscrews. The "Two-O-Two" was the first twin-engine airliner of postwar design to receive certification for airline use. Accommodations provided for a crew of three or four plus 36 to 40 passengers. Another version of the 202 was outfitted with larger fuel tanks to increase its range to 2,365. The subsequent 4-0-4 was introduced in 1950 with a fuselage 39 inches longer, slightly more powerful engines, and pressurization.

As the name implies, Martin's 404 was a bigger and better version of the popular Martin 202. The four-engine airliner was unveiled in 1949 and immediately ordered by a variety of air carriers. The onset of the Korean War suddenly made airplane materials significantly more expensive, and Martin found itself filling orders at a loss and stopped production.

MITSUBISHI MU-2
1967–85

STANDARD DATA: (MU-2L) Seats 6-14. Gross wt. 11,575. Empty wt. 6,975. Fuel capacity 366. Engines two 715-shp AiResearch turboprops. PERFORMANCE: Cruise mph 340. Stall mph 115. Initial climb rate 2,630. Ceiling 29,600. Range 1,450. Takeoff distance (50') 2,170. Landing distance (50') 1,880.

Mitsubishi Solitaire

Mitsubishi Marquise

STANDARD DATA: (MU-2M) Seats 7-11. Gross wt. 10,470. Empty wt. 6,090. Fuel capacity 366. Engines two 724-shp AiResearch turboprops. PERFORMANCE: Cruise mph 365. Stall mph 112. Initial climb rate 2,840. Ceiling 32,200. Range 1,680. Takeoff distance (50') 1,800. Landing distance (50') 1,600.

STANDARD DATA: (Solitaire) Seats 8-9. Gross wt. 10,470. Empty wt. 7,010. Fuel capacity 403. Engines two 727-shp AiResearch turboprops. PERFORMANCE: Top mph 370. Cruise mph 360. Stall mph 84. Initial climb rate 2,350. Ceiling 33,500. Range 1,840. Takeoff distance (50') 1,800. Landing distance (50') 1,950.

STANDARD DATA: (Marquise) Seats 9-11. Gross wt. 11,575. Empty wt. 7,650. Fuel capacity 403. Engines two 778-shp AiResearch turboprops. PERFORMANCE: Top mph 355. Cruise mph 340. Stall mph 87. Initial climb rate 2,200. Ceiling 29,750. Range 1,600. Takeoff distance (50') 2,170. Landing distance (50') 2,200.

The Mitsubishi MU-2 is a high-performance turboprop with an extraordinary top speed of 370 mph. It can cruise at an exceptional 360 mph. Much of this outstanding performance apparently is the result of rather compact overall dimensions for a turboprop twin. Before the earlier versions of the MU-2 had established a substantial penetration of the United States market, certain features of the aircraft were modified to make it more suitable and competitive. The Japanese manufacturer, Mitsubishi, made highly successful aircraft of its own design and of the designs of United States plane makers. The MU-2 is unusual in that it is one of the few high-wing turboprops.

Models B and D were powered by 605 shp and seated 7-9 passengers. The Model F represented a boost in power to 705 shp, and the Model G featured increased seating capacity for up to 11 people. In 1972, Models J and K were added to the line, both utilizing 724-shp turboprops and offering seating arrangements that corresponded to Models F and G, respectively. The MU-2L is powered by 776-shp Garrett AiResearch turboprops and carries nine passengers. Its counterpart, the MU-2M, is a continuation of the Model K. The MU-2L and MU-2M were discontinued in 1976 and replaced by the MU2N and MU-2P, which evolved into the Solitaire (standard fuselage) and Marquise (stretched fuselage), respectively.

The Solitaire is powered by two turboprops producing 727 shp at maximum continuous power or 689 shp at recommended cruise power of 96% RPM. Each engine turns a Hartzell 98-inch four-blade prop and provides a 475-fpm single-engine rate of climb when loaded to full gross. With a cabin pressurization differential of 6.0 psi, a sea-level cabin can be maintained up to 14,000. The Marquise, which is 6 feet 2 inches longer, is powered by two turboprops, each producing 778-shp for takeoff or maximum continuous operation and 738 shp at recommended cruise power. Single-engine rate-of-climb is 410 fpm at full gross, and cabin pressurization differential is the same as the Solitaire.

NORTH AMERICAN B-25 "MITCHELL"
1942

STANDARD DATA: Crew 6. Gross wt. 33,500. Empty wt. 21,100. Engines two 1,708-hp Wright Cyclones. PERFORMANCE: Top mph 303. Cruise mph 230. Landing mph 95. Initial climb rate 1,110. Range 1,350. Ceiling 24,200.

The prototype of the B-25 was flown for the first time in 1940. It and the first few B-25s off the production line had wings with a constant dihedral from the fuselage to the tips. Only after the 10th one were the wings redesigned with the characteristic gull configu-

ration. Its armament included four .30-caliber machine guns, one in the nose and three amidships, and a single .50-caliber gun in the tail. The usual bomb load was 2,000 pounds with a maximum overload of 3,600 pounds. Several models of the B-25 were produced in subsequent years. The B-25A was fitted with self-sealing fuel tanks and armor for the pilot. The B replaced the midship and tailguns with electrically operated turrets. Each turret had two .50-caliber machine guns. The lower turret was remote-controlled.

The C and D were provided with automatic flight control equipment. The E and F were fitted with experimental deicing equipment. The G was the first model to carry a 70mm cannon. The H increased its armament to four .50-caliber guns in an armored nose and two pairs of.50-caliber guns on each side of the fuselage. The B-25J was produced in the largest numbers. It was the precision bomber version of the H; the crew increased to six to include a bombardier.

PARTENAVIA "P-68"
1974−Present

Partenavia P-68B

Partenavia P-68TC

STANDARD DATA: P-68B Seats 7. Gross wt. 4,321. Empty wt. 2,645. Engines two 200-hp Lycoming IO-360-A1B. PERFORMANCE: Max Speed 174 kts. Max Cruise 165 kts. Initial climb rate 1,160 fpm. Range 920 nm. Ceiling 20,000'.

STANDARD DATA: P-68TC Seats 7. Gross wt. 4,387. Empty wt. 2,866. Fuel capacity 137-196. Engines two 210-hp turbocharged Lycoming IO-360C-1A6D. PERFORMANCE: Max Speed 190 kts. Max Cruise 175 kts. Initial climb rate 1,130. Range 1,040 nm. Ceiling 27,000.

Partenavia built the P-68 as a multi-role utility airplane. Despite its fixed gear, the big-bodied twin compared favorably to many conventional aircraft with retractable gear. A retractable gear version was developed but provided so little improvement over the rock-solid workhorse that it never went into production. In 1980, turbocharging was added for a slight increase in speed and a significant boost in service ceiling. The P68 also comes in a clear-nose "observer" option for increased forward/down visibility.

PIAGGIO AERO P.180 AVANTI
1990–Present

STANDARD DATA: P.180 Avanti Seats 7-11. Gross wt. 11,550. Empty wt. 7,500. Engines two 850-shp Pratt & Whitney PT6A 66. PERFORMANCE: Max Speed 395 kts. Max Cruise 348 kts. Initial climb rate 2,950 fpm. Range 1,400 nm. Ceiling 41,000'.

The Piaggio Avanti began as a collaboration between the Italian company and Gates Learjet in 1981, but by 1986 was all Italian. The first prototype flew in 1986 and deliveries began in late 1990 certified for single pilot operation. The forward canard allowed the Avanti's wing to be positioned at the rear of the fuselage, allowing maximum cabin space for six passengers. The empennage, engine nacelles, outboard wing flaps, gear doors and canard are carbon composite construction.

PILATUS BRITTEN-NORMAN "ISLANDER"
1967–Present

STANDARD DATA: (Islander) Seats 10. Gross wt. 6,600. Empty wt. 3,738. Fuel capacity 137-196. Engines two 300-hp Lycomings. PERFORMANCE: Top mph 180. Cruise mph 164. Stall mph 49. Initial climb rate 1,130. Range 900. Ceiling 18,000. Takeoff distance (50') 1,100. Landing distance (50') 1,170.

STANDARD DATA: (Trislander) Seats 18. Gross wt. 10,000. Empty wt. 5,843. Fuel capacity 197. Engines three 260-hp Lycomings. PERFORMANCE: Top mph 180. Cruise mph 166. Initial climb rate 980. Ceiling 13,150. Takeoff distance (50') 1,950. Landing distance (50') 1,445.

The Britten-Norman Islander is a popular, fixed-gear twin for commuter/feeder work. With accommodations for up to nine passengers plus a pilot, the Islander can also be operated as a freighter carrying more than a ton of cargo. The high-wing twin has three forward opening doors, two on the port side and one on the starboard. Passenger baggage is stored in a large 30 cu.ft. bin behind the cabin with an access door on the port side. Delivery of the Islander began in August 1967, but the great number of orders from over 50 countries forced Britten-Norman to subcontract manufacture of a number of the mini-airliners to the British Hovercraft Corporation. Others were produced in Romania by IRMA. Buyers were able to choose Lycoming engines: 260 or 300 hp. A Rajay turbocharging unit increased the Islander's twin-engine ceiling to 26,000.

A choice of wings was offered, so the plane could be fitted with the standard 49-foot-span wings or extended 53-foot wings, using raked tips and auxiliary fuel tanks. In 1970, Britten-Norman introduced an enlarged version of the twin-engine Islander with a third engine mounted high on the tail in a tractor position. The three engines were 260-hp 0-540-E4C flat-sixes turning Hartzell two-blade constant-speed fully feathering propellers. Three versions of the Trislander are the BN-2A Mk 111-2 (a standard version with extended nose baggage compartment), the BN-2A Mk 111-3 (with an automatic feathering system for the props), and the BN-2A Mk 111-4 (with a rocket engine for additional thrust if an engine fails on takeoff). In 1978, Pilatus Aircraft Ltd. of Switzerland acquired all the assets of Britten-Norman Ltd., including the facilities on the Isle of Wright. BN-2B-20 and BN-2B-26 remain in production. The turboprop (Allison 250) powered BN-2T has been built since 1981.

In July 1998 it was renamed back to Britten-Norman, and from April 2000 it became B-N Group.

PIPER "APACHE"
1954–66

STANDARD DATA: (160 hp). Seats 4-5. Gross wt. 3,800. Empty wt. 2,280. Fuel capacity 72-108. Engines two 160-hp Lycomings. PERFORMANCE: Top mph 183. Cruise mph 173. Stall mph 61. Initial climb rate 1,260. Range 1,260. Ceiling 17,000. Takeoff run 1,190. Landing roll 750.

STANDARD DATA: (235 hp). Seats 4-5. Gross wt. 4,000. Empty wt. 2,735. Fuel capacity 144. Engines 235-hp Lycomings. PERFORMANCE: Top mph 202. Cruise mph 191. Stall mph 62. Initial climb rate 1,450. Range 980. Ceiling 17,200. Takeoff run 830. Landing roll 880.

The Piper Apache is generally credited as being the first successful light twin. While Apaches are no longer in production, they were made in such great numbers that the supply is plentiful, and they should be plentiful for many years to come.

It all began in 1952 with the introduction of the Twin-Stinson, the first Piper of Stinson lineage to be produced since the Piper/Stinson Flying Station Wagon. It was powered by twin 125-hp Lycoming engines. The following year Piper introduced the PA-23 Apache, a vast improvement on the Twin-Stinson concept.

The Apache featured a conventional single rudder tail unit rather than the Twin-Stinson's twin-tail configuration, and power was boosted with the use of 150-hp Lycomings. The new Piper also utilized all-metal construction and retractable landing gear. In 1958, 160-hp engines were added, and in 1963, the 235-hp Lycoming became the standard powerplant to meet requirements for better single-engine performance. This later model was the first to sport swept tail surfaces and was quite similar to the Aztec of the same vintage, except for the Apache's smaller engines and shorter nose.

The Apache became the "basic bread-and-butter" light twin for trainer use; quite a few have been modified with higher performance engines or other improvements. Not only are Apaches inexpensive to purchase, but operating costs are low.

PIPER PA-30/39 "TWIN COMANCHE"
1963–72

STANDARD DATA: Seats 4. Gross wt. 3,725. Empty wt. 2,210. Fuel capacity 30. Engines two 160-hp Lycomings. PERFORMANCE: Top mph 205. Cruise mph 194. Stall mph 69. Initial climb rate 1,460. Range 948. Ceiling 18,600. Takeoff run 950. Landing roll 700.

The Twin Comanche was a derivative of the single-engine Comanche and was introduced in 1963 as a replacement for the Apache H. Little was done to the original Comanche fuselage when it was adapted for use in the Twin Comanche in order to simplify tooling and assembly operations. The PA-30 was offered in four models: Standard, Custom, Sportsman, and Turbo. The latter differed in engine power, and the rest contained different interior appointments, electronics, and instrumentation. Piper announced the end of PA-30 production in 1970 and introduced a new PA-39 line. The new Twin Comanche was fitted with counter-rotating props to simplify engine-out procedures. A starboard engine that was a mirror image of the port engine equalized the single-engine performance of both powerplants. Piper also claimed improved flight characteristics due to a balanced airflow over each wing.

PIPER PA-44 "SEMINOLE"/ "TURBO SEMINOLE"
1978–Present

STANDARD DATA: Seats 4. Gross wt. 3,800. Empty wt. 2,354. Fuel capacity 110. Engines two 180-hp Lycomings. PERFORMANCE: Top mph 193. Cruise mph 191. Stall mph 63. Initial climb rate 1,340. Ceiling 17,100. Range 898. Takeoff distance (50') 1,400. Landing distance (50') 1,190.

STANDARD DATA: (Turbo) Seats 4. Gross wt. 3,925. Empty wt. 2,430. Fuel capacity 110. Engines two 180-hp turbocharged Lycomings. PERFORMANCE: Top mph 224. Cruise mph 211. Stall mph 64. Initial climb rate 1,290. Ceiling 20,000+. Range 903. Takeoff distance (50') 1,500. Landing distance (50') 1,190.

In the light-twin field, Piper has always dominated the industry with the Apache, Twin Comanche, and Senecas. While the Seminole was more than a simple homogenization of existing Piper components, it did borrow most of its fuselage from the Arrow III, from what would be the forward firewall to the aft cabin bulkhead. The T-tail was actually developed on the Seminole first, but introduced on the Lance II. The wings are basically beefed-up versions of the semi-tapered Arrow III to within four feet of the tip. Like the Seneca II and the Navajo C/R, the Seminole uses counter-rotating propellers for balanced thrust, and optional three-blade propellers in 1979 provided a quieter ride. Also in the same year, a propeller synchrophaser further reduced cabin noise levels.

Two 54-gallon fuel tanks are fitted in the engine nacelles. At 75% power and 7,000 feet, the Seminole cruises at 191 mph. When leaned to 65%, best-economy power cruise speed is 181 mph, and range is 898 miles with a 45-minute reserve. At 3,800 pounds gross, the Seminole weighs the same as Gulfstream American's Cougar, which flies between a pair of 160-hp engines; thus, each Seminole horsepower must heft only 10.6 pounds compared to the Cougar's 11.9 pounds/hp loading. From the beginning, Piper intended the Seminole as a relatively inexpensive alternative to high-performance singles.

In the middle of 1980, Piper introduced a turbocharged version of the Seminole powered by twin Lycoming TO-360 counter-rotating engines. At 65-percent power economy cruise, the Turbo Seminole can travel at 194 mph over a distance of 920 miles burning fuel at a rate of 19 gph. Standard equipment includes a built-in oxygen system that consists of a rear-mounted bottle with easy-to-reach overhead outlets, night-lighted

pressure gauge, oxygen masks, and a control-wheel mike button.

Piper's financial troubles brought Seminole production to an end in 1990. Five years later, New Piper Aircraft resumed making the entry-level twin, the only remaining T-tail aircraft in the line.

PIPER SENECA /II/III/IV/V
1972–Present

Seneca II

Seneca V

STANDARD DATA: Seneca II Seats 6. Gross wt. 4,570. Empty wt. 2,839. Fuel capacity 98-128. Engines two 200-hp turbocharged counter-rotating Continentals. PERFORMANCE: Top mph 226. Cruise mph 219. Stall mph 70. Initial climb rate 1,340. Ceiling 25,000. Range 627-903. Takeoff distance (50') 1,240. Landing distance (50') 1,860.

STANDARD DATA: Seneca V Seats 5-6. Gross wt. 4,570. Empty wt. 3,413. Fuel capacity 122. Engines two 220-hp turbocharged Continental TSIO-360-RB. PERFORMANCE: Top Cruise 197 kts. Stall 61 kts. Initial climb rate 1,550 fpm. Ceiling 25,000. Range 730-820 nm. Takeoff distance (50') 1,707. Landing distance (50') 2,180'.

The Piper Seneca was first produced in 1972 and was sold alongside the Twin Comanche until 1973 when the latter was discontinued. More Senecas are powered by twin Teledyne Continental counter-rotating engines with full-time turbocharging. The engines are rated at

200 hp at sea level and develop 215 hp at 12,000 feet, which allows for a 75-percent cruise speed of 218 mph. With the extended-range tanks, it's possible to travel 900 miles and arrive with a 45-minute fuel reserve. At economy power it's possible for the Seneca to get 55 seat miles per gallon with a load of six. Full-time turbocharging helps increase the Seneca's gross weight and climb performance. With turbocharging, power output is actually increased as the airplane gains altitude. Piper did away with the costly hydraulic wastegate system often found on other turbochargers and uses a low-cost fixed-bypass instead.

The ailerons were also lengthened to improve handling and slow-speed characteristics. A large utility door was located aft of the rear passenger door. The Seneca III added positive slow-speed characteristics. A new bobweight in the stabilator control system has heightened dynamic stability and reduced downspring forces. In the rudder, an antiservo tab helps increase directional stability and rudder effectiveness. The ailerons are long and aerodynamically balanced. Senecas also offered conference seating in a wide-ride cabin, measuring four feet in width. Five standard and four optional interior packages were available with several new aerodynamic speed enhancers.

Major additions in 1979 included optional three-blade propellers and a propeller synchrophaser. The three-blade props reduced cabin noise and vibration. The synchrophaser electronically seeks and maintains synchronization of the propellers to further reduce cabin noise levels. The Seneca II and III are certified for flight into known icing conditions when equipped with the appropriate optional deice package, which was available for both two- and three-blade models. A heavy-duty brake option reduced landing distance over a 50-foot obstacle from a standard 2,110 feet to 1,860 feet.

The Seneca III was replaced by the IV in 1994, when New Piper added some aerodynamic refinements (including axisymmetric engine inlets in the cowlings) and some upgrades to the interior. In 1997, the Seneca V was introduced with its turbocharged, intercooled L/TSIO-360-RB engines. The turbos allowed the Seneca to produce its rated power all the way up to 19,500'. In an effort to make the Seneca V more marketable as both personal and corporate transportation, New Piper replaced a seat with a workstation/entertainment center with an optional phone/fax.

PIPER AZTEC
1960–81

STANDARD DATA: (Aztec) Seats 6. Gross wt. 5,200. Empty wt. 3,183. Fuel capacity 137-177. Engines two 250-hp Lycomings. PERFORMANCE: Top mph 216. Cruise mph 206. Stall mph 62. Initial climb rate 1,400. Range 909-1,219. Ceiling 17,600. Take-

off distance (50') 1,980. Landing distance (50') 1,585.

STANDARD DATA: (Turbo) Seats 6. Gross wt. 5,200. Empty wt. 3,322. Fuel capacity 137-177. Engines two 250-hp turbocharged Lycomings. PERFORMANCE: Top mph 256. Cruise mph 247. Stall mph 62. Initial climb rate 1,470. Ceiling 24,000. Range 800-1,090. Takeoff distance (50') 1,980: Landing distance (50') 1,585.

The Piper Aztec grew from the Piper Apache design, and the two aircraft share the same model numerical designation of PA-23 established during the original Apache certification. The earliest versions of the Aztec differed only slightly in appearance from the Apache, although early Aztecs featured higher performance obtained from 150-hp engines. In 1964, these differences became greater with the Aztec C featuring fuel injection, a new configuration, and improved landing gear. The 1966 Aztec C was also the first model to offer turbocharging as an option.

The Aztec F is equipped with flap-to-stabilator trim interconnect to automatically retrim to neutral pitch-control pressures when the flaps are extended or retracted. Also, improved slow-flight characteristics give a more positive climb/approach control. The Aztec probably ranks as one of the most docile of the conventional low-wing light twins. While its maximum and cruise speeds compare favorably with the swiftest competitor, the short, thick wing permits slow and safe airspeeds. This means excellent short-field capabilities for critical situations. Both Aztecs can clear the equivalent of a five-story building in just 1,700 feet from brake release. The normally aspirated Aztec's 75-percent best-power cruise is 206 mph with a range of 1,134 miles and 45-minute reserve. Optional tanks stretch that range to 1,519 miles. The Turbo model has a cruise speed of 242 mph at 22,000 feet, 961 miles with standard fuel, or 1,318 miles with optional fuel.

PIPER AEROSTAR 600/601/700P
1969–84

STANDARD DATA: (600A) Seats 6. Gross wt. 5,500. Empty wt. 3,735. Fuel capacity 165. Engines two 290-hp Lycomings. PERFORMANCE: Top mph 260.

Piper Aerostar 600A

Piper Aerostar 601B

Piper Aerostar 700P

Cruise mph 253. Stall mph 85. Initial climb rate 1,800. Range 1,131. Ceiling 21,200. Takeoff distance (50') 1,950. Landing distance (50') 1,840.

STANDARD DATA: (601B) Seats 6. Gross wt. 6,000. Empty wt. 3,958. Fuel capacity 165. Engines two 290-hp turbo-charged Lycomings. PERFORMANCE: Top mph 302. Cruise mph 296. Stall mph 89. Initial climb rate 1,460. Ceiling 30,000. Range 1,178. Takeoff distance (50') 2,490. Landing distance (50') 2,030.

STANDARD DATA: (601P) Seats 6. Gross wt. 6,000. Empty wt. 4,056. Fuel capacity 165. Engines two 290-hp Lycomings. PERFORMANCE: Top Cruise 257 kts. Stall 77 kts. Initial climb rate 1,460. Ceiling 26,350. Range 1,178. Takeoff distance (50') 2,490. Landing distance (50') 2,030'.

STANDARD DATA: (700 P) Seats 6. Gross wt. 6,315. Empty wt. 4,275. Fuel capacity 165-210. Engines two 350-hp Lycoming TIO-540-U2A. PERFORMANCE: Top Cruise 264 kts. Stall 80 kts. Initial climb rate 1,820 fpm. Ceiling 25,000. Range 868 nm (w/o optional fuel). Takeoff distance (50') 3,080'. Landing distance (50') 2,100'.

The Aerostar is another outstanding design by Ted Smith. Originally built by the Ted Smith Aircraft Co. (a subsidiary of the American Cement Corp.), production began in 1967 on a limited basis. In 1969, the assets of the company were purchased by Butler Aviation International, which also acquired Mooney Aircraft Corp. one year later. The Aerostars built under this management were referred to as Aerostar Mooneys, but the project was soon suspended. In 1972 Ted R. Smith and Associates Inc. was formed, and production of the Aerostar executive transport resumed.

The Model 600 is powered by two 290-hp six-cylinder normally aspirated engines. Its basic structure consists of innovations to reduce weight and improve strength. The airframe contains only half as many components as that of many other comparable aircraft. Also, the Aerostar components are interchangeable with those of other sister ships. The Model 601 is the turbocharged version, and the 601P features pressurization. A slightly larger and more powerful development is designated the Aerostar 700 and is powered by two 350-hp Lycomings. Its speed is increased to 275 mph at sea level and its gross weight is boosted to 6,300 pounds. The latest 601B features wings extended 15 inches on each side to result in an increased gross weight, which has, in turn, boosted useful load by about 270 pounds.

Piper took over production of the Aerostars in 1979. The fastest Aerostar also has the distinction of being the fastest six-place general aviation piston twin in the world: the 601B. All three Piper Aerostars can attribute their performance to a sleek aerodynamically advanced design that features a radically aft-swept horizontal stabilizer, reduced and swept vertical stabilizer, mid-fuselage wings with trailing-edge taper, and an elongated pointed nose. Purchasing the Aerostars was a quick way for Piper to expand its twin lineup and fill the gap between the 250-hp Aztec and the 310- to 425-hp Navajos. For 1981, the Aerostar 601B and 601P were approved for flight into icing conditions to enhance their usefulness to corporate, commuter, and air-taxi operations.

The final version of the Aerostar, the model 700P, added more powerful engines, 350-hp turbocharged and counter rotating TIO540U2As, and an option for additional fuel. The 700P also had a higher takeoff weight. Only 25 of what many consider the best of the Aerostars were ever produced before Piper took the twin out of production.

PIPER PA-31 "NAVAJO"
1967–84

STANDARD DATA: (C) Seats 5-8. Gross wt. 6,500. Empty wt. 4,003. Fuel capacity 187. Engines two 310-hp turbocharged Lycomings. PERFORMANCE: Top mph 261. Cruise mph 248. Stall mph 81. Initial climb rate 1,220. Range 1,125. Ceiling 24,000. Takeoff distance (50') 2,290. Landing distance (50') 1,818.

STANDARD DATA: (CR) Seats 5-8. Gross wt. 6,500. Empty wt. 4,099. Fuel capacity 183-237. Engines two 325-hp turbocharged Lycomings, counterrotating. PERFORMANCE: Top mph 265. Cruise mph 253. Stall mph 80. Initial climb rate 1,220. Range 1,082-1,485. Ceiling 24,000+. Takeoff distance (50') 2,440. Landing distance (50') 1,818.

STANDARD DATA: (Chieftain) Seats 5-10. Gross wt. 7,000. Empty wt. 4,221. Fuel capacity 182-236. Engines two 350-hp turbocharged Lycomings, counterrotating. PERFORMANCE: Top mph 267. Cruise mph 254. Stall mph 85. Initial climb rate 1,120. Range 1,018-1,392. Ceiling 27,200. Takeoff distance (50') 2,780. Landing distance (50') 1,880.

STANDARD DATA: (Pressurized) Seats 6-8. Gross wt. 7,800. Empty wt. 4,842. Fuel capacity 192-242. Engines two 425-hp turbocharged Lycomings. PERFORMANCE: Top mph 280. Cruise mph 272. Stall mph 83. Initial climb rate 1,740. Range 995. Ceiling 29,000. Takeoff distance (50') 2,200. Landing distance (50') 2,700.

Taking to the air for the first time in 1964, the Piper Navajo was the first of a series of large executive airplanes to be produced by Piper. The Navajo is known for its excellent performance, easy-to-fly characteristics, and dependable systems. It was the first in its class

to offer factory air-conditioning and the longest cabin interior available: 16 feet. Piper's exclusive engine nacelle was designed to house an extended shaft that put the prop blades well ahead of the cowling. This allowed the blades to bite into undisturbed air for greater propulsion efficiency.

Another feature of the Navajo was Altimatic VF/D, a truly automatic flight control at an economical price. To simplify flight operations, the Navajo's full-time turbochargers have no special controls, and safety devices prevent overboost or turbine overspeeding. The early Navajos were powered by 310-hp turbocharged Lycoming engines.

At one time, the Navajo family of aircraft included four models. The Navajo C, powered by 310-hp Lycomings, has accommodations for five passengers plus pilot in a standard or executive arrangement and up to eight persons with its optional commuter interior. The Navajo CR, introduced in 1975, offers stepped-up performance during takeoff, climb, and cruise, due to the increase in power brought about by its 325-hp Lycomings. Counterrotating three-blade props neutralize torque and eliminate the "critical engine." With either engine feathered, equal rate of climb and ceiling are assured. The Pressurized Navajo is powered by twin 425-hp Lycomings and provides executive class travel for six to eight. Optional pressurization was first offered in 1970.

The Chieftain's super-stretched 18-foot cabin allows it to perform as either an executive transport or light airliner. Powered by 350-hp Lycomings, it offers seating for six in an executive configuration or up to 10 in a commuter configuration. This latter aircraft was initially introduced as simply the PA-31-350 in 1973. The Navajo line was recertified for flight into icing conditions under newer more stringent standards in 1980. The Navajo family of aircraft was eventually trimmed to three models: basic Navajo, CR, and the Chieftain. Optional nacelle tanks on the Navajo CR and Chieftain in 1981 offered 54 gallons of extra fuel capacity, increasing the range of the Chieftain by 391 miles to a maximum range of 1,485 miles and boosting the range of the Navajo CR by 432 miles for a maximum range of 1,628 miles. The system incorporates two bladder tanks with non-icing fuel vents. The fuel simply gravity-feeds into main inboard tanks.

PIPER "MOJAVE"
1983–86

STANDARD DATA: Mojave Seats 7. Gross wt. 7,200. Empty wt. 5,070. Fuel capacity 238. Engines two turbocharged and fuel injected Lycoming TIO-540-V2AD. PERFORMANCE: Top Cruise 242 kts. Stall 75 kts. Range 1,190 nm. Ceiling 26,500'. Takeoff distance (50') 3,035'. Landing distance (50') 2,305'.

Piper Cheyenne II XL

The Mojave was the swansong for the pressurized models of the PA-31, produced for only about three years. The aircraft was a transition from the pressurized Chieftain version of the popular Navajo to the Cheyenne I. The Chieftain and the Mojave gave way to the production of the Cheyenne series, Piper's most powerful twins.

PIPER PA-31T "CHEYENNE" I/II/III/XL
1975–85

Piper Cheyenne I

Piper Cheyenne III

Engines two 720-shp Pratt & Whitney turboprops. PERFORMANCE: Top mph 336. Cruise mph 332. Stall mph 96. Initial climb rate 2,300. Ceiling 32,800. Range 1,415-2,106. Takeoff distance (50') 3,100. Landing distance (50) 2,650.

STANDARD DATA: (I) Seats 6. Gross wt. 8,700. Empty wt. 4,907. Fuel capacity 300-382. Engines two 500-shp Pratt & Whitney turboprops. PERFORMANCE: Top mph 290. Stall mph 83. Initial climb rate 1,750. Ceiling 28,020. Range 1,248-1,548. Takeoff distance (50') 2,444. Landing distance (50) 2,263.

STANDARD DATA: (II) Seats 6. Gross wt. 9,000. Empty wt. 4,983. Fuel capacity 382. Engines two 620-shp Pratt & Whitney turboprops. PERFORMANCE: Top mph 325. Stall mph 86. Initial climb rate 2,710. Ceiling 31,600. Range 1,588. Takeoff distance (50') 1,980. Landing distance (50) 2,480.

STANDARD DATA: (III) Seats 6. Gross wt. 10,500. Empty wt. 5,621. Fuel capacity 392. Engines two 680-shp Pratt & Whitney turboprops. PERFORMANCE: Top mph 330. Stall mph 92. Initial climb rate 2,450. Ceiling 30,500. Range 1,973-2,071. Takeoff distance (50') 2,320. Landing distance (50') 2,610.

STANDARD DATA: (1981 III) Seats 8-11. Gross wt. 11,000. Empty wt. 6,389. Fuel capacity 390-540.

Piper's first turboprop, the Cheyenne was based upon the Navajo airframe but powered by twin Pratt & Whitney turbines flat-rated at 620-shp and certified up to 680 shp. Flat-rating these free (as opposed to fixed-shaft) turboprops has the advantage of lowering gas temperature, prolonging engine life, lowering operating costs, and simplifying operation. Inside the cabin, six can sit in the comfort of a fully air-conditioned and pressurized atmosphere. The cabin can be maintained at sea level pressure up to 12,300 feet. Further, the Cheyenne offers an extraordinary ratio between useful load and weight of the aircraft (a ratio of almost 1 to 1.2).

Piper expanded the Cheyenne line in 1978 to include three versions: the Cheyenne I, II, and III. The I and II models are powered by smaller engines than the original Cheyenne. The Model III retained the original 680-shp powerplant but was equipped with a new T-tail for improved stability by keeping the horizontal control surfaces clear of propwash. The Cheyenne III was introduced in late 1979 and was five feet longer than the Cheyenne II. The Cheyenne III is powered by twin flat-rated 720-shp Pratt & Whitney turboprops. It's the first turboprop to incorporate nacelle baggage lockers and the first to use Q-tip propellers that provide a quieter cabin and increased ground clearance.

Maximum range of the Cheyenne III is in excess of 2,300 miles, and maximum certificated altitude is 33,000 feet. A 6.3 psi differential will give the Cheyenne III a 10,000-foot cabin at 33,000 feet. Also in 1980, the Cheyenne I and 11 received a higher and 20-percent larger windshield. Headlining the 1981 changes among Piper turboprops were the addition of the Cheyenne II XL, introduced in late 1980, and extended range for the Cheyenne III. The Model II XL is a stretched version of the Model II and provides an additional two feet of cabin room for maximum passenger and pilot comfort. The Cheyenne III benefits from extended range as a result of an increase in gross takeoff weight. The increased rate allowance for Model IIIs equipped with optional nacelle tanks makes it possible to carry 30 extra gallons of fuel for a six-percent improvement in range.

PIPER PA-35 "POCONO"
1968–71

STANDARD DATA: Seats 11-18. Gross wt. 9,500. Empty wt. 4,900. Fuel capacity 200. Engines two 500-hp turbocharged Lycomings. PERFORMANCE: Top mph 242. Cruise mph 230. Stall mph 74. Initial climb rate 1,630. Range 650.

The Piper Pocono PA-35 was designed to serve as a high-capacity commuter airline, an unusually spacious executive aircraft, or a versatile cargo carrier. Its airframe incorporates a large circular hull measuring 88 inches in diameter. This large capacity hull makes it possible to install a variety of seating configurations or handle bulky cargo loads. Passenger accommodations include seating for 17 plus pilot or 14 with toilet facilities. With a gross weight of 9,000 pounds, the Pocono has a useful load of 4,100 to 4,300 pounds. Its turbocharged 470-hp engines allow it to operate at cruising speeds in the 200- to 230-mph range, depending upon altitude. The Pocono is easily identified by a fuselage shape that retains a large diameter for a substantial distance aft of the wing trailing edge. There is minimal fuselage taper toward the tail.

ROCKWELL COMMANDER "SHRIKE" (AERO COMMANDER 500)
1958–80

STANDARD DATA: (Shrike) Seats 4-7. Gross wt. 6,750. Empty wt. 4,635. Fuel capacity 156. Engines two 290-hp Lycomings. PERFORMANCE: Top mph 215. Cruise mph 203. Stall mph 68. Initial climb rate 1,340. Range 950. Ceiling 17,500. Takeoff distance (50') 1,915. Landing distance (50) 2,235.

STANDARD DATA: (500U) Seats 4-7. Gross wt. 6,750. Empty wt. 4,635. Fuel capacity 156. Engines two 290-hp Lycomings. PERFORMANCE: Top mph 230. Cruise mph 215. Stall mph 68. Initial climb rate 1,340. Range 1,230. Takeoff distance (50') 1,375. Landing distance (50') 1,235.

STANDARD DATA: (500A) Seats 5-7. Gross wt. 6,250. Empty wt. 4,255. Fuel capacity 156. Engines two 260-hp Lycomings. PERFORMANCE: Top mph 228. Cruise mph 218. Stall mph 62. Initial climb rate 1,400. Ceiling 22,500. Range 1,225. Takeoff distance (50) 1,210. Landing distance (50) 1,150.

STANDARD DATA: (500) Seats 5-7. Gross wt. 6,000. Empty wt. 3,850. Fuel capacity 156. Engines two 250-hp Lycomings. PERFORMANCE: Top mph 218. Cruise mph 205. Stall mph 63. Initial climb rate 1,400. Ceiling 22,500. Range 1,100. Takeoff distance (50') 1,250. Landing distance (50) 1,350.

The Shrike Commander is the latest version of the well-known Aero Commander 500 with an extended nose and other features that deal mainly with styling and extras. The 500 is unsurpassed in many ways and enjoys pilot respect. The profusion of controls and gauges makes the Shrike appear complicated to operate when it is actually very easy by light-twin standards. Engines can be run at full throttle without restriction. All fuel tanks are interconnected, so no tank selection or cross-feeding is required. One-engine flight is managed without any particular fuss. The cabin is spacious, and there is freedom of movement almost on a par with an airliner.

The Shrike is a big plane with a span of about 50 feet, which makes it a handful on narrow taxiways and in tie-down areas for a pilot accustomed to small aircraft. Aero Commander was eventually bought by Rockwell International. One distinguishing feature of the Rockwell Shrike is its eyebrow windows for improved cockpit visibility. This business twin was certified in the utility category partly because the landing gear was designed for use on aircraft nearly twice the Shrike's gross weight. Such steady legs make landings on unimproved airstrips easy.

ROCKWELL COMMANDER 685
1972–74

STANDARD DATA: Seats 9. Gross wt. 9,000. Empty wt. 6,021. Fuel capacity 250-322. Engines two 435-hp Continentals. PERFORMANCE: Top mph 279. Cruise mph 256. Stall mph 86. Initial climb rate 1,490. Range 976-1,284. Ceiling 27,500. Takeoff distance (50) 1,943. Landing distance (50') 2,312.

The Rockwell Commander 685 is a turbocharged high-performance piston-powered airplane designed to meet the business requirements of room and speed normally found in propjet aircraft. The seven- to nine-place 685 is powered by twin turbocharged 435-hp Continental engines with Hartzell constant-speed full-feathering three-blade props. It can cruise at speeds of 255 mph at 24,000 feet. Its cabin can be arranged in no less than 12 different ways and can maintain sea-level cabin pressure at altitudes up to 9,000 feet. The Commander's high wing, sturdy landing gear, and 75-knot stall speed allow it to operate from short unimproved strips. With 322 gallons of fuel, the 685 has a range of 1,731 miles with a 45-minute reserve. Its simple fuel system requires no crossfeeding. All fuel feeds into a central fuselage tank.

ROCKWELL TURBO COMMANDER 690A/B
1966–79

STANDARD DATA: (690B) Seats 7-10. Gross wt. 10,250. Empty wt. 6,195. Fuel capacity 389. Engines 700-shp Garrett AiResearch turboprops. PERFORMANCE: Top mph 330. Cruise mph 321. Stall mph 89. Initial climb rate 2,849. Range 1,458. Ceiling 33,000. Takeoff distance (50') 1,666. Landing distance (50') 2,084.

STANDARD DATA: (681B) Seats 8-9. Gross wt. 9,400. Empty wt. 5,647. Fuel capacity 286-337. Engines two 605-shp AiResearch turboprops. PERFORMANCE: Top mph 290. Cruise mph 278. Stall mph 94. Initial climb rate 2,007. Ceiling 25,600. Range 1,062-1,315. Takeoff distance (50') 2,016. Landing distance (50') 1,200.

STANDARD DATA: (Hawk) Seats 8-10. Gross wt. 9,400. Empty wt. 5,783. Fuel capacity 286-337. Engines two 605-shp AiResearch turboprops. PERFORMANCE: Top mph 290. Cruise mph 280. Stall mph 94. Initial climb rate 2,025. Ceiling 25,000. Range 1,094. Takeoff distance (50') 1,975. Landing distance (50') 1,200.

The Turbo Commander first appeared in 1965 as a pressurized version of the Grand Commander. Power was supplied by twin 605-shp AiResearch turboprop engines, each driving a three-blade constant-speed reversible-pitch propeller. This model became known as the Turbo Hawk and was built until 1971 when it was replaced by the Turbo Commander 681B, another pressurized version similar to the Shrike Commander. A pair of 605-shp turboprops were still used until the 690 was introduced in 1972 with 717-shp powerplants.

The Turbo Commander cabin can be pressurized to 5.2 psi. and the operational ceiling is 31,000 feet. Interior temperature is controlled by a high-volume climate system, and heated windshields provide maximum visibility in all weather conditions. The Turbo Commander is also certified for flight into known-icing conditions, and all deicing equipment is standard. While the 690A is just minutes slower that most business jets on a 900- to 1,000-mile business trip, fuel consumption is about 50% less.

The combination of reversible props, tough landing gear, high-wing, and 14-inch prop clearance are custom-tailored for short, rough landing strips. Engines that are flat-rated from 840 shp, to a nominal 700 shp help the 690A climb directly to the best cruise altitude without lengthy step climbing. The 690B was offered in the Executive I and Executive II models. Many features that are usually considered optional are standard equipment in the Executive I, including avionics and cabin accommodations. The Executive II was for owners who wanted to select their own avionics and interior appointments.

ROCKWELL COMMANDER 700
1977–80

STANDARD DATA: Seats 6. Gross wt. 6,947. Empty wt. 4,704. Fuel capacity 210. Engine two 340-hp turbocharged Lycomings. PERFORMANCE: Top mph 254. Cruise mph 244. Stall mph 79. Initial climb rate 1,578. Ceiling 25,000. Range 1,214. Take-off distance (50') 2,264. Landing distance (50') 2,154.

The pressurized 700 was designed and produced under a joint development agreement between Fuji Heavy Industries and Rockwell. The Model 700 was powered by two 340-hp Lycoming engines and was to be the first in a series of wide-bodied twin-engine aircraft to be produced by the two companies. The airframe subassemblies and major assemblies were to be manufactured by Fuji, and the aircraft were to be assembled by Rockwell using avionics, powerplants, brakes, wheels, and tires manufactured in the United States. The Rockwell 700 provides sea-level comfort up to 12,500 feet with a useful load of up to 2,283 pounds. Rockwell and Fuji Jet Industries terminated their agreement on the Commander 700 in December 1979.

ROCKWELL COMMANDER 840/980
1980–85

Commander Jetprop 840

Commander Jetprop 98W

STANDARD DATA: (840) Seats 8. Gross wt. 10,325. Empty wt. 6,120. Fuel capacity 425. Engines two 717-shp Garrett AiResearch jetprops. PERFORMANCE: Cruise mph 335. Stall mph 86. Initial climb rate 1,000. Ceiling 31,000. Range 2,047. Takeoff distance (50') 1,830. Landing distance (50') 2,050.

STANDARD DATA: (980) Seats 8. Gross wt. 10,325. Empty wt. 6,271. Fuel capacity 425. Engines two 733-shp Garrett AiResearch jetprops. PERFORMANCE: Cruise mph 364. Stall mph 86. Initial climb rate 1,010. Ceiling 31,000. Range 2,079. Takeoff distance (50') 1,830. Landing distance (50') 2,150.

In 1980, Rockwell experienced an unprecedented increase in turboprop sales led by the Jetprop 980 and Jetprop 840. The former carries up to eight persons and is powered by Garrett TPE-10501K turboprops. It is characterized by a 309 knot cruise, a 3,176-pound useful load, 5.2 psi pressurization, and enough fuel for a mission-efficient range of 2,040 nm with reserves.

The 840, powered by twin Garrett TPE-331-5-254K turboprops, boasts speeds up to 290 knots and a maximum range of 1,780 nm with reserves. Rockwell-developed high-technology sound control permits an easy conversation level in the cabins of both aircraft. Standard and custom cabin appointments permit the owner to outfit the interiors with hideaway tables, beverage servers, reclining chairs, telephones, and stereo systems.

ROCKWELL COMMANDER "JETPROP 1000"
1981

STANDARD DATA: Seats 6-10. Gross wt. 11,200. Empty Weight 7,289. Engines two 730-shp Garrett TPE3310501K. PERFORMANCE: Top Speed 308 kts. Max Cruise 256 kts. Initial climb rate 2,800 fpm. Ceiling 35,000'. Range 2,080 nm.

The 10-passenger Jetprop 1000 is the third in the series of winglet-tipped fuel-efficient models from Rockwell's General Aviation Division. This Commander represented the company's entry into the larger turboprop market because the 1000 has an 11,250-pound gross ramp weight. The 1000's 6.7 psi pressurization provides a 10,000-foot altitude cabin at flight altitudes up to an operation ceiling of 35,000 feet. In terms of fuel and mission efficiency, it is equal to Rockwell's 10,375-pound models.

Upon its announcement, the Commander 1000 was expected to cruise at 307 knots at 22,000 feet. Climb with both Garrett-AiResearch TPE 331-10 powerplants operating was supposed to exceed 2,800 fpm: single-engine climb 1,000 fpm. Range with normal reserves was predicted to be about 2,000 nm.

Rockwell claimed that the aerodynamic wing treatment, including winglets, supercritical propellers from Dowty Rotol, and new nacelle configurations, would reduce high-speed induced drag at altitude by as much as 17% over earlier models. The Model 1000's interior has separate crew, passenger, and lavatory compartments with additional space for refreshment consoles and a pressurized baggage area convenient to the passenger cabin.

SWEARINGEN MERLIN III
1969–81

STANDARD DATA: (III) Seats 8-11. Gross wt. 12,500. Empty wt. 7,400. Fuel capacity 648. Engines two 840-shp AiResearch turboprops. PERFORMANCE: Top mph 325. Cruise mph 288. Stall mph 96. Initial climb rate 2,530. Range 2,860. Ceiling 28,900. Takeoff distance (50') 2,150. Landing distance (50') 1,570.

STANDARD DATA: (IIIB) Seats 8-11. Gross wt. 12,500. Empty wt. 7,800. Fuel capacity 648. Engines two 900-shp AiResearch turboprops. PERFORMANCE: Top mph 355. Cruise mph 345. Stall mph 95. Initial climb rate 2,825. Ceiling 32,500. Range 2,790. Takeoff distance (50') 2,790. Landing distance (50') 2,874.

In 1971, a Swearingen Merlin III placed first in the 5,851-mile transatlantic and transcontinental London to Victoria (British Columbia) air race. The Merlin III is an eight to 11 seat executive transport that offers near-jet speed while consuming less than half the fuel. It also claims the longest range (2,860 miles) of any business propjet with cruising speeds up to 325 mph. The luxury interior in the Merlin is one of the most lavish of any

business airplane, and the cabin is a spacious 5 feet wide with 23 feet of usable length. Sea-level pressurization can be maintained up to 16,800 feet, and at 31,000 feet, the cabin atmosphere is still equivalent to that at 7,400. Power is provided by two AiResearch turboprops rated at 840 shp and equipped with single shafts, a negative torque sensing system, and full beta control reversing. Complete deicing gear is also provided.

Swearingen introduced the Merlin IIIB in September 1978 with new AiResearch powerplants producing 900-shp each and turning four-blade propellers equipped with synchrophasers. The IIIB has a 2,425-nm IFR range and a service ceiling of 32,500 feet. To the typical business user, this range capability permits a number of average 300- to 500-mile trips during one day without the need to refuel at out-of-the-way places. Subsequent models featured a reshaped fairing between the wing root and fuselage for better aerodynamic flow and a new horizontal stabilizer leading edge contour for more efficient trim capability.

SWEARINGEN MERLIN IVA/ "METRO II"
1971–81

STANDARD DATA: (Merlin IVA) Seats 12-15. Gross wt. 12,500. Empty wt. 8,200. Fuel capacity 554. Engines two 840-shp AiResearch turboprops. PERFORMANCE: Top mph 310. Cruise 276. Stall mph 99. Initial climb rate 2,400. Range 2,095. Ceiling 27,000. Takeoff distance (50') 2,050. Landing distance (50') 1,970.

STANDARD DATA: (Metro II) Seats 19. Gross wt. 12,500. Empty wt. 7,450. Fuel capacity 648. Engines two 940-shp AiResearch turboprops. PERFORMANCE: Top mph 294. Cruise 278. Stall mph 99. Initial climb rate 2,400. Range 2,150. Ceiling 27,000. Takeoff distance (50') 2,050. Landing distance (50') 1,970.

The Merlin IVA is an executive version of the Metro with 689 cu. ft. of pressurized cabin area and a large baggage compartment. It can carry up to 15 people in smooth over-the-weather flight with 7.0-psi pressurization. As an executive aircraft, it can be equipped with bar, galley, cabinets, and couch. Baggage capacity is 30 cu. ft. in the nose and 113 cu. ft. in the cabin. The

Metro, introduced in 1974, is a 19-passenger turbo-prop airliner designed specifically for commuter service. It combines 300-mph cruise with a roomy air-conditioned pressurized cabin. A rear cargo door and optional movable cargo bulkhead provide passenger/cargo flexibility. Power is supplied by twin 940-shp turboprops.

WING "DERRINGER"

1965/1976/1981

STANDARD DATA: Seats 2. Gross wt. 3,050. Empty wt. 2,070. Fuel capacity 88. Engines two 160-hp Lycomings. PERFORMANCE: Top mph 232. Cruise mph 219. Stall mph 72. Initial climb rate 1,700. Range 1,160. Ceiling 19,600. Takeoff distance (50') 1, 180. Landing distance (50') 2,100.

The Wing Derringer was powered by twin 160-hp engines driving Hartzell constant-speed full-feathering propellers, and was awarded FAA type certification in 1966. The Derringer made use of unique manufacturing techniques with a patented wing construction uti-

lizing a stretch-formed chemically milled exterior skin. All exterior surfaces were aerodynamically smooth. The Derringer's wings featured integral fuel tanks. After a delay of many years, it appeared as though the Derringer would reenter production in the early 1980s. The airplane's target was travelers who usually commuted in pairs. If the Model I had been a success, designer George Wing planned to add turbocharging and then possibly go to a four-place turbofan. Unfortunately, the Derringer never found its way into further production.

Jet-Engine Aircraft

ince the airplane's inception, development of lighter, smaller, and more powerful propulsion has been a major focal point. During the 1930s, jet-engine technology really began to take shape with English and German scientists leading the way. With the advent of World War II, development was kicked into high gear in an effort to gain the upper hand against the respective foe. By that time, it had been well established that the secret to winning warfare was in air power. The side that controlled the skies would be the eventual victor. Unfortunately, usable jet-engine technology evolved too late during the war to be of any consequence.

As jet-engine research gained momentum, the power that was unleashed in these compact powerplants pushed aviation and aircraft into realms that were never even dreamed of by the Wrights. Load-carrying capabilities have jumped to staggering levels and have effectively shrunk the size of our planet by making travel to faraway places commonplace.

While the final chapter is far from being written, there is little doubt that jet propulsion will become increasingly more important. Breakthroughs in size, weight, and thrust in the last decade alone have been remarkable, and a continuing advance of newer jet-engine technologies is all but certain. Jet engines are now small enough and reliable enough to have begun a migration from military, commercial carriers and business aircraft to the smaller and more robust general aviation fleet. There will no doubt be a place for the piston engine for years to come; but the more than ever before, turbojet power is pushing its way to the forefront of aviation.

AEROSPATIALE SE 210 "CARAVELLE-12"

1959–81

STANDARD DATA: Seats 104-140. Gross wt. 127,870. Empty wt. 70,100. Fuel capacity 5,808. Engines two 14,500-lb. s.t. Pratt & Whitney turbofans. PERFORMANCE: Top cruise mph 505. Range 2,367. Takeoff run 8,070. Landing roll 4,985.

As one of the first jet airliners, the French-built twinjet Caravelle has provided short- to medium-range service to more than 30 airlines since 1959. The first Model I Caravelles carry 61-80 passengers. Nine models later, the last produced, the Caravelle 12 carries 104-140 passengers and is almost 14 feet longer than the original design. Turbojet and turbofan powerplants have been provided by Rolls-Royce, General Electric, and Pratt & Whitney. Thrust increased from approximately 10,600 pounds to 14,500 pounds. As the Caravelle's capacities increased, not only was there the usual increase in fuselage strength and wing and tail surface areas, but the windshield area also expanded for greater cockpit visibility. An auxiliary power unit (APU) was added to provide for self-contained air-conditioning and other power needs while on the ground. Many Caravelles were equipped with the Aerospatiale/Lear-Seigler all-weather landing system.

AEROSPATIALE/BRITISH AEROSPACE "CONCORDE"

1969–2003

STANDARD DATA: Seats 128-144. Gross wt. 385,000. Empty wt. 169,000. Fuel capacity 30,985. Engines four 38,050-lb. s.t. Olympus 593 turbojets. PERFORMANCE: Top cruise mph 1,450. Initial climb rate 5,000. Range 4,500 nm. Ceiling 60,000.

As a joint venture between the French company Aerospatiale and British Aircraft Corporation, the Concorde Super Sonic Transport (SST) took the lead in sales orders over its rival, the Russian TU-144. With costs, responsibility, and work on the Concorde divided fairly between the two partners, deliveries of the four-engine airliner started in 1974. Production finally got underway after extensive testing on prototypes over the first four years of development.

With the very look of speed, the shark-nosed giant was designed to cruise at Mach 2.05 for a maximum range of 4,020 miles. Accommodation for 100 economy-class passengers was available, although most airlines reduced seating and included a first-class section.

Construction of the Concorde prototypes began in 1965 with the first flight on March 2, 1969. Aerospatiale was responsible for the following Concorde items: rear cabin section, wings and wing control surfaces, hydraulic system, flight controls, navigation systems, and radio and air-conditioning systems. BAC was responsible for the rest of the airliner except engines and the autopilot. The Olympus engines were produced jointly by Rolls-Royce and SNECMA; the autopilot was designed jointly by Elliott in the UK and SFENA in France. Due to noise restrictions and environmental activist groups, flights into U.S. airspace were restricted during its transcontinental flight career.

A typical subsonic trip from New York to London takes 7-8 hours on a conventional airliner. On February 8, 1996, the Concorde made the trip in 2 hours 52 minutes and 59 seconds.

20 Concordes were built and 14 entered airline service. After more than two decades of safe service, in July 2000 a Concorde crashed after runway debris ruptured the left main tires, which ultimately lead to fire and engine failure. After modifications to bolster the tires and to protect the fuel cells, the Concorde returned to service between New York, London and Paris in November of 2001 for less than two years before retirement.

AEROSPATIALE SN-601 "CORVETTE"

1970–1977

STANDARD DATA: Seats 6-14. Gross wt. 14,550. Empty wt. 7,738. Engines two 2,500-lb. Pratt & Whitney JT15D-4 turbofans. PERFORMANCE: Max speed 410 kts. Cruise 306 kts. Ceiling 41,000+. Range 800-1,380 nm.

The Corvette was Aerospatiale's first and only attempt to compete in the light jet market. The model's

Airbus A300-600

first prototype flew in 1970 and completed only 270 hours before it crashed. In 1972, Aerospatiale began again, this time with a stretched fuselage and more powerful turbofan engines. French certification came in May on 1974, but production was plagued by supply troubles and languid acceptance of the Corvette in the market. Only 39 production aircraft were ever built, though many remain in service today.

Airbus A318

AERO VODOCHODY L-39 "ALBARTOS"
1972–Present

Airbus A330-200

STANDARD DATA: Seats 2 . Gross wt. 11,618. Empty wt. 7,340. Engine one 3,792 lb. Ivchenko AI-25TL turbofan. PERFORMANCE: Max speed 485 mph. Ceiling 37,730'. Range 528-995 nm.

The Czechoslovakian L-39 was an evolved improvement over the L-29 Delfin, and was the primary advanced jet trainer in Soviet Block countries for more than twenty years. Variants of the L-39 were also flown as close-support and ground-attack aircraft. A modernized version, the L-59 is now in production. After the end of the Cold War, a number of the trainers have been exported, with hundreds flying as private aircraft in the United States alone.

Airbus A330-300

STANDARD DATA: (A310) Seats 236. Gross wt. 330,690. Empty wt. 169,842. Fuel capacity 13,746. Engines two 50,000-lb. s.t. Pratt & Whitney JT9D-7R4E turbofans. PERFORMANCE: Top mph 557. Cruise mph 532. Ceiling 41,000+. Range 5,240. Takeoff distance 7,575. Landing distance 5,000.

STANDARD DATA: (A320) Seats 179. Gross wt. 158,730. Empty wt. 84,171. Fuel capacity 3,380. Engines two 25,000-lb. s.t. CFM CFM56-5 turbofans. PERFORMANCE: Top mph 560. Cruise mph 522. Ceiling 31,000+. Range 2,640. Takeoff distance 5,630. Landing distance 4,750.

AIRBUS A300
1974–Present

STANDARD DATA: Seats 281-331. Gross wt. 302,000. Empty wt. 168,259. Fuel capacity 11,361-15,324. Engines two 51,008-lb. s.t. General Electric turbofans. PERFORMANCE: Top mph 582. Cruise mph 570. Approach mph 154. Range 1,000-2,190. Ceiling 35,000. Takeoff run 6,150. Landing roll 5,600.

STANDARD DATA: (A330-300) Seats 300-440. Gross wt. 450,000. Empty wt. 145,000. Fuel capacity 24,500. Engines two 64,000-lb. s.t. General Electric CF6-80C2 turbofans. PERFORMANCE: Max cruise 475 kts. Economy cruise 464 kts. Ceiling 41,000'. Range 4,640-5,500 nm.

Production of the A300 Airbus is truly an international effort. Aerospatiale is responsible for building the nose section, flight deck, lower center fuselage, and engine pylons. Deutsche Airbus of Germany, made up of MBB and VFW-Fokker, manufactures the forward fuselage from the flight deck to the wings, the upper center fuselage, the rear fuselage and the vertical tail. Hawker Siddeley makes the wings, while VFW-Fokker of the Netherlands manufactures the moving wing surfaces. CASA of Spain is responsible for the horizontal tail surfaces, landing gear doors, and the main doors. The General Electric turbofans are built under license by SNECMA and MTU. The A300B1 was the initial version powered by 49,000-lb. s.t. engines. The B2 is the first production model and the B4 is the long-range version of the wide-bodied transport. Standard all-tourist seating accommodations are for 281 passengers, and a high-density arrangement allows for 331 passengers.

The 300 series Airbus has a huge array of variants, each modified for a market niche.

- A300-600—Medium range widebody airliner
- A300-600ST (Super Transporter)—Oversize cargo freighter
- A300 B2/B4—Medium range widebody airliner
- A310—Medium to long range widebody airliner
- A318—100 seat regional airliner
- A320—Short to medium range airliner
- A321—Short to medium range narrow body airliner
- A330-200—Large capacity medium to long range airliner
- A330-300—Long range widebody airliner

AIRBUS A319CJ
1999–Present

Airbus A319CJ

STANDARD DATA: Seats 2-39. Gross wt. 166,450. Empty wt. 129,000. Engines two 26,500-lb. International Aero Engines IAE V2527M-A5. PERFORMANCE: Max speed Mach 0.82. Ceiling 41,000'. Range 6,300 nm.

When Boeing announced its Boeing Business Jet (BBJ), a personalized version of its 737 airframe,

Aerospatiale countered with the A319CJ (Corporate Jet), a private Airbus 319. The first version was rolled out at the Paris Air Show in 1997 and Airbus immediately began taking orders. The CJ was also designed to be easily refitted as airliner and thus providing more flexibility for resale, which can be important since the jet cost $35 million in 1999 dollars—before the additional $5–15 million interior finishing price. Airbus also offers the A319 configured for traditional airline service.

AIRBUS 340 A340-200–800
1991–Present

Airbus A340-200

Airbus A340-500

STANDARD DATA: A340-300 Seats 335. Gross wt. 606,275. Empty wt. 287,050. Engines four 32,550-lb. International CFM56-5C3 turbofans. PERFORMANCE: Max speed 494 kts. Economy cruise 475 kts. Ceiling 41,000'. Range 7,450 nm.

The 330 and 340 Airbus were developed at the same time, and both aircraft have the same flightdeck with side stick controllers and fly-by-wire controls. The shortened A340-200 first flew in April 1992, and trades seating capacity (263-303 passengers) for greater range. The A340 can carry about 330 passengers with a range of 7,100-7,450 nm.

The 500 and 600 series are currently the world's longest-range airliners. The 500 can travel 8,500 nm, enabling nonstop flights like Los Angeles to Singapore.

The A600's first flight was in April of 2001, and was certified 13 months later. The A500's maiden flight was in February of 2002 and received its certification just 10 months later. Both models are direct competition for Boeing's long range 747-400.

The A340-800 is a variant of the 200, but with extra fuel capacity in the cargo holds, which extends the range to a whopping 8,000 nm. All versions are offered with the underfloor passenger sleepers.

AIRBUS 380
2006–Present

Airbus A380

STANDARD DATA: Seats 555. Gross wt. 1,234,600. Empty wt. 610,700. Engines four 84,000-lb. Rolls-Royce Trent 900 turbofans. PERFORMANCE: Max speed Mach 0.88. Long range cruise Mach 0.85. Initial climb rate 2,300. Range 8,000-13,100 nm. Ceiling 43,000'.

The two-deck, 555 seat A380 is the largest airliner in the world. Like other Airbus projects, the A380 comes from a composite of contributors, not only in France, but Germany, the United Kingdom, Spain, Australia, Austria, Belgium, Finland, Italy, Japan, South Korea, Malaysia, Netherlands, Sweden, Switzerland and even the United States. In its 550-seat version, the A380 can carry 35% more passengers than the largest Boeing 747-400, and the A380-900 is on the drawing boards to carry 656 passengers.

BAC VC-10
1964–70

STANDARD DATA: (Super VC-10) Seats 131-174. Gross wt. 335,000. Empty wt. 155,380. Fuel capacity 23,257. Engines four 22,500-lb. s.t. Rolls-Royce turbofans. PERFORMANCE: Top mph 581. Cruise mph 550. Initial climb rate 2,300. Range 4,720. Ceiling 42,000. Takeoff distance (35') 8,300. Landing distance (50) 7,000.

The British Aircraft Corp. VC-10 is a long-range high payload jetliner. With all four of its turbofan engines mounted in two sets below the tail and its horizontal stabilizer mounted on top of the rudder, the airliner presents a picture of strength and speed. First flown in

June 1962, four years after the introduction of the DC-8 in America, the airliners initially went into commercial service on a route to West Africa from London. The airliner was built in Weybridge, England, by the former Vickers of Rome Aircraft. The four powerful Rolls-Royce engines, with a total of 18,000 pounds more than the International 707, permit a maximum takeoff weight of 312,000 pounds for the standard VC-10 and over one-third of a million pounds for the later Super VC-10. The Super VC-10 is 13 feet longer than standard and has an increased range and payload. Both the VC-10 and the Super VC-10 will cruise at 86% of the speed of sound.

BAC 111
1965–81

STANDARD DATA: (Series 500) Seats 97-119. Gross wt. 104,500. Empty wt. 54,582. Fuel capacity 3,705. Engines two 12,550-lb. s.t. Rolls-Royce turbofans. PERFORMANCE: Top mph 541. Cruise mph 461. Stall mph 121. Initial climb rate 2,280. Range 1,705. Ceiling 35,000. Takeoff distance (35') 7,300. Landing distance (50') 4,720.

The BAC 111, built by the British Aircraft Corp., was designed for both short- and medium-range operation. This twin-engine airliner was first certified for United States operation in April 1964, and orders were placed by Mohawk, Braniff, and American Airlines. The first production model, the Series 200, flew for the first time in December 1963 and was powered by the smaller Rolls-Royce 10,330-lb. s.t. engines. The 300 Series were fitted with larger engines, greater fuel capacity, and a stronger landing gear. The 400 Series came equipped with a fuel dump system and was the first model certified for United States operation. The 475 series is fitted with low-pressure tires to permit operation on low-strength runways with surfaces of poorer grade. The final series, the 500, is a stretched version that can carry up to 119 passengers. Executive and freighter versions of the BAC 111 are also available. National Aircraft Leasing Ltd. offers a modified version for executive use; it features a redesigned interior.

BEECHCRAFT "PREMIER I"
2001-Present

STANDARD DATA: Seats 2+6. Gross wt. 12,500. Empty wt. 8,470. Fuel capacity 548. Engines two 2,300-lb. Williams FJ-44 2A. PERFORMANCE: Max cruise 451 kts. Range 826-1,502 nm. Ceiling 41,000 nm. Takeoff 3,792'. Landing 3,170'.

After the problems of developing the composite Beech Starship, it is to Raytheon's credit they had the courage to take on another composite project, the Premier I. The entry-level jet has a composite fuselage, empennage and control surfaces, built of graphite and epoxy laminates with honeycomb construction, totaling more than a million miles of carbon-fiber filaments. The wings are aluminum.

Unlike many entry level jets which typically settle for 300 knots and a ceiling of 30,000', the Premier offers typical jet speed and altitudes. The Premier I is also certified for single pilot operation.

BEECHJET
See Hawker 400XP

BOEING 707
1954-81

STANDARD DATA: (707-320C) Seats 219. Gross wt. 333,680. Empty wt. 146,000. Fuel capacity 23,855. Engines four 19,000-lb. s.t. Pratt & Whitneys. PERFORMANCE: Top mph 627. Cruise mph 600. Stall mph 121. Initial climb rate 3,550. Range 7,475.

Ceiling 38,500. Takeoff distance (35) 10,900. Landing distance (50') 6,250.

The prototype of the Boeing 707 was the first jet transport to be completed and flown in the United States. Its first run was on July 15, 1954, and was known as the Model 36780. Under the designation of KC-135, it was used by the U.S. Air Force for air-to-air refueling. In 1955, the Air Force permitted Boeing to produce commercial versions of the transport. These became known as the 707 and 720. The 707-120 was the first production version and was primarily designed for domestic use, though capable of over-ocean operations. Power was provided by four 13,000-lb. s.t. turbojets. The 707-220 followed with its 15,800-lb. s.t. Pratt & Whitneys. The 707-320 was the first intercontinental version and featured increased fuselage length and was powered by either 15,800- or 16,800-lb. s.t. turbofans. Accommodations provided for 195 to 219 economy class passengers. The usual arrangement was 14 first-class seats with 133 coach seats.

BOEING 717
1999-2006

STANDARD DATA: Seats 106-117. Gross wt. 110,000. Empty wt. 69,830. Engines two 18,500-lb. Rolls-Royce BR715-A1-30 turbofans. PERFORMANCE: Max cruise 438 kts. Range 1,375-2,060 nm. Ceiling 41,000'.

After its merger with McDonnell Douglas 1997, Boeing retained the MD-80/90/95 product line as the Boeing 717. The aircraft was designed for high-cycle, short haul regional airline applications and received FAA certification in September 1999.

Variants of the B717 include the 80-seat 717-100, the stretched 717-200, and the 120-seat 717 300. All models feature the Honeywell six-screen EFIS flightdeck.

BOEING 720
1960-69

STANDARD DATA: (720B) Seats 153. Gross wt. 234,000. Empty wt. 112,883. Fuel capacity 14,880.

Engines four 17,000-lb. s.t. Pratt & Whitneys. PER-FORMANCE: Top mph 627. Cruise mph 611. Stall mph 116. Initial climb rate 4,080. Range 4,155. Ceiling 42,000. Takeoff distance (35') 6,450. Landing distance (50') 6,350.

Produced in two models, the 720 and the 720B, this intermediate-range Boeing transport looks very much like the Boeing 707. The first model, the 720, uses four Pratt & Whitney JT3D-7 turbojet engines rated at 12,500 pounds of thrust each. The 720B is powered by JT3D-3 turbofan engines with a thrust rating of 18,000 pounds each. The difference in thrust allows the 720B to carry almost 15,000 pounds more payload than the 720. One way to tell the difference between the 720 and its big brother the 707 is to count the overwing emergency-exit doors. The 707 has two doors over each wing, but the 720's smaller passenger capacity allows for only one over-wing door on each side. Another way to distinguish the two jetliners is to look at the engine housings. A large hump on top of the engine indicates the presence of a turbocompressor, or "TC," used for cabin pressurization and air conditioning. The 720 is equipped with two TCs; the 707 has three.

BOEING 727
1963–1990

STANDARD DATA: (727-200) Seats 163-189. Gross wt. 184,800. Empty wt. 99,398. Fuel capacity 8,186-10,666. Engines three 14,500-lb. s.t. Pratt & Whitney turbofans. PERFORMANCE: Top mph 632. Cruise mph 592. Stall mph 122. Initial climb rate 2,500. Range 1,670. Ceiling 33,000. Takeoff distance (35') 9,340. Landing distance (50') 4,690.

The Boeing 727 was built with the intention of producing a short- to medium-range jet transport. It was flown for the first time in February 1963. A major innovation, compared with the company's earlier designs, was the choice of a rear-engine layout. The 727 is powered by three Pratt & Whitney turbofans; one is mounted at the base of the T-tail assembly. In all other respects, the 727 resembles the 707 and 720 series. Not only are the upper fuselages identical, but many parts are interchangeable. The 727-200 is the stretched version and was announced in 1965. It had a maximum capacity of 189 passengers compared to the earlier model's seating for 114. Optional turbofans rated at 15,000 lbs. s.t., 15,500 lbs. s.t., and 16,000 pounds s.t. can be installed. Since 1972, Hawker-de Havilland of Australia has been the sole supplier of rudders and main wing ribs for the 200 series.

Production of commercial 707s ended in 1978 after 878 had been built. Limited production of military variants continued until 1990. A number of 707 are still in service, many as freighters, some as corporate transport. The Boeing 707 is still very active in its various military roles.

BOEING 737 200–900
1967–Present

STANDARD DATA: (737-200) Seats 115-130. Gross wt. 115,500-150,000. Empty wt. 60,210-138,500. Fuel capacity 5,151-5,311. Engines two 14,500-lb. s.t. Pratt & Whitney turbofans. PERFORMANCE: Top mph 586. Cruise mph 576. Stall mph 111. Initial climb rate 3,760. Range 1,545-2,370. Takeoff distance (35) 6,150-7,760. Landing distance (50) 4,300.

STANDARD DATA: (737-300) Seats 121-149. Gross wt. 135,800. Empty wt. 74,490. Fuel capacity 5,096. Engines two 20,000-lb. CFM CFM56-3bl turbofans. PERFORMANCE: Max speed 491 kts. Long range cruise 429 kts. Ceiling 35,000+. Range 1,815-3,400 nm. Takeoff distance 6,360. Landing distance 4,580.

STANDARD DATA: (737-400) Seats 121-188. Gross wt. 138,500. Empty wt. 76,200. Engines two 22,000-lb. CFM CFM56-3B2 turbofans. PERFORMANCE: Max speed 492 kts. Long range cruise 439 kts. Ceiling 41,000. Range 2,080-2,160 nm.

STANDARD DATA: (737-600/700) Seats 110-149. Gross wt. 124,000. Empty wt. 81,800. Engines two 22,700-lb. CFM CFM56-7B18 turbofans. PERFORMANCE: Max cruise speed Mach 0.785. Ceiling 41,000'. Range 1,340-3,260 nm.

STANDARD DATA: (737-800/900) Seats 162-189. Gross wt. 174,200. Empty wt. 90,710. Engines two 27,300-lb. CFM CFM56-7B24 turbofans. PERFORMANCE: Max cruise speed Mach 0.785. Ceiling 41,000'. Range 1,990-2,940 nm.

The Boeing 737 was initially designed as a short-range twin-jet transport as a replacement to the popular 727. Since its introduction in 1967, the 737 family has become the best-selling commercial jetliner in history with orders totaling more than 3,044 by 1993 from 159 customers in 81 countries. It differs in appearance from the 727 in that its two engines are mounted on the wings. The decision to build the 737 was announced in February 1965, and seven versions have been produced. The basic model 737-100 provides accommodations for 81-101 passengers plus baggage. The 737-200 has a lengthened fuselage and accommodates up to 130 passengers with standard seating for 115. In addition to the basic JT8139 turbofan rated at 14,500 lbs., other available turbofans are the JT813-15 (15,500 lbs.) and J1813-17 (16,000 lbs.).

The 727-300 came along in late 1984 as a stretched version of the 200. The new design would also incorporate more economical and quieter GE engines. This was also the first Boeing to show off its new flattened, oval-shaped engine nacelles.

The 737-400 added another ten feet to the fuselage and upped the maximum number of seats to 188. The model entered service in 1988.

The 737-500 received FAA certification in 1990, making it the last of the 737-300/400/500 variants. It was originally to be called the 737-1000, but was re-named the 500 before entering service. Only a foot longer than the 300 model, the 500 was offered as a replacement to the older fleet of 300s.

The 737-600/700 models are the smallest of Boeing's Next Generation family. They featured a new wing, a new tail section the more efficient CFM56-7B turbofans. The larger wing had more fuel capacity, allowing the 737 to become transcontinental.

Model 800/900s are the largest of the 737 family. Stretched fuselages allowed more seating, and more efficient engines, combined with an increase in fuel capacity made these model an immediate success. The cockpit crew of two also enjoys the same six LCD flat panel displays as found on the Boeing 777. The first deliver of an 800 came in April of 1998, and the first 900 was delivered in May 2001.

BOEING BUSINESS JET "BBJ/BBJ2"
1998–Present

STANDARD DATA: BBJ/BBJ2 Seats 2-63. Gross wt. 171,000/174,200. Empty wt. 94,570/100,815. Engines two 26,400-lb. CFM International CFM 56-7

turbofans. PERFORMANCE: Max cruise Mach 0.82. Long range cruise Mach 0.79. Range 4,935-6,200 nm. Ceiling 41,000.

The BBJ was co-developed by Boeing and General Electric as long-range corporate transportation, and is based on the 737 airframe. The first delivery took place in September 1999. A stretched version (19' longer) of the original BBJ, the BBJ2 offers 25% more cabin space and 100% more baggage space. First delivery of the larger Boeing Business Jet was in early 2001.

The BBJ features the same panel as the formidable Boeing 777 and also adds a heads-up display. A variety of fuel tank configurations allow the BBJ to have a more than 6,000 nm range. With a customized interior, some of which feature a conference room and a gymnasium, the BBJ approaches a $50m total acquisition cost.

BOEING 747
1969–Present

Boeing 747-200

Boeing 747-400

STANDARD DATA: (747-200) Seats 385-500. Gross wt. 785,000. Empty wt. 363,068. Fuel capacity 51,000. Engines four 48,570-lb. s.t. Pratt & Whitney turbofans. PERFORMANCE: Top mph 608. Cruise mph 595. Stall mph 115. Initial climb rate 2,000. Range 6,218. Ceiling 45,000. Takeoff distance (35) 10,500. Landing distance (50') 6,170.

STANDARD DATA: (747-300) Seats 400+. Gross wt. 833,000. Empty wt. 384,480. Fuel capacity 44,953. Engines four 54,750-lb. s.t. Pratt & Whitney JT9D-7R4G2 turbofans. PERFORMANCE: Top mph 583. Cruise mph 564. Ceiling 45,000+. Range 5,650. Takeoff distance 10,450. Landing distance 6,920.

STANDARD DATA: (747-400ER) Seats 416-568. Gross wt. 910,000. Empty wt. 401,800. Engines four 58,000-lb. Rolls-Royce RB-211-524G turbofans. PERFORMANCE: Max cruise 507 kts. Long range cruise 490 kts. Ceiling 45,000+. Range 5,650. Takeoff distance 10,450. Landing distance 6,920.

The Boeing 747 was designed to carry large numbers of passengers at low cost. The basic passenger design, designated 747-200B, is capable of carrying up to 500 passengers in a 10-abreast seating arrangement. Basic accommodations are for 385 passengers made up of 48 first-class and 337 economy-class. The aircraft is powered by four Pratt & Whitney turbofan engines in pods and pylon-mounted to the underside of the wings. All current 747s can be outfitted with either 43,500, 45,000, 46,950, 48,570, or 49,000-lb. engines. A General Electric turbofan rated at 52,500 lbs. can also be used.

The first 747s to be delivered were received by Pan American in 1969. The 747-100 was the first model with a maximum takeoff weight of 713,000 pounds. Later, the 747-200 was introduced with a maximum takeoff weight of 775,000 pounds. The latest version, the 400, is the world's largest commercial jetliner and offers greater range, better fuel economy, and lower operating costs than previous 747 models. The 400's range is boosted 1,150 statute miles over the 300, giving a maximum range of 8,290 miles.

The 747-400ER rolled out in 2002 with even more range and payload capabilities. MTOW increased to 910,000 lbs and range increased an additional 435 nm.

BOEING 757 "200/300"
1982–Present

STANDARD DATA: Seats 239. Gross wt. 240,000. Empty wt. 126,250. Fuel capacity 9,370. Engines two 40,100-lb. s.t. Pratt & Whitney PW2037 turbofans. PERFORMANCE: Top mph 581. Cruise mph 528. Ceiling 40,000+. Range 4,570. Takeoff distance 10,450. Landing distance 4,600.

The Boeing 757-200 is a medium-sized, twin-engine jetliner designed for medium-to-long-range service and takes advantage of advanced technology for exceptional fuel economy, increased passenger comfort, lower noise levels, and elevated operating performance. The 757 also offers great versatility with a wide weight range (220,000-255,500 pounds) for greater payload capability. A freighter version is also available. The 757 is designed to carry 194 passengers in a typical mixed-class configuration and can carry an additional 45 passengers for charter service, which brings the 757's overall capacity between that of the 737-400 and the 767.

The 757-300 made its debut in at the Farnsborough Airshow in 1996. Though the aircraft shares the same wing and fuselage as the original 757, a fuselage stretch of just over 23' allowed 20% more seats, and freight increase of 40%. The first model 757-300 went into service in 1999.

BOEING 767 "200/300/400"
1982–Present

STANDARD DATA: B-757-200 Seats 290. Gross wt. 300,000. Empty wt. 176,200. Fuel capacity 13,900. Engines two 48,000-lb. s.t. Pratt & Whitney JT9D-7R4D. PERFORMANCE: Top mph 557. Cruise mph 528. Ceiling 40,000+. Range 6,210. Takeoff distance 5,650. Landing distance 4,750.

STANDARD DATA: B-757-300 Seats 210-350. Gross wt. 401,000. Empty wt. 198,800. Engines two 52,500-lb. CF6-80C2B2 turbofans. PERFORMANCE: Max cruise speed 486 kts. Long range cruise 460 kts. Ceiling 40,000+. Range 4,230-5,875 nm.

STANDARD DATA: B-757-400 Seats 245. Gross wt. 450,000. Empty wt. 227,400. Engines two 48,000-lb. s.t. Pratt & Whitney JT9D-7R4D. PERFORMANCE: Max cruise Mach 0.80. Ceiling 40,000+. Range 5,625 nm.

The 767 makes use of advanced technology to offer exceptional efficiency to help offset rising operational costs while bringing twin-aisle passenger-cabin convenience to routes that were never served by wide-bodied aircraft in the past. Because of its twin-aisle design, the 767 offers 87% of available seating either at a window or on an aisle.

The 767-200 was developed at the same time as the Boeing 757; in fact the Boeing 767-100 (the first model) was never launched, due its similar capacity to the 757. The 200 model was awarded FAA certification on July 30, 1982 just a few months earlier than the 757. Both aircraft share early EFIS flightdecks.

After release of the 200, Boeing immediately announced the development of the stretched 767, the 300. The model entered service in late 1986. Both the 200 and 300 series 757 were made in an ER (extended range) version, which increased fuel capacity and higher MTOWs.

The 767-300ER made way for the yet another fuselage stretch—the 767-400. This Boeing model was designed to compete more directly with the Airbus A330-200. This was the first project for Boeing after merging with McDonnell Douglas in 1997. The 400 featured the same flightdeck as the B-777 and made its first flight in 1999.

BOEING 777 "200/300"
1995–Present

STANDARD DATA: Seats 375-400. Gross wt. 506,000-580,000. Empty wt. 306,492 lbs. Fuel capacity 31,000. Engines two 77,000-lb. s.t. Pratt & Whitney PW4000 turbofans. PERFORMANCE: Top cruise 508 kts. Ceiling 43,000'. Range 4,560-8,490. Takeoff distance 10,600. Landing distance 6,000.

The 777 was initially imagined to be a variant of the 767, but eventually morphed into a whole new design. It was to become Boeing's most advanced aircraft, using fly-by-wire technology, a glass flightdeck and composite construction. The 777 was also designed to have folding wings to accommodate cramped airport facilities. The four-year development effort culminated on October 29, 1990, with the announcement that the 777 would indeed see production. Flight testing began in June 1994. Orders and options for more than 250 aircraft were tallied within a year.

Models of the B-777 include the 200LR, capable of 18 hours aloft, and the 300 and 300ER. This latest model features a 33' fuselage stretch, and can seat up to 550 passengers. The model 300 was awarded both FAA and JAA type certification on May 4, 1998. The 300ER, which uses the powerful General Electric GE90-115B engines, increased the B-777's range to 7,250 nm.

BOMBARDIER CHALLENGER 300
2002–Present

STANDARD DATA: Seats 8-9. Gross wt. 38,500. Empty wt. 23,350. Engines two 6,826-lb. Honeywell HTF7000 turbofans. PERFORMANCE: Max cruise 470 kts. Normal cruise 460 kts. Ceiling 45,000'. Range 3,100 nm. Landing distance 2,600'.

The Challenger 300 is mid-range corporate jet, sitting between Bombardier's large Learjet 60 and the Challenger 604. The Challenger 300 is made of a light-alloy structure, with composites used for some non-structural items. The fuselage is of a semi-monocoque construction with frames and stringers. The 300 was originally named the 'Continental', but became the Challenger 300 in 2002.

BOMBARDIER CHALLENGER "600/601/604/800"
1977–Present

Challenger 604

Challenger 800

STANDARD DATA: (604) Seats 9-19. Gross wt. 32,650. Empty wt. 13,567. Engines two 8,729-lb General Electric CF34-1B1 turbofans. PERFORMANCE: High speed cruise 459 kts. Typical cruise 442 kts. Ceiling 41,000. Range 4,027 nm. Landing distance 2,910'.

STANDARD DATA: (800) Seats 8-13. Gross wt. 24,040. Empty wt. 15,377. Engines two 8,729 lb General Electric CF34-1B1 turbofans. PERFORMANCE: High speed cruise 459 kts. Typical cruise 442 kts. Ceiling 41,000. Range 3,590'. Landing distance 2,910'.

In 1977, Canadair unleashed its Challenger series of business jets to go head to head with the Gulfstream, Dassault Falcon 50, and the Lockheed JetStar II. Canadair's goal was to make a competitive aircraft that would fly faster, farther, more economically, and with greater comfort than its competitors. The original design came from none other than Bill Lear, and was originally called the LearStar 600. Certification for the new Canadair jet was in August 1980.

An aerodynamically cleaned-up and lighter design followed, the Challenger 601, employing the General Electric CF-34 turbofan engines. The upgrade was so successful that the original 600 model was dropped from production a year later in 1983. In 1986 Canadair was acquired by Bombardier.

The Challenger 604 entered service in early 1996, sporting an all new Collins ProLine glass panel flightdeck and a variety of improvements, including a higher MTWO, more fuel capacity and new CF-34-3B turbofan engines.

The stretched Challenger 800 can seat up to 19 plus a crew of two and can cruise almost 3,600 nm nonstop.

BOMBARDIER CRJ "REGIONAL JET"
1992–Present

STANDARD DATA: (CRJ200) Seats 50. Gross wt. 47,450. Engines two 8,729-lb General Electric CF34-3B1 turbofans. PERFORMANCE: High speed cruise 464 kts. Typical cruise Mach 0.81. Ceiling 41,000. Range 2,005 nm.

STANDARD DATA: (CRJ700) Seats 64-75. Gross wt. 75,250. Empty wt. 45,023. Engines two 12,670-lb General Electric CF34-8C turbofans. Max fuel 3,405. PERFORMANCE: High speed cruise Mach 0.825. Ceiling 41,000. Range 2,000 nm.

STANDARD DATA: (CRJ900) Seats 86-90. Gross wt. 80,500. Empty wt. 47,500. Fuel 3,250. Engines two 13,123-lb General Electric CF34-8C5 turbofans. PERFORMANCE: High speed cruise 464 kts. Typical cruise 442 kts. Ceiling 41,000. Range 2,005 nm. Takeoff 2,887'. Landing 5,134'.

The idea of producing a "regional jet," a smaller jet purposefully designed for shorter hauls with fewer passengers has made a huge impact on airline travel worldwide. Bombardier's CRJ100 began service in Europe, quickly followed by the CRJ200, which featured more powerful engines. In 1999, the CRJ700 entered the fleet, and in 2003 the CRJ900 joined the family. Even though all three are different size, CRJs require only a single type rating, maximizing the benefits of common crew qualifications.

The largest, the CRJ900, typically features 86-90 seats, the CRJ700 64-70 seats and the CRJ 200 accommodates 50 passengers.

BOMBARDIER GLOBAL EXPRESS BD-700
1998–Present

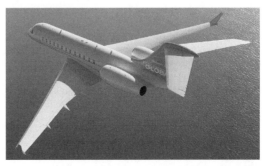

STANDARD DATA: (5000) Seats 8-19. Gross wt. 95,000. Empty wt. 48,800. Engines two 14,750-lb BMW Rolls-Royce BR-710-220 turbofans. PERFOR-

MANCE: High speed cruise 505 kts. Typical cruise 488 kts. Ceiling 41,000. Range 5,325-6,700 nm. Landing distance 2,700'.

The Global Express 5000 is Bombardier's crown jewel in corporate jets, competing handily with the Airbus A319CJ, the Gulfstream V and the Boeing BBJ. The BD-700 has enough range that it can fly between any two points in the world nonstop. The XRS version can travel 6,700 nm without refueling. Corporate shuttle variants can seat as many as 30.

Three Bombardier divisions, Canadair, Shorts and de Havilland all participate in producing the jet, while Japan's Mitsubishi constructs the wing and center fuselage. Cockpits are all glass and can feature heads-up display and enhanced vision as options. Passengers can enjoy satellite telephone/fax, datalink, on-board local area network and single channel high-speed data.

BRITISH AEROSPACE "BAe-146"
1983–1993

STANDARD DATA: (146-300) Seats 128. Gross wt. 97,500. Empty wt. 54,848. Engines four 6,970-lb. ALF 502-5 turbofans. PERFORMANCE: Max speed Mach 0.73. Cruise 426 kts. Range 1,040-1,520 nm. Ceiling 35,000.

One of Britain's most successful airliners, the HS-146 began in 1973 under the leadership of Hawker Siddeley under subsidy from the British government. Economic pressures made development slow, and was not until 1978, under the larger umbrella of British Aerospace, that the four-engine airliner really took shape. The version -200, a stretch of the prototype -100, featured more cargo space and allowed for the resulting increase in gross weights. Later a -300 model was certified, with even more such increases. The BAe-146s flew two roles, as both passenger and freight haulers. Military versions were also operated by the Royal Air Force.

BRITISH AEROSPACE RJ70/85/100
1993–2002

STANDARD DATA: (RJ70) Seats 70. Gross wt. 95,000. Empty wt. 52,690. Engines four 6,130-lb.

RJ85

Allied Signal LF-507 turbofans. PERFORMANCE: Max speed Mach 0.73. Cruise 412 kts. Range 1,440-1,660 nm. Ceiling 40,000'.

The Avro RJ series were upgrades from the BAe-146 series. The RJ variants came in three fuselage lengths, all with glass cockpits and super-efficient FADEC-equipped Allied Signal engines. British Aerospace also planned on offering an RJ115, with extra emergency exits and a higher seat capacity, but none were built before production ended in 2002.

CESSNA "CITATION"
1971–Present

Citation I

Citation CJ1

STANDARD DATA: (Citation I) Seats 5-7. Gross wt. 11,850. Empty wt. 6,631. Fuel capacity 564. Engines two 2,200-lb. Pratt & Whitney JT15D-1AB turbofans. PERFORMANCE: Max cruise 357 kts. Stall mph 98. Initial climb rate 2,220. Range 1,328 nm. Ceiling 38,400'. Takeoff distance (50') 3,275. Landing distance (50') 2,300.

STANDARD DATA: (CJ1/CJ2+) Seats 4-6. Gross wt. 10,400/12,300. Empty wt. 6,160. Engines two 1,900/2,300-lb. Williams Rolls-Royce FJ44-1A/FJ44-2C tur-

Citation CJ2

Citation CJ3

Citation Bravo

Citation Encore

Citation XLS

Citation Sovereign

Citation X

bofans. PERFORMANCE: Max cruise 380/412 kts. Initial climb rate 3,311 fpm. Stall speed 86 kts. Range 1,250-1,580 nm. Ceiling 41,000/45,000'.

STANDARD DATA: (CJ3) Seats 6. Gross wt. 13,870. Empty wt. 8,160. Engines two 2,780-lb. Williams Rolls-Royce FJ44-3A turbofans. PERFORMANCE: Max cruise 417 kts. Stall speed 86 kts. Range 1,875 nm. Ceiling 45,000'.

STANDARD DATA: (Bravo) Seats 7-10. Gross wt. 14,800. Empty wt. 8,750. Engines two 2,885-lb. Pratt & Whitney PW503A turbofans. PERFORMANCE: Max cruise 401 kts. Initial climb rate 3,195 fpm. Range 1,739-1,900 nm. Ceiling 45,000.

STANDARD DATA: (Encore) Seats 7-8. Gross wt. 16,630. Empty wt. 9,977. Engines two 3,360-lb. Pratt & Whitney PW535 A turbofans. PERFORMANCE: Max cruise 431 kts. Initial climb rate 4,100 fpm. Range 1,700-1,960 nm. Ceiling 45,000.

STANDARD DATA: (XLS) Seats 6-10. Gross wt. 20,200. Empty wt. 11,910. Engines two 3,804-lb. Pratt & Whitney PW545 A turbofans. PERFOR-MANCE: Max cruise 429 kts. Initial climb rate 4,100 fpm. Range 1,700-2,080 nm. Ceiling 45,000.

STANDARD DATA: (Sovereign) Seats 6-12. Gross wt. 30,000. Engines two 5,690-lb. Pratt & Whitney PW 306C turbofans. PERFORMANCE: Max cruise

444 kts. Initial climb rate 4,100 fpm. Range 1,750-2,820 nm. Ceiling 47,000.

STANDARD DATA: (X) Seats 6-12. Gross wt. 36,100. Empty wt. 21,400. Engines two 6,764-lb. Rolls-Royce AE 3007C1 turbofans. PERFORMANCE: Max cruise Mach 0.92. Initial climb rate 4,000 fpm. Range 3,390 nm. Ceiling 51,000. Take-off distance 5,140'. Landing distance 3,400'.

Cessna had experience with military-jet building under contracts for the T-37 (Tweet) jet trainer, but the Cessna Fanjet 500, later renamed the Citation 500, marked the first attempt any general aviation manufacturer had made into the pure jet market. Deliveries of the Citation began in late 1971, and it soon became the best-selling business jet in the world. The Cessna Citation provided the starting point for world's largest family of personal/corporate jets.

By 1976 the Citation 500 was ready to mature, and Cessna added JT15D-1A engines, thrust reversers, and a slightly increased wingspan. The new model became the Citation I. The straight wing jets could get in and out or runways typically used by singles and light twins. The safety and simplicity of the Citation's systems help make the airplane remarkably easy to fly and led to its universal acceptance. More important, the Citation could be flown by a single pilot. The current model CessnaJet (CJ) is the legacy of the first Citations.

The remarkable success of the Citation led Cessna to look at building larger and faster versions. First out of the chute was the Citation II in 1978, nearly 4 feet longer, faster and higher flying. The Citation II has now become Cessna Bravo.

The largest of the Cessna straight-wing jets was the Citation V (model 560), certified in 1988. Production ended in 1994 as the model morphed once again into the Citation Excel (XLS).

The Citation III (model 650) was Cessna's transition from the small to medium-sized jets and received certification in April of 1982. The all-new jet had swept wings and Garrett TFE731 engines, which allowed the 650 to set time-to-climb records, performance not immediately associated with the original Citations. A model IV Citation was contemplated but shelved to make room for the Citations VI and VII. Ultimately the 600 series Citations translated to the Model 680 Sovereign.

Still producing an entry-level jet, the CJ1, and the progressively larger and more powerful 2 and 3 models, have proven even more successful than the original Citation. All CJs are powered by Williams Rolls-Royce engines.

At the other end of the spectrum is the Citation X (Model 750), the fastest civil airplane in service with the retirement of the Concorde. The 750 can fly from LA to New York in just over four hours. And just as remarkable, the Citation X cruises alone at 51,000' where conflicts with other air traffic are improbable.

CONVAIR 880
1960–64

STANDARD DATA: Seats 88-110. Gross wt. 184,500. Empty wt. 88,615. Fuel capacity 12,534. Engines four 11,650-lb. s.t. General Electric turbojets. PERFORMANCE: Top mph 615. Cruise mph 501. Stall mph 121. Initial climb rate 3,565. Range 3,995. Ceiling 41,000. Takeoff run 8,050. Landing roll 6,150.

First of General Dynamics jet passenger airplanes, the Convair 880 began to set speed records soon after its introduction into airline service. Still considered one of the fastest jetliners, the medium-range transport achieves much of its speed through the use of a comparatively thin wing swept back at 35 degrees. Powered by four General Electric engines, an advanced version of the engine used on the supersonic B-58 "Hustler" bomber, the 880 cruises at 615 mph. The combined power of the engines permits an airline operation at 89% of the speed of sound.

The FAA certified the 880 for airline use on May 1, 1960, and 15 days later Delta Airlines put the liner into commercial service. TWA began 880 service in January 1961. Airplane spotters can differentiate the Convair 880 from other transports with four engines mounted on the wings by its nose, engines, air scoops, and tail. The tip of the empennage is formed with a right angle, giving the appearance of being sharply cut off, unlike the smooth flare to a point as seen on other airliners. The engines of the 880 are narrow compared to those on Boeing or Douglas aircraft, and the long sleek nose comes almost to a point. Other features of the 880 not seen on the 707 or DC-8 are two air scoops located underneath the wing root on each side. These scoops collect air that is compressed and conditioned for cabin use.

CONVAIR 990
1962–64

STANDARD DATA: Seats 96-121. Gross wt. 244,200. Empty wt. 113,000. Fuel capacity 15,119-15,675. Engines four 16,100-lb. General Electric tur-

bofans. PERFORMANCE: Top mph 640. Cruise mph 610. Stall mph 105. Initial climb rate 3,250. Range 4,300-5,445. Ceiling 41,000. Takeoff run 5,350. Landing roll 4,770.

Nicknamed the "San Diego Anteater," the Convair 990 does look a bit like it's searching for ants on the runway. Its nose has a high slope from the cockpit window to the tip, which, aided by a short nose gear strut, gives the aircraft a rakish appearance. Easily identified in the air and on the ground by four large pods mounted on the top of the wing, the 990 was not widely accepted by United States airlines. Four General Electric aft-fan engines, each with a thrust of over 16,000 lbs., provide the push to cruise at 621 mph, the fastest airliner made when the FAA certification was awarded in 1962. But the G.E. engines were one reason for the small number of 990s purchased. Most airlines felt it was uneconomical to have an airplane that didn't use the almost-standard Pratt & Whitney engines.

The aircraft's long range came about by using the four wing pods as fuel tanks. The 24-foot-long pods, known as "antishock bodies," reduce the intensity of shock waves generated when an airplane reaches the speed of sound. In essence, they control the air flowing over the wing and therefore reduce drag. Although passengers enjoy the quiet and luxurious 990, the economics of having an oddball plane in the fleet has caused the disappearance of the airliner from the lucrative routes. Convair stopped producing passenger liners after making the 990, leaving that specialized business to Douglas and Boeing.

DASSAULT MYSTERE FALCON 10/20/30 FALCON 100-200

1973–1990

STANDARD DATA: (Falcon 20) Seats 8-14. Gross wt. 28,660. Empty wt. 15,970. Fuel capacity 1,385. Engines two 4,315-lb. s.t. General Electric turbofans. PERFORMANCE: Top mph 465. Cruise mph 405. Stall mph 95. Range 2,200. Ceiling 42,000. Takeoff distance (35') 3,790. Landing distance (50) 1,930.

The Dassault Mystere 20/Falcon is a lightweight, pressurized, twin-engine business jet that took to the air for the first time in 1963. Developed as a joint effort between Dassault and Aerospatiale, the aircraft was powered by two Pratt & Whitney turbojets rated at 3,300 lbs. s.t.; however, it was soon re-engined with General Electric turbofans. Deliveries began in 1965, and Pan American placed the first orders. Several versions were built, differing by more powerful engines. The Series F featured high-lift devices (to improve takeoff and landing performance), more powerful engines, and increased fuel capacity. Standard passenger accommodations provide seating for 8 to 10, while a maximum of 12 to 14 is optional. The Falcon 200 replaced the Falcon 20 starting in 1981. The re-engined Falcon had more fuel capacity and upgraded avionics. The last Falcon 200 was produced in 1988.

The Falcon 10 is merely a scaled down version of the Falcon 20F, and the model 10 seats four to seven in executive-like accommodations. Power is supplied by two 3,230-lb. s.t. Garrett AiResearch turbofans. The Falcon 30 and Mystere 40100 are both further developments of the original airframe and provide for 30 to 40 passengers, respectively. The prototype for these aircraft first flew in 1973 and was fitted with 6,070lb. s.t. Lycoming turbofans fed by a 1,400-gallon fuel supply. The Falcon 100 replaced the Falcon 10 in production during the 1980s. Changes included a high MTOW and an early EFIS glass cockpit. The model ended production in 1990.

DASSAULT FALCON 50

1977–Present

STANDARD DATA: Falcon 50EX Seats 12-19. Gross wt. 39,700. Empty wt. 21,270. Engines three 3,700-lb. Allied Signal TFE73140 turbofans. PERFORMANCE: Max cruise 475 kts. Ceiling 45,000'. Takeoff run 5,415. Landing roll 3,280.

Development of the new Falcon 50 began in May 1974. Some of the components of the Falcon 50 are modeled after those of the earlier Falcon 20, such as the front and center fuselage sections. The Falcon 50 makes use of advanced high-lift devices such as double-slotted trailing-edge flaps; the wings are designed to

perform well at high Mach numbers. This luxurious jet is powered by three Garrett AiResearch turbofan engines, each flat-rated at 3,700 lbs. s.t. for takeoff. Two are mounted separately in pods on each side of the rear fuselage; the third is located in the tailcone with its intake just forward of the base of the vertical stabilizer. In order to make room for this third engine, the fuselage was lengthened and the fin was enlarged over that of the Falcon 20.

The three-engine Falcon 50 was designed for long range jet transport (originally 3,500 nm), and Dassault continued to refine that theme. In 1995, they announced the even longer range Falcon 50EX featuring TFE73140 engines which added another 400 nm to the airliner's range. The first models came off the production line in 1996.

DASSAULT FALCON 900
1986–Present

STANDARD DATA: Falcon 900EX Seats 8-15. Gross wt. 48,300. Empty wt. 23,875. Engines three 5,000-lb. Allied Signal TFE731-60 turbofans. PERFORMANCE: Max cruise Mach 0.80. Range 3,840-4,500 nm. Ceiling 51,000'.

Though the Falcon 900 drew its basis from the Falcon 50, it is essentially an all-new airplane. To demonstrate its even more improved long range capability, in 1985, Dassault flew a prototype of the Falcon 900 nonstop from Paris to Little Rock, Arkansas. The new de-

sign was wider and longer than the model 50 and could seat passengers three abreast.

In 1991, the Falcon 900B became the standard production model, with an increase in power and range. The model B was upgraded to the model C in 2000, and the Falcon 900EX in 2004. The primary changes offered more sophisticated avionics.

DASSAULT FALCON 2000
1994–Present

STANDARD DATA: Falcon 900EX Seats 8-12. Gross wt. 35,800. Empty wt. 20,735. Engines two 5,918-lb. General Electric/Allied Signal CFE738 turbofans. PERFORMANCE: Max cruise Mach 0.85. Range 3,000-3,125 nm. Ceiling 47,000'.

The Falcon 2000 derived from the Falcon 900, but was designed as a smaller transcontinental jet with a reduction in range. That factor allowed Dassault to remove one engine, and make the Falcon 2000 more economical to operate and maintain. Its two remaining engines were developed in partnership with General Electric and Allied Signal specifically for the new jet design.

DE HAVILLAND DH-115 "VAMPIRE"
1944–1961

STANDARD DATA: Seats 1-2. Gross wt. 11,150. Empty wt. 7,380. Engine one 3,350-lb. Goblin 3 Centrifugal flow turbojet. PERFORMANCE: Max speed

538 mph. Cruise speed 316 mph. Range 840 nm. Ceiling 40,000'

The twin-tailed Vampire was too late to see service in World War II, but quickly became Britain's home defense fighter. By 1951 the Vampire was being replaced by the Meteor, so in 1950 de Havilland offered a two-seat training version of the jet. Training and tactical versions of the jet remained in service in a number of countries throughout the world until the 1970s.

DOUGLAS DC-8
1959–81

STANDARD DATA: (Super 61) Seats 259. Gross wt. 325,000. Empty wt. 148,897. Fuel capacity 23,390. Engines four 18,000-lb. s.t. Pratt & Whitney turbofans. PERFORMANCE: Top mph 600. Landing mph 153. Initial climb rate 2,270. Range 3,750. Takeoff run 9,980. Landing roll 6,140.

The DC-8 has been produced in eight versions that can be divided into two groups: the first five standard versions and the Super Sixty line. The Series 10, introduced in 1958, was powered by 13,500-lb. s.t. turbojets and had a 17,600-gallon fuel capacity. In the same year, the Series 20 flew with its 15,800-lb. s.t. turbojets and similar fuel tankage. The long-range Series 30 flew in 1959 and was outfitted with 16,800- or 17,500-lb. s.t. turbojets and 23,079 gallons of fuel. The long-range Series 40 was introduced in the same year and differed from the Series 30 by utilizing Rolls-Royce engines. The Series 50 was the first to employ turbofans: either 17,000 or 18,000 lbs. s.t.

The Series 61 was the first of the Super Sixties. It and the Series 62 were introduced in 1966 and were powered by 18,000-lb. s.t. turbofans. The 61 was the extended-fuselage version, and the 62 was designed for long-range routes. The Series 63 used 19,000-lb. s.t engines and combined the features of the 61 and 62.

Despite the company's optimism over the development of the DC-8, by the mid-1960s it became clear that Douglas Aircraft was in need of capital, and in the view of some, new management as well. In 1967, Douglas accepted an offer from McDonnell Aircraft Corporation, and McDonnell Douglas began operations on April 28, 1967.

DOUGLAS DC-9
1965–86

STANDARD DATA: (Series 50) Seats 139. Gross wt. 121,000. Empty wt. 55,700. Fuel capacity 3,700. Engines two 15,500- or 16,000-lb. s.t. Pratt & Whitney turbofans. PERFORMANCE: Top mph 576. Cruise mph 561. Initial climb rate 2,850. Range 932. Takeoff distance (35') 7,750. Landing distance (50') 4,720.

The DC-9 is the McDonnell Douglas short-to-medium-range rear-engine jet transport. It was designed to operate on shorter routes in and out of smaller airports. It stands lower to the ground than its larger brother, the DC-8. This facilitates passenger and baggage access at airports where there are no large terminal complexes with built-in loading and unloading ramps. The DC-8 Series 10 was the initial version powered by 12,250-lb. s.t. turbofans. The Series 20 was designed for operation in hot climates or high-altitude conditions with a longer wingspan similar to the Series 30 but with a shorter body similar to the Series 10. The Series 30 increased in size with 14,000-lb. turbofans and larger 150-passenger load. The Series 40 with still larger engines, 14,500 lbs. s.t., had increased fuel capacity and accommodations for up to 125 passengers.

DOUGLAS DC 10
1971–91

STANDARD DATA: (Series 30) Seats 225-380. Gross wt. 555,000. Empty wt. 263,500. Fuel capacity 35,800. Engines 49,008-lb. s.t. General Electric turbofans. PERFORMANCE: Top mph 610. Cruise mph 578. Landing mph 167. Initial climb rate 3,000.

Range 4,375. Ceiling 34,000. Takeoff distance (35')
11,670. Landing distance (50') 5,960.

The Douglas DC-10 is designed to carry more passengers for less cost while still retaining a capability for
utilizing airports with shorter runways. It is capable of
operating economically over ranges from 300 to 3,200
miles. Standard seating accommodations are for 270
mixed-class passengers or for a maximum of 380. The
DC-10 is powered by three turbofan engines; two are
mounted on pylons beneath the wings and the third is
installed above the aft fuselage at the base of the rudder. Four versions were built. The initial Series 10 had
40,000lb. s.t. General Electric turbofans. The extended-
range Series 20 had Pratt & Whitneys rated at 47,000
or 50,000 lbs. s.t. wet. The Series 30 was the same as
the Series 20 but with General Electric engines. The
Series 40 was a convertible freighter with Pratt &
Whitney engines.

EMBRAER ERJ-135/140/145
1996–Present

Embraer ERJ-135

STANDARD DATA: ERJ-145LR Seats 37-50. Gross
wt. 48,500. Empty wt. 26,470. Engines two 7,426-
lb. AE-3007A1 turbofans. PERFORMANCE: Max
cruise 450 kts. Range 1,550. Ceiling 37,000'.

Embraer's regional airliners have become some of
the world's most popular short haulers. Drastically redesigned from its popular Brasilia, the ERJ-145 first
went into service in 1996. The model's success spawned
instant variants, including the shorter ERJ-135 and 140
which were flying a year and a half later. Upgraded versions of each model have followed. The ERJ-145LR
came in 1998 and the XR came in 2002, both with larger
more efficient engines, an increase in takeoff weight and
more fuel capacity for extended range. The ERJ-135
has also translated into Embraer's Legacy corporate jet.

EMBRAER ERJ-170/175/190/195
2004–Present

STANDARD DATA: ERJ-170 Seats 78. Gross wt.
78,153. Empty wt. 44,422. Engines two 14,000-lb.
General Electric CF34-8E. PERFORMANCE: Max
cruise 470 kts. Range 1,800-2,100 nm. Ceiling

Embraer ERJ-170

37,000'. Takeoff field length 5,499'. Landing field
length 399'.

Embraer's success in regionals is manifested in its
largest and most capable models in the fleet, the ERJ
170-195. As the numbers imply, each model of the ERJ
is bigger that the predecessor. The original ERJ-170 has
70 seats, the ERJ-175 is five feet longer with 78, the
190 holds 98 passengers and the 195 will seat up to
108. Each version of Embraer's biggest regional jets
come in a standard and long range version, plus the
company is looking at a variant of the ERJ-170 as a
corporate jet.

FAIRCHILD AEROSPACE
328JET/528JET/728JET
1999–Present

STANDARD DATA: 728JET Seats 7-110. Gross wt.
83,754. Engines two 12,500-lb. General Electric
CF343-3D1 turbofans. PERFORMANCE: Max cruise
460 kts. Range 1,400-4,000 nm. Ceiling 41,000'.
Takeoff 4,800'. Landing 4,659'.

When Fairchild Dornier became Fairchild Aerospace, the basic 328 turboprop was soon to become
the 328JET. FADEC Pratt & Whitneys were hung under
the wings, the landing gear was strengthened, and new
Honeywell Primus 2000 EFIS panels were installed in
the cockpit. The new airplane was thus brought to
market in record time. Fairchild is developing the En-
voy, a private jet variant of the 328JET, and the 528JET,
a 55-63 seat stretch. A larger 728Jet was planned until
the company declared bankruptcy in 2002.

FOKKER F28 "FELLOWSHIP"

1980–90

STANDARD DATA: (4000) Seats 55-85. Gross wt. 73,000. Empty wt. 38,269. Fuel capacity 2,558-3,430. Engines two 9,908-lb. s.t. Rolls-Royce turbofans. PERFORMANCE: Top mph 380. Cruise mph 523. Threshold mph 127. Ceiling 35,000. Range 1,036-1,611. Takeoff distance 5,217. Landing distance 3,166.

In 1980, Empire Airlines, based in Utica, New York, entered into an agreement to purchase F28 Mk 4000s to put into commuter service. The F28 Fellowship short/medium-haul transport was originally developed by Fokker in collaboration with other European aircraft manufacturers. Production is shared by Fokker-VFW of the Netherlands in association with MBB and VFW-Fokker in Germany and Short Brothers in Great Britain. The first flight of the prototype occurred in May 1967. The Mk 300 is similar to the Mk 400 with a short fuselage and seating for 65. The Mk 4000 is a long-fuselage version with high-density seating for up to 85. The Mk 6000 is a long version with slatted wings and seating for up to 79 passengers.

FOKKER F100

1988–Present

STANDARD DATA: Seats 85-107. Gross wt. 98,000. Empty wt. 58,645. Engines two Rolls-Royce Tay Mk 650-15 turbofans. PERFORMANCE: Max cruise 456 kts. Long range cruise 453 kts. Range 1,323 nm. Ceiling 35,000.

The F100 is based on the F28 Mk 4000, but with noticeable differences. The fuselage is longer, the wing is redesigned, and power comes from more modern Rolls-Royce engines. The panel is all glass as well. In 1993, the F100 came with a higher MTOW and more fuel capacity. In 1994, one option was a quick-change model featuring a cargo door on the left side behind the cockpit.

FOUGA MAGISTER "CM-170"

1952–1972

STANDARD DATA: Seats 2. Gross wt. 7,055. Empty wt. 4,740. Engines two 882-lb Turbomeca Marbore IIA turbojets. PERFORMANCE: Max cruise 444 mph. Range 575 nm. Ceiling 36,090'.

Developed in France, the butterfly-tail Fouga won instant praise from the French Air Force. The two-seat trainer was exported to a number of other countries, and even flew ground attack missions during the Six Day War in 1967. While France retired the Fouga during the 1980s, the Irish Air Corps used the aircraft as a light attack/trainer well into the 1990s. As a war bird, the Fouga Magister is relatively inexpensive to own and operate. Consequently dozens are now in private hands.

GRUMMAN AMERICAN GULFSTREAM II/III/IV/V

1967–Present

STANDARD DATA: (II) Seats 19. Gross wt. 62,000. Empty wt. 29,000. Fuel capacity 3,478. Engines two 11,440-lb. s.t. Rolls-Royce Spey turbofans. PERFORMANCE: Top mph 588. Cruise mph 526. Stall mph 116. Initial climb rate 4,350. Range 3,886. Ceiling 43,000. Takeoff run 5,000. Landing roll 3,190.

STANDARD DATA: (III) Seats 19. Gross wt. 68,200. Empty wt. 38,300. Fuel capacity 4,400. Engines two

Gulfstream II

Gulfstream III

Gulfstream V

11,400-lb. s.t. Rolls-Royce Spey turbofans. PERFORMANCE: Top speed Mach 0.85. Cruise speed Mach 0.77. Stall mph 121. Ceiling 45,000. Range 4,330. Takeoff run 5,850. Landing roll 3,400.

STANDARD DATA: (IV) Seats 14-24. Gross wt. 70,200. Empty wt. 33,400. Fuel capacity 4,340. Engines two 12,420-lb. s.t. Rolls-Royce Tay turbofans. PERFORMANCE: Top mph 564. Economy cruise mph 528. Stall mph 121. Ceiling 45,000. Range 4,952. Takeoff run 5,100. Landing roll 3,200.

STANDARD DATA: (V) Seats 14-24. Gross wt. 70,200. Empty wt. 33,400. Fuel capacity 4,340. Engines two 12,420-lb. s.t. Rolls-Royce Tay turbofans. PERFORMANCE: Top mph 564. Economy cruise mph 528. Stall mph 121. Ceiling 45,000. Range 4,952. Takeoff run 5,100. Landing roll 3,200.

The Grumman Gulfstream II was originally designed as a business jet, but an enlarged version would eventually serve in feeder airline use. This aircraft evolved from the Gulfstream I turboprop, which was introduced in 1958. Production of the swept-wing Model II version with turbofan engines started in 1965, and the first delivery was in 1967. It is one of the larger business jets, with a gross weight of 58,000 pounds. It is also one of the fastest, with a top speed of 589 mph, and it has a long-range capability of up to 3,600 miles.

The Gulfstream II is at the upper limit of size for business jets. The next step upward is into the Boeing 737 or the Douglas DC-9. It ranks as the fastest of the jets in this class by a margin of nearly 10 mph. Engines are by Rolls-Royce. The single-engine ceiling is 37,000 feet. The Gulfstream at gross weight has a range of slightly fewer than 3,000 miles.

The Gulfstream III was certified in September 1980. Using a supercritical-wing design and powered by Rolls-Royce engines, the Model III has a long-range cruising speed of 555 mph.

The Gulfstream IV has seating for 24. Set at economy cruise of 528 mph and at 45,000 feet, the G-IV is capable of flying nonstop almost 5,000 miles.

The Gulfstream G V entered service in 1997 and was designed as a competitor to the Boeing BBJ, the Bombardier Global Express and the Airbus A319CJ. The fuselage is 8 feet longer than the preceding G IV, and features a new wing design built by Northrop Grumman for high speed flight. Six Honeywell EFIS screens on the panel make the G V one of the fastest, most sophisticated means of travel on earth.

HAWKER SIDDELEY DH 125
1964–81

STANDARD DATA: Seats 9. Gross wt. 25,000. Empty wt. 12,700. Fuel capacity 1,416. Engines two 3,750-lb. s.t. Rolls-Royce Viper 601 turbofans. PERFORMANCE: Top mph 524. Stall mph 94. Initial climb rate 4,500. Range 1,959. Ceiling 41,000. Takeoff distance (50') 5,350. Landing distance (50') 2,550.

Beech Aircraft Corp. began to market the Hawker Siddeley DH 125 corporate jet in the United States in 1970. Designated the Beech Hawker, it featured a center cabin aisle recessed below the level of the floor supporting the seats on either side. This gave sufficient cabin height to allow a passenger stand-up headroom. Such an arrangement was made possible by a wing attachment technique opposite to that used in the Japanese-built Mitsubishi MU-2. The wing spar crosses the fuselage above the cabin on the MU-2 and below the fuselage on the Beech Hawker 125. On later models, a faired auxiliary fuel tank is tucked up below the fuselage and behind the wing, simultaneously improving streamlining and increasing range.

The DH 125 met with considerable success as a corporate executive transport because of its cruising range beyond 2,000 miles, its ability to operate above 41,000 feet, and its ability to operate from runways that are fewer than 4,000 feet long. The DH 125 was selected for production as a standard Royal Air Force machine under the name "Dominie." Hawker Siddeley continued to build the jet in Great Britain, but its agreement with Beech was terminated in middle of 1975. Development of the DH 125 included a "700" series powered by Garrett AiResearch TFE-731-3-IH engines.

HAWKER SIDDELEY COMET 4
1956–64

STANDARD DATA: Seats 68-81. Gross wt. 162,000. Empty wt. 74,900. Fuel capacity 10,686. Engines four 10,509-lb. s.t. Rolls-Royce Avon turbojets. PERFORMANCE: Top mph 526. Cruise mph 500. Range 4,030. Takeoff run 6,750. Landing distance (50') 6,880.

A BOAC Comet 4 was put into service Oct. 4, 1958, on the world's first transatlantic jet service. It was a long-range version of the basic Comet design and was easily recognized by the projection of the two-pod fuel tanks on the leading edge of each wing. Most of the flight tests for the Comet 4 were conducted on the one and only Comet 3 built by Hawker. A great deal of structural knowledge was gained through the unfortunate accidents of four of the original nine Comet I models. This knowledge was later tested on the model 3 and applied to the model 4. Following the model 4, the Comet 4B was produced for intermediate-range flights carrying a high-density passenger load. The model C-2 was a military cargo airplane and was structurally far superior to the original Comet 1.

HAWKER SIDDELEY TRIDENT
1964–81

STANDARD DATA: Seats 97-180. Gross wt. 150,000. Empty wt. 81,778. Fuel capacity 6,750. Engines three 11,960-lb. s.t. turbofans and one 5,250-lb. s.t Rolls-Royce Spey turbojet. PERFOR-

MANCE: Top mph 601. Cruise mph 533. Stall mph 129. Range 1,785. Takeoff distance (35') 8,900. Landing distance

The British tri-engine short- to medium-range jet first flew in airline service in 1964. It has been produced in four models. The IE featured accommodations for a maximum of 115 passengers and was powered by 11,400-lb. s.t. turbofans. The 2F featured increased fuel capacity and takeoff weight and was fitted with 11,960-lb. s.t. turbofans. The 3B was a high-capacity short-haul transport with a lengthened fuselage and the addition of a 5,250-lb. s.t. turbojet in the tail for better takeoff performance. The Super 3B was an upgraded version of the 3B. The first automatic landing at London Airport was made with a Trident in 1965.

HAWKER 400XP

STANDARD DATA: Seats 7-9. Gross wt. 16,500. Empty wt. 10,550. Fuel capacity 733. Engines two 2,965-lb. Pratt & Whitney JT15D-5 turbofans. PERFORMANCE: Max cruise 450 kts. Long range cruise 414 kts. Range 874-1,687 nm. Ceiling 45,000'. Takeoff distance 3,906'. Landing distance 3,514'.

The design began as the Mitsubishi MU-300 Diamond in 1978. In 1985 Beechcraft acquired the rights, and the Diamond II became the Beechjet 400. In 2003 its name changed once again to the Hawker 400XP (for 'extended performance') for a better fit into the Raytheon family of bizjets.

Newest Hawker 400XPs belie the airframe's age. The flight deck is equipped with a Rockwell Collins Pro Line 4 EFIS plus a V-speed indicator, airspeed trend indicator and a Doppler radar turbulence detector. Military variants of the 400s airframe fly with the United States Air Force and the Japan Air Self Defense Force for pilot training.

HAWKER 800XP
1995–Present

STANDARD DATA: Seats 8-15. Gross wt. 28,120. Empty wt. 16,245. Fuel capacity 1,492. Engines two 4,669-lb. Honeywell TFE731-5BR turbofans. PERFORMANCE: Max cruise 447 kts. Long range cruise 402 kts. Range 2,285-2,621 nm. Ceiling 41,000. Takeoff distance 5,030'. Landing distance 2,650'.

The series 800 Hawkers were built in the UK until Raytheon purchased the production rights from Hawker Siddeley in 1993, and two years later the 800XP went into service. Over 1,000 of both models are now flying.

The 800XP got an interior upgrade in 1999. Pilots got the Honeywell SPZ 8000 avionics suite or can choose the Rockwell Collins EFIX-86 system as an option. The Hawker 800XP has been extremely well received for fractional aircraft ownership programs, as well as finding service with the U.S. Air Force, the Republic of China and in Japan.

HAWKER HORIZON
2004–Present

STANDARD DATA: Seats 8-14. Gross wt. 37,700. Empty wt. 21,555. Fuel capacity 2,134. Engines two 6,900-lb. Pratt & Whitney PW308A turbofans. PERFORMANCE: Max cruise 470 kts. Long range cruise 430 kts. Range 2,763-3,477 nm. Ceiling 45,000. Takeoff distance 5,088'. Landing distance 2,907'.

Raytheon's biggest Hawker design (30% larger than the 800XP) originated at roughly the same time as the initial work began on the Premier I. The Horizon would

be an effort to blend high technology with earlier Hawker flight characteristics. The composite construction, clean-sheet design received FAA certification in 2004.

On the flight deck is a Primus Epic flight control system and flight management system. The navigation comes from a dual VHF omnidirectional radio navigation system, dual distance measuring equipment, dual inertial navigation system and a dual global positioning system.

Preliminary performance specifications for the 37,500-pound-MTOW, P&WC PW308A-powered twinjet include a 470-knot high-cruise speed, 3,366 nm NBAA IFR range (two crew and six passengers), and a 5,088' balanced field length.

ILYUSHIN IL-62
1967–81

STANDARD DATA: Seats 168-186. Gross wt. 357,000. Empty wt. 146,390. Fuel capacity 26,420. Engines four 23,150-lb. s.t. Kuznetsov turbofans. PERFORMANCE: Top mph 560. Cruise mph 510.

Landing mph 137. Range 4,160. Takeoff run 10,660. Landing roll 9,185.

Produced in Kazan, Russia (formally U.S.S.R.), the 174-foot airliner first flew to North America on September 15, 1967, on a maiden flight from Moscow to Montreal. It replaced the older TU-114, the giant turboprop transport, on Aeroflot's intercontinental routes. In July 1968, the IL-62 began service from Moscow to New York and would subsequently fly on all of Aeroflot's long-range flights, such as Moscow to Tokyo. The airliner is capable of carrying more than 150 passengers and reserve fuel on a flight of more than 4,800 miles. The basic IL-62 was announced in September 1962 during Khrushchev's regime; the aircraft will carry up to 186 passengers, but other seating arrangements provide more leg room with 114 or 168 passengers.

Shown first at the Paris Air Show in 1971, the IL-62M200 is a high-density version of the IL-62 that seats a maximum 198 economy-class passengers or 161 in a mixed-class configuration. The newer deluxe model has the same outer dimensions as those found on the basic model, but an additional fuel tank in the tail of the plane plus improved turbofan engines give the airplane greater range and payload.

Looking very much like the British VC-10, the IL-62 has its four engines horizontally mounted on the fuselage at the tail. Aside from airline markings, the easiest way to tell the two aircraft apart is by the two tail wheels mounted on a tall spindly strut just aft of the engine exhaust on the IL-62. The Russian airliner has two airflow guide vanes on the forward section of the fuselage, while the VC-10 builders placed airguide vanes on the top wing surface.

ISRAEL COMMODORE/ WESTWIND JET
1968–87

STANDARD DATA: (Westwind) Seats 10. Gross wt. 20,700. Empty wt. 9,370. Fuel capacity 1,330. Engines two 3,109-lb. s.t. General Electric turbojets. PERFORMANCE: Top mph 428. Cruise mph 420. Stall mph 112. Initial climb rate 4,040. Range 1,600. Ceiling 45,000. Takeoff distance (35') 4,100. Landing distance (50') 3,400.

The Jet Commander originated with Aero Commander in 1967 when the Rockwell Company, then making Aero Commanders, was merged with North American. One of the conditions imposed by the government on approval of the merger was Aero Commander disposing of its jet. The purchaser turned out to be the State of Israel. Manufacturing in Israel began in 1969. The Jet Commander is one of the most frequently seen of the business jets along with the Lear. The Commander's appearance is also unique with a long, slim fuselage and short wings set far back. It is also one of the smaller of the business jets and one of the most economical to operate, consuming only about 225 gallons per hour.

The Jet Commander is so easy to control that flight controls are not boosted hydraulically and there is no artificial stall-warning device. In a deliberate stall, the Jet Commander will not fall off either wing. When Israel Aircraft industries began production of the Commodore Jet, several improvements were added: increased takeoff weight, strengthened landing gear, greater fuel capacity, and improved performance.

The 1123 Westwind features a longer cabin, auxiliary wingtip fuel tanks, more powerful engines, two additional cabin windows, and modified wing leading edges. The 1124 Westwind is the long-range version utilizing two 3,700-lb. s.t. Garrett turbofans with an 8,620-gallon fuel capacity.

The 1123 converted to the 1124 when Garrett TFE731 turbofans were added. That model changed to the 1124A Westwind 2 with improved hot and high performance, better fuel economy and longer range. The Westwind 2 also had a modified wing, winglets, and upgrades to the interior.

LEARJET
1964–95

Learjet 25D

STANDARD DATA: (24E) Seats 6-8. Gross wt. 12,499. Empty wt. 7,025. Fuel capacity 715. Engines two 2,950-lb. s.t. General Electric turbojets. PERFORMANCE: Top mph 534. Cruise mph 507. Stall mph 101. Initial climb rate 7,220. Ceiling 45,000. Range 1,455. Balanced field length 3,000.

Learjet 36A

STANDARD DATA: (24F) Seats 6-8. Gross wt. 13,500. Empty wt. 7,130. Fuel capacity 840. Engines two 2,950-lb. s.t. General Electric turbojets. PERFORMANCE: Top mph 534. Cruise mph 507. Stall mph 101. Initial climb rate 7,100. Ceiling 51,000. Range 1,695. Balanced field length 3,297.

STANDARD DATA: (25D) Seats 8-10. Gross wt. 15,000. Empty wt. 7,640. Fuel capacity 910. Engines 2,950-lb. s.t. General electric turbojets. PERFORMANCE: Top mph 534. Cruise mph 507. Stall mph 107. Initial climb rate 6,300. Ceiling 51,000. Range 1,765. Balanced field length 3,937.

STANDARD DATA: (25F) Seats 6-8. Gross wt. 15,000. Empty wt. 7,575. Fuel capacity 1,103. Engines two 2,958-lb. s.t. General Electric turbojets. PERFORMANCE: Top mph 534. Cruise mph 507. Stall mph 107. Initial climb rate 6,300. Ceiling 51,000. Range 1,910. Balanced field length 3,937.

STANDARD DATA: (35A) Seats 6. Gross wt. 17,300. Empty wt. 9,110. Fuel capacity 931. Engines two 3,500-lb. s.t. AiResearch turbofans. PERFORMANCE: Top mph 534. Cruise mph 507. Stall mph 110. Initial climb rate 4,900. Ceiling 45,000. Range 2,785. Balanced field length 4,224.

STANDARD DATA: (36A) Seats 6. Gross wt. 18,300. Empty wt. 9,154. Fuel capacity 1,110. Engines two 3,500-lb. s.t. AiResearch turbofans. PERFORMANCE: Top mph 534. Cruise mph 507. Stall mph 110. Initial climb rate 4,525. Ceiling 45,000. Range 3,285. Balanced field length 4,784.

By name, the LearJet is probably the most recognized private jet in the world. Indeed, the name is almost synonymous with executive jet aircraft. The first model 23 was delivered in 1964 with seating for eight. Two years later, the improved model 24 with airline transport category certification was introduced, and in 1968, a stretched 10-seat model 25 was offered. This aircraft has the most exceptional climb rate in its class. The model 23 at gross weight will climb at 6,900 fpm. All Learjets are approved for operation at 45,000 feet, and they have much better short-field performance than is common in this category of aircraft. One reason for the climb and takeoff advantage is weight: The model 23, which needs only 2,300 feet to clear a 50-foot obstacle at gross-weight takeoff, weighs only 6,500 pounds empty and grosses at 12,500 pounds. It can fly at 26,000 feet with one engine inoperable.

Models include the 24E with seats for six to eight and featuring a short balanced field length of 2,590 feet. The 24F has the same accommodations as the 24E but with a larger gross weight by 1,001 pounds. The 25D offers seating for eight to 10 and a 15,000-pound gross weight. The 25F with the same 15,000 gross weight has provisions for fewer passengers to allow for a greater fuel load. The 35A is a transcontinental version with a 17,000-pound maximum takeoff weight and a 2,858-mile range. The transoceanic 36A features a farther than 2,000-mile range and an 18,000-pound weight when fully loaded.

The 24- and 25-series models are powered by General Electric turbojets with 2,950 lbs. s.t. for takeoff. The 35A and 36A are outfitted with 3,500-lb. s.t. Garrett AiResearch turbofan engines; the 55, 55ER, and 55LR are all powered by two 3,700-lb. s.t. Garrett AiResearch turbofans and can carry 1,001 gallons of fuel for ranges up to 3,003 miles.

All models feature a new modified wing design to reduce approach speeds and balanced field length without sacrificing Mach cruise and range. In conjunction with the Dee Howard Co., Gates Learjet developed a new 20-series model with extended range capabilities, the Century III 25G. The 30-series has its takeoff weight increased by 300 pounds and its landing weight boosted by 1,000 pounds. The TBO for the 20-series General Electric engine was increased from 4,000 to 5,000 hours.

LEARJET LONGHORN 54/55/56
1978–94

Learjet Longhorn

STANDARD DATA: (54) Seats 12. Gross wt. 10,216. Fuel capacity 825. Engines two 3,650-lb. s.t. Garrett AiResearch fanjets. PERFORMANCE: Top mph 550. Stall mph 100. Initial climb rate 5,380. Ceiling 51,000. Range 2,300. Balanced field length 3,520.

STANDARD DATA: (55) Seats 12. Gross wt. 18,500. Empty wt. 10,216. Fuel capacity 985. Engines two 3,650-lb. s.t. Garrett AiResearch fanjets. PERFORMANCE: Top mph 550. Stall mph 100. Initial climb rate 5,020. Ceiling 51,000. Range 2,825. Balanced field length 3,900.

STANDARD DATA: (56) Seats 12. Gross wt. 20,000. Empty wt. 10,257. Fuel capacity 1,194. Engines two 3,650-lb. s.t. Garrett AiResearch fanjets. PERFORMANCE: Top mph 550. Stall mph 100. Initial climb rate 4,700. Ceiling 51,000. Range 3,380. Balanced field length 4,160.

STANDARD DATA: (28) Seats 12. Gross wt. 15,000. Empty wt. 7,895. Fuel capacity 697. Engines two 2,950-lb. s.t. General Electric turbojets. PERFORMANCE: Top mph 550. Stall mph 91. Initial climb rate 6,350. Ceiling 51,000. Range 1,525. Balanced field length 2,520.

STANDARD DATA: (29) Seats 10. Gross wt. 15,000. Empty wt. 7,824. Fuel capacity 786. Engines two 2,950-lb. s.t. General Electric turbojets. PERFORMANCE: Top mph 550. Stall mph 91. Initial climb rate 6,110. Ceiling 51,000. Range 1,780. Balanced field length 2,700.

Learjet's Longhorn series combines a revolutionary wing design, two of the most advanced engines introduced to the market, and 51,000-foot performance. The line of five aircraft has been designated the Learjet 28 and Learjet 29, both powered by General Electric turbojets, and the Learjet 54/55/56, and those three are powered by twin Garrett AiResearch fanjets. All the models are designed with a larger wing incorporating near-vertical winglets that have replaced the traditional Learjet tiptanks.

The wing's increased aspect ratio and super-critical winglets provide substantial aerodynamic improvements that in turn produce greater fuel efficiency and improved flight performance at high and low altitudes. The wing also has been responsible for significantly improved short-field performance. The balanced field length for the 28/29 series is only 2,520 feet and 3,520 feet for the 54/55/56 series. In addition, the 28/29 is able to climb from takeoff directly to 51,000 feet, something no other business jet can do.

LEARJET 40/45
1998–Present

STANDARD DATA: Seats 9. Gross wt. 20,750. Empty wt. 13,888. Engines two 3,500-lb. Honeywell TFE731-20-AR turbofans. PERFORMANCE: Max cruise 464 kts. Long range cruise 430 kts. Range 2,032 nm. Ceiling 51,000. Takeoff distance (50) 5,250. Landing distance 2,660'.

Learjet 40

In early 1990, Learjet was purchased by Bombardier. The high performing jets fit perfectly into the company's growing family of personal/corporate/airline transportation. The Lear 45 is Bombardier's medium-size jet market contender, with the first deliveries starting in 1998. As its number designator implies, the Learjet 45 is larger than the model 31, and smaller than the Learjet 60. The flightdeck has been all glass since day one. FADEC-equipped Allied Signal engines make this later version easier to maintain and more fuel efficient than all previous models.

In 2002, Bombardier offered a smaller version of the Learjet 45, the model 40. The aircraft is designed for shorter hops with maximum Lear performance. The Learjet 40 features the same engines, cockpit and systems as the Learjet 45, but with a slightly shorter fuselage. The Learjet 40 offers a 36% larger cabin and 35% more range than the Learjet 31 for only a 10% higher price. The 40 can fly with a full passenger load of seven and full fuel. With four passengers, it will travel from New York to Chicago in one hour and 35 minutes.

LEARJET 60
1993–Present

Learjet 60

STANDARD DATA: Seats 10. Gross wt. 23,500. Empty wt. 13,850. Engines two 4,300-lb. Pratt & Whitney PW305A turbofans. PERFORMANCE: Max Cruise 453 kts. Long range cruise 420 kts. Range 2,409 nm. Ceiling 51,000'.

The Learjet 60 is a follow-up to the Lear 55, the largest of the Learjet fleet. It is a direct evolution of the Longhorn wing mated to an extended 10-passenger fuselage. The Learjet 60 first flew in 1991 with final certification coming in 1993. The big Learjet has complete cross-continental range, and as the showpiece of the line, features an amazing array of interior options and accoutrements.

LOCKHEED "JETSTAR"
1961–81

STANDARD DATA: Seats 10. Gross wt. 43,750. Empty wt. 24,178. Fuel capacity 2,660. Engines four 3,700-lb. s.t. Garrett AiResearch turbofans. PERFORMANCE: Top mph 552, Cruise mph 508. Stall mph 142. Initial climb rate 2,450. Range 3,189. Ceiling 38,000. Takeoff distance (50) 5,250. Landing distance (50) 3,900.

The Lockheed Georgia JetStar was the first of the executive jets and was uniquely the only four-engine jet of its type in the class. In its time, the JetStar had many features that were normally found only on larger jet commercial airliners such as dual landing gear, thrust reversers, standing headroom throughout the cabin, backup systems, a complete lavatory, galley, and superior pressurization. This jet is rated as having a cruise speed of 550 mph. It can carry a maximum of 10 persons plus a crew of two. The Lockheed JetStar is capable of taking off on runways as short as 5,000 feet.

The JetStar II was introduced in 1974. The main difference between the two being the use of Garrett AiResearch turbofans flat rated at 3,700 lbs. s.t. instead of the previous 3,300-lb. Pratt & Whitney turbojets.

LOCKHEED L-1011 "TRISTAR"
1972–83

STANDARD DATA: Seats 250-400. Gross wt. 430,000. Empty wt. 222,941. Fuel capacity 23,814. Engines three 42,000-lb. s.t. Rolls-Royce three-shaft turbofans. PERFORMANCE: Top mph 500. Cruise mph 474. Stall mph 144. Initial climb rate 2,800. Range 2,677. Ceiling 42,000. Takeoff run 7,590. Landing roll 5,660.

Early in 1966 Lockheed became interested in the short- to medium-haul airliner market. The Model L-1011 was designed to enter this category with optimum payload-range performance and short-field characteristics. The Model L-1011 is powered by three 42,000-lb. s.t. turbofan engines, two of which are mounted in pods underneath each wing, and the third is located in the rear of the fuselage at the base of the tail unit. Fuel is carried in two integral wing tanks and an inboard tank. With a full load, the TriStar can travel a maximum of 4,467 miles. Accommodations provide for 256 passengers in a mixed coach and first-class arrangement or a maximum of 400 passengers in a high-density all-economy configuration.

LOCKHEED T-33
1946–1959

STANDARD DATA: T-33A Seats (ejection) 2. Gross wt. 16,800. Empty wt. 8,440. Engine one 5,400-lb. Allison J-33-A/4 turbojet with w/water-alcohol injection. PERFORMANCE: Max Speed 525 mph. Long range cruise 455 mph. Range 1,000 nm. Ceiling 47,000'.

The 'T-Bird' was the first widely used jet trainer, a design evolved from the P-80 Shooting Star that flew briefly at the end of World War II. Original engines were Allison J33-35 single-shaft turbojet engines with a thrust rating of 5,200 lbs. Almost 6,000 T-33s were built in the United States, 210 in Japan (by Kawasaki) and 656 in Canada featuring the Rolls-Royce Nene engines. By the end of 2000, 7 nations in the world still listed the T-33 as "in service."

LOCKHEED SR-71 "BLACKBIRD"
1964–1990

STANDARD DATA: Seats 2. Gross wt. 170,000. Empty wt. 60,000. Fuel capacity 13,000+ gallons.

Engines two 32,500-lb Pratt & Whitney J-58 turbofans operating in continuous afterburn. PERFORMANCE: Max cruise Mach 3.5+. Range 2,982 nm. Ceiling 85,000+.

Though it was conceived and designed back in the early 1960s, no air-breathing aircraft on earth can match the speed of the Lockheed's SR-71 Blackbird. As a Cold War reconnaissance aircraft, it spent more time in hostile airspace than any other aircraft. Its development under the hand of Kelly Johnson at the Lockheed Skunk Works required the development of a variety of new technologies, including the titanium aircraft skin and the Mach 3+ powerplants. Though NASA flew the Blackbirds through 1999, the SR-71 left US Air Force service in January 1990. On a flight from the West Coast to the East Coast, where the aircraft was to retire to permanent static display at the Smithsonian, the Blackbird set a new transcontinental speed record, flying from Los Angeles to Washington D.C. in 1 hour, 4 minutes, and 20 seconds, averaging a speed of 2,124 mph.

MCDONNELL DOUGLAS MD80/90
1981–2000

MD90

STANDARD DATA: MD-81 Seats 142-172. Gross wt. 140,000. Empty wt. 78,420. Fuel capacity 4,812. Engines two 18,550-lb. s.t. Pratt & Whitney JT8D turbofans. PERFORMANCE: Max cruise 500 kts. Long range cruise 440 kts. Ceiling 35,000+. Range 1,563-2,630 nm. Takeoff distance 7,250. Landing distance 4,860.

STANDARD DATA: MD-90 Seats 141-187. Gross wt. 156,000. Empty wt. 88,000. Engines two 25,000-lb. International Aero V2525D5 turbofans. PERFORMANCE: Cruise speed 437 kts. Range 2,085-3,022 nm.

The MD-80 series of aircraft were a stretched improvement of the DC-9. The first version of the jet was literally a re-engined DC-9. After a fuselage stretch, the aircraft became the DC-9 Super 80. In 1993, McDonnell Douglas renamed the aircraft the MD-80. Over the years, a number of variants would arrive, starting with the MD-81 and ending with the MD-88. All were more capable than their predecessors, all except the MD-87 which was smaller.

The largest of the line, the MD-90 came in 1993. Four and a half feet longer than the MD-88, it allowed for ten more passenger seats. The MD series of aircraft evolved into what is now the Boeing 717.

MCDONNELL DOUGLAS MD11
1990–2001

MD11

STANDARD DATA: Seats 315-400. Gross wt. 602,500. Empty wt. 277,000. Fuel capacity 32,185. Engines three 58,000-lb. s.t. Pratt & Whitney PW4358 turbofans. PERFORMANCE: Top mph 644. Cruise mph 588. Ceiling 45,000+. Range 5,010. Takeoff distance 10,100. Landing distance 6,470.

The MD-11 is a direct descendent from the DC-10. Certification came in 1990 and deliveries began the same year. Several variants included long range MD-11ER, the MD11CF freighter and two combination freighter/passenger aircraft. After the Boeing/McDonnell Douglas merger, the MD-11 was removed from production.

MESSERSCHMITT ME 262 "SWALLOW/STORMBIRD"
1942–1945

STANDARD DATA: Seats 1-2. Gross wt. 14,110. Empty wt. 8,378. Engines one BMW 003 turbojet. PERFORMANCE: Max cruise 540 mph. Range 652 nm. Ceiling 37,565'.

The ME 262 holds the distinction as the first turbojet aircraft to ever fly in combat. Developed by the Nazis beginning in 1939 and first flown in 1941, the new concept showed remarkable promise. The ME 262 had significant limitations. Huge fuel burns severely limited mission lengths, and the early jet engines were forever troublesome. As amazing as the new jet aircraft was, however, it was too little, too late. The Allied Air Force had been developed to incredible strength, and the war crippled Germany could not make enough ME 262s for the airplane to have much impact in the war. Only 1,433 ME 262s were built, 500 of those destroyed during Allied bombings, leaving less than 300 jets to enter into the final days of combat.

MESSERSCHMITT MBB HFB 320 "HANSA"
1966–74

STANDARD DATA: Seats 15. Gross wt. 20,280. Empty wt. 11,960. Fuel capacity 1,099. Engines two 3,108-lb. s.t. General Electric turbojets. PERFORMANCE: Top mph 513. Cruise mph 420. Stall mph 111. Initial climb rate 4,250. Range 1,472. Ceiling 40,000. Takeoff distance (50') 2,740. Landing distance (50') 4,429.

The first production Hansa Jet flew on February 2, 1966, and received FAA certification on April 7, 1967. The Hansa 320 is one of the most distinctive commercial jet designs and is easily identified by the 15-degree forward sweep of the wings. Aerodynamically, the forward sweep of the wings performs the same function as the rearward sweep. The forward sweep forestalls the undesirable control problems that occur as the upper-wing airflow reaches transsonic speed by directing the airflow spanwise. The Hansa can be used as an executive transport or as a 15-passenger feeder liner. Production of the Hansa was initiated by Hamburger Flugzeugbau and carried the name of Messerschmitt-Bolkow-Blohm (MBB) when the two large German aircraft companies merged in 1969.

MIKOYAN GUREVICH MIG 15 "FAGOT"
1949–1957

STANDARD DATA: Seats 1-2. Gross wt. 12,000. Empty wt. 8,115. Engine one 7,452-lb Klimov VK-1F turbojet. PERFORMANCE: Max speed 668 mph. Range 450 nm. Ceiling 50,855.

The Mikoyan Gurevich MiG 15 was a formidable fighter in the Korean War, flown primarily by Russian and Chinese pilots. It had good speed and maneuverability, plus two cannons. They were effective enough to inflict sufficient damage on American B-29 bombers that daylight raids were suspended. It met its match, however, against the North American F-86 Sabre. MiG 15 was gradually replaced throughout the late 1950s by the MiG 17, although it remained extremely popular throughout the Cold War in many East Block and Communist nations. Many MiG 15s are now flying as private aircraft in the United States.

MIKOYAN GUREVICH MIG 21 "FISHBED"
1956–1988

STANDARD DATA: Seats 1-2. Gross wt. 20,720. Empty wt. 8,115. Engine one 14,550-lb Turmanski R-13-300 turbojet. PERFORMANCE: Max speed 1,385 mph (Mach 2.1). Range 685 nm. Ceiling 50,000'.

The delta-wing MiG-21 fought the American F-4 Phantom during the Vietnam war, and was given the name 'Fishbed' by NATO allies. Variants of the Russian fighter became all-weather interceptors with increasingly powerful Soyuz engines. The MiG 21 was last made in India, but another variant, the F-7 is still in production in China. Dozens of air forces around the world still fly the Fishbed, and several are in private hands in the United States.

MITSUBISHI DIAMOND I/II/III
1979–94

STANDARD DATA: Seats 9-11. Gross wt. 13,890. Empty wt. 8,050. Fuel capacity 662. Engines two 2,500-lb. s.t. Pratt & Whitney Aircraft of Canada JT-15D-4 turbofans. PERFORMANCE: Top speed 0.78 Mach. Cruise mph 322. Minimum control mph 103. Range 1,800. Takeoff run 4,100. Landing roll 2,700.

The Diamond I was introduced in 1979 as Mitsubishi's example of a 500-mph-plus executive fanjet. Its twin turbofans are rated at 2,500 lbs. s.t. for takeoff and 2,375 lbs. s.t. for maximum continuous operation. The two Diamond I prototypes underwent 350 hours of test flying in Japan before their arrival in the United States for FAA certification. A Diamond offers the performance characteristics, cabin size, and comfort level of the medium-class swept-wing jets plus the low cost and economy associated with light jets and some turboprops. The Diamond I wing design, with its advanced flight control system of full-span flaps, wing spoilers, and T-tail empennage, is built for optimum performance. (For more, see HAWKER 400XP).

NORTH AMERICAN F-86 "SABRE"
1948–1956

STANDARD DATA: Seats 1. Gross wt. 13,791. Engines one 5,200-lb. General Electric J-47 turbojets. PERFORMANCE: Max speed 685 mph. Cruise speed 540 mph. Range 1,200 nm. Ceiling 49,000'.

The Sabre was the USAF's first swept wing fighter. Just six months after it was assigned to duty, the F-86 set a world speed record of 670.9 mph. Later the Sabre beat its own record, upping the bar to 715 mph. This fighter was the prime contender against the North Korean MiG-15, typically flown by Russian and Chinese pilots. The tally at the end of the war was telling, both about American technology and pilot skills. By the end of hostilities, it had shot down 729 MiGs, loosing only 76 Sabres—a victory ration of 10:1.

NORTHROP T-38 "TALON"
1961–Present

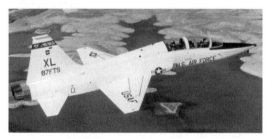

STANDARD DATA: Seats (ejection) 2. Gross wt. 12,000. Empty wt. 7,615. Engines two 3,850-lb. General Electric J-85-GE-5A turbojets. PERFORMANCE: Max speed 858 mph. Cruise Mach 0.9. Range 1,090. Ceiling 53,500'.

Though aging, the T-38 is still in heavy use around the world, from advanced jet training for the U.S. military to research applications with NASA, as well as in various roles in a variety of countries. The aircraft boasts a 720° per second roll rate. The T-38A ended production in 1971. A variant, the T-38B has a gunsight and a centerline pylon which can be fitted with a gun pod or bombs. The latest variant, the T-38C employed older airframes retrofitted with new, electronic instrumentation. Several T-38s have made their way back into the U.S. in private hands.

PIAGGIO-DOUGLAS PD808 VESPA-JET
1964–81

STANDARD DATA: Seats 5-9. Gross wt. 18,000. Empty wt. 10,650. Fuel capacity 984. Engines two 3,368-lb. s.t. Rolls-Royce Bristol Viper turbojets. PERFORMANCE: Top mph 529. Cruise mph 497. Stall mph 104. Initial climb rate 5,400. Range 1,332. Ceiling 45,000. Takeoff distance (35') 3,180. Landing distance (50') 2,990.

Under an agreement signed in 1961, Piaggio and Douglas Aircraft developed the PD-808 for military and commercial use. The aircraft was designed at Douglas and constructed by Piaggio. Taking to the air for the first time in 1964, the PD-808 was powered by Bristol Siddeley Viper turbojets mounted on the sides of the rear fuselage. Accommodations provided for a crew of one or two, five passengers in individual seats, bar, toilet, and baggage space.

Power increased in 1966 to 3,300 lbs. s.t. The PD-808 differed from the original model by having larger tip tanks, a longer dorsal fin, and a forward-sliding nose fairing. By 1972, the aircraft was available in several versions: a five-seat executive version, a seven-seat executive transport, a six-seat version for the Italian Air Force, and one powered by 3,500-lb. s.t. AiResearch turbofans. Other PD-808s are powered by twin 3,360-lb. s.t. turbojets drawing from two integrated tanks of 511 gallons total capacity and wingtip tanks with 473 gallons total capacity.

ROCKWELL 75A "SABRE"
1963–83

STANDARD DATA: Seats 10. Gross wt. 23,000. Empty wt. 13,000. Fuel capacity 1,102. Engines two 4,315-lb. s.t. General Electric turbofans. PERFORMANCE: Top mph 563. Cruise mph 527. Stall mph 99. Initial climb rate 4,500. Range 1,938. Ceiling 45,000. Takeoff run (balanced) 4,900. Landing roll 2,525.

As the North American Sabreliner, this executive jet bore a famous name. It actually began as a military utility transport aircraft and dates back to 1958. The commercial version emerged in 1963 as the Sabreliner. In its civilian form as an airliner and business jet, the Sabreliner ranks as medium sized. Its speed by jet standards is modest with a cruise of 489 knots. Because the Sabreliner was originally designed as a military T-39 and was designed to meet military specifications, it shows unmistakable signs of its origin. It is larger and more rugged and powerful than jets that have been designed solely for civilian use. The Sabreliner has excellent climb performance and a ceiling of 45,000 feet. Rockwell also built a Sabre 60 jet equipped with 3,300-lb.-thrust engines. Both the 74 and 60 models were fitted with thrust reversers to aid in shorter landings and assist in braking on icy or wet runways.

TUPOLEV TU-144
1972–81

STANDARD DATA: Seats 140. Gross wt. 396,830. Empty wt. 187,400. Fuel capacity 209,440 lbs. Engines four 44,090-lb. s.t. Kuznetsov turbofans. PERFORMANCE: Top mph 1,550. Cruise mph 1,430. Operating altitude 59,000. Range 4,030. Take-off distance (balanced) 9,845. Landing roll 8,530.

First shown at the 1965 Paris Air Show in model form, the TU-144 supersonic transport was the Soviet Union's rival for the British-French Concorde. The TU-144 was reported to be in production with design changes incorporated following the tragic crash of a prototype aircraft at the 1973 Paris Show. With a configuration similar to the Concorde, the Russian jetliner also featured a nose that is lowered hydraulically 12 degrees to improve cockpit vision during takeoff and landing. The wings are of double-delta design with a sweep-back of 70-75 degrees on the inboard portions and about 40 degrees on the outboard sections. The main landing gear had 12 tires each (three rows of four). The tall, spindly nose gear had just two wheels. A maximum 130 passengers could be accommodated in an all-economy version, but the initial model seated 98 in mixed classes (18 in first class and 80 in tourist). On May 26, 1970, the Russian aircraft became the first commercial transport to exceed Mach 2.

Homebuilt/Kitbuilt Aircraft

The inventor's spirit has long lived in the heart of the aviation enthusiast. The dream has been alive since perhaps the dawn of man, but building a flying machine that can carry man into the skies to fly with the birds has only recently become a reality. It is this spirit that drives certain individuals to plan and build their own aircraft regardless of the availability of production aircraft. There has never really been a lull in the experimental movement. As time and technology marches on, the movement continues to gain in popularity and numbers. Design innovation and the availability and use of the most technologically advanced materials has kept the fire burning while opening up doors to efficient structural and aerodynamic design.

During the energy crunch of the early 1970s, homebuilders began to focus on efficiency aspects of design, developing aircraft that could go farther, faster, and more economically than before. This led to the use of more innovative building materials and aerodynamic concepts. Innovative, efficient, state-of-the-art kit/homebuilt aircraft have now become commonplace.

In many ways, kitbuilt and homebuilt aircraft have always represented the "skinny branches" of aviation, the zone where new green sprigs of innovation can grow uninhibited from the temporal and financial obligations of production certification. Where once homebuilt aircraft were the realm of the hobbyist, many of these home-grown designs now leave certified aircraft in the dust in terms of price and performance. In that light, it is not surprising that one of the most celebrated homebuilders, Burt Rutan, was the first to put a civilian in space. And he did it with a *homebuilt* aircraft, SpaceShipOne.

ACE MODEL D "BABY ACE"

STANDARD DATA: Gross wt. 950. Empty wt. 575. Fuel capacity 17. Wingspan 26'5". Length 17'9". PERFORMANCE: Top mph 110. Cruise mph 100. Stall mph 34. Climb rate 1,200. Takeoff run 200. Landing roll 250. Range 350.

The Baby Ace is an ultralight monoplane specially designed for the amateur builder. It is the successor to the original Corben Baby Ace, which first flew in 1931 and was extensively redesigned in 1955 as the Model D. Baby Aces usually carry Continental engines rated from 65 to 85 hp, and owners consider their performance excellent. Construction consists of a steel-tube fuselage, all-wood wings, and fabric covering. Kits for model D and E are still offered.

ACE MODEL E "JUNIOR ACE"

STANDARD DATA: Gross wt. 1,335. Empty wt. 809. Fuel capacity 22. Wingspan 26'. Length 18'. PERFORMANCE: Top mph 130. Cruise mph 105. Stall mph 65. Climb rate 500. Ceiling 10,000. Takeoff run 400. Landing roll 600. Range 350.

The Junior Ace is the successor to the Baby Ace. This side-by-side two-seater version is powered by a Continental 85-hp engine. Construction is the same, consisting of a steel tube fuselage structure, all-wood wings, and fabric covering.

AERO AT-3

STANDARD DATA: Gross wt. 1,282. Empty wt. 771. Fuel capacity 18.5. Engine 100-hp Rotax 912S. PER-FORMANCE: Top cruise 116 kts. Cruise 108 kts. Stall 44 kts. Climb rate 807 fpm. Ceiling 13,123. Takeoff run 689'. Landing roll 656'. Range 429 nm.

The AT-3 is available in Europe as both a certified pre-built aircraft or as a kit. Its design originated in France as the Pottier P220, who also spawned the Czech Evektor. The AT-3 was ultimately improved by Polish designer Tomasz Antoniewski. He was also responsible for a single-seat taildragger, the AT-1. The Aero AT-3 hopes to compete in the US in the Light Sport Aircraft category.

AEROCOMP COMP AIR MERLIN

Comp Air Merlin

Comp Air 7

STANDARD DATA: Gross wt. 1,300. Empty wt. 650. Fuel capacity 16. Wingspan 32'. Length 20'. PERFORMANCE: Top cruise mph 95. Stall mph 35. Climb rate 1,500 fpm. Takeoff roll 100-200'. Landing roll 200'.

The Merlin is an impressive STOL aircraft, ideal for wheels or floats. The two-seater has a roomy cabin and typically has a 600-700 lb. useful load. Tube and fabric construction, it's an easy, straightforward design, at home on wheels or floats. The Merlin is the entry level kit for Aerocomp, which continues the line to larger and higher performing designs, the Comps 3-12, including turbine models.

AEROCOMP COMP AIR 10XL

STANDARD DATA: Gross wt. 5,200-6,000 lbs. Empty wt. 2,750-3,150 lbs. Fuel capacity 120-180. Wingspan 36'6". Length 31'. PERFORMANCE: Top cruise 192 kts. Stall mph 46-54. Climb rate 800-2,000 fpm. Takeoff roll 250-500'. Landing roll 700'. Range 672-795 nm.

This composite 7-10-seater has as much as 3,000 lbs. of useful load. Powered by a Walter M601D turbine engine, the big experimental category single can cruise at 200 mph without breaking a sweat. Because of the power-to-weight ratio, the 10XL can hop off the ground in just a few hundred feet and climb at 1,500-2,000 fpm. An even larger Comp Air 12 is already flying.

AEROCOMP COMP AIR JET

STANDARD DATA: Gross wt. 10,900. Useful load 5,900 lbs. Fuel capacity 480. Wingspan 36'6". Length 31'. PERFORMANCE: Top cruise 400 mph.

This pressurized single engine jet is all carbon composite fiber and offers one of the least expensive entries into pure jet flight. Power comes from a 3,400-lb. thrust AI-25 jet engine used in the L-39 Albatross and the Yak 40. The big cabin (70" tall and 68" wide) can be configured in a variety of seating arrangements for up to 8 people. Cabin altitude of 10,000' is available at the aircraft's maximum certified ceiling of 29,900'.

AERO DESIGN DG-1

STANDARD DATA: Gross wt. 2,300. Empty wt. 1,700. Fuel capacity 55-90. Wingspan 19'7". Length 20'4". Engines two 330-hp Mazda rotaries (automotive). PERFORMANCE: Top mph 400. Cruise 345.

Stall mph 98. Climb rate (estimated) 3,000. Ceiling (estimated) 24,000.

The DG-1 holds the distinction of being the first custom-built Unlimited Class racer to be built in the United States after the 1930s. It is intended for competition in that category as recognized by the United States Air Racing Association of the National Aeronautic Association. The prototype flew in 1978, and in addition to racing, the design is adaptable for follow-up production of two-place, tandem seating models. It can be modified easily to a remotely piloted vehicle, and design studies examined the use of a J-85 series GE turbojet propulsion unit. The wings are the cantilevered mid-wing type with a fiberglass reinforced plastic spar, and the wings are foam-filled internally. The fuselage is a steel-tube frame covered by plywood and is fiberglass reinforced. Power is supplied by fore and aft Mazda rotary auto engines modified to produce in excess of 330 hp each. Both are fuel injected and turbocharged by custom AiResearch units and turn 68-inch three-blade propellers. This kit is no longer available.

AERO DESIGNS "PULSAR"

(*See Also* Pulsar Aircraft Company, Tri-R Technologies)

STANDARD DATA: Seats 2. Gross wt. 1,000. Empty wt. 460. Fuel capacity 17. Engine Rotax 582. PERFORMANCE: Top mph 160. Cruise mph 130. Initial climb rate 1,000. Ceiling 15,000. Range 500. Takeoff distance (50') 800. Landing distance (50') 800.

The Pulsar is a popular aircraft in the kitbuilding world for many of the right reasons. It's sleek, fast, economical, docile, and relatively inexpensive to build. The majority of the Pulsar kit is made of "prepreg" fiberglass, which enables the Pulsar to maintain its very high strength. The company manufactures the Super Pulsar 100, Super Cruiser Four-Place, Pulsar III, Pulsar 150.

AEROSPORT "QUAIL"

STANDARD DATA: Gross wt. 792. Empty wt. 534. Fuel capacity 10. Wingspan 24'. Length 15'11". Engine 1600cc Volkswagen. PERFORMANCE: Top mph 130. Cruise mph 115. Stall mph 48. Climb rate

850. Ceiling 12,000. Takeoff run 300. Landing roll 400. Range 230.

The Quail is a stubby little single-seater with an enclosed cabin that can be powered by a variety of engines, the KAM525 Kiekhaefer, the Volkswagen 1600, 1700, or a two-cylinder Franklin. This high-wing plane is constructed of all metal and stands on tricycle landing gear. The Quail's wing is similar to that of the Rail, and its tricycle gear can be equipped with optional wheel fairings. This aircraft kit is no longer available.

AEROSPORT "RAIL"

STANDARD DATA: Gross wt. 730. Empty wt. 446. Fuel capacity 10. Wingspan 23'4". Length 15'9". Engine modified Volkswagen. PERFORMANCE: Top mph 90. Cruise mph 80. Stall mph 45. Ceiling 12,000. Range 220.

The original open-air pusher was powered by twin Aerosport 600 engines rated at 25 hp each. Top speed was about 80 mph, while standard cruise was cited at 66 mph. The Mk II Rail has been changed to take a modified Volkswagen powerplant mounted behind the pilot's head. The all-metal Rail seats only one, stands on a tricycle gear, and makes use of a T-tail assembly. The Rail has always emphasized easy construction, simplified tools, and economy of operation.

AEROSPORT "SCAMP"

STANDARD DATA: Gross wt. 768. Empty wt. 520. Fuel capacity 30. Wingspan 17'6". Length 14'. PERFORMANCE: Top mph 95. Cruise mph 85. Stall mph 45. Ceiling 12,000. Takeoff run 300. Landing roll 400. Range 150.

The Scamp can be used for limited acrobatics and is stressed to +3G and -3G. The single-seat biplane is powered by a modified Volkswagen engine (1,600 to 2,100cc) turning a fixed-blade prop. Standing on tricycle landing gear, it utilizes a T-tail, a lightweight-metal two-spar wing structure, and a semi-monocoque lightweight-alloy fuselage. First flown in 1973, the Scamp can be built from either plans or a kit and is still on the market.

AEROSPORT "WOODY'S PUSHER"

STANDARD DATA: Gross wt. 1,150. Empty wt. 630. Fuel capacity 12. Wingspan 29'. Length 20'5". PERFORMANCE: Top mph 98. Cruise mph 87. Stall mph 45. Climb rate 600. Takeoff run 300. Landing roll 400. Range 190.

The Woody's Pusher was designed by H.L. Woods, a former engineer at Bensen Aircraft Corp. He later founded Aerosport, Inc. to continue to market his plans and kits. The Woody's Pusher is a tandem two-seater with a parasol-mounted wing. The engine, which may range in power from 65 to 85 hp, is carried on top of the wing in a pusher fashion and turns a wooden fixed-blade prop. Originally, the Pusher was designed with a fuselage of wood covered with plywood and fabric. Later models of the lightweight open-cockpit plane feature a steel-tube fabric-covered fuselage and metal leading edges on its wood-and-fabric wing assemblies. The landing gear is conventional. Kits are no longer available.

AERO-SYSTEMS "CADET STF"

STANDARD DATA: Seats 2. Gross wt. 1,350. Empty wt. 785. Fuel capacity 25. Engine 85-115 hp Teledyne Continental. PERFORMANCE: Top mph 175. Cruise mph 130. Initial climb rate 800. Ceiling 15,000. Range 520. Takeoff distance (50') 800. Landing distance (50') 800.

The Cadet STF is a replica of the very popular Culver Cadet of the early 1940s; however, this new version of the Cadet has done away with some of the inherent long-term frailties that were found to affect the original. The most notable improvement is the steel-tube fuselage (STF) structure. Steel tube construction has done away with the dreaded wood-rotting problem that plagued the original all-wood fuselage and in turn has significantly increased strength and structural integrity without altering the racy lines of the aircraft. Overall weight has been reduced, increasing overall performance figures and providing more versatility within the finished product.

AIRCRAFT DESIGNS, INC. "STALLION"

STANDARD DATA: Seats 4. Gross wt. 3,200. Empty wt. 1,920. Fuel capacity 90. Engine 230-hp Continental 10-520-G. PERFORMANCE: Top mph 239. Cruise mph 228. Initial climb rate 1,119. Ceiling 28,000. Range 1,540. Takeoff distance (50') 600. Landing distance (50') 500.

The Stallion is one of a string of composite kit aircraft that makes available advanced-technology building techniques to the kit builder. What makes the Stallion stand out among the other aircraft in its class is its method of construction, configuration, and multipurpose focus. Although the construction is largely composite, the Stallion utilizes a steel-tube inner fuselage cage that surrounds the cabin providing an integral high-strength central structure. The Stallion utilizes the same basic wing assembly as the Lancair IV and also uses the same retractable-gear mechanism. The configuration of the Stallion differs from the norm in its class by featuring a high-wing design that looks a lot like a Cessna 210 Centurion. The Stallion possesses a large payload capacity with quick-disconnect seats and features a large 72 x 36" right-side fuselage panel that removes for bulky cargo loading.

AIRCRAFT SPRUCE & SPECIALTY IAC "ONE DESIGN"

STANDARD DATA: Seats 1. Gross wt. 1,140. Empty wt. 740. Fuel capacity 18. Engine 160-hp Lycoming 10-320. PERFORMANCE: Top mph 184. Cruise mph 160. Initial climb rate 2,000. Ceiling n/a. Range 350. Takeoff distance n/a. Landing distance n/a.

One Design was designed by Dan Rihn to develop a single-class of affordable acrobatic competition for the sportsman pilot. The development of such a class would allow pilots to compete in a more controlled environment thus virtually eliminating the "have and the have

One Design

Christavia MK I

Acrosport

Acrosduster II

nots" that seem to have infiltrated all competitions. This class will bring aerobatic competition back to the pilot's ability to perform well by providing a very capable aircraft within which to perform—and in the same aircraft type. Construction is standard mixed with steel-tube fuselage, wood wing, all fabric covered, with aluminum forward of the cockpit and fiberglass to cowl the engine.

Since that time, Aircraft Spruce & Specialty has expanded the kit projects it represents to include the

Acroduster, Acrolite, Acrosport, Barracuda, Breezy, Christavia, Cozy, GP4 and Osprey, Cozy, KR, Prober, Skybolt, Sonex, Starduster, Volksplane and Wittman.

AIRDALE FLYER COMPANY "AVID FLYER"/ "AVID MAGNUM"/ "MARK IV"

Mark IV

Magnum

STANDARD DATA: AVID FLYER Gross wt. 1,400. Empty wt. 700. Fuel capacity 28-36. Wingspan 30'. Engine 100-hp Rotax 912S. Length 18.9' PERFOR-MANCE: Top cruise mph 115. Initial climb rate 900-1,200 fpm. Stall 37 mph. Range 750-1,000 nm. Takeoff distance (50') 800'.

Avid Aircraft Inc. made its reputation with the original Avid Flyer and Heavy Hauler kit planes. Despite manufacturing well-received kits, the company began to evaporate in the late 1990s. After a series of ownership shuffles, Avid is Airdale Avid, with a line of kits that include the entry level Mark IV and the Magnum, which has Cub-like performance.

AMERICAN GHILES AIRCRAFT

STANDARD DATA: AGA Lafayette Texan Seats 2. Gross wt. 992. Empty wt. 606. Fuel capacity 19. Engine 80-hp Rotax 912S. PERFORMANCE: Top mph 140. Cruise mph 124. Initial climb rate 1180 fpm. Ceiling 10,000. Takeoff distance 490'. Landing distance 460'.

AGA makes a series of carbon fiber high performance kit planes, including the Sportster, Bushplane, Revolution 4S, Stork, Texan and Wallaby. The aircraft often feature carbon composite spars derived directly

Bushplane

Lafayette Sportster

Texan

Wallaby

from competition airplanes, with multiple foam ribs for structural strength. Fuselages are typically carbon monocoque. AGA aircraft come with a variety of options and in quick-built configurations.

ANDERSON "KINGFISHER"

STANDARD DATA: Gross wt. 1,500. Empty wt. 1,032. Fuel capacity 20. Wingspan 36'1". Length 24'. PERFORMANCE: Top mph 122. Cruise mph 90. Stall mph 42. Climb rate 550. Takeoff time 16 sec. Range 275.

Designer Anderson credits the highly popular VJ-22 Sportsman as the inspiration behind his own creation, the Kingfisher. There are many similarities between the two. Both use wings from production airplanes, the J-3 Cub in the case of the Kingfisher. Both use 100-hp Continental engines. General structural technique is similar with the fuselage built of spruce longerons and braces with mahogany plywood skin and an overall lightweight covering of fiberglass. The biggest difference is Anderson's choice of a tractor engine mounting rather than a pusher. In this way the engine mounts on its proper pads, the cooling, induction, and exhaust systems are standard, and there is no necessity to have the propeller custom made. Plans are still available.

ARISTOCRAFT III

STANDARD DATA: Gross wt. 2,650-3,300. Empty wt. 1,600-1,800. Wingspan 36'10". Length 25'10". PERFORMANCE: Top mph 135. Cruise mph 120. Stall mph 55. Climb rate 500. Takeoff run 1,000. Landing roll 1,000. Range 800.

The Aristocraft was originally the last plane designed and built by the Waco Airplane Company. It was aimed at the cabin-class ultra-safe market. Terrence O'Neill bought the rights, simplified its design, and increased its payload. The all-metal high-wing ship is one of the largest homebuilts and can seat up to six persons. Its speed and range make it excellent for cross-country travel. Plans are no longer available.

AVIATION ADVENTURES "MUSTANG"

This 2/3-scale Mustang is fully acrobatic, seats two, and is powered by a Geschwender 351 CID Ford engine producing 300 to 350 hp. Because the original fighter had a liquid-cooled Rolls-Royce Merlin engine with an external radiator affixed to the underside of its fuse-lage, Aviation AdVentures chose to go the liquid-cooled route with the same automobile engine/reduction gear system by Geschwender Aeromotive that has been flying successfully on crop dusters. The conventional automobile distributor has been replaced with a dual magneto system that is more reliable and efficient during high engine RPM. Likewise, the automobile carburetor has been exchanged for a Bendix PS SC pressure carburetor to meet the in-flight requirements of changing altitudes.

AVID AIRCRAFT
(*See* Airdale Avid)

AVIPRO "BEARHAWK"

STANDARD DATA: Seats 4. Gross wt. 2,500. Empty wt. 1,150-1,350. Fuel capacity 50-68. Engine 150-260 hp. PERFORMANCE: Cruise mph 150. Initial climb rate 1,500-1,700 fpm. Takeoff distance 200-500'.

One of the best kit planes out there, the Bearhawk is slightly larger on the inside than the popular Cessna 172, but scores much higher in an overall utility rating. Useful load ranges from 1,000-1,300 lbs. and can carry four adults and full fuel. The back seat can be removed resulting in a huge cargo area with unobstructed access. Not only does the back seat have its own door, but also the door combines with the cargo door to allow a six-foot loading area. The Bearhawk is available in a "quick build" kit.

BAKENG "DUCE"

STANDARD DATA: Gross wt. 1,500. Empty wt. 898. Fuel capacity 28. Wingspan 30'4". Length 20'9". Engine 120-hp Lycoming. PERFORMANCE: Top mph 145. Cruise mph 105. Stall mph 36. Climb rate 2,000. Ceiling 17,000. Takeoff run 150. Landing roll 150. Range 300.

The high-performance parasol-wing homebuilt received the "Outstanding New Design" and "Design Improvement" awards from the EAA in 1971. The V-strut braced wing utilizes both metal and spruce construction and is covered with fabric. The fuselage is also fabric covered but is built from steel tubes. The landing gear is the conventional tailwheel type, and the two seats are arranged in tandem fashion. Bakeng has also designed a biplane version of the Duce, called the Double Duce. Horizontally opposed and radial engines can be used.

"BANTAM"

STANDARD DATA: Gross wt. 790. Empty wt. 535. Fuel capacity 11.5. Wingspan 18'5". Length 13'9". PERFORMANCE: Top mph 140. Cruise mph 115. Stall mph 52. Climb rate 1,000. Takeoff run 550. Landing roll 500.

Designed for simple fabrication, Bill Warwick's Bantam uses no compound curves and very few simple ones. The cockpit area is a steel-tube structure taking all the wing, gear, and engine-mount loads. The remaining is wood construction with a plywood cover. The Bantam is a single-seat, low-wing plane that can use any engine from 65 to 100 hp. Plans are no longer available.

BARNETT J-4B GYROPLANE

STANDARD DATA: Gross wt. 750. Empty wt. 441. Fuel capacity 15. Main rotor length 24'. Length 12'2". Engine 65-hp Continental. PERFORMANCE: Top mph 115. Cruise mph 90. Climb rate 700. Ceiling 14,000. Takeoff run 200. Landing roll 0-20. Range 250.

The Barnett Gyroplane is a single-place craft constructed of tubular steel, fiberglass, and aluminum. Its pusher prop is powered by a 65-hp Continental engine. The pilot sits inside an enclosed cabin shell. The J3-M differs from the J-4B by replacing the molded fiberglass cockpit nacelle with a flat-sided fabric-covered structure. Both models are fitted with tricycle gear and disc brakes. The company has changed its name to Barnett Rotorcraft and currently markets the J-4B.

BEDE BD-4

STANDARD DATA: Gross wt. 2,000. Empty wt. 1,080. Fuel capacity 57.6. Wingspan 25'7". Length 21'4". PERFORMANCE: Top mph 183. Cruise mph 174. Stall mph 63. Climb rate 1,400. Takeoff run 600. Landing roll 600. Range 750.

The BD-4 was designed to be built by homebuilders who have only simple shop tools and no previous experience; however, the finished product is a high-performance, low-cost, all-metal aircraft capable of carrying two to four persons. Only the wings are constructed of fiberglass. The BD-4 can use any Lycoming engine from 108 to 200 hp. It is a high-wing enclosed-cabin design.

BEDE BD-5 "MICRO"

STANDARD DATA: Gross wt. 850. Empty wt. 410. Fuel capacity 35. Wingspan 17'. Length 13'3". Engine 70-hp Xenoah. PERFORMANCE: Top mph 230. Cruise mph 210. Stall mph 69. Climb rate 1,750. Ceiling 18,800. Takeoff run 820. Range 1,130.

The Bede Aircraft Co. did not compromise high performance and aerodynamic design for simple tooling and ease of construction in its snappy little single-seater BD-5. Originally it was powered by a 40-hp Hirth snowmobile engine and was fitted with a wingspan of 14 feet. The wingspan was stretched to 17 feet, and the more powerful Xenoah three-cylinder two-stroke engine was installed. The pilot is seated under a transparent canopy forward of the engine in a heated cockpit. The landing gear is fully retractable, and the entire fuselage/wing structure is constructed of lightweight alloy

materials. The BD-5 was also designed in a jet version; the BD-5J became a regular air show performer and appeared in a James Bond movie. BD Micro-Technologies, Inc. developed a support group to help builders of the BD-5s complete their projects.

BEDE BD-6

STANDARD DATA: Gross wt. 605. Empty wt. 375. Fuel capacity 21. Wingspan 21'6". Length 16'9". Engine 55-hp Hirth. PERFORMANCE: Top mph 140. Cruise mph 130. Stall mph 50. Climb rate 900. Ceiling 14,000. Takeoff run 600. Landing roll 400. Range 450.

The BD-6 was another in the line of "build-it-yourself" airplanes from Bede Aircraft. Essentially a single-seat version of the BD-4, it incorporated the same ease of construction aimed at the novice builder while utilizing the same German-made Hirth engine originally used in the BD-5. This high wing all-metal ship seats one person in an enclosed cockpit and stands on non-retractable tricycle gear.

BEDE JET CORP. "BD-10"

STANDARD DATA: Seats 2. Gross wt. 4,140. Empty wt. 1,580. Fuel capacity 263. Engine 2,950-lb. s.t. GE CJ-610 fanjet. PERFORMANCE: Top mph 926. Cruise mph 620. Initial climb rate 30,000. Ceiling 45,000. Range 1,840. Takeoff distance (50') 600. Landing distance (50') 1,500.

One of the most significant developments in

homebuilt aircraft, the BD-10 Jet has brought the fantasy almost within reach for most pilots: streaking around the sky in your own pocket-sized jet at Mach speeds and being the fastest kid on the block. The aircraft is "almost within reach" because along with being the hottest kit on wings it also carries the highest price tag (approximately $250,000 less engine, avionics, and finishing products). As fast as this bird is, it still remains very docile at slow speeds and is simple enough for most competent prop pilots to fly. Construction of the BD-10 is made largely of state-of-the-art honeycomb-sandwich aluminum and is designed with all the seriousness of today's frontline fighter aircraft. The aircraft is complex in structure but not beyond the means of competent builders exhibiting the proper building skills. Build time is around 6,000 hours, and it does take a large amount of change, but in the grand scheme it is a lot less expensive to build and operate than most military surplus jets available to the serious gen-av pilot.

BEETS G/B SPECIAL

STANDARD DATA: Gross wt. 925. Empty wt. 603. Fuel capacity n/a. Wingspan 25'. Length 16'4". Engine 70-hp Volkswagen. PERFORMANCE: Top mph 156. Cruise mph 120. Stall mph 35. Climb rate 2,000. Takeoff run 200. Landing roll 300. Range 600.

The G/B is a single-seat open-cockpit sporting plane featuring a high parasol-braced wing and conventional landing gear. While the fuselage is a fabric-covered steel-tube structure, the wing is built with spruce spars and ribs, also fabric covered. All plans, kits, and components are sold through the Stolp Starduster Corp.

BENSEN GYROCOPTER

STANDARD DATA: Gross wt. 500. Empty wt. 247. Fuel capacity 6. Main rotor length 21'. Length 11'3". PERFORMANCE: Top mph 85. Cruise mph 60. Maximum climb rate 1,000. Range 100.

There are more than 20,000 active rotorcraft fans in the United States. Originator of the sport is Bensen

Aircraft Corp. With purchase of the plans and component kits, it is possible to build a machine in a few weeks of spare time with only a drill press and a few wrenches. Bensen Gyrocopters can be towed behind a car or boat or flown under their own power. Float models are also available. The simple glider models are available as one- or two-seaters. The powered gyrocopters are available only with a single seat. Bensen's Gyrocopter is capable of climbing to 12,500 feet. (It is said "for each 500 feet in altitude, the seat gets two inches narrower.") The powerplant is a 72- to 90-hp McCulloch. Bensen Aircraft is no longer in business.

"BIG COOTIE"

STANDARD DATA: Gross wt. 750. Empty wt. 467. Fuel capacity 12. Wingspan 18'9". Length 14'. PERFORMANCE: Top mph 140. Cruise mph 120. Stall mph 63. Takeoff run 500. Landing roll 500. Range 300.

The single-place "Powell Racer" is a tail-dragging biplane design constructed of wood, fabric, and tubular metal. Stressed for an engine up to 80 hp, the Big Cootie is usually pulled by a 65- to 80-hp Lycoming engine.

BIRDMAN TL-1

STANDARD DATA: Gross wt. 350. Empty wt. 100. Fuel capacity 4. Wingspan 34'. Length 20'. Engine 15-hp Tally Aircraft M.C.101 DT. PERFORMANCE:

Top mph 60. Cruise mph 54. Stall mph 19. Climb rate 350. Ceiling 12,500. Takeoff run 75. Landing roll 25. Range 200.

Because it is a mere 100 pounds, there is no debate that the Birdman TL-1 is an ultralight craft. In an effort to emphasize ease of construction and light weight, an unusual heat-shrink-to-fit synthetic mylar skin, Monokote, is used to cover the wood and foam-reinforced wings. The fuselage is a standard plywood monocoque, and the tail section is a V-type. While the main gear is attached underneath the wing, the pilot's legs and feet take the place of a nose wheel.

BOREDOM FIGHTER

STANDARD DATA: Gross wt. 770. Empty wt. 473. Wingspan 20'. Length 15.7". PERFORMANCE: Top mph 110. Cruise mph 100. Stall mph 42. Climb rate 1,200 fpm. Takeoff run 150'. Landing roll 300'.

The Boredom Fighter is constructed entirely from wood. Designed by Don Wolf, the aircraft's raison d'etre is flying for fun. Available as a plan only, more than 300 have been sold. Like many homebuilts, the Boredom Fighters can employ a variety of engines. Most versions use the Continental A-65.

BOWERS "FLY BABY"

STANDARD DATA: Gross wt. 924. Empty wt. 605. Fuel capacity 16. Wingspan 28'. Length 18'10". PERFORMANCE: Top mph 120. Cruise mph 110. Stall mph 45. Climb rate 1,100. Takeoff run 200. Landing roll 300. Range 300.

For novice wooden-plane builders, the Fly Baby is one of the best. This single-place monoplane won the 1962 EAA competition for the best amateur plane with

a C-85 engine. The Fly Baby has the distinction of being one of the most enduring designs in the homebuilt field. It has been tested with floats and in 1968 was fitted with biplane wings that were interchangeable with the single wings. The wings are a wooden structure covered with Dacron fabric, and the fuselage is a conventional plywood-covered wooden structure with a single open-cockpit seat. The 85-hp engine drives a two-blade fixed-pitch propeller. Options include a two-seat version and an enclosed canopy for additional comfort. Kits are still available.

BOWERS "FLY BI-BABY"

STANDARD DATA: Gross wt. 970. Empty wt. 652. Fuel capacity 16. Wingspan 22'. Length 18'10". PERFORMANCE: Top mph 100. Cruise mph 90. Stall mph 40. Climb rate 900. Takeoff run 150. Landing roll 250. Range 275.

The Fly Baby is also distinguished by the fact that it can be flown as a monoplane or biplane, the biplane being named the Bi-Baby. The switch from monoplane to biplane wings takes only one hour.

BOWERS "NAMU II"

STANDARD DATA: Gross wt. 1,850. Empty wt. 1,200. Fuel capacity 32. Wingspan 33'. Length 21'6". Engine 125-hp Lycoming. PERFORMANCE: Top mph 140. Cruise mph 126. Stall mph 50. Climb rate 950. Ceiling 15,000. Range 500.

The Namu, named after the famous whale, first flew in 1975. The side-by-side two-seater features an en-

closed canopy, dual con[trols] wheel type gear. Its low structed from wood. Da[cron] and tail section. Plywood the rear decking. Fuel is aft of the firewall.

BROKAW "BULLE[T"

STANDARD DATA: (Equipped with the 380-hp Lycoming.) Gross wt. 3,142. Empty wt. 2,033. Fuel capacity 47-92. Wingspan 24'4". Length 23'10". PERFORMANCE: Top mph 322. Cruise mph 293. Stall mph 86. Climb rate 2, 100. Ceiling 28,000. Takeoff run (50) 2,000. Landing run (50) 1,300. Range 1,323.

Dr. D.F. Brokaw, with the aeronautical engineering help of Dr. Ernest R. Jones, developed a high-speed homebuilt with good cross-country capability, comfortable seating for two in tandem fashion, retractable gear, full-IFR capability, and the ability to perform aerobatics. The prototype took Brokaw seven years to build, but offspring can be built in about three years working from plans. The original powerplant was a 285-hp Continental, but the most common options are a 310-hp Continental or the 380-hp Lycoming turning a Sensenich three-blade propeller. Standard fuel capacity is 47 gallons with 45 auxiliary gallons, and all fuel is carried in the wings. The fuselage, wings, tail, and all control surfaces are built from lightweight alloy. The tricycle landing gear is retractable. The Bullet ranks as one the highest performance homebuilts in the skies because it is stressed to 6G for aerobatics with a 322 mph top speed and a service ceiling of 28,000 feet.

BUSHBY "MIDGET MUSTANG"

STANDARD DATA: Gross wt. 900. Empty wt. 580. Fuel capacity 15. Engine 125-hp Lycoming. PERFORMANCE: Top mph 225. Cruise mph 215. Stall mph

60. Climb rate 2,200. Takeoff run 400. Landing roll 750. Range 400.

Another sport plane inspired by the famous North American Mustang is the Bushby Midget Mustang. This little single-seater attains incredible speeds propelled by a Lycoming 125-hp powerplant. Its sleek appearance is due to its all-metal construction. Fabrication is simple. Only two simple wooden jigs are required, but Bushby can supply components or full kits that eliminate virtually all metal bending.

BUSHBY "MUSTANG II"

STANDARD DATA: Gross wt. 1,500. Empty wt. 975. Fuel capacity 25. Wingspan 24'4". Length 19'5". Engine 180-hp Lycoming. PERFORMANCE: Top mph 245. Cruise mph 220. Stall mph 63. Climb rate 1,800. Takeoff run 500. Range 650.

Kin to the Midget Mustang, this frisky tail-dragger seats two in side-by-side fashion and was developed as a cross country/sport plane. There is enough panel to accommodate full IFR gear. The Mustang II is a slightly slower ship using a 150-hp Lycoming engine. Construction is all-metal with stressed skin. There are no complicated fittings or parts that require special skills or tools. The Mustang II can be equipped with the 180-hp Lycoming and Ray-Jay Ri 0325 turbocharger to offer 250-mph cruise with 30-gph economy.

CASSUTT SPECIAL II

STANDARD DATA: Gross wt. 800. Empty wt. 500. Fuel capacity 15. Wingspan 15'0". Length 16'. Engine 85-hp Continental. PERFORMANCE: Top mph 235. Cruise mph 180. Stall mph 62. Climb rate 2,000. Takeoff run 600. Landing roll 525. Range 600.

The Cassutt Formula I racer and sport plane is a little mid-wing flash that commonly wrings 200-plus mph out of 85-hp engines. This speedy ship performs well using either Continental, Lycoming, or Volkswagen engines. Its construction uses a welded steel-tube fuselage, wood wings, and flat spring steel landing gear. Professionally designed for racing, aerobatics, and sport use, the Cassutt is stressed to positive 12 Gs. The design is now marketed by National Aeronautics Company as the Cassutt IIIM.

CAVALIER

STANDARD DATA: Gross wt. 1,500. Empty wt. 900. Fuel capacity 34. Wingspan 26'10". Length 18'4". PERFORMANCE: Top mph 2,200. Cruise mph 155. Stall mph 50. Climb rate 1,500. Range 850. Landing roll 800.

The Cavalier is a sporty side-by-side two-seater of all wood-and-fabric construction. It can use any four-cylinder Continental, Lycoming, or Franklin engine up to 235 pounds in weight and rated in the 85- to 135-hp range. The ship can be switched from tricycle to conventional gear in a few minutes. Other options include wingtip fuel tanks and a third jump seat.

CHRISTEN "EAGLE II"

STANDARD DATA: Gross wt. 1,578. Empty wt. 1,025. Fuel capacity 26. Wingspan 19'11". Length 18'6". Engine 200-hp Lycoming. PERFORMANCE: Top mph 184. Cruise mph 165. Stall mph 58. Climb

rate 2,100. Ceiling 17,000. Takeoff distance (50) 1,250. Landing distance (50') 1,575. Range 380.

The Eagle II is a two-seat sporting biplane that can be used for unlimited-class aerobatics as well as for advanced training. The Eagle II and II-F have a full electrical system (starter-alternator-battery). The Eagle II uses a 200-hp engine with constant-speed propeller. The Eagle II-F uses a 260-hp engine with fixed-pitch propeller. Characterized by their startling paint scheme, the Eagles feature swept symmetrical wings, a strong fuselage, and a blown canopy that covers both cockpits. With a roll rate of 187 degrees/second and a power loading of 7.89 lbs./hp, the Eagle is a strong performer.

The fuselage is finished in metal from the cowling back to the rear cockpit. The midsection, all the way to the empennage, is covered in fabric. The fabric-covered wings are built with aluminum ribbing over spruce spars. The amateur builder has the option of buying 25 kits in sequence, starting with the ailerons, to test his or her dexterity. The intention of the Eagle is to provide the homebuilder with an easy-to-build unlimited-aerobatic airplane. Currently available through Aviat Aircraft.

CIRRUS DESIGN "VK30"

Alan and Dale Klapmeier, progenitors of the Cirrus SR20 and SR22 certified aircraft, offered a kit aircraft in 1987 called the VK30. The five-seater was powered by a 300-hp Continental pusher engine and had a cruise speed of over 200 mph. The Klapmeiers sold the rights to an Israeli company with intentions to certify the design, but the plan never moved forward. The kit is no longer available and only 5 models were ever built.

CONDOR K-10 "SHOESTRING"

STANDARD DATA: Gross wt. 800. Empty wt. 525. Fuel capacity 10. Wingspan 19'. Length 17'8". PERFORMANCE: Top mph 225. Cruise mph 180. Stall mph 65. Climb rate 3,000. Takeoff run 500. Range 360.

One of the more successful Formula I racers is the Shoestring. Constructed from the conventional combination of steel tubing, wood, and fabric, the tiny racer houses a 100-hp 0-200 Continental engine. The aircraft first flew in 1949 and entered its first competition in 1950. By 1974, the Shoestring racer had accumulated 14 first places in major air race competitions. Other recommended engines are the Continental 85- and 90-hp versions.

CORBY CJ-1 "STARLET"

STANDARD DATA: Gross wt. 650. Empty wt. 420. Fuel capacity 11. Wingspan 18'6". Length 14'9". PERFORMANCE: Top mph 160. Cruise mph 123. Stall mph 34. Climb rate 775. Takeoff run 1,100. Landing roll 1,100. Range 370.

The Starlet is a single-place semi-acrobatic monoplane of wood, fabric, and tubular steel construction.

It is designed to handle any Volkswagen or Continental engine up to 75 hp. This aircraft is currently sold by CSN.

COZY "MARK IV"

STANDARD DATA: Gross wt. 2,050. Empty wt. 1,050. Engine 180-hp Lycoming 0-360. PERFORMANCE: Top Cruise mph 220. Stall mph 42. Climb rate 1,200. Ceiling 20,000'+. Range 900-1,300 nm.

Designed by Burt Rutan, the Cozy Mark IV is one of the most popular four place composites in the air. The Cozy features forward canards, which provide two lifting surfaces. With canards, wings can have less area, less span and a lower weight loading. Drag is reduced and the performance is enhanced. The Cozy resembles the Velocity, but is completely plan built. The rear pusher-propeller makes the aircraft unsuitable for un-improved landing surfaces. Rutan no longer sells his plans or kits, but offers full support for current owners at the Mojave, California airport.

CRI-CRI

STANDARD DATA: (Single-seater) Gross wt. 374 lbs. Empty wt. 138 lbs. Wingspan 15'. Length 12'5". Engines: various. PERFORMANCE: Top Cruise mph 124. Standard cruise mph 105. Climb rate 1,000 fpm. G-limits +9/-4.5G Take off run 450'. Ceiling 15,000'. Range 400 nm.

Michele Colmban thought up the unique twin-engine design in 1971 and ultimately named it after his daughter's nickname. Construction is all metal with standard stick-n-rudder controls. Ailerons span the entire length of the wing allowing the airplane to be considered acrobatic. Almost two hundred Cri-Cris have been built and registered. Plans are no longer available.

CVJETKOVIC CA-61 "MINI ACE"

STANDARD DATA: (Single-seater) Gross wt. 950. Empty wt. 606. Fuel capacity 17. Wingspan 27'6". Length 18'11". Engine 65-hp Continental. PERFORMANCE: Top mph 120. Cruise mph 100. Stall mph 42. Climb rate 1,200. Takeoff run 200. Landing roll 300. Range 425.

The CA-61 can be built as either a single-seat or side-by-side low-wing monoplane. It is designed for amateur builders with little or no previous experience in building light airplanes. With a minimum of tools, the plane can be assembled in less than 1,000 working hours. The structure is light with reduced wing loading, so in addition to the standard Continental powerplant, a VW conversion can be substituted. Another option is the availability of either fixed tricycle landing gear or retractable tailwheel type. Construction is all wood, and the wing is made in one piece with a main and auxiliary spar. Current plans sold by Anton Cvjetkovic himself.

CVJETKOVIC CA-65

STANDARD DATA: Gross wt. 1,500. Empty wt. 900. Fuel capacity 28. Wingspan 25'. Length 19'. Engine 125-hp Lycoming. PERFORMANCE: Top mph 180. Cruise mph 155. Stall mph 55. Climb rate 1,000. Ceiling 15,000. Takeoff run 450. Landing roll 600. Range 500.

This airplane represents a further development of the CA-61 Mini Ace. The CA-65 is a low-wing monoplane with retractable landing gear and dual controls. The high degree of efficiency produced by its design yields economic performance at all speeds. It features a streamlined canopy, enclosed engine, tapered wing, and fully retractable gear. Its wood construction cuts requirements for tooling and special jigs to a minimum. For easy storage the wings fold up in an "aircraft carrier" style.

fuselage and wire-braced steel-tube tail section. Fabric covers the entire airplane. The fuel supply and the front seat passenger are very close to the center of gravity, so trim is little affected by expending fuel or by the presence or absence of a passenger. A variety of engines can be used from 190 to 260 hp.

D'APUZZO "JUNIOR AERO SPORT"

STANDARD DATA: Gross wt. 1,275. Empty wt. 840. Fuel capacity 20. Wingspan 21'8", Length 18'3". Engine 180-hp Lycoming. PERFORMANCE: Top mph 160. Cruise mph 140. Stall mph 55. Climb rate 2,500. Ceiling 20,000. Takeoff run 400. Landing roll 550 Range 300.

This single-seat sporting biplane is a smaller version of the Senior Aero Sport and is built from the standard combination of a fabric-covered wooden wing and a fabric-covered steel-tube fuselage. The powerplant drives a constant-speed metal propeller to produce a maximum speed of 160 mph. Plans are no longer available.

D'APUZZO "SENIOR AERO SPORT"

STANDARD DATA: Gross wt. 2,050. Empty wt. 1,450. Fuel capacity 36-62. Wingspan 27'0". Length 21'0". Engine 260-hp Lycoming. PERFORMANCE: Top mph 155. Cruise mph 140. Stall mph 52. Climb rate 2,000. Takeoff distance (50') 700. Landing distance (50) 900. Range 400.

The acrobatic Senior Aero Sport is available as either a single- or two-seater. One example is the grand champion homebuilt at the 1968 EAA Fly-In at Rockford, Illinois. This sport biplane has a wood-faired steel-tube

D'APUZZO "SPORTWING"

STANDARD DATA: Gross wt. 1,845. Empty wt. 1,185. Fuel capacity 30. Wingspan 27'. Length 21'7". Engine 160-hp Lycoming. PERFORMANCE: Top mph 142. Cruise mph 127. Stall mph 47. Climb rate 1,500. Takeoff distance (50) 790. Landing distance (50') 850. Range 380.

The D-201 Sportwing is a completely redesigned version of the Senior Aero Sport. Of special interest is the attention that was given to reducing the cost and complexity of building the airplane without sacrificing the safety aspects of the previous models. The fuselage is a conventional steel-tube structure with aluminum-alloy panels used for covering forward of the cockpit and fabric used aft of the cockpit. The wings are the conventionally braced biplane type with long-span ailerons on the lower wings. Power is supplied by Lycoming engines ranging from 150 to 200 hp; the most common powerplant is the 160-hp Lycoming. Seating is in tandem fashion with a canopy as an option.

DAVIS DA-2A

STANDARD DATA: Gross wt. 1,125. Empty wt. 610. Fuel capacity 20. Wingspan 19'3". Length 17'10". PERFORMANCE: Top mph 120. Cruise mph 115.

Stall mph 62. Climb rate 400. Takeoff run 800. Landing roll 700. Range 450.

In 1966, the Davis all-metal design was voted the most popular at the Rockford EAA Fly-In. It requires little work on the part of the builder because of its simple construction with no compound curves or expensive fittings. The Davis design uses a 100-hp Continental and is one of the few do-it-yourself planes with a V-tail.

DAVIS DA-5A

STANDARD DATA: Gross wt. 775. Empty wt. 460. Fuel capacity 17. Wingspan 15'7". Length 15'9". Engine 65-hp Continental. PERFORMANCE: Top mph 160. Cruise mph 140. Stall mph 60. Climb rate 800. Ceiling 14,500. Takeoff run 600. Landing roll 600. Range 450.

This single-seat low-wing monoplane makes use of the same V-type tail as the DA-2A. The pilot sits inside an enclosed canopy behind a 65-hp Continental turning a fixed-pitch prop. Both the wings and fuselage are a lightweight alloy structure with stressed skins, and the landing gear is the non-retractable tricycle type.

DIAMANT C.P. 60

STANDARD DATA: Gross wt. 1,880. Empty wt. 1,100. Fuel capacity 45. Wingspan 31'6". Length 22'. PERFORMANCE: Top mph 134. Cruise mph 118. Stall mph 51. Climb rate. 492. Takeoff run 850. Landing roll 900. Range 450.

The Diamant is a three- or four-seat version of the Emeraude. This low-wing high-performance mono-

plane is powered by a 100-hp Continental engine. It is also available in a fourplace model propelled by a 150-hp Lycoming designated the Super Diamant. Both were created by designer Claude Piel.

DIRECT FLY "ALTO"

STANDARD DATA: Seats 2. Gross wt. 998. Empty wt. 637. Fuel capacity 14. Wingspan 24'1". Length 21'3". Engine 120-hp Javibu 3300. PERFORMANCE: Top mph 146. Cruise mph 121. Stall mph 31. Climb rate 1,450 fpm. Takeoff run 260'. Landing roll 490'.

The Alto is registered in the Czech Republic and is an all-metal two-seater. Builders can buy the aircraft almost completely assembled, less engine and instruments, making the Alto one of the shortest waits to get flying.

DOODLE BUG

STANDARD DATA: Gross wt. 970. Empty wt. 616. Fuel capacity 25. Wingspan 18'. Length 16'6". PERFORMANCE: Top mph 196. Cruise mph 170. Stall mph 70. Climb rate 2,000. Takeoff run 1,000. Landing roll 800. Range 700.

This fast single-seater picked up three trophies when it flew to the 1955 EAA Fly-In at Oshkosh, Wisconsin. With its 12-gallon main fuel tank and a pair of 6.5 gallon fiberglass tip tanks, the Doodle Bug boasts an amazing 700-mile range. It is built from welded steel tube. The fuselage and tail group is fabric covered. The wings are all metal. It is powered by a 90-hp Continental.

DSK-1 "HAWK"

STANDARD DATA: Gross wt. 893. Empty wt. 525. Fuel capacity 9-14. Wingspan 20'4". Length 15'. Engine 65-hp Lycoming. PERFORMANCE: Top mph 156. Cruise mph 141. Stall mph 50. Climb rate 1,500. Ceiling 12,000. Takeoff run 600. Landing roll 550. Range (14 gals) 480.

The Hawk is a single-seat low-wing monoplane stressed to 9 Gs. Originally it was designed to be built around a surplus 200-gallon drop-tank, but plans also provide for a bulkhead and stressed-skin structure. The

wings are built with twin light-alloy spars, and the landing gear is the non-retractable tricycle type. Fuel is carried in a forward tank with the capacity of nine gallons, but an optional 14-gallon tank can be added in the aft section.

DURAND MARK V

STANDARD DATA: Gross wt. 1,840. Empty wt. 1,210. Fuel capacity 24.5. Wingspan 24'6". Length 20'3". Engine 150-hp Lycoming. PERFORMANCE: Top mph 170. Cruise mph 135. Stall mph n/a. Climb rate 1,200. Ceiling 15,000. Range 520. Takeoff run 550. Landing roll 450.

The Durand biplane features a negative-stagger configuration so that it does not produce a full stall, only a very short period of "nibbling" with little loss of altitude. The structure is rated at +3.8Gs and -1.5Gs. Roll is produced by a combination of effects when a spoiler is activated, instead of by use of ailerons. According to its designer, a spoiler for roll control actually helps an airplane turn in the direction of the bank, while ailerons do not. The trailing edges of the wings are taken up by full-span flaps. With a standard 150-hp Lycoming, the Durand can carry two people with 128 pounds of baggage at 135 mph over a range of 520 miles. Cockpit controls are basic, with dual sticks in lieu of standard control wheels. The cabin features exceptional visibility by using a forward sliding canopy instead of side doors normally associated with high-wing and biplane cabin aircraft.

DYKE DELTA

STANDARD DATA: Gross wt. 1,750. Empty wt. 1,000. Fuel capacity 41. Wingspan 22'. Length 19'. PERFORMANCE: Top mph 190. Cruise mph 170. Stall mph (no stall). Climb rate 2,000. Takeoff run 700. Landing roll 1,500. Range 700.

John Dyke wanted a high-speed airplane with folding wings that would be compact enough to tow home for garage storage-thus the unique delta design. The basic fuselage skeleton, vertical stabilizer, and wing spars are of welded steel tube. The wings have an all-metal frame and have been tried with either fiberglass or aluminum covering. Virtually the entire planform surface of the Delta provides lift at cruise speeds. A 180-hp Lycoming provides the power. Plans are available through Dyke Aircraft.

EAA "ACRO-SPORT"

STANDARD DATA: Gross wt. 1,178. Empty wt. 739. Fuel capacity 20. Wingspan 19'7". Length 17'6". Engine 100-200 hp. PERFORMANCE: Top mph 180. Cruise mph 130. Stall mph 50. Climb rate 3,500. Ceiling 14,000. Takeoff run 350. Landing roll 800. Range 350.

The original Experimental Aircraft Association's designs are no longer available from the EAA, but many are now sold by a company called Acro-Sport.

The Acro-Sport is a hot little acrobatic ship that is also delightful to handle. Some say that it flies similarly to the two-place Pitts, but since the Acro-Sport is a single-seater and much lighter, it is easier to land, has a shorter roll at takeoff, and has an improved glide ratio.

This bipe was designed by EAA President Paul Poberezny, who wanted to come up with a plane that could be used in high school industrial arts programs and Civil Air Patrol groups as an educational tool. The Acro-Sport can be fabricated with tools normally found in a high-school shop. It is built with steel tube covered by fabric and 100- to 200-hp engines.

EAA "ACRO-SPORT II"

STANDARD DATA: Gross wt. 1,520. Empty wt. 875. Fuel capacity 25. Wingspan 21'8". Length 18'11". Engine 180-hp Lycoming. PERFORMANCE: Cruise mph 123. Range 400.

The Acro II, a two-place larger version of the single-place Acro Sport, can be constructed for little more than its single-place siblings. With its larger wheels, wide landing gear, and light gross weight, the Acro II is a fun, docile sport airplane designed for engines ranging in power from 115 to 200 hp. When fitted with a 180-hp Lycoming, its empty weight of 875 pounds makes it one of the lightest custom-built airplanes. Like all Acro Sports, its cockpit is designed to be comfortable for pilots up to 66" and 240 pounds. The airframe is somewhat larger than the really "midget" biplanes to avoid "touchy" flight characteristics and allow for more baggage. Designed by Paul Poberezny, the Acro II features an M-6 airfoil with a 43-inch chord.

EAA "SUPER ACRO-SPORT"

STANDARD DATA: Gross wt. 1,350. Empty wt. 884. Fuel capacity 20. Wingspan 19'7". Length 17'6". Engine 200-hp Lycoming. PERFORMANCE: Top mph 156. Cruise mph 135. Stall mph 50. Climb rate 3,700. Ceiling 15,000. Takeoff run 1,025. Landing roll 800. Range 300.

This further development of the Acro-Sport is intended for unlimited international-class aerobatic competition. Though basically similar in appearance to its counterpart, the Super Acro-Sport takes advantage of a more powerful engine turning a fixed-pitch prop, an improved roll rate, and inverted flight capabilities. Its two wings have almost symmetrical airfoil sections. Also added was a trim tab on the starboard elevator and a servo tab on the port side.

EAA BIPLANE

STANDARD DATA: Gross wt. 1,023. Empty wt. 640. Fuel capacity 12. Wingspan 20'. Length 17'. PERFORMANCE: Top mph 125. Cruise mph 110. Stall mph 55. Climb rate 1,000. Takeoff run 500. Landing roll 550. Range 200.

The EAA decided in 1955 to develop a single-seat sport biplane as a service to its members. The prototype was built as a classroom project by students of St. Rita's High School in Chicago. It flew for the first time in 1960. The plane is, in a sense, the predecessor to the Acro-Sport, the difference being that the A-1 Biplane is lighter and uses a smaller engine, an 85-hp Continental. Construction is the same. Plans are no longer marketed.

EAA HEATH PARASOL

Heath Parasol

STANDARD DATA: Gross wt. 700. Empty wt. 450. Fuel capacity 9. Wingspan 31'3". Length 17'3". PERFORMANCE: Top mph 73. Cruise mph 62. Stall mph 30. Climb rate 500. Takeoff run 400. Landing roll 400. Range 350.

The Heath Parasol was one of the more distinctive lightweight homebuilt aircraft designs in the late 1920s and early 1930s. That makes it one of the oldest designs still being built. This single-seater is powered by either a Volkswagen conversion or a 65-hp Continental and is constructed of wood, fabric, and tubular steel. At present, the plans for the Parasol are no longer marketed by EAA.

EAA NESMITH "COUGAR"

STANDARD DATA: Gross wt. 1,250. Empty wt. 624. Fuel capacity 25. Wingspan 20'6". Length 18'11". Engine 115-hp Lycoming. PERFORMANCE: Top mph 195. Cruise mph 166. Stall mph 53. Climb rate 1,300. Ceiling 13,000. Takeoff run 450. Landing roll 350. Range 750.

Plans for the Cougar were first handled by its designer, Robert Nesmith, and subsequently by EAA. First flown in 1957, the Cougar is a high-wing, enclosed-cabin, sporting monoplane that resembles the Whitman Tailwind to a small degree. The wing's all-wood two-spar structure is covered with plywood and fabric. The fuselage is a fabric-covered steel-tube framework. The conventional landing gear can be fitted with optional main-gear fairings. Inside the cabin, seating is for two in a side-by-side fashion with dual controls.

EAA "POBER PIXIE"

STANDARD DATA: Gross wt. 900. Empty wt. 543. Fuel capacity 12.3. Wingspan 29'10". Length 17'3". Engine 50-hp VW conversion. PERFORMANCE: Top mph 130. Cruise mph 85. Stall mph 30. Climb rate 500. Ceiling 13,000. Takeoff run 300. Landing roll 300.

The single-seat Pober Pixie is another homebuilt designed by Paul Poberezny. It originally started as an effort to help pilots beat high operational costs and was designated "Project Econoplane" in 1974. Inspired by a Heath Parasol LN, the Pixie is a parasol monoplane powered by a Limbach VW engine rated at 50 to 75 hp. Full-span ailerons give excellent roll with little yaw on entry and recovery.

EDI "EXPRESS 90"

STANDARD DATA: Seats 4. Gross wt. 2,895. Empty wt. 1,700. Fuel capacity 92. Engine 260-hp Lycoming 10-540. PERFORMANCE: Top mph 240. Cruise mph 210. Initial climb rate 1,300. Ceiling 22,000. Range 1,450. Takeoff distance (50') 650. Landing distance (50') 1,100.

Originally designed and built as the Wheeler Express by Ken Wheeler, Wheeler Technology, the Express 90 is a four to six-place, all composite, low-wing, fixed-gear monoplane that subscribes to the high-tech school of kit-built aircraft. Express Design, Inc., acquired the rights to manufacture the Express 90 and is one of the more popular multipurpose cross-country aircraft. Two major features of the Express are its load-carrying capabilities and the versatile seating options available to the owner/builder. Ownership of the EDI Express 90 currently belongs to Express Aircraft.

EOS

STANDARD DATA: Gross wt. 1,000. Empty wt. 670. Fuel capacity 15. Wingspan 26'. Length 16'8". Engine 55-hp Volkswagen. PERFORMANCE: Top cruise 200 mph. Stall mph 55. Climb rate 1,100. Takeoff run 500'. Landing roll 800. Range 1,000 nm.

The EOS SFA is a single-seater with retractable gear and a tractor-thrust configuration. The fuselage is built from lightweight alloy pop-riveted and epoxy-resin bonded with a fiberglass engine cowling. It is not intended to be the simplest aircraft to build but rather to provide a mix between maximum design efficiency and minimum construction complexity. No compound forming is necessary. There's a castering nose gear, and the tricycle landing gear are manually retracted. Steering is via rudder and differential braking. The 1,834cc VW drives a 50-inch diameter ground-adjustable wooden propeller with three blades.

EUROPA "TRI-GEAR/MONOWHEEL"

Europa Monowheel

STANDARD DATA: TRI-GEAR Seats 2. Gross wt. 1,370. Empty wt. 780. Fuel capacity 18-28. Engine Rotax 914 turbo. PERFORMANCE: Top mph 191. Stall mph 51. Takeoff run 500. Landing roll 600. Range 732-1,094 nm.

The Europa is one of the most popular kit planes in the world, with examples now flying more than three dozen countries worldwide. The two-place, low-wing monoplane is available in a variety of configurations. Two-seater is comfortable, friendly to fly and offers remarkable performance. The Europa's wings can stow in a matter of minutes allowing the aircraft to be trailered home.

EVANS VP-1 "VOLKSPLANE"

STANDARD DATA: Gross wt. 700. Empty wt. 480. Fuel capacity 8. Wingspan 24'. Length 18'. PERFORMANCE: Top mph 95. Cruise mph 75. Stall mph 45. Climb rate 600. Takeoff run 500. Landing roll 400. Range 200.

Ultra-simple wooden construction and the familiar VW engine mean low-cost flying fun and ease of construction. The fuselage of the VP-1 is little more than a plywood box. The wings use a spruce frame covered with fabric. Any stock VW engine from 1,500cc to 2,100cc can be used; only small changes need to be made. The VP-1 is available as a single-seater and as a side-by-side two-seater. It has been said that the VP-1 handles similarly to the Piper Cub. Minimal welding is in the control-stick assembly, the flying struts, and the stabilator horn. The VP-1 and VP-2 can be stowed at home and require no trailer for highway towing.

EVANS VP-2

STANDARD DATA: Gross wt. 1,040. Empty wt. 640. Fuel capacity 14. Wingspan 27'. Length 19'. Engine 60-hp Volkswagen. PERFORMANCE: Top mph 100. Cruise mph 75. Stall mph 45. Climb rate 500. Ceiling 10,000. Takeoff run 700. Landing roll 400. Range 200.

The VP-2 is generally similar to its smaller brother, the VP-1, except for an increased span and chord measurement, and the fuselage width is 12 inches wider to make room for the extra passenger. Any stock VW engine from 1,834cc to 2,100cc can be used. The VP-2 with a passenger aboard is designed for "normal category" use, which allows non-aerobatic operation and all maneuvers incident to normal flying. Without a passenger, "utility category" use is permitted, which includes stalls, lazy eights, chandelles, and steep turns with a bank angle of more than 60 degrees. Aerobatics are not approved in either the VP-1 or VP-2.

EVEKTOR "SPORTSTAR"

STANDARD DATA: Gross wt. 1,212. Empty wt. 668. Fuel capacity 17.2 Wingspan 28'7". Length 19'7". Engine Rotax 912. PERFORMANCE: Top cruise 115 kts. Normal cruise 110 kts. Stall 39 kts. Climb rate 840 fpm. Ceiling 13,100'. Takeoff run 560. Landing roll 540. Range 350 nm.

This Czech-built two-seater is a popular trainer and leisure flyer with a semi-monocoque fuselage and a large, high visibility canopy. The SportStar is operating in more than thirty countries around the world. The aircraft is equipped with four cylinder four stroke 80 hp Rotax 912 UL engine, optionally 100 hp Rotax 912 ULS and can be ordered in a "quick build" configuration. This aircraft is certified in the United States as a Light Sport Aircraft.

EXPERIMENTAL AVIATION "BERKUT"

STANDARD DATA: Seats 2. Gross wt. 2,000. Empty wt. 1,035. Fuel capacity 55. Engine 205-hp IO-36-B1A Lycoming. PERFORMANCE: Top mph 250. Cruise mph 220. Initial climb rate 2,000. Ceiling 29,500. Range 1,228. Takeoff distance 1,000. Landing distance 1,000.

Since Burt Rutan made the advantages of a canard design configuration so apparent with his line of composite aircraft, builders have been taking the ball and running with it in order to improve a good thing. The Berkut is perhaps the epitome of the design evolution. The structure has evolved from the carved, foam-core with applied wet-lay-up fiberglass into vacuum-formed wet-lay-up composite sandwich construction. This method of component construction greatly increases part integrity and strength, and it significantly reduces weight of the finished product. The Berkut has a fully retractable landing gear and many other significant changes that have improved the original concept. The Berkut is no longer available as a kit or in plan form.

FALCONAR

STANDARD DATA: FLYING FLEA Gross wt. 700. Empty wt. 410. Fuel capacity 12. Wingspan 20'. Length 14'. PERFORMANCE: Top mph 105. Cruise mph 8,085. Stall mph 35. Climb rate 500-600. Ceiling 16,400. Range 275.

STANDARD DATA: AMF S-14 Gross wt. 1,500. Empty wt. 1,000. Fuel capacity 18. Wingspan 32'. Length 23'. PERFORMANCE: Top mph 150. Cruise mph 115. Stall mph 35. Climb rate 1,200. Takeoff run 100. Landing roll 250. Range 400.

STANDARD DATA: MUSTANG P-51 Gross wt. 1,985. Wingspan 24'8". PERFORMANCE: Top cruise mph 170+. Stall mph 60. Climb rate 1,200. Takeoff run 700'. Landing roll 700'. Range 575 nm.

For Chris Falconar, what began as a simple introduction in 1935 to the H14 Flying Flea in a Montreal department store, resulted in a lifelong fascination with aircraft design. Falconar added a fleet of flying homebuilts to the world, ranging from the most simple to high performance variants of the North American P-51 Mustang. He was awarded for outstanding achievements from the Experimental Aircraft Association in Oshkosh.

The first Flying Flea took to the air back in 1933 and quickly earned a reputation for being temperamental. The version pictured here is an authentic copy of the original biplane built by Mignet except for installation of a McCulloch 72-hp engine and two minor rigging changes. Mignet was a furniture manufacturer, and he impishly named his creation "LePou de Ciel," or "Louse of the Sky." It started out to be "Everyman's Airplane" that could be built for $500 (complete) in the Great Depression years. Mignet's Flea carried a 17-hp engine and had a speed range from 25 to 62 mph.

The AMF S-14 is a two-place taildragger modeled after the Adam RA-14. The S-14 was first flown in 1961. It is powered by 85- to 150-hp engines. Its fuselage is a conventional wooden box-girder structure covered with plastic-coated fabric. The 514's wings are a braced high-wing design of all-wood and fabric with STOL characteristics.

The kit Mustang is composed from wood and fabric, but includes a jettisonable canopy, removable fiberglass belly scoop, electrical or manual flaps and a retractable tail wheel.

The most common Falconar are still the more conventional "F" series. The simplest construction begins with the single-seat F9A, which often flies with small two stroke engines. The F10A is a beefier model designed to use a Continental engine. The F11A "Sporty" adds a side-by-side two-seat cockpit, and the F12A "Cruiser" adds a third seat.

F.E.W. "P-51D/TF"

STANDARD DATA: Seats 1-2. Gross wt. 2,000. Empty wt. 1,100. Fuel capacity 58. Engine 300-hp automotive conversion V8. PERFORMANCE: Top mph 250. Cruise mph 210. Initial climb rate 2,000. Ceiling 16,000. Range 750. Takeoff distance (50') 900. Landing distance (50') 1,000.

For years, many experimental aircraft builders have strived to re-create their favorite World War II fighters in miniature. For most, many hurdles had to be negotiated to get the right look, feel, sound, and of course, performance all at the right cost of ownership. Until the advent of composite building techniques, forming all those compound curves of a fighter in metal just wasn't within the means of your average builder. Then, getting the proper powerplant to look and sound like "the real thing" was next to impossible with the technology and funds at hand. Now with automotive/aviation V-8 conversions attaining a respectable degree of reliability, cost, and power coupled with these modern, prepreg, composite techniques, the right combination has been reached. F.E.W.'s P-51D is a 67% scale version of the most famous fighter of World War II, and it looks the part, sounds the part, and flies the part. The P-51D is stressed to ±6Gs for aerobatics and is available in a dual-control version, the P-51TF.

FIKE MODEL E

STANDARD DATA: Gross wt. 1,150. Empty wt. 690. Fuel capacity 15. Wingspan 22'5". Length 19'7". Engine 80-hp Continental. PERFORMANCE: Top mph 110. Cruise mph 100. Stall mph 37. Climb rate 800. Ceiling 10,000+, Takeoff run 400. Landing roll 600. Range 280.

William Fike, designer and Alaska airline pilot, created this two-place cabin monoplane. The Model E's airframe structure includes a Piper J-3 tail assembly, a welded steel-tube fuselage, and an all-wood fabric-covered wing. Power is supplied by an 85-hp Continental engine. The wing can be removed within 10 minutes to enable the plane to be towed.

FISHER FLYING PRODUCTS

STANDARD DATA: FP-202 Seats 1. Gross wt. 500. Empty wt. 250. Fuel capacity 13. Wingspan 29'. Length 18'. Engine 28-hp PERFORMANCE: Top

FP202

FP303

FP Youngster

FP RS Tiger Moth

cruise mph 60. Stall mph 26. Climb rate 900 fpm. Takeoff run 95'. Landing roll 125. Range 135 nm.

STANDARD DATA: FP-303 Seats 1. Gross wt. 450. Empty wt. 235. Fuel capacity 13. Wingspan 27.8'. Length 16.6'. Engine 25-hp. PERFORMANCE: Top mph 60. Cruise mph 45. Stall mph 25. Climb rate 800 fpm. Takeoff run 125. Landing roll 125.

STANDARD DATA: YOUNGSTER Seats 1. Gross wt. 650. Empty wt. 400. Fuel capacity 12. Wingspan 18'. Length 15.6'. Engine 50-hp Rotax. PERFORMANCE: Cruise mph 90. Stall mph 32. Climb rate 700 fpm. Takeoff run 200. Landing roll 250.

This North Dakota company manufacturers 15+ airplane kits, including a replica of the classic Tiger Moth. Products run the gamut from the FP-202, a Piper Cub look-alike to low wing cruisers and traditional biplane designs. Fisher Flying Products' entire line of aircraft is sold throughout the United States and in 30 foreign countries.

FLAGLOR "SCOOTER"

STANDARD DATA: Gross wt. 650. Empty wt. 390. Fuel capacity 5. Wingspan 28'. Length 15'8". Engine 40-hp Volkswagen. PERFORMANCE: Top mph 90. Cruise mph 80. Stall mph 34. Climb rate 600. Takeoff run 250. Landing roll 250. Range 175.

The Scooter was originally powered by a Cushman golf cart engine, which was ultimately replaced by a 1,500cc VW engine rated at 40 hp. At the 1967 EAA meet, this tiny, high-wing, enclosed-cabin taildragger received both "Outstanding Ultralight" and "Outstanding Volkswagen Powered" awards. Construction is of wood with a plywood covering, except for the aft section of the fuselage, which is fabric covered. The VW engine is mounted over the cabin and turns a two-blade propeller. The Scooter is now marketed by Rotor Wings & Flying Machines.

FLIGHT DYNAMICS "FLIGHTSAIL VII"

STANDARD DATA: Gross wt. 1,600. Empty wt. 1,100. Fuel capacity 12. Wingspan 39'. Length 29'. PERFORMANCE: Top mph 95. Cruise mph 80. Stall mph 35. Climb rate 500. Takeoff time 20 sec. Range 200.

What makes this bird truly different is that it can either be towed behind a 70-hp ski boat or it can have a 90-hp Continental pylon mounted above the fuselage to fly the Flightsail under its own power. The structure is built from bolted aluminum, foam, and epoxy. This two-seater amphibian features twin booms and twin tails.

GARRISON OM-1 "MELMOTH"

STANDARD DATA: Gross wt. 2,950. Empty wt. 1,500. Fuel capacity 154. Wingspan 23'. Length 21'6". Engine 195-hp Continental. PERFORMANCE: Top mph 209. Cruise mph 201. Stall mph 80. Climb rate 1,800. Takeoff distance (50') 2,500. Landing distance (50') 2,500. Range 3,400.

The Melmoth first flew in 1973 and was developed by Peter Garrison from the British Practavia Sprite (also partly a Garrison project). The Melmoth represented considerably more work than the average homebuilder would like to tackle. In fact, it was more of a research prototype than a backyard project. The Melmoth was conceived and designed as an exercise in extreme efficiency in all aspects of flight. It carried an unusually large amount of fuel for an aircraft of its size with a 41-gallon main tank and two 35-gallon tip tanks on each wing, which yielded the exceptional range. Some of the Melmoth's extras included double-slotted flaps, adjustable incidence ailerons, autopilot, and retractable landing gear. Unfortunately, the aircraft was destroyed in a highly unusual accident in which a landing aircraft struck Melmoth while waiting on the ground at the end of a runway. Garrison survived the accident and proceeded to design and construct a replacement.

HARMON "DER DONNERSCHLAG"

STANDARD DATA: Gross wt. 600. Empty wt. 350. Fuel capacity 10. Wingspan 19'6". Length 14'6". Engine 75-hp Volkswagen. PERFORMANCE: Top mph 120. Cruise mph 110. Stall mph 55. Climb rate 800. Ceiling 10,000. Takeoff run 150. Landing roll 250. Range 500.

The language translation of this open-cockpit sport plane's name is "The Thunderclap." The airframe of this plane was used as the foundation for "Mr. America." Both share similar wings, fuselage, tail unit, and landing gear. The wings are a wire-braced shoulder type with two simple beam spars. As with the Mr. America, seating is for one behind a modified Volkswagen engine turning a two-blade wooden prop.

HARMON "MR. AMERICA"

STANDARD DATA: Gross wt. 650. Empty wt. 430. Fuel capacity 9. Wingspan 19'8". Length 15'2". Engine 60- to 70-hp Volkswagen. PERFORMANCE: Top mph 125. Cruise mph 110. Stall mph 48. Climb rate 800. Ceiling 12,000. Takeoff run 200. Landing roll 300. Range 400.

Harmon chose the long-established combination of a welded steel-tube fuselage and tail surfaces with a wooden spar and rib wings. In addition, the wings can be easily removed for storage and towing. The entire aircraft can be built with hand tools, except for the use of a welding rig. Mr. America's powerplant is a nearly stock 1,600cc Volkswagen engine bored to 1,650cc. The engine develops an honest 60 hp to produce what is said to be rapid acceleration on takeoff to about 800 fpm at 90 mph during initial climb.

HARRIS GEODETIC LW-108

STANDARD DATA: Gross wt. 1,000. Empty wt. 585. Fuel capacity 16. Wingspan 28'1". Length 19'4". Engine 80-hp Continental. PERFORMANCE: Top mph 150. Cruise mph 130. Stall mph 40. Climb rate 1,500. Takeoff run 500. Range 400.

The LW-108 offers the comfort of side-by-side seating underneath an enclosed canopy. Possibly the most outstanding feature of this low-wing tail-dragger is its unique geodetically constructed fuselage. It is said to be both lightweight and economical to build while providing exceptional strength without sacrificing a low-

drag fuselage shape. The framework is all spruce and plywood.

HATZ CB-1 BIPLANE

STANDARD DATA: Gross wt. 1,400. Empty wt. 850. Fuel capacity 18. Wingspan 25'4". Length 19'. Engine 100-hp Lycoming. PERFORMANCE: Top mph 100. Cruise mph 80. Stall mph 40. Climb rate 600. Takeoff run 400. Landing roll 300. Range 200.

The first flight of this tandem, two-seat, and open-cockpit biplane took place in 1968. The wings are a fabric-covered wooden structure, while the fuselage is built from welded-steel tubing. The design weight of the Hatz (850 pounds) makes it the lightest two-place biplane available. It performs well with the 85-hp Continental and is stressed to take engines up to 150 hp. The Hatz can be trimmed to fly hands off (more or less), which helps out when trying to read a map in an open cockpit. Control response is slow enough to give a feeling of a much larger aircraft, and it is capable of all aerobatic maneuvers in its power range.

HILLMAN "HORNET"

STANDARD DATA: Gross wt. 1,400. Empty wt. 800. Fuel capacity 22. Rotor span 25'5". Length 21'2". Engine 150-hp Lycoming. PERFORMANCE: Top mph 100. Cruise mph 90. Climb rate 1,000. Ceiling 12,000. Range 200.

The Hornet was the 1978 "Overall Award" winner at Oshkosh and received the "Best Helicopter Design Award" at the Popular Rotorcraft Convention in Rockford, Illinois. Standard features include a comfortable cockpit for two, excellent visibility, room for a variety of avionics, and dual controls. Flight performance has been favorably compared with that of the Hughes 300.

HOLLMAN HA-2M "SPORTSTER"

STANDARD DATA: Gross wt. 1,050. Empty wt. 620. Fuel capacity 12. Rotor diameter 28'. Length 13'. Engine 135-hp Lycoming. PERFORMANCE: Top mph 90. Cruise mph 75. Minimum mph 28. Climb rate 500. Ceiling 7,000. Takeoff run 350. Landing roll 0. Range 90.

The Sportster is the world's first two-place gyroplane designed for the homebuilder who has limited access to power tools. Ninety percent of the structure is bolted or riveted together, and a minimum of machined parts are used. For convenience, the Sportster is designed to be towed behind a car. Two average people, 350 pounds combined, can fly comfortably inside its nearly enclosed cockpit for up to 90 miles on a cross-country trip. A 130-hp Franklin, 135-hp Lycoming, or 150-hp Lycoming engine can be used. With the engine cut, the Sportster has a 1,000-fpm sink rate. The Sportster is now marketed by Aircraft Designs, Inc.

HOVEY "BETA BIRD"

STANDARD DATA: Gross wt. 6'6". Length 16'11". PERFORMANCE: Top mph 85. Cruise mph 80. Stall mph 40. Climb rate 500. Takeoff run (50) 400. Landing run (50') 400. Range 180.

The single-seat "Beta Bird" was first flown at Mojave, California, in April 1979. It is powered by a 1,385cc converted VW engine and offers the homebuilder-simplified methods of construction. The wings fold for transport or storage. The fuselage pod is plywood and spruce construction with a stiffened aluminum tailboom to support the tail. The wings are spruce in a two-spar configuration, and the ribs are single-piece aluminum tubes. The tail group is fabricated from aluminum tubing, pop-riveted together with gussets, and covered with Dacron. Only 250 feet are needed for takeoff and landing, and the 7.5 gallons of fuel yield 180 miles.

HOVEY "WHING-DING II"

STANDARD DATA: Gross wt. 310. Empty wt. 122. Fuel capacity 1/2 gallon. Wingspan 16'4". Length 12'11". PERFORMANCE: Top mph 45. Cruise mph 45. Stall mph 26. Climb rate 200. Takeoff run (50') 300. Landing run (50') 300. Range 22.

This 15-hp, 300-pound gross-weight biplane is the ultimate in lightness and simplicity. The tail surfaces are constructed from 1/2-inch-thick Styrofoam art board faced with high-strength craft paper on both sides; the critical areas are reinforced with 1/8-inch plywood gussets. The tail boom is a 3-inch aluminum pipe filled with foam to resist buckling. The fuselage is basically a 6-inch wide box of plywood filled with foam that serves as an engine mount and a mast support for the wings. The prop is chain driven from a 15-hp McCulloch, two-cycle, go-kart engine. The wings have two spars and are fabric covered.

HU-GO CRAFT

STANDARD DATA: Gross wt. 848. Empty wt. 558. Fuel capacity 12. Wingspan 17'. Length 14'8". PERFORMANCE: Top mph 115. Cruise mph 105. Stall

mph 55. Climb rate 1,000. Takeoff run 500. Landing roll 500. Range 250.

With a lot of lift for its small size and light weight, the HUGO Craft wrings a 105-mph cruise speed out of a mere 65-hp Continental. This single-seater bipe is largely conventional in construction with fuselage and tail group of welded-steel tubing and wings of wood. All surfaces are fabric covered.

INTERNATIONAL COMMUTER IIA "SAFARI"

STANDARD DATA: Gross wt. 1,300. Empty wt. 700. Fuel capacity 22. Rotor span 25'. Length 29'. Engine 150-hp Lycoming. PERFORMANCE: Top mph 100. Cruise mph 90. Climb rate 1,071. Ceiling 13,000. Range 200.

The Commuter was designed by Harold "Pop" Emigh who includes among his accomplishments the Navajo and Polaris ballistic missile systems and the Emigh Trojan (see the single-engine section). He stressed safety and reliability in every component of this two-seater to assure the safest helicopter possible. The main rotor and tail rotor are gear driven, so there are no rubber belts or chains to readjust or fail. It is powered by the proven 150-hp Lycoming aircraft engine with a dual ignition. Such complicated parts as the main rotor transmission, tail rotor gear box, rotor blades, and the like are assembled at the factory. The airframe is Chrome-Moly steel tubing and can be constructed with a minimum of common tools. The Com-

muter will auto-rotate better than most helicopters; with engine off, it descends at a rate of only 1,200 to 1,400 fpm. The aircraft is now marketed by Canadian Home Rotors, Inc.

JANOWSKI "DON QUIXOTE"

STANDARD DATA: Gross wt. 600. Empty wt. 291. Wingspan 24.93'. Length 16'. Engine 25-50-hp Volkswagen. PERFORMANCE: (23 hp). Top mph 84. Cruise mph 77. Stall mph 39. Climb rate 244. Ceiling 6,820. Range 310. Takeoff run 761. Landing run (50) 1,256.

The prototype Don Quixote designed and built by M.R. Janowski was powered by a 230-hp two-stroke Saturn engine, also designed by Janowski. However, several problems were inherent in the two-stroke engine, and so the more readily available Volkswagen engine was settled upon. A heavier engine called for strengthening the airplane's structure. To cover the widest range of homebuilders in various countries, it was decided that the Don Quixote would make use of conventional wood and fabric along with more modern polyurethane foam and epoxy/fiberglass. The J-113 can withstand loading of +4G and -2G, but in the fiberglass version of the plane, +6G and -3G are possible. Construction of the plane follows conventional building rules with spruce wood, birch plywood, and flat sheets of Plexiglas as basic materials.

JAVELIN "WICHAWK"

STANDARD DATA: Gross wt. 2,000. Empty wt. 1,280. Fuel capacity 39. Wingspan 24'. Length 19'3". Engine 180-hp Lycoming. PERFORMANCE: Top mph 140. Cruise mph 127. Stall mph 45. Climb rate 1,700. Takeoff run 150.

The Wichawk is structurally similar to the Boeing Stearman biplane and is stressed for up to 12 Gs positive and 6 Gs negative. Standard seating is for two in a side-by-side configuration, which is rather unusual for a sport biplane of its type. Optional tandem seating is also available. While the 180-hp Lycoming is most often used, the ship can be adapted to house various horizontally opposed or radial engines. The wings make use of wooden spars with lightweight alloy ribs, and the fuselage is constructed from welded steel tubes. Javelin no longer sells the Wichawk. It is now marketed by its designer, Dave Blanton.

JEFFAIR "BARRACUDA"

STANDARD DATA: Gross wt. 2,200. Empty wt. 1,495. Fuel capacity 44. Wingspan 24'9". Length 21'6". Engine 220-hp Lycoming. PERFORMANCE: Top mph 218. Cruise mph 200. Stall mph 62. Climb rate 2,200.

The Barracuda is a sophisticated enclosed-cabin two-seater in the image of the Thorp T-18 but with tricycle landing gear, all-wood construction, and a three-blade controllable pitch propeller. It was designed by former RAF fighter pilot Geoffrey Siers. The landing gear features electro-hydraulic retraction. The cabin is fitted with dual controls, gull-wing doors, and two armchair-type seats. Siers Flight Systems owns the rights to the Barracuda.

JODEL D-11 "CLUB"

STANDARD DATA: Gross wt. 1,290. Fuel capacity 10. Wingspan 26'11". Length 20'6". PERFORMANCE: Top mph 124. Cruise mph 114. Stall mph 35. Climb rate 800. Ceiling 16,000. Takeoff run 500. Landing roll 800. Range 300.

This low-wing taildragger of all-wood construction comes from France where homebuilding was flourishing long before the movement took hold in the United States. The distinguishing feature of the Jodel is the bent wing with a straight center section and dihedral in the outer panels only. It is powered by Continental engines

of 65 to 90 hp and seats two in side-by-side fashion. The company also made the Jodel D-9 "Bebe," a single-seat monoplane. The Jodel aircraft are now owned by Avions Jodel.

"JUNGSTER I"

STANDARD DATA: Gross wt. 1,000. Empty wt. 605. Fuel capacity 16. Wingspan 16'8". Length 16'. PERFORMANCE: Top mph 200. Cruise mph 150. Stall mph 52. Climb rate 2,500+. Takeoff run 300. Landing roll 800. Range 300.

The Jungster I was developed as an 8/10-scale version of the famous Jungmeister aerobatic airplane. The intention was to capture many of the flying qualities of the Jungmeister in a smaller size. This all-wood and fabric-covered biplane has a sweptback wing design of about 11 degrees to keep the center of lift close to the center of gravity. It can handle engines rated from 85 to 150 hp, and is a frisky single-place aerobatic plane.

"JUNGSTER II"

STANDARD DATA: Gross wt. 1,375. Empty wt. 739. Fuel capacity 16. Wingspan 22'4". Length 16'11". PERFORMANCE: Top mph 170. Cruise mph 148. Stall mph 5. Climb rate 3,500. Takeoff run 200. Landing roll 800.

The Jungster II is a follow-up design that grew out of experience with the Jungster I. The intent was to create a plane with the same open-cockpit concept, but to increase speed and capacity so that it would be an acceptable cross-country airplane. The Jungster II uses the same design and construction concepts, except that it is just a little bit bigger, has a single extended parasol-type wing, and uses a welded steel-tube center section. Engines rated from 85 to 180 hp are used. Plans are no longer available.

JURCA MJ-2 "TEMPETE"

STANDARD DATA: Gross wt. 950. Empty wt. 639. Fuel capacity 16. Wingspan 19'6". Length 18'6". PERFORMANCE: Top mph 120. Cruise mph 102. Stall mph 41. Climb rate 555. Takeoff run 820. Range 375.

Marcel Jurca incorporated many Jodel components in the design of the MJ-2 Tempete. The Tempete is a cantilevered low-wing monoplane that can be fitted with engines ranging in horsepower from 65 to 125. The standard version is powered by a 65-hp engine. Another common version powered by a 90-hp engine cruises at 120 mph and climbs to 3,280 in three minutes. It can perform aerobatics without loss of altitude.

JURCA MJ-5 "SIROCCO"

STANDARD DATA: Gross wt. 1,300. Empty wt. 726. Fuel capacity 36. Wingspan 21'6". Length 20'6". PERFORMANCE: Top mph 190. Cruise mph 162. Stall mph 60. Climb rate 2,500. Takeoff run 820. Landing roll 750. Range 570.

The Sirocco is an all-wood, fiberglass- or fabric-covered, and low-wing aircraft that can give the homebuilding enthusiast the wild performance of a small fighter ship. Identified by its "rooster tail," the

Sirocco seats two in tandem fashion and sports retractable landing gear for adding speed. Any 85- to 150-hp engine can be used.

JURCA MJ-7 "BABY MUSTANG"

STANDARD DATA: Gross wt. 2,000. Empty wt. 1,175. Fuel capacity 30. Wingspan 25'10". Length 22'4". PERFORMANCE: Top mph 225. Cruise mph 175. Stall mph 65. Takeoff run 900. Landing roll 800. Range 570.

Sportplane enthusiasts have always shown an interest in building replicas of fighter planes. Unlike planes from World War I, World War II ships have been difficult to re-create due to their massive engines, complex metal structure, and sheer size. To facilitate homebuilding, designer Marcel Jurca created scaled-down versions of the P-51 Mustang, the Supermarine Spitfire, and the Focke-Wulf FW-190. The Mustang was designed in 2/3 or 3/4 scale. Only the relative size of a pilot's head identifies the baby P-51 from its bigger ancestor. The ship first flew with a 200-hp Ranger inline engine. Other engines that can be used include: any of the six-cylinder Rangers, the 125-hp Menasco, the 130-hp Gipsy Major, the 125- to 160-hp Canadian Rambler, or the General Motors Buick F-58. Materials used are wood and fabric.

JURCA MJ-8 "BABY FOCKE-WULF"

STANDARD DATA: Gross wt. 2,400. Empty wt. 400. Fuel capacity 32. Wingspan 25'10". Length 21'8". PERFORMANCE: Top mph 225. Cruise mph 150.

Stall mph 50. Climb rate 2,000. Takeoff run 380. Landing roll 800. Range 575.

The replica of the German Focke-Wulf 190, the finest piston-engine fighter developed for the Luftwaffe, is available in 3/4-scale only. Engines from 220 to 350 hp can be used.

JURCA MJ-10 "BABY SPITFIRE"

STANDARD DATA: Gross wt. 2,000. Empty wt. 900. Fuel capacity 34. Wingspan 27'8". Length 23'4". PERFORMANCE: Top mph 225. Cruise mph 140. Stall mph 60. Climb rate 1,650. Takeoff run 740. Landing roll 700. Range 630.

This scaled-down version of the hero of the Battle of Britain is available in 3/4-scale only. As with all Jurca World War II fighters, the materials used are wood and fabric. Retractable landing gear is also a common feature. Engines for the Spitfire range from 220 to 350 hp.

KELEHER JK-1 "LARK"

STANDARD DATA: Gross wt. 855. Empty wt. 555. Fuel capacity 12. Wingspan 23'. Length 17'. PERFORMANCE: Top mph 135. Cruise mph 122. Stall mph 55. Climb rate 1,000. Takeoff run 550. Landing roll 700. Range 300.

The Lark is an enclosed-cockpit mid-wing monoplane. This single-seat taildragger is relatively unusual with its strut-braced mid-wing configuration. The fuselage is of steel-tube construction, and the wing uses wooden spars and ribs. The whole aircraft is fabric covered. Engines vary from 65 to 100 hp.

"KITTIWAKE"

STANDARD DATA: Gross wt. 1,350. Empty wt. 925. Fuel capacity 26. Wingspan 24'. Length 19'8". PERFORMANCE: Top mph 135. Cruise mph 115. Stall mph 48. Climb rate 950. Range 500.

The Kittiwake single-seat low-wing monoplane was designed to make full use of all-metal materials and modern construction while retaining a simple design that lends itself to homebuilding. The wings attach directly to the sides of the fuselage so that the Kittiwake can be constructed or stored in a garage. The Kit-

tiwake stands on tricycle landing gear and is used as a sporting light aircraft and a glider tow plane. Power is supplied by a 100-hp Continental.

KRAFT "SUPER FLI"

STANDARD DATA: Gross wt. 1,450. Empty wt. 1,060. Fuel capacity 23. Wingspan 24'6". Length 20'. Engine 200-hp Lycoming. PERFORMANCE: Top mph 185. Cruise mph 135. Stall mph 48. Climb rate 1,800. Ceiling 12,000. Takeoff run 800. Landing roll 1,000. Range 400.

World-champion model builder and radio-control-system manufacturer Phil Kraft used his know-how to design and construct the Super Fli. This unlimited aerobatic low-winger has seating for one under a transparent canopy. Fuselage construction is a steel-tube frame covered by aluminum, while the wings are a spruce and plywood structure covered with plywood.

LACEY M-10

STANDARD DATA: Gross wt. 1,118. Empty wt. 638. Fuel capacity 20. Wingspan 20'. Length 20'. PERFORMANCE: Top mph 140. Cruise mph 120. Stall mph 55. Climb rate 1,000. Takeoff run 600. Landing roll 600. Range 400.

The Lacey is one of the simplest designs for the homebuilder to construct. In the words of its designer, "There are no compound curves and very few simple ones. The wing has no wash-in, no wash-out, no dihedral, and no incidence angle; the wing's bottom is flat and fits flat on top of the fuselage. It has no taper, no slots, no flaps, no spoilers, no wingtips, no struts, no wires, no braces, and no spars." The two-place towable Lacey is propelled by a 90-hp Continental.

LACO-125

STANDARD DATA: Gross wt. 1,400. Empty wt. 860. Fuel capacity 24. Wingspan 22'9". Length 19'6". Engine 125-hp Continental. PERFORMANCE: Top mph 124. Cruise mph 113. Stall mph 50. Climb rate 900. Range 300.

Legacy FG

The Laco-25 is a sturdy two-seat biplane that is easy to fly yet very agile. To aid the builder, there are no castings, forgings, or other difficult-to-build-or-obtain parts. The fuselage is a Warren truss type of chrome-moly tubing with wooden formers and stringers. The wings are conventional two-spar construction with wooden ribs and chrome-moly fittings for strength. This homebuilt derives its designation from the use of a 125-hp Continental in the prototype, which is interchangeable with the 145-hp engine. The weight distribution of the Laco-125 is such that larger four-cylinder powerplants can be substituted.

LANCAIR "200/235/320/360" "LEGACY"

Legacy

STANDARD DATA: LEGACY Seats 2. Gross wt. 2,200. Empty wt. 1,500. Fuel capacity 65. Engine 310-hp Continental IO-550-N. PERFORMANCE: Top Cruise mph 276. Stall 67 mph. Initial climb rate 2,700. Ceiling 18,000. Range 1,200 nm. Takeoff distance 800'. Landing distance 900'.

The first model Lancair 200 was developed in 1984 and today, that prototype resides in the Experimental Aircraft Association (EAA) Museum in Oshkosh, WI. In the past decade, the name Lancair has come to represent industry leadership, a success based on an unrelenting commitment to quality and innovation. Lancair has played a key role in defining the actual character of this growing kit plane industry, a market segment that now outsells the production market fleet by more than 3 to 1. Today, there are more than 1,870 Lancairs sold in more than 34 countries, on 5 continents.

In 1985 Lance Neibauer designed the retractable-gear Lancair 235. The 235 was designed to go as fast as possible and provide economical operation in cross-country comfort for two full-size adults. As if this wasn't enough, Neibauer wanted the slippery-looking craft to have very docile flight characteristics and do it all powered by the Lycoming 0-235 which put out only 100-115 hp. Results of the finished product were astounding. Not only did the 235 stand up to its expectations, it also cruised at better than 200 mph and burned something in the neighborhood of 6 gph. The design evolved into the Lancair 320/360 and then finally into the Legacy. A fixed gear version, the Legacy FG is also available.

LANCAIR "IV/IV-P/PROPJET"

STANDARD DATA: IV Seats 4. Gross wt. 3,200. Empty wt. 1,750. Fuel capacity 82. Engine 350-hp Continental TSIO-550. PERFORMANCE: Top mph 361. Cruise mph 341. Initial climb rate 2,600. Ceiling 35,000. Range 1,450. Takeoff distance 1,200. Landing distance 1,900.

STANDARD DATA: IV-P Seats 4. Gross wt. 3,550. Empty wt. 2,000. Fuel capacity 82. Engine 350-hp Continental TSIO-550. PERFORMANCE: Cruise

Lancair IVP

Lancair Turbine IVP

mph 331. Initial climb rate 2,600. Ceiling 35,000. Range 1,550 sm. Takeoff distance 1,500. Landing distance 1,900.

STANDARD DATA: PROPJET Seats 4. Gross wt. 3,550. Empty wt. 2,200. Fuel capacity 125. Engine 750-hp Walter 601E turbine. PERFORMANCE: Cruise mph 370. Initial climb rate 4,000-7,000 fpm. Ceiling 35,000. Range 1,400 sm. Takeoff distance 1,200. Landing distance 1,400.

The Lancair IV was a natural progression from the 235 and the 320. Lance Neibauer wanted to build a four-place retractable that would give him and the kitbuilder the most bang for the buck. The IV is essentially a scaled-up version of the 320 with a 30-ft. wingspan and a twin-turbo 350-hp Continental swinging a three-blade constant-speed prop. The aircraft is faster, lighter, roomier, has more useful load, and is less expensive than any aircraft in its class. Since its introduction in 1991, the Lancair IV has broken many speed and altitude records for its class type and at altitude has reached sustained speeds in excess of 395 mph with no tailwind. The entire airframe is constructed of vacuum-formed, oven-cured, prepreg carbon fiber. Building time is approximately 2,500 hours.

A pressurized version, the Lancair IV-P is also available, only the fourth single engine piston with that achievement. The IV-P is structurally quite different and is designed to operate with an impressive 5.0 psi cabin differential pressure. This equates to a "cabin altitude" of just 8,500 ft. when you're cruising at FL240 (24,000 ft.).

In 2000, Lancair began testing the ultimate IV-P by replacing the piston engine with a Walter 601E tur-

bine. By 2001, the idea was flying and became available to kit builders shortly afterward. As expected, the turbine-powered performance is remarkable.

LANCAIR "ES/SUPER ES/ES-P"

Lancair ES

STANDARD DATA: ES Seats 4. Gross wt. 2,800. Empty wt. 1,600. Fuel capacity 76. Engine 200-hp Continental 10-360-ES. PERFORMANCE: Top mph 200. Cruise mph 192. Initial climb rate 1,200. Ceiling 18,000. Range 1,360. Takeoff distance (50') 800. Landing distance (50') 800.

STANDARD DATA: SUPER ES Seats 4. Gross wt. 3,200. Empty wt. 1,900. Fuel capacity 98. Engine 310-hp Continental IO-550-N. PERFORMANCE: Top cruise mph 293. Initial climb rate 2,000 fpm. Stall 65 mph. Ceiling 18,000. Range 1,900 sm. Takeoff distance 600. Landing distance 800.

STANDARD DATA: ES-P Seats 4. Gross wt. 3,550. Empty wt. 2,200. Fuel capacity 105. Engine 310-hp Continental IO-550-N. PERFORMANCE: Top mph 225. Cruise mph 215. Initial climb rate 1,550-2,000 fpm. Stall 65 mph. Ceiling 18,000. Range 1,200 sm. Takeoff distance 600. Landing distance 900.

The Lancair ES is essentially a fixed gear, lesser horsepower version of the Lancair IV. Although the appearance is basically the same for both aircraft, they are really quite different from one another. The concept of the ES was to give the kitbuilder a fast, economical, and roomy four-seater without the complexity and expense of a retractable. The ES provides exceptional performance and flight characteristics with its 35ft. wingspan and 200-hp engine. Construction is advanced composite prepreg that has been vacuum-formed and autoclaved to give unparalleled uniformity and component integrity throughout the airframe. The ES will accommodate four full-sized adults comfortably and contains 20 cubic feet of baggage space and a load limit of 175 pounds. Kits are sold less engine, avionics, and finishing products.

The Lancair Super ES is available with a 310-hp

Continental IO-550-N, the same engine used in the certified Columbia 350.

Add pressurization to the Super ES and you get the ES-P. Lancair publishes performance numbers of 293 mph at FL240.

LARKIN "SKYLARK"

STANDARD DATA: Gross wt. 1,246. Empty wt. 790. Fuel capacity 17. Wingspan 26'6". Length 19'6". Engine 100-hp Volkswagen. PERFORMANCE: Top mph 115. Cruise mph 105. Stall mph 42. Climb rate 550. Ceiling 12,000. Takeoff run 600. Landing roll 400. Range 525.

The Skylark is a beautifully designed two-seater that looks more like it was intended to land on water than return to Earth. Its configuration includes an enclosed cabin with a pusher engine and prop mounted overhead and centered between twin booms. The booms are attached to the wings and connected by one single elevator surface at the rear between twin vertical stabilizers. One unique feature of the airplane's structure is the use of a square tubular aluminum keel that is responsible for the loads from the landing gear and the main fuselage. An optional V-shaped lower hull of fiberglass can be added for amphibious operations.

LEVI RL3 "MONSOON"

STANDARD DATA: Gross wt. 1,500. Empty wt. 870. Fuel capacity 28. Wingspan 25'10". Length 20'3". PERFORMANCE: Top mph 130. Cruise mph 115. Stall mph 45. Climb rate 800. Takeoff run 500. Landing roll 700. Range 600.

This two-place low-wing taildragger was first built in India by an Italian engineer who studied in England and France. A Canadian company brought it to the United States. The Monsoon is of conventional all-wood construction and covered with fabric. The prototype was powered by a Continental 85-hp engine, and other versions have a 125-hp Lycoming.

LEZA AIRCAM CORP. "AIRCAM"

STANDARD DATA: Gross wt. 1,680. Empty wt. 1,040. Fuel capacity 28. Wingspan 36'. Length 27'. Engines two 100-hp Rotax 912S. PERFORMANCE: Cruise mph 50-100. Stall mph 39. Climb rate 1500 fpm. Takeoff run 200. Landing roll 300. Range 340 nm.

The twin-engine kit plane is a hybrid, an evolution from an ultralight toward airplane. Many of the AirCams feature a full cockpit of avionics. Factory kits require no fabrication, just assembly of pre-machined parts. The AirCam is equally at home on floats as on wheels.

LOVING'S "LOVE"

STANDARD DATA: Gross wt. 885. Empty wt. 613. Fuel capacity 15. Wingspan 20'. Length 17'2". PERFORMANCE: Top mph 215. Cruise mph 142. Stall mph 58. Climb rate 2,100. Takeoff run 500. Landing roll 1,200. Range 450.

The Love racer features reverse gull wings and full wheel covers. It is built from fabric around a wooden frame. With an 85-hp Continental powerplant, it is capable of speeds in excess of 200 mph.

LUTON "MAJOR"

STANDARD DATA: Gross wt. 1,030. Empty wt. 600. Fuel capacity 13. Wingspan 35'2". Length 23'9". PERFORMANCE: Top mph 120. Cruise mph 105. Stall mph 35. Climb rate 750. Takeoff run 250. Landing roll 150. Range 300.

The Luton Major was first flown in 1939. This two-seat high-wing monoplane features an airframe that is similar to the Luton Minor. Its wings are vee-bracing struts and fold back along the fuselage for towing. The fuselage is an all wood structure covered with plywood. Power is provided by a 55- to 65-hp Lycoming or 65- to 85-hp Continental.

LUTON "MINOR"

STANDARD DATA: Gross wt. 750. Empty wt. 450. Fuel capacity 7.5. Wingspan 25'. Length 20'9". PERFORMANCE: Top mph 85. Cruise mph 75. Stall mph 28. Climb rate 450. Takeoff run 250. Landing roll 120. Range 180.

This single-seat strut-braced parasol monoplane carries Volkswagen air-cooled engines rated from 30 to 65 hp. First flown in 1936, the design was upgraded in 1960 to handle 55-hp engines and up. The Luton Minor's wings are built around a wooden two-spar structure in two halves and supported by a tubular center-section pylon structure. The wings are removable for transporting and storage. The fuselage is an all-wood plywood-covered structure. Plans are now being sold by Popular Flying Association.

MACDONALD S-20

STANDARD DATA: Gross wt. 720. Empty wt. 456. Fuel capacity 10. Wingspan 25'. Length 18'6". Engine 53-hp Volkswagen. PERFORMANCE: Top mph 110. Cruise mph 90. Stall mph 38. Climb rate 850. Takeoff run 300. Landing roll 300. Range 250.

The S-20 utilizes all-metal construction but keeps it simple by the extensive use of pop rivets. It features open-cockpit seating for one, low wings, and conventional landing gear. The fuselage is of steel-tube truss construction with a lightweight alloy skin. The constant-chord wings are also covered with the same lightweight alloy skin.

MAVERICK JET "LEADER"

STANDARD DATA: Gross wt. 5,800. Empty wt. 2,900. Fuel capacity 300. Engine two 1,100-lb. Williams Jet FJ33-4. PERFORMANCE: Top cruise 412 kts. Stall 78 kts. Climb rate 3,000 fpm. Takeoff run 1,800. Landing roll 1,900. Range 1,508 nm.

The Maverick Jet Leader is a twin-engine, kit-built very light jet that debuted in 1999. Made of carbon-fiber/fiberglass/Nomex, the 5-seater uses two lightweight Williams Jet FADEC fanjet engines. The cockpit is pressurized for flight to FL310.

MEAD "ADVENTURE"

STANDARD DATA: Gross wt. 800. Empty wt. 460. Fuel capacity 20. Wingspan 20'. Length 13'. Engine 65- to 85-hp Continental. PERFORMANCE: Top mph 188. Cruise mph 180. Stall mph 57. Climb rate 1,600. Takeoff run 800. Landing roll 700. Range 650.

The Model 100 Adventure's simplicity of operation is equaled only by its simplicity in construction: a modern higher performance sandwich-composite structure. The materials and working techniques are descendants of Rutan's VariEze technology. The Adventure is a stunning performer with a combination of high-speed cruise, slow stall speeds, and good climb performance. The general configuration is a single-seat, low mid-wing, tractor-monoplane with fixed tricycle landing gear. The aircraft can be powered by any of the Continental Motors A- or C-series engines of 65 to 85 hp, driving a fixed-pitch wooden propeller. The wing is a two-piece assembly to minimize the space required to build and to facilitate its removal from the fuselage. The fuselage is built from flat sheets of half-inch-thick polystyrene foam and is constructed from the inside out. The canopy is a single-piece free-blown unit.

MERKEL MARK II

STANDARD DATA: Gross wt. 1,540. Empty wt. 1,200. Fuel capacity 18. Wingspan 25'6". Length 22'9". Engine 220-hp Franklin. PERFORMANCE: Top mph 206. Cruise mph 160. Stall mph 55. Climb rate 2,500. Takeoff run 300. Landing roll 300. Range 250.

This two-seat aerobatic biplane is stressed to a +6Gs and -3Gs limit, and +9Gs to -4.5Gs ultimate. It was first flown in 1973, and its designer, Edwin Merkel, planned to produce the biplane in a two-seater trainer version and a single-place competition model. The Mark

II has a lightweight alloy skin on a welded-steel tube fuselage; the wings feature a single-spar torsional structure. Other extras include an anti-servo tab, ground-adjustable trim tab, and optional cockpit canopy.

MEYERS "LITTLE TOOT"

STANDARD DATA: Gross wt. 1,230. Empty wt. 914. Fuel capacity 18. Wingspan 19'. Length 16'6". Engine 160 hp. PERFORMANCE: Top mph 200. Cruise mph 125. Stall mph 55. Climb rate 2,500. Takeoff run 300. Landing roll 300. Range 250.

George Meyers' "Little Toot" has long been one of the nation's most popular homebuilt sport biplanes. It is constructed with a sheet-metal-covered steel-tube cockpit section and monocoque sheet-metal rear fuselage. The Little Toot uses two-spar wooden wings covered with fabric. The original was fitted with a Continental 90-hp engine, but the airplane is capable of housing engines up to 200 hp. The Little Toot has an eight-degree sweepback on the upper wing. The straight lower wing carries wide, almost full-span ailerons that give the ship an unusually high roll rate. A fiberglass engine cowling is available. Plans are marketed by Tommy Meyers.

MILLER JM-2

STANDARD DATA: Gross wt. 1,100. Empty wt. 630. Fuel capacity 12. Wingspan 15'. Length 19'. Engine 100-hp Continental. PERFORMANCE: Top mph 235. Cruise mph 190. Stall mph 70. Climb rate 1,600. Takeoff run 1,500. Landing roll 2,000. Range 300.

Designed by J.W. Miller, the JM-2 took a different approach to Formula I airplane racing. Both the engine and main wings are set aft of the pilot's enclosed cockpit. A Continental drove a pusher prop; the spinner took the place of the tailcone. Two sections of the vertical propeller shroud act as the vertical stabilizer, and the elevators are placed in T-tail fashion. The wings are covered with honeycomb material reinforced by fiberglass and resin. The fuselage is constructed from four fiberglass panels.

MILLER "LIL' RASCAL"

STANDARD DATA: Gross wt. 1,100. Empty wt. 600. Fuel capacity 12. Wingspan 20'8". Length 15'3". Engine 85-hp Continental. PERFORMANCE: (estimated) Top mph 110. Cruise mph 90. Stall mph 58.

The Lil' Rascal by Merle B. Miller began flight testing in early 1978. This biplane makes use of a steel-tube fuselage and tail section covered with Stits Poly-Fibre Dacron. The wings are constructed of spruce and plywood and are covered with the same fabric. The landing gear is the non-retractable tailwheel type, and seating is for two persons in a side-by-side open cockpit. The standard 85-hp engine turns a fixed-pitch prop.

MINI COUPE

STANDARD DATA: Gross wt. 850. Empty wt. 497. Fuel capacity 13. Wingspan 22'4". Length 16'4". PERFORMANCE: Top mph 145. Cruise mph 119. Stall mph 400. Climb rate 850. Ceiling 12,500. Takeoff run 300. Landing roll 400. Range 300.

The Mini Coupe made its first flight in 1971 and was certified in 1972. By late 1975, approximately 150 sets of plans had been sold. The Mini Coupe is a lightweight all-metal single-seat sporting aircraft powered by a 65-hp modified Volkswagen 1,600cc engine. Its wings are of constant-chord design with all-metal stressed-skin construction, metal ailerons, and no flaps or trim tabs. Its landing gear is the non-retractable tricycle type with oversize tires. The single-seat can be either covered by a canopy or open. Plans are now sold by DCS, Inc.

MINI-HAWK "TIGER HAWK"

STANDARD DATA: Gross wt. 800. Empty wt. 525. Fuel capacity 12. Wingspan 18'. Length 13'3". Engine 72-hp Revmaster Volkswagen. PERFOR-MANCE: Top mph 175. Cruise mph 160. Stall mph

50. Climb rate 1,000. Ceiling 10,000. Takeoff run 400. Landing roll 400. Range 700.

The Mini-Hawk combines the economy of the Volkswagen engine with that of detachable wings for towing or storage. Standard VW engines up to 67 hp are applicable. The wings can be removed in under 10 minutes. Its all-metal construction is built around a configuration that includes low wings with trailing-edge flaps and seating for one under an enclosed canopy. The tricycle landing gear includes a steerable nosewheel with disc brakes and wheel fairings all around.

MONNETT "MONEX"

Monnett Monex

Monnett Moni

STANDARD DATA: Gross wt. 650. Empty wt. 380. Wingspan 16'8". Length 15'2". Fuel capacity 10. Engine Monnett "AeroVee" VW 2,180cc. PERFORMANCE: Top mph 230. Climb rate 2,000+. Range 400+.

The Monex made its maiden flight on September 30, 1980, to begin the testing program. It is a very high-performance single-place conventionally geared aircraft designed for amateur builders with limited building experience. Design limits are +6Gs and -4Gs. The Moni is a tricycle version.

MONNETT "SONERAI"

STANDARD DATA: Gross wt. 750. Empty wt. 440. Fuel capacity 11. Wingspan 16'8". Length 16'8". PERFORMANCE: Cruise mph 150. Stall mph 40. Climb rate 1,200. Takeoff run 500. Landing roll 500. Range 300.

The 150-mph Sonerai is a real "spark plug" in the VW/racing picture. This midwing sport plane/racer was designed to meet all PRPA Formula VEE requirements for 1,600cc VW-powered aircraft. Its wings are aluminum, built with folding panels so the aircraft can be towed tail-first on its own gear. Fuselage and tail are of standard chrome-moly tubing. Cowling is fiberglass, and fuselage and tail surfaces are fabric covered.

MONNETT "SONERAI II"

STANDARD DATA: Gross wt. 925. Empty wt. 506. Fuel capacity 10. Wingspan 18'8". Length 18'10". Engine 65- to 70-hp Volkswagen. PERFORMANCE: Top mph 165. Cruise mph 140. Stall mph 45. Climb rate 750. Takeoff run 900. Landing roll 500. Range 420.

After enjoying success with his original VW-powered Sonerai, John Monnett decided to develop the Sonerai II, a tandem-seated version. Both pilot and passenger sit under a bubble canopy that is hinged on the right side. The Sonerai II differs mainly by being slightly larger, making use of a somewhat more powerful engine, and by being stressed for aerobatics when flown by the pilot alone. The Sonerai II is now manufactured by Great Plains Aircraft, Inc.

MOONEY "MITE"

STANDARD DATA: Gross wt. 780. Empty wt. 500. Fuel capacity 11-17. Wingspan 26'10". Length 17'8". PERFORMANCE: Top mph 143. Cruise mph 130. Stall mph 43. Climb rate 1,000+. Takeoff run 300. Landing roll 275. Range 600.

The Mooney Mite, first flown in 1947, was constructed by Mooney Aircraft, a company formed by the executives of the Culver Aircraft Corp. This single-seat monoplane was originally powered by a 25-hp Crosley converted automobile engine. The Mooney Mite is built with, a combination of steel tube, wood, and fabric materials. The most common engine is the 65-hp Continental. Mooney no longer sells the plans for the Mite.

NEW GLASAIR "GLASAIR"

Glasair, Fixed Gear

Glasair II

STANDARD DATA: Gross wt. 2,400. Empty wt. 1,625. Fuel capacity 65-84. Wingspan 23.3'. Length 21.3'. Engine 300-hp Lycoming IO-540-K. PERFORMANCE: Top speed mph 327. Stall mph 73. Climb rate 2,140-2,990 fpm. Ceiling 24,000-30,000' (turbocharged). Range 1,060-1,421 nm.

This impressive design has evolved considerably since its inception with Stoddard Hamilton. The latest version, the Glasair III, has grown 30" in overall

Glasair III

fuselage length, both forward and aft of the cockpit. The increased length has given the III markedly improved longitudinal and directional stability, making it an impressive platform for serious cross-country and IFR flying.

The Glasair II, in both a retractable and fixed gear version, is a less powerful version of the airframe, but with many of the same characteristics as the top-of-the-line Glasair III.

With years of refinements to the airframe and its components, the Glasair kits are extremely well designed and thought out. The resulting performance is truly remarkable.

NEW GLASAIR "GLASTAR"

STANDARD DATA: SPORTSMAN 2+2. Gross wt. 2,300. Empty wt. 1,300. Fuel capacity 50. Wingspan 35'. Length 23'. Baggage capacity 300 lbs. Engine 200-hp Continental. PERFORMANCE: Top mph 161. Cruise mph 153. Stall mph 48. Climb rate 1,000-1,950 fpm. Ceiling 21,500'. Range 573 nm.

The GlaStar design combines aluminum sheetmetal, fiberglass composite and welded steel-tube structures into one integrated package. The two-seat design has become a hugely popular, easy to fly airplane, offering a variety of options and configurations.

Glastar

Sportsman 2+2

The most impressive of the GlaStar family may be the Sportsman 2+2, the only four-place general aviation aircraft on the market that is a tail-dragger, trike, float ready, wing folding, trailerable, high-utility aircraft, all rolled into a single airframe. The Sportsman 2+2 flies in both a 180 and 200-hp version and combines good performance with an impressive useful load.

All GlaStar models are available in a "jump start" version that greatly reduces construction time. The factory also offers a widely acclaimed assisted owner building program.

OLDFIELD "BABY LAKES"

STANDARD DATA: Gross wt. 850. Empty wt. 475. Fuel capacity 12. Wingspan 16'8". Length 13'9". Engine 80-hp Continental. PERFORMANCE: Top mph 135. Cruise mph 118. Stall mph 50. Climb rate 2,000. Takeoff run 300. Landing roll 400. Ceiling 17,000. Range 250.

Barney Oldfield's Baby Great Lakes flies much like its big brother, the Great Lakes Sport Trainer. The "Baby Lakes" was designed to get the same sort of flying ease

and performance at lower cost. It uses a steel-tube fuselage, wooden wings, and fabric cover, and it offers unusually lively aerobatic performance when powered by an 80-hp Continental engine. The "Baby Lakes" can also be fitted with a 50- to 100-hp Continental, a 108-hp Lycoming, or a 125-hp Lycoming. Its makers say it will outfly aircraft with twice the horsepower, and it is the least-expensive high-performance biplane available to the homebuilder.

OSPREY

STANDARD DATA: Gross wt. 900. Empty wt. 600. Fuel capacity 16. Wingspan 24'9". Length 17'9". PERFORMANCE: Top mph 120. Cruise mph 105. Stall mph 55. Climb rate 2,000. Takeoff run 200. Range 350.

The Osprey is a tiny single-place flying boat. It is built from fir and pine; the vertical fin is an integral part of the structure. The hull is skinned with mahogany plywood and fiberglass. The steel-tube pylon mount for the engine is bolted to the wing center section. A simple wing-folding mechanism holds the wings in position with the same steel pin that locks them in the extended position. Power is provided by a 90-hp Continental.

OSPREY II

STANDARD DATA: Gross wt. 1,570. Empty wt. 960. Fuel capacity 38. Wingspan 26'. Length 21'. Engine 150-hp Lycoming. PERFORMANCE: Top mph 145. Cruise mph 130. Stall mph 60. Climb rate 1,100. Takeoff run (land) 300. Takeoff run (water) 520. Landing roll 600. Range 550.

The Osprey II is a considerably improved enclosed cockpit version of the original Osprey. It boasts one of the most streamlined designs in the homebuilt amphibian class. George Pereira achieves the necessary aquadynamics of the hull in a rather unique way. After the fuselage is complete, urethane foam is attached to the bottom and then sculptured into shape before several layers of fiberglass are added. The wings are an all-wood structure with a single box-spar. The hull or fuselage is also an all-wood structure of marine plywood. The engine is mounted in a pusher fashion atop a steel-tube pylon. The landing gear is a retractable tricycle type.

PAYNE "KNIGHT TWISTER IMPERIAL"

STANDARD DATA: Gross wt. 900-1,100. Empty wt. 694. Fuel capacity 35. Wingspan 17'. Length 16'1". Engine 140-hp Lycoming. PERFORMANCE: Top mph 170. Cruise mph 120. Stall mph 50. Climb rate 1,000. Takeoff run 475. Landing roll 800. Range 680.

The Knight Twister Imperial is actually a Knight Twister upgraded to race in the Sport Biplane class. Piloted by Don Fairbanks, it won the Silver Biplane Race at Reno in 1971. The differences in the Imperial version were a redesigned wing section and an increase in wingspan, tailplane span, and fuel capacity. The fuel is carried in two tanks, a 21-gallon upper and a 15-gallon bottom. The wings are fabric-covered wood structures, and the fuselage is a fabric-covered steel-tube truss structure with wood stringers. Plans are now sold by Steen Aero Lab.

PAZMANY PL-1

STANDARD DATA: Gross wt. 1,326. Empty wt. 800. Fuel capacity 25. Wingspan 28'. Length 18'11". Engine 95-hp Continental. PERFORMANCE: Top mph 120. Cruise mph 115. Stall mph 51. Climb rate 1,000. Ceiling 18,000. Takeoff run 550. Landing roll 175. Range 600.

The prototype PL-1 was stressed to 9Gs for aerobatics and featured a low-wing tricycle-gear configuration with a sliding canopy. In 1968, the Chinese Nationalist Air Force in Taiwan presented a PL-1 which they built

for Generalissimo Chiang Kai-Shek. Nearly 400 sets of plans were sold for the PL-1 before sales were discontinued. The fuselage of the plane is all-metal with only flat or single-curvature skins. The wings are built around a single all-metal spar with a leading edge torsion box. In the cabin, seating is side-by-side with dual controls, and there is room for 40 pounds of baggage.

PAZMANY PL-2

STANDARD DATA: Gross wt. 1,416. Empty wt. 875. Fuel capacity 25. Wingspan 28'. Length 19'4". Engine 100-hp Lycoming. PERFORMANCE: Top mph 138. Cruise mph 119. Stall mph 52. Climb rate 1,280. Takeoff run 700. Landing roll 700. Range 492.

Along with the PL-1, the PL-2 is the only design for amateur builders that is also used for military trainers. The PL-2 is simply an advanced version of the PL-1. The external shape and flight characteristics are almost identical, but the construction has been simplified. The PL-2 offers a wider cockpit, better canopy and fuselage lines, simplified dihedral, and the possibility of using engines from 90 to 150 hp. Despite its aerodynamically clean lines, there are no compound curves anywhere in the skin. This is partly the result of the use of a fiberglass cowl to streamline the nose. Pilots who have flown the PL-2 say it is an airplane flown with the fingers and not the fist. And, like the PL-1, it is stressed for aerobatics.

PAZMANY PL-4A

STANDARD DATA: Gross wt. 850. Empty wt. 578. Fuel capacity 12. Wingspan 26'8". Length 16'6". PERFORMANCE: Top mph 120. Cruise mph 98. Stall mph 48. Climb rate 650. Takeoff run 485. Landing roll 435. Range 375.

When designer Ladislao Pazmany was encouraged to come up with an easy-to-build, simple, safe, and inexpensive metal plane that could carry a Volkswagen 1,500cc engine, he came up with the PL-4A. Not the least part of its attractiveness is economy of operation and roadability; folding wings make it a cinch to trail home and park in the family garage. Pazmany supplied the fiberglass pieces, Plexiglas windscreen and canopy, landing gear, welded engine mount, and control stick.

PIETENPOL "AIR CAMPER"

STANDARD DATA: Gross wt. 1,150. Empty wt. 622. Fuel capacity 15. Wingspan 29'. Length 18'5". PERFORMANCE: Top mph 100. Cruise mph 80. Stall mph 40. Climb rate 500. Takeoff run 400. Landing roll 600. Range 320.

The do-it-yourself craze was just getting started as a Depression-born phenomenon when the Air Camper replaced the earlier primary glider as aviation's favorite backyard building project. In 1930, Modern Mechanics magazine featured the Ford Model A engine as the perfect powerplant for the little homebuilt (and named this version the Sky Scout). The two-seat open-cockpit monoplane is said to land like a Luscombe and handle like a J-3 Cub. Modern Air Campers are powered by Corvair, Lycoming, or Continental engines. Plans are now sold by Pietenpol BHP and Sons.

PITTS S-1S "SPECIAL"

STANDARD DATA: Gross wt. 1,950. Empty wt. 710. Fuel capacity 19. Wingspan 17'4". Length 14'3". PERFORMANCE: Top mph 156. Cruise mph 140. Stall mph 57. Climb rate 2,600. Takeoff run 450. Landing roll 1,000. Range 350.

Originally designed and designated "Lil' Stinker" by aircraft-design legend Curtis Pitts, the Pitts Special is one of the world's most outstanding aerobatic aircraft. It was no mere coincidence that the U.S. Acrobatic Team members, which outflew all competition in the 1972 world acrobatic meet and established themselves as virtually unbeatable champions, flew only Pitts biplanes. While there are a number of fine aerobatic ships around the sky, there's got to be a reason why so many of the top performers fly the Pitts. The plans called for installation of a 180-hp engine, but it is not uncommon to find aircraft powered by a 200-hp engine.

POLLIWAGEN

STANDARD DATA: Gross wt. 1,250. Empty wt. 600. Fuel capacity 19. Wingspan 26'. Length 16'. Engine 78-hp Revmaster VW. PERFORMANCE: (designer figures) Top mph 200+. Cruise mph 180. Stall mph

38. Climb rate 700. Ceiling 28,000. Range 1,000. Takeoff run 450. Landing roll 550.

Designed by Argentine-born Joseph Alvarez, the Polliwagen derives its name from its appearance and its engine type. It is powered by a Revmaster R-2 100 turbocharged Volkswagen conversion. The Revmaster powers a two-position constant-speed Maloof metal propeller of 59 inches diameter. The Polliwagen's exceptionally clean lines give it an excellent speed-to-power ratio as well as fine aerodynamic handling characteristics. The wings are Wortmann FX-67-K-150 wing section with full-span trailing-edge flaps and ailerons. The wings and fuselage make use of foam/epoxy composite construction. Kits included prefabricated parts: molded windshield and canopy, landing gear, disc brakes, complete panels, composite-structure wingtip fuel tanks, outward-breaking cabin structure, T-tail, and the like.

POWELL "ACEY DEUCY"

STANDARD DATA: Gross wt. 1,275. Empty wt. 750. Fuel capacity 14. Wingspan 32'6". Length 20'9". PERFORMANCE: Top mph 104. Cruise mph 87. Stall mph 27. Climb rate 650-700. Takeoff run 250. Landing roll 250. Range 250.

This parasol-type tandem-seat monoplane was designed by John Powell, who was formerly a commander in the U.S. Navy. It is powered by a Continental A65 four-banger and features a combination of wood, fabric, and tubular-steel construction.

PROWLER AVIATION "PROWLER/JAGUAR"

STANDARD DATA: Seats 2. Gross wt. 2,500. Empty wt. 1,560. Fuel capacity 72. Engine 350-hp Rodeck V-8. PERFORMANCE: Top mph 300. Cruise mph 250. Initial climb rate 2,500. Ceiling n/a. Range 1,200. Takeoff distance (50') 1,100. Landing distance (50') 1,200.

Back in 1973, George Morse, the founder of Prowler Aviation, saw the need for an alternative aircraft powerplant that was economical, lightweight, powerful, efficient, and wouldn't break the bank at overhaul time. Morse settled on the Rodeck automotive racing engine. This customized, all-aluminum, and liquid-cooled V-8 develops 350 hp and burns 13 gallons of 100-octane avgas per hour. Prowler Aviation became a reality in 1985, and after three years of development, the Prowler I prototype took to the skies. The World War II fighter-esque homebuilt aircraft began to receive its share of notice and the first kit was sold in 1988. The beautiful lines of the Prowler/Jaguar are very reminiscent of the Spitfire from World War II, and the combination air-frame/powerplant gives the airplane fighter-like flight characteristics. The aircraft cruises at 250 mph and is fully aerobatic.

PULSAIR AIRCRAFT CORPORATION "PULSAR XP"/"SUPER PULSAR 100"/ "SUPER CRUISER"/"PULSAR III"/ "PULSAR 150"

(*See* Tri-R Technologies)

Pulsar XP

STANDARD DATA: PULSAR XP Seats 2. Gross wt. 1,235. Empty wt. 700. Fuel capacity 28-38. Engine 120-hp Rotax 912/914T. PERFORMANCE: Top cruise mph 206. Initial climb rate 1,750 fpm. Range 1,400 sm. Stall mph 47. Takeoff distance 500. Landing distance 800.

The Pulsar Aircraft Corporation obtained the rights to Tri-R Technologies' Pulsar kit aircraft designs, including the Pulsar XP, the Super Pulsar 100, the 4-place Super Cruiser and two-seat Pulsar 150. Kits are composite and have been refined for simplified construction.

QUESTAIR "SPIRIT"

STANDARD DATA: Seats 2-3. Gross wt. 1,700. Empty wt. 1,025. Fuel capacity 40. Engine 210-hp Continental 10-360. PERFORMANCE: Top mph 287. Cruise mph 228. Initial climb rate 2,000. Range 1,180.

The Spirit is actually the second of two extremely fast aircraft from Questair. The Spirit is a toned-down fixed-gear version of the record-setting Venture design. The Spirit's unusually stubby design is very reminiscent of an egg with wings. Nonetheless, the Spirit and the Venture are very popular with kit builders primarily for their exceptional performance and relatively forgiving flight characteristics. The airframe structure is all-aluminum with all of the compound curve components provided in the kit to ease the building process. Approximate building time is 2,000 hours.

QUESTAIR "VENTURE"

STANDARD DATA: Seats 2. Gross wt. 2,000. Empty wt. 1,240. Fuel capacity 56. Engine 280-hp Continental 10-550. PERFORMANCE: Top mph 345. Cruise mph 276. Initial climb rate 2,600. Ceiling 25,000. Range 1,150. Takeoff distance (50') 1,000. Landing distance (50') 1,600.

When the Venture was introduced, few could believe the performance figures that were being claimed by this stubby little plane. But seeing is believing, and as the records fell, more and more people started taking Questair's Venture as an aircraft to be reckoned with. The basic formula is really quite simple and is one that has held fast since the airplane was invented: largest engine + smallest practical airframe = speed. Of course, the trick is to simultaneously keep it safely flyable and easy to build. This speedy little two-seater is of all-aluminum, construction with a retractable tricycle landing gear. There's ample room in the cockpit for two full-sized adults and about 50 pounds of baggage.

"QUICKIE"

STANDARD DATA: Gross wt. 480. Empty wt. 240. Fuel capacity 8. Wingspan 16'8". Length 17'4". Engine 18-hp Onan two-cylinder. PERFORMANCE: Top mph 126. Cruise mph 121. Stall mph 49. Climb rate 425. Ceiling 12,300. Takeoff run 660. Landing roll 835. Range 550.

The "Quickie" is an unusual design that can cruise at 121 mph and actually fly for 100 miles on a single gallon of avgas. The design work was accomplished by Burt Rutan of VariEze and VariViggen fame. The project was masterminded by Tom Jewett and Gene Sheehan. Basic to the Quickie's economy is the 18-hp Onan horizontally opposed flat four-stroke engine commonly used to power lawn mowers and RV generators. The wide canard of the Quickie carries the main landing wheels at each end, and a tiny tailwheel at the rear end is covered with a small rudder. Complete kits include engine, prefabricated cowling, canopy, all the machined parts, all the welded parts, and some of the tools in an effort to save construction time for the inexperienced builder. Construction is from composite materials. The cockpit is suitable for one pilot up to 210 pounds.

"QUICKIE Q2"

STANDARD DATA: Gross wt. 960. Empty wt. 537. Wingspan 16'8". Engine 63-64 Revmaster Volkswagen. PERFORMANCE: Top mph 180. Climb rate 1,000. Range 750. Takeoff run 500.

The Q2 is a newer two-place side-by-side version of the composite-construction Quickie canard-platform aircraft. It is designed for high performance on low horsepower with high efficiency. The proven Revmaster 2100-D was detuned to just under 65 hp by removing the blower and running the engine RPM back down to 3,200. Typical cruise for the Q2 is 155 mph at a 12,000-foot density altitude burning 3.6 gph for 45 mpg. According to its designers, the Q2's equivalent flatplate area is 1.37, cleaner than the Glasair or the original VW-powered VariEze prototype. Like the Quickie, the Q2 is built from basic foam and epoxy/fiberglass composite construction and is similar in configuration.

RAND KR-1

STANDARD DATA: Gross wt. 600. Empty wt. 310. Fuel capacity 7.5. Wingspan 17'2". Length 12'6". PERFORMANCE: Top mph 140. Cruise mph 130. Stall mph 42. Climb rate 700 fpm. Takeoff run 300. Landing roll 800. Range 500.

The Taylor Monoplane with a wingspan of almost 22 feet prompted Rand's original concept. Rand ended up with a wing that had a wider chord but spanned only 17 feet, and the airplane weighed 150 pounds less than the Monoplane. Powered by a Volkswagen engine, it can squeeze 32 miles out of a gallon of automotive gas. The structure of the KR-1 combines both conventional and unconventional materials. The ship is basically a wooden box with polystyrene foam to round out the aerodynamic shape; it is covered with 4-ounce Dynel fabric and epoxy resins. The wings are modeled after the airfoil of the British Spitfire. Retractable gear adds to its performance.

RAND KR-2

STANDARD DATA: Gross wt. 900. Empty wt. 480. Fuel capacity 12-60. Wingspan 20'8". Length 14'6". Engine 2,100cc VW. PERFORMANCE: Top mph 200. Cruise mph 180. Stall mph 45. Climb rate 1,200. Takeoff run 350. Landing run 500. Range 2,000.

The KR-2 is a two-place version of the KR-1 and is generally similar in construction. The low wings are removable, the main gear is retractable, and the tailwheel is steerable. With a stock 1,600cc engine, cruise speed is 140 mph. With a 2,100cc turbocharged VW conversion, cruise is 180 mph at 3,200 RPM. To achieve simplicity of construction, the airplane is designed so that no machining or welding is required in building the airframe. The cost and construction time is minimized by using a combination of wood, polyurethane foam, Dynel fabric, and epoxy resin. The result is a structurally strong, clean, and hard surface to make the airplane exceptionally fast for the power used.

REDFERN FOKKER DRI

STANDARD DATA: Gross wt. 1,485. Empty wt. 1,100. Fuel capacity 30. Wingspan 23'5". Length 19'. Engine 160- to 145-hp Warner radial. PERFORMANCE: Top mph 115. Cruise mph 105. Stall mph 50. Climb rate 2,500. Takeoff run 150. Landing roll 300. Range 350.

This replica of the Red Baron's famed fighter is not one of the easier-to-build homebuilts. The cost of materials, a good deal of skill in using hand tools and a torch, several years of spare time, and a lot of scrounging for props, wheels, and the like are necessary to end up with a show-stopper like the Fokker. The fuselage is built from steel tube and plywood, then fabric covered. The all-wood wings are fabric covered. The 145-hp Warner Radial is usually the recommended engine.

REDFERN NIEUPORT 21

STANDARD DATA: Gross wt. 1,391. Empty wt. 1,006. Fuel capacity 30. Wingspan 27'5". Length 19'. Engine 145- to 165-hp Warner. PERFORMANCE: Top mph 120. Cruise mph 110. Stall mph 45. Climb rate 1,500. Takeoff run 100. Landing roll 300. Range 350.

This replica of the famous World War I Nieuport 21 is powered by a seven-cylinder Warner radial engine in the 145 to 165-hp range. A single open cockpit is situated close under the trailing edge of the upper wing.

RENEGADE

STANDARD DATA: Gross wt. 652. Empty wt. 400. Fuel capacity 7.5. Wingspan 16'. Length 14'. PERFORMANCE: (40 hp) Top mph 130. Cruise mph 120. Stall mph 49. Climb rate 1,000. Takeoff run 560. Landing roll 400. Range 375.

This Formula-V sport racer features a straight-line wing design. Its designer, Charles Lasher, chose steel-tube construction for the fuselage and tail because of its ability to withstand the shock of a crash better than other materials. The wings are a wooden-frame structure with fabric covering. The ship is made to handle any Volkswagen engine from 35 to 65 hp.

RICHARD COMMUTER

STANDARD DATA: Gross wt. 1,500. Empty wt. 805. Fuel capacity 50. Wingspan 25'. Length 19'9". PERFORMANCE: Top mph 150. Cruise mph 140. Stall mph 40. Climb rate 900. Takeoff run 1,200. Landing roll 1,500. Range 900.

The Commuter is a high-wing cabin monoplane that features all-metal construction with no complicated compound-curve skin panels. The two-place taildragger carries 125- to 150-hp Lycoming powerplants. Occupants sit side-by-side.

RLU-1 "BREEZY"

STANDARD DATA: Gross wt. 1,200. Empty wt. 700. Fuel capacity 18. Wingspan 33'. Length 22'6" PERFORMANCE: Top mph 105. Cruise mph 75. Stall mph 25. Climb rate 500. Takeoff run 450. Landing roll 450. Range 250.

Minimum structure and maximum open-air fun are the formula for the Breezy. It is a three-place airplane with two seated abreast on the second seat, but it can easily be adapted as a single-seater or tandem two-seater. Apart from the welding, nothing much about the construction of the Breezy would trouble the average craftsman. The original design utilizes a Piper Super Cruiser wing. The ship is pushed by a 90-hp Continental.

ROTORWAY INTERNATIONAL "SCORPION"/"EXEC"

Exec 162F

STANDARD DATA: SCORPION Gross wt. 1,250. Empty wt. 800. Fuel capacity 10. Rotor diameter 25'. Length 27'. Engine 133-hp RotorWay. PERFORMANCE: Top mph 95. Cruise mph 80-90. Climb rate 800. Range 120. Ceiling 10,000. Hover I.G.E. 6,500.

STANDARD DATA: EXEC 162F Gross wt. 1500. Empty wt. 975. Fuel capacity 17. Rotor diameter 25'. Engine 162 cu. in. RotorWay RI 162F. PERFORMANCE: Top mph 115. Cruise mph 95. Stall mph. Climb rate 800. Range 180. Ceiling 10,000. Hover I.G.E. 7,000.

RotorWay is one of the great aviation stories, beginning in the mid-sixties and continuing today to offer one of the most time-tested kit built helicopters. The open-cabin single-seat Scorpion I came out in 1967, and in 1970, a two-cycle powerplant rated at 125 hp became available. In 1975, RotorWay developed its own four-cylinder engine to better meet the helicopter's requirements for a two-person load and an empty-vehicle weight of less than 700 pounds. The Scorpion rotor system incorporates an elliptical hub plate designed to withstand stresses many times those encountered during operation. Its enclosed cabin is constructed of light-weight fiberglass.

In 1980, a whole new look evolved with the birth of the Exec, the grandfather of the current model, the Exec 162F. Helicopters from RotorWay International's customers have won top EAA Awards almost every year since 1990. The company is now employee owned.

RUTAN "DEFIANT"

STANDARD DATA: Gross wt. 2,900. Empty wt. 1,610. Fuel capacity 90. Wingspan 29'7". Engines two 160-hp Lycomings. PERFORMANCE: Top mph 214. Cruise mph 210. Stall mph 75. Climb rate 1,600. Range 1,128. (No plans available.)

The Rutan Defiant is a four-seat twin-engine proof-of-concept offshoot of the other Rutan canard designs. The Defiant was intended for eventual mass production. It made use of the VariEze rear-mounted swept cantilever wings with winglet surfaces, canard foreplane, and a retractable nose wheel with a fixed main landing gear. The two engines were mounted in tractor and pusher positions feeding off a 45-gallon tank for each. The Defiant was intended to be a simple aircraft with no flaps, fixed-pitch propellers, and few complex systems. Its designers claimed that the Defiant had no minimum controllable airspeed.

RUTAN "LONG-EZ"

STANDARD DATA: Gross wt. 1,325. Empty wt. 700. Fuel capacity 52. Wingspan 26'3". Length 100". Engine 108- to 115-hp Lycoming. PERFORMANCE:

Top mph 220. Cruise mph 185. Stall mph 66. Climb rate 1,150. Ceiling 26,900. Range 1,298. Takeoff run 775. Landing roll 780.

Rutan's Long-EZ is a larger and heavier version of the VariEze built around the 115-hp Lycoming engine. It has over four feet more wingspan and nearly half again the wing area of the VariEze. It takes off in 100 feet less distance and lands in only slightly more than half the distance of the original VariEze. While identical in length-100 inches-the long version is two inches wider. During one record flight, Dick Rutan logged 52.2 hours on a two-week round-trip to Florida from Mojave, averaging a 183-mph airspeed.

RUTAN "VARIEZE"

STANDARD DATA: Gross wt. 1,050. Empty wt. 570. Fuel capacity 26. Wingspan 22'2". Length 15'. Engine 100-hp Continental. PERFORMANCE: Top mph 195. Cruise mph 190. Stall mph 65. Climb rate 1,600. Takeoff run 900. Landing roll 900. Range 700.

This sleek, fast, and lightweight homebuilt is capable of achieving a top speed of 175 mph with a 1,600cc VW conversion or 210 mph with Continental's 100-hp engine. The unusual aircraft combines the use of a NASA GA (W)-l airfoil with Whitcomb winglets and was actually the first aircraft to fly with the latter. The wing is a non-laminar flow airfoil optimized for good lift and stall qualities. The ship's low induced drag lets the pilot negotiate steep, 90-degree banks with strong spiral stability.

RUTAN "VARIVIGGEN"

STANDARD DATA: Gross wt. 1,700. Empty wt. 950. Fuel capacity 25. Wingspan 19'. Length 19'. Engine 150-hp Lycoming. PERFORMANCE: Top mph 160. Cruise mph 152. Stall mph. 53. Climb rate 800. Takeoff run 800. Landing roll 500. Range 450.

One of the most unusual homebuilts ever designed also has an unusual name. Despite the unique appearance of the VariViggen, its basic design was actually the first shape that ever managed powered flight. The tail-

first pusher configuration was also employed by the Wright brothers. This two-seat tandem pusher is named after the Swedish Saab 37 Viggen, a faster-than-Mach 2 delta-wing fighter with a canard surface. The airframe is all wood and fabric with the exception of a tubular-steel engine mount.

SAPPHIRE C.P. 80

STANDARD DATA: Gross wt. 770. Empty wt. 525. Fuel capacity 10. Wingspan 23'8". Length 20'10". Engine 90 hp. PERFORMANCE: Top mph 190. Cruise mph 150. Stall mph 67. Climb rate 2,300. Ceiling 19,000+. Takeoff run 650. Landing roll 650. Range 300.

The Sapphire is a single-seat racing airplane of all-wood construction designed by Claude Piel, who is famous for his Emeraude Diamant and Beryl designs. The airplane is stressed for the load factors of +12Gs and -9Gs at the maximum takeoff weight of 770 pounds. The Sapphire can accommodate any engine from 50 to 100 hp. Its wing is fully cantilevered and tapered for minimum drag and has a tip-to-tip laminated box spar to avoid heavy root fittings and wing alignment problems. The fuselage consists of three bulkheads and is entirely plywood covered. The cockpit offers plenty of room for any pilot.

SAWYER "SKYJACKER II"

STANDARD DATA: Gross wt. 2,250. Empty wt. 1,650. Fuel capacity 50. Wingspan 18'. Length 18'. Engine 200-hp Lycoming. PERFORMANCE: Top mph 130. Cruise mph 105. Stall mph 45. Climb rate 400. Takeoff run 1,200. Landing roll 1,000. Range 525.

Sawyer's objective for constructing this vehicle was to prove the stability, controllability, and capability of such a radical low-aspect-ratio aircraft. The size for this type of aircraft is unlimited due to the nature of its lifting-body design. The Skyjacker is cheap to build because there are no compound curves, highly stressed areas, or complex control systems. The design will not stall or spin and has no rudders. The Skyjacker is not yet marketed as a sporting aircraft, but is a two-seat research vehicle of all-metal construction.

"SCRAPPY"

STANDARD DATA: Gross wt. 1,428. Empty wt. 981. Fuel capacity 28. Wingspan 20'8". Length 16'8". PERFORMANCE: Top mph 188. Cruise mph 151. Stall mph 55. Climb rate 3,700. Takeoff run 950. Landing roll 1,250. Range 500.

The UAC-200 Scrappy is a single-place sport biplane constructed of steel tubing, wood, and fabric. A 200-hp Lycoming engine provides the power.

S.E.5A REPLICA

STANDARD DATA: Gross wt. 1,100. Empty wt. 900. Fuel capacity 24. Wingspan 22'. Length 18'. PERFORMANCE: Top mph 95. Cruise mph 85. Stall mph 50. Climb rate 600. Takeoff run 200. Range 250.

This little single-seat biplane is a 4/5-scale model of the famous British S.E.5A fighter of World War I. Designed by William Wienberg of Kansas City, Missouri, it is constructed of wood and fabric. The wing structure consists of conventional wooden spars and ribs with center-section bracing struts and fabric covering. The fuselage is an all-wooden box structure covered with plywood. The tail assembly is a wire-braced steel-tube structure also covered with Ceconite fabric. Accommodations include a single-seat cockpit and a small baggage compartment behind the headrest.

SEQUOIA F. 8L "FALCO"

STANDARD DATA: Gross wt. 1,808. Empty wt. 1,212. Fuel capacity 31. Wingspan 26'3". Length 21'4". Engine 160-hp Lycoming. PERFORMANCE: Top mph 212. Cruise mph 190. Stall mph 62. Climb rate 1,140. Ceiling 19,000. Takeoff run (50') 1,150. Landing roll (50') 1,150. Range 870.

The Falco is a two-place aircraft (with an optional third seat for a child) that offers an unbeatable combination of high-speed cross-country travel with complete acrobatic capability. Designed by an Italian, Stelio Frati, a Falco equipped with an optional Christen inverted fuel and oil system is capable of unlimited inverted flight and the full range of aerobatic maneuvers. Landing gear are fully retractable, activated by a simple mechanical system. Designer Frati has been responsible for such airplanes as the Waco Meteor/SF 260 and the F20 Pegaso. Between 1956 and 1968, 101 Falcos were built as production aircraft. Earmarked for homebuilt construction in the United States through Sequoia Aircraft Corp., the Falco is made of wood, except for the firewall forward, the landing gear, and the sliding canopy. Fuselage and wing skins are Dacron. Power is supplied by either a 150- or 160-hp Lycoming behind a fixed-pitch or constant-speed prop. Gear and flaps are operated electrically.

SHEFFIELD "SKEETER X-1"

STANDARD DATA: Gross wt. 730. Empty wt. 500. Fuel capacity 5.5. Wingspan 22'. Length 13'6". PERFORMANCE: Top mph 85. Cruise mph 75. Stall mph 42. Climb rate 600. Takeoff run 600. Landing 600. Range 160.

The Skeeter is a lightweight sporting plane featuring a single seat and a single strut-braced wing mounted in parasol fashion. The wing is constructed from wooden spars and fabric covering with the exception

of the leading edge, which is covered with metal. The fuselage is constructed from a steel-tube frame that is paneled with either wood or metal in the cockpit area only. The airframe is not covered aft of the cockpit. Power is supplied by Volkswagen engines rated from 50 to 72 hp.

SINDLINGER "HAWKER HURRICANE"

STANDARD DATA: Gross wt. 1,375. Empty wt. 984. Fuel capacity 32. Wingspan 25'. Length 19'8". Engine 180-hp Lycoming. PERFORMANCE: Top mph 200. Cruise mph 170. Stall mph 62. Climb rate 1,850. Ceiling 21,000. Takeoff run 490. Landing roll 550. Range 575.

Sindlinger's 5/8-scale version of the British Hawker Hurricane first flew in 1972. The wings and fuselage are constructed of wood with a fabric covering. The powerplant turns a metal constant-speed prop. A 14-gallon fuel tank is located just aft of the firewall; optional 10-gallon tanks can be built into the wing root. The landing gear is a steerable tailwheel type with the main gear retracting into the wings. The pilot sits under a sliding canopy.

"SIZZLER"

STANDARD DATA: Gross wt. 1,350. Empty wt. 950. Fuel capacity 33. Wingspan 18'4". Length 20'7". PERFORMANCE: Top mph 180. Cruise mph 160. Stall mph 70. Climb rate 900. Takeoff run 1,200. Landing roll 700. Range 600.

The two-place Sizzler features a T-tail arrangement and gets a fair amount of lift from its fuselage. The low-wing monoplane is built entirely of metal and is flush-riveted throughout. Compound curves are no problem on the Sizzler, which uses flat panels. It stands on tricycle landing gear and carries a 125-hp Continental engine.

SKYSTAR "KITFOX"

STANDARD DATA: Seats 2. Gross wt. 1,200-1,400. Empty wt. 495-705. Fuel capacity 21-25. Engine 50- to 80-hp Rotax 503, 582, or 912. PERFORMANCE: Top mph 95-135. Cruise mph 85-125. Initial climb rate 880-1,200. Ceiling n/a. Range 170-640. Takeoff distance (50) 200. Landing distance (50') 200-240.

The SkyStar Kitfox series became one of the most popular kitplane lines of the 1980s and 1990s. The popularity is largely due to the fact that the Kitfox Classic IV or Speedster can be bought for comparatively reasonable prices in the kitbuilding marketplace. This enables the builder/pilot to construct and own an hon-

est sportplane that can double as a light-utility aircraft on a budget. Kitfoxes have been optioned with floats and skis and can operate well in tight confines with good short-field capabilities.

Newest versions of the SkyStar, Series 7, makes room for a Continental 0-200, IO-235 and the fuel-injected IO-240 engines. The model can also convert from tricycle gear to taildragger configuration. Wings also fold for easy storage and transport.

SKYSTAR "VIXEN"

STANDARD DATA: Seats 2. Gross wt. 1,400. Empty wt. 725. Fuel capacity 26. Engine 80-hp Rotax 912. PERFORMANCE: Top mph 123. Cruise mph 112. Initial climb rate 1,200. Ceiling n/a. Range 618. Takeoff distance (50) 230. Landing distance (50) 220.

Now sold as the SkyStar Vixen, this is a two-place fixed-trigear sportplane designed to give the sport flier a newer and more up-to-date look as well as good performance with STOL capabilities. Construction is conventional steel-tube, wood, and fabric covering.

A 32-foot wing is available as an option. Two adults and more than 150 pounds of baggage can be accommodated.

SMITH "MINIPLANE"

STANDARD DATA: Gross wt. 1,000. Empty wt. 616. Fuel capacity 17. Wingspan 17'. Length 15'3". Engine 65- to 85-hp, Continental or 100- to 125-hp Lycoming. PERFORMANCE: Top mph 130. Cruise mph 122. Stall mph 56. Climb rate 1,600. Ceiling 13,000. Takeoff run 375. Landing roll 500. Range 275.

The primary appeals of the Smith Miniplane are its small-size construction simplicity and open-cockpit romance, which is a combination that not all homebuilt biplanes can offer. The fuselage framework is a conventional truss structure of welded steel tubing, faired to shape with wooden stringers. As on most similar designs, the vertical stabilizer is welded up as part of the rear fuselage structure. The wings are made from spruce spars and ribs. Several engines can provide the power: 65- to 85-hp Continentals or 100- to 125-hp Lycomings.

SMYTH "SIDEWINDER"

STANDARD DATA: Gross wt. 1,450. Empty wt. 867. Fuel capacity 17. Wingspan 24'10". Length 19'4". Engine 125-hp Lycoming. PERFORMANCE: Top mph 185. Cruise mph 160. Stall mph 55. Climb rate 900. Ceiling 15,000. Takeoff run 800. Landing roll 1,500. Range 425.

In order to simplify construction of the Sidewinder, several standard components are borrowed from other established aircraft. The bubble canopy is from a Thorp T-18. The landing gear is taken from a Wittman. This fully enclosed two-seater has all-metal wings with aluminum skin and an all-metal steel-tube fuselage also covered with aluminum skin. Though the prototype was fitted with a 125-hp powerplant, engines from 65 to 125 hp can be used.

SONEX

STANDARD DATA: Gross wt. 1,000. Empty wt. 620. Fuel capacity 16. Wingspan 22'10". Length 20'10". Engine 8-hp 2180 VW. PERFORMANCE: Top mph 150. Cruise mph 110. Stall mph 40. Climb rate 800-1,000 fpm. Range 475.

The Sonex is a relatively inexpensive two-seater of all metal construction. It uses a variety of engines from 80 to 120 hp, including the 2180cc Volkswagon, 2200 Jabiru, and 3300 Jabiru. Plans include mods for a tailwheel or a nose wheel, and kits can be ordered in an "easy build" configuration that includes pre-formed wing ribs, fuse formers, and control surface ribs.

SORRELL "HIPERBIPE"

STANDARD DATA: Gross wt. 1,911. Empty wt. 1,236. Fuel capacity 39. Wingspan 22'10". Length 20'10". Engine 180-hp Lycoming. PERFORMANCE: Top mph 170. Cruise mph 160. Stall mph 49. Climb rate 1,500. Ceiling 20,000. Takeoff run 400. Landing roll 595. Range 502.

Even the most advanced aerobatic maneuvers are possible in the Hiperbipe, such as vertical eight-point rolls or inside/outside vertical eights, and the like. But the Hiperbipe doesn't sacrifice the comforts usually missing with open-cockpit aerobatic models, such as complete carpeting, full electrical system, lights, and radio. Welded steel tubes are used for the fuselage, tail group, engine and landing gear mounts, interplane struts, and flight control systems. Wing construction is all-wood with a stressed skin. Landing gear is the

Wittman type. The engine cowling and wheel fairings are fiberglass. The entire airframe is covered with fabric, including the plywood-covered wings.

SPACE SHIP ONE

STANDARD DATA: Gross wt. 6,800. Empty wt. 2,500. Engine, hybrid rocket motor, 18,000 lbs. of thrust. Initial rate of climb, 198,000 fpm. Max speed Mach 3.3. Landing distance 3,000'.

Burt Rutan's Scaled Composites built the composite three-seater with a hybrid rocket propulsion system provided by SpaceDev of Poway, California. Hybrid propulsion uses nitrous oxide—also dubbed laughing gas—and HTPB (tire rubber). On October 24, 2004, civilian astronaut Mike Melville piloted SpaceShipOne into history, flying the first private manned spacecraft to exceed an altitude of 328,000. A few days later, fellow astronaut Brian Binnie repeated the flight into suborbital space claiming the ten million dollar Ansari X-Prize.

SPENCER "AIR CAR"

STANDARD DATA: Gross wt. 3,200. Empty wt. 2,190. Fuel capacity 94. Wingspan 37'4". Length 26'5". Engine 285-hp Continental. PERFORMANCE: Top mph 147. Cruise mph 135. Stall mph 43. Climb rate 1,000. Takeoff time 16 sec. Range 700.

The Air Car is a four-place retractable with a strong family resemblance to the old Republic Seabee. The resemblance is no accident because the Air Car was designed by the same man, P.H. Spencer. The Seabee was designed in metal, but Spencer has gone back to wood covered with fiberglass for the basic Air Car hull structure. Extensive use is made of molded fiberglass for the fuselage, cabin section, engine cowl, wing root fairings, tips, floats, and miscellaneous parts. The heart of the Air Car design is a single steel-tube weldment combining the engine mount, wing-spar carry-throughs, and lift strut attach points. This steel skeleton attaches to the hull and carries all major flight loads. The all-wooden wings have a mahogany three-ply skin. The original powerplant was a 260-hp Lycoming; a 210- or 285-hp Continental may also be mounted on the airframe.

SPEZIO "TUHOLER"

STANDARD DATA: Gross wt. 1,400. Empty wt. 810. Fuel capacity 23. Wingspan 24'9". Length 18'3". PERFORMANCE: Top mph 160. Cruise mph 128. Stall mph 45. Climb rate 2,000. Takeoff run 160. Landing roll 300. Range 400.

After a day of flying, you can take the folding Spezio Tuholer home behind your car. Offering the thrill of open cockpit flying, this two-seat monoplane is powered by a 125-hp Lycoming. (The name Tuholer means "two-holer," for two cockpits). The ship should not be built by anyone who is afraid to weld. The fuselage and tail structure call for the use of steel tubing. Its large center section, supporting the folding-wing mechanism, is fashioned from a trio of one-inch .049 tubing with end plates, fittings, and large bolts that allow the wings to fold for storage.

"SPORTAIRE"

STANDARD DATA: Gross wt. 1,600. Empty wt. 984. Fuel capacity 22. Wingspan 26'4". Length 20'6". PERFORMANCE: Top mph 160. Cruise mph 150. Stall mph 55. Climb rate 1,000. Takeoff run 750. Landing roll 500. Range 400.

This two-place low-wing monoplane stands on tricycle gear and is propelled by a Lycoming 125-hp engine. Building materials include tubular steel, wood, and fabric.

"SPRITE"

STANDARD DATA: Gross wt. 1,400. Empty wt. 850. Fuel capacity 12. Wingspan 24'. Length 20'. Engine 130-hp Continental. PERFORMANCE: Top mph 138. Cruise mph 128. Stall mph 55. Climb rate 800. Takeoff roll 750. Landing roll 800.

The Sprite was designed to the United Kingdom's semi-aerobatic certification category with a positive load factor of 4.5 Gs and allowing legal spins and maneuvers past 60 degrees of banking. To go fully aerobatic would be self-defeating, adding extra load not needed for training, touring, or sport flying. Metal was selected instead of wood because it offered a better potential for mass-production kits. Sprite builders start off making the wings based upon a strong main spar of thick webbing, capped on the top and bottom with standard-size extrusion and backing plates. Wing ribs come from a single jig. The fuselage sides are bowed to prevent drumming of flat panels. Many parts of Sprites can be borrowed from other types of commercial aircraft: gear legs, brakes, wheels, fuel tanks, and the like. The standard powerplant is the Rolls-Royce 130-hp Continental driving a fixed-pitch two-blade prop.

"STARDUST II"

STANDARD DATA: Gross wt. 790. Empty wt. 520. Fuel capacity 15. Wingspan 16'. Length 18'. PERFORMANCE: Top mph 258. Cruise mph 178. Stall mph 58. Takeoff run 900. Landing roll 1,800. Range 500.

The Stardust is a single-seat homebuilt Formula 1 racer designed by John Scoville. It accommodates engines rated from 65 to 100 hp. The fuselage is built from molybdenum steel tube with lightweight alloy and fabric covering. Its wings feature a composite structure of steel and wood, with a wood-and-fabric covering.

"STARDUST JS-2"

STANDARD DATA: Gross wt. 790. Empty wt. 520. Fuel capacity 15. Wingspan 16'. Length 18'. PERFORMANCE: Top mph 250. Cruise mph 178. Stall mph 58. Takeoff run 1,500. Landing roll 1,800. Range 500.

The Stardust is a single-place Formula I sport racer constructed from conventional wood, fabric, and tubular steel. It is propelled by the regulation 85- or 100-hp Continental.

STEEN "SKYBOLT"

STANDARD DATA: Gross wt. 1,680. Empty wt. 1,080. Fuel capacity 340. Wingspan 24'. Length 19'. Engine 180-hp Lycoming. PERFORMANCE: Top mph 145. Cruise mph 130. Stall mph 50. Climb rate 2,500. Ceiling 18,000. Takeoff run 400. Range 450.

The Skybolt is a two-seat acrobatic biplane designed by Lamar Steen. It first flew in 1970 and received the EAA award for "Best School Project." The Skybolt is stressed to +12Gs and -10Gs. The fabric-covered wings are built around two spruce spars. The fuselage is a fabric-covered welded steel tube structure. The aircraft can be fitted with engines ranging in size from 125 to 260 hp.

STEPHENS "AKRO"

STANDARD DATA: Gross wt. 1,100. Empty wt. 830. Fuel capacity 21. Wingspan 24'4". Length 19'. Engine 180-hp Lycoming. PERFORMANCE: Top mph 192. Cruise mph 175. Stall mph 54. Climb rate 2,100. Ceiling 22,000. Takeoff run 400. Landing roll 900. Range 375.

The Akro was designed to meet the requirements of unlimited aerobatic competition. It is stressed to +12Gs and -11Gs. The Akro's wing is a one-piece all-wood structure with two spars, and its fuselage is a fabric-covered steel-tube frame. Seating is for one under a sliding bubble canopy. The Model B fuel and oil systems are designed for inverted flight. The Akro is one of the most popular aerobatic ships in the monoplane class. All control surfaces are fully static balanced. Plans for the Akro are no longer available.

STEWART "FOO FIGHTER"

STANDARD DATA: Gross wt. 1,100. Empty wt. 720. Fuel capacity 19. Wingspan 20'8". Length 18'9".

PERFORMANCE: Top mph 145. Cruise mph 115. Stall mph 45. Climb rate 1,200. Takeoff run 450. Landing roll 550. Range 345.

It's not difficult to mistake the Foo Fighter for a Pfalz, a Spad, or an Albatross, but the plane that actually inspired this design was the Alcock A-1, a World War I warbird that resembles the Sopwith Pup. One distinguishing feature of the Foo Fighter is its lower wing that crosses below the fuselage, aft of the gear, and attaches on the centerline. The airframe is built from steel tubing and covered with fabric. A Ford Falcon auto engine was installed first, but a 130-hp Franklin Sport Four also can be used.

STEWART "HEADWIND"

STANDARD DATA: Gross wt. 750. Empty wt. 450. Fuel capacity 6. Wingspan 28'3". Length 17'. PERFORMANCE: Top mph 110. Cruise mph 80. Stall mph 35. Climb rate 600. Takeoff run 300. Landing roll 400. Range 195.

The virtue of the Headwind is not high speed or altitude performance but utter simplicity of design and construction and ease of handling. In the words of the designer, Don Stewart, "It's not quick and skittish like a lot of homebuilts, but in fact flies a lot like a J-3 or Champ with a very docile stall." The Headwind is described as an extremely simple airplane of steel tubing construction for the fuselage and tail. The wings are two wooden spars with either sawed plywood or formed aluminum ribs. All the fittings are flat, and only two of them require any preassembly. The engine bolts directly to the front of the fuselage, saving a separate engine mount. A 36- to 65-hp VW engine is used.

STEWART "S-51D"

STANDARD DATA: Seats 2. Gross wt. 2,960. Empty wt. 2,200. Fuel capacity 70. Engine 400-c.i.d. 300-600-hp liquid-cooled automotive V-8. PERFORMANCE: Top mph 265. Cruise mph 235. Initial climb rate 2,380. Ceiling 23,600. Range 660. Takeoff distance (50') 1,370. Landing distance (50') 2,080.

The S-51D is the culmination of over 25 years in development. Jim Stewart's dream was to develop the most accurate reduced-scale P-51D to hit the homebuilt circuit. Many times the project was put on hold due to many obstacles that producing an aircraft of this type can throw at you. Stewart, an aeronautical engineer by trade, made great strides to make the S-51 as close to the real thing in looks, structure, and performance as possible. Stewart chose aluminum for the entire airframe. Stewart also quickly realized that a kit was required to market the aircraft because very few homebuilders had the tools or the talent to form all of the compound-curved panels. All of the panels in the kit are hydro-formed to obtain the distortion-free curves that make this kit a successful endeavor. Kits are available in a variety of packages to save time and/or money for the builder. The basic kit requires about 3,500 hours of work, and a fast-build kit reduces the required time by about 1,200 hours.

STITS FLUT-R-BUG

STANDARD DATA: Gross wt. 1,032. Empty wt. 575. Wingspan 26'. Length 18'. PERFORMANCE: Top mph 100. Climb rate 1,100 fpm. Stall speed mph 38. Takeoff roll 125'.

Wonderfully simple mid-wing two-seat fabric kit. Pre-welded kits sold for $1,100 and plans cost $35 a set. Plans were sold from August 1956 through April 1968. The Flut-R-Bug is credited with starting amateur-built aviation in Australia and is still quite popular in the United States.

STITS "PLAYBOY"

STANDARD DATA: Gross wt. 700. Empty wt. 430. Wingspan 26'. Engine Continental A75. PERFOR-

MANCE: Top mph 95. Cruise mph 130. Climb rate 1,050. Range 400.

One of the more popular designs by Ray Stits, the Playboy was designed for backyard builders to construct from easy-to-follow plans or simple-to-do work kits. The Playboy can handle any one of several four-cylinder engines with 85 to 160 hp. Probably the most common is the 85-hp Continental. Construction is mixed: wooden wings and a steel-tube fuselage. All surfaces are fabric covered. The Playboy is easily recognizable because of its sliding canopy and strut-braced low-wing design.

STODDARD-HAMILTON

(*See* New Glasair)

STODDARD-HAMILTON "TURBINE 250/III"

STANDARD DATA: Seats 2. Gross wt. 2,500. Empty wt. 1,650. Fuel capacity 86. Engine 450-shp Allison turbine. PERFORMANCE: Top mph 330. Cruise mph 280. Initial climb rate 4,200. Ceiling 25,000. Range 1,200. Takeoff distance (50') 600. Landing distance (50') 1,000.

In 1994, Stoddard-Hamilton decided to take the airframe of its Glasair III and strap on 450 slip of an Allison 250 turbine. The combination gave the ship exceptional performance with regards to straight-and-level flight speeds and rate of climb. Speeds in excess of 340 mph have been recorded and the climb to ceiling can be accomplished in under eight minutes.

STOLP "ACRODUSTER 1"

STANDARD DATA: Gross wt. 1,190. Empty wt. 750. Fuel capacity 25. Wingspan 19'. Length 15'9". PERFORMANCE: Top mph 180. Cruise mph 165. Stall mph 70. Climb rate 3,000. Takeoff run 300. Landing roll 800. Range 360.

First introduced in 1973, the SA-700 Acroduster I is a single-seat fully aerobatic biplane suitable for engines in the 125- to 200-hp range. Its fuselage is an all-metal structure constructed from lightweight alloy,

and the wings are conventional two-spar structures with spruce spars, plywood ribs, and fabric covering. A unique feature of the Acroduster I is that when the stick is pulled back, all four ailerons are raised slightly to help maintain aileron control when the airplane is stalled in a normal attitude. The opposite happens when the stick is pushed forward to aid control when the airplane is in an inverted stall.

STOLP "ACRODUSTER TOO"

STANDARD DATA: Gross wt. 1,800. Empty wt. 1,100. Fuel capacity 37. Wingspan 21'5". Length 18'6". Engine 200-hp Lycoming. PERFORMANCE: Top mph 210. Cruise mph 150. Stall mph 55. Climb rate 2,400. Takeoff run (50') 1,200. Landing run (50) 1,800. Range 450.

The Acroduster Too, originally called the Schrack-Stolp Super Starduster Too, is a scaled-down 9/10-scale version of the highly successful Starduster Too, which was designed by Lou Stolp. The Acroduster's designer, Morgan Schrack, beefed up the little ship to withstand up to 9 Gs. He made it possible to remove the front windscreen, cover the front cockpit with a hatch cover, and add a sliding bubble canopy over the rear hole. The fuselage was also metalized back to the rear of the cockpit. Lycoming engines from 180 to 200 hp provide the power.

STOLP SA-100 "STARDUSTER"

STANDARD DATA: Gross wt. 1,080. Empty wt. 700. Fuel capacity 24. Wingspan 19'. Length 16'6". PERFORMANCE: Top mph 147. Cruise mph 132. Stall mph 50. Climb rate 2,000. Takeoff run 200. Landing roll 300. Range 450.

This single-place member of the Stolp family is the younger brother to the two-place Starduster Too. The Starduster is intended for the 125-hp Lycoming engine, but it has been built with engines ranging from 85 to 170 hp with a constant-speed prop. Good visibility, very tame stall and landing characteristics, and something called "charisma" are all traits of the Starduster.

STOLP "STARDUSTER TOO"

STANDARD DATA: Gross wt. 1,704. Empty wt. 1,200. Fuel capacity 42. Wingspan 24'. Length 19'8". Engine 180-hp Lycoming. PERFORMANCE: Top mph 180. Cruise mph 130. Stall mph 56. Climb rate 1,800. Takeoff run (50') 450. Landing run (50) 900. Range 500.

The Starduster Too is the two-place member of the Stolp family. Though not specifically designed or offered as an aerobatic airplane, this graceful flyer can handle the stunts when in competent hands. Stolp recommends the 180-hp Lycoming with a constant-speed prop as the optimum powerplant. The fuselage is welded-steel tubing with wooden fairings and a fabric covering. The wings use two spruce spars, ribs of quarter inch plywood, and a fabric cover. All four wings carry ailerons.

STOLP SA500 "STARLET"

STANDARD DATA: Gross wt. 1,000. Empty wt. 630. Fuel capacity 20. Wingspan 25'. Length 17'. Engine 100-hp Continental. PERFORMANCE: Top mph 150. Cruise mph 130. Stall mph 55. Climb rate 1,500. Takeoff run (50) 500. Landing run (50') 900. Range 500.

The little sister of the Stolp family is the Starlet, a single-place parasol-winged monoplane. This ship was

originally designed to handle a Volkswagen engine (1,500cc) but was subsequently modified to house small aircraft engines such as a 108-hp Lycoming.

STOLP "V-STAR"

STANDARD DATA: Gross wt. 1,000. Empty wt. 650. Fuel capacity 20. Wingspan 23'. Length 17'2". Engine 100-hp Continental. PERFORMANCE: Top mph 150. Cruise mph 90. Stall mph 35. Climb rate 1,800. Takeoff run (50') 300. Landing run (50') 500. Range 359.

In response to demand for a low-cost and low-horse-power aerobatic homebuilt, Stolp designed the V-Star, which is basically a biplane version of the parasol-winged Starlet. Stressed to 9Gs, the V-Star was originally powered by a 65-hp Continental turning a fixed-pitch propeller; however, the airplane is certified to be outfitted with engines from 60 to 125 hp.

STUKA JU 87-82

STANDARD DATA: Gross wt. 2,260. Engine 220-hp Lycoming. PERFORMANCE: Top mph 132. Cruise mph 124. Stall mph 64. Climb rate 1,000. Takeoff roll 750.

The original Junkers became synonymous with the abbreviation "Stuka," from the word Sturzkampfflugzeug, which is a term applicable to all dive bombers. Like the original, the Langhurst replica Stuka is a two-place aircraft with a single control from the front seat. The rear seat faces the tail, which makes flying in that location quite an experience. The replica is completely of metal construction with an inner steel-tube frame and an aluminum skin. Because the original rib type was unknown, Langhurst utilized the NACA 2415, which looks very much like the original. The Yio Stuka is actually a full-sized airplane by most homebuilt standards. It has a full electrical system, full hydraulic system, and complete fuel management system. The landing gear and tailwheel unit are standard from a PT-19.

SUNSHINE CLIPPER

STANDARD DATA: Gross wt. 1,500. Empty wt. 1,100. Hull length 14'. Engine 85-hp Continental. Fuel 18. PERFORMANCE: Top cruise mph 58.

This creation was born in November 1987, growing out of the hull of a 1948 Orlando Clipper. And yes, it really flies.

SUPER EMERAUDE C.P. 328

STANDARD DATA: Gross wt. 1,540. Empty wt. 850. Fuel capacity 232. Wingspan 26'6". Length 21'. Engine 100-hp Continental. PERFORMANCE: Top mph 172. Cruise mph 120. Stall mph 52. Climb rate 700. Ceiling 14,000. Takeoff run 600. Landing roll 850. Range 620.

Besides designing the Super Emeraude, Claude Piel has also created the Diamant and Beryl. The Emeraude is a low-wing monoplane that achieves excellent per-

formance from a 100-hp Continental with a fixed-pitch prop. It features an enclosed cockpit for two in side-by-side fashion. Construction materials consist of wood and fabric. The most significant improvement in the Super Emeraude is a reinforced structure to allow the use of engines up to 150 hp and to be fully aerobatic when flown solo. It is distinguished by a larger and swept-back vertical tail, which improves directional stability. The airplane has all modern features including slotted flaps, slotted ailerons, single-leg landing gear, steerable tailwheel, and sliding canopy. The Super Emeraude is approved for categories N, U, and A.

"SYLKIE"

STANDARD DATA: Gross wt. 1,650. Empty wt. 1,020. Fuel capacity 28. Wingspan 24'11". Length 20'7". Engine 150-hp Lycoming. PERFORMANCE: Top mph 234. Cruise mph 182. Stall mph 48. Climb rate 1,800. Ceiling 19,000. Range 960. Takeoff run 1,850. Landing run 1,200.

Designer Wayne Barton used a beefed-up Emeraude fuselage and a Minicab wing of 24'11" span and 110 sq.ft. area (fully cantilevered with 15-percent rib chord at the root) for the Sylkie. In building the fuselage, the standard right side and left side frame construction method was used. In building the Minicab wing, the spar center sections were strengthened to provide a 9+G ultimate load factor for a 1,200-pound frame. Landing gear retracts, and dual controls are called for with brakes on the left side only. Three fuel tanks are located inside the fuselage with a 28-gallon fiberglass main tank aft of the passenger seats below the baggage compartment. The stabilator was designed with a 12-degree rotation capability around its single spar, which is built in two units. The engine is enclosed in a conventional fiberglass cowling with the nose gear door hinged to the aft part of the cowl. Dacron covering and Randolph's fabric dope finish everything off.

TAYLOR MODEL A "COOT" (AMPHIBIAN)

STANDARD DATA: Gross wt. 1,950. Empty wt. 1,200. Fuel capacity 24-50. Wingspan 36-37'. Length

20'-22'. PERFORMANCE: Cruise mph 100-130. Stall mph 45-50. Climb rate 600-1,000. Takeoff run (land) 200. Takeoff time (water) 10-12 sec.

The Model A differs from the Model B in that it can be fitted with a fiberglass hull; the Model B has a twin-boom tail. The amphibian is basically of wood construction and can be built by anyone with basic manual training experience using ordinary tools. Power can be supplied by any engine from 150 to 220 hp with a controllable propeller. The Coot is a comfortable two-place ship with side-by-side seating and dual controls. The folding wings make road towing and home storage possible. (Molt Taylor emphasizes with all his aircraft designs that performance and specification figures are greatly dependent on such variables as engine size, fuel capacity, etc.)

TAYLOR "MINI-IMP"

STANDARD DATA: (60 hp) Gross wt. 800. Empty wt. 500. Fuel capacity 12+. Wingspan 25'. Length 16'. PERFORMANCE: Cruise mph 150+. Stall mph 48. Climb rate 1,200. Takeoff run 800. Range 500.

The Mini-Imp is a single-seat version of the two-seat Imp. It features an unusual configuration with a pusher prop aft of an inverted V-type tail assembly and cantilevered high wing that folds back for towing and storage. The wing is the latest NASA design with a spoiler and flaps. The retractable gear is the tricycle spring-legged type. A controllable propeller is available. Power is provided by any engine from 60 to 115 hp. The most common engines are the 60-hp Franklin, 60-hp Limbach VW, 70-hp Turbo Revmaster VW, 80-hp Turbo Kawasaki (1,000cc), 100-hp Continental, and 115-hp Avco Lycoming Modification. The aluminum and fiberglass Mini-Imp requires a minimum of tools to construct, and all hard-to-build parts are available.

It offers unequaled safe flyability and stability, positive spiral stability, limited aerobatic capability (stressed to 9 Gs), and good fuel economy (3.5 gph).

TAYLOR "MONOPLANE"

STANDARD DATA: Gross wt. 620. Empty wt. 410. Fuel capacity 7.5. Wingspan 21'. Length 15'. PERFORMANCE: Top mph 105. Cruise mph 90. Stall mph 38. Climb rate 950. Takeoff run 200. Landing roll 150. Range 230.

The Monoplane single-place taildragger was designed to house low-powered engines in the 30- to 65-hp range, like the English JAP or the German VW (both air-cooled). Some say that the Taylor Monoplane bears a striking resemblance to the World War II Spitfire. It features all-wood construction and is covered with a 1/16-inch plywood stressed skin. The ribs are conventional built-up-truss type in a basic box design. The aircraft was designed especially for the amateur builder who does not have a comprehensive workshop at his or her disposal. The airfoil section was carefully chosen for its high-lift and gentle stall characteristics. Since the first prototype flew in June 1960, no modifications of any kind have been incorporated.

TAYLOR "TITCH"

STANDARD DATA: Gross wt. 745. Empty wt. 500. Fuel capacity 10. Wingspan 18'9". Length 16'2". PERFORMANCE: Top mph 170. Cruise mph 155. Stall mph 53. Climb rate 1,100. Takeoff run 140. Landing roll 120. Range 380.

The Taylor Titch has a reputation as a pleasant-to-fly aerobatic plane. Stall occurs at a very high angle of attack, and the airplane recovers straight forward with no wing drop and a height loss of only 50 feet. This single-place monoplane features all-wood wings with plywood and fabric covering. Its fuselage is also an all-wood structure that includes a double-curvature plywood covering and aluminum cockpit side panels. When the low-powered Taylor Monoplane became

known in the United States, requests were made for permission to fit larger engines than the design permitted. This led to the introduction of the Titch (English for anything small). The Titch is stressed for any engine from 40 to 90 hp, the only provision being a reposition of the engine bulkhead for engines with 65 hp or more. This allows for the use of VW, Lycoming, or Continental powerplants.

TEAM TANGO

STANDARD DATA: Seats 2. Gross wt. 2,000. Empty wt. 1,150. Fuel capacity 57-85. PERFORMANCE: Top cruise mph 220. Cruise mph 210. Stall mph 60. Climb rate 1,800-3,000 fpm. Ceiling 24,000'. Range 1,200 sm.

From Williston, Florida, this gull-wing homebuilt is a good performer with a snappy 120°-per-second roll rate. With miserly fuel management, the company claims the Tango has a west-to-east coast-to-coast range.

TECNAM "P92 ECHO"/"P96 GOLF"

P96 Golf 100

STANDARD DATA: P96 GOLF Seats 2. Gross wt. 990. Empty wt. 581. Fuel capacity 16. PERFORMANCE: Top cruise mph 130. Cruise mph 100. Stall mph 40. Climb rate 1,000 fpm. Takeoff run 650. Landing roll 700.

Luigi Pascale, who designed the Partenavia twin, designed and built both the P92 and P96. The Echo first flew in 1992, and its low-wing variant, the P96 Echo made its maiden flight in 1996. Designed to fly with a Jabiru 2200 engine, the two-seaters are immensely popular in Europe, Australia and New Zealand.

"TEENIE TWO"

STANDARD DATA: Gross wt. 585. Empty wt. 310. Fuel capacity 9. Wingspan 18'. Length 12'11". Engine 1,600cc Volkswagen. PERFORMANCE: Top mph 140. Cruise mph 110. Stall mph 50. Climb rate 1,000. Takeoff run 600. Landing roll 800. Range 400.

One of the smallest homebuilts around, the Teenie Two is an all-metal single-place monoplane that measures slightly under 13 feet in length. Built entirely from aluminum except for the landing gear and controls, it needs no bending brake nor is any metal or riveting experience required. Most of the sheet-metal bending to build the Teenie Two is done by hand, and the design is close to optimum simplicity. Power is provided by a Volkswagen conversion.

"TERMITE"

STANDARD DATA: Gross wt. 658. Empty wt. 432. Wingspan 23'6". Length 15'1". PERFORMANCE: Top mph 95. Cruise mph 83. Landing mph 38. Climb rate 450. Ceiling 6,000. Takeoff run 350. Landing roll 400. Range 150.

The original Termite, designed by Wilbur Smith, was powered by a 36-hp, Aeronca engine, but since then other engines such as the 38-hp Continental and the 65-hp Lycoming have been used. The Termite is a single-seat sporting monoplane with a braced parasol-type wing. Its wing structure is built with two wooden spars, an aluminum leading edge, and fabric covering aft of the front spar. The fuselage is an all-wood structure with plywood covering from the rear of the cockpit forward and fabric covering aft. The tail section is also fabric covered. The Termite's landing gear is a Piper Cub type.

THORP T-18

STANDARD DATA: Gross wt. 1,500. Empty wt. 900. Fuel capacity 29. Wingspan 20'10". Length 18'. PERFORMANCE: Top mph 200. Cruise mph 175. Stall mph 65. Climb rate 2,000. Takeoff run 300. Landing roll 900. Range 500.

The Thorp T-18 is without a doubt one of the most popular homebuilts in existence. This two-place speedster can wring 160 mph out of a 125-hp engine. Its monoplane design with slightly upturned wings is clean and streamlined in appearance. A tight cowling, sleek canopy, very clean exterior metalwork, and light weight help explain its speed. John Thorp, designer of the T-18, removed the plans from the market.

TINKER TOY

STANDARD DATA: Gross wt. 1,650. Empty wt. 1,188. Fuel capacity 20. Wingspan 28'3". Engine 140-hp Corsa. PERFORMANCE: Cruise mph 100. Stall mph 60. Range 300.

Powered by a 140-hp Corsa engine, the Tinker Toy was built around a Fly Baby wing and makes use of a pusher prop to keep the cabin quiet. The powerplant burns 4.5 gph at 3,500 RPM and turns a Warrike ground-adjustable prop. The Fly Baby wing was selected for Tinker Toy because it was a high lift wing. To get away from a long drive shaft running back to behind the tail, the engine was hung underneath the wing at CG position with the prop spinning right behind the trailing edge. A bottom spar and top member were then used to carry a large vertical fin, leaving clearance for the propeller blades. It took some engineering to design the top spar that attached the tail to the center point of the spinning propeller hub. Landing-gear legs were made from heat-treated truck leaf-spring stock with the wheels encased in fiberglass pants.

TOURBILLION YC-12

STANDARD DATA: Gross wt. 952. Empty wt. 628. Fuel capacity 16. Wingspan 22'. Length 19'. PERFORMANCE: Top mph 146. Cruise mph 127. Stall mph 47. Climb rate 900 fpm. Takeoff run 855. Landing roll 900. Range 500.

The Tourbillion (Whirlwind) is a single-seat, amateur-built, and lightweight low-wing plane that comes from France. It is available in several models that differ only in their engine size. Most common is the 65-hp Continental. Airframe construction includes wood and fabric wings and a plywood-covered fuselage structure.

TRI-R TECHNOLOGIES "KIS"/"TR-1"/ "PULSAR"/"PULSAR 150"

Pulsar

Pulsar 150

STANDARD DATA: Seats 2. Gross wt. 1,200. Empty wt. 680. Fuel capacity 20. Engine 80-hp Limbach L 2000. PERFORMANCE: Top mph 150. Cruise mph 135. Initial climb rate 1,000. Ceiling 14,000. Range 600. Takeoff distance (50') 1,000. Landing distance (50') 1,100.

The KIS (keep it simple) series of aircraft became a vision of designer Rich Trickel when he was commissioned by Lance Neibauer (Lancair) to design and develop the molds and structural techniques used in the building of the Lancair series of aircraft. Trickel designed the KIS as a high-performance entry- or training-level aircraft that could reap the benefits of the composite technology that he had accomplished with the Lancair. Using epoxy preimpregnated glass cloth (prepreg), combined with high-density foam core and honeycomb Nomex, the vacuum-formed components for the KIS could become reality. The extreme light weight and high strength from this type of composite construction allows for the use of smaller engines to get superior performance for an aircraft. The KIS series is available with a number of options for configuration and powerplants. The KIS TD is a taildragger; the KIS Super and TR-1 are higher horsepower versions of the KIS with 120 hp and 125 hp respectively. All four of the kits are sold less engine, upholstery, avionics, and paint.

TRI-R TECHNOLOGIES "KIS TR-4 CRUISER"/"SUPER CRUISER"

Super Cruiser

STANDARD DATA: Seats 4. Gross wt. 2,300. Empty wt. 1,200. Fuel capacity 50. Engine 180-hp Lycoming 10-360. PERFORMANCE: Top mph 185. Cruise mph 165. Initial climb rate 1,200. Ceiling 17,000. Range 800. Takeoff distance (50') 1,200. Landing distance (50') 1,500.

Rich Trickel's addition to the Tri-R Technologies family, the TR-4 Cruiser, is a four-place fixed-gear aircraft that follows the form of the previous KIS models. The Cruiser made its debut at Oshkosh 1994 and was well received as a practical, kitbuilt, family aircraft that was inexpensive to build and operate. The Cruiser can accommodate four full-sized adults, full fuel, carry 66 pounds of baggage, and cruise at 165 mph anywhere within an 800-mile range. Any way you slice it, this is one practical aircraft. The Cruiser requires around 1,500 hours to complete.

TROYER SPORTPLANE VX

STANDARD DATA: Gross wt. 456. Empty wt. 306. Fuel capacity 5. Wingspan 23'9". Length 15'9". PERFORMANCE: Top mph 95. Cruise mph 85. Stall mph 34. Climb rate 600. Takeoff run 195. Landing roll 150. Range 200.

Few homebuilts weigh less than this VW-powered mid-wing model. The Troyer Sportplane weighs only 306 pounds empty. Oddly enough, it has a welded steel-tube fuselage and tail assembly. Its wings use spruce spars and ribs built from 1/4-inch square spruce, ply gusseted. Steel tubing also forms the flying struts for the wing, but a little balsa wood is used for fairing. Power is supplied by either the Heath B4 or a converted VW engine.

"TURBULENT"

STANDARD DATA: Gross wt. 620. Empty wt. 342. Fuel capacity 10.5. Wingspan 21'6". Length 17'. PERFORMANCE: Top mph 100. Cruise mph 85. Stall mph 29. Climb rate 500. Takeoff run 440. Landing roll 300. Range 350.

This brainchild of Roger Druine is so good that Rollason Aircraft in England and Flugzeubau in Germany started manufacturing them. The Turbulent's airframe is an all-wood structure covered with fabric. It uses a box spar with a built-up rear spar, conventional ribs, and a plywood-skinned leading edge forming a rigid D section. A happy feature of the Turbulent wing is leading edge slots and Friese-type ailerons that bring the stall down to around 29 mph with full aileron control all the way. Volkswagen engines from 30 to 40 hp are commonly used.

TURNER T-40

STANDARD DATA: Gross wt. 1,050. Empty wt. 750. Fuel capacity 18. Wingspan 22'3". Length 19'5". PERFORMANCE: Top mph 170. Cruise mph 145. Stall mph 52. Climb rate 900. Takeoff run 850. Landing roll 750. Range 450.

The Turner airplane family got started in 1958. First aircraft in the series was the T-40, a sleek, hot little single-seater that won the 1961 "Outstanding Design" trophy at the Experimental Aircraft Association Fly-in. Of all-wood construction and featuring a sliding-hood canopy, the T-40 was first powered by a 65-hp engine and did without all the frills associated with an electrical system. In this form, it cruised at 128 mph and blitzed along at 145 mph with the throttle fire walled. Later, an 85-hp, package was added.

TURNER T-40A

STANDARD DATA: Gross wt. 1,500. Empty wt. 950. Fuel capacity 20. Wingspan 24'11". Length 19'5". PERFORMANCE: Top mph 170. Cruise mph 150.

Stall mph 56. Climb rate 1,600. Takeoff run 865. Landing roll 760. Range 520.

The T-40 was so successful that it collected 18 awards and convinced Turner that the only thing wrong with it was that nobody could ride along to enjoy the reading on the airspeed indicator; thus, he created the T-40A. It is a two-place version of the predecessor. Turner simply divided the entire fuselage of the T-40 down the middle and increased the cabin width from 24 to 40 inches. Flight tests showed that the 85-hp engine would still deliver 163 mph top speed with a fuselage nearly twice as wide as before and with considerably more airframe weight. Both Turners feature folding wings.

TURNER T-40B

STANDARD DATA: Gross wt. 1,600. Empty wt. 828. Fuel capacity 20. Wingspan 22'3". Length 19'9". PERFORMANCE: Top mph 175. Cruise mph 155. Stall mph 57. Climb rate 1,200. Takeoff run 850. Landing roll 500. Range 475.

The Turner T-40B is basically the same as the T-40A, but with tricycle landing gear and other improvements. Development of the prototype began in 1966 and the first flight was made in 1969. Originally an 85-hp engine was used, but it was replaced by a 125-hp Lycoming in order to improve high-altitude performance. Other refinements on the basic T-40A frame included a bubble canopy, hydraulically operated double-slotted flaps, and a fixed leading-edge droop.

VAN'S AIRCRAFT, INC. "RV-3"

STANDARD DATA: Gross wt. 1,050. Empty wt. 695. Fuel capacity 24. Wingspan 19'11". Length 19'.

Engine 125-hp Lycoming. PERFORMANCE: Top mph 195. Cruise mph 185. Stall mph 48. Climb rate 1,900. Ceiling 21,000. Takeoff run 200. Landing roll 300. Range 600.

Richard Van Grunsven's all-metal single-seat monoplane won the "Best Aerodynamic Detailing" award at the 1972 EAA Fly-in. The wings are built around a single I-beam spar and a lighter rear spar. The fuselage and tail unit are built of light alloy, and the engine is covered with a fiberglass cowling. The conventional landing gear has Cleveland brakes and fiberglass wheel fairings.

VAN'S AIRCRAFT, INC. "RV-4 – RV10"

RV-4

STANDARD DATA: (RV-4) Seats 2. Gross wt. 1,500. Empty wt. 905. Fuel capacity 32. Engine 160-hp 0-320 Lycoming. PERFORMANCE: Top mph 205. Cruise mph 194. Initial climb rate 2,050. Ceiling 25,000. Range 650. Takeoff distance 300. Landing distance 300.

STANDARD DATA: (RV-6 and 6A) Seats 2. Gross wt. 1,600. Empty wt. 965. Fuel capacity 38. Engine 160-hp 0-320 Lycoming. PERFORMANCE: Top mph 202. Cruise mph 191. Initial climb rate 1,900. Ceiling 21,500. Range 775. Takeoff distance 300. Landing distance 300.

RV-6

RV9A

RV10

STANDARD DATA: RV9A Seats 2. Gross wt. 1750. Empty wt. 1075 Fuel capacity 36. Engine 160-hp Lycoming. PERFORMANCE: Top cruise mph 194. Cruise mph 186. Stall 50 mph. Initial climb rate 1,400 fpm. Ceiling 18,500'. Takeoff distance 475'. Landing distance 450'. Range 700-850 nm.

STANDARD DATA: RV10 Seats 4. Gross wt. 2700. Empty wt. 1520. Fuel capacity 60. Engine 260-hp IO-540 Lycoming. PERFORMANCE: Top cruise mph 208. Cruise mph 197. Stall 63 mph. Initial climb rate 1,450 fpm. Ceiling 20,000'. Takeoff distance 500'. Landing distance 650'. Range 825-1,000 nm.

Van's RV series of home and kit-built aircraft are among the most popular kit airplanes. The combination of performance, low cost, case of construction, and overall good looks seems to be a winning one. Construction is conventional aluminum alloy riveted together without complex panels or compound curves. All of the RV aircraft are capable of sport aerobatics and have exceptional STOL capabilities. The RV-3 is an all-metal single-seat sportplane with a conventional gear. The RV-4 is the two-place tandem version of the RV-3 with a slightly longer wingspan. The RV-6 and RV-6A are side-by-side two-seat sportplanes that are designed for excellent touring and sport flying. The RV-6A has the exact airframe as the RV-6 but incorporates a tricycle rather than a conventional gear.

Further evolution brought the side-by side RV7 and RV7A, the tandem-seat RV8/RV8A and RV9/V9A (with both conventional and tricycle gear). In 2003, Van's Aircraft introduced their first four-seat design, the RV10.

VCA-1

STANDARD DATA: Gross wt. 1,100. Empty wt. 710. Fuel capacity 24.5. Wingspan 20'. Length 18'. Engine 100-hp Continental. PERFORMANCE: Top mph 150. Cruise mph 130. Stall mph 57. Climb rate 1,100. Range 200.

The VCA-l is a tiny single-seat low-wing monoplane of all-metal construction. The wing section is NASA GA (W)-1 with no sweepback. It has a constant chord with plain ailerons and electrically operated flaps. The fuselage uses 2024-T3 aluminum alloy. The tricycle landing gear is non-retractable. A Continental 0-200 flat-four engine drives a two-blade Sensenich fixed-pitch propeller. The cockpit is enclosed and sweeps back to a combination fuselage and T-tail empennage.

"VELOCITY"

STANDARD DATA: (Fixed gear) Seats 4. Gross wt. 2,250. Empty wt. 1,250. Fuel capacity 65. Engine 200-hp Lycoming IO-360. PERFORMANCE: Top mph 215. Cruise mph 200. Initial climb rate 1,400. Ceiling 20,000. Range 1,200. Takeoff distance (50') 850. Landing distance (50') 800.

STANDARD DATA: (Retractable gear) Seats 4. Gross wt. 2,250. Empty wt. 1,250. Fuel capacity 65. Engine 200-hp Lycoming IO-360. PERFORMANCE: Top mph 230. Cruise mph 220. Initial climb rate 1,500. Ceiling 20,000. Range 1,320. Takeoff distance (50') 850. Landing distance (50') 800.

The first Velocity took to the sky in 1985 and followed with its public debut at the Sun-N-Fun Fly-in at Lakeland, Florida, in early 1986. The Velocity made quite an impression, and kits for this four-place canard-design pusher were served up like hotcakes. Construction is all-composite, and the systems are simple with no complex jigs or advanced tooling necessary.

VIKING "DRAGONFLY"

STANDARD DATA: Gross wt. 1,075. Empty wt. 590. Wingspan 22'. Engine 1,600cc Volkswagen. PERFORMANCE: Top mph 150. Climb rate 800. Range 500 (estimated). Takeoff run 450.

Winner of the "Outstanding New Design" award at Oshkosh 1980, the Dragonfly is another canard-configured composite homebuilt in the same vein as the Quickie and VariEze. With two-place side-by-side seating under a bubble canopy, the Dragonfly is powered by a stock 1,600cc VW engine. The intention of the aircraft is to provide builders with a project that is inexpensive to build and also inexpensive to operate on a readily available engine. The wing and canard are built as a single piece in a jig, and the job can be accomplished in a normal two-car garage. The cockpit width is 43 inches, like that of a Cessna 172. A molded canopy was selected to avoid the soap-bubble effect of a free-blown canopy. A typical 140-mph cruise burns gas at the rate of 45 mpg. A Great American-brand propeller has a 4-inch pitch and 52-inch diameter. The designers have claimed that there will never be an authorization to use a 1,200cc VW, any certified aircraft engine, or any turbocharged powerplant.

VOLMER VJ-22 "SPORTSMAN"

STANDARD DATA: Gross wt. 1,500. Empty wt. 1,000. Fuel capacity 20. Wingspan 36'6". Length 24'. Engine 85- to 100-hp Continental. PERFORMANCE: Top mph 95. Cruise mph 85. Stall mph 45. Climb rate 600. Ceiling 13,000. Takeoff time 20 sec. Range 320.

Volmer Jensen's two-place Sportsman amphibian has to be called one of the more successful homebuilt designs around. Building it costs about a tenth as much as buying a comparable airplane. Saltwater can't hurt its fiberglass plywood hull, so corrosion is no problem. The Sportsman uses fabric-covered Aeronca Chief or Champion wings. It is essentially a small flying boat fitted with wheels that can be exchanged for skis. Power is supplied by a 100-hp Continental mounted in pusher fashion.

WAG-AERO "CUBy"

(Now renamed the Sport Trainer)

STANDARD DATA: Gross wt. 1,400. Empty wt. 720. Fuel capacity 12-26. Wingspan 35'2". Length 22'4". Engine 65- to 125-hp Continental. PERFORMANCE: Top mph 102. Cruise mph 94. Stall mph 39. Climb rate 490. Ceiling 11,200. Takeoff run 375. Range 220-455 (with auxiliary).

The CUBy is a replica of the ever-popular Piper J-3 Cub. It was designed by Dick Wagner, president of Wag-Aero, the nation's biggest homebuilder's supply house in Lyons, Wisconsin. Wagner was well aware of the demand for a kit version of the venerable puddle jumper whose name has become a household word. Power is supplied by an 85-hp Continental. There is very little

difference between the CUBy and the original J-3, except for a crank-operated elevator trim tab instead of the jackscrew adjustment that moved the stabilizer plane.

WAG-AERO "WAG-A-BOND"

STANDARD DATA: (Classic) Gross wt. 1,250. Empty wt. 640. Fuel capacity 26. Wingspan 29'4". Length 18'9". Engine 65- to 100-hp Continental. PERFORMANCE: Top mph 105. Cruise mph 95. Stall mph 45. Climb rate 625.

The Wag-A-Bond can be built in either of two versions, the Classic (performance figures above) or the Traveler. The Classic is a replica of the Piper PA-15 Vagabond, and the Traveler is a modified and updated version of the Vagabond with port and starboard doors, overhead skylight window, extended sleeping deck, extended baggage area, and provisions for engines up to 115 hp. The wings are strut-braced, high-wing, and all-wood structures covered with fabric. The spar and ribs are spruce with mahogany plywood gussets. The ailerons are fabric-covered aluminum. The fuselage is welded steel-tube. With a 108-hp Lycoming, the Traveler has a top speed of 122 mph, a cruise speed of 115 mph, and a climb rate of 850 fpm.

WAR "CORSAIR"

STANDARD DATA: Gross wt. 900. Empty wt. 600. Fuel capacity 12-15. Wingspan 20'. Length 16'6". Engine 100-hp Continental. PERFORMANCE: Top mph 170. Cruise mph 145. Stall mph 55. Climb rate 1,200. Range 400-500. Takeoff run 800-1,000.

The half-scale Corsair is built around a plywood box core and covered with styrofoam and fiberglass, in the manner of the KR-1 and KR-2 homebuilts. The fuselage is a standard four-longeron torsion box, while the tail and wings use conventional wooden structure. The wing is made from a laminated plywood-covered hollow front spar. The rear spar is laminated as a solid single-piece unit faced with plywood. Plywood ribs are used at the root, the center-section joints, and the tip sections. For landing gear, an air-oil oleo system is used, with either an electrical or manual ratchet system for retraction. Engines in the 65- to 125-hp range can be used, so performance varies greatly.

WAR "FOCKEWULF"

STANDARD DATA: Gross wt. 900. Empty wt. 610. Fuel 12. Wingspan 20'. Length 16'7". PERFORMANCE: Top mph 165. Cruise mph 140. Stall mph 55. Climb rate 1,000. Ceiling 12,500. Takeoff run 1,000. Landing roll 1,200. Range 400.

WAR Aircraft Replicas is a company formed to market kits and plans for 1/2-scale World War II aircraft replicas. The FockeWulf 190 was singled out to be the first prototype, and development started in 1973. The first flight was made in 1974. Subsequent versions were to be the F4U Corsair, Hawker Sea Fury, and the Republic Thunderbolt. All were to use the same common wooden fuselage box and wing spar construction. To duplicate various fighter aircraft, polyurethane foam was shaped and converted with high-strength laminating fabric and epoxy resin to form a rigid yet lightweight structure.

The tailwheel is retractable and even has an emergency system to manually deploy the gear. Power is supplied by a modified 70-hp 1,600cc Volkswagen engine turning a three-blade fixed-pitch prop.

WARNER AEROCRAFT "REVOLUTION II/SPORTSTER"

STANDARD DATA: Gross wt. 1,500. Empty wt. 850. Fuel capacity 12. Wingspan 26'. Length 20.4'. PER-FORMANCE: Top cruise mph 130. Stall mph 45. Climb rate 1,175 fpm. Ceiling 12,500. Takeoff run 425. Landing roll 400.

The Revolution (also marketed as the Space Walker II) is an open cockpit, two-place tandem amenable to engines from 85 to 150 hp. The Sportster is a new variant of the design, with the addition of a removable canopy. Construction calls for chrome-moly steel tubes, spruce wing spars and Dacron fabric covering. The Sportster can handle up to a 160-hp engine and is available in kit form only.

WATSON "WINDWAGON"

STANDARD DATA: Gross wt. 485. Empty wt. 273. Fuel capacity 4. Wingspan 18'. Length 12'6". Engine 30-hp Watson 1/2 VW. PERFORMANCE: Top mph 110. Cruise mph 90. Stall mph 40. Climb rate 500. Ceiling 10,000. Range 300. Takeoff run 250. Landing roll 300.

The Windwagon measures 18 feet from wingtip to wingtip, and it features all-aluminum construction with pop rivets. The tricycle gear is non-retractable. Wings are removable for storage or transportation. The powerplant is a modified 900cc half-Volkswagen engine that drives a four-blade propeller. On just two cylinders, top speed is 110 mph, and climb rate is 450 to 500 fpm. The wing features a Clark Y wing section with constant chord. There are conventional ailerons and no flaps. The fuselage is a conventional semi-monocoque structure made from pop-riveted aluminum.

WELSH WR-3 "RABBIT"

STANDARD DATA: Gross wt. 1,050. Empty wt. 640. Fuel capacity 12. Wingspan 28'. Length 17'8". Engine 100-hp Continental. PERFORMANCE: Top mph 108. Cruise mph 98. Stall mph 48. Climb rate 500. Ceiling 10,500. Takeoff distance (50') 480. Landing roll 500. Range 290.

The Welsh Rabbit, designed by George Welsh, is a two-place trigeared homebuilt with a single high wing. Construction of the fuselage and tail group is welded-steel tube covered by Dacron. The wings have externally strut-braced metal spars and metal ribs covered by Dacron and fitted with corrugated-skin aluminum ailerons.

WENDT WH-1 "TRAVELER"

STANDARD DATA: Gross wt. 1,400. Empty wt. 900. Fuel capacity 22. Wingspan 30'. Length 19'6". Engine 65- to 85-hp Continental. PERFORMANCE: Top mph 131. Cruise mph 115. Stall mph 65. Climb rate 750. Range 580. Ceiling 13,000. Takeoff run 800. Landing roll 700.

The intention was that Wendt Traveler would be a high performance cross-country ship with a max range of more than 500 miles, a sea-level rate of climb of 700 fpm, and a ceiling of 17,000 feet. The prototype was built largely of wood to make it simple for homebuilders. Seating was tandem style to reduce form drag. At 2,450 RPM, the WH-1 Traveler cruised at better than 120 mph at 300 feet MSL, stalled at 65 IAS, clean and climbed at 500 fpm with two people onboard. The wings were detachable using NACA 643A-418 with an 18-percent thickness. Both the fuselage and wings were built of wood, the tailcone formed of 1/8-inch mahogany plywood over 7/8-inch spruce longerons. Wooden wing spars were used, and the forward 37 percent of chord covered with mahogany ply forming a D-box. The spring-steel landing gear is similar to the Wittman type, bolted to the wing carry-through structure. Wendt originally used a McCauley cruise prop of 71-inch diameter and 48-inch pitch.

WHITE "DER JAGER"

STANDARD DATA: Gross wt. 888. Empty wt. 534. Fuel capacity 24. Wingspan 20'. Length 17'. PERFORMANCE: Top mph 145. Cruise mph 133. Stall mph 54. Climb rate 2,000. Takeoff run 175. Landing roll 250. Range 532.

Though modeled after World War I fighters, the Der Jager is not a replica. Its builder, Marshall White, patterned the wing shape after that of the German Albatross. The tail assembly is patterned after that of the Fokker D-7, and the gear after that of the FockeWulf "Strosser." The frameworks of the fuselage and the tail group are of welded-steel tube that is fabric covered. The wings are wood with no flaps. The prototype was

fitted with a 115-hp Lycoming, but the airplane is so light that anything down to the Volkswagen 1,600cc engine will fly it nicely.

"WHITE LIGHTNING"

STANDARD DATA: Seats 4. Gross wt. 2,400. Empty wt. 1,400. Fuel capacity 70. Engine 210-hp Continental 10-360. PERFORMANCE: Top mph 280. Cruise mph 265. Initial climb rate 1,900. Ceiling 20,000. Range 1,600. Takeoff distance (50) 1,300. Landing distance (50) 1,300.

During the past 15-20 years, composite construction of homebuilt aircraft has taken a firm hold of the technology and rewritten the rules regarding form and function. Now it is feasible to let the imagination fly and allow the most fluid and streamlined of aerodynamic shapes to become reality. One of these products is the White Lightning. This craft falls into the sleek-and-speedy four-place-composite dream-machine group. The configuration is conventional, but frontal area and overall wetted area are greatly trimmed to the minimum thanks to composite technology. This makes for great performance and efficiency specs as well as being quite pleasing aesthetically. Seating is for four with the two rear passengers facing aft with legs pointing to the tail. This seating arrangement allows for a less-critical CG. Although the White Lightning is a tight package, there is ample room for any avionics complement a pilot should need. The Jackson Fields Mathews Company announced it has acquired the rights to the White Lightning and will re-launch the aircraft plans.

WILLIAMS-CANGIE "SUNDANCER"

STANDARD DATA: Gross wt. 1,115. Empty wt. 835. Fuel capacity 16. Wingspan 19'9". Length 16'1". Engine 135-hp Lycoming. PERFORMANCE: Top mph 235. Stall mph 65.

The Sundancer is built around the basic fuselage and tail unit of the Bushby Midget Mustang. The single-seat racing biplane was co-designed by Art Williams and Carl Cangie, built by Ralph Thenhaus, and flown by Sidney White. It set a national class record of faster than 194 mph the first time that it was flown. It won the championship at Reno in 1973, then went on to

victories in the five races in which it was entered in 1974. The fuselage of the Sundancer has a flush-riveted stressed skin. The wings are a conventional lightweight alloy structure with no flaps.

WILLIAMS "STINGER"

STANDARD DATA: Gross wt. 835. Empty wt. 385. Fuel capacity 8. Wingspan 19'. Length 15'10". Engine 100-hp Continental. PERFORMANCE: Top mph 260. Stall mph 65.

This single-seat Formula I racing monoplane was designed by Art Williams. The wings are an all-wood structure with laminated spruce spars. The fuselage is built from lightweight alloy and employs a monocoque structure. Flown by John Paul Jones, it captured second place at the 1973 Reno Air Races. In the same year it recorded the best single-lap speed of 234.7 mph. The craft was then sold to the late former astronaut Deke Slayton who continued racing Stinger for the next 20 years. Stinger, like its related ships Falcon and Sundancer, is a one-of-a-kind custom racing plane. Arthur Williams offers no plans or drawings for sale to the homebuilding public.

WITTTMAN "TAILWIND"

STANDARD DATA: (100-hp version) Gross wt. 1,300. Empty wt. 700. Fuel capacity 25. Wingspan 22'6". Length 19'3". Engine 80-, 90-, and 100-hp Continental, or 100- to 135-hp Lycoming. PERFORMANCE: (100-hp version) Top mph 165. Cruise mph 150. Stall mph 55. Climb rate 900. Ceiling 16,000+. Takeoff run 800. Landing roll 600. Range 600+.

Aviation legend Steve Wittman's idea in 1953 was to create a fast and economical cross-country airplane

that could tote two people and 60 pounds of baggage. Additionally, the airplane would fly with the greatest of ease and would have gentle stall characteristics at the low end of the speed spectrum. The first five airplanes built were loaded to gross weight and subjected to 4Gs. So successful did the Tailwind design turn out that for some years it stood alone in its class for its cruise speed as well as for its acrobatic-quality handling, though Wittman considers it to be a utility aircraft. Not until John Thorp came along with his low-wing T-18 could any two-place homebuilt match the Tailwind's performance. Improvements to the design include a modified airfoil, which is longer than the original wing by 19 inches. The modified airfoil slows landing and takeoff speeds, improves rate of climb, gives high ceilings, and boosts cruise speed at altitude. Also, revisions have been made to allow the use of a 150-hp Lycoming, a 145-hp Continental, and the Olds/Buick 215-cu. in. V-8s.

WITTMAN "WITT'S VEE"

STANDARD DATA: Gross wt. 700. Empty wt. 430. Fuel capacity 10. Wingspan 166". Length 182". PERFORMANCE: Top mph 170. Cruise mph 150. Stall mph 48. Climb rate 1,000. Takeoff run 800. Range 400.

The real bomb in the Formula VEE circuit is Steve Wittman's Witt's V. The amazing thing about this racing ship is its speed. Wittman has had it up to 170 mph (not quite supersonic, but three miles a minute). Wittman made "Bonzo" a household word back in the Goodyear Racedays.

ZENAIR MONO-Z

STANDARD DATA: Gross wt. 960. Empty wt. 630. Fuel capacity 15. Wingspan 22'. Length 19'6". Engine 100-hp Continental. PERFORMANCE: Top mph 125. Cruise mph 110. Stall mph 48. Climb rate 820. Takeoff run (50') 1,000. Landing run (50') 1,000. Range 400.

The Mono-Z is a single-place scaled-down version of the original Zenith. It offers maximum operating economy with VW power at a 3-gph cruise. Detachable wings leave an 8-footwide section for easy road towing; only 20 minutes are required to install both wings. It is stressed for 9Gs, and it becomes a powerful aerobatic performer with a 100-hp engine. Powerplant possibilities range from the VW 1,600cc to 100-hp Continental.

ZENAIR "TRI-Z"

STANDARD DATA: Gross wt. 1,850. Empty wt. 1,100. Fuel capacity 34. Wingspan 26'6". Length 21'6". Engine 150 hp. PERFORMANCE: Top mph 160. Cruise mph 143. Stall mph 53. Climb rate 1,000. Takeoff run (50') 1,400. Landing run (50') 1,400. Range 530.

The natural step up from the Zenith is this three-passenger version. Designed primarily to satisfy the need for a good cross-country performer that falls into the sportplane category, the Tri-Z can be fitted with medium power engines in the 125 to 180-hp category. With only two persons in the front seats, the rear bench can be covered with 210 pounds of baggage. The Tri-Z easily adapts to floats or taildragger options and is easy to fly. It has docile handling characteristics.

ZENAIR "ZENITH"

STANDARD DATA: Gross wt. 1,500. Empty wt. 930. Fuel capacity 24. Wingspan 23'. Length 20'6". Engine 125 hp. PERFORMANCE: Top mph 151. Cruise mph 141. Stall mph 54. Climb rate 1,100. Takeoff run (50') 1,400. Landing run (50') 1,400. Range 450.

The French-born designer Chris Heintz graduated from E.T.H. (engineering institute) in Zurich, Switzerland, worked on the Concorde at Aerospatiale, and joined Avion's Pierre Robin (famous for the Jodel series) as chief engineer before he started work on the Zenith. This homebuilt has a split personality in that with 100 hp it will cruise for four hours at 130 mph carrying two passengers and baggage. A 150-hp engine and an acrobatic option turns the Zenith into a powerful performer. The Zenith is stressed for T-engines from 85 to 160 hp, with two-place seating under a sliding canopy in a fuselage formed by four longerons with stiffened skins blind-riveted to longerons. Five bulkheads carry the top skin. The constant-chord wings have a single cantilevered spar with three sections and electronically operated flaps. One-piece all-moving horizontal and vertical control surfaces constitute the tail.

ZENITH AIRCRAFT COMPANY "STOL CH 701/801"

STANDARD DATA: STOL CH 701 Seats 2. Gross wt. 1,100. Empty wt. 580. Fuel capacity 30-60. Engine 100-hp. Rotax 912S. PERFORMANCE: Top mph 95. Cruise mph 85. Stall mph 34. Climb rate 1,200. Ceiling 15,000+. Takeoff run 50. Landing run 80. Range 350.

STANDARD DATA: STOL CH 801 Seats 4. Gross wt. 2,200. Empty wt. 1,150. Fuel capacity 24. Wingspan 23'. Length 20'6". Engine 125 hp. PERFORMANCE: Top mph 110. Cruise mph 105. Stall mph

CH 701

CH 801

39. Climb rate 720 fps. Ceiling 14,000'. Takeoff run 390. Landing run 345. Range 315-630 sm.

As their names imply, the CH 701/801 are utility aircraft kits made to come and go from tight places. The CH 701 emerged in 1986 with fixed leading-edge slats for high lift, full-span flaperons (both ailerons and flaps) and an all-flying rudder. A four-seat version, the CH 801, is also flying. Both aircraft are designed to fly on wheels, floats and skis.

ZENITH AIRCRAFT COMPANY "ZODIAC 601/640"

Zodiak 601

STANDARD DATA: ZODIAK 601XL Gross wt. 1,300. Empty wt. 800. Fuel capacity 24. Engine 116-hp Lycoming 0-235. PERFORMANCE: Top mph 138. Cruise mph 141. Stall mph 44. Climb rate 930 fpm. Takeoff run 500'. Landing run 500'. Range 575 sm.

STANDARD DATA: ZODIAK 640 Gross wt. 2,200. Empty wt. 1,147. Fuel capacity 38-46. Wingspan 23'. Length 20'6". Engine 125 hp. PERFORMANCE: Top mph 157. Cruise mph 150. Stall mph 47. Climb rate 950 fpm. Ceiling 12,800. Takeoff run 990. Landing run 1,150. Range 510 sm.

The long wing Zodiac originated in 1984 as an all-metal two-seater. The design evolved to the 601XL with an enlarged cockpit and baggage area. The CH 640 is larger, conventional four-seater, with a 2+2 seating configuration derived from the CH 2000 production aircraft. The four-seater has a 180-hp Lycoming O-360 engine, fixed tricycle landing gear, large dual gull-wing doors, a wing span of 31.5 feet and an overall length of 23 feet.

Sailplane and Motorglider Aircraft

For its feeling of pure flight, soaring is likened by enthusiasts to bird flight—quiet, without the aid of power to keep you aloft. It's just you and your piloting skill, riding the rising currents of air. When a sailplane or glider is towed or winched to altitude, it is truly a balance of the skill of energy transfer and light touch, of being at one with your surroundings and making the most of the natural environment's influence. As with other form of aircraft, the sailplane has enjoyed marked improvement and development throughout history from the wood- and linen-craft built and flown by Otto Lilienthal to the modern, sleek composite craft that seem to capture the smallest of rising air currents with little effort.

Motorgliders gained prominence in Europe where rising columns of warm air and large expansive landing strips are available less frequently. The concept was to produce a glider or sailplane with a small air-cooled engine that could be utilized for takeoffs and for regaining lost altitude. This proved particularly handy on cool days or when there was no available towplane in the vicinity. Motorgliders are not as prominent in the United States, where weather is cooperative more often, but they can be spotted from time to time. The motorglider has proven to be a very efficient form of personal transport by only requiring miserly amounts of fuel to cover great distances.

SAILPLANE/MOTORGLIDER SPECIFICATIONS

Manufacturer and model	Wingspan: ft. in.	Wing aspect ratio	Length overall: ft. in.	Empty: lbs.	Max. T/O: lbs.	Best glide ratio	At (speed): mph	Stall speed: mph	Max. speed mph
Aeromot Ximango	57'4"	NA	26.5'	1370	NA	31	67	48	140
ASW 28-15	49'2"	21.4	21.6'	569	1157	45	60	39	161
Alisport DU Light	39.3'	10.3m	21'	297	528	31	53	34	120
Ahrens AR 124	42'7.75"	13.5	20'	350	640	26	69	34.5	150
AmEagle	36'	18	16'	160	360	27	52	38	115
Apis 15	49'2"	NA	22'	327	661	40	49	29	72
Blanik LAK 17A	49'2"	24.8	23'	474	500	46	51	37	110
Briegleb BG-12	50'	17.9	21'11"	525	750	34	NA	35	136
Bryan RS-15	49'2 1/2"	21.4	22'	440	940	38	NA	46	150
Bryan HP-18	49'2 1/2"	21.1	23'6"	420	920	40	NA	40	150
Caproni Vizzola A21S	66.9'	25.7	30'6"	961	1164	43	65	43	156
Caproni Vizzola A21SJ	66.9'	25.7	30'6"	1464	1781	43	75	43	156
DG 800	49'2"	21	23.1'	736	1156	45	63	39	146
DSK BJ-1b Duster	42'7 3/4"	17.4	NA	390	620	NA	NA	NA	NA
Explorer PG-I	16'	5	13'8"	180	400	6.5	45	35	65
Flight Dynamics	34'	6.96	20'	165	500	6	NA	NA	NA
G-D DG200	49'2 1/2"	22.5	23'	570	990	44.6	68	41	168
Glasflügel Hornet C	49'2 1/2"	23	21'	461	992	38.2	66.5	37.3	155
Glasflügel 304	49'2 1/2"	22.78	21'2"	519	994	43	72	37	155
Grob Acro 103	57'4"	NA	17'2"	811	1279	35	65	44	117
Hornet 304C	49'2"	22.8	21.6'	517	990	45	72	46	112
Katana X-Treme	53'5"	NA	23.8'	1221	1694	27	NA	NA	124
Marske Monarch C	42'	9.5	11'6"	220	450	19	40	24	70
Monnett Monerai	36'	16.6	19'7"	220	450	28	60	38	120
Oldershaw 0-3	55'	24.1	23'	780	1000	37	68	50	125
Orlik 2	49'2"	19	15.2'	353	540	24	44	NA	108
PIK-20E	49'2 1/2"	22.5	21'5"	660	1036	40	73	47	174
Pilatus B4	49'5"	21 7	NA	508	773	35	53	37	149
Rand KR-1B	27'	NA	12'10"	484	800	21.12	NA	38	144
Ryson ST-100	57'8"	15.61	25'6"	1212	1650	28	NA	NA	NA
SF-H34	51'8"	17	24'6"	660	1100	35	59	40	156
SF-25	59'	17.8	24'7"	970	1430	29	53	42.5	112
SF-28	53'5"	14.5	26'1"	860	1300	27	53	40	112
SGS 1-26	40'	10	21'6 1/2"	430	700	23	NA	33	114
SGS 2-32	57'1"	18.05	26'9"	850	1430	34	59	50	140
SGS 2-33A	51'	11.85	25'9"	600	1040	22.25	NA	35	98
SGS 1-34B	49'2"	16.04	25'9"	550	800	34	52	NA	135
SGS 1-35	49'1/2"	23.29	19'2"	440	930	39	NA	32	139
Schweizer Sprite	46'2"	15.2	20'7"	475	710	31	53	36	125
Shempp-Hirth Nimbus	66'7"	28.6	23'11"	770	1278	49	56	40	168
Shempp-Hirth Janus	59'8"	20	28'2"	805	1370	39.5	68	40	137
Shempp-Hirth Janus C	65'4"	23	28'3"	783	1543	43.5	68	43	155
Shempp-Hirth Janus CM	65'4"	23	28'3"	1025	1543	42.5	68	43	155
Shempp-Hirth Ventus	49'2"	23.7	20'1"	474	949	43.5	62	41	155
Shempp-Hirth Ventus B	49'2"	23.7	21'5"	486	949	43.5	62	41	155
Sonex	22"	NA	22'	620	1100	NA	NA	40	150
Stemme S10	75'5 1/2"	27 7	29'3"	1455	1874	50	66	48	168
Volpar-Spencer Drag-N-Fly	17'	2.56	15'11"	225	425	NA	NA	NA	75
Woodstock	39'	14.5	NA	235	450	24	NA	35	NA

AEROMOT "XIMANGO"

Ximango Motorglider

The Brazilian company Grupo Aeromot makes three sleek motorgliders, the Ximango Sport, the Super Ximango and the Turbo Ximango. Designed by Rene Fournier, the aircraft feature wide-track landing gear, powerful spoilers and power on demand from the liquid cooled Rotax engine. The Super Ximango has a L/D ratio of 31:1 and a minimum sink rate of 184 fpm. Under power, the motorglider can cruise at 115 knots. The turbocharged version steps up to the 115-hp Rotax 914. With redesigned ailerons and the addition of winglets, the 140 KTAS Turbo Ximango is hard to beat.

AHRENS AR 124

Design of this single-seat sailplane began in 1974, and the first flight of the prototype was that same year. The cantilevered mid-wing has a constant chord with ailerons and upper-surface spoilers but no tabs or flaps. The fuselage is all-aluminum with a flush-riveted skin, and the swept T-tail has a one-piece elevator. One unsprung nosewheel with a disc brake and a tailwheel comprise the landing gear. Seating is for one pilot under a molded one-piece canopy.

ALEXANDER SCHLEICHER

Founded by Alexander Schleicher in 1927, the company is the world's oldest sailplane manufacturer. The company makes both pure sailplanes and motorgliders, with entries in every category, from the entry level ASW 21 to the remarkable ASW 28 and its 48:1 glide ratio. The ASW 28 series also offers a retracting engine and optional solar panels for in-flight recharging of avionics or engine battery.

ALISPORT

Alisport's sailplane division produces the Silent Club and Silent 2 series of light sailplanes. The Silent Club is available as a pure sailplane or as a self-launcher, with either fuel-injected or electric power. The Silent 2 is available with a fuel-injected engine. Both aircraft series offer exceptional handling and performance. Alisport Srl is based in Cremella (Lecco) located in northern Italy near Milan.

AmEAGLE "AMERICAN EAGLET"

The American Eaglet is a self-launching sailplane designed to eliminate the need for two planes, ground crews, and the requirement to operate out of a regular glider port. Its in-air-restartable engine reduces the need for off-field landings. The wings and inverted-V tailfeathers are built from spruce spars surrounded by urethane foam and covered with pre-cured fiberglass skins. The fuselage is comprised of two preformed fiberglass shells pop-riveted to an aluminum-tube framework and tailboom. The Eaglet's powerplant is not designed for sustained powered flight. The MC 101 engine and folding propeller are provided for takeoff, in-flight restarts, and climbs only. Fuel tank capacity is five gallons and is generally sufficient for one takeoff and climb to 2,000 feet AGL and three airborne restarts and climbs from 500 feet back up to 2,000 feet.

APIS

The Apis series includes both a 13 and 15-meter sailplane, is a combination of composite construction and old world craftsmanship. The Apis is intended for the sport flyer, but still holds several world records. They offer a forward-hinged canopy, automatic control hook-ups, in-flight adjustable rudder pedals, full-span flaperons, blended winglets, and Schempp-Hirth type airbrakes. They also make the Apis M, a 15 meter motorglider.

BLANIK

L13

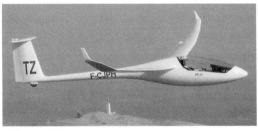

L19

The original L13 Blanik was built in 1958 and several thousands of them are flying worldwide. The two-seat, all-metal L13 evolved into the L23 Super Blanik. The new glider retains the excellent flying and maintenance characteristics of the L13, while visibility and handling are further refined. Among the many improvements are the new T-tail (to minimize damage during land-outs), the swiveling tail wheel (for easier ground handling), and the new canopy (enhancing visibility to the sides and back). The L23 has been approved for all stages of flight training from basic to advanced cross-country, aerobatic, stunt, and instrument flying. Removable wing tip extensions of one meter each may be installed. The USAF Academy uses the Blanik gliders exclusively. Blanik also makes the LAK-17A in the 15-18 meter racing category, the LAK-17AT motorglider, the LAK-19 standard class racer, the LAK-19T motorglider and the LAK-20 two-place glider.

BRIEGLEB BG-12

Gus Briegleb began designing and building sailplanes in the 1930s. In 1940, he came up with his sixth design, the BG-6, and initially sold it in kit form. As a utility-training glider, it had a lift-to-drag ratio of 16

and a minimum sink of about 3 fps. The BG-7 was an improved version using the same fuselage and tail but with a tapered wing 123 sq. ft. in area and 40 feet in span. Finally, the BG-12 was designed in 1956 with a 50-foot span and 141 sq. ft. of wing area. Empty weight was 525 pounds. Its full-cantilever wing was fitted with trailing edge flaps. It was built entirely of wood, and its lift-to-drag ratio was an excellent 34 and minimum sink rate was 2.3 fps. The BG-12-16 used the same wing but has a low-profile fuselage of reduced cross-section dimensions. Its fin and rudder sweep forward (ala Mooney), and the BG-12 elevator/horizontal stabilizer is replaced with an all-flying stabilator fitted with anti-servo tabs. The flaps are longer and the sailplane has a better lift-to-drag ratio.

BRYAN (SCHREDER) RS-15

Designer R.E. Schreder built the RS-15 to OSTIV Standard Class specifications. Licensed in the amateur-built experimental category, its assembly is relatively simple with most major components pre-made to cut building time to about 500 hours. The shoulder-type wings are all-metal with the exception of polyurethane foam ribs. Provision for a 200-pound water ballast is inside the wing's box spars. Seating is for one pilot in a prefabricated fiberglass pod from which an aluminum-tube tailboom stretches back to an all-metal V tail. The tail and wings can be folded and removed for storage or travel.

BRYAN (SCHREDER) HP-18

Intended to be an improved competition sailplane stressed to 12 Gs, the HP-18 is basically a larger version of the RS-15. Its longer fuselage has been revamped to reduce drag. Refinements to the aircraft include improved gap seals, redesigned wingtips, a removable tail-wheel, and overall better aerodynamics.

CAPRONI VIZZOLA CALIF A-21S/A-21SJ

A quick glance at the gross weight or wingspan of the Calif motorglider or sailplane should tell the enthusiast that the pair are not ordinary aircraft. With 66.9 feet of wingspan, the A-21SJ is the only production turbojet-powered sailplane in the world. It offers side-by-side seating and all-metal construction. The engine retracts into the fuselage just aft of the cockpit. Cruise speed is 124 mph and climb is 945 fpm. On 36 gallons of fuel, range is about 217 miles, with a ceiling of 43,300 feet. Takeoff run requires only 1,181 feet. Up to 90 percent of the parts between the sailplane and the motorglider are common to both, so the glider can be transformed easily into a jet glider, even in retrofit. The landing gear for both aircraft features dual main gear that retract into the undercarriage. Two small wheels are built into the wingtips. The wing is all-metal with a single spar, stressed skin, and fiberglass tips; the wing is fitted with top-hinged, differentially operated ailerons plus lower-hinged, aerodynamically balanced flaps/spoilers. The fuselage has a monocoque forward section of fiberglass with a load-carrying lightweight alloy structure. The tailboom is an all-metal stressed-skin unit ending in an all-metal single-spar tailplane.

DG FLUGZEUGBAU

DG300

DG600

DG800

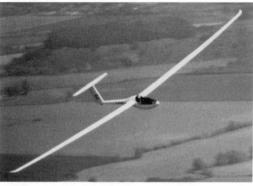

DG1000

Gerhard Glaser, owner of a civil engineering business, and Diplom Ingenieur Wilhelm Dirks, founded the Glaser-Dirks Flugzeugbau GmbH company. In 1972, they built their first glider, the DG-100. Glaser-Dirks produced 105 DG-100 and another 222 units have been produced later at the Elan factory.

In 1977 the 15-meter class sailplane DG-200 entered the market. In 1978 the DG-200 was updated with 17-meter wingtip extensions. The DG-200/17 is one of the most sought-after gliders on the secondhand market.

By 1980 Glaser-Dirks pushed into carbon fiber construction with the DG-200/17C motorglider. The DG-400 followed the next year and quickly became one of the best-selling motorgliders of all time.

In 1983, version DG-300 Club Elan was designed to replace the DG-100 in the production line, and the

LS10

fully aerobatic version DG-300 Elan Acro contributed to its popularity. The DG-300 is still in production; up until today 484 DG-300s have been delivered. In 1987 the two-seat DG-500 made its first flight, and the motorized DG-500M followed only 4 weeks later. Next came the 15m class sailplane DG-600. In 1989 a motorized self-launching version, the DG-600M followed.

The latest product family is the DG-800, which was optimized for 18m span with wing flaps and equipped with modern wing sections designed by L.M. Boermans from the TU Delft. In May 1993, the self-launching version DG-800A and the pure sailplane DG-800S made their maiden flights.

The newest projects are the DG-1000 in both sailplane and motorglider variations, along with the high-performance two-seat LS10.

DIAMOND AIRCRAFT KATANA X-TREME

The Katana X-Treme was born in Austria in 1990. The all-composite two-seater flies with 80, 100, and 115-hp Rotax engines, operating as both a sport plane (under the name HK36 Super Dimona in Europe) and as the Eco Dimona, a variant modified for surveillance and observation. This model features a movable Wescam camera and cockpit monitor.

Roughly a thousand of these motorgliders are flying worldwide, owing its origin to the H36 Dimona developed in 1981. The big wings or the HK36 Super Dimona can also be found flying the company's powered aircraft, the Katana C1 and the Diamond DA40 four-seater.

DSK "DUSTER"

The BJ-1b Duster is designed for amateur builders with an estimated construction time of 700 hours. Both plans and kit components are available. Its shoulder-type wings have a single wooden spar with plywood ribs and plywood covering. Wing features include washed-out tips, trailing-edge flaps, airbrakes, and ailerons. The fuselage is also built from plywood, with straight sides for simplified construction. Only the nose and fairings are fiberglass. Seating is for one pilot with the option of an open or closed cockpit. Also, optional power can be added without altering the design of the aircraft. Duster manufacturers are looking at a number of refinements and additions, including a 26-hp powerplant.

EXPLORER PG-1 "AQUA GLIDER"

The Explorer Aircraft Aqua Glider can be towed behind any powerboat capable of speeds in excess of 35 mph. The biplane wings have a forward stagger and make use of a conventional single wooden spar and balance floats on the tips of the lower wing. The hull is built from spruce and mahogany plywood, then covered with fiberglass up to the waterline. Standard twin jumper skis are attached to the bottom of the hull.

FLIGHT DYNAMICS "SEASPRITE"

Because the Flightsail (or unpowered Seasprite) can be fitted with a 90-hp engine as well as towed behind a 70-hp powerboat, it is listed in the homebuilt aircraft section of this book. Glider specifications are included in the specifications and performance chart in this section.

GLASER-DIRKS
(*See* DG Flugzeugbau)

GROB G-103

The biggest improvement for the G-103, the successor to the Twin Astir, came from modifications to the ailerons. Pilots reported a substantial improvement in feel (with the steel control pushrods) and overall roll re-

sponse for greater aerobatic performance. The mains, which sits aft of the aircraft's center of gravity in a fairing, features a hydraulic brake. Final descent comes from the Schempp-Hirth-type airbrakes. The FAA has also approved the Grob 103 for handicapped flight ops when equipped with all-hand control.

HpH GLASFLUGEL

Libelle 205

Kestrel

Hornet 206

Glasflügel was founded by Eugen Hänle in 1962 and carried the logo of a dragonfly (in German "Libelle"). In May 1975, financial problems lead to a co-operation with the firm Schempp-Hirth. Until 1979 Glasflügel carried the name "Holighaus & Hillenbrand" and was then dissolved in 1982 as a German-Brazilian Aircraft

Mosquito 303

Glasflügel 304

Consortium. The founder, Eugen Hänle, was killed in a flight accident on the 21st of September, 1975.

Glasflügel began building the H-301 Libelle in mass-production in 1963, a 15m glider with wing flaps, which achieved performance far ahead of the others in the newly created 15m class in 1975. Between 1964 and 1969 more than 100 gliders of this type, known as the Open Libelle, were mass-produced. This was the first time in history that an aircraft of fiberglass construction was mass-produced! There were other famous gliders built at Glasflügel: the BS-1, Standard Libelle, Kestrel, Glasflügel 604, Club Libelle, Hornet, Mosquito, Glasflügel 304 and Glasflügel 402. In addition to these, there were some more prototypes, the 202, 203 and 204 were the predecessors of Club Libelle and Hornet.

The company's most lasting design comes in the form of the Hornet, the top standard-class sailplane at the 1979 nationals contest. The 304 is a 15-meter-class smaller version of the 604. The Hornet offers a retractable monowheel, water ballast, and a large flush-fitting canopy. It is a shoulderwing cantilever monoplane with a T-tail and Wortmann wing section. The entire structure is a fiberglass monocoque and fiberglass/foam sandwich. Its carbon-fiber wing construction reduces the empty weight to 463 pounds compared to previous models. The Glasflugel 304 is a racing-class aircraft with a two-part double-tapered wing built with a fiberglass/hard-foam sandwich shell. The fuselage is a pure fiberglass shell with a one-piece canopy, and the empennage has a T-tail constructed of fiberglass and hard foam in a sandwich.

When Czech company HpH Ltd took over production of the Glasflugel 304, they introduced the 304CZ, and added winglets to the design. They also extended the 304's wing span to 17.43 meters. Their latest introduction is the 304C Standard Class sailplane, popularly called the Wasp.

Newest variants include a totally new carbon-fiber 15-meter 304S and a 15/18-meter 304SE.

MARSKE "MONARCH"

Plans and kits are available to the homebuilder for the Monarch C ultralight motorglider. Power is supplied by a 12-hp McCulloch engine located behind the pilot's seat; however, engines up to 20 hp can be used. The high wing makes use of a wooden rear spar with wood-and-foam ribs. Fiberglass covers the leading edge, and the remainder of the wing is covered with fabric. Despite its fragile appearance, the Monarch C is stressed to +8Gs and -4Gs. The fuselage pod is molded in two pieces then joined at the centerline; there are no horizontal tail surfaces. A single landing wheel is beneath the pilot.

MONNETT "MONERAI"

The Monerai follows the precedents set by its VW-powered sportplane siblings Sonerai I and II by offering simplified construction and economy with high performance. Designed for the first-time builder or the expert, the Monerai can be either a true sailplane for the purist or, with the addition of a podmounted engine, a self-launching sailplane for those who wish to operate independent of towplanes. A chrome-moly-tubing primary-fuselage structure combines with a molded fuselage shell and extruded aluminum tail boom to make up a lightweight and ultrasmooth exterior with integral structural integrity for pilot safety. If any damage should be suffered by the fuselage structure, the molded shell can be easily removed to facilitate repairs. The preformed canopy, molded ABS components, sewn seat sling, and simplified control-system components

are offered to make construction easier. The optional engine is designed to be removed easily so that the ship can be used as a pure sailplane at the pilot's whim. The wing uses a single-piece skin bonded to an extruded main spar and completely formed ribs.

OLDERSHAW O-3

Vernon Oldershaw's motorglider features a retractable powerplant that can be used for takeoff and climb to soaring altitude. A 31-hp Yamaha snowmobile two-stroke flat-twin engine drives a wooden pusher propeller and feeds from a N-gallon fuel supply. The shoulder-type wings are built with a spruce spar, plywood ribs, and plywood skin; the wing does feature ailerons and airbrakes. The fuselage is all-wood except for fiberglass skin from the nose back to the wing.

ORLIK

The Orlik 2 first flew in 1938, and an improved variation, the Orlik 3 competed in the 1940 Olympic Games. It had airbrakes beneath the wings. The design briefly held a world altitude record in 1948 of 30,000 feet.

PIK-20E

The PIK motorized glider has a manually retractable engine and propeller. The Rotax 503 500cc two-stroke two-cylinder engine produces 43 hp at 6,200 RPM. With double carburetors and resonance exhaust system, the whole snowmobile engine has been redesigned and built to aircraft requirements. The propeller is belt-driven giving a 1:2 reduction. When not in use, the powerplant is retracted into the fuselage by a manual crank and lever in the cockpit wall. The glider features fiberglass monocoque construction. Half of the fuselage/wing fairing has been taken to the wing so that the main rib and wing spar are 20 nm higher in order to save weight. The wings, flaps, and complete tail are of sandwich construction with fiberglass skin and PVC-foam core. Wing spars are made of carbon fiber. The PIK boasts a maximum L/D ratio of 40 to 1. With power on, takeoff can be accomplished in less than 1,000 feet if a 50' obstacle has to be cleared and rate of climb is 787 fpm. Cruising speed is 84 mph at 75 percent power, burning 4.4 gph from the 8.7-gallon fuel tank.

PILATUS B4

The only glider manufactured by Swiss aircraft manufacturer Pilatus was the B4. About 300 were produced beginning in 1972 until the Japanese company Nippi bought the rights to the design. The P4 is all metal and economical to maintain, and has good acro capabilities.

PIPISTREL

The Sinus-Sport and Virus-Sport models are the certified composite two-seat motorgliders designed for the Sport Pilot category. Both models use Rotax engines and offer a range of about 650 miles under power. Side by side seating makes them attractive as trainers. With its prop feathered, the Sinus has an impressive 30:1 glide ratio.

RAND KR-1B

This sleek motorglider is essentially a stock KR-1 with longer wings and a bigger tail. For a wing curve, an RAF-48 standard KR-1 airfoil was used for the center section and the GA(W)-2 airfoil for the replacement outer panels. The outer wing section provides a clean and responsive curve for use with a spoiler/flap control, permitting deadstick landings at 70 mph TAS. Where the stock KR-1 wingspan is 172", the motorglider wingspan measures 27' from tip to tip, thereby increasing square footage from 64 to 91. Power is supplied by a 60-hp VW engine. Maximum cruise is 130 mph, and with 33 gallons of fuel, range is 950 miles while getting 29 mpg. At the standard 4-gph burn rate, 33 gallons should deliver 8.25 hours of flying at 120 mph for a range of 1,020 miles.

RYSON ST-100 "CLOUDSTER"

The Cloudster is a powered sailplane or an airplane that soars, whichever you prefer. The all-metal airplane is fitted with a 100-hp Continental and a Wortmann FX 67-170/17 airfoil. The flaps, which also serve as airbrakes, are electrically actuated, and the ailerons and flaps are interconnected to operate together from -12 degrees to +8 degrees. After that, the flaps continue down to any desired position. The two-wheel fixed landing gear is extremely clean and gives a gliding performance as good as if they were retractable. The tailwheel is steerable. Both seats are designed to accommodate parachutes, and the cockpit is heated and ventilated. A full-vision one-piece canopy hinges on the right side.

As a touring airplane, it cruises at 135 mph (75-percent power) using just 6 gph to yield a range of 690 miles. At lower power settings, the range can be greatly increased. Only 20-percent power is required to keep the Cloudster in level flight.

SCHEIBE-FLUGZEUGBAU
SF-H34/SF 25/SF 28

SF-25

SF-28A

The two-place all-fiberglass SF-H34 has pleasant flight characteristics and a low construction weight. Schempp-Hirth airbrakes on the top surface of the wings are provided for glide-angle control. The nosewheel is fixed, and the main landing wheel is sprung. A disc brake is mounted with the main landing wheel. Visibility is excellent through the one-piece blown plexiglass canopy. Both seats offer adjustable rudder pedals and backrests. Due to the sailplane's low weight, small size, and rearward placed mainwheel, it is quite easy to handle on the ground, an important consideration for training. Other motorgliders are the SF 25 and SF 28. The SF 25 is powered by a 65-hp Limbach engine, which is based upon well-proven Volkswagen components and is mounted forward of the cockpit in conventional tractor style. The gliding performance has been improved by an increased wingspan and modified fuselage. Seating is side by side. The SF 28 is powered by the same Limbach engine, but offers tandem seating; the front

pilot is seated ahead of the wing, and the rear pilot sits over the main spar. The SF 25 cruises at 93 mph, climbs at 450 fpm, and takes off in 500-650 feet. The SF 28 cruises at 100 mph, climbs at 450 fpm, and takes off in 500-650 feet.

SCHEMPP-HIRTH

Cirrus 75

Discus 2A

Discus 2C

Martin Schempp and Wolf Hirth first met in 1928. Their life-long collaborations would bring about some of the world's most respected sailplane designs. Beginning in 1935, the team developed the Minimoa, the first high performance glider to sell more than a 100 models. In 1967 the company produced the first glass fiber glider, the Cirrus. Today thousands of their gliders are flying around the world.

Schempp-Hirth sailplanes include the Ventus A, an advanced 15-meter-class plane with carbon-fiber technology, thin wings, and a low-profile fuselage. The Ventus B is a 15-meter-class craft with a larger cockpit for tail pilots. The Nimbus 2C (open class) has a 20.3-

Duo Discus

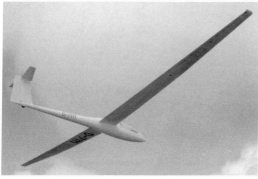

Nimbus 2

Nimbus 3

Nimbus 4

meter wingspan with either carbon or carbon/fiberglass construction. The Janus B has an 18.2-meter wingspan for high-performance tandem two-place flying. The Janus C has a 20-meter span with carbon wings, seating for two, and competition-type performance. The Janus CM, with a 20-meter span, is a two-place motorglider with carbon wings and fully retractable engine.

Schempp-Hirth's newest sailplanes include the Discus, Duo Discus, Ventus and Nimbus, available in a variety of variations, including pure gliders and powered sailplanes.

Ventus 2AX

Ventus 2BX

Ventus 2C

SCHWEIZER AIRCRAFT CORPORATION "SGS"

SGU 1-7

SGS 1-26

SGS 2-32

SGS 2-33

SGS 1-35

In December 1999, Schweizer Aircraft celebrated its 60th Anniversary. Since the three Schweizer brothers built their first glider in 1930 and incorporated Schweizer Aircraft in 1939, the company has manufactured more than 2,160 sailplanes. Schweizer is now a major U.S. aerospace contractor and no longer manufactures gliders. Historically significant Schweizer sailplanes include the following:

SGU 1-7—the first of the gliders, this one for Harvard's Altosqurus Glider Club, in 1937.

SGS 2-8—established a new American two-place distance record of 219 miles.

SGS 1-2—set a new glider distance record of 303 miles.

SGS 1-26—the single-seat SGS 1-26 was originally designed to be marketed in kit form to homebuilders.

The later SGS 1-26E is the production version that introduced an all-metal fuselage. The all-metal mid-wing has fabric-covered ailerons and airbrakes.

SGS 2-32—this high-performance sailplane had a cockpit large enough to carry a pilot and either one large or two smaller passengers. Production began in 1964, and national gliding records were established by pilots flying this aircraft. The wings have speed-limiting brakes; only the tail fin has a fabric-covered control surface.

SGS 2-33—designed for training, the SGS 2-33A flew for the first time in 1966 and entered production in 1967. The two-seater has a strut-braced high-wing built entirely from metal. The fuselage is constructed of welded steel tube, the nose covered with fiberglass, and the remainder is covered with fabric.

SGS 1-36

SGS 1-34—this high-performance single-seat sail-plane was designed to meet Standard Class specifications and is stressed to +8.33Gs and -5.33 Gs. The all-metal aluminum wings were the shoulder type with a Wortmarm FX-61-163 at the root and Wortmann FX-60-126 at the tip. The SGS 1-34B features doubleflap speed-limiting airbrakes and an optional retractable nosewheel. The standard nonretractable nosewheel is fitted with a Cleveland brake and is balanced by a forward skid and tailwheel.

SGS 1-35A/1-35C—the SGS 1-35 was available in two models. The Model A is an unrestricted 15-meter-class sailplane with interconnected flaps and ailerons and an empty weight of 490 pounds. The Model C was a less expensive spin-off intended for club use with no provision for water ballast. The C has a nonretractable nosewheel and a 425-pound empty weight.

SGS 1-36—The Sprite was an all-metal one-design sailplane, compact, lightweight and intended for clubs and schools or individual owners who want Diamond "C" performance. With a 46-foot wingspan, it has an all-aluminum structure with standard effective dive brakes, T-tail, a large cockpit, and good visibility. Two landing gear positions are offered: a forward-wheel position, which makes the ship a "taildragger," or an aft-wheel position with a nonspring tailwheel and an aluminum nose skid. The latter is recommended for school and club operation. Standard equipment includes tip wheels, deluxe seat cushions, headrest, and rudder pedal adjusters.

SONEX

Sonex, Ltd. is a kit manufacturer in Oshkosh, Wisconsin. Their original design, the all-metal, two-seat Sonex single engine monoplane morphed into the V-tailed Waiex. Add a 45' wingspan to that airplane, and a

motorglider, the Xenos, is born. The company boasts the talents of John Monnett, creator of the Monerai sailplane and the Moni motorglider.

STEMME S10

Stemme's S10 is one of the truly remarkable combinations of power and glide. The big-winged aircraft has a 50:1 sink rate. The mid-engine-front propeller drive was somewhat of an evolutionary moment for motorgliders and has set a number of world records. The two-seater has carbon-fiber wings and solar panels for 30W of electrical power once airborne. Power comes from Rotax 914 and Stemme offers both a normally aspirated and a turbocharged model.

VOLPAR-SPENCER "DRAG-N-FLY"

This single-seat water glider is built from plastic and foam materials and designed to be controlled easily by the nonpilot. The Drag-N-Fly is towed behind a ski boat and can be disconnected by the pilot. The fuselage is hinged to facilitate storage or travel. The cockpit is located forward of the biplane wings, and two floats are located underneath the lower wing. The airfoils are shaped from styrofoam blocks, reinforced by plywood spars, and covered with fiberglass. The fuselage and floats are made from plywood and are also covered with fiberglass.

"WOODSTOCK"

No special jigs or fixtures are needed to build the Woodstock. Every effort has been made to keep the

Woodstock

hardware simple. The Woodstock weighs only 235 pounds empty and can be launched by auto tow, aero tow, winch tow, or bungee-launched off a hill. The wing is built around a single main spar formed as a hollow box and plywood ribs. The fuselage is also framed with plywood, and both wings (forward of the spar) and fuselage are covered with plywood. The wings pin to the fuselage with three Y-inch pins and to each other with two 1/2-inch pins. Plans for this aircraft are no longer marketed.

Aviation Manufacturers

Ace Aircraft Inc.
8506 E. Tugalo-Aviation Way
Toccoa,GA 30577
Tel: (706) 886-6341
Fax: (706) 886-6341
E-mail: aceair@alltel.net
Website: www.aceaircraft.net

Acro Sport Inc.
PO Box 462
Hales Corners, WI 53130
Tel: (414) 529-2609

Adam Aircraft Industries
12876 E. Jamison Circle
Englewood, CO 80112
Tel: (303) 406-5900
Website: www.adamaircraft.com

Aermacchi
21040 Venegono Superiore (VA)
Via Ing. P. Foresio, 1
Tel: (+39) 0331 813111
Fax: (+39) 0331 827595 / 813450
E-mail: info@aermacchi.it
Website: www.aermacchi.it

Aero AT-3
(*see* Aero Limited)

Aero Commander
(*see* Commander Aircraft Company)

Aero Designs Pulsar
(*see* Pulsar Aircraft Corporation)

Aero Limited
Wal Miedzeszynski 844
03-942 Warsaw, Poland
Tel: +48 22 616 20 87
Fax: +48 22 617 85 28
E-mail: aero@post.pl
Website: www.aero.com.pl

Aero Vodochody a.s.
U Letiste 374
250 70 Odolena Voda
Czech Republic
Tel: +420 255 76 3173
Fax: +420 283 97 0038
Website: www.aero.cz

Aerocomp Inc.
800 Kemp Street
Merritt Island, FL 32952
Tel/Fax: (321) 453-6641
E-mail: info@aerocompinc.com
Website: http://aerocompinc.com

Aeromot Industria Mecanico-Metalurgica Ltda.
Av. das Industrias, 1210 - Bairro Anchieta
90200-290 Porto Alegre - RS - Brasil
Tel: +55 51 3371 1644
Fax: +55 51 3371 1655
Website: www.aeromot.com.br

Aerospatiale
(*see* Socata Aircraft, Inc.)

Aerosport Inc.
1200 Campwoods Ct.
New Ark, DE 19711-3449
Tel: (302) 234-1196

Aerosport Woody's Pusher
(*see* Sirius Aviation)

Airbus
Taxiway, 10 Avenue Guynemer
31770 Colomiers
Toulouse, France
Tel: +33 (0)5 61 18 06 01
Website: www.airbus.com

Aircraft Designs, Inc.
5 Harris Court Bldg S
Monterey, CA 93940
Tel: 831-649-6212
Fax: 831-649-5738
E-mail: aircraft@mbay.net
Website: www.aircraftdesigns.com

Aircraft Manufacturing & Development Co., Inc.
Heart of Georgia Regional Airport
P.O. Box 639
Eastman, GA 31023
Tel: (478) 374-2-SKY
Fax: (478) 374-2793
Website: www.newplane.com

Aircraft Spruce & Specialty Inc.
P.O. Box 4000
Corona, CA 91718-9961
Tel: (877) 477-7823
Fax: (909) 372-0555
E-mail: info@aircraft-spruce.com
Website: www.aircraft-spruce.com

Airdale Flyer Company
20274-B Ward Lane
Caldwell, ID 83605
Tel: (208) 459-6254
Website: www.airdale.com

Albatros
(*see* Aero Vodochody a.s.)

Alexander Schleicher GmbH and Co. Segelflugzeugbau
P.O. Box 60 D-36161
Alexander-Schleicher-Str. 1, Germany
Tel: +49 (0) 6658/89-0
Fax: +49 (0) 6658/89-40
E-mail: info@alexander-schleicher.de
Website: www.alexander-schleicher.de

Alisport Srl
Via Confalonieri, 22
Cremella (Lecco), Italy
Tel: +39 039 9212128
Fax: +39 039 9212130
Website: www.alisport.com

Alto
(*see* Direct Fly Limited)

AMD
(*see* Aircraft Manufacturing & Development Co., Inc.)

American Champion Aircraft Corporation
P.O. Box 37
32032 Washington Ave.
Rochester, WI 53167
Tel: (262) 534-6315
Fax: (262) 534-2395
Website: www.amerchampionaircraft.com

American Ghiles Aircraft
1270 Biscayne Blvd, Suite 7 & 8
Deland, FL 32724
Tel: (386) 740-7140
Fax: (386) 740-8621
Website: www.aircraftkit.com

American Hatz Association
P.O. Box 10
Weyauwega, WI 54983
E-mail: admin@weebeastie.com
Website: www.weebeastie.com/hatzcb1

Anderson Kingfisher
(*see* Wings Unlimited)

Angel Aircraft Corporation
1410 Arizona Place SW
Orange City, IA 51041
Tel: (712) 737-3344
Fax: (712) 737-3399
Website: www.angelaircraft.com

Anton Cvjetkovic
5324 W. 121 St.
Hawthorne, CA 90250
Tel: (310) 643-6931
E-mail: tcvjetkovic@yahoo.com
Website: www.cvjetkovic-aircraft.com

Apex Aircraft
1, route de Troyes
21121 Darois
France
E-mail: info@apex-aircraft.com
Website: www.apex-aircraft.com

Apis Sailplanes, Inc.
P.O. Box 2010
Moriarty Municipal Airport
Hangar C-L
Moriarty, NM 87035
Tel: (505) 269-8234
E-mail: apisgliders@aol.com
Website: www.apisgliders.com

Aquila Technische Entwicklungen GmbH
Flugplatz D14959
Schoenhagen, Germany
Tel: +49 (0) 33731 707 0
Fax: +49 (0) 33731 707-11
Website: www.aquila-aero.com

Arctic Tern
(*see* Interstate Aircraft Company)

Astec Enterprises, Inc.
7921 Tierney's Woods Rd.
Bloomington MN, 55438
Tel: (952) 942-0105
Fax: (952) 941-8042
E-mail: arthendricks@uswest.net

ATR
(*see* Avions de Transport Regional)

Aviat Aircraft Inc.
672 S. Washington
P.O. Box 1240
Afton, WY 83110
Tel: (307) 885-3151
Fax: (307) 885-9674
E-mail: aviat@aviataircraft.com
Website: www.aviataircraft.com

Avid Aircraft
(*see* Airdale Flyer Company)

Avions de Transport Regional
1, allée Pierre Nadot
31712 Blagnac cedex, France
Tel: +33 (0) 5 62 21 62 21
Fax :+33 (0) 5 62 21 68 00
Website: www.atraircraft.com

Avions Jodel
Aerodrome Beaune Challenges
Beaune F-21200, France
03-80-22-01-51
03-80-24-19-43

AviPro Aircraft, Limited
3536 East Shangri-La Rd.
Phoenix, AZ 85028
Tel: (602) 971-3768
E-mail: info@bearhawkaircraft.com
Website: www.bearhawkaircraft.com

Bakeng Deuce Airplane Factory
9850 52nd Street
Kenosha, WI 53144
Tel: (262) 658-9286
Fax: (262) 658-9285
Website: www.bakengdeuce.com

BAE Systems
1601 Research Boulevard
Rockville, MD 20850
Tel: (301) 838-6000
Fax: (301) 838-6925
Website: www.baesystems.com

Barnett Rotorcraft
4307 Olivehurst Ave.
Olivehurst, CA 95961
Tel: (530) 742-7416
Fax: (530) 743-6866
E-mail: barnett@syix.com

BD-5 Micro
(*see* BD-Micro Technologies, Inc.)

BD-Micro Technologies, Inc.
1260 Wade Rd.
Siletz, OR 97380
Tel: (541) 444-1343
Fax: (541) 444-1343
E-mail: sales@bd-micro.com
Website: www.bd-micro.com

BedeCorp, LLC
6440 Norwalk Rd.
Medina, OH 44256
Tel: (330) 721-9999
Fax: (330) 721-9998
E-mail: jim@bedecorp.com
Website: www.bedecorp.com

Beechcraft
(*see* Raytheon Aircraft Company)

Blanik America, Inc.
P.O. Box 1124
Wenatchee, WA 98807-1124
Tel: (509) 884-8305
Fax: (509) 884-9198
E-mail: mailto:blanikam@nwi.net
Website: www.nwinternet.com/~blanikam/ba/
home.htm

Boeing
100 North Riverside
Chicago, IL 60606
Tel: (312) 544-2000
Website: www.boeing.com

Bombardier
800 Rene-Levasque Blvd. West
Montreal, Quebec
Canada H3B 1Y8
Tel: (514) 861-9481
Fax: (514) 861-7053
Website: www.bombardier.com

Britten-Norman Aircraft Limited
Hangar 2, Bembridge Airport
Isle of Wight, PO35 5PR
United Kingdom
Tel: +44 (0) 870 881 5064
Fax: +44 (0) 870 881 5065
E-mail: aircraft@britten-norman.com
Website: www.britten-norman.com

Bryan Aircraft, Inc.
Williams County Airport
Bryan, OH 43506

Calvin Parker
P.O. Box 928
Claremont, NC 28610
Tel: (828) 464-8371

Canadian Home Rotors, Inc.
P. O. Box 370, 4 Roy Street
Ear Falls, Ontario, P0V 1T0, Canada
Tel: (807) 222-2474
Website: www.acehelicopter.com

CAP
(*see* Apex Aircraft)

Caproni
11465 Perkle Road
Lakeland, FL 33809
Tel: (941) 858-0224

Cassutt IIIM
(*see* National Aeronautics Company)

Cavalier
(*see* Stan McLeod)

Cessna Aircraft Company
P.O. Box 7706
Wichita, KS 67277
Tel: (800) 4-CESSNA (in the U.S.),
(316) 517-6056 (outside the U.S.)
Website: www.cessna.com

Christen Eagle II
(*see* Aviat Aircraft Inc.)

Cirrus Design Corporation
4515 Taylor Circle
Duluth, MN 55811
Tel: (218) 727-2737
Fax: (218) 727-2148
Website: www.cirrusdesign.com

Commander Aircraft Company
7200 Northwest 63rd Street
Bethany, OK 73008
Tel: (405) 495-8080
Fax: (405) 495-8383
Website: www.commanderair.com

Coot-Builders
6958 Applewood Drive
Madison, WI 53719
Tel: (608) 833-5586
E-mail: coot42@charter.net
Website: www.coot-builders.com

Corby CJ-1 Starlet
(*see* CSN)

Cri-Cri
(*see* Michael Colomban)

CSN
1335 Robinhood Lane S.
Lakeland, FL 33813
Tel: (941) 646-9446
E-mail: corbystarlet@juno.com

Cvjetkovic CA-65
(*see* Anton Cvjetkovic)

Dassault Aviation
Teterboro Airport, Box 2000
South Hackensack, NJ 07606
Tel: (201) 440-6700
Fax: (201) 541-4700
Website: www.dassault-aviation.com

Dave Blanton
14 Hawthorne Road
Valley Center, KS 67147
Tel: (316) 755-0659

DCS, Inc.
12618 Millstream Drive
Bowie, MD 20715-1618
Tel: (301) 262-0446
Website: www.theminicoupe.com

Derringer Aircraft Company LLC
558 S. Broad St.
Mobile, AL 36603
Tel: (661) 824-2222
Fax: (661) 824-2202
E-mail: derringer@derringeraircraft.com
Website: www.derringeraircraft.com

DG Flugzeugbau GmbH
Otto Lilienthal Weg 2/Am Flugplatz
D-76646 Bruchsal, Germany
Tel: +49 (0) 7251 3020 0
Fax: +49 (0) 7251 3020 0
E-mail: dg@dg-flugzeugbau.de
Website: www.dg-flugzeugbau.de

Diamond Aircraft Industries
1560 Crumlin Sideroad
London, Ontario
Canada N5V 1S2
Tel: (519) 457-4000
Fax: (519) 457-4021
Website: www.diamondair.com

Direct Fly Limited
Fax: +420 5 4124 8512
E-mail: sportplanes@directmedia.cz
Website: www.ultralights.cz

Don Wolf
53 Cedar Drive
Huntington, NY 11743
E-mail: dwolf@optonline.net

Douglas
(*see* Boeing)

Dyke Aircraft
2840 Old Yellow Spring Road
Fairborn, OH 45324
E-mail: dykedelta1@aol.com

EADS
(*see* Socata Aircraft, Inc.)

Eagle Aircraft
P.O. Box 38
Maitland NSW 2320, Australia
Tel: 0414 683377
Fax: 02 49343205
Website: www.eagleaircraft.webcentral.com.au

Eclipse Aviation Corp.
2503 Clark Carr Loop SE
Albuquerque, NM 87106
Tel: (505) 245-7555
Fax: (505) 241-8800
Website: www.eclipseaviation.com

Eklund Engineering, Inc.
P.O. Box 1510
Lockeford, CA 95237-1510
Tel: (209) 727-0318
Fax: (209) 727-0873

Embraer
276 S.W. 34th Street
Fort Lauderdale, FL 33315
Tel: (954) 359-3700
Fax: (954) 359-8170
Website: www.embraer.com

EU-WISH Aircraft
RR 2, EU-WISH Airport
Hermann, MO 65041
Tel: (573) 486-3215
E-mail: euwish@ktis.net

Europa Aircraft (2004) Limited
7 Dove Way, Kirkby Mills Industrial Estate
Kirkbymoorside, York
YO62 6QR, UK
Tel: +44 (0) 1751 431773
Fax: +44 (0) 1751 431706
E-mail: john@europa-aircraft.com
Website: www.europa-aircraft.co.uk/

Evans Aircraft
Evans Aircraft
P.O. Box 231762
Encinitas, CA 92023
Website: www.evansair.com

Evektor Sportstar
(*see* Sport Flight, Inc.)

Explorer Aqua Glider
(*see* VULA)

Extra Aircraft, LLC
1935 Fruitville Pike, #104
Lancaster, PA 17601-3996
Tel: (717) 394-9797
Fax: (717) 394-5106
Website: www.extraaircraft.com

Falconar Avia Inc.
7739-81 Ave.
Edmonton, Alberta
T6C OV4, Canada
Tel: (780) 465-2024
Fax: (780) 465-2029
E-mail: sales@falconaravia.com
Website: www.falconaravia.com

F.E.W. P-51D/TF
(*see* Fighter Escort Wings)

Fighter Escort Wings
948 Tourmaline Dr.
Newbury Park, CA 91320
Tel: (805) 402-1554
Fax: (805) 499-0118
E-mail: info@fighterescortwings.com
Website: www.fighterescortwings.com

Fisher Flying Products
P.O. Box 468
Edgeley, ND 58433
Tel: (701) 493-2286
Fax: (701) 493-2539
E-mail: ffp@fisherflying.com
Website: www.fisherflying.com

Flaglor Scooter
(*see* Rotor Wings And Flying Machines)

Found Aircraft
RR#2, Site 12, Box 10
Parry Sound, Ontario
P2A 2W8, Canada
Tel: (705) 378-0530
Fax: (705) 378-1264
Website: www.foundair.com

Glaser-Dirks
(*see* DG Flugzeugbau GmbH)

Great Plains Aircraft Supply Co. Inc.
P.O. Box 545
Boys Town, NE 68010
Tel: (800) 922-6507
E-mail: gpasc@earthlink.net
Website: www.greatplainsas.com

Grob Aerospace
Lettenbachstr. 9
86874 Tussenhausen-Mattsies
Germany
Tel: +49 (0) 82 68 9 98 0
Fax: +49 (0) 82 68 9 98 1 14
E-mail: sales@grob-aerospace.de
Website: www.grob-aerospace.com

Gulfstream Aerospace Corporation
500 Gulfstream Road M/S C-10
Savannah, GA 31407
Tel: (912) 965-5555
Fax: (912) 965-3084
Website: www.gulfstream.com

Heath Parasol
(*see* Loehle Aircraft Company)

Helio Aircraft
6487 Wilkinson Drive
Prescott, AZ 86301
Tel: (928) 717-1069
Fax: (928) 717-0999
Website: www.helioaircraft.com

Hollman HA-2M Sportster
(*see* Aircraft Designs, Inc.)

Hovey Whing-Ding
(*see* VULA)

HpH Glasflugel
(*see* HpH Limited)

HpH Limited
Caslavska 126
P.O. Box 112
CZ-284 01 Kutna Hora
Czech Republic
Tel: +420 327 512 633
Fax: +420 327 513 441
E-mail: hph@hph.cz
Website: www.hph.cz

IndUS Aviation, Inc.
5681 Apollo Drive
Dallas Executive Airport
Dallas, TX 75237
Tel: 877-GO INDUS
Website: www.indusav.com

Interstate Aircraft Company
43 Airpark Road
West Lebanon, NH 03784
Tel: (603) 298-9644
Fax: (603) 298-9648
Website: www.interstateaircraft.com

Jeffair Barracuda
(*see* Siers Flight Systems, Inc.)

Jodel D-11 Series
(*see* Avions Jodel)

John C. Powell
4032 76th Lane
Riviera Beach, FL 33404-5836

Jungster I/II
(*see* Stan McLeod)

Jurca Air Force
Comite Marcel Jurca
Aerodrome de Nagis-les-loges (LFAI)
77370 Clos Fontaine, France
Fax: +33 1 64 60 68 59
E-mail: cmj@marcel-jurca.com
Website: www.marcel-jurca.com

K2NE
E-mail: vince-q@k2nesoft.com
Website: www.netk2ne.net/webstores/chl

Lafayette
(*see* American Ghiles Aircraft)

Lake Aircraft
1396 Grandview
Kissimmee, FL 34744
Tel: (407) 847-8080
Website: www.lakeamphib.com

Lancair Company
Certified Aircraft Division
22550 Nelson Road
Bend, OR 97701
Tel: (541) 318-1144
Fax: (541) 318-1177
Website: www.flycolumbia.com

Lancair International Inc.
Kit Aircraft Division
2244 Airport Way
Redmond, OR 97756
Tel: (541) 923-2244
Fax: (541) 923-2255
E-mail: sales@lancair-kits.com
Website: www.lancair-kits.com

Leza AirCam Corporation
1 Leza Drive
Sebring, FL 33870
Tel: (863) 655-4242
Fax: (863) 655-0310
E-mail: aircam@ct.net
Website: www.leza-aircam.com

Liberty Aerospace, Inc.
General Aviation Drive
Melbourne, FL 32935
Tel: (800) 759-5953
Fax: (321) 752-0377
Website: www.libertyaircraft.com

Lockheed Martin Corporation
6801 Rockledge Drive
Bethesda, MD 20817
Tel: (301) 897-6000
Website: www.lockheedmartin.com

Loehle Aircraft Corporation
380 Shippmans Creek Road
Wartrace, TN 37183-3302
Tel: (931) 857-3419
E-mail: info@loehle.com
Website: www.loehle.com

Luscombe Aircraft
5333 N. Main St.
Altus, OK 73521
Tel: (580) 477-3355
Fax: (580) 477-3368
E-mail: sales@luscombeaircraft.com
Website: www.luscombeaircraft.com

Luton Minor
(*see* Popular Flying Association)

Mark Sorrell Co., LLC
18702 Old Hwy 99 SW
Rochester, WA 98579
Tel: (360) 858-8105
Website: www.sorrellco.com

Marske
3007 Harding Highway East
Marion, OH 43302
Tel: (740) 223-3550
E-mail: marske@continuo.com
Website: www.continuo.com

Maverick Jets
1371 General Aviation Drive
Melbourne, FL 32935
Tel: (321) 752-4111
Fax: (321) 752-4455
Website: www.maverickjet.com

Maule Air, Inc.
2099 Ga. Hwy. 133 S.
Moultrie, GA 31768
Tel: (229) 985-2045
Fax: (229) 890-2402
Website: www.mauleairinc.com

McDonnell Douglas
(*see* Boeing)

Merlin
(*see* Aerocomp Inc.)

Meyer's Little Toot
(*see* Tommy Meyer)

Meyers Aircraft Company
E-mail: pwhetstone@meyersaircraft.com
Website: www.meyersaircraft.com

Micco
(*see* Meyers Aircraft Company)

Michel Colomban
37 Bis Rue La Kanol
92500 Rueil Malmaison, France
Fax: 0033 147 51 8876

Mini Coupe
(*see* DCS, Inc.)

Mini-Imp Aircraft Company
P.O. Box 2011
Weatherford, TX 76086
Tel: (817) 596-3278
E-mail: info@mini-imp.com
Website: www.mini-imp.com

Monnett
(*see* Great Plains Aircraft Supply Co. Inc.)

Mooney Mite Site
E-mail: mooneymite@mooneymite.com
Website: www.mooneymite.com

Mooney Airplane Company, Inc.
165 Al Mooney Road North
Kerrville, TX 78028
Tel: 800-456-3033 (in the U.S.),
1-830-896-6000 (outside the U.S.)
E-mail: sales@mooney.com
Website: www.mooney.com

Mustang Aeronautics Inc.
1470 Temple City
Troy, MI 48084
Tel: (248) 649-6818
Fax: (248) 588-6788
Email: mustair@wwnet.com
Website: www.mustangaero.com

National Aeronautics Company
5611 Kendall Court, Unit 4
Arvada, CO 80002
Tel/Fax: (303) 940-8442
E-mail: cassutts@aol.com

NewGlasair LLC and NewGlaStar LLC
18810 59th Ave. NE
Arlington, WA 98223
Tel: (360) 435-8533
Fax: (360) 435-9525
E-mail: info@glasairaviation.com
Website: www.newglasair.com

New Piper Aircraft, Inc.
2926 Piper Drive
Vero Beach, FL 32960
Tel: (772) 567-4361
Fax: (772) 978-6584
Website: www.newpiper.com

Northrup Grumman
Air Combat Systems
Integrated Systems
One Northrop Grumman Avenue
El Segundo, CA 90245-2804
Website: www.is.northrupgrumman.com

NuVenture Aircraft
Tel: (559) 447-1112
E-mail: alantolle@earthlink.net
Website: www.nuventureaircraft.com

O'Neill Aircraft Company
791 Livingston Street
Carlyle, IL 62231
Tel: (618) 594-2681
E-mail: troneill@charter.net
Website: www.oneillairplane.com

Osprey Aircraft
3741 El Ricon Way
Sacramento, CA 95864
Tel: (916) 483-3004
Fax: (916) 978-9813
E-mail: info@ospreyaircraft.com
Website: www.ospreyaircraft.com

PAC 750 XL
(*see* Pacific Aerospace Corporation Limited)

Pacific Aerospace Corporation Limited
Private Bag HN 3027
Hamilton, New Zealand
Tel: +64 7 843 6144
Fax: +64 7 843 6134
Email: pacific@aerospace.co.nz
Website: www.aerospace.co.nz

Partenavia
(*see* Vulcanair S.p.A)

Payne Knight Twister Imperial
(*see* Steen Aero Lab)

Pazmany Aircraft Corporation
P.O. Box 80051
San Diego, CA 92138
Fax: (619) 224-7358
Website: www.pazmany.com

Peter M. Bowers Company
458 16th Avenue South
Seattle, WA 98168
Tel: (206) 242-2582

Piaggio Aero Industries S.p.A.
Via Cibrario 4-16154
Genova, Italy
Tel: +39 010 64811
Fax: +39 010 6481234-309
Website: www.piaggioamerica.com

Pietenpol B.H.P. And Sons Engineering Companies Inc.
W12351 848th Avenue
River Falls, WI 54022
E-mail:
pietenpol_bhp_and_sons_aviation@yahoo.com
Website: www.pressenter.com/~apietenp

Pilatus Aircraft Ltd.
P.O. Box 992
6371 Stans, Switzerland
Tel: +41 41 619 61 11
Fax: +41 41 610 92 30
E-mail: info@pilatus-aircraft.com
Website: www.pilatus-aircraft.com

Pilatus Britten-Norman
(*see* Britten-Norman Aircraft Limited)

Piper
(*see* New Piper Aircraft, Inc.)

Pipistrel d. o. o. Ajdovscina
Goriska Cesta 50 A
5270 Ajdovscina, Slovenija
Tel: + 386 5 36 63 873
Fax: +386 5 36 61 263
E-mail: pipistrel@siol.net
Website: www.pipistrel.si

Pitts S-1T
(*see* Aviat Aircraft Inc.)

Polliwagen
(*see* K2NE)

Popular Flying Association
Terminal Building, Shoreham Airport
Shoreham By Sea, West Sussex
BN43 5FF, UK
E-mail: office@pfa.org.uk

Powell Acey Deucy
(*see* John C. Powell)

Pulsar Aircraft Corporation
4233 N. Santa Anita Avenue
El Monte, CA 91731
Tel: (626) 443-1019
Fax: (626) 443-1311
E-mail: info@pulsaraircraft.com
Website: www.pulsaraircraft.com

Questair Venture
(*see* NuVenture Aircraft)

Rand-Robinson Engineering, Inc.
7071 Warner Ave., #F
PMB 724
Huntington Beach, CA 92647-5492
Tel: (714) 898-3811
Fax: (714) 890-1658
Website: www.fly-kr.com

Raytheon Aircraft Company
P.O. Box 85
Wichita, KS 67201-0085
Tel: (316) 676-5034
Fax: (316) 676-6614
Website: www.raytheonaircraft.com

Redfern Plans
Colorado Springs, CO 80907
Tel: (719) 634-6505
E-mail: redfernplans@earthlink.net

Reflex Fiberglass Works
538 Rentz Road
Walterboro, SC 29488
Tel: (843) 538-6682
Fax: (843) 538-6683

Replica Plans
4366 Eckert St.
Chilliwack, BC
V2R 5J5 Canada
Tel: (604) 823-6428

RLU-1 Breezy
(*see* Aircraft Spruce And Specialty, Inc.)

Robin
(*see* Apex Aircraft)

Rotor Wings and Flying Machines
8215 Racing Trail
Austin, TX 78717-5325
Tel: (512) 341-7930

RotorWay International
4140 W. Mercury Way
Chandler, Arizona 85226 USA
Tel: (480) 961-1001
Fax: (480) 961-1514
Email: rotorway@rotorway.com
Website: www.rotorway.com

Rotorway Scorpion 133
(*see* Vortech, Inc.)

S. Littner
432 Hamel
St-Eustache, Quebec
J7P 4M3, Canada
Tel: (450) 974-7001
Email: slittner@e-scape.net
Website: www.homebuilt.org/kits/littner/littner.html

Safari
(*see* Canadian Home Rotors, Inc.)

Scaled Composites, LLC
1624 Flight Line
Mojave, CA 93501
Website: www.scaled.com/projects/tierone

Scheibe
August-Pfaltz Strasse 23
85221 Dachau
Germany
Tel: +49 (0) 8131 72084/4
Fax: +49 (0) 8131 736 985

Schempp-Hirth
Krebenstrae 25, D-73230
Kirchheim/Tech, Germany
Tel: +49 7021/7298 0
Fax: +49 7021/7298 199
E-mail: info@schempp-hirth.com
Website: www.schempp-hirth.com

Schweizer
P.O. Box 147
Elmira, NY 14814
Tel: (607) 739-3821
Fax: (607) 796-2488
E-mail: schweizer@sacusa.com
Website: www.schweizer-aircraft.com

S.E. 5A Replica
(*see* Replica Plans)

Sequoia Aircraft Corporation
2000 Tomlynn Street
Richmond, VA 23230
Tel: (804) 353-1713
Fax: (804) 359-2618
Email: support@seqair.com
Website: www.sequair.com

SIAI Marchetti
(*see* Aermacchi)

Siers Flight Systems, Inc.
P.O. Box 6533
Lynnwood, WA 98036-0533
Tel: (425) 478-3655
E-mail: barracuda@siersflight.com
Website: www.siersflight.com

Sirius Aviation
1717 Wheatfield Dr.
Mesquite, TX 75149
Tel: (214) 457-1760
Fax: (214) 432-0659
E-mail: info@sirius-aviation.com
Website: www.sirius-aviation.com

Sky Classic Aircraft
108 Jefferson Ave.
Des Moines, IA 50314
Tel: (515) 243-0094
Fax: (515) 243-3915
E-mail: miniplane@skyclassic.net
Website: www.skyclassic.net

Skystar Aircraft Corporation
3901 Aviation Way
Caldwell, ID 83605
Tel: (208) 454-2444
Fax: (208) 454-6464
E-mail: info@skystar.com
Website: www.skystar.com

Smith Miniplane
(*see* Sky Classic Aircraft)

Socata Aircraft, Inc.
North Perry Airport
7501 South Airport Rd.
Pembroke Pines, FL 33023
Tel: (954) 893-1400
Fax: (954) 964-0805
E-mail: sales@socataaircraft.com
Website: www.socata.eads.net

Solaris Aviation Inc.
Palm Beach North County Airport
11250-4 Aviation Boulevard
West Palm Beach, FL 33412
Tel: (954) 757-5480
Fax: (954) 757-5182
Website: www.solarisaviation.com

Sonex, Limited
P.O. Box 2521
Oshkosh, WI 54903-2521
Tel: (920) 231-8297
Fax: (920) 426-8333
E-mail: info@sonex-ltd.com
Website: www.sonex-ltd.com

Sorrell Hiperbipe
(*see* Mark Sorrell Co., LLC)

SpaceShipOne
(*see* Scaled Composites, LLC)

Spencer Amphibian Air Car
P.O. Box 327
Kansas, IL 61933
Tel: (847) 882-5678
Fax: (847) 882-0123
Website: www.geocities.com/Paris/Concorde/7563/
page3.html

Sport Flight, Inc.
560 Anne Street North
Barrie, Ontario, Canada
Stan McLeod
Tel: (403) 563-5517
E-mail: mcleodsk@shaw.ca

Steen Aero Lab
1451 Clearmont St., NE
Palm Bay, FL 32905
Tel: (321) 725-4160
Fax: (321) 725-3058
Website: www.steenaerolab.com

StemmeWest, LLC
c/o Sky Sailing, Inc.
31930 Highway 79
Warner Springs, CA 92086
Tel: (760) 782-0404
E-mail: info@stemmewest.com
Website: www.stemmewest.com

Stewart Aircraft Corporation
W8923 North Lake Road
Vulcan, MI 49892
E-mail: info@stewartaircraft.com
Website: www.stewartaircraft.com

Stoddard-Hamilton
(*see* New Glasair LLC and New GlaStar LLC)

Stolp
(*see* Aircraft Spruce and Specialty, Inc.)

Super Diamant C.P. 60
(*see* S. Littner)

Super Emeraude C.P. 328
(*see* S. Littner)

Symphony Aircraft Industries
3005 Lindbergh, Three Rivers
Quebec, Canada G91 5E1
Tel: (819) 377-3979
Fax: (819) 377-7928
Website: www.symphonyaircraft.com

Taylor Mini-Imp
(*see* Mini-Imp Aircraft Company)

Taylor Model A Coot
(*see* Coot-Builders)

Taylor Monoplane
(*see* Terry Taylor)

Taylorcraft Aviation, Inc.
4495 W. State Hwy. 71
La Grange, TX 78945-5150
Tel: (800) 217-1399
Website: www.taylorcraft.com

Team Tango
1990 SW 19th Avenue
Williston, FL 32696
Tel: (352) 528-0982
E-mail: info@teamtango.com
Website: www.teamtango.com

TECNAM, Ltd.
121, Victa Lane
Ardmore Airport, Private Bag 14
Papakura, Auckland
New Zealand
Tel: +64 9 298 9144
Fax: +64 9 298 9148
E-mail: info@tecnam.net
Website: www.tecnam.co.nz/index.htm

Teenie Two
(*see* Calvin Parker)

Terry Taylor
79 Springwater Road
Leigh-on-Sea, Essex
England SS9 5BW

Thorp T211
(*see* IndUS Aviation, Inc.)

Tiger Aircraft
226 Pilot Way
Martinsburg, WV 25401
Tel: (304) 267-1000
Website: www.tigeraircraft.com

Tommy Meyer
170 Park Lane
Double Oak, TX 75077
Tel: (817) 430-3507
E-mail: tommy@littletootbiplane.com
Website: www.littletootbiplane.com

Tri-R Technologies KIS
(*see* Pulsar Aircraft Company)

Tri-R Technologies KIS TR-4 Cruiser
(*see* Pulsar Aircraft Company)

Trident 320 Trigull
(*see* Viking Air Limited)

Turner Aircraft, Inc.
P.O. Box 74
Cleburne, TX 76033
Tel/Fax: 817-556-3535
E-mail: GenenJean@aol.com

Van's Aircraft, Inc.
14401 NE Keil Road
Aurora, OR 97002
Tel: (503) 678-6545
Fax: (503) 678-6560
E-mail: info@vansaircraft.com
Website: www.vansaircraft.com

Velocity Inc.
200 W Airport Dr.
Sebastian, FL 32958
Tel: (772) 589-1860
Fax: (772) 589-1893
Website: www.velocityaircraft.com

Viking Aircraft
P.O. Box 646
Elkhorn, WI 53121
Tel: (414) 723-1048
Fax: (414) 723-1049

Volmer Club of America, Inc.
536 Oak Ave.
Bridge City, LA 70094
E-mail: rjaflys@aol.com
Website: www.volmeraircraft.com

Vortech, Inc.
P.O. Box 511-W
Fallston, MD 21047
Website: www.vortechonline.com/bensen

VULA
74 Brookwood Drive
Marietta, GA 30064
Tel: (678) 290-0507
Website: http://vulatalk.zdwebhosting.com/
blueprint_pricelist.htm

Vulcanair S.p.A.
Via G. Pascoli, 7
Casoria, Naples
80026 Italy
Tel: +39 081.5918111
Fax: +39 081.5918172
Website: www.vulcanair.com

WACO Classic Aircraft Corporation
P.O. Box 1229
Battle Creek, MI 49016-1229
Tel: (269) 565-1000
Fax: (269) 565-1100
E-mail: flywaco@wacoclassic.com
Website: www.wacoclassic.com

Wag-Aero Group
1216 North Road
Lyons, Wisconsin 53148
Phone: 262-763-9586
Fax: 262-763-7595
E-mail: wagaero-sales@wagaero.com
Website: www.wagaero.com

WAR Aircraft Replicas International, Inc.
P.O. Box 79007
Tampa, FL 33619

Warner Aerocraft
9415 Laura Ct.
Seminole, FL 33776-1625
Tel: (727) 595-2382
E-mail: mike@warnerair.com
Website: www.warnerair.com

White Lightning
(*see* Reflex Fiberglass Works)

Wichawk
(*see* Dave Blanton)

Wings Unlimited
6230 Rock Island Rd.
Charlotte, NC 28278
Tel/Fax: (704) 588-9249

Wittman
(*see* Aircraft Spruce & Specialty, Inc.)

Zenair Ltd.
PO Box 235
Huronia Airport
Midland, Ontario
Canada L4R 4K8
Website: www.zenair.com

Zenith Aircraft Company
Mexico Airport, P.O. Box 650
Mexico, MO 65265-0650
Tel: (573) 581-9000
Fax: (573) 581-0011
E-mail: info@zenithair.com
Website: www.zenithair.com

Aviation Clubs and Organizations

Aero Commander
(*see* Twin Commander Aircraft LLC)

Aeronca Aviators Club
P.O. Box 66
Coxsackie, NY 12051
E-mail: staff@aeronca.org
Website: www.aeronca.org

Aircoupe
(*see* Ercoupe Owners Club)

Aluminum Overcast
Tel: (800) FLY-NB17
E-mail: b17reservations@eaa.org
Website: www.b-17.org

American Bonanza Society
P.O. Box 12888
Wichita, KS 67277
Tel: (316) 945-1700
Fax: (316) 945-1710
Website: www.bonanza.org

American Champion
(*see* Bellanca-Champion Club)

American Navion Society
16420 SE McGillivray, #103
Vancouver, WA 98683-3461
Tel: (360) 833-9921
Fax: (360) 833-1074
E-mail: flynavion@yahoo.com
Website: www.navionsociety.org

American Waco Club, Inc.
28415 Springbrook Drive
Lawton, MI 49065
Tel: (269) 624-6490
Website: www.americanwacoclub.com

American Yankee Association
P.O. Box 1531
Cameron Park, CA 95682-1531
Tel: (403) 932-4323
E-mail: pres@aya.org
Website: www.aya.org

Auster
(*see* International Auster Club)

B-17 Combat Crewmen and Wingmen
P.O. Box 1102
Simi Valley, CA 93062
Website: www.b-17combatcrewmen.org

BAC VC-10
(*see* A Little VC10derness Website)

BD-4.org
780 Pebble Beach Ct.
Lake Oswego, OR 97034
Tel: (503) 534-2898
E-mail: webmaster@bd-4.org
Website: www.bd-4.org

Beagle Pup
(*see* De Havilland Support Ltd. and Beagle Pup and Bull Dog Club)

Beagle Pup and Bull Dog Club
E-mail: paulfowler@pigeonhouse1.demon.co.uk
Website: www.beaglepupandbulldogclub.org

Beechcraft
(*see* World Beechcraft Society)

Beechcraft Bonanza
(*see* American Bonanza Society)

Beechcraft Bonanza, twins
(*see* Twin Bonanza Association)

Bellanca-Champion Club
P.O. Box 100
Coxsackie, NY 12051
E-mail: staff@bellanca-championclub.com
Website: www.bellanca-championclub.com

Bensen Gyrocopter
(*see* Vortech, Inc.)

Berkut
3025 Airport Avenue
Santa Monica, CA 90405
Tel: (310) 391-0179
Fax: (310) 391-8645
Website: www.berkutengineering.com

Boeing B-17 Flying Fortress
(*see* Aluminum Overcast and B-17 Combat Crewmen and Wingmen)

Boeing/Stearman
(*see* Stearman Restorers Association)

Boredom Fighter
(*see* Unofficial Wolf W-11 Boredom Fighter Web Page)

Bowersflybaby.com
Website: www.bowersflybaby.com

Bryan (Schreder)
(*see* Schreder Sailplane Designs)

Bucker
(*see* International Aerobatics Club)

Camair
(*see* Navion Skies)

Cessna, twins
(*see* Twin Cessna Flyer)

Cessna 172-182 Club
P.O. Box 22631
Oklahoma City, OK 73123
Tel: (405) 495-8664
Fax: (405) 495-8666
E-mail: scott@cessna172-182club.com
Website: www.cessna172-182club.com

Cessna Pilots Association
P.O. Box 5817
Santa Maria, CA 93456
Tel: 805-922-2580
Fax: 805-922-7249
E-mail: info@cessna.org
Website: www.cessna.org

Champion
(*see* Bellanca-Champion Club)

Chance-Vought
(*see* Vought Heritage)

CHL Associates
Bob Rudolph
123 Mt. Kennedy Dr.
Martinez, CA 94553
E-mail: brudolph@chlassociates.com
Website: www.chlassociates.com

Christen Eagle II
(*see* Eagle Owners Exchange Forum)

Commander Owners Group
E-mail: gmores@microdata.com
Website: www.commander.org

Continental Luscombe Association
10251 E. Central Ave.
Del Rey, CA 93616
Tel: (559) 888-2745
E-mail: cla-jim-patti@pacbell.net
Website: www.luscombe-cla.org

Cozy
(*see* Unofficial Cozy Builders Website)

Culver Aircraft Association
723 Baker Dr.
Tomball, TX 77375
Tel: (281) 351-0114
E-mail: dann@gie.com

Culver Club
P.O. Box 127
Blakesburg, IA 52536
Tel: (641) 938-2773
Fax: (641) 938-2093
E-mail: antiqueairfield@sirisonline.com

Culver Dart Club
2656 East Sand Road
Port Clinton, OH 43452-2741
Tel: (419) 734-6685

Culver PQ-14 Association
29621 Kensington Drive
Laguna Niguel, CA 92677
Tel: (949) 495-4540

Davis DA-2A
(*see* Leeon Davis)

Davis DA-5A
(*see* Leeon Davis)

DC-3 Vennerne
P.O. Box 16
DK-3500 Værlose, Denmark
Website: www.dc3vennerne.dk

De Havilland Support Ltd.
Building 213, Duxford Airfield
Cambridgeshire, CB2 4QR, England
Tel: +44 (0) 1223 830090
Fax: +44 (0) 1223 830085
Website: www.dhsupport.com

Delta Builders Network
964 New Haven Ave.
Milford, CT 06460
E-mail: deltad@astrosurf.net
Website: http://dbn.astrosurf.net/dbn454.html

Douglas DC-3
(*see* DC-3 Vennerne)

Dyke Delta
(*see* Delta Builders Network)

EAA Biplane Group
E-mail: swenson@eaabiplane.org
Website: www.eaabiplane.org

EAA Vintage Aircraft Association
P.O. Box 3086
Oshkosh, WI 54903-3086
Tel: (920) 426-4825
Fax: (920) 426-6865
E-mail: membership@eaa.org
Website: www.vintageaircraft.org

Eagle Owners Exchange Forum
1760 Montara Avenue
Sacramento, CA 95835
Tel: (916) 825-3102
Website: http://musclebiplane.org/htmlfile/
eaglehm.htm

EDI Express 90
(*see* Express Aircraft LLC)

Ercoupe Owners Club
7263 Schooners Ct. SW A2
Ocean Isle Beach, NC 28469
Tel/Fax: (910) 575-2758
E-mail: coupeclub@aol.com
Website: www.ercoupe.org

Experimental Aviation Berkut
(*see* Berkut)

Express Aircraft LLC
P.O. Box 14666
Tumwater, WA 98501
Website: www.express-aircraft.com

Fairchild Club
7645 Echo Point Road
Cannon Falls, MN 55009
Tel: (507) 263-2414
E-mail: fchld@rconnect.com
Website: www.fairchildclub.com

Fleet
(*see* International Fleet Club)

Globe Temco Swift Homepage
E-mail: arbeau@napanet.net
Website: www.napanet.net/~arbeau/swift

Grumman-American Yankee
(*see* American Yankee Association)

Gulfstream-American
(*see* American Yankee Association)

Helio
(*see* EAA Vintage Aircraft Association)

Howard Aircraft Foundation
E-mail: howardclub@aol.com
Website: http://members.aol.com/HowardClub

International Aerobatics Club
EAA Aviation Center
P.O. Box 3086
Oshkosh, WI 54903-3086
Tel: (920) 426-4800
Website: www.iac.org

International Auster Club
Greystones, Widmerpool,
Nottingham NG12 5PY, England
Tel: +0115 937 4518
Website: www.austerclub.com

International Fleet Club
P.O. Box 511
Marlborough, CT 06447
Tel: (860) 267-6562
E-mail: flyboy@ntplx.net
Website: http://users.ntplx.net/~flyboy

International Republic Seabee Owner's Club
E-mail: hjpoel@aol.com
Website: www.republicseabee.com

International Ryan Club
6749 Sproul Lane
Colorado Springs, CO 80918
Tel: (719) 637-0978
E-mail: editor@ryanclub.org
Website: www.ryanclub.org

International Stinson Club
1658 E. Capitol Expressway, #344
San Jose, CA 95121
Tel: (408) 229-2386
E-mail: patsmith@americanclassicaeroplane.com
Website: www.aeromar.com/swsc.html

Interstate Club
P.O. Box 127
Blakesburg, IA 52536
Tel/Fax: (515) 938-2773

Janowski Aircraft
Website: www.angelfire.com/ks2/janowski/j1.html

Jim Maupin, Limited
E-mail: maupin@jcpress.com
Website: www.jcpress.com/jmaupinltd/home.htm

Leeon Davis
2201 SCR 1060
Midland, TX 79706

A Little VC10derness Website
E-mail:
vickers_vc10@zonnet.nl.removethisbeforesending
Website: www.vc10.net

Lockheed Club
P.O. Box 62275
Boulder City, NV 89006-2275
Fax: (702) 293-0652

Luscombe
(*see* Continental Luscombe Association, Luscombe
Association and Luscombe Endowment)

Luscombe Association
1002 Heather Lane
Hartford, WI 53027
Tel: (262) 966-7627
Fax: (262) 966-9627
E-mail: sskrog@aol.com
Website: www.luscombeassoc.org

Luscombe Endowment
15815 E. Melrose Street
Gilbert, AZ 85296
Tel: (480) 650-0883
E-mail: dcombs@luscombesilvaire.info
Website: www.luscombe.org

MAPA Safety Foundation
Website: www.mapasafety.com

Maule Aircraft Association
5630 South Washington Road
Lansing, MI 48911-4999
Tel: (800) 594-4634
Fax: (800) 596-8341

Messerschmitt Owners Club
33 Church Road
Kelvedon, Colchester C05 9JH
Essex, UK
Tel/Fax: +01376 570851

Meyers OTW
(*see* Russell-Aire)

Mini Nimbus Owners Group
E-mail: bergrath.alfred@gmx.de
Website: www.nimbus.org.uk

Monocoupe Club
E-mail: monocoupe@sbcglobal.net
Website: http://monocoupe.com

Mooney Mite
(*see* Western Association of Mooney Mites)

Mooney Owners of America
P.O. Box 1748
Nokomis, FL 34275-1748
Tel: (877) JOIN-MOA
Fax: (941) 412-0551
Website: www.mooneyowners.com

N3N Owners and Restorers Association
2380 Country Road, #217
Cheyenne, WY 82009
Tel: (307) 638-2210
E-mail: wyn3n@aol.com

Naval Aircraft Factory N3N
(*see* N3N Owners and Restorers Association)

Navion
(*see* American Navion Society, Navion Pilots
Association, Navion Skies and Navion Type Club)

Navion Pilots Association
P.O. Box 6656
Ventura, CA 93006-6656
Tel: (805) 320-3924
E-mail: jon@navionpilots.org
Website: www.navionpilots.org

Navion Skies
Website: www.navionskies.com

Navion Type Club
P.O. Box 2678
Lodi, CA 95241-2678
Tel: (209) 367-9390
E-mail: Navion1@inreach.com
Website: www.navionskies.com

Noorduyn Norseman Website
E-mail: noorduynnorseman@comcast.net
Website: www.noorduynnorseman.com

North American AT-6
(*see* T-6 Racing Association)

Official Spezio Tuholer Website
Website: www.tuholer.com

Piper Owner Society
Website: www.piperowner.org

Piper, short wings
(*see* Short-Wing Piper Club, Inc.)

Porterfield Airplane Club
91 Hickory Loop
Ocala, FL 34472
Tel: (352) 687-4859

Quickie
(*see* Unofficial Quickie, Q-2 And Q-200 Webiste)

Rearwin Register
P.O. Box 127
Blakesburg, IA 52536
Tel/Fax: (515) 938-2773

Republic Seabee
(*see* International Republic Seabee Owner's Club)

Rockwell Commander
(*see* Commander Owners Group)

Rotorway Owners Group
E-mail: rogadmin@rotorwayownersgroup.com
Website: www.rotorwayownersgroup.com

Russell-Aire
E-mail: dick@russellaire.com
Website: www.russellaire.com

Rutan Aircraft Factory
1654 Flight Line
Mojave, CA 93501
E-mail: raf@antelecom.net
Website: www.rutanaircraft.com

Ryan
(*see* International Ryan Club)

Schempp-Hirth Cirrus 75
(*see* Standard Cirrus Sailplanes Website)

Schempp-Hirth Mini Nimbus
(*see* Mini Nimbus Owners Group)

Schempp-Hirth Open Cirrus Sailplane Website
E-mail: jim@kellett.com
Website: http://classicsailplane.org/Cirrus

Schempp-Hirth Standard Cirrus
(*see* Standard Cirrus Sailplanes Website)

Schreder Sailplane Designs
2212 South Chicago Avenue
Nampa, ID 83686
Fax: (208) 463-9239
E-mail: wayne@soaridaho.com
Website: www.soaridaho.com/Schreder

Short-Wing Piper Club, Inc.
309 Main Street, Suite 4
P.O. Box 166
Halstead, KS 67056
Website: www.shortwing.org

SIAI-Marchetti SF-260 Association
3538 Veteran Ave.
Los Angeles, CA 90034
Tel/Fax: 310-559-7131
Website: www.geocities.com/Nashville/7348

Standard Cirrus Sailplanes Website
Website: www.standardcirrus.org

Stearman Restorers Association
7000 Merrill Ave., Box 90
Chino Airport, Chino, CA 91710-8800
Website: www.stearman.net

Stewart S-51D
(*see* Unofficial Stewart 51 Builders Page)

Stinson
(*see* International Stinson Club)

Swift
(*see* Globe Temco Swift Homepage)

T-6 Racing Association
P.O. Box 1612
Southaven, MS 38671
E-mail: at61942@aol.com
Website: www.racingt-6.org

Taylorcraft Owner's Club and Foundation
Website: www.taylorcraft.org

Temco (Globe Temco Swift Homepage)

Travel Air Club
P.O. Box 127
Blakesburg, IA 52536
Tel/Fax: (515) 938-2773

Twin Bonanza Association
19684 Lakeshore Dr.
Three Rivers, MI 49093
Tel/Fax: (269) 279-2540
Email: forward@twinbonanza.com
Website: www.twinbonanza.com

Twin Cessna Flyer
912 Summit St., Ste. A
New Haven, IN 46774
Tel: (260) 749-2520
Fax: (260) 749-6140
E-mail: twinces@aol.com
Website: www.twincessna.org

Twin Commander Aircraft LLC
19010 59th Dr. N.E.
Arlington, WA 98223-7832
Tel: (360) 435-9797
Fax: (360) 435-1112
Website: www.twincommander.com

Unofficial Cozy Builders Website
E-mail: marc_zeitlin@alum.mit.edu
Website: www.cozybuilders.org

Unofficial Dragonfly Page
E-mail: kevinh@geeksville.com
Website: www.geeksville.com/~kevinh/dragonfly/

Unofficial Quickie, Q-2 and Q-200 Website
P.O. Box 11929
Prescott, AZ 86304-1929
Website: www.siinc-sources.com/q-bird

Unofficial Stewart 51 Builders Page
E-mail: osmith@seas.ucla.edu
Website: www.seas.ucla.edu/~osmith/s51

Unofficial Wolf W-11 Boredom Fighter Web Page
E-mail: webmaster@adap.com
Website: http://adap.com/index.htm

Viking Dragonfly
(*see* Unofficial Dragonfly Page)

Vortech, Inc.
P.O. Box 511-W
Fallston, MD 21047
Website: www.vortechonline.com/bensen

Vought Heritage
E-mail: heritage@voughtaircraft.com
Website: www.vought.com/heritage

Waco
(*see* American Waco Club, Inc.)

Western Association of Mooney Mites
100 S. Westwood St., #2
Porterville, CA 93257-7704
Tel: (559) 784-1980
E-mail: t35flyer@sosinet.net
Website: www.mooneymite.com

Wittman Tailwind
(*see* CHL Associates)

Woodstock
(*see* Jim Maupin, Limited)

World Beechcraft Society
8609 S. 212th St.
Kent, WA 98031
Tel: (866) 732-3927
Website: www.worldbeechcraft.com

Zlin
(*see* International Aerobatics Club)

Index